In Praise of *Engineering Software as a Service*

It is a pleasure to see a student text that emphasizes the production of real useful software. I also applaud the emphasis on getting results early in the process. Nothing stimulates student morale and activity more.

—Frederick P. Brooks, Jr., Turing Award winner and author of *The Mythical Man-Month*

I'd be far more likely to prefer graduates of this program than any other I've seen.

—Brad Green, Engineering Manager, Google Inc.

A number of software engineers at C3 Energy consistently report that this book and its companion online course enabled them to rapidly attain proficiency in SaaS development. I recommend this unique book and course to anyone who wants to develop or improve their SaaS programming skills.

—Thomas M. Siebel, CEO, C3 Energy, and founder and former CEO, Siebel Systems (the leading Customer Relationship Management software company)

A wide and deep coverage of all you need to get started in the SaaS business.

—Vicente Cuellar, Chief Executive Officer, Wave Crafters, Inc.

The book filled a gap in my knowledge about cloud computing and the lectures were easy to follow. Perhaps the most exciting part was to write a cloud application, upload, and deploy it to Heroku.

—Peter Englmaier, University of Zürich, Switzerland

An excellent kickstart into Ruby, Rails and test driven approaches. The fundamentals have been covered with great depth and experience, it's the perfect introduction to modern web development. It should be a requisite for new engineers.

—Stuart Corbishley, Clue Technologies/CloudSeed, South Africa.

An excellent book that will have you up and running building SaaS apps progressively in a few short days. The screencasts and the Pastebin sections are invaluable. A very practical approach to Agile software development. You won't know it but you would have picked up software engineering techniques without even knowing you are doing it!

—Rakhi Saxena, Assistant Professor, Delhi University, India

The authors have accomplished a very welcome juxtaposition of theory and practice for any modern beginning to advanced Software Engineering course. On the one hand, they cover key Software Engineering fundamentals including development processes, requirements engineering, testing, software architecture, configuration management, implementation, and deployment. On the other hand, they convey all of this grounded in a "real-world" approach centered around Ruby/Rails and its rich ecosystem of agile, test- and behavior-driven development tools and techniques, with a direct avenue to cloud deployment of running, quality software. I have used the Beta Edition of this book very successfully in my advanced undergraduate software engineering course, where it beautifully complements both my lectures and the team project.

—Ingolf Krueger, Professor, University of California at San Diego

A really good introduction book to practical Agile development. All you need is gathered in one book with lots of practical examples.

—Dmitrij Savicev, Sungard Front Arena, Sweden

Engineering Software as a Service: An Agile Approach Using Cloud Computing
First Edition, 1.1.1

Armando Fox and David Patterson

Edited by Samuel Joseph

September 18, 2014

Book version: 1.1.1

The cover background is a photo of the **Aqueduct of Segovia**, Spain. We chose it as an example of a beautiful, long-lasting design. The full aqueduct is about 20 miles (32 km) long and was built by the Romans in the 1st or 2nd century A.D. This photo is from the half-mile (0.8 km) long, 92 feet (28 m) high above ground segment built using unmortared granite blocks. The Roman designers followed the architectural principles in the ten-volume series **De Architectura** ("On Architecture"), written in 15 B.C. by Marcus Vitruvius Pollio. It was untouched until the 1500s, when King Ferdinand and Queen Isabella performed the first reconstruction of these arches. The aqueduct was in use and delivering water until recently.

Both the print book and ebook were prepared with LaTeX, tex4ht, and Ruby scripts that use Nokogiri (based on **libxml2**) to massage the XHTML output and HTTParty to automatically keep the Pastebin and screencast URIs up-to-date in the text. The necessary Makefiles, style files and most of the scripts are available under the BSD License at `http://github.com/armandofox/latex2ebook`.

Arthur Klepchukov designed the covers and graphics for all versions.

Publisher's Cataloging-in-Publication

Fox, Armando.
    Engineering software as a service : an agile approach using cloud computing / Armando Fox and David Patterson.
    -- First edition.
    page cm
    Includes bibliographical references and index.
    ISBN 978-0-9848812-4-6
    ISBN 978-0-9848812-3-9

    1. Software engineering. 2. Cloud computing.
I. Patterson, David A. II. Title.
        QA76.758.F69 2014   005.1
                    QBI14-600139

About the Authors

Armando Fox is a Professor of Computer Science at UC Berkeley and the Faculty Advisor to the UC Berkeley MOOCLab. During his previous time at Stanford, he received teaching and mentoring awards from the Associated Students of Stanford University, the Society of Women Engineers, and Tau Beta Pi Engineering Honor Society. He was named one of the "Scientific American 50" in 2003 and is the recipient of an NSF CAREER award and the Gilbreth Lectureship of the National Academy of Engineering. In previous lives he helped design the Intel Pentium Pro microprocessor and founded a successful startup to commercialize his UC Berkeley dissertation research on mobile computing, which included the world's first graphical web browser running on a mobile device (Top Gun Wingman on the Palm Pilot). He received his other degrees in electrical engineering and computer science from MIT and the University of Illinois and is an ACM Distinguished Scientist. He is also a classically-trained musician and freelance Music Director, and a bilingual/bicultural (Cuban-American) New Yorker transplanted to San Francisco.

David Patterson is the Pardee Professor of Computer Science at UC Berkeley. In the past, he served as Chair of Berkeley's Computer Science Division, Chair of the Computing Research Association, and President of the Association for Computing Machinery. His best-known research projects are Reduced Instruction Set Computers (RISC), Redundant Arrays of Inexpensive Disks (RAID), and Networks of Workstations (NOW). This research led to many papers, 6 books, and more than 35 honors, including election to the National Academy of Engineering, the National Academy of Sciences, and the Silicon Valley Engineering Hall of Fame as well as being named a Fellow of the Computer History Museum, ACM, IEEE, and both AAAS organizations. His teaching awards include the Distinguished Teaching Award (UC Berkeley), the Karlstrom Outstanding Educator Award (ACM), the Mulligan Education Medal (IEEE), and the Undergraduate Teaching Award (IEEE). He received all his degrees from UCLA, which awarded him an Outstanding Engineering Academic Alumni Award. He grew up in California, and for fun he enters sporting events with his two adult sons, including weekly soccer games, annual charity bike rides and sprint triathlons, and the occasional weight-lifting contest.

About the Editor

Samuel Joseph is an Associate Professor at Hawaii Pacific University (HPU) and was previously an Associate Researcher at University of Hawaii at Manoa (UHM). He is a recipient of the Raymond Hide Prize for Astrophysics and a Toshiba Fellowship. He teaches fully-online courses on game and mobile programming and design, software engineering, and scientific research methods, from London, UK. He runs the "funniest computer ever" competition as part of his research on creating humorous chatbots, which dovetails nicely with his other research interests in software to support online collaborative learning, especially remote pair programming. He runs the Agile Ventures group which coordinates learning developers contributing to open source projects for non-profit organizations. His degrees in Astrophysics, Cognitive Science and Computer Science are from the University of Leicester, the University of Edinburgh, and UHM. He grew up in the UK and lived in Japan and Hawaii before returning to the UK with his Japanese wife and three Hawaiian born sons. His spare time is taken up biking, jogging and trying to keep up with his guitar, drum and soccer playing sons.

i

Dedication

Armando Fox dedicates this book to his wife and best friend Tonia, whose support while writing it made all the difference, and to Pogo, under whose careful supervision much of it was written and whose feisty spirit will always inhabit our home and our hearts.

David Patterson dedicates this book to his parents and all their descendants:
—To my father David, from whom I inherited inventiveness, athleticism, and the courage to fight for what is right;
—To my mother Lucie, from whom I inherited intelligence, optimism, and my temperament;
—To our sons David and Michael, who are friends, athletic companions, and inspirations for me to be a good man;
—To our daughters-in-law Heather and Zackary, who are smart, funny, and caring mothers to our grandchildren;
—To our grandchildren Andrew, Grace, and Owyn, who give us our chance at immortality (and who helped with marketing for this book);
—To my younger siblings Linda, Don, and Sue, who gave me my first chance to teach;
—To their descendants, who make the Patterson clan both large and fun to be with;
—And to my beautiful and understanding wife Linda, who is my best friend and the love of my life.

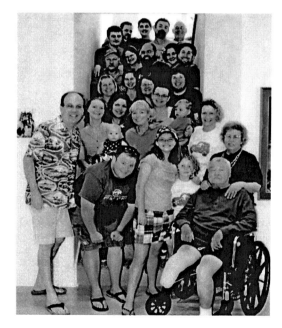

Quick Contents

Contents

II Software Development: Agile vs. Plan-and-Document   217

7 Requirements: BDD and User Stories   218

8 Testing: Test-Driven Development   258

9 Maintenance: Legacy, Refactoring, and Agile   298

Preface

If you want to build a ship, don't drum up the men to gather wood, divide the work and give orders. Instead, teach them to yearn for the vast and endless sea.

—Antoine de Saint-Exupéry, *Citadelle*, 1948

Welcome!

There have been two dramatic software advances in the last decade that an an up-to-date textbook must include. These twin advances constitute the two halves of this book.

The first half explains **Software as a Service** (**SaaS**), which is revolutionizing the software industry. Having a single copy of the program in the cloud with potentially millions of customers places different requirements and offers new opportunities versus conventional shrink-wrap software, in which customers install millions of copies of the program on their own computers.

The enthusiasm for SaaS by developers and customers has led to new highly-productive frameworks for SaaS development. We use **Ruby on Rails** in this book because it is widely believed to have the best tools for SaaS, but there are many other good examples of languages and frameworks for SaaS: for example, Python/Django, JavaScript/Sails, and Java/Enterprise Java Beans.

The question then is which software development methodology is best for SaaS. As there is only one copy of the program and it is deployed in a controlled environment, it is easy to deploy new features quickly and incrementally, and so SaaS evolves much more rapidly than shrink-wrap software. Thus, we needed a software methodology in which change is the norm rather than the exception.

Since industry often complains about weaknesses in software education, we also spoke to representatives from many leading software companies including Amazon, eBay, Facebook, Google, and Microsoft. We were struck by the unanimity of the number one request from each company: that students learn how to enhance sparsely-documented legacy code. In priority order, other requests were making testing a first-class citizen, working with non-technical customers, and working in teams. The social skills needed to work effectively with nontechnical customers and work well in teams surely are helpful for the developers' whole careers; the question is how to fit them into one book. Similarly, no one questions the emphasis on testing; the question is how to get novices to embrace it. Thus, we needed an up-to-date software methodology that also works well with legacy code, emphasizes testing, integrates non-technical customers, and embraces working in teams rather than as lone wolves.

Coincidentally, about the same time that SaaS appeared on the scene, a group of developers proposed the **The Agile Manifesto**, which was a radical change from prior methods. One of the founding tenets of Agile is "responding to change over following a plan," so it is a much better match to the quickly evolving nature of SaaS than traditional "Plan-and-Document" methodologies like Waterfall, Spiral, or RUP. Another Agile tenet is "customer collaboration over contract negotiation," which leads to weekly meetings with non-technical customers. Two critical Agile foundations are **behavior-driven design** and **test-driven development**, which means tests are written *before* the code, so testing really is a first class citizen in Agile. Agile ideas like **pair programming** and **scrum** emphasize working with others. Agile techniques are even a good match to evolving legacy code, as well shall see.

Therefore, the second half of the book explains Agile in the context of building and deploying a SaaS application implemented using Ruby on Rails. In addition, each chapter gives the perspective of the Plan-and-Document methodologies on topics like requirements, testing, management, and maintenance. This contrast allows readers to decide for themselves when each methodology is appropriate for SaaS and non-SaaS applications.

Fulfilling the Most Recent Curriculum Standard

From an instructor's perspective, these dual views of software development allow the book to be used for software engineering courses. For example, we've made sure that the material fulfills all the requirements of the 2013 ACM/IEEE curriculum standard for Software Engineering; in fact, roughly 45 of the end-of-chapter exercises come directly from the learning outcomes in the standard. (We label them with a special margin icon, at right.) Stated alternatively, about 40% of the learning outcomes of the standard are specific exercises and another 40% map directly onto book chapters or sections, which in combination far exceed the 45% minimum that a course needs to conform to the standard.

The Instructors' Manual, downloadable from http://esa.as, treats the instructor-facing topics of this chapter in depth.

Massive Open Online Course (MOOC) to Aid Teachability

We had already decided to write a textbook when we were recruited in October 2011 to offer the first part of the UC Berkeley course as a free Massive Online Open Course (MOOC). We ultimately developed two MOOCs through BerkeleyX (the UC Berkeley partnership with the nonprofit edX) covering the introductory and advanced material: CS169.1x and CS169.2x, available at saas-class.org[1]. As a result of the co-development of the book and the MOOCs, they are complementary: the video segments of MOOCs map nearly one-to-one with sections of the book, and like the MOOC segments, each book section ends with one or two short "Self-Check" questions. Enrollment is free; to date, over 100,000 learners have experienced the MOOCs and over 10,000 have gained certificates of completion, giving the book and materials a much bigger Beta test than we could ever have envisioned!

The MOOCs are also a valuable instructor aid. Some instructors have had their students co-enroll in the MOOC to take advantage of its automatically-graded programming assignments. Some instructors have "flipped their classrooms," having students watch the MOOC videos and devoting class time to problem solving and other activities, while other instructors have used the videos to prepare their own material. The autograders are constantly being enhanced and new assignments created that take advantage of them.

In fact, interested instructors can even get a private version of the MOOC—a SPOC, or Small Private Online Course—which they can customize to their needs and still take advantage of autograded programming assignments and other MOOC features. The Instructor Resources page[2] on the book's website has information on how to request a SPOC, as well as a report describing other instructors' experience with SPOCs in their own classrooms. SPOC instructors can even participate in a biweekly conference call to discuss problems and ideas with colleagues using the same material, such as creating new assignments that take advantage of the autograders.

Organization

The book is organized into two main parts: the first covers the big ideas and essential technologies of Agile+SaaS, while the second focuses on the tools and techniques for practicing the Agile lifecycle and effectively managing SaaS design, construction, and deployment.

These parts correspond to two main units of material, with an optional but recommended student project providing a third unit. Unit 1, which corresponds roughly to the content of the CS169.1x MOOC, covers the basics of building a simple SaaS app using Rails and the Agile lifecycle. Unit 2 introduces more advanced software engineering concepts such as design patterns, working with legacy code, and basics of SaaS performance and security ("DevOps"), corresponding roughly to the content of BerkeleyX CS169.2x. Each of these units includes autogradable assignments, supplementary online materials for instructors such as question banks and exams, and so on. In Unit 3, students use the skills acquired in the first and/or second parts to develop an open-ended team project. At present there is no corresponding MOOC (though we are exploring ideas) but the Instructors' Manual distills the lessons we've learned facilitating successful (and less-successful) student projects.

At Berkeley, we cover all three components in a single, aggressive 14-week course (3 hours of lecture, 1 hour of seminar/recitation, and 8 non-classroom hours of work per week), in which four Agile iterations of the group project partially overlap unit 2. The Instructors' Manual describes our syllabus as well as many other possible options, for example:

- A two-course sequence, covering Units 1 and 2 in the first course and devoting the second course to a semester-long or quarter-long project

- A single course covering only Units 1 and 3, limiting the project's complexity to the skills learned in Unit 1

- A single course covering all the units but omitting specific elements to meet a length constraint, such as omitting JavaScript (Chapter 6) or DevOps (Chapter 12).

However the course is factored, the nearly one-to-one correspondence between book sections and MOOC/SPOC lecture videos makes it easy to recombine course modules in whatever way works best for your classroom.

Student Projects and Learning By Doing

The ACM/IEEE software engineering curriculum guidelines emphasize the value of an iterative approach in which students assess and revise their work continuously. We have found that students are much more likely to actually follow the Agile methodology because the

Ruby on Rails tools, which we introduce in this book, make it easy and because the advice is genuinely helpful for their projects. We believe Agile offers learning skills that transfer to non-agile projects, should need arise. We even show how to use Agile techniques on legacy code that wasn't developed that way to begin with; that is, Agile is good for more than just writing new code from scratch. To facilitate such learning by doing, the book's website provides links to a freely downloadable preconfigured virtual machine (VM) image, deployable on students' own computers or in the cloud. The free screencasts[3] may be useful to both instructors and students as demonstrations of how to use these tools.

The ACM/IEEE curriculum guidelines also highlight team projects as a critical learning mechanism for software engineering students. The experience of many instructors (including ourselves) is that students enjoy learning and using Agile in projects. Its iteration-based, short-planning-cycle approach is a great fit for the reality of crowded undergraduate schedules and fast-paced courses. Busy students will by nature procrastinate and then pull several all-nighters to get a demo cobbled together and working by the project deadline; Agile not only thwarts this tactic (since students are evaluated on progress being made each iteration) but in our experience actually leads to real progress using responsible practices on a more regular basis.

To help you run successful projects, the Instructors' Manual contains detailed suggestions for organizing and scheduling project milestones in a classroom course, and gives example rubrics for grading the projects based on both the artifacts produced and the processes used to produce them, taking full advantage of being able to do multiple iterations in a single course. We also survey each generation of students to determine what they learned from the projects and where they had difficulty; the Instructors' Manual distills these "seven habits of highly effective projects" based on several offerings of the course at UC Berkeley and elsewhere.

Why Write a New Book?

Prospective authors wouldn't write a new book if they thought the old ones were up-to-date and easy to teach from. Our dissatisfaction differs depending on the part of the book.

For Part 1, the problem isn't that there are too few good books on the SaaS topics, but that there are too many! Our first step in writing was to read them. Figures 1 and 2 show just 24 of the 50+ books we consulted, and just these 24 represent more than 10,000 pages! The sheer mass of these books can intimidate beginners. Therefore, one reason we wrote a new book is simply to offer a coherent introduction and up-to-date overview of all SaaS topics within a single relatively slim, inexpensive volume. As one reviewer of the Alpha edition complained, there is nothing new in Part 1, as long as you have the budget and time to buy and read dozens of books. We can live with that critique!

Regarding Part 2, there are a few choices of textbooks on software engineering, but none that you would call up-to-date, slim, or inexpensive. While the reviews of the SaaS books we consulted are often excellent—4 out of 5 stars or higher on Amazon.com—that is not the case for these software engineering textbooks. The two most widely-used textbooks get ratings between 2 and 3 stars, and the reviewer comments are unkind.

One reason may be that these books are primarily long, qualitative surveys of the literature—listing many options on each topic based published research papers and books—but offer few concrete clues or methods on how to pick from among them. Another reason may be that the first editions were written long before SaaS and Agile appeared on the scene, and it is difficult to gracefully integrate up-to-date perspectives into older material.

Figure 1: These 12 books contain more than 5000 pages. Your authors read more than 50 books to prepare this text. Most of these books are listed in the **To Learn More** sections at the end of the appropriate chapters.

Figure 2: Another 12 books your authors read also contain more than 5000 pages. Most of these books are listed in the To Learn More sections at the end of the appropriate chapters.

This is déjà vu, as one of your authors had the same feelings about computer architecture textbooks 25 years ago; they were just long, qualitative surveys of related products and research papers with no framework for readers to pick between the implementation options. Moreover, there had been a dramatic and (at the time) controversial change in computer architecture that was not reflected in these books. This dissatisfaction led one of your authors and a friend to write a book that was very different from conventional computer architecture textbooks.

Repeating history, then, Part 2 is very different from conventional software engineering textbooks. It treats Agile as a first class citizen and gives concrete, hands on examples of code and tools to follow the Agile process that can really lead to products that match customers' needs. As mentioned above, each chapter in Part 2 also presents the Plan-and-Document perspective to help readers appreciate Agile and to see where it should and should not be used.

Our goal for each part is to bring a diverse set of topics together into a *single narrative,* to help you understand the most important ideas by giving concrete examples. We can then imagine someone already familiar with Agile in Part 2 to read the book just to learn about SaaS in Part 1, or vice versa. If you're new to the topic—or if your education precedes the development of SaaS and Agile—then you get a double-barreled, synergistic introduction to this new and exciting software era. This sharp focus led to a book that covers both of the recent advances of SaaS and Agile software development in approximately half of the chapters and half of the pages at a quarter of the price of conventional software engineering textbooks.

Errata and Supplementary Content

From an author's perspective, one delightful feature of electronic textbooks is that we can update all electronic copies of an edition when readers find mistakes in the book. We have been collecting the Errata together and released updates a few times a year. The book's website shows the latest version of the book and a brief description of the changes since the previous version. Previous errata can be reviewed, and new ones reported, on the book's website. We apologize in advance for the problems you find in this edition, and look forward to your feedback on how to improve this material.

History of this Book

The material in this book started as a byproduct of a Berkeley research project[4] that was developing technology to make it easy to build the next great Internet service. We decided that young people were more likely to come up with such a service, so we started teaching Berkeley undergraduates about Software as a Service using Agile techniques in 2007. Each year the course improved in scope, ambition, and popularity, embracing the rapid improvements in the Rails tools along the way. Between 2007 and 2013, our enrollments followed Moore's Law: 35, 50, 75, 115, 165, and 240.

A colleague suggested that this would be excellent material for the software engineering course that has long been taught at Berkeley, so one of us (Fox) taught that course with this new content. The results were so impressive that the other of us (Patterson) suggested that writing a textbook would let others benefit from this powerful curriculum.

These ideas crystallized with the emerging viability of electronic textbooks and the possibility of avoiding the costs and delays of a traditional publisher. In March 2011, we made a pact to write the book together. We were equally excited by making the material more widely available and about rethinking what an electronic textbook should be, since up until then they were essentially just the PDFs of print books.

We talked to others about the content. We attended conferences such as SIGCSE (Special Interest Group in Computer Science Education), the Conference on Software Engineering Education and Training, and the Federated Computing Research Conference both to talk with colleagues and to send them a survey to get their feedback.

Given the perspective of educators and industrial colleagues, we proposed an outline that we thought addressed all these concerns, and started writing in June 2011. Given Fox's much greater expertise on the subject, the plan was for him to write roughly two-thirds of the chapters and Patterson the rest. Both of us collaborated on the organization and were first reviewers for each other's chapters. We've ended up writing some sections each other's chapters, so it's a little more mixed than we expected. Fox authored Chapters 2, 3, 4, 5, 6, 8, 9, 11, 12, Appendix A, and Sections 10.4 to 10.6, while Patterson wrote Chapters 1,7, 10, the Preface, the Afterword, the Instructors' Manual, and the Plan-and-Document Perspectives in Sections 7.10, 8.9, 9.7, 10.7, 11.8, and 12.10. Fox also created the LaTeX pipeline[5] that let us produce the many formats of the book for the various electronic and print targets.

We offered an Alpha edition of the textbook for 115 UC Berkeley students and thousands of MOOC students in the Spring semester 2012. Based on their feedback, the Beta edition was ready by Fall 2012, when it was used at Berkeley and several other schools. A Second Beta edition in May 2013, with new material based on careful study of the 2013 ACM/IEEE Computer Society curriculum standard, was tested again by Berkeley and MOOC students in Fall of 2013, leading to this (very well tested!) first edition.

Specific SaaS Companies and Products

Where possible, we focus on free and/or open-source software and services so that students can get hands-on experience with the examples without incurring additional out-of-pocket costs. A number of companies in the SaaS ecosystem have agreed to provide special trial offers of useful tools and services; the book's website lists the constantly-evolving set of special offers available to instructors and students using this book. None of this affected the book's content, which was frozen long before these arrangements were made.

Therefore, when we use specific Web sites, tools, products, or trade names to ground the book's examples in reality, unless specifically noted we have no formal connection to any of these sites, tools, or products, and the examples are for informational purposes only and not meant as commercial endorsements. Any trademarked names mentioned are the property of their respective owners and mentioned here for informational purposes only.

The authors' opinions are their own and not necessarily those of their employer.

Acknowledgments

We thank our industrial colleagues who gave us feedback on our ideas about the course and the book, especially these awesome individuals, listed alphabetically by company: Peter Vosshall, Amazon Web Services; Tony Ng, eBay; Tracy Bialik, Brad Green, and Russ Rufer, Google Inc.; Peter Van Hardenberg, Heroku; Jim Larus, Microsoft Research; Brian

Cunnie, Edward Hieatt, Matthew Kocher, Jacob Maine, Ken Mayer, and Rob Mee, Pivotal Labs; Jason Huggins, SauceLabs; and Raffi Krikorian, Twitter.

We thank our academic colleagues for their feedback on our approach and ideas, especially Fred Brooks, University of North Carolina at Chapel Hill; Marti Hearst and Paul Hilfinger, UC Berkeley; Timothy Lethbridge, University of Ottawa; John Ousterhout, Stanford University; and Mary Shaw, Carnegie-Mellon University.

We deeply thank the content experts who reviewed specific chapters: Danny Burkes, Pivotal Labs; Timothy Chou, Stanford; Daniel Jackson, MIT ; Jacob Maine, Pivotal Labs; John Ousterhout, Stanford University; and Ellen Spertus, Mills College.

Thanks to Alan Fekete, University of Sydney, for pointing us to the 2013 ACM/IEEE Computer Society Curriculum on Software Engineering in time for us to consider it.

We're especially grateful to the Beta testers who used early versions of our book in their own classrooms, starting with Samuel Joseph, Hawaii Pacific University, who also serves as Lead Facilitator for the CS169.1x and CS169.2x MOOCs[6] and whose extensive contributions to the development and improvement of both the course materials and the textbook material made it clear that we should ask him to assume the official mantle of Editor. Other early adopters who continue to give valuable feedback and contribute to the course materials include Daniel Jackson, MIT; Richard Ilson, University of North Carolina at Charlotte; Ingolf Krueger, University of California, San Diego; Kristen Walcott-Justice, University of Colorado–Colorado Springs; Rose Williams, Binghamton University; and Wei Xu, Tsinghua University, who was the first to test this material in a classroom outside the United States and who facilitated our relationship with Tsinghua University Press to produce the Chinese language edition of the book.

Part of the "bookware" is the collection of excellent third-party sites supporting SaaS development. For their help in connecting us with the right products and services that could be offered free of charge to students in the class, and valuable discussion on how to use them in an educational setting, we thank Ann Merrihew, Kurt Messersmith, Marvin Theimer, Jinesh Varia, and Matt Wood, Amazon Web Services; Kami Lott and Chris Wanstrath, GitHub; Maggie Johnson and Arjun Satyapal, Google Inc.; James Lindenbaum, Heroku; Juan Vargas and Jennifer Perret, Microsoft; Rob Mee, Pivotal Labs; Dana Le, Salesforce; and John Dunham, SauceLabs.

We thank our graduate student instructors Kristal Curtis and Shoaib Kamil for helping us reinvent the on-campus class that led to this effort, and graduate student instructors Michael Driscoll and Richard Xia for helping us make scalable automatic grading a reality for the thousands of students that enrolled in the online course. Last but far from least, we thank our dedicated undergraduate lab staff over various iterations of the class since 2008: Alex Bain, Aaron Beitch, Allen Chen, James Eady, David Eliahu, Max Feldman, Amber Feng, Karl He, Arthur Klepchukov, Jonathan Ko, Brandon Liu, Robert Marks, Jimmy Nguyen, Sunil Pedapudi, Omer Spillinger, Hubert Wong, Tim Yung, and Richard Zhao.

We'd also like to thank Andrew Patterson, Grace Patterson, and Owyn Patterson for their help in marketing the book, as well as to their managers Heather Patterson, Michael Patterson, David Patterson, and Zackary Patterson.

Finally, we thank the hundreds of UC Berkeley students and the tens of thousands of MOOC students for their debugging help and their continuing interest in this material!

Armando Fox and David Patterson
March, 2014
Berkeley, California

Notes

[1] http://www.saas-class.org
[2] http://www.saasbook.info/instructors
[3] http://screencast.saasbook.info
[4] http://radlab.cs.berkeley.edu
[5] http://github.com/armandofox/latex2ebook
[6] http://saas-class.org

1

Introduction to Software as a Service and Agile Software Development

It was on one of my journeys between the EDSAC room and the punching equipment that "hesitating at the angles of stairs" the realization came over me with full force that a good part of the remainder of my life was going to be spent finding errors in my own programs.

—Maurice Wilkes, Memoirs of a Computer Pioneer, 1985

Concepts

Each chapter opening starts with a one-page summary of that chapter's big concepts. For this introductory chapter, they are:

- **Plan-and-Document** software development processes or *lifecycles* rely on careful, up-front planning that is extensively documented and carefully managed to make software development more predictable. Prominent examples are *Waterfall*, *Spiral*, and the *Rational Unified Process* (*RUP*) lifecycles.

- In contrast, the *Agile* lifecycle relies on incrementally developed prototypes that involve continuous feedback from the customer on each *iteration*, each of which takes between one to four weeks.

- *Service Oriented Architecture* (*SOA*) creates apps from components that act as interoperable services, which allows new systems to be built from these components with much less effort. More importantly, from a software engineering perspective, SOA enables the construction of large services from many small ones, which history teaches us is more likely to be successful than a single large project. One reason is that smaller size allows use of Agile development, which has a superior track record.

- *Software as a Service* (*SaaS*) is a special case of SOA that deploys software at a single site but makes it available to millions of users over the Internet on their personal mobile devices, which provides benefits to both users and developers. The single copy of the software and the competitive environment for SaaS products leads to more rapid *software evolution* for SaaS than for shrink-wrapped software.

- *Legacy Code* evolution is vital in the real world, yet often ignored in software engineering books and courses. Agile practices enhancing code each iteration, so the skills gained also apply to legacy code.

- *Cloud Computing* supplies the dependable and scalable computation and storage for SaaS by utilizing **Warehouse Scale Computers** containing as many as 100,000 servers. The economies of scale allow Cloud Computing to be offered as a utility, where you pay only for actual use.

- *Software quality* is defined as providing business value to both customers and developers. Software *Quality Assurance* (*QA*) comes from many levels of testing: *unit*, **module**, *integration*, *system*, and *acceptance*.

- **Clarity via conciseness**, *synthesis*, *reuse*, and **automation via tools** are four paths to improving *software productivity*. The programming framework *Ruby on Rails* follows them to make SaaS developers productive. **Don't Repeat Yourself (DRY)** warns not to use repetition to achieve reuse, as there should be one representation of each piece of knowledge.

Since change is the norm for Agile, it is an excellent SaaS lifecycle, and the one on which the book focuses.

Topic	Amazon.com	ACA Oct	ACA Nov	ACA Dec
Customers/Day (Goal)	–	50,000	50,000	30,000
Customers/Day (Actual)	>10,000,000	800	3,700	34,300
Average Response time (seconds)	0.2	8	1	1
Downtime/Month (hours)	0.07	446	107	36
Availability (% up)	99.99%	40%	85%	95%
Error Rate	–	10%	10%	–
Secure	Yes	No	No	No

Figure 1.1: Comparing Amazon.com and Healthcare.gov during its first three months. (Thorp 2013) After its stumbling start, the deadline was extended from December 15, 2013 to March 31, 2014, which explains the lower goal in customers per day in December. Note that availability for ACA does *not* include time for "scheduled maintenance," which Amazon does include (Zients 2013). The error rate was for significant errors on the forms sent to insurance companies (Horsley 2013). The site was widely labeled by security experts as insecure, as the developers were under tremendous pressure to get proper functionality, and little attention was paid to security (Harrington 2013).

1.1 Introduction

Now, this is real simple. It's a website where you can compare and purchase affordable health insurance plans, side-by-side, the same way you shop for a plane ticket on Kayak or the same way you shop for a TV on Amazon...Starting on Tuesday, every American can visit HealthCare.gov to find out what's called the insurance marketplace...So tell your friends, tell your family...Make sure they sign up. Let's help our fellow Americans get covered. (Applause.)

—President Barack Obama, Remarks on the Affordable Care Act, Prince George's Community College, Maryland, September 26, 2013

...it has now been six weeks since the Affordable Care Act's new marketplaces opened for business. I think it's fair to say that the rollout has been rough so far, and I think everybody understands that I'm not happy about the fact that the rollout has been, you know, wrought with a whole range of problems that I've been deeply concerned about.

—President Barack Obama, Statement on the Affordable Care Act, The White House Press Briefing Room, November 14, 2013

When the *Affordable Care Act* (*ACA*) was passed in 2010, it was seen as the most ambitious US social program in decades, and it was perhaps the crowning achievement of the Obama administration. Just as millions shop for items on Amazon.com, HealthCare.gov—also known as the Affordable Care Act website—was supposed to let millions of uninsured Americans shop for insurance policies. Despite taking three years to build, it fell flat on its face when it debuted on October 1, 2013. Figure 1.1 compares Amazon.com to Heathcare.gov in the first three months of operation, demonstrating that not only was it slow, error prone, and insecure, it was also down much of the time.

Why is that companies like Amazon.com can build software that serves a much large customer base so much better? While the media uncovered many questionable decisions, a surprising amount of the blame was placed on the *methodology* used to develop the software (Johnson and Reed 2013). Given their approach, as one commentator said, "The real news would have been if it actually did work." (Johnson 2013a)

We're honored to have the chance to explain how Internet companies and others build successful software services. As this introduction illustrates, this field is not some dreary academic discipline where few care what happens; failed software projects can become infamous, and can even derail Presidents. On the other hand, successful software projects can create services that millions of people use every day, leading to companies like Amazon, Facebook, and Google that become household names. All involved with such services are proud to be associated with them, unlike the ACA.

Moreover, this book is *not* just the traditional well-intentioned survey of do's and don'ts for each phase of software development. It makes recent concepts concrete with a hands-on demonstration of how to design, implement, and deploy an application in the cloud. The virtual machine image associated with this book comes pre-loaded with all the software you'll need to do it (see Appendix A). In addition to reading what we wrote, you can see our demonstrations and hear our voices as part of the 27 screencasts in the following chapters. You can even *watch* us teach this material, for this book is associated with a free **Massive Open Online Course** (**MOOC**) from EdX.org[2]. CS169.1x and CS169.2x offer 6- to 10-minute video segments that generally correspond one-to-one with all the sections of this book, including this one. These MOOCs offer quick autograding of programming assignments and quizzes to give you feedback on how well you've learned the material plus an online forum to ask and answer questions.

The rest of this chapter explains why disasters like ACA can happen and how to avoid repeating this unfortunate history. We start our journey with the origins of software engineering itself, which began with software development methodologies that placed a heavy emphasis on planning and documenting. We next review the statistics on how well the **Plan-and-Document** methodologies worked, alas documenting that project outcomes like ACA are all too common, if not as well known. The frequently disappointing results of following conventional wisdom in software engineering inspired a few software developers to stage a palace revolt. While the **Agile Manifesto** was quite controversial when it was announced, over time Agile software development has trumped its critics. Agile allows small teams to outperform the industrial giants, especially for small projects. Our next step in the journey demonstrates how **service-oriented architecture** allows the successful composition of large software services like Amazon.com from many smaller software services developed by small Agile teams.

As a final but critical point, it's rare in practice for software developers to do "green field" development, in which they start from a blank slate. It's much more common to enhance large existing code bases. The next step in our journey observes that unlike Plan-and-Document, which aims at a perfect design up front and then implements it, the Agile process spends almost all of its time enhancing working code. Thus, by getting good at Agile, you are also practicing the skills you need to evolve existing code bases.

To start us on our journey, we introduce the software methodology used to develop HealthCare.gov.

1.2 Software Development Processes: Plan and Document

> *If builders built buildings the way programmers wrote programs, then the first woodpecker that came along would destroy civilization.*

> —Gerald Weinberg, *Weinberg's Second Law*

The general unpredictability of software development in the late 1960s, along with the software disasters similar to ACA, led to the study of how high-quality software could be developed on a predictable schedule and budget. Drawing the analogy to other engineering fields, the term **software engineering** was coined (Naur and Randell 1969). The goal was to discover methods to build software that were as predictable in quality, cost, and time as those used to build bridges in civil engineering.

One thrust of software engineering was to bring an engineering discipline to what was often unplanned software development. Before starting to code, come up with a plan for the project, including extensive, detailed documentation of all phases of that plan. Progress is then measured against the plan. Changes to the project must be reflected in the documentation and possibly to the plan.

The goal of all these "Plan-and-Document" software development processes is to improve predictability via extensive documentation, which must be changed whenever the goals change. Here is how textbook authors put it (Lethbridge and Laganiere 2002; Braude 2001):

> *Documentation should be written at all stages of development, and includes requirements, designs, user manuals, instructions for testers and project plans.*
>
> —Timothy Lethbridge and Robert Laganiere, 2002

> *Documentation is the lifeblood of software engineering.*
>
> —Eric Braude, 2001

This process is even embraced with an official standard of documentation: IEEE/ANSI standard 830/1993.

CGI Group won the contract for the backend of the ACA website. The initial estimate ballooned from US$94M to $292M (Begley 2013). This same company was involved in a Canadian firearms registry whose costs skyrocketed, from an initial estimate of US$2M to $2B. When MITRE investigated the problems with Massachusetts' ACA website, it said CGI Group did not have the expertise to build the site, lost data, failed to adequately test functions, and managed the project poorly (Bidgood 2014).

Governments like that of the US have elaborate regulations to prevent corruption when acquiring new equipment, which lead to lengthy specifications and contracts. Since the goal of software engineering was to make software development as predictable as building bridges, including elaborate specifications, government contracts were a natural match to Plan-and-Document software development. Thus, like many countries, US acquisition regulations left the ACA developers little choice but to follow a Plan-and-Document lifecycle.

Of course, like other engineering fields, the government has escape clauses in the contracts that let it still acquire the product even if it is late. Ironically, the contractor makes more money the longer it takes to develop the software. Thus, the art is negotiating the contract and the penalty clauses. As one commentator on ACA noted (Howard 2013), "The firms that typically get contracts are the firms that are good at getting contracts, not typically good at executing on them." Another noted that the Plan-and-Document approach is not well suited to modern practices, especially when government contractors focus on maximizing profits (Chung 2013).

An early version of this Plan-and-Document software development process was developed in 1970 (Royce 1970). It follows this sequence of phases:

1. Requirements analysis and specification

2. Architectural design

3. Implementation and Integration

4. Verification

5. Operation and Maintenance

Given that the earlier you find an error the cheaper it is to fix, the philosophy of this process is to complete a phase before going on to the next one, thereby removing as many errors as early as possible. Getting the early phases right could also prevent unnecessary work downstream. As this process could take years, the extensive documentation helps to ensure that important information is not lost if a person leaves the project and that new people can get up to speed quickly when they join the project.

Because it flows from the top down to completion, this process is called the **Waterfall** software development process or Waterfall software development **lifecycle**. Understandably, given the complexity of each stage in the Waterfall lifecycle, product releases are major events toward which engineers worked feverishly and which are accompanied by much fanfare.

> **Windows 95** was heralded by a US$300 million outdoor party[3] for which Microsoft hired comedian Jay Leno, lit up New York's Empire State Building using the Microsoft Windows logo colors, and licensed "Start Me Up" by the Rolling Stones as the celebration's theme song.

In the Waterfall lifecycle, the long life of software is acknowledged by a maintenance phase that repairs errors as they are discovered. New versions of software developed in the Waterfall model go through the same several phases, and take typically between 6 and 18 months.

The Waterfall model can work well with well-specified tasks like NASA space flights, but it runs into trouble when customers change their minds about what they want. A Turing Award winner captures this observation:

> *Plan to throw one [implementation] away; you will, anyhow.*

—Fred Brooks, Jr.

That is, it's easier for customers to understand what they want once they see a prototype and for engineers to understand how to build it better once they've done it the first time.

This observation led to a software development lifecycle developed in the 1980s that combines prototypes with the Waterfall model (Boehm 1986). The idea is to iterate through a sequence of four phases, with each iteration resulting in a prototype that is a refinement of the previous version. Figure 1.2 illustrates this model of development across the four phases, which gives this lifecycle its name: the **Spiral model**. The phases are

1. Determine objectives and constraints of this iteration

2. Evaluate alternatives and identify and resolve risks

3. Develop and verify the prototype for this iteration

4. Plan the next iteration

Rather than document all the requirements at the beginning, as in the Waterfall model, the requirement documents are developed across the iteration as they are needed and evolve with the project. Iterations involve the customer before the product is completed, which reduces chances of misunderstandings. However, as originally envisioned, these iterations were 6 to 24 months long, so there is plenty of time for customers to change their minds during an iteration! Thus, Spiral still relies on planning and extensive documentation, but the plan is expected to evolve on each iteration.

> **Big Design Up Front**, abbreviated **BDUF**, is a name some use for software processes like Waterfall, Spiral, and RUP that depend on extensive planning and documentation. They are also known variously as **heavyweight**, **plan-driven**, **disciplined**, or **structured** processes.

Given the importance of software development, many variations of Plan-and-Document methodologies were proposed beyond these two. A recent one is called the **Rational Unified Process** (**RUP**) (Kruchten 2003), which combines features of both Waterfall and Spiral lifecycles as well standards for diagrams and documentation. We'll use RUP as a representative of the latest thinking in Plan-and-Document lifecycles. Unlike Waterfall and Spiral, it is more closely allied to business issues than to technical issues.

Like Waterfall and Spiral, RUP has phases:

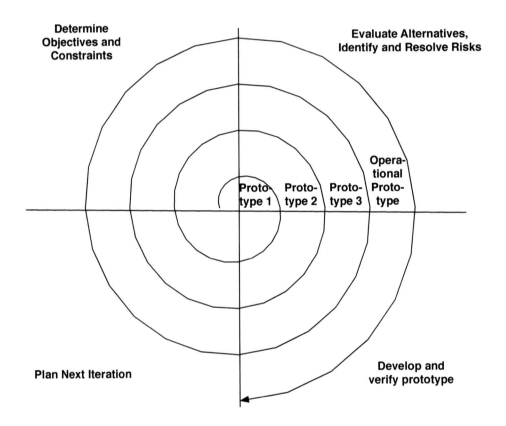

Figure 1.2: The Spiral lifecycle combines Waterfall with prototyping. It starts at the center, with each iteration around the spiral going through the four phases and resulting in a revised prototype until the product is ready for release.

1. Inception: makes the business case for the software and scopes the project to set the schedule and budget, which is used to judge progress and justify expenditures, and initial assessment of risks to schedule and budget.

2. Elaboration: works with stakeholders to identify use cases, designs a software architecture, sets the development plan, and builds an initial prototype.

3. Construction: codes and tests the product, resulting in the first external release.

4. Transition: moves the product from development to production in the real environment, including customer acceptance testing and user training.

Unlike Waterfall, each phase involves iteration. For example, a project might have one inception phase iteration, two elaboration phase iterations, four construction phase iterations, and two transition phase iterations. Like Spiral, a project could also iterate across all four phases repeatedly.

In addition to the dynamically changing phases of the project, RUP identifies six "engineering disciplines" (also known as workflows) that people working on the project should collectively cover:

1. Business Modeling

2. Requirements

3. Analysis and Design

4. Implementation

5. Test

6. Deployment

These disciplines are more static than the phases, in that they nominally exist over the whole lifetime of the project. However, some disciplines get used more in earlier phases (like business modeling), some periodically throughout the process (like test), and some more towards the end (deployment). Figure 1.3 shows the relationship of the phases and the disciplines, with the area indicating the amount of effort in each discipline over time.

An unfortunate downside to teaching a Plan-and-Document approach is that students may find software development tedious (Nawrocki et al. 2002; Estler et al. 2012). Given the importance of predictable software development, this is hardly a strong enough reason not to teach it; the good news is that there are alternatives that work just as well for many projects that are a better fit to the classroom, as we describe in the next section.

Summary: The basic *activities* of software engineering are the same in all the software development process or **lifecycles**, but their interaction over time relative to product releases differs among the models. The Waterfall lifecycle is characterized by much of the design being done in advance of coding, completing each phase before going on to the next one. The Spiral lifecycle iterates through all the development phases to produce prototypes, but like Waterfall, the customers may only get involved every 6 to 24 months. The more recent Rational Unified Process lifecycle includes phases, iterations, and prototypes, while identifying the people skills needed for the project. All rely on careful planning and thorough documentation, and all measure progress against a plan.

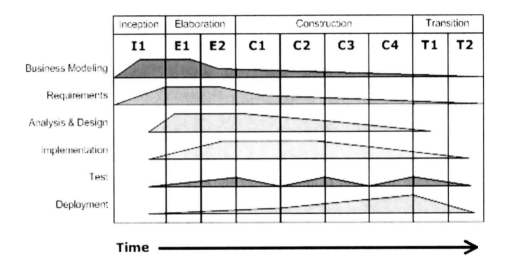

Figure 1.3: The Rational Unified Process lifecycle allows the project to have multiple iterations in each phase and identifies the skills needed by the project team, which vary in effort over time. RUP also has three "supporting disciplines" not shown in this figure: Configuration and Change Management, Project Management, and Environment. (Image from Wikipedia Commons by Dutchgilder.)

Self-Check 1.2.1. *What are a major similarity and a major difference between processes like Spiral and RUP versus Waterfall?*

◇ All rely on planning and documentation, but Spiral and RUP use iteration and prototypes to improve them over time versus a single long path to the product. ∎

Self-Check 1.2.2. *What are the differences between the phases of these Plan-and-Document processes?*

◇ Waterfall phases separate planning (requirements and architectural design) from implementation. Testing the product before release is next, followed by a separate operations phase. The Spiral phases are aimed at an iteration: set the goals for an iteration; explore alternatives; develop and verify the prototype for this iteration; and plan the next iteration. RUP phases are tied closer to business objectives: inception makes business case and sets schedule and budget; elaboration works with customers to build an initial prototype; construction builds and test the first version; and transition deploys the product. ∎

∎ *Elaboration: SEI Capability Maturity Model (CMM)*

The Software Engineering Institute at Carnegie Mellon University proposed the **Capability Maturity Model** (CMM) (Paulk et al. 1995) to evaluate organizations' software-development processes based on Plan-and-Document methodologies. The idea is that by modeling the software development process, an organization can improve them. SEI studies observed five levels of software practice:

1. Initial or Chaotic—undocumented/*ad hoc*/unstable software development.

2. Repeatable—not following rigorous discipline, but some processes repeatable with consistent results.

3. Defined—Defined and documented standard processes that improve over time.

4. Managed—Management can control software development using process metrics, adapting the process to different projects successfully.

5. Optimizing—Deliberate process optimization improvements as part of management process.

CMM implicitly encourages an organization to move up the CMM levels. While not proposed as a software development methodology, many consider it one. For example, (Nawrocki et al. 2002) compares CMM Level 2 to the Agile software methodology (see next section).

1.3 Software Development Processes: The Agile Manifesto

If a problem has no solution, it may not be a problem, but a fact—not to be solved, but to be coped with over time.

—Shimon Peres

While plan-and-development processes brought discipline to software development, there were still software projects that failed so disastrously that they live in infamy. Programmers have heard these sorry stories of the **Ariane 5 rocket explosion**, the **Therac-25** lethal radiation overdose, and the FBI **Virtual Case File** project abandonment so frequently that they are clichés. No software engineer would want these projects on their résumés.

Ariane 5 flight 501. On June 4, 1996, an overflow occurred 37 seconds after liftoff in a guidance system, with spectacular consequences[4], when a floating point number was converted to a shorter integer. This exception could not occur on the slower Ariane 4 rocket, so reusing successful components without thorough system testing was expensive: satellites worth $370M were lost.

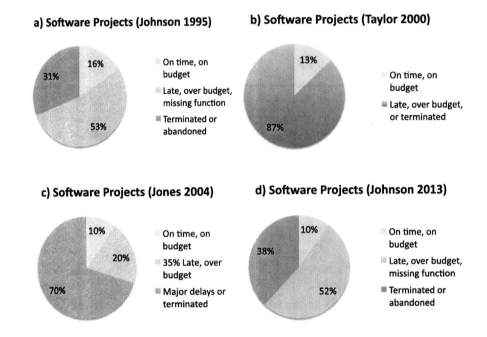

Figure 1.4: a) Study of software projects found that 53% of projects exceeding their budgets by a factor of 2.9 and overshot their schedule by a factor of 3.2 and another 31% of software projects were cancelled before completion (Johnson 1995). The estimated annual cost in the United States for such software projects was $100B. b) Survey of members of the British Computer Society found that only 130 of 1027 projects met their schedule and budget. Half of all projects were maintenance or data conversion projects and half new development projects, but the successful projects divided into 127 of the former and just 3 of the latter (Taylor 2000). c) Survey of 250 large projects, each with the equivalent of more than a million lines of C code, found similarly disappointing results (Jones 2004). d) Survey listing just the large examples of 50,000 projects, in that they cost at least $10M in development (Johnson 2013b). It has the most dismal outcomes, suggesting that HealthCare.gov had just a 10% chance of success.

One article even listed a "Software Wall of Shame" with dozens of highly-visible software projects that collectively were responsible for losses of $17B, with the majority of these projects abandoned (Charettte 2005).

Figure 1.4 summarizes four surveys of software projects. With just 10% to 16% on time and on budget, more projects were cancelled or abandoned than met their mark. A closer look at the 13% success of survey b) is even more sobering, as fewer than 1% of new development projects met their schedules and budgets. Although the first three surveys are 10 to 25 years old, survey d) is from 2013. Nearly 40% of these large projects were cancelled or abandoned, and 50% were late, over budget, and missing functionality. Using history as our guide, poor President Obama had only a one in ten chance that HealthCare.gov would have a successful debut.

Perhaps the "Reformation moment" for software engineering was the **Agile Manifesto** in February 2001. A group of software developers met to develop a lighter-weight software lifecycle. Here is exactly what the **Agile Alliance** nailed to the door of the "Church of Plan and Document":

Agile is also known variously as a **lightweight** or **undisciplined** process.

"We are uncovering better ways of developing software by doing it and helping others do it. Through this work we have come to value:

- **Individuals and interactions** *over processes and tools*

- **Working software** *over comprehensive documentation*

- **Customer collaboration** *over contract negotiation*

- **Responding to change** *over following a plan*

That is, while there is value in the items on the right, we value the items on the left more."

This alternative development model is based on embracing change as a fact of life: developers should continuously refine a working but incomplete prototype until the customer is happy with the result. In addition the customer should offer feedback on each iteration. Agile emphasizes **test-driven development (TDD)** to reduce mistakes by writing the tests *before* writing the code, **user stories** to reach agreement and validate customer requirements, and **velocity** to measure project progress. We'll cover these topics in detail in later chapters.

Variants of Agile There are many variants of Agile software development (Fowler 2005). The one we use in this book is **Extreme Programming**, which is abbreviated **XP**, and credited to Kent Beck.

Regarding software lifetimes, the Agile software lifecycle is so quick that new versions are available every week or two—with some even releasing every day—so they are not even special events as in the Plan-and-Document models. The assumption is one of basically continuous improvement over its lifetime.

We mentioned in the prior section that newcomers can find Plan-and-Document processes tedious, but this is not the case for Agile. This perspective is captured by a software engineering instructor's early review of Agile:

> *Remember when programming was fun? Is this how you got interested in computers in the first place and later in computer science? Is this why many of our majors enter the discipline—because they like to program computers? Well, there may be promising and respectable software development methodologies that are perfectly suited to these kinds of folks. ... [Agile] is fun and effective, because not only do we not bog down the process in mountains of documentation, but also because developers work face-to-face with clients throughout the development process and produce working software early on.*
>
> —Renee McCauley, "Agile Development Methods Poised to Upset Status Quo," *SIGCSE Bulletin*, 2001

	Question: A no answer suggests Agile; a yes suggests Plan and Document
1	Is specification required?
2	Are customers unavailable?
3	Is the system to be built large?
4	Is the system to be built complex (e.g., real time)?
5	Will it have a long product lifetime?
6	Are you using poor software tools?
7	Is the project team geographically distributed?
8	Is team part of a documentation-oriented culture?
9	Does the team have poor programming skills?
10	Is the system to be built subject to regulation?

Figure 1.5: Ten questions to help decide whether to use an Agile lifecycle (the answer is no) or a Plan-and-Document lifecycle (the answer is yes) (Sommerville 2010). We find it striking that when asking these questions for projects done by student teams in a class, virtually all answers point to Agile. As this book attests, open source software tools are excellent, thus available to students (question 6). Our survey of industry (see Preface) found that graduating students do indeed have good programming skills (question 9). The other eight answers are clearly no for student projects.

By de-emphasizing planning, documentation, and contractually binding specifications, the Agile Manifesto ran counter to conventional wisdom of the software engineering intelligentsia, so it was not universally welcomed with open arms (Cormick 2001):

> [The Agile Manifesto] is yet another attempt to undermine the discipline of software engineering... In the software engineering profession, there are engineers and there are hackers... It seems to me that this is nothing more than an attempt to legitimize hacker behavior... The software engineering profession will change for the better only when customers refuse to pay for software that doesn't do what they contracted for... Changing the culture from one that encourages the hacker mentality to one that is based on predictable software engineering practices will only help transform software engineering into a respected engineering discipline.
>
> —Steven Ratkin, "Manifesto Elicits Cynicism," *IEEE Computer*, 2001

One pair of critics even published the case against Agile as a 432-page book! (Stephens and Rosenberg 2003)

The software engineering research community went on to compare Plan-and-Document lifecycles to the Agile lifecycle in the field and found—to the surprise of some cynics—that Agile could indeed work well, depending on the circumstances. Figure 1.5 shows 10 questions from a popular software engineering textbook (Sommerville 2010) whose answers suggest when to use Agile and when to use Plan-and-Document methods.

Recall that the last and most recent survey in Figure 1.4 shows the disappointing results for large software projects, which do not use Agile. Figure 1.6 shows the success of small software projects—defined as costing less than $1M—that typically do use Agile. With three-fourths of these projects on time, on budget, and with full functionality, the results are in stark contrast to Figure 1.4. Success has fanned Agile's popularity, and recent surveys peg Agile as the primary development method for 60% to 80% of all programming teams in 2013 (ET Bureau 2012, Project Management Institute 2012). One paper even found Agile was used by the majority of programming teams that are geographically distributed, which is much more difficult to pull off (Estler et al. 2012).

Software Projects (Johnson 2013)

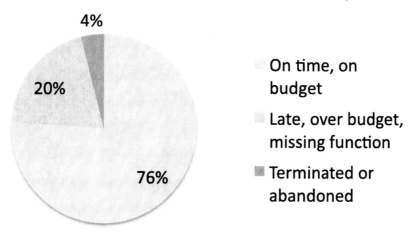

4%

20%

76%

On time, on budget

Late, over budget, missing function

Terminated or abandoned

Figure 1.6: This survey of small examples of 50,000 projects, in that they cost less than $1M in development (Johnson 2013b). These projects work tremendously better than those of Figure 1.4.

Thus, we concentrate on Agile in the six software development chapters in Part II of the book, but each chapter also gives the perspective of the Plan-and-Document methodologies on topics like requirements, testing, project management, and maintenance. This contrast allows readers to decide for themselves when each methodology is appropriate.

While we now see how to build some software successfully, not all projects are small. We next show how to design software to enable composition into services like Amazon.com.

Summary: In contrast to the Plan-and-Document lifecycles, the Agile lifecycle works with customers to continuously add features to working prototypes until the customer is satisfied, allowing customers to change what they want as the project develops. Documentation is primarily through user stories and test cases, and it does not measure progress against a predefined plan. Progress is gauged instead by recording **velocity**, which essentially is the rate that a project completes features.

Self-Check 1.3.1. *True or False: A big difference between Spiral and Agile development is building prototypes and interacting with customers during the process.*
◇ False: Both build working but incomplete prototypes that the customer helps evaluate. The difference is that customers are involved every two weeks in Agile versus up to two years in with Spiral. ∎

■ *Elaboration: Versions of Agile*

There is not just a single Agile lifecycle. We are following **Extreme Programming** (XP), which includes one- to two-week iterations, behavior driven design (see Chapter 7), test-driven development (see Chapter 8), and pair programming (see Section 10.2). Another popular version is **Scrum** (see Section 10.1), where self-organizing teams use two- to four-week iterations called *sprints*, and then regroup to plan the next sprint. A key feature is daily standup meetings to identify and overcome obstacles. While there are multiple roles in the scrum team, the norm is to rotate the roles over time. The **Kanban** approach is derived from Toyota's just-in-time manufacturing process, which in this case treats software development as a pipeline. Here the team members have fixed roles, and the goal is to balance the number of team members so that there are no bottlenecks with tasks stacking up waiting for processing. One common feature is a wall of cards that to illustrate the state of all tasks in the pipeline. There are also hybrid lifecycles that try to combine the best of two worlds. For example, **ScrumBan** uses the daily meetings and sprints of Scrum but replaces the planning phase with the more dynamic pipeline control of the wall of cards from Kanban.

■ *Elaboration: Reforming Acquisition Regulations*

Long before the ACA website, there were calls to reform software acquisition, as in this US National Academies study of the Department of Defense (DOD):

"The DOD is hampered by a culture and acquisition-related practices that favor large programs, high-level oversight, and a very deliberate, serial approach to development and testing (the waterfall model). Programs that are expected to deliver complete, nearly perfect solutions and that take years to develop are the norm in the DOD...These approaches run counter to Agile acquisition practices in which the product is the primary focus, end users are engaged early and often, the oversight of incremental product development is delegated to the lowest practical level, and the program management team has the flexibility to adjust the content of the increments in order to meet delivery schedules...Agile approaches have allowed their adopters to outstrip established industrial giants that were beset with ponderous, process-bound, industrial-age management structures. Agile approaches have succeeded because their adopters recognized the issues that contribute to risks in an IT program and changed their management structures and processes to mitigate the risks."

(National Research Council 2010)

Even President Obama belatedly recognized the difficulties of software acquisition. On November 14, 2013, he said in a speech: "...when I do some Monday morning quarterbacking on myself, one of the things that I do recognize is since I know how we purchase technology in the federal government is cumbersome, complicated and outdated ...it's part of the reason why, chronically, federal IT programs are over budget, behind schedule...since I [now] know that the federal government has not been good at this stuff in the past, two years ago as we were thinking about this...we might have done more to make sure that we were breaking the mold on how we were going to be setting this up."

1.4   Service Oriented Architecture

SOA had long suffered from lack of clarity and direction.....SOA could in fact die—not due to a lack of substance or potential, but simply due to a seemingly endless proliferation of misinformation and confusion.

—Thomas Erl, *About the SOA Manifesto*, 2010

The success of small projects in Figure 1.6 can be repeated for larger ones by using a software architecture designed to make composible services: **Service Oriented Architecture (SOA)**.

Alas, SOA was one of those terms that was ill defined, over used, and so over hyped that some thought it was just an empty marketing phrase, like **modular**. SOA actually means that components of an application act as interoperable services, and can be used independently and recombined in other applications. The contrasting implementation is considered a "software silo," which rarely has externalizable **Application Programming Interfaces** (**APIs**) to internal components.

If you mis-estimate what the customer really wants, the cost is much lower with SOA than with "siloed" software to recover from that mistake and try something else or to produce a similar-but-not-identical variant to please a subset of users.

For example, Amazon started in 1995 with siloed software for its online retailing site. According to the blog of former Amazonian Steve Yegge[5], in 2002 the CEO and founder of Amazon mandated a change to what we would today call SOA. Yegge claims that Jeff Bezos broadcast an email to all employees along the following lines:

1. *All teams will henceforth expose their data and functionality through service interfaces.*

2. *Teams must communicate with each other through these interfaces.*

3. *There will be no other form of interprocess communication allowed: no direct linking, no direct reads of another team's data store, no shared-memory model, no back-doors whatsoever. The only communication allowed is via service interface calls over the network.*

4. *It doesn't matter what technology they use. HTTP, CORBA, Pub/Sub, custom protocols—doesn't matter. Bezos doesn't care.*

5. *All service interfaces, without exception, must be designed from the ground up to be externalizable. That is to say, the team must plan and design to be able to expose the interface to developers in the outside world. No exceptions.*

6. *Anyone who doesn't do this will be fired.*

7. *Thank you; have a nice day!*

A similar software revolution happened at Facebook in 2007—three years after the company went online—when **Facebook Platform** was launched. Relying on SOA, Facebook Platform allowed third party developers to create applications that interact with core features of Facebook such as what people like, who their friends are, who is tagged in their photos, and so on. For example, the New York Times was one of the early Facebook Platform developers. Facebook users reading the New York Times online on May 24, 2007 suddenly noticed that they could see which articles their friends were reading and which articles their friends liked. As a contrasting example of a social networking site using a software silo, Google+ had no APIs when it was launched on June 28, 2011 and had just one heavyweight API three months later: following the complete stream of everything a Google+ user sees.

To make these notions more concrete, suppose we wanted to create a bookstore service first as a silo and then as a SOA. Both will contain the same three subsystems: reviews, user profiles, and buying.

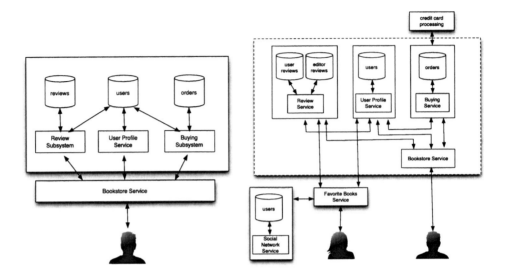

Figure 1.7: Left: Silo version of a fictitious bookstore service, with all subsystems behind a single API. Right: SOA version of a fictitious bookstore service, where all three subsystems are independent and available via APIs.

The left side of Figure 1.7 shows the silo version. The silo means subsystems can internally share access to data directly in different subsystems. For example, the reviews subsystem can get user profile info out of the users subsystem. However, all subsystems are inside a single external API ("the bookstore").

The right side of Figure 1.7 shows the SOA version of the bookstore service, where all subsystems are separate and independent. Even though all are inside the "boundary" of the bookstore's datacenter, which is shown as a dotted rectangle, the subsystems interact with each other as if they were in separate datacenters. For example, if the reviews subsystem wants information about a user, it can't just reach directly into the users database. Instead, it has to ask the users *service*, via whatever API is provided for that purpose. A similar restriction is true for buying.

The "bookstore app" is then just one particular composition of these services. Consequently, others can recombine the services with others to create new apps. For example, a "my favorite books" app might combine the users service and reviews service with a social network, so you can see what your social-network friends think about the books you have reviewed (see Figure 1.7).

The critical distinction of SOA is that no service can name or access another service's data; it can only make requests for data through an external API. If the data it wants is not available through that API, then too bad. Note that SOA does not match the traditional layered model of software, in which each higher layer is built directly from the primitives of the immediately lower layer as in siloed software. SOA implies vertical slices through many layers, and these slices are connected together to form a service. While SOA usually means a bit more work compared to building a siloed service, the payback is tremendous reusability. Another upside of SOA is that the explicit APIs make testing easier.

There are two widely accepted downsides to SOA. First, each invocation of a service involves the higher cost of wading through the deeper software stack of a network interface, so there is a performance hit to SOA. Second, while a siloed system is very likely to be completely down on a failure, software engineers using SOA must deal with the sticky case of partial failures, so SOA makes dependability planning a bit more challenging.

The huge upside of SOA is that we use successfully built small services, in part because we can use Agile to build them, and then compose them together into bigger ones.

Alas, if only President Obama had read this chapter in time to send a Bezos-style email to the ACA contractors before its launch, history might record him as a more successful president. For the future presidents among our readers: forewarned is forearmed!

Summary: Although the term was nearly lost in a sea of confusion, **Service Oriented Architecture** (**SOA**) just means an approach to software development in which all the subsystems are only available as external services, which means others can recombine them in different ways. Following the tools and guidelines in this book ensures that your apps will be a good fit to SOA.

Self-Check 1.4.1. *Another take on SOA is that it is just a common sense approach to improving programmer productivity. Which productivity mechanism does SOA best exemplify: Clarity via conciseness, Synthesis, Reuse, or Automation and Tools?*
⋄ Reuse! The purpose of making internal APIs visible is so that programmers can stand on the shoulders of others. ∎

1.5 Software as a Service

The power of SOA combined with the power of the Internet led to a special case of SOA with its own name: **Software as a Service (SaaS)**. It delivers software and data as a service over the Internet, usually via a thin program such as a browser that runs on local client devices instead as an application binary that must be installed and runs wholly on that device. Examples that many use every day include searching, social networking, and watching videos. The advantages for the customer and for the software developer are widely touted:

1. Since customers do not need to install the application, they don't have to worry whether their hardware is the right brand or fast enough, nor whether they have the correct version of the operating system.

2. The data associated with the service is generally kept with the service, so customers need not worry about backing it up, losing it due to a local hardware malfunction, or even losing the whole device, such as a phone or tablet.

3. When a group of users wants to collectively interact with the same data, SaaS is a natural vehicle.

4. When data is large and/or updated frequently, it may make more sense to centralize data and offer remote access via SaaS.

5. Only a single copy of the server software runs in a uniform, tightly-controlled hardware and operating system environment selected by the developer, which avoids the compatibility hassles of distributing binaries that must run on wide-ranging computers and

SaaS Programming Framework	Programming Language
Active Server Pages (ASP.NET)	C#, VB.NET
Django	Python
Enterprise Java Beans (EJB)	Java
JavaServer Pages (JSP)	Java
Rails	Ruby
Sinatra	Ruby
Spring	Java
Zend	PHP

Figure 1.8: Examples of SaaS programming frameworks and the programming languages they are written in.

operating systems. In addition, developers can test new versions of the application on a small fraction of the real customers temporarily without disturbing most customers. (If the SaaS client runs in a browser, there still are compatibility challenges, which we describe in Chapter 2.)

SaaS: Innovate or Die? Lest you think the perceived need to improve a successful service is just software engineering paranoia, the most popular search engine used to be AltaVista and the most popular social networking site used to be MySpace.

6. SaaS companies compete regularly on bringing out new features to help ensure that their customers do not abandon them for a competitor who offers a better service.

7. Since only developers have a copy of the software, they can upgrade the software and underlying hardware frequently as long as they don't violate the external application program interfaces (API). Moreover, developers don't need to annoy users with the seemingly endless requests for permission to upgrade their applications.

Combining the advantages to the customer and the developer together explains why SaaS is rapidly growing and why traditional software products are increasingly being transformed to offer SaaS versions. An example of the latter is Microsoft Office 365, which allows you to use the popular Word, Excel, and PowerPoint productivity programs as a remote service by paying for use rather than pre-purchasing software and installing it on your local computer. Another example is TurboTax Online, which offers the same deal for another shrink-wrap standard-bearer.

Unsurprisingly, given the popularity of SaaS, Figure 1.8 lists the many programming frameworks that claim to help. In this book, we use Ruby on Rails ("Rails"), although the ideas we cover will work with other programming frameworks as well. We chose Rails because it came from a community that had already embraced the Agile lifecycle, so the tools support Agile particularly well.

Ruby is typical of modern scripting languages in including automatic memory management and dynamic typing. By including important advances in programming languages, Ruby goes beyond languages like Perl in supporting multiple programming paradigms such as object oriented and functional programming.

Useful additional features that help productivity via reuse include *mix-ins*, which collect related behaviors and make it easy to add them to many different classes, and *metaprogramming*, which allows Ruby programs to synthesize code at runtime. Reuse is also enhanced with Ruby's support for *closures* via *blocks* and *yield*. Chapter 3 is a short description of Ruby for those who already know Java, and Chapter 4 introduces Rails.

In addition to our view of Rails being technically superior for Agile and SaaS, Ruby and Rails are widely used. For example, Ruby routinely appears among top 10 most popular programming languages. A well-known SaaS app associated with Rails is Twitter, which began as a Rails app in 2006 and grew from 20,000 tweets per day in 2007 to 200,000,000 in 2011, during which time other frameworks replaced various parts of it.

If you are not already familiar with Ruby or Rails, this gives you a chance to practice an important software engineering skill: use the right tool for the job, even if it means learning a new tool or new language! Indeed, an attractive feature of the Rails community is that its contributors routinely improve productivity by inventing new tools to automate tasks that were formerly done manually.

Note that frequent upgrades of SaaS—due to only having a single copy of the software— perfectly align with the Agile software lifecycle. Hence, Amazon, eBay, Facebook, Google, and other SaaS providers all rely on the Agile lifecycle, and traditional software companies like Microsoft are increasingly using Agile in their product development. The Agile process is an excellent match to the fast-changing nature of SaaS applications.

Summary: *Software as a Service (SaaS)* is attractive to both customers and providers because the universal client (the Web browser) makes it easier for customers to use the service and the single version of the software at a centralized site makes it easier for the provider to deliver and improve the service. Given the ability and desire to frequently upgrade SaaS, the Agile software development process is popular for SaaS, and so there are many frameworks to support Agile and SaaS. This book uses Ruby on Rails.

Self-Check 1.5.1. *Which of the examples of Google SaaS apps—Search, Maps, News, Gmail, Calendar, YouTube, and Documents—is the* best *match to each of the six arguments given in this section for SaaS, reproduced below.*

◇ While you can argue the mappings, below is our answer. (Note that we cheated and put some apps in multiple categories)

1. No user installation: Documents

2. Can't lose data: Gmail, Calendar.

3. Users cooperating: Documents.

4. Large/changing datasets: Search, Maps, News, and YouTube.

5. Software centralized in single environment: Search.

6. No field upgrades when improve app: Documents.

∎

Self-Check 1.5.2. *True or False: If you are using the Agile development process to develop SaaS apps, you could use Python and Django or languages based on the Microsoft's .NET framework and ASP.NET instead of Ruby and Rails.*

◇ True. Programming frameworks for Agile and SaaS include Django and ASP.NET. ∎

Given the case for SaaS and the understanding that it relies on a Service Oriented Architecture, we are ready to see the underlying hardware that makes SaaS possible.

1.6   Cloud Computing

John McCarthy
(1927–2011) received the
Turing Award in 1971 and
was the inventor of Lisp and
a pioneer of timesharing
large computers. Clusters of
commodity hardware and
the spread of fast
networking have helped
make his vision of
timeshared "utility
computing" a reality.

The gold standard set
by the US public phone
system is 99.999%
availability ("five nines"), or
about 5 minutes of downtime
per year. Amazon.com aims
for four nines.

If computers of the kind I have advocated become the computers of the future, then computing may someday be organized as a public utility just as the telephone system is a public utility … The computer utility could become the basis of a new and important industry.

—John McCarthy, at MIT centennial celebration in 1961

SaaS places three demands on our information technology (IT) infrastructure:

1. Communication, to allow any customer to interact with the service.

2. Scalability, in that the central facility running the service must deal with the fluctuations in demand during the day and during popular times of the year for that service as well as a way for new services to add users rapidly.

3. Availability, in that both the service and the communication vehicle must be continuously available: every day, 24 hours a day ("24×7").

The Internet and broadband to the home easily resolve the communication demand of SaaS. Although some early web services were deployed on expensive large-scale computers—in part because such computers were more reliable and in part because it was easier to operate a few large computers—a contrarian approach soon overtook the industry. Collections of commodity small-scale computers connected by commodity Ethernet switches, which became known as **clusters**, offered several advantages over the "big iron" hardware approach:

- Because of their reliance on Ethernet switches to interconnect, clusters are much more scalable than conventional servers. Early clusters offered 1000 computers, and today's datacenters contain 100,000 or more.

- Careful selection of the type of hardware to place in the datacenter and careful control of software state made it possible for a very small number of operators to successfully run thousands of servers. In particular, some datacenters rely on **virtual machines** to simplify operation. A virtual machine monitor is software that imitates a real computer so successfully that you can even run an operating system correctly on top of the virtual machine abstraction that it provides (Popek and Goldberg 1974). The goal is to imitate with low overhead, and one popular use is to simplify software distribution within a cluster.

- Two senior architects at Google showed that the cost of the equivalent amount of processors, memory, and storage is much less for clusters than for "big iron," perhaps by a factor of 20 (Barroso and Hoelzle 2009).

- Although the cluster components are less reliable than conventional servers and storage systems, the cluster software infrastructure makes the whole system dependable via extensive use of redundancy in both hardware and software. The low hardware cost makes the redundancy at the software level affordable. Modern service providers also use multiple datacenters that are distributed geographically so that a natural disaster cannot knock a service offline.

As Internet datacenters grew, some service providers realized that their per capita costs were substantially below what it cost others to run their own smaller datacenters, in large part due to economies of scale when purchasing and operating 100,000 computers at a time. They also benefit from higher utilization given that many companies could share these giant datacenters, which (Barroso and Hoelzle 2009) call **Warehouse Scale Computers**, whereas smaller datacenters often run at only 10% to 20% utilization. Thus, these companies realized they could profit from making their datacenter hardware available on a pay-as-you-go basis.

The result is called **public cloud services** or **utility computing**, which offers computing, storage, and communication at pennies per hour (Armbrust et al. 2010). Moreover, there is no additional cost for scale: Using 1000 computers for 1 hour costs no more than using 1 computer for 1000 hours. Leading examples of "infinitely scalable" pay-as-you-go computing are Amazon Web Services, Google AppEngine, and Microsoft Azure. The public cloud means that today anyone with a credit card and a good idea can start a SaaS company that can grow to millions of customers without first having to build and operate a datacenter.

Today, we call this long held dream of computing as a utility **Cloud Computing**. We believe that Cloud Computing and SaaS are transforming the computer industry, with the full impact of this revolution taking the rest of this decade to determine. Indeed, this revolution is one reason we decided to write this book, as we believe engineering SaaS for Cloud Computing is radically different from engineering shrink-wrap software for PCs and servers.

Rapid growth of FarmVille The prior record for number of users of a social networking game was 5 million. FarmVille had 1 million players within 4 days after it was announced, 10 million after 2 months, and 28 million daily players and 75 million monthly players after 9 months. Fortunately, FarmVille used the Elastic Compute Cloud (EC2) from Amazon Web Services, and kept up with its popularity by simply paying to use larger clusters.

Summary

- The Internet supplies the communication for SaaS.

- **Cloud Computing** provides the scalable and dependable hardware computation and storage for SaaS.

- Cloud computing consists of **clusters** of commodity servers that are connected by local area network switches, with a software layer providing sufficient redundancy to make this cost-effective hardware dependable.

- These large clusters or **Warehouse Scale Computers** offer economies of scale.

- Taking advantage of economies of scale, some Cloud Computing providers offer this hardware infrastructure as low-cost **utility computing** that anyone can use on a pay-as-you-go basis, acquiring resources immediately as your customer demand grows and releasing them immediately when it drops.

Self-Check 1.6.1. *True or False: Internal datacenters could get the same cost savings as Warehouse Scale Computers (WSCs) if they embraced SOA and purchased the same type of hardware.*

◇ False. While imitating best practices of WSC could lower costs, the major cost advantage of WSCs comes from the economies of scale, which today means 100,000 servers, thereby dwarfing most internal datacenters. ∎

1.7 Beautiful vs. Legacy Code

*To me programming is more than an important practical art. It is also a gigantic
undertaking in the foundations of knowledge.*

—Grace Murray Hopper

Unlike hardware, software is expected to grow and evolve over time. Whereas hardware designs must be declared finished before they can be manufactured and shipped, initial software designs can easily be shipped and later upgraded over time. Basically, the cost of upgrade in the field is astronomical for hardware and affordable for software.

Hence, software can achieve a high-tech version of immortality, potentially getting better over time while generations of computer hardware decay into obsolescence. The drivers of *software evolution* are not only fixing faults, but also adding new features that customers request, adjusting to changing business requirements, improving performance, and adapting to a changed environment. Software customers expect to get notices about and install improved versions of the software over the lifetime that they use it, perhaps even submitting bug reports to help developers fix their code. They may even have to pay an annual maintenance fee for this privilege!

Just as novelists fondly hope that their brainchild will be read long enough to be labeled a classic—which for books is 100 years!—software engineers should hope their creations would also be long lasting. Of course, software has the advantage over books of being able to be improved over time. In fact, a long software life often means that others maintain and enhance it, letting the creators of original code off the hook.

This brings us to a few terms we'll use throughout the book. The term *legacy code* refers to software that, despite its old age, continues to be used because it meets customers' needs. Sixty percent of software maintenance costs are for adding new functionality to legacy software, vs. only 17% for fixing bugs, so legacy software is successful software.

The term "legacy" has a negative connotation, however, in that it indicates that the code is difficult to evolve because of inelegance of its design or use of antiquated technology. To contrast to legacy code, we use the term *beautiful code* to indicate long-lasting code that is easy to evolve. The worst case is not legacy code, however, but *unexpectedly short-lived code* that is soon discarded because it doesn't meet customers' needs. We'll highlight examples that lead to beautiful code with the Mona Lisa icon. Similarly, we'll highlight text that deals with legacy code using an abacus icon, which is certainly a long-lasting but little changed calculating device. In the following chapters, we show examples of both beautiful code and legacy code that we hope will inspire you to make your designs simpler to evolve.

Surprisingly, despite the widely accepted importance of enhancing legacy software, this topic is traditionally ignored in college courses and textbooks. We feature such software in this book for three reasons. First, you can reduce the effort to build a program by finding existing code that you can reuse. One supplier is open source software. Second, it's advantageous to learn how to build code that makes it easier for successors to enhance, as that increases software's chances of a long life. Finally, unlike Plan-and-Document, in Agile you revise code continuously to improve the design and to add functionality starting with the second iteration. Thus, the skills you practice in Agile are exactly the ones you need to evolve legacy code—no matter how it was created—and the dual use of Agile techniques makes it much easier for us to cover legacy code within a single book.

Summary: Successful software can live decades and is expected to evolve and improve, unlike computer hardware that is finalized at time of manufacture and can be considered obsolete within just a few years. One goal of this book is to teach you how to increase the chances of producing beautiful code so that your software lives a long and useful life.

We next define software quality and see how to test for it to increase our chances of writing beautiful code.

1.8 Software Quality Assurance: Testing

And the users exclaimed with a laugh and a taunt:
"It's just what we asked for, but not what we want."

—Anonymous

We start this topic with a definition of quality. A standard definition of **quality** for any product is "fitness for use," which must provide business value for both the customer and the manufacturer (Juran and Gryna 1998). For software, quality means both satisfying the customer's needs—easy to use, gets correct answers, does not crash, and so on—*and* being easy for the developer to debug and enhance. **Quality Assurance** (**QA**) also comes from manufacturing, and refers to processes and standards that lead to manufacture of high-quality products and to the introduction of manufacturing processes that improve quality. Software QA, then, means both ensuring that products under development have high quality and creating processes and standards in an organization that lead to high quality software. As we shall see, some Plan-and-Document software processes even use a separate QA team that tests software quality (Section 8.9).

Determining software quality involves two terms that are commonly interchanged but have subtle distinctions (Boehm 1979):

- **Verification**: Did you build the thing *right*? (Did you meet the specification?)

- **Validation**: Did you build the right *thing*? (Is this what the customer wants? That is, is the specification correct?)

Software prototypes that are the lifeblood of Agile typically help with validation rather than verification, since customers often change their minds on what they want once they begin to see the product work.

The main approach to verification and validation is **testing**; the motivation for testing is that the earlier developers find mistakes, the cheaper it is to repair them. Given the vast number of different combinations of inputs, testing cannot be exhaustive. One way to reduce the space is to perform different tests at different phases of software development. Starting bottom up, **unit testing** makes sure that a single procedure or method does what was expected. The next level up is **module testing**, which tests across individual units. For example, unit testing works within a single class whereas module testing works across classes. Above this level is **integration testing**, which ensures that the interfaces between the units have consistent assumptions and communicate correctly. This level does not test the functionality of the units. At the top level is **system testing** or **acceptance testing**, which tests to see if the integrated program meets its specifications. In Chapter 8, we'll describe an alternative to testing, called **formal methods**.

Infeasibility of exhaustive testing
Suppose it took just 1 nanosecond to test a program and it had just one 64-bit input that we wanted to test exhaustively. (Obviously, most programs take longer to run and have more inputs.) Just this simple case would take 2^{64} nanoseconds, or 500 years!

As mentioned briefly in Section 1.3, the approach to testing for the XP version of Agile is to write the tests *before* you write the code. You then write the minimum code you need to pass the test, which ensures that your code is always tested and reduces the chances of writing code that will be later discarded. XP splits this test-first philosophy into two parts, depending on the level of the testing. For system, acceptance, and integration tests, XP uses **Behavior-Driven Design** (**BDD**), which is the topic of Chapter 7. For unit and module tests, XP uses **Test-Driven Development** (**TDD**), which is the topic of Chapter 8.

Summary: Testing reduces the risks of errors in designs.

- In its many forms, testing helps **verify** that software meets the specification and **validates** that the design does what the customer wants.

- Attacking the infeasibility of exhaustive testing, we divide in order to conquer by focusing on **unit testing**, **module testing**, **integration testing**, and full **system testing** or **acceptance testing**. Each higher-level test delegates more detailed testing to lower levels.

- Agile attacks testing by writing the tests before writing the code, using either **Behavior Driven Design** or **Test Driven Design**, depending on the level of the test.

Self-Check 1.8.1. *While all of the following help with verification, which form of testing is most likely to help with validation: Unit, Module, Integration, or Acceptance?*

◇ Validation is concerned with doing what the customer really wants versus whether code met the specification, so acceptance testing is most likely to point out the difference between doing the thing right and doing the right thing. ■

■ Elaboration: Testing: Plan-and-Document vs. Agile lifecycles

For the Waterfall development process, testing happens after each phase is complete and in a final verification phase that includes acceptance tests. For Spiral, it happens on each iteration, which can last one or two years. Assurance for the XP version of Agile comes from test-driven development, in that the tests are written *before* the code when coding from scratch. When enhancing existing code, test-driven design means writing the tests before writing the enhancements. The amount of testing depends on whether you are enhancing beautiful code or legacy code, with the latter needing a lot more.

After this review of quality assurance, let's see how to make developers productive.

1.9   Productivity: Conciseness, Synthesis, Reuse, and Tools

Most software today is very much like an Egyptian pyramid with millions of bricks piled on top of each other, with no structural integrity, but just done by brute force and thousands of slaves.

—Alan Kay, *ACM Queue*, 2005

Moore's Law meant hardware resources have doubled every 18 months for nearly 50 years. These faster computers with much larger memories could run much larger programs.

To build bigger applications that could take advantage of the more powerful computers, software engineers needed to improve their productivity.

Engineers developed four fundamental mechanisms to improve their productivity:

1. Clarity via conciseness

2. Synthesis

3. Reuse

4. Automation via Tools

One of the driving assumptions of improving productivity of programmers is that if programs are easier to understand, then they will have fewer bugs and to be easier to evolve. A closely related corollary is that if the program is smaller, it's generally easier to understand. We capture this notion with our motto of "clarity via conciseness."

Programming languages do this two ways. The first is simply offering a syntax that lets programmers express ideas naturally and in fewer characters. For example, below are two ways to express a simple assertion:

```
assert_greater_than_or_equal_to(a, 7)
a.should be >= 7
```

Unquestionably, the second version (which happens to be legal Ruby) is shorter and easier to read and understand, and will likely be easier to maintain. It's easy to imagine momentary confusion about the order of arguments in the first version in addition to the higher cognitive load of reading twice as many characters (see Chapter 3).

The other way to improve clarity is to raise the level of abstraction. That initially meant the invention of higher-level programming languages such as Fortran and COBOL. This step raised the engineering of software from assembly language for a particular computer to higher-level languages that could target multiple computers simply by changing the compiler.

As computer hardware performance continued to increase, more programmers were willing to delegate tasks to the compiler and runtime system that they formerly performed themselves. For example, Java and similar languages took over memory management from the earlier C and C++ languages. Scripting languages like Python and Ruby have raised the level of abstraction even higher. Examples are ***reflection***, which allows programs to observe themselves, and ***metaprogramming***, which allows programs to modify their own structure and behavior at runtime. To highlight examples that improve productivity via conciseness, we will use this "Concise" icon.

The second productivity mechanism is synthesis; that is, the implementation is generated rather than created manually. Logic synthesis for hardware engineers meant that they could describe hardware as Boolean functions and receive highly optimized transistors that implemented those functions. The classic software synthesis example is ***Bit blit***. This graphics primitive combines two bitmaps under control of a mask. The straightforward approach would include a conditional statement in the innermost loop to chose the type of mask, but it was slow. The solution was to write a program that could synthesize the appropriate special-purpose code *without* the conditional statement in the loop. We'll highlight examples that improve productivity by generating code with this "CodeGen" gears icon.

The third productivity mechanism is to reuse portions from past designs rather than write everything from scratch. As it is easier to make small changes in software than in hardware,

John Backus (1924–2007) received the 1977 Turing Award in part for "profound, influential, and lasting contributions to the design of practical high-level programming systems, notably through his work on Fortran," which was the first widely used high-level language.

software is even more likely than hardware to reuse a component that is almost but not quite a correct fit. We highlight examples that improve productivity via reuse with this "Reuse" recycling icon.

Procedures and functions were invented in the earliest days of software so that different parts of the program could reuse the same code with different parameter values. Standardized libraries for input/output and for mathematical functions soon followed, so that programmers could reuse code developed by others.

Procedures in libraries let you reuse implementations of individual tasks. But more commonly, programmers want to reuse and manage **collections** of tasks. The next step in software reuse was therefore **object-oriented programming**, where you could reuse the same tasks with different objects via the use of inheritance in languages like C++ and Java.

While inheritance supported reuse of implementations, another opportunity for reuse is a general strategy for doing something even if the implementation varies. **Design patterns**, inspired by work in civil architecture (Alexander et al. 1977), arose to address this need. Language support for reuse of design patterns includes **dynamic typing**, which facilitates composition of abstractions, and **mix-ins**, which offer ways to collect functionality from multiple methods without some of the pathologies of multiple inheritance found in some object oriented programming. Python and Ruby are examples of languages with features that help with reuse of design patterns.

Note that reuse does *not* mean copying and pasting code so that you have very similar code in many places. The problem with copying and pasting code is that you may not change all the copies when fixing a bug or adding a feature. Here is a software engineering guideline that guards against repetition:

> *Every piece of knowledge must have a single, unambiguous, authoritative representation within a system.*

> —Andy Hunt and Dave Thomas, 1999

This guideline has been captured in the motto and acronym: **Don't Repeat Yourself (DRY)**. We'll use a towel as the "DRY" icon to show examples of DRY in the following chapters.

A core value of computer engineering is finding ways to replace tedious manual tasks with tools to save time, improve accuracy, or both. Obvious Computer Aided Design (CAD) tools for software development are compilers and interpreters that raise the level of abstraction and generate code as mentioned above, but there are also more subtle productivity tools like Makefiles and version control systems (see Section 10.4) that automate tedious tasks. We highlight tool examples with the hammer icon.

Learning new tools
Proverbs 14:4 in the King James Bible discusses improving productivity by taking the time to learn and use tools: *Where there are no oxen, the manger is clean; but abundant crops come by the strength of oxen.*

The tradeoff is always the time it takes to learn a new tool versus the time saved in applying it. Other concerns are the dependability of the tool, the quality of the user experience, and how to decide which one to use if there are many choices. Nevertheless, one of the software engineering tenets of faith is that a new tool can make our lives better.

Your authors embrace the value of automation and tools. That is why we show you several tools in this book to make you more productive. The good news is that any tool we show you will have been vetted to ensure its dependability and that time to learn will be paid back many times over in reduced development time and in the improved quality of the final result. For example, Chapter 7 shows how **Cucumber** automates turning user stories into integration tests and it also demonstrates how **Pivotal Tracker** automatically measures **Velocity**, which is a measure of the rate of adding features to an application. Chapter 8 introduces **RSpec** that automates the unit testing process. The bad news is that you'll need to learn several new tools. However, we think the ability to quickly learn and apply new tools is a requirement for success in engineering software, so it's a good skill to cultivate.

Thus, our fourth productivity enhancer is automation via tools. We highlight examples that use automation with the robot icon, although they are often also associated with tools.

Summary: Moore's Law inspired software engineers to improve their productivity by:

- Coveting conciseness, in using compact syntax and by raising the level of design by using higher-level languages. Recent advances include **reflection** that allows programs to observe themselves and **metaprogramming** that allows programs to modify their own structure and behavior at runtime.

- Synthesizing implementations.

- Reusing designs by following the principle of **Don't Repeat Yourself (DRY)** and by relying upon innovations that help reuse, such as procedures, libraries, object-oriented programming, and design patterns.

- Using (and inventing) CAD tools to automate tedious tasks.

Self-Check 1.9.1. *Which mechanism is the weakest argument for productivity benefits of compilers for high-level programming languages: Clarity via conciseness, Synthesis, Reuse, or Automation and Tools?*

◇ Compilers make high-level programming languages practical, enabling programmers to improve productivity via writing the more concise code in a HLL. Compilers do synthesize lower-level code based on the HLL input. Compilers are definitely tools. While you can argue that HLL makes reuse easier, reuse is the weakest of the four for explaining the benefits of compilers. ∎

> ∎ *Elaboration: Productivity: Plan-and-Document vs. Agile lifecycles*
>
> Productivity is measured in the engineer-hours to implement a new function. The difference is the cycles are much longer in Waterfall and Spiral vs. Agile—on the order of 6 to 24 months vs. 1/2 month—so much more work is done between releases that the customer sees, and hence the chances are greater that more work will ultimately be rejected by the customer.

1.10 Guided Tour of the Book

I hear and I forget. I see and I remember. I do and I understand.

—Confucius

With this introduction behind us, we can now explain what follows and what paths you might want to take. To do and understand, as Confucius advises, begin by reading Appendix A. It explains how to obtain and use the "bookware," which is our name for the software associated with the book.

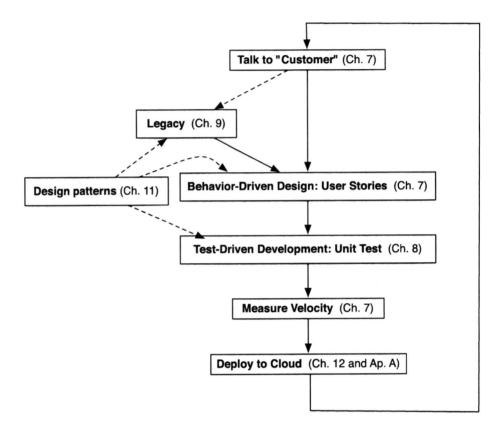

Figure 1.9: An iteration of the Agile software lifecycle and its relationship to the chapters in this book. The dashed arrows indicate a more tangential relationship between the steps of an iteration, while the solid arrows indicate the typical flow. As mentioned earlier, the Agile process applies equally well to existing legacy applications and new applications, although the customer may play a smaller role with legacy apps.

The rest of the book is divided into two parts. Part I explains Software as a Service, and Part II explains modern software development, with a heavy emphasis on Agile.

Chapter 2 starts Part I with an explanation of the architecture of a SaaS application, using an altitude analogy of going from the 100,000-foot view to the 500-foot view. During the descent you'll learn the definition of many acronyms that you may have already heard—APIs, CSS, IP, REST, TCP, URLs, URIs, and XML—as well as some widely used buzzwords: cookies, markup languages, port numbers, and three-tier architectures. More importantly, it demonstrates the importance of design patterns, particularly Model-View-Controller that is at the heart of Rails.

Rather than just tell you how to build long lasting software and watch you forget, we believe you must do to understand. It is much easier to try good guidelines if the tools encourage it, and we believe today the best SaaS tools support the Rails framework, which is written in Ruby. Thus, Chapter 3 introduces Ruby. The Ruby introduction is short because it assumes you already know another object-oriented programming language well, in this case Java. As mentioned above, we believe successful software engineers will need to routinely learn new languages and tools over their careers, so learning Ruby and Rails is good practice.

Chapter 4 next introduces the basics of Rails and the more advanced features of Rails in Chapter 5. We split the material into two chapters for readers who want to get started writing an app as soon as they can, which just requires Chapter 4. While the material in Chapter 5 is more challenging to learn and understand, your application can be DRYer and more concise if you use concepts like partials, validations, lifecycle callbacks, filters, associations, and foreign keys. Readers already familiar with Ruby and Rails should skip these chapters.

Building on the familiarity with Ruby and Rails by this point in the book, Chapter 6 introduces the programming language JavaScript, its productive framework jQuery, and the testing tool Jasmine. Just as the Rails framework amplifies the power and productivity of the Ruby language for creating the server side of SaaS apps, the jQuery framework amplifies the power and productivity of JavaScript for enhancing its client side. And just as RSpec makes it possible to write powerful automated tests to increase our confidence in our Ruby and Rails code, Jasmine makes it possible to write similar tests to increase our confidence in our JavaScript code.

Given this background, the next six chapters of Part II illustrate important software engineering principles using Rails tools to build and deploy a SaaS app. Figure 1.9 shows one iteration of the Agile lifecycle, which we use as a framework on which to hang the next chapters of the book.

Chapter 7 discusses how to talk to the customer. **Behavior-Driven Design (BDD)** advocates writing acceptance tests that customers without a programming background can understand, called **user stories**, and Chapter 7 shows how to write them so that they can be turned into integration tests as well. It introduces the **Cucumber** tool to help automate this task. This testing tool can be used with any language and framework, not just Rails. As SaaS apps are often user facing, the chapter also covers how to prototype a useful user interface using "Lo-Fi" prototyping. It also explains the term **Velocity** and how to use it to measure progress in the rate that you deliver features, and introduces the SaaS-based tool **Pivotal Tracker** to track and calculate such measurements.

Chapter 8 covers **Test-Driven Development (TDD)**. The chapter demonstrates how to write good, testable code and introduces the **RSpec** testing tool for writing unit tests, the **Autotest** tool for automating test running, and the **SimpleCov** tool to measure test coverage.

Chapter 9 describes how to deal with existing code, including how to enhance legacy code. Helpfully, it shows how to use BDD and TDD to both understand and refactor code and how to use the Cucumber and RSpec tools to make this task easier.

Chapter 10 gives advice on how to organize and work as part of an effective team using the **Scrum** principles mentioned above. It also describes how the version control system **Git** and the corresponding service **GitHub** can let team members work on different features without interfering with each other or causing chaos in the release process.

To help you practice Don't Repeat Yourself, Chapter 11 introduces design patterns, which are proven structural solutions to common problems in designing how classes work together, and shows how to exploit Ruby's language features to adopt and reuse the patterns. The chapter also offers guidelines on how to write good classes. It introduces just enough **UML** (**Unified Modeling Language**) notation to help you notate design patterns and to help you make diagrams that show how the classes should work.

Note that Chapter 11 is about software architecture whereas prior chapters in Part II are about the Agile development process. We believe in a college course setting that this order will let you start an Agile iteration sooner, and we think the more iterations you do, the better you will understand the Agile lifecycle. However, as Figure 1.9 suggests, knowing design patterns will be useful when writing or refactoring code, since it is fundamental to the BDD/TDD process.

Chapter 12 offers practical advice on how to first deploy and then improve performance and scalability in the cloud, and briefly introduces some reliability and security techniques that are uniquely relevant to deploying SaaS.

We conclude with an Afterword that reflects on the material in the book and projects what might be next.

1.11   How *NOT* to Read this Book

Don't skip the screencasts. The temptation is to skip sidebars, elaborations, and screencasts to just skim the text until you find what you want to answer your question.

While elaborations are typically for experienced readers who want to know more about what is going on behind the curtain, and sidebars are just short asides that we think you'll enjoy, screencasts are *critical* to learning this material. While we wouldn't say you could skip the text and just watch the screencasts, we would say that they are some of the most important parts of the book. They allow us to express a lot of concepts, show how they interact, and demonstrate how you can do the same tasks yourself. What would take many pages and be difficult to describe can come alive in a two to five minute video. Screencasts allow us to follow the advice of Confucius: "I see and I remember." So please watch them!

Learn by doing. Have your computer open with the Ruby interpreter ready so that you can try the examples in the screencasts and the text. We even make it easy to copy-and-paste the code using the service Pastebin[7], (If you're reading the ebook, the link accompanying each code example will take you to that code example on Pastebin.) This practice follows the "I do and I understand" observation of Confucius. Specific opportunities to learn by doing are highlighted by a bicycle icon.

There are topics that you will need to study to learn, especially in our buzzword-intensive ecosystem of Agile + Ruby + Rails + SaaS + Cloud Computing. Indeed, Figure 13.2 in the Afterword lists nearly 120 new terms introduced in just the first three chapters. To help you identify important terms, text formatted *like this* refers to terms with corresponding Wikipedia entries. (In the ebook, such terms are links to Wikipedia itself.) We also use icons to remind you of the common themes throughout the book, which Figure 1.10 summarizes as a single handy place to look them up.

Depending on your background, we suspect you'll need to read some chapters more than once before you get the hang of it. To help you focus on the key points, each chapter starts with a 1-page *Concepts* summary, which lists the big concepts of each chapter, and each chapter ends with *Fallacies and Pitfalls*, which explains common misconceptions or problems that are easy to experience if you're not vigilant. Each section concludes with a *summary* of the key concepts in that section and *self-check questions* with answers. *Projects* at the end of each chapter are more open-ended than the self-check questions. To give readers a perspective about who came up with these big ideas that they are learning and that information technology relies upon, we use sidebars to introduce 20 Turing Award winners. (As there is no Nobel Prize in IT, our highest honor is known as the "Nobel Prize of Computing." Or better yet, we should call the Nobel Prize the "Turing Award of Physics.")

We deliberately chose to keep the book concise, since different readers will want additional detail in different areas. Links are provided to the Ruby and Rails online documentation for built-in classes or methods, to definitions of important concepts you may be unfamiliar

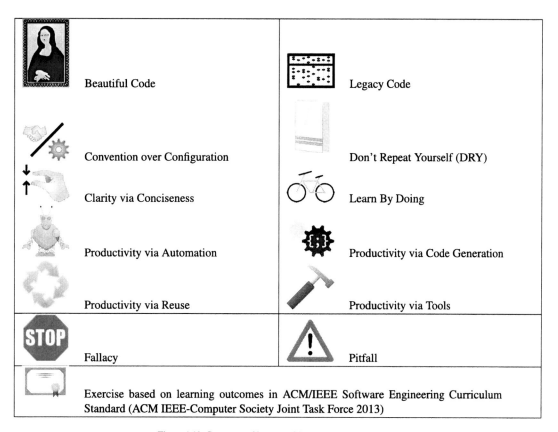

Figure 1.10: Summary of icons used in the book.

with, and to the Web in general for further reading related to the material. If you're using the Kindle edition, the links should be live if you're connected to the Internet; in the print version, the link URIs appear at the end of each chapter.

1.12 Fallacies and Pitfalls

> *Lord, give us the wisdom to utter words that are gentle and tender, for tomorrow we may have to eat them.*
>
> —Sen. Morris Udall

As mentioned above, this section near the end of a chapter explains ideas of a chapter from another perspective, and gives readers a chance to learn from the mistakes of others. *Fallacies* are statements that seem plausible (or are actually widely held views) based on the ideas in the chapter, but they are not true. *Pitfalls*, on the other hand, are common dangers associated with the topics in the chapter that are difficult to avoid even when you are warned.

 Fallacy: **The Agile lifecycle is best for all software development.**

Agile is a nice match to many types of software, particularly SaaS, which is why we use it in this book. However, Agile is *not* best for everything. Agile may be ineffective for safety-critical apps, for example.

Our experience is that once you learn the classic steps of software development and have a positive experience in using them via Agile, you will use these important software engineering principles in other projects no matter which methodology is used. Each chapter in Part II concludes with contrasting Plan-and-Document perspective to help you understand these principles and to help you use other lifecycles should the need arise

Nor will Agile be the last software lifecycle you will ever see. We believe that new development methodologies develop and become popular in response to new opportunities, so expect to learn new methodologies and frameworks in your future.

 Pitfall: **Ignoring the cost of software design.**

Since there is no cost to manufacture software, the temptation is to believe there is almost no cost to changing it so that it can be remanufactured the way the customer wants. However, this perspective ignores the cost of design and test, which can be a substantial part of the overall costs for software projects. Zero manufacturing cost is also one rationalization used to justify pirating copies of software and other electronic data, since pirates apparently believe no one should pay for the cost of development, just for manufacturing.

1.13 Concluding Remarks: Engineering Software is More Than Programming

> *But if Extreme Programming is just a new selection of old practices, what's so extreme about it? Kent's answer is that it takes obvious, common sense principles and practices to extreme levels. For example:*
> *— If short iterations are good, make them as short as possible—hours or minutes or*

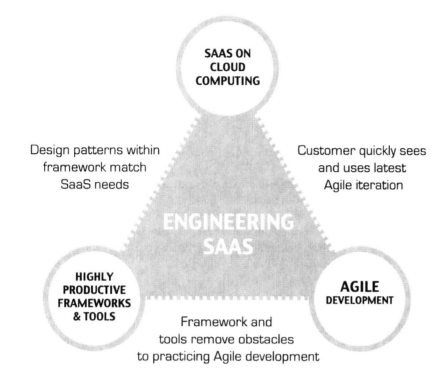

Figure 1.11: The Virtuous Triangle of Engineering SaaS is formed from the three software engineering crown jewels of (1) SaaS on Cloud Computing, (2) Agile Development, and (3) Highly Productive Framework and Tools.

seconds rather than days or weeks or years.
— If simplicity is good, always do the simplest thing that could possibly work.
— If testing is good, test all the time. Write the test code before you write the code to test.
— If code reviews are good, review code continuously, by programming in pairs, two programmers to a computer, taking turns looking over each other's shoulders.

—Michael Swaine, interview with Kent Beck, (Swaine 2001)

This single quote gives a good deal of the rationale behind the extreme programming (XP) version of Agile that we cover in this book. We keep iterations short, so that the customer sees the next version of the incomplete but working prototype every week or two. You write the tests *before* you write the code, and then you write the least amount of code it takes to make it pass the test. Pair programming means the code is under continuous review, rather than just on special occasions. Agile has gone from software methodology heresy to the dominant form of programming in just a dozen years, and when combined with service oriented architecture, allows complex services to be built reliably.

While there is no inherent dependency among SaaS, Agile, and highly productive frameworks like Rails, Figure 1.11 suggests there is a synergistic relationship among them. Agile development means continuous progress while working closely with the customer, and SaaS on Cloud Computing enables the customer to use the latest version immediately, thereby closing the feedback loop (see Chapters 7 and Chapter 12). SaaS on Cloud Computing matches the Model–View–Controller design pattern (see Chapter 11), which Highly-Productive SaaS

Frameworks expose (see Chapters 2, 4, and 5). Highly Productive Frameworks and Tools designed to support Agile development remove obstacles to practicing Agile (see Chapters 7, 8, and 10). We believe these three "crown jewels" form a "virtuous triangle" that leads to on-time and on-budget engineering of beautiful Software as a Service, and they form the foundation of this book.

This virtuous triangle also helps explain the innovative nature of the Rails community, where new important tools are frequently developed that further improve productivity, simply because it's so easy to do. We fully expect that future editions of this book will include tools not yet invented that are so helpful that we can't imagine how we got our work done without them!

As teachers, since many students find the Plan-and-Document methods tedious, we are pleased that the answers to the 10 questions in Figure 1.5 strongly recommend using Agile for student team projects. Nevertheless, we believe it is worthwhile for readers to be familiar with the Plan-and-Document methodology, as there are some tasks where it may be a better match, some customers require it, and it helps explain parts of the Agile methodology. Thus, we include sections near the end of all chapters in Part II that offer the Plan-and-Document perspective.

As researchers, we are convinced that software of the future will increasingly be built and rely on services in the Cloud, and thus Agile methodology will continue to increase in popularity in part given the strong synergy between them. Hence, we are at a happy point in technology where the future of software development is more fun both to learn and to teach. Highly productive frameworks like Rails let you understand this valuable technology by *doing* in a remarkably short time. The main reason we wrote this book is to help more people become aware of and take advantage of this extraordinary opportunity.

We believe if you learn the contents of this book and use the "bookware" that comes with it, you can build your own (simplified) version of a popular software service like FarmVille or Twitter while learning and following sound software engineering practices. While being able to imitate currently successful services and deploy them in the cloud in a few months is impressive, we are even more excited to see what *you* will invent given this new skill set. We look forward to your beautiful code becoming long-lasting and to becoming some of its passionate fans!

1.14 To Learn More

ACM IEEE-Computer Society Joint Task Force. Computer science curricula 2013, Ironman Draft (version 1.0). Technical report, February 2013. URL http://ai.stanford.edu/users/sahami/CS2013/.

C. Alexander, S. Ishikawa, and M. Silverstein. *A Pattern Language: Towns, Buildings, Construction (Cess Center for Environmental)*. Oxford University Press, 1977. ISBN 0195019199.

M. Armbrust, A. Fox, R. Griffith, A. D. Joseph, R. Katz, A. Konwinski, G. Lee, D. Patterson, A. Rabkin, I. Stoica, and M. Zaharia. A view of cloud computing. *Communications of the ACM (CACM)*, 53(4):50–58, Apr. 2010.

L. A. Barroso and U. Hoelzle. *The Datacenter as a Computer: An Introduction to the Design of Warehouse-Scale Machines (Synthesis Lectures on Computer Architecture)*. Morgan and

Claypool Publishers, 2009. ISBN 159829556X. URL `http://www.morganclaypool.com/doi/pdf/10.2200/S00193ED1V01Y200905CAC006`.

S. Begley. As Obamacare tech woes mounted, contractor payments soared. *Reuters*, October 17, 2013. URL `http://www.nbcnews.com/politics/politics-news/stress-tests-show-healthcare-gov-was-overloaded-v21337298`.

J. Bidgood. Massachusetts appoints official and hires firm to fix exchange problems. *New York Times*, February 7, 2014. URL `http://www.nytimes.com/news/affordable-care-act/`.

B. W. Boehm. Software engineering: R & D trends and defense needs. In P. Wegner, editor, *Research Directions in Software Technology*, Cambridge, MA, 1979. MIT Press.

B. W. Boehm. A spiral model of software development and enhancement. In *ACM SIGSOFT Software Engineering Notes*, 1986.

E. Braude. *Software Engineering: An Object-Oriented Perspective*. John Wiley and Sons, 2001. ISBN 0471692085.

R. Charettte. Why software fails. *IEEE Spectrum*, 42(9):42–49, September 2005.

L. Chung. Too big to fire: How government contractors on HealthCare.gov maximize profits. *FMS Software Development Team Blog*, December 7, 2013. URL `http://blog.fmsinc.com/too-big-to-fire-healthcare-gov-government-contractors`.

M. Cormick. Programming extremism. *Communications of the ACM*, 44(6):109–110, June 2001.

H.-C. Estler, M. Nordio, C. A. Furia, B. Meyer, and J. Schneider. Agile vs. structured distributed software development: A case study. In *Proceedings of the 7th International Conference on Global Software Engineering (ICGSE'12))*, pages 11–20, 2012.

ET Bureau. Need for speed: More it companies switch to agile code development. *The Economic Times*, August 6, 2012. URL `http://articles.economictimes.indiatimes.com/2012-08-06/news/33065621_1_thoughtworks-software-development-iterative`.

M. Fowler. The New Methodology. *martinfowler.com*, 2005. URL `http://www.martinfowler.com/articles/newMethodology.html`.

E. Harrington. Hearing: Security flaws in Obamacare website endanger AmericansHealthCare.gov. *Washington Free Beacon*, 2013. URL `http://freebeacon.com/hearing-security-flaws-in-obamacare-website-endanger-americans/`.

S. Horsley. Enrollment jumps at HealthCare.gov, though totals still lag. *NPR.org*, December 12, 2013. URL `http://www.npr.org/blogs/health/2013/12/11/250023704/enrollment-jumps-at-healthcare-gov-though-totals-still-lag`.

A. Howard. Why Obama's HealthCare.gov launch was doomed to fail. *The Verge*, October 8, 2013. URL `http://www.theverge.com/2013/10/8/4814098/why-did-the-tech-savvy-obama-administration-launch-a-busted-healthcare-website`.

C. Johnson and H. Reed. Why the government never gets tech right. *New York Times*, October 24, 2013. URL `http://www.pmi.org/en/Professional-Development/Career-Central/Must_Have_Skill_Agile.aspx`.

J. Johnson. The CHAOS report. Technical report, The Standish Group, Boston, Massachusetts, 1995. URL `http://blog.standishgroup.com/`.

J. Johnson. HealthCare.gov chaos. Technical report, The Standish Group, Boston, Massachusetts, October 22, 2013a. URL `http://blog.standishgroup.com/images/audio/HealthcareGov_Chaos_Tuesday.mp3`.

J. Johnson. The CHAOS manifesto 2013: Think big, act small. Technical report, The Standish Group, Boston, Massachusetts, 2013b. URL `http://www.standishgroup.com`.

C. Jones. Software project management practices: Failure versus success. *CrossTalk: The Journal of Defense Software Engineering*, pages 5–9, Oct. 2004. URL `http://cross5talk2.squarespace.com/storage/issue-archives/2004/200410/200410-Jones.pdf`.

J. M. Juran and F. M. Gryna. *Juran's quality control handbook*. New York: McGraw-Hill, 1998.

P. Kruchten. *The Rational Unified Process: An Introduction, Third Edition*. Addison-Wesley Professional, 2003. ISBN 0321197704.

T. Lethbridge and R. Laganiere. *Object-Oriented Software Engineering: Practical Software Development using UML and Java*. McGraw-Hill, 2002. ISBN 0072834951.

National Research Council. *Achieving Effective Acquisition of Information Technology in the Department of Defense*. The National Academies Press, 2010. ISBN 9780309148283. URL `http://www.nap.edu/openbook.php?record_id=12823`.

P. Naur and B. Randell. *Software engineering*. Scientific Affairs Div., NATO, 1969.

J. R. Nawrocki, B. Walter, and A. Wojciechowski. Comparison of CMM level 2 and extreme programming. In *7th European Conference on Software Quality*, Helsinki, Finland, 2002.

M. Paulk, C. Weber, B. Curtis, and M. B. Chrissis. *The Capability Maturity Model: Guidelines for Improving the Software Process*. Addison-Wesley, 1995. ISBN 0201546647.

G. J. Popek and R. P. Goldberg. Formal requirements for virtualizable third generation architectures. *Communications of the ACM*, 17(7):412–421, 1974.

Project Management Institute. Must-have skill: Agile. *Professional Development*, February 28, 2012. URL `http://www.pmi.org/en/Professional-Development/Career-Central/Must_Have_Skill_Agile.aspx`.

W. W. Royce. Managing the development of large software systems: concepts and techniques. In *Proceedings of WESCON*, pages 1–9, Los Angeles, California, August 1970.

I. Sommerville. *Software Engineering, Ninth Edition*. Addison-Wesley, 2010. ISBN 0137035152.

M. Stephens and D. Rosenberg. *Extreme Programming Refactored: The Case Against XP*. Apress, 2003.

M. Swaine. Back to the future: Was Bill Gates a good programmer? What does Prolog have to do with the semantic web? And what did Kent Beck have for lunch? *Dr. Dobb's The World of Software Development*, 2001. URL http://www.drdobbs.com/back-to-the-future/184404733.

A. Taylor. IT projects sink or swim. *BCS Review*, Jan. 2000. URL http://archive.bcs.org/bulletin/jan00/article1.htm.

F. Thorp. 'Stress tests' show HealthCare.gov was overloaded. *NBC News*, November 18, 2013. URL http://www.nbcnews.com/politics/politics-news/stress-tests-show-healthcare-gov-was-overloaded-v21337298.

J. Zients. HealthCare.gov progress and performance report. Technical report, Health and Human Services, December 1, 2013. URL http://www.hhs.gov/digitalstrategy/sites/digitalstrategy/files/pdf/healthcare.gov-progress-report.pdf.

Notes

[1] http://en.wikipedia.org/wiki/Turing_Award
[2] https://www.edx.org/
[3] http://www.youtube.com/watch?v=DeBi2ZxUZiM
[4] http://www.youtube.com/watch?v=kYUrqdUyEpI
[5] https://plus.google.com/112678702228711889851/posts/eVeouesvaVX
[6] http://developers.slashdot.org/story/08/05/11/1759213/
[7] http://www.pastebin.com/u/saasbook

1.15   Suggested Projects

Project 1.1. *(Discussion) Identify the principal issues associated with software evolution and explain their impact on the software life cycle. Note: We use this margin icon to identify all projects that from come come from the ACM/IEEE 2013 Computer Science Curriculum for Software Engineering standard (ACM IEEE-Computer Society Joint Task Force 2013).*

Project 1.2. *(Discussion) Discuss the challenges of evolving systems in a changing environment.*

Project 1.3. *(Discussion) Explain the concept of a software life cycle and provide an example, illustrating its phases including the deliverables that are produced.*

Project 1.4. *(Discussion) Referring to Figure 1.5, compare the process models from this chapter with respect to their value for development of particular classes of software systems: information management, embedded, process control, communications, and web applications.*

Project 1.5. *(Discussion) In your opinion, how would you rank the software disasters in this chapter from most terrible to the least? How did you rank them?*

Project 1.6. *(Discussion) The closest hardware failure to the software disasters mentioned in the first section is probably the Intel Floating Point Divide bug[1]. Where would you put this hardware problem in the ranked list of software examples from the exercise above?*

Project 1.7. *(Discussion) Measured in lines of code, what is the largest program in the world? For purposes of this exercise, assume it can be a suite of software that is shipped as a single product.*

Project 1.8. *(Discussion) Which programming language has the most active programmers?*

Project 1.9. *(Discussion) In which programming language is the most number of lines of code written annually? Which has the most lines of active code cumulatively?*

Project 1.10. *(Discussion) Make a list of, in your opinion, the Top 10 most important applications. Which would best be developed and maintained using the four lifecycles from this chapter? List your reasons for each choice.*

Project 1.11. *(Discussion) Given the list of Top 10 applications from the exercise above, how important are each of the four productivity techniques listed in this chapter?*

Project 1.12. *(Discussion) Given the list of Top 10 applications from the exercise above, what aspects might be difficult to test and need to rely on formal methods? Would some testing techniques be more important for some applications than others? State why.*

Project 1.13. *Distinguish between program validation and program verification.*

Project 1.14. *(Discussion) What are the Top 5 reasons that SaaS and Cloud Computing will grow in popularity and the Top 5 obstacles to its growth?*

Project 1.15. *(Discussion) Discuss the advantages and disadvantages of software reuse.*

Project 1.16. *(Discussion) Describe and distinguish among the different types and levels of testing (unit, integration, module, system, and acceptance).*

Project 1.17. *Describe the difference between principles of the waterfall model and Plan-and-Document models using iterations.*

Project 1.18. *Describe the different practices that are key components of Agile and various Plan-and-Document process models.*

Project 1.19. *Differentiate among the phases of software development of Plan-and-Document models.*

Part I

Software as a Service

2 The Architecture of SaaS Applications

Dennis Ritchie (left, 1941–2011) and Ken Thompson (right, 1943–) shared the 1983 Turing Award for fundamental contributions to operating systems design in general and the invention of Unix in particular.

I think the major good idea in Unix was its clean and simple interface: open, close, read, and write.

—Unix and Beyond: An Interview With Ken Thompson, IEEE Computer 32(5), May 1999

Concepts

Software architecture describes how the subsystems that make up a piece of software are connected together to meet the application's functional and non-functional requirements. A *design pattern* describes a general architectural solution to a family of similar problems, obtained by generalizing from the experience of developers who have solved those problems before. Examining SaaS apps, design patterns are evident at all levels of detail:

- SaaS apps follow the *client-server* pattern, in which a client makes requests and a server responds to the requests of many clients.

- A SaaS server follows the *three-tier architecture* pattern, which separates the responsibilities of different SaaS server components and enables **horizontal scaling** to accommodate millions of users.

- SaaS app code lives in the **application tier**. Many SaaS apps, including those based on Rails, follow the *Model-View-Controller* design pattern, in which Models deal with the app's *resources* such as users or blog posts, Views present information to the user via the browser, and Controllers map the user's browser actions to application code.

- For Models, Rails uses the *Active Record pattern* because it is a good fit to *relational databases*, the most popular way of storing SaaS data. For Views, Rails uses the **Template View pattern** to create Web pages to send to the browser. For Controllers, Rails follows the *Representational State Transfer* or REST principle, in which each controller action describes a single self-contained operation on one of the app's *resources*.

Modern SaaS frameworks such as Rails capture a decade's worth of developer experience by encapsulating these SaaS design patterns so that SaaS app writers can easily apply them.

1. A Web client (Firefox) requests the Rotten Potatoes home page from a Web server (WEBrick).

2. WEBrick obtains content from the Rotten Potatoes app and sends this content back to Firefox

3. Firefox displays the content and closes the HTTP connection.

Figure 2.1: 100,000-foot view of a SaaS client-server system.

2.1   100,000 Feet: Client-Server Architecture

Since the best way to learn about software is by doing, let's jump in right away.

If you haven't done so already, turn to Appendix A and get this book's "bookware" running on your own computer or in the cloud. Once it is ready, Screencast 2.1.1 shows how to deploy and login to your Virtual Machine and try an interaction with the simple educational app RottenPotatoes, which aspires to be a simplified version of the popular movie-rating Web site RottenTomatoes[2].

> **Screencast 2.1.1: Getting Started.**
> http://vimeo.com/34754478
> Once logged in to your VM, the screencast shows how to open a Terminal window, cd (change to) the directory Documents/rottenpotatoes, and start the RottenPotatoes app by typing rails server. We then opened the Firefox web browser and entered http://localhost:3000/movies into the address bar and pressed Return, taking us to the RottenPotatoes home page.

What's going on? You've just seen the simplest view of a Web app: it is an example of the *client-server architecture*. Firefox is an example of a client: a program whose specialty is asking a server for information and (usually) allowing the user to interact with that information. WEBrick, which you activated by typing rails server, is an example of a server: a program whose specialty is waiting for clients to make a *request* and then providing a *reply*. WEBrick waits to be contacted by a Web browser such as Firefox and routes the browser's requests to the RottenPotatoes app. Figure 2.1 summarizes how a SaaS application works, from 100,000 feet.

Distinguishing clients from servers allows each type of program to be highly specialized to its task: the client can have a responsive and appealing user interface, while the server concentrates on efficiently serving many clients simultaneously. Firefox and other browsers (Chrome, Safari, Internet Explorer) are clients used by millions of people (let's call them *production clients*). WEBrick, on the other hand, is not a production server, but a "miniserver" with just enough functionality to let one user at a time (you, the developer) interact with your Web app. A real Web site would use a production server such as the Apache web server[3] or the Microsoft Internet Information Server[4], either of which can be deployed on hundreds of computers efficiently serving many copies of the same site to millions of users.

Before the Web's open standards were proposed in 1990, users would install separate and mutually-incompatible proprietary clients for each Internet service they used: Eudora (the ancestor of Thunderbird) for reading email, AOL or CompuServe for accessing proprietary content portals (a role filled today by portals like MSN and Yahoo!), and so on. Today, the Web browser has largely supplanted proprietary clients and is justifiably called the "universal

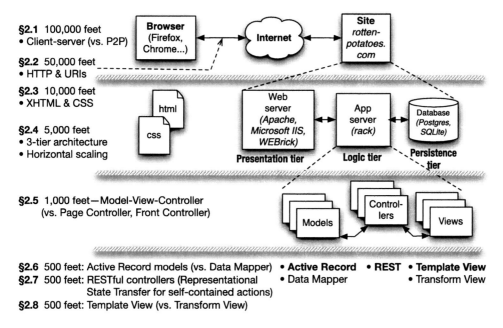

§2.1 100,000 feet
• Client-server (vs. P2P)

§2.2 50,000 feet
• HTTP & URIs

§2.3 10,000 feet
• XHTML & CSS

§2.4 5,000 feet
• 3-tier architecture
• Horizontal scaling

§2.5 1,000 feet—Model-View-Controller
(vs. Page Controller, Front Controller)

§2.6 500 feet: Active Record models (vs. Data Mapper)   • **Active Record**   • **REST**   • **Template View**
§2.7 500 feet: RESTful controllers (Representational   • Data Mapper   • Transform View
State Transfer for self-contained actions)
§2.8 500 feet: Template View (vs. Transform View)

Figure 2.2: Using altitude as an analogy, this figure illustrates important structures in SaaS at various levels of detail and serves as an overall roadmap of the discussion in this chapter. Each level is discussed in the sections shown.

client." Nonetheless, the proprietary clients and servers still constitute examples of client-server architecture, with clients specialized for asking questions on behalf of users and servers specialized for answering questions from many clients. Client-server is therefore our first example of a *design pattern*—a reusable structure, behavior, strategy, or technique that captures a proven solution to a collection of similar problems by *separating the things that change from those that stay the same*. In the case of client-server architectures, what stays the same is the separation of concerns between the client and the server, despite changes across implementations of clients and servers. Because of the Web's ubiquity, we will use the term SaaS to mean "client-server systems built to operate using the open standards of the World Wide Web."

In the past, the client-server architecture implied that the server was a much more complex program than the client. Today, with powerful laptops and Web browsers that support animation and 3D effects, a better characterization might be that clients and servers are comparably complex but have been specialized for their very different roles. In this book we will concentrate on server-centric applications; although we cover some JavaScript client programming in Chapter 6, its context is in support of a server-centric application rather than for building complex in-browser applications such as Google Docs[5].

Of course, client-server isn't the only architectural pattern found in Internet-based services. In the *peer-to-peer architecture*, used in BitTorrent, every participant is both a client and a server—anyone can ask anyone else for information. In such a system where a single program must behave as both client and server, it's harder to specialize the program to do either job really well.

Summary:

- SaaS Web apps are examples of the ***client-server architectural pattern***, in which client software is typically specialized for interacting with the user and sending requests to the server on the user's behalf, and the server software is specialized for handling large volumes of such requests.

- Because Web apps use open standards that anyone can implement royalty-free, in contrast to proprietary standards used by older client-server apps, the Web browser has become the "universal client."

- An alternative to client-server is peer-to-peer, in which all entities act as both clients and servers. While arguably more flexible, this architecture makes it difficult to specialize the software to do either job really well.

Self-Check 2.1.1. *What is the primary difference between a client and a server in SaaS?*
◇ A SaaS client is optimized for allowing the user to interact with information, whereas a SaaS server is optimized for serving many clients simultaneously. ■

Self-Check 2.1.2. *What element(s) in Figure 2.2 refer to a SaaS client and what element(s) refer to a SaaS server?*
◇ The **Browser** box in the upper-left corner refers to a client. The **html** and **css** document icons refer to content delivered to the client. All other elements are part of the server. ■

2.2   50,000 Feet: Communication—HTTP and URIs

Vinton E. "Vint" Cerf (left, 1943–) and Bob Kahn (right, 1938–) shared the 2004 Turing Award for their pioneering work on networking architecture and protocols, including TCP/IP.

A ***network protocol*** is a set of communication rules on which agents participating in a network agree. In this case, the agents are Web clients (like Firefox) and Web servers (like WEBrick or Apache). Browsers and Web servers communicate using the ***HyperText Transfer Protocol***, or ***HTTP***. Like many Internet application protocols, HTTP relies on ***TCP/IP***, the venerable ***Transmission Control Protocol/Internet Protocol***, which allows a pair of agents to communicate ordered sequences of bytes. Essentially, TCP/IP allows the communication of arbitrary character strings between a pair of network agents.

In a TCP/IP network, each computer has an ***IP address*** consisting of four bytes separated by dots, such as 128.32.244.172. Most of the time we don't use IP addresses directly—another Internet service called ***Domain Name System*** (***DNS***), which has its own protocol based on TCP/IP, is automatically invoked to map easy-to-remember ***hostnames*** like www.eecs.berkeley.edu to IP addresses. Browsers automatically contact a DNS server to look up the site name you type in the address bar, such as www.eecs.berkeley.edu, and get the actual IP address, in this case 128.32.244.172. A convention used by TCP/IP-compatible computers is that if a program running on a computer refers to the name localhost, it is referring to the very computer it's running on. That is why typing localhost into Firefox's address bar at the beginning of Section 2.1 caused Firefox to communicate with the WEBrick process running on the same computer as Firefox itself.

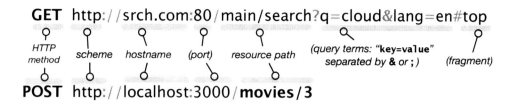

Figure 2.3: An HTTP request consists of an *HTTP method* plus a *URI*. A *full URI* begins with a scheme such as `http` or `https` and includes the above components. Optional components are in parentheses. A *partial URI* omits any or all of the leftmost components, in which case those components are filled in or *resolved* relative to a *base URI* determined by the specific application. Best practice is to use full URIs.

■ *Elaboration: Networking: multi-homing, IPv6 and HTTPS.*

We have simplified some aspects of TCP/IP: technically each **network interface device** has an IP address, and some **multi-homed** computers may have multiple network interfaces. Also, for various reasons including the exhaustion of the address space of IP numbers, the current version of IP (version 4) is slowly being phased out in favor of version 6 (IPv6), which uses a different format for addresses. However, since most computers have only one network interface active at a time and SaaS app writers rarely deal directly with IP addresses, these simplifications don't materially alter our explanations. We also defer discussion of the Secure HTTP protocol (HTTPS) until Chapter 12. HTTPS uses **public-key cryptography** to encrypt (encode) communication between an HTTP client and server, so that an eavesdropper sees only gibberish. From a programmer's point of view, HTTPS behaves like HTTP, but only works if the Web server has been configured to support HTTPS access to certain pages. "Mini" servers like WEBrick typically don't support it.

What about the `:3000` we appended to `localhost` in the example? Multiple agents on a network can be running at the same IP address. Indeed, in the example above, both the client and server were running on your own computer. Therefore, TCP/IP uses **port numbers** from 1 to 65535 to distinguish different network agents at the same IP address. All protocols based on TCP/IP, including HTTP, must specify both the host and port number when opening a connection. When you directed Firefox to go to `localhost:3000/movies`, you were indicating that on the computer called `localhost` (that is, "this computer"), a server program was monitoring port 3000 waiting for browsers to contact it. If we didn't specify the port number (3000) explicitly, it would default to 80 for `http` or 443 for `https` (secure) connections.

> **The IANA.** The Internet Assigned Numbers Authority[6] assigns official default port numbers for various protocols and manages the top-level or "root" zone of DNS.

To summarize, communication in HTTP is initiated when one agent *opens a connection* to another agent by specifying a hostname and port number; an HTTP server process must be *listening for connections* on that host and port number.

The string `http://localhost:3000/movies` that you typed into Firefox's address bar is a **URI**, or **Uniform Resource Identifier**. A URI begins with the name of the communication *scheme* by which the information may be retrieved, followed by a hostname, optional port number, and a *resource* on that host that the user wants to retrieve; as shown in Figure 2.3. A resource generally means "anything that can be delivered to the browser": an image, the list of all movies in HTML format, and a form submission that creates a new movie are all examples of resources. Each SaaS application has its own rules for interpreting the resource name, though we will soon see one proposal called REST that strives for simplicity and consistency in resource naming across different SaaS apps.

> **URI or URL?** URIs are sometimes referred to as URLs, or Uniform Resource Locators. Despite subtle technical distinctions, for our purposes the terms can be used interchangeably. We use URI because it is more general and matches the terminology used by most libraries.

1. A Web client (Firefox) requests the Rotten Potatoes home page from a Web server (WEBrick).
    a) Firefox constructs an HTTP request using the URI *http://localhost:3000* to contact an HTTP
       server (WEBrick) listening on port 3000 on the same computer as Firefox itself (*localhost*).
    b) WEBrick, listening on port 3000, receives the HTTP request for the resource '/movies' (the list of
       all movies in Rotten Potatoes).

2. WEBrick obtains content from the Rotten Potatoes app and sends this content back to Firefox

3. Firefox displays the content and closes the HTTP connection.

Figure 2.4: At 50,000 feet, we can expand Step 1 from Figure 2.1.

HTTP is a **stateless protocol** because every HTTP request is independent of and un-related to all previous requests. A web app that keeps track of "where you are" (Have you logged in yet? What step of the checkout process are you on?) must have its own mechanisms for doing so, since nothing about an HTTP request remembers this information. HTTP **cookies** associate a particular user's browser with information held at the server corresponding to that user's **session**, but it is the browser's responsibility, not HTTP's or the SaaS app's, to make sure the right cookies are included with each HTTP request. Stateless protocols therefore simplify server design at the expense of application design, but happily, successful frameworks such as Rails shield you from much of this complexity.

Screencast 2.2.1: Cookies.
`http://vimeo.com/33918630`
SaaS frameworks simplify working with cookies, which are used to establish that two independent requests actually originated from the same user's browser, and can therefore be thought of as part of a session. On the first visit to a site, the server includes a long string (up to 4 KBytes) with the `Set-Cookie:` HTTP response header. It is the browser's responsibility to include this string with the `Cookie:` HTTP request header on subsequent requests to that site. The cookie string, which is usually not encrypted but is protected by a "fingerprint" or **message authentication code**, contains enough information for the server to associate the request with the same user session.

We can now express what's happening when you load the RottenPotatoes home page in slightly more precise terms, as Figure 2.4 shows.

To drill down further, we'll next look at how the content itself is represented.

Summary

- Web browsers and servers communicate using the **HyperText Transfer Protocol**. HTTP relies on **TCP/IP** (Transmission Control Protocol/Internet Protocol) to reliably exchange ordered sequences of bytes.

- Each computer connected to a TCP/IP network has an **IP address** such as 128.32.244.172, although the **Domain Name System** (DNS) allows the use of human-friendly names instead. The special name localhost refers to the local computer and resolves to the special IP address 127.0.0.1.

- Each application running on a particular computer must "listen" on a distinct **TCP port**, numbered from 1 to 65535 ($2^{16} - 1$). Port 80 is used by HTTP (Web) servers.

- To run a SaaS app locally, you activate an HTTP server listening on a port on localhost. WEBrick, Rails' lightweight server, uses port 3000.

- A **Uniform Resource Identifier** (URI) names a resource available on the Internet. The interpretation of the resource name varies from application to application.

- HTTP is a stateless protocol in that every request is independent of every other request, even from the same user. **HTTP cookies** allow the association of HTTP requests from the same user. It's the browser's responsibility to accept a cookie from an HTTP server and ensure that the cookie is included with future requests sent to that server.

■*Elaboration: Client Pull vs. Server Push.*

The Web is primarily a *client pull* client-server architecture because the client initiates all interactions—HTTP servers can only wait for clients to contact them. This is because HTTP was designed as a **request-reply protocol**: only clients can initiate anything. Evolving standards, including WebSockets and HTML5, have some support for allowing the server to *push* updated content to the client. In contrast, true *server push* architectures, such as text messaging on cell phones, allow the server to initiate a connection to the client to "wake it up" when new information is available; but these cannot use HTTP. An early criticism of the Web's architecture was that a pure request-reply protocol would rule out such **push-based** applications. In practice, however, the high efficiency of specialized server software supports creating Web pages that frequently *poll* (check in with) the server to receive updates, giving the user the illusion of a push-based application even without the features proposed in WebSockets and HTML5.

Self-Check 2.2.1. *What happens if we visit the URI http://google.com:3000 and why?*

◇ The connection will eventually "time out" unable to contact a server, because Google (like almost all Web sites) listens on TCP port 80 (the default) rather than 3000. ■

Self-Check 2.2.2. *What happens if we try to access RottenPotatoes at (say) http://localhost:3300 (instead of :3000) and why?*

◇ You get a "connection refused" since nothing is listening on port 3300. ■

2.3   10,000 Feet: Representation—HTML and CSS

If the Web browser is the universal client, **HTML**, the HyperText Markup Language, is the universal language. A **markup language** combines text with markup (annotations about the text) in a way that makes it easy to syntactically distinguish the two. Watch Screencast 2.3.1 for some highlights of HTML 5, the current version of the language, then continue reading.

Screencast 2.3.1: HTML Introduction.

`http://vimeo.com/34754506`

HTML consists of a hierarchy of nested elements, each of which consists of an opening tag such as `<p>`, a content part (in some cases), and a closing tag such as `</p>`. Most opening tags can also have attributes, as in `<a href="http://...">`. Some tags that don't have a content part are self-closing, such as `<br clear="both"/>` for a line break that clears both left and right margins.

The use of angle brackets for tags comes from **SGML** (Standard Generalized Markup Language), a codified standardization of IBM's Generalized Markup Language, developed in the 1960s for encoding computer-readable project documents.

There is an unfortunate and confusing mess of terminology surrounding the lineage of HTML[7]. HTML 5 includes features of both its predecessors (HTML versions 1 through 4) and XHTML (eXtended HyperText Markup Language), which is a subset of **XML**, an eXtensible Markup Language that can be used both to represent data and to describe other markup languages. Indeed, XML is a common data representation for exchanging information *between* two services in a Service-Oriented Architecture, as we'll see in Chapter 8 when we extend RottenPotatoes to retrieve movie information from a separate movie database service. The differences among the variants of XHTML and HTML are difficult to keep straight, and not all browsers support all versions. Unless otherwise noted, from now on when we say HTML we mean HTML 5, and we will try to avoid using features that aren't widely supported.

Of particular interest are the HTML tag attributes `id` and `class`, because they figure heavily into connecting the HTML structure of a page with its visual appearance. The following screencast illustrates the use of Firefox's Web Developer toolbar to quickly identify the ID's and Classes of HTML elements on a page.

Screencast 2.3.2: Inspecting the ID and Class attributes.

`http://vimeo.com/34754568`

CSS uses **selector notations** such as `div#`*name* to indicate a `div` element whose `id` is *name* and `div.`*name* to indicate a `div` element with class *name*. Only one element in an HTML document can have a given `id`, whereas many elements (even of different tag types) can share the same `class`. All three aspects of an element—its tag type, its `id` (if it has one), and its `class` attributes (if it has any)—can be used to identify an element as a candidate for visual formatting.

For an extreme example of how much can be done with CSS, visit the CSS Zen Garden[8].

As the next screencast shows, the **CSS** (**Cascading Style Sheets**) standard allows us to associate visual "styling" instructions with HTML elements by using the elements' classes and IDs. The screencast covers only a few basic CSS constructs, which are summarized in Figure 2.5. The Resources section at the end of the chapter lists sites and books that describe CSS in great detail, including how to use CSS for aligning content on a page, something designers used to do manually with HTML tables.

Selector	What is selected
h1	Any h1 element
div#message	The div whose ID is message
.red	Any element with class red
div.red, h1	The div with class red, or any h1
div#message h1	An h1 element that's a child of (inside of) div#message
a.lnk	a element with class lnk
a.lnk:hover	a element with class lnk, when hovered over

Attribute	Example values	Attribute	Example values
font-family	"Times, serif"	background-color	red, #c2eed6 (RGB values)
font-weight	bold	border	1px solid blue
font-size	14pt, 125%, 12px	text-align	right
font-style	italic	text-decoration	underline
color	black	vertical-align	middle
margin	4px	padding	1cm

Figure 2.5: A few CSS constructs, including those explained in Screencast 2.3.3. The top table shows some CSS *selectors*, which identify the elements to be styled; the bottom table shows a few of the many attributes, whose names are usually self-explanatory, and example values they can be assigned. Not all attributes are valid on all elements.

Screencast 2.3.3: Introduction to CSS.
http://vimeo.com/34754607
There are four basic mechanisms by which a selector in a CSS file can match an HTML element: by tag name, by class, by ID, and by hierarchy. If multiple selectors match a given element, the rules for which properties to apply are complex, so most designers try to avoid such ambiguities by keeping their CSS simple. A useful way to see the "bones" of a page is to select *CSS>Disable Styles>All Styles* from the Firefox Web Developer toolbar. This will display the page with all CSS formatting turned off, showing the extent to which CSS can be used to separate visual appearance from logical structure.

Using this new information, Figure 2.6 expands steps 2 and 3 from the previous section's summary of how SaaS works.

1. A Web client (Firefox) requests the Rotten Potatoes home page from a Web server (WEBrick).
    a) Firefox constructs an HTTP request using the URI **http://localhost:3000** to contact an HTTP server (WEBrick) listening on port 3000 on the same computer as Firefox itself (**localhost**).
    b) WEBrick, listening on port 3000, receives the HTTP request for the resource '/movies' (the list of all movies in Rotten Potatoes).

2. WEBrick obtains content from the Rotten Potatoes app and sends this content back to Firefox
    a) WEBrick returns content encoded in HTML, again using HTTP. The HTML may contain references to other kinds of media such as images to embed in the displayed page. The HTML may also contain a reference to a CSS stylesheet containing formatting information describing the desired visual attributes of the page (font sizes, colors, layout, and so on).

3. Firefox displays the content and closes the HTTP connection.
    a) Firefox fetches any referenced assets (CSS, images, and so on) by repeating the previous four steps as needed but providing the URIs of the desired assets as referenced in the HTML page.
    b) Firefox displays the page according to the CSS formatting directives and including any referenced assets such as embedded images.

Figure 2.6: SaaS from 10,000 feet. Compared to Figure 2.4, step 2 has been expanded to describe the content returned by the Web server, and step 3 has been expanded to describe the role of CSS in how the Web browser renders the content.

Summary

- An **HTML** (HyperText Markup Language) document consists of a hierarchically nested collection of elements. Each element begins with a **tag** in <angle brackets> that may have optional **attributes**. Some elements enclose content.

- A **selector** is an expression that identifies one or more HTML elements in a document by using a combination of the element name (such as body), element id (an element attribute that must be unique on a page), and element class (an attribute that need not be unique on a page).

- **Cascading Style Sheets** (CSS) is a stylesheet language describing visual attributes of elements on a Web page. A stylesheet associates sets of visual properties with selectors. A special link element inside the head element of an HTML document associates a stylesheet with that document.

- The Firefox Web Developer toolbar is invaluable in peeking under the hood to examine both the structure of a page and its stylesheets.

Pastebin is the service we use to make it easy to copy-and-paste the code. You need to type in the URI if you're reading the print book.

Self-Check 2.3.1. *True or false: every HTML element must have an ID.*

⋄ False—the ID is optional, though must be unique if provided. ∎

Self-Check 2.3.2. *Given the following HTML markup:*

http://pastebin.com/4ATW3CJd

```
1  <p class="x" id="i">I hate <span>Mondays</span></p>
2  <p>but <span class="y">Tuesdays</span> are OK.</p>
```

Write down a CSS selector that will select only *the word* Mondays *for styling.*

◇ Three possibilities, from most specific to least specific, are: **#i span**, **p.x span**, and **.x span**. Other selectors are possible but redundant or over-constrained; for example, **p#i span** and **p#i.x span** are redundant with respect to this HTML snippet since at most one element can have the ID **i**. ∎

Self-Check 2.3.3. *In Self-Check 2.3.2, why are* **span** *and* **p span** *not valid answers?*
◇ Both of those selector also match *Tuesdays*, which is a **span** inside a **p**. ∎

Self-Check 2.3.4. *What is the most common way to associate a CSS stylesheet with an HTML or HTML document? (HINT: refer to the earlier screencast example.)*

◇ Within the HEAD element of the HTML or HTML document, include a LINK element with at least the following three attributes: REL="STYLESHEET", TYPE="text/css", and HREF="*uri* ", where *uri* is the full or partial URI of the stylesheet. That is, the stylesheet must be accessible as a resource named by a URI. ∎

2.4   5,000 Feet: 3-Tier Architecture & Horizontal Scaling

So far we've seen how the client communicates with the server and how the information they exchange is represented, but we haven't said anything about the server itself. Moving back to the server side of Figure 2.2 and zooming in for additional detail on the second level, Web apps are structured as three logical *tiers*. The **presentation tier** usually consists of an **HTTP server** (or simply "**Web server**"), which accepts requests from the outside world (i.e., users) and usually serves static assets. We've been using WEBrick to fulfill that role.

The web server forwards requests for dynamic content to the **logic tier**, where the actual application runs that generates dynamic content. The application is typically supported by an **application server** whose job is to hide the low-level mechanics of HTTP from the app writer. For example, an app server can route incoming HTTP requests directly to appropriate pieces of code in your app, saving you from having to listen for and parse incoming HTTP requests. Modern application servers support one or more **Web application frameworks** that simplify creation of a particular class of Web applications in a particular language. We will be using the Rails framework and the Rack application server, which comes with Rails. WEBrick can "speak" to Rack directly; other Web servers such as Apache require additional software modules to do so. If you were writing in PHP, Python, or Java, you would use an application server that handles code written in those languages. For example, Google AppEngine, which runs Python and Java applications, has proprietary middleware that bridges your app's Python or Java code to the Google-operated infrastructure that faces the outside world.

Because application servers sit between the Web server (presentation tier) and your actual app code, they are sometimes referred to as *middleware*.

Finally, since HTTP is stateless, application data that must remain stored across HTTP requests, such as session data and users' login and profile information, is stored in the **persistence tier**. Popular choices for the persistence tier have traditionally been databases such as the open-source MySQL or PostgreSQL, although prior to their proliferation, commercial databases such as Oracle or IBM DB2 were also popular choices.

The "tiers" in the three-tier model are *logical* tiers. On a site with little content and low traffic, the software in all three tiers might run on a single physical computer. In fact, Rotten-Potatoes has been doing just this: its presentation tier is just WEBrick, and its persistence tier is a simple open-source database called SQLite, which stores its information directly in files on your local computer. In production, it's more common for each tier to span one or more

LAMP. Early SaaS sites were created using the Perl and PHP scripting languages, whose availability coincided with the early success of Linux, an open-source operating system, and MySQL, an open-source database. Thousands of sites are still powered by the *LAMP Stack*—Linux, Apache, MySQL, and PHP or Perl.

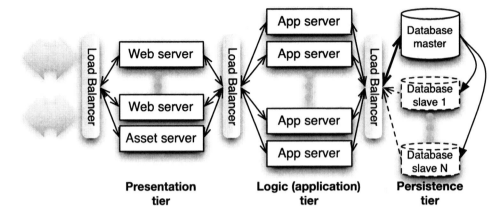

Figure 2.7: The 3-tier *shared-nothing* architecture, so called because entities within a tier generally do not communicate with each other, allows adding computers to each tier independently to match demand. *Load balancers*, which distribute workload evenly, can be either hardware appliances or specially-configured Web servers. The statelessness of HTTP makes shared-nothing possible: since all requests are independent, any server in the presentation or logic tier can be assigned to any request. However, scaling the persistence tier is much more challenging, as the text explains.

physical computers. As Figure 2.7 shows, in a typical site, incoming HTTP requests are directed to one of several Web servers, which in turn select one of several available application servers to handle dynamic-content generation, allowing computers to be added or removed from each tier as needed to handle demand.

However, as the Fallacies and Pitfalls section explains, making the persistence layer shared-nothing is much more complicated. Figure 2.7 shows the ***master-slave*** approach, used when the database is read much more frequently than it is written: any slave can perform reads, only the master can perform writes, and the master updates the slaves with the results of writes as quickly as possible. However, in the end, this technique only postpones the scaling problem rather than solving it. As one of Heroku's[9] founders wrote:

> *A question I'm often asked about Heroku is: "How do you scale the SQL database?"*
> *There's a lot of things I can say about using caching, sharding, and other techniques*
> *to take load off the database. But the actual answer is: we don't. SQL databases are*
> *fundamentally non-scalable, and there is no magical pixie dust that we, or anyone, can*
> *sprinkle on them to suddenly make them scale.*

—Adam Wiggins, Heroku[10]

We can now add one more level of detail to our explanation; step 2a is new in Figure 2.8.

1. A Web client (Firefox) requests the Rotten Potatoes home page from a Web server (WEBrick).
   a) Firefox constructs an HTTP request using the URI ***http://localhost:3000*** to contact an HTTP server (WEBrick) listening on port 3000 on the same computer as Firefox itself (***localhost***).
   b) WEBrick, listening on port 3000, receives the HTTP request for the resource '/movies' (the list of all movies in Rotten Potatoes).

2. WEBrick obtains content from the Rotten Potatoes app and sends this content back to Firefox
   a) Via the Rack middleware (written in Ruby), WEBrick calls Rotten Potatoes code in the application tier. This code generates the page content using movie information stored in the persistence tier implemented by a SQLite database using local files.
   b) WEBrick returns content encoded in HTML, again using HTTP. The HTML may contain references to other kinds of media such as images to embed in the displayed page. The HTML may also contain a reference to a CSS stylesheet containing formatting information describing the desired visual attributes of the page (font sizes, colors, layout, and so on).

3. Firefox displays the content and closes the HTTP connection.
   a) Firefox fetches any referenced assets (CSS, images, and so on) by repeating the previous four steps as needed but providing the URIs of the desired assets as referenced in the HTML page.
   b) Firefox displays the page according to the CSS formatting directives and including any referenced assets such as embedded images.

Figure 2.8: SaaS from 5,000 feet. Compared to Figure 2.6, step 2a has been inserted, describing the actions of the SaaS server in terms of the three-tier architecture.

Summary

- The three-tier architecture includes a presentation tier, which renders views and interacts with the user; a logic tier, which runs SaaS app code; and a persistence tier, which stores app data.

- HTTP's statelessness allows the presentation and logic tiers to be ***shared-nothing***, so cloud computing can be used to add more computers to each tier as demand requires. However, the persistence tier is harder to scale.

- Depending on the scale (size) of the deployment, more than 1 tier may be hosted on a single computer, or a single tier may require many computers.

■ *Elaboration: Why Databases?*

While the earliest Web apps sometimes manipulated files directly for storing data, there are two reasons why databases overwhelmingly took over this role very early. First, databases have historically provided high *durability* for stored information—the guarantee that once something has been stored, unexpected events such as system crashes or transient data corruption won't cause data loss. For a Web app storing millions of users' data, this guarantee is critical. Second, databases store information in a structured format—in the case of ***relational databases***, by far the most popular type, each kind of object is stored in a table whose rows represent object instances and whose columns represent object properties. This organization is a good fit for the structured data that many Web apps manipulate. Interestingly, today's largest Web apps, such as Facebook, have grown so far beyond the scale for which relational databases were designed that they are being forced to look at alternatives to the long-reigning relational database.

Self-Check 2.4.1. *Explain why cloud computing might have had a lesser impact on SaaS if most SaaS apps didn't follow the shared-nothing architecture.*

◇ Cloud computing allows easily adding and removing computers while paying only for what you use, but it is the shared-nothing architecture that makes it straightforward to "absorb" the new computers into a running app and "release" them when no longer needed. ∎

Self-Check 2.4.2. *In the ____ tier of three-tier SaaS apps, scaling is much more complicated than just adding computers.*

◇ Persistence tier ∎

2.5 1,000 Feet: Model-View-Controller Architecture

So far we've said nothing about the structure of the app code in RottenPotatoes. In fact, just as we used the client-server architectural pattern to characterize the "100,000-foot view" of SaaS, we can use an architectural pattern called **Model-View-Controller** (usually shortened to MVC) to characterize the "1,000-foot view."

An application organized according to MVC consists of three main types of code. **Models** are concerned with the data manipulated by the application: how to store it, how to operate on it, and how to change it. An MVC app typically has a model for each type of entity manipulated by the app. In our simplified RottenPotatoes app, there is only a Movie model, but we'll be adding others later. Because models deal with the application's data, they contain the code that communicates with the storage tier.

Views are presented to the user and contain information about the models with which users can interact. The views serve as the interface between the system's users and its data; for example, in RottenPotatoes you can list movies and add new movies by clicking on links or buttons in the views. There is only one kind of model in Rotten Potatoes, but it is associated with a variety of views: one view lists all the movies, another view shows the details of a particular movie, and yet other views appear when creating new movies or editing existing ones.

Finally, **controllers** mediate the interaction in both directions: when a user interacts with a view (e.g. by clicking something on a Web page), a specific controller **action** corresponding to that user activity is invoked. Each controller corresponds to one model, and in Rails, each controller action is handled by a particular Ruby method within that controller. The controller can ask the model to retrieve or modify information; depending on the results of doing this, the controller decides what view will be presented next to the user, and supplies that view with any necessary information. Since RottenPotatoes has only one model (Movies), it also has only one controller, the Movies controller. The actions defined in that controller can handle each type of user interaction with any Movie view (clicking on links or buttons, for example) and contain the necessary logic to obtain Model data to *render* any of the Movie views.

Given that SaaS apps have always been view-centric and have always relied on a persistence tier, Rails' choice of MVC as the underlying architecture might seem like an obvious fit. But other choices are possible, such as those in Figure 2.9 excerpted from Martin Fowler's *Catalog of Patterns of Enterprise Application Architecture*[11]. Apps consisting of mostly static content with only a small amount of dynamically-generated content, such as a weather site, might choose the *Template View* pattern. The *Page Controller* pattern works well for an application that is easily structured as a small number of distinct pages, effectively giving each

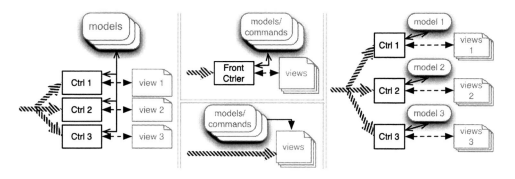

Figure 2.9: Comparing Web app architectural patterns. Models are rounded rectangles, controllers are rectangles, and views are document icons. Page Controller (left), used by Sinatra, has a controller for each logical page of the app. Front Controller (top center), used by Java 2 Enterprise Edition (J2EE) servlets, has a single controller that relies on methods in a variety of models to generate one of a collection of views. Template View (bottom center), used by PHP, emphasizes building the app around the views, with logic in the models generating dynamic content in place of part of the views; the controller is implicit in the framework. Model-View-Controller (right), used by Rails and Java Spring, associates a controller and a set of views with each model type.

page its own simple controller that only knows how to generate that page. For an application that takes a user through a sequence of pages (such as signing up for a mailing list) but has few models, the *Front Controller* pattern might suffice, in which a single controller handles all incoming requests rather than separate controllers handling requests for each model.

Figure 2.10 summarizes our latest understanding of the structure of a SaaS app.

Summary

- The ***Model-View-Controller*** or MVC design pattern distinguishes *models* that implement business logic, *views* that present information to the user and allow the user to interact with the app, and *controllers* that mediate the interaction between views and models.

- In MVC SaaS apps, every user action that can be performed on a web page—clicking a link or button, submitting a fill-in form, or using drag-and-drop—is eventually handled by some controller action, which will consult the model(s) as needed to obtain information and generate a view in response.

- MVC is appropriate for interactive SaaS apps with a variety of model types, where it makes sense to situate controllers and views along with each type of model. Other architectural patterns may be more appropriate for smaller apps with fewer models or a smaller repertoire of operations.

Self-Check 2.5.1. *Which tier(s) in the three-tier architecture are involved in handling each of the following: (a) models, (b) controllers, (c) views?*

⋄ (a) models: logic and persistence tiers; (b) controllers: logic and presentation tiers; (c) views: logic and presentation tiers. ∎

1. A Web client (Firefox) requests the Rotten Potatoes home page from a Web server (WEBrick).
   a) Firefox constructs an HTTP request using the URI *http://localhost:3000* to contact an HTTP server (WEBrick) listening on port 3000 on the same computer as Firefox itself (*localhost*).
   b) WEBrick, listening on port 3000, receives the HTTP request for the resource '/movies' (the list of all movies in Rotten Potatoes).

2. WEBrick obtains content from the Rotten Potatoes app and sends this content back to Firefox
   a) Via the Rack middleware (written in Ruby), WEBrick calls Rotten Potatoes code in the application tier. This code generates the page content using movie information stored in the persistence tier implemented by a SQLite database using local files.
      i) Rack routes the request to the *index* action of the Movies controller; the resource named by this route is the list of all movies
      ii) The Ruby function implementing the *index* action in the Movies controller asks the *Movie* model for a list of movies and associated attributes.
      iii) If successful, the controller identifies a View that contains the HTML markup for presenting the list of movies, and passes it the movie information so that an HTML page can be constructed. If it fails, the controller identifies a View that displays an error message.
      iv) Rack passes the constructed view to WEBrick, which sends it back to Firefox as the HTTP reply.
   b) WEBrick returns content encoded in HTML, again using HTTP. The HTML may contain references to other kinds of media such as images to embed in the displayed page. The HTML may also contain a reference to a CSS stylesheet containing formatting information describing the desired visual attributes of the page (font sizes, colors, layout, and so on).

3. Firefox displays the content and closes the HTTP connection.
   a) Firefox fetches any referenced assets (CSS, images, and so on) by repeating the previous four steps as needed but providing the URIs of the desired assets as referenced in the HTML page.
   b) Firefox displays the page according to the CSS formatting directives and including any referenced assets such as embedded images.

Figure 2.10: Step 2a has been expanded to show the role of the MVC architecture in fulfilling a SaaS app request.

id	title	rating	release_date	description
1	Gone with the Wind	G	1939-12-15	An American classic ...
2	Casablanca	PG	1942-11-26	Casablanca is a...

Figure 2.11: A possible RDBMS table for storing movie information. The `id` column gives each row's *primary key* or permanent and unique identifier. Most databases can be configured to assign primary keys automatically in various ways; Rails uses the very common convention of assigning integers in increasing order.

2.6 500 Feet: Active Record for Models

How do the models, views, and controllers actually do their jobs? Again, we can go far by describing them in terms of patterns.

Every nontrivial application needs to store and manipulate persistent data. Whether using a database, a plain file, or other persistent storage location, we need a way to convert between the data structures or objects manipulated by the application code and the way that data is stored. In the version of RottenPotatoes used in this chapter, the only persistent data is information about movies. Each movie's *attributes* include its title, release date, MPAA rating, and short "blurb" summarizing the movie. A naive approach might be to store the movie information in a plain text file, with one line of the file corresponding to one movie and attributes separated by commas:

http://pastebin.com/FYLxpiAT

```
1 | Gone with the Wind,G,1939-12-15,An American classic ...
2 | Casablanca,PG,1942-11-26,Casablanca is a classic and...
```

To retrieve movie information, we would read each line of the file and split it into *fields* at the commas. Of course we will run into a problem with the movie *Food, Inc.* whose title contains a comma:

http://pastebin.com/LFSX4LSH

```
1 | Food, Inc.,PG,2008-09-07,The current method of raw...
```

We might try to fix this by surrounding each field with quote marks:

http://pastebin.com/KubsyZHq

```
1 | "Food, Inc.","PG","2008-09-07","The current method of raw..."
```

...which will be fine until we try to enter the movie *Waiting for "Superman"*. As this example shows, devising even a simple storage format involves tricky pitfalls, and would require writing code to convert an in-memory object to our storage representation (called **marshalling** or **serializing** the object) and vice versa (*unmarshalling* or *deserializing*).

Fortunately, the need to persist objects is so common that several design patterns have evolved to fulfill it. A subset of these patterns makes use of **structured storage**—storage systems that allow you to simply specify the desired structure of stored objects rather than writing explicit code to create that structure, and in some cases, to specify relationships connecting objects of different types. *Relational database management systems* (RDBMSs) evolved in the early 1970s as elegant structured storage systems whose design was based on a formalism for representing structure and relationships. We will discuss RDBMSs in more detail later, but in brief, an RDBMS stores a collection of *tables*, each of which stores entities with a common set of *attributes*. One row in the table corresponds to one entity, and the columns in that row correspond to the attribute values for that entity. The `movies` table for RottenPotatoes includes columns for `title`, `rating`, `release_date`, and `description`, and the rows of the table look like Figure 2.11.

Edgar F. "Ted" Codd (1923–2003) received the 1981 Turing Award for inventing the **relational algebra** formalism underlying relational databases.

Since it is the responsibility of the Models to manage the application's data, some correspondence must be established between the operations on a model object in memory (for example, an object representing a movie) and how it is represented and manipulated in the storage tier. The in-memory object is usually represented by a class that, among other things, provides a way to represent the object's attributes, such as the title and rating in the case of a movie. The choice made by the Rails framework is to use the **Active Record architectural pattern**. In this pattern, a single instance of a model class (in our case, the entry for a single movie) corresponds to a single row in a specific table of an RDBMS. The model object has built-in behaviors that directly operate on the database representation of the object:

- Create a new row in the table (representing a new object),

- Read an existing row into a single object instance,

- Update an existing row with new attribute values from a modified object instance,

- Delete a row (destroying the object's data forever).

This collection of four commands is often abbreviated **CRUD**. Later we will add the ability for moviegoers to review their favorite movies, so there will be a one-to-many relationship or *association* between a moviegoer and her reviews; Active Record exploits existing mechanisms in the RDBMS based on foreign keys (which we'll learn about later) to make it easy to implement these associations on the in-memory objects.

Summary

- One important job of the Model in an MVC SaaS app is to persist data, which requires converting between the in-memory representation of an object and its representation in permanent storage.

- Various design patterns have evolved to meet this requirement, many of them making use of structured storage such as Relational Database Management Systems (RDBMSs) to simplify not only the storage of model data but the maintenance of relationships among models.

- The four basic operations supported by RDBMSs are Create, Read, Update, Delete (abbreviated CRUD).

- In the ActiveRecord design pattern, every model knows how to do the CRUD operations for its type of object. The Rails ActiveRecord library provides rich functionality for SaaS apps to use this pattern.

Self-Check 2.6.1. *Which of the following are examples of structured storage: (a) an Excel spreadsheet, (b) a plain text file containing the text of an email message, (c) a text file consisting of names, with exactly one name per line.*

◇ (a) and (c) are structured, since an app reading those files can make assumptions about how to interpret the content based on structure alone. (b) is unstructured. ∎

2.7 500 Feet: Routes, Controllers, and REST

Active Record gives each model the knowledge of how to create, read, update, and delete instances of itself in the database (CRUD). Recall from Section 2.5 that in the MVC pattern, controller actions mediate the user's Web browser interactions that cause CRUD requests, and in Rails, each controller action is handled by a particular Ruby method in a controller file. Therefore, each incoming HTTP request must be mapped to the appropriate controller and method. This mapping is called a ***route***.

As Figure 2.3 showed, an HTTP request is characterized by the combination of its URI and the ***HTTP method***, sometimes also called the ***HTTP verb***. Of the roughly half dozen methods defined by the HTTP standard, the most widely used in Web apps and service-oriented architecture are GET, POST, PUT, and DELETE. Since the term ***method*** can mean either a function or the HTTP method of a request, when discussing routes we will use *method* to mean the HTTP verb associated with a request and *controller action* or simply *action* to mean the application code (method or function) that handles the request.

A route, then, associates a URI plus an HTTP method with a particular controller and action. In 2000, Roy Fielding proposed, in his Ph.D. dissertation, a consistent way to map requests to actions that is particularly well suited to a service-oriented architecture. His idea was to identify the various entities manipulated by a Web app as ***resources***, and design the routes so that any HTTP request would contain all the information necessary to identify both a particular resource and the action to be performed on it. He called the idea ***Representational State Transfer***, or REST for short.

Although simple to explain, REST is an unexpectedly powerful organizing principle for SaaS applications, because it makes the app designer think carefully about exactly what conditions or assumptions each request depends on in order to be self-contained and how each type of entity manipulated by the app can be represented as a "resource" on which various operations can be performed. Apps designed in accordance with this guideline are said to expose RESTful APIs (Application Programming Interfaces), and the URIs that map to particular actions are said to be RESTful URIs.

In Rails, the route mappings are generated by code in the file `config/routes.rb`, which we'll learn about in Chapter 4. While Rails doesn't mandate that routes be RESTful, its built-in support for routing assumes REST by default. Figure 2.12 explains the information displayed when you type `rake routes` in a terminal window while in the `rottenpotatoes` directory. In a URI such as `/movies/:id`, the tokens beginning with ':' are parameters of the route; in this case `:id` represents the `id` attribute (primary key) of a model instance. For example, the route GET `/movies/8` will match the second row of Figure 2.12 with `:id` having the value 8; therefore it is a request to display the details for the movie whose ID in the Movies table is 8, if such a movie exists. Similarly, the route GET `/movies` matches the first row, requesting a list of all the movies (the Index action), and the route POST `/movies` matches the fourth row and creates a new movie entry in the database. (The POST `/movies` route doesn't specify an `id` because the new movie won't have an ID until after it's created.) Note that the Index and Create actions have the same URI but different HTTP methods, which makes them distinct routes.

Critically, a RESTful interface simplifies participating in a Service-Oriented Architecture because if every request is self-contained, interactions between services don't need to establish or rely on the concept of an ongoing session, as many SaaS apps do when interacting with human users via a Web browser. This is why Jeff Bezos's mandate (Section 1.4) that all

`rake` runs maintenance tasks defined in RottenPotatoes' `Rakefile`. `rake --help` shows other options.

Operation on resource	Method & URI	Controller action
Index (list) movies	`GET` `/movies`	**index**
Read (show) existing movie	`GET` `/movies/:id`	**show**
Display fill-in form for new movie	`GET` `/movies/new`	**new**
Create new movie from filled-in form	`POST` `/movies`	**create**
Display form to edit existing movie	`GET` `/movies/:id/edit`	**edit**
Update movie from fill-in form	`PUT` `/movies/:id`	**update**
Destroy existing movie	`DELETE` `/movies/:id`	**destroy**

Figure 2.12: A summary of the output of `rake routes` showing the routes recognized by RottenPotatoes and the CRUD action represented by each route. The rightmost column shows which Rails controller action in the Movies controller would be called when a request matches the given URI and HTTP method. The mapping of routes to methods relies heavily on convention over configuration, as we'll see in Chapter 4.

internal Amazon services have "externalizable" APIs was so forward-looking.

Indeed, modern practice suggests that even when creating a user-facing SaaS app designed to be used via a browser, we should think of the app primarily as a collection of resources accessible via RESTful APIs that happen to be accessed via a Web browser. Unfortunately, this presents a minor problem, which you may have already spotted if you have prior Web programming experience. The routes in Figure 2.12 make use of four different HTTP methods—GET, POST, PUT and DELETE—and even use different methods to distinguish routes with the same URI. However, for historical reasons, Web browsers only implement GET (for following a link) and POST (for submitting forms). To compensate, Rails' routing mechanism lets browsers use POST for requests that normally would require PUT or DELETE. Rails annotates the Web forms associated with such requests so that when the request is submitted, Rails can recognize it as special and can internally change the HTTP method "seen" by the controller to PUT or DELETE as appropriate. The result is that the Rails programmer can operate under the assumption that PUT and DELETE are actually supported, even though browsers don't implement them. The advantage, as we will see, is that the same set of routes and controller methods can be used to handle either requests coming from a browser (that is, from a human being) and requests coming from another service in a SOA.

Actually, most browsers also implement HEAD, which requests metadata about a resource, but we needn't worry about that here.

Exploring this important duality further, observe in Figure 2.12 that the new and create routes (third and fourth rows of the table) both appear to be involved in handling the creation of a new movie. Why are two routes needed for this action? The reason is that in a user-facing Web app, two interactions are required to create a new movie, as Screencast 2.7.1 shows; whereas in a SOA, the remote service can create a single request containing all the information needed to create the new movie, so it would never need to use the new route.

> **Screencast 2.7.1: Create and Update each require two interactions.**
> `http://vimeo.com/34754622`
> Creating a new movie requires two interactions with RottenPotatoes, because before the user can submit information about the movie he must be presented with a form in which to enter that information. The empty form is therefore the resource named by the route in the third row of Figure 2.12, and the submission of the filled-in form is the resource named by the route in the fourth row. Similarly, updating an existing movie requires one resource consisting of an editable form showing the existing movie info (fifth row) and a second resource consisting of the submission of the edited form (sixth row).

RESTfulness may seem an obvious design choice, but until Fielding crisply characterized the REST philosophy and began promulgating it, many Web apps were designed non-

	Non-RESTful site URI	RESTful site URI
Login to site	`POST /login/dave`	`POST /login/dave`
Welcome page	`GET /welcome`	`GET /user/301/welcome`
Add item ID 427 to cart	`POST /add/427`	`POST /user/301/add/427`
View cart	`GET / cart`	`GET /user/301/cart`
Checkout	`POST /checkout`	`POST /user/301/checkout`

Figure 2.13: Non-RESTful requests and routes are those that rely on the results of previous requests. In a Service-Oriented Architecture, a client of the RESTful site could immediately request to view the cart (line 6), but a client of the non-RESTful site would first have to perform lines 3–5 to set up the implicit information on which line 6 depends.

RESTfully. Figure 2.13 shows how a hypothetical non-RESTful e-commerce site might implement the functionality of allowing a user to login, adding a specific item to his shopping cart, and proceeding to checkout. For the hypothetical non-RESTful site, every request after the login (line 3) relies on implicit information: line 4 assumes the site "remembers" who the currently-logged-in user is to show him his welcome page, and line 7 assumes the site "remembers" who has been adding items to their cart for checkout. In contrast, each URI for the RESTful site contains enough information to satisfy the request without relying on such implicit information: after Dave logs in, the fact that his user ID is 301 is present in every request, and his cart is identified explicitly by his user ID rather than implicitly based on the notion of a currently-logged-in user.

Summary: Routes and RESTfulness

- A route consists of an HTTP method (`GET`, `POST`, `PUT`, or `DELETE`) and a URI, which may include some parameters. App frameworks such as Rails map routes to controller actions.

- An app designed in accordance with REST (REpresentational State Transfer) can be seen from the outside as a collection of entities on which specific operations can be performed, with each operation having a corresponding RESTful request that includes all the information necessary to complete the action.

- When routes and resources are RESTful, the same controller logic can usually serve user-facing pages via a Web browser or requests arriving from other services in a SOA. Although web browsers only support the `GET` and `POST` HTTP methods, framework logic can compensate so that the programmer can work under the assumption that all methods are available.

■ *Elaboration: REST vs. SOAP vs. WS-**
_____

In the late 1990s, as interest in SOA increased, vendors and standards bodies created committees to develop standards for SOA interoperation. One approach resulted in a collection of elaborate protocols for **Web** Services including WS-Discovery, WS-Description, and others, sometimes collectively called ***WS-**** and jokingly called "WS-Deathstar" by David Heinemeier Hansson, the creator of Rails. The competing ***SOAP*** standard (Simple Object Access Protocol) was a bit simpler but still far more complex than REST. By and large, practicing developers perceived SOAP and WS-* as overdesigned committee-driven standards burdened by the archaic design stance of enterprise-based interoperation standards such as CORBA and DCOM, which preceded them. In contrast, although REST is dramatically simpler and is more of a philosophy than a standard, it appealed immediately to developers, so that is how the majority of SOA apps are built today.
_____

Self-Check 2.7.1. *True or false: If an app has a RESTful API, it must be performing CRUD operations.*

◇ False. The REST principle can be applied to any kind of operation, as long as the app represents its entities as resources and specifies what operations are allowed on each type of resource. ■

Self-Check 2.7.2. *True or false: Supporting RESTful operations simplifies integrating a SaaS app with other services in a Service-Oriented Architecture.*

◇ True. ■

2.8 500 Feet: Template Views

We conclude our brief tour with a look at views. Because user-facing SaaS applications primarily deliver HTML pages, most frameworks provide a way to create a page of static markup (HTML or otherwise) interspersed with variables or very brief snippets of code. At runtime, the variable values or results of code execution are substituted or ***interpolated*** into the page. This architecture is known as Template View, and it is the basis of many SaaS frameworks including Rails, Django, and PHP.

We prefer Haml's conciseness to Rails' built-in *erb* templating system, so Haml is preinstalled with the bookware.

We will use a templating system called Haml (for HTML Abstraction Markup Language, pronounced "HAM-ell") to streamline the creation of HTML template views. We will learn more details and create our own views in Chapter 4, but in the interest of visiting all the "moving parts" of a Rails app, open `app/views/movies/index.html.haml` in the RottenPotatoes directory. This is the view used by the Index controller action on movies; by convention over configuration, the suffixes `.html.haml` indicate that the view should be processed using Haml to create `index.html`, and the location and name of the file identify it as the view for the **index** action in the **movies** controller. Screencast 2.8.1 presents the basics of Haml, summarized in Figure 2.14.

Haml	HTML
`%br{:clear => 'left'}`	`<br clear="left"/>`
`%p.foo Hello`	`<p class="foo">Hello</p>`
`%p#foo Hello`	`<p id="foo">Hello</p>`
`.foo`	`<div class="foo">...</div>`
`#foo.bar`	`<div id="foo" class="bar">...</div>`

Figure 2.14: Some commonly used Haml constructs and the resulting HTML. A Haml tag beginning with % must either contain the tag and all its content on a single line, as in lines 1–3 of the table, or must appear by itself on the line as in lines 4–5, in which case all of the tag's content must be indented by 2 spaces on subsequent lines. Notice that Haml specifies `class` and `id` attributes using a notation deliberately similar to CSS selectors.

Screencast 2.8.1: Interpolation into views using Haml.

`http://vimeo.com/34754654`

In a Haml template, lines beginning with % expand into the corresponding HTML opening tag, with no closing tag needed since Haml uses indentation to determine structure. Ruby-like hashes following a tag become HTML attributes. Lines **–beginning with a dash** are executed as Ruby code with the result discarded, and lines **=beginning with an equals sign** are executed as Ruby code with the result interpolated into the HTML output.

According to MVC, views should contain as little code as possible. Although Haml technically permits arbitrarily complex Ruby code in a template, its syntax for including a multi-line piece of code is deliberately awkward, to discourage programmers from doing so. Indeed, the only "computation" in the Index view of RottenPotatoes is limited to iterating over a collection (provided by the Model via the Controller) and generating an HTML table row to display each element.

In contrast, applications written using the PHP framework often mingle large amounts of code into the view templates, and while it's possible for a disciplined PHP programmer to separate the views from the code, the PHP framework itself provides no particular support for doing this, nor does it reward the effort. MVC advocates argue that distinguishing the controller from the view makes it easier to think first about structuring an app as a set of RESTful actions, and later about rendering the results of these actions in a separate View step. Section 1.4 made the case for Service-Oriented Architecture; it should now be clear how the separation of models, views and controllers, and adherence to a RESTful controller style, naturally leads to an application whose actions are easy to "externalize" as standalone API actions.

■ *Elaboration: Alternatives to Template View*

Because all Web apps must ultimately deliver HTML to a browser, building the output (view) around a static HTML "template" has always made sense for Web apps, hence the popularity of the Template View pattern for rendering views. That is, the input to the view-rendering stage includes both the HTML template and a set of Ruby variables that Haml will use to "fill in" dynamic content. An alternative is the Transform View pattern (Fowler 2002), in which the input to the view stage is *only* the set of objects. The view code then includes all the logic for converting the objects to the desired view representation. This pattern makes more sense if many different representations are possible, since the view layer is no longer "built around" any particular representation. An example of Transform View in Rails is a set of Rails methods that accept ActiveRecord resources and generate pure-XML representations of the resources—they do not instantiate any "template" to do so, but rather create the XML starting with just the ActiveRecord objects. These methods are used to quickly convert an HTML-serving Rails app into one that can be part of a Service-Oriented Architecture.

Self-Check 2.8.1. *What is the role of indentation in the Index view for Movies described in Screencast 2.8.1?*

◇ When one HTML element encloses other elements, indentation tells Haml the structure of the nesting so that it can generate closing tags such as `</tr>` in the proper places. ■

Self-Check 2.8.2. *In the Index view for Movies, why does the Haml markup in line 11 begin with −, while the markup in lines 13–16 begins with =?*

◇ In line 10 we just need the code to execute, to start the for-loop. In lines 13–16 we want to substitute the result of executing the code into the view. ■

2.9   Fallacies and Pitfalls

 Fallacy: **Rails doesn't scale (or Django, or PHP, or other frameworks).**

With the shared-nothing 3-tier architecture depicted in Figure 2.7, the Web server and app server tiers (where Rails apps would run) can be scaled almost arbitrarily far by adding computers in each tier using cloud computing. The challenge lies in scaling the database, as the next Pitfall explains.

 Pitfall: **Putting all model data in an RDBMS on a single server computer, thereby limiting scalability.**

The power of RDBMSs is a double-edged sword. It's easy to create database structures prone to scalability problems that might not emerge until a service grows to hundreds of thousands of users. Some developers feel that Rails compounds this problem because its Model abstractions are so productive that it is tempting to use them without thinking of the scalability consequences. Unfortunately, unlike with the Web server and app tiers, we cannot "scale our way out" of this problem by simply deploying many copies of the database because this might result in different values for different copies of the same item (the **data consistency** problem). Although techniques such as master-slave replication and database **sharding** help make the database tier more like the shared-nothing presentation and logic tiers, extreme database scalability remains an area of both research and engineering effort.

⚠️ **Pitfall: Prematurely focusing on per-computer performance of your SaaS app.**

Although the shared-nothing architecture makes horizontal scaling easy, we still need physical computers to do it. Adding a computer used to be expensive (buy the computer), time-consuming (configure and install the computer), and permanent (if demand subsides later, you'll be paying for an idle computer). With cloud computing, all three problems are alleviated, since we can add computers instantly for pennies per hour and release them when we don't need them anymore. Hence, until a SaaS app becomes large enough to require hundreds of computers, SaaS developers should focus on *horizontal scalability* rather than per-computer performance.

2.10 Concluding Remarks: Patterns, Architecture, and Long-Lived APIs

An API that isn't comprehensible isn't usable.

—James Gosling

To understand the architecture of a software system is to understand its organizing principles. We did this by identifying patterns at many different levels: client-server, three-tier architecture, model-view-controller, Active Record, REST.

Patterns are a powerful way to manage complexity in large software systems. Inspired by Christopher Alexander's 1977 book *A Pattern Language: Towns, Buildings, Construction* describing design patterns for civil architecture, Erich Gamma, Richard Helm, Ralph Johnson and John Vlissides (the "Gang Of Four" or GOF) published the seminal book *Design Patterns: Elements of Reusable Object-Oriented Software* in 1995 (Gamma et al. 1994). It described what are now called the 23 GOF Design Patterns focusing on class-level structures and behaviors. Despite design patterns' popularity as a tool, they have been the subject of some critique; for example, Peter Norvig, currently Google's Director of Research, has argued that some design patterns just compensate for deficiencies in statically-typed programming languages such as C++ and Java, and that the need for them disappears in dynamic languages such as Lisp or Ruby. Notwithstanding some controversy, patterns of many kinds remain a valuable way for software engineers to identify structure in their work and bring proven solutions to bear on recurring problems.

Indeed, we observe that by choosing to build a SaaS app, we have predetermined the use of some patterns and excluded others. By choosing to use Web standards, we have predetermined a client-server system; by choosing cloud computing, we have predetermined the 3-tier architecture to permit horizontal scaling. Model–View–Controller is not predetermined, but we choose it because it is a good fit for Web apps that are view-centric and have historically relied on a persistence tier, notwithstanding other possible patterns such as those in Figure 2.9. REST is not predetermined, but we choose it because it simplifies integration into a Service-Oriented Architecture and can be readily applied to the CRUD operations, which are so common in MVC apps. Active Record is perhaps more controversial—as we will see in Chapters 4 and 5, its powerful facilities simplify apps considerably, but misusing those facilities can lead to scalability and performance problems that are less likely to occur with simpler persistence models.

If we were building a SaaS app in 1995, none of the above would have been obvious because practitioners had not accumulated enough examples of successful SaaS apps to "extract" successful patterns into frameworks like Rails, software components like Apache, and

In fact, Rails itself was
originally extracted from a
standalone app written by
the consulting group
37signals.

middleware like Rack. By following the successful footsteps of software architects before us, we can take advantage of their ability to *separate the things that change from those that stay the same* across many examples of SaaS and provide tools, frameworks, and design principles that support building things this way. As we mentioned earlier, this separation is key to enabling reuse.

Lastly, it is worth remembering that a key factor in the Web's success has been the adoption of well-defined protocols and formats whose design allows separating the things that change from those that stay the same. TCP/IP, HTTP, and HTML have all gone through several major revisions, but all include ways to detect which version is in use, so a client can tell if it's talking to an older server (or vice versa) and adjust its behavior accordingly. Although dealing with multiple protocol and language versions puts an additional burden on browsers, it has led to a remarkable result: A Web page created in 2011, using a markup language based on 1960s technology, can be retrieved using network protocols developed in 1969 and displayed by a browser created in 1992. Separating the things that change from those that stay the same is part of the path to creating long-lived software.

Tim Berners-Lee, a
computer scientist at
CERN[12], led the
development of HTTP and
HTML in 1990. Both are
now stewarded by the
nonprofit vendor-neutral
World Wide Web
Consortium (W3C)[13].

2.11   To Learn More

- W3Schools[14] is a free (advertising-supported) site with tutorials on almost all Web-related technologies.

- Nicole Sullivan[15], a self-described "CSS ninja," has a great blog with indispensable CSS/HTML advice for more sophisticated sites.

- The World Wide Web Consortium (W3C)[16] stewards the official documents describing the Web's open standards, including HTTP, HTML, and CSS.

- The XML/XHTML Validator[17] is one of many you can use to ensure the pages delivered by your SaaS app are standards-compliant.

- The Object-Oriented Design web site[18] has numerous useful resources for developers using OO languages, including a nice catalog of the GoF design patterns with graphical descriptions of each pattern, some of which we will discuss in detail in Chapter 11.

M. Fowler. *Patterns of Enterprise Application Architecture*. Addison-Wesley Professional, 2002. ISBN 0321127420. URL `http://martinfowler.com/eaaCatalog/`.

E. Gamma, R. Helm, R. Johnson, and J. M. Vlissides. *Design Patterns: Elements of Reusable Object-Oriented Software*. Addison-Wesley Professional, 1994. ISBN 0201633612.

Notes

[1] `http://en.wikipedia.org/wiki/Pentium_FDIV_bug`
[2] `http://rottentomatoes.com`
[3] `http://projects.apache.org/projects/http_server.html`
[4] `http://www.iis.net`
[5] `http://docs.google.com`
[6] `http://iana.org`

[7] http://www.w3.org/TR/html5/introduction.html#history-1
[8] http://csszengarden.com
[9] http://heroku.com
[10] http://adam.heroku.com/past/2009/7/6/sql_databases_dont_scale/
[11] http://martinfowler.com/eaaCatalog
[12] http://info.cern.ch
[13] http://w3.org
[14] http://w3schools.com
[15] http://www.stubbornella.org/content
[16] http://w3.org
[17] http://validator.w3.org
[18] http://oodesign.com

2.12 Suggested Projects

Project 2.1. *If the DNS service stopped working, would you still be able to surf the Web? Explain why or why not.*

Project 2.2. *Suppose HTTP cookies didn't exist. Could you devise another way to track a user across page views? (HINT: it involves modifying the URI and was a widely-used method before cookies were invented.)*

Project 2.3. *Find a Web page for which the W3C's online XHTML validator[1] finds at least one error. Sadly, this should be easy. Read through the validation error messages and try to understand what each one means.*

Project 2.4. *What port numbers are implied by each of the following URIs and why:*

1. *https://paypal.com*

2. *http://mysite.com:8000/index*

3. *ssh://root@cs.berkeley.edu/tmp/file (HINT: recall that the IANA establishes default port numbers for various network services.)*

Project 2.5. *As described on the DuckDuckGo Search API documentation[2], you can do query the DuckDuckGo search engine for a term by constructing a URI that includes the search query as a parameter named q, for example, http://api.duckduckgo.com/?q=saas to search for the term "saas". However, as Figure 2.3 showed, some characters are not allowed in URIs because they are "special," including spaces, '?', and '&'. Given this restriction, construct a legal URI that searches DuckDuckGo for the terms "M&M" and "100%?".*

String#ord returns the string's first **codepoint** (numeric value corresponding to a character in a character set). If the string is encoded in **ASCII**, **ord** returns the first character's ASCII code. So **"%".ord** shows the ASCII code for **%**, and **"%".ord.to_s(16)** shows its hexadecimal equivalent.

Project 2.6. *Why do Rails routes map to controller actions but not model actions or views?*

Project 2.7. *Given a high-level design, identify the software architecture by differentiating among common software architectures such as three-tier, pipe-and-filter, and client-server.*

Project 2.8. *Investigate the impact of software architectures selection on the design of a simple system. Look at alternatives to client-server, alternatives to request-reply, and so on.*

3

SaaS Framework: Introduction to Ruby for Java Programmers

Jim Gray (1944–Lost at sea 2007) was a friendly giant in computer science. He was the first PhD in Computer Science from UC Berkeley, and he mentored hundreds of PhD students and faculty around the world. He received the 1998 Turing Award for contributions to database and transaction processing research and technical leadership in system implementation.

Well, the <omitted> paper is in good company (and for the same reason).
The B-tree paper was rejected at first.
The Transaction paper was rejected at first.
The data cube paper was rejected at first.
The five-minute rule paper was rejected at first.
But linear extensions of previous work get accepted.
So, resubmit! PLEASE!!!

—Jim Gray, Email to Jim Larus about a rejected paper, 2000

Concepts

This chapter introduces both the Ruby equivalents of basic object-oriented techniques in other languages such as Java and some Ruby mechanisms with no Java counterparts that help with reuse and DRYness.

- *Everything* is an object in Ruby, even a lowly integer, and all Ruby operations are accomplished by method calls on objects.

- *Reflection* lets your code inspect itself at runtime and *metaprogramming* allows it to generate and execute new code at runtime.

- Ruby borrows great ideas from *functional programming*, especially the use of *blocks*—parameterized chunks of code called *lambda expressions* that carry their scope around with them, making them *closures*.

- Ruby's **yield** statement, which has no Java counterpart, enables reuse by separating the traversal of data structures from operations on their elements using a *coroutine*-like mechanism.

- Because of Ruby's *dynamic typing*, to determine whether you can call a certain method on a certain object, you don't consider the object's type—only whether it can respond to the method. Some call this feature *duck typing*: "If it looks like an array, walks like an array, and quacks like an array, then you can treat it like an array."

Metaprogramming, reflection, dynamic typing, and blocks using **yield** can be tastefully combined to write DRYer, more concise, and more beautiful code.

3.1   Overview and Three Pillars of Ruby

Programming can only be learned by doing, so we've placed this icon in the margin in places where we strongly encourage you to try the examples yourself. Since Ruby is interpreted, there's no compile step—you get instant gratification when trying the examples, and exploration and experimentation are easy. Each example has a link to Pastebin[3], where you can copy the code for that example with a single click and paste it into a Ruby interpreter or editor window. (If you're reading the ebook, these links are live.) We also encourage you to check the official documentation for much more detail on many topics we introduce in Section 3.11.

Ruby is a minimalist language: while its libraries are rich, there are few mechanisms *in the language itself*. Three principles underlying these mechanisms will help you read and understand idiomatic code:

1. Everything is an object. In Java, some primitive types like integers must be "boxed" to get them to behave like objects.

2. Every operation is a method call on some object and returns a value. In Java, operator overloading is different from method overriding, and it's possible to have **void** functions that return no value.

3. All programming is metaprogramming: classes and methods can be added or changed at any time, even while a program is running. In Java, all classes must be declared at compile time, and base classes can't be modified by your app even then.

Each of these three principles will be covered in its own section. #1 and #2 are straightforward. #3 gives Ruby much of its productivity-enhancing power, but must be qualified with the admonition that with great power comes great responsibility. Using Ruby's metaprogramming features tastefully will make your code elegant and DRY, but abusing them will make your code brittle and impenetrable.

Ruby's basic syntax should be unsurprising if you're familiar with other modern scripting languages. Figure 3.1 shows the syntax of basic Ruby elements. Statements are separated by newlines (most commonly) or semicolons (rarely). Indentation is insignificant. While Ruby is concise enough that a single line of code rarely exceeds one screen line, breaking up a single statement with a newline is allowed if it doesn't cause a parsing ambiguity. An editor with good syntax highlighting can be very helpful if you're not sure whether your line break is legal.

A *symbol*, such as :octocat, is an immutable string whose value is itself; it is typically used in Ruby for enumerations, like an **enum** type in C or Java, though it has other purposes as well. However, a symbol is not the same as a string—it is its own primitive type, and string operations cannot be performed on it, though it can easily be converted to a string by calling **to_s**. For example, :octocat.to_s gives "octocat", and "octocat".to_sym gives :octocat.

Regular expressions or *regexps* (often *regex* and *regexes* in order to be pronounceable) are part of every programmer's toolbox. A regular expression allows matching a string against a pattern containing possible "wildcards." Ruby's regular expression support resembles that of other modern programming languages: regexes appear between slashes and may be followed by one or more letters modifying their behavior, for example, /*regex*/i to indicate that the regex should ignore case when matching. As Figure 3.2 shows, special constructs embedded in the regex can match multiple types of characters and can specify the number of times

Variables	local_variable, @@class_variable, @instance_variable
Constants	ClassName, CONSTANT, $GLOBAL, $global
Booleans	**false, nil** are false; **true** and *everything else* (zero, empty string, etc.) is true.
Strings and Symbols	**"string", 'also a string', %q{like single quotes}, %Q{like double quotes}, :symbol** special characters (**\n**) expanded in double-quoted but not single-quoted strings
Expressions in *double-quoted* strings	**@foo = 3 ; "Answer is #{@foo}"; %Q{Answer is #{@foo+1}}**
Regular expression matching	**"hello" =~ /lo/** or **"hello".match(Regexp.new 'lo')**
Arrays	**a = [1, :two, 'three'] ; a[1] == :two**
Hashes	**h = {:a =>1, 'b' =>"two"} ; h['b'] == "two" ; h.has_key?(:a) == true**
Hashes (alternate notation, Ruby 1.9+)	**h = {a: 1, 'b': "two"}**
Instance method	**def method(***arg, arg***)...end** (*use ***args** *for variable number of arguments*
Class (static) method	**def ClassName.method(***arg, arg***)...end,** **def self.method(***arg, arg***)...end**
Special method names *Ending these methods' names in* ? *and* ! *is optional but idiomatic*	**def setter=(***arg, arg***)...end** **def boolean_method?(***arg, arg***)...end** **def dangerous_method!(***arg, arg***)...end**

Conditionals	**Iteration** (see Section 3.6)	**Exceptions**
if *cond* (or **unless** *cond*) 　*statements* [**elsif** *cond* 　*statements*] [**else** 　*statements*] **end**	**while** *cond* (or **until** *cond*) 　*statements* **end** **1.upto(10) do |i|**...**end** **10.times do**...**end** *collection*.**each do |elt|**...**end**	**begin** 　*statements* **rescue AnError => e** 　**e** *is an exception of class* **AnError**; 　　*multiple* **rescue** *clauses OK* [**ensure** 　*this code is always executed*] **end**

Figure 3.1: Basic Ruby elements and control structures, with optional items in [square brackets].

	Symbol	Meaning	Example	Matches	Example	Mismatch
Count	*	0 or more	a*		aaaa	b
	+	1 or more	a+	a	aaaa	
	?	0 or 1	a?	a	a	aaaa
Anchors, Sets, Range, Append	^	start of line, also NOT in set	^a	a	ab	ba
	$	end of line	a$	a	dcba	ab
	()	group, also captures that group in Ruby	(ab)+	ababab	ab	b
	[]	set	[ab]	a	b	ab
	[x-y]	character range	[0-9]	3	9	a
	|	OR	(It's|It is)	It's	It is	Its
	[^	NOT (opposite) in set	[^"]	b	9	"
	.	any character (except newline)	.{3}	abc	1+2	aa
	\	used to match meta-characters, also for classes	\.$	The End.	.	a
	i	append to pattern to specify case insensitive match	\ab\i	Ab	ab	a
Classes	\d	decimal digit ([0-9])	\d	3	9	a
	\D	not decimal digit ([^0-9])	\D	a	=	3
	\s	whitespace character	\s			a
	\S	not whitespace character	\S	a	=	
	\w	"word" character ([a-zA-Z0-9_])	\w	a	9	=
	\W	"nonword" character ([^a-zA-Z0-9_])	\W	=	$	a
	\n	newline	\n	--	--	a

Figure 3.2: Review of Ruby's regular expressions.

a match must occur and whether the match must be "anchored" to the beginning or end of the string. For example, here is a regex that matches a time of day, such as "8:25pm", on a line by itself:

http://pastebin.com/S61dtePp

```
1 | time_regex = /^\d\d?:\d\d\s*[ap]m$/i
```

This regexp matches a digit at the beginning of a string (^\d), optionally followed by another digit (\d?), followed by a colon, exactly two digits, zero or more whitespace characters (\s*), either **a** or **p**, then **m** at the end of the string (**m$**) and ignoring case (the **i** after the closing slash). Another way to match one or two digits would be **[0-9][0-9]?** and another way to match *exactly* two digits would be **[0-9][0-9]**.

Ruby allows the use of parentheses in regexes to *capture* the matched string or substrings. For example, here is the same regexp with three capture groups:

http://pastebin.com/zFfnSRCG

```
1 | x = "8:25 PM"
2 | x =~ /(\d\d?):(\d\d)\s*([ap])m$/i
```

The second line attempts to match the string **x** against the regex. If the match succeeds, the =~ operator will return the position in the string (with 0 being the first character) at which the match succeeded, the global variable **$1** will have the value **"8"**, **$2** will be **"25"**, and **$3** will be **"P"**. The last-match variables are reset the next time you do another regex match. If the match fails, =~ will return **nil**. Note that **nil** and **false** are not actually equal to each other, but both evaluate to "false" when used in a conditional expression (in fact, they are the *only* two values in Ruby that do so). Idiomatically, methods that are truly Boolean (that is, the only possible return values are "true" or "false") return **false**, whereas methods that return an object when successful return **nil** when they fail.

Lastly, note that =~ works on both strings and **Regexp** objects, so both of the following are legal and equivalent, and you should choose whichever is easiest to understand in the context of your code.

http://pastebin.com/8kKJZKpb

```
1  "Catch 22" =~ /\w+\s+\d+/
2  /\w+\s+\d+/ =~ "Catch 22"
```

Summary

- A distinguishing primitive type in Ruby is the symbol, an immutable string whose value is itself. Symbols are commonly used in Ruby to denote "specialness," such as being one of a set of fixed choices like an enumeration. Symbols aren't the same as strings, but they can easily be converted back and forth with the methods **to_s** and **to_sym**.

- Ruby statements are separated by newlines, or less commonly, by semicolons.

- Ruby's regular expression facilities are comparable to those of other modern languages, including support for capture groups using parentheses and for match modifiers such as a trailing **i** for "ignore case when matching."

Self-Check 3.1.1. *Which of the following Ruby expressions are equal to each other: (a)* **:foo** *(b)* **%q{foo}** *(c)* **%Q{foo}** *(d)* **'foo'.to_sym** *(e)* **:foo.to_s**

◇ (a) and (d) are equal to each other; (b), (c), and (e) are equal to each other ∎

Self-Check 3.1.2. *What is captured by* **$1** *when the string* **25 to 1** *is matched against each of the following regexps:*
(a) **/(\d+)$/**
(b) **/^\d+([^0-9]+)/**

◇ (a) the string "**1**" (b) the string " **to** " (including the leading and trailing spaces) ∎

Self-Check 3.1.3. *When is it correct to write*
Fixnum num=3
to initialize the variable **num***: (a) on its first use; (b) on any use, as long as it's the same class* **Fixnum** *each time; (c) never*

◇ Never; variable declarations aren't used in Ruby. ∎

3.2 Everything is an Object

Ruby supports the usual basic types—fixed-point integers (class **Fixnum**), floating-point numbers (class **Float**), strings (class **String**), linear arrays (class **Array**), and associative arrays or hashmaps (class **Hash**). But in contrast to Java, Ruby is *dynamically typed*: the type of a variable is generally not inferable until runtime. That is, while objects have types, the variables that reference them do not. So **s = 5** can follow **s = "foo"** in the same block of code. Because variables do not have types, an array or hash can consist of elements of all different types, as Figure 3.1 suggests. We speak only of "an array" rather than "an array of Ints" and of "a hash" rather than "a hash with keys of type Foo and values of type Bar."

Ruby's object model descends from Smalltalk, whose design was inspired by ideas in Simula. Everything in Ruby, even a plain integer, is an object that is an instance of some class. All operations, without exception, are performed by calling a method on an object, and every such call (indeed, every Ruby statement) returns a value. The notation **obj.meth()** calls method **meth** on the object **obj**, which is said to be the *receiver* and is hopefully able to *respond to* **meth**. As we will see shortly, parentheses around method arguments are often optional. For example:

http://pastebin.com/Pu0uULN8

```
1 | 5.class      # => Fixnum
```

(We strongly recommend you start up a Ruby interpreter by typing irb in a Terminal window in your VM so you can try these examples as you go.) The above call *sends* the method call **class** to the object **5**. The **class** method happens to return the class that an object belongs to, in this case **Fixnum**. (We will use the notation $\#\ =>$ in code examples to indicate what the interpreter should print as the result of evaluating a given expression.)

Even a class in Ruby is itself an object—it's an instance of **Class**, which is a class whose instances are classes (a *metaclass*).

Every object is an instance of some class. Classes can inherit from superclasses as they do in Java, and all classes ultimately inherit from **BasicObject**, sometimes called the *root class*. Ruby does not support multiple inheritance, so every class has exactly one superclass, except for **BasicObject**, which has no superclass. As with most languages that support inheritance, if an object receives a call for a method not defined in its class, the call will be passed up to the superclass, and so on until the root class is reached. If no class along the way, including the root class, is able to handle the method, an *undefined method* exception is raised.

Try **5.class.superclass** to find out what **Fixnum**'s superclass is; this illustrates *method chaining*, a very common Ruby idiom. Method chaining associates to the left, so this example could be written **(5.class).superclass**, meaning: "Call the **class** method on the receiver **5**, and whatever the result of that is, call the **superclass** method on that receiver."

Object-orientation (OO) and class inheritance are *distinct properties*. Because popular languages such as Java combine both, many people conflate them. Ruby also happens to have both, but the two features do not necessarily interact in all the same ways they would in Java. In particular, compared to Java, reuse through inheritance is much less important, but the implications of object-orientation are much more important. For example, Ruby supports comprehensive *reflection*—the ability to ask objects about themselves. **5.respond_to?('class')** tells you that the object **5** would be able to respond to the method **class** if you asked it to. **5.methods** lists all methods to which the object **5** responds including those defined in its ancestor classes. Given that an object responds to a method, how can you tell if the method is defined in the object's class or an ancestor class? **5.method(:+)** reveals that the + method is defined in class **Fixnum**, whereas **5.method(:ceil)** reveals that the **ceil** method is defined in **Integer**, an ancestor class of **Fixnum**. Determining which class's methods will handle a method call is called *looking up a method* on a receiver, and is analogous to virtual method dispatch in Java.

Summary

- The notation **a.b** means "call method **b** on object **a**." Object **a** is said to be the *receiver*, and if it cannot handle the method call, it will pass the call to its superclass. This process is called *looking up a method* on a receiver.

- Ruby has comprehensive **reflection**, allowing you to ask objects about themselves.

■ *Elaboration: Looking up a method*

Previously we said that if method lookup fails in the receiver's class, the call is passed up to the ancestor (superclass). The truth is a bit more subtle: mix-ins, which we'll describe shortly, can handle a method call *before* punting up to the superclass.

Self-Check 3.2.1. *Why does* **5.superclass** *result in an "undefined method" error? (Hint: consider the difference between calling* **superclass** *on 5 itself vs. calling it on the object returned by* **5.class**.*)*

◇ **superclass** is a method defined on classes. The object **5** is not itself a class, so you can't call **superclass** on it. ■

3.3 Every Operation is a Method Call

To cement the concept that every operation is a method call, note that even basic math operations such as **+**, *****, **==** (equality comparison) are **syntactic sugar** for method calls: the operators are actually method calls on their receivers. The same is true for array dereferences such as **x[0]** and array assignment such as **x[0]="foo"**.

The table in Figure 3.3 shows the de-sugared versions of these expressions and of the regex syntax introduced in Section 3.1, as well as showing how Ruby's core method **send** can be used to send any method call to any object. Many Ruby methods including **send** accept either a symbol or a string argument, so the first example in the table could also be written **10.send('modulo',3)**.

A critical implication of "every operation is a method call" is that concepts such as **type casting** rarely apply in Ruby. In Java, if we write **f+i** where **f** is a float and **i** is an integer, the type casting rules state that **i** will be converted internally to a float so it can be added to **f**. If we wrote **i+s** where **s** is a **String**, a compile-time error would result.

In contrast, in Ruby **+** is just like any other method that can be defined differently by each class, so its behavior depends entirely on the receiver's implementation of the method. Since **f+i** is syntactic sugar for **f.+(i)**, it's entirely up to the **+** method (presumably defined in **f**'s class or one of its ancestor classes) to decide how to handle different types of values for **i**. Thus, both **3+2** and **"foo"+"bar"** are legal Ruby expressions, evaluating to **5** and **"foobar"** respectively, but the first one is calling **+** as defined in **Numeric** (the ancestor class of **Fixnum**) whereas the second is calling **+** as defined in **String**. As above, you can verify that **"foobar".method(:+)** and **5.method(:+)** refer to distinct methods. Although this might resemble operator overloading in other languages, it's more general: since only the method's name matters for dispatching, we'll see in Section 3.7 how this feature enables a powerful reuse mechanism called a mix-in.

In Ruby the notation **ClassName#method** is used to indicate the instance method

Sugared	De-sugared	Explicit send
10 % 3	10.modulo(3)	10.send(:modulo, 3)
5+3	5.+(3)	5.send(:+, 3)
x == y	x.==(y)	x.send(:==, y)
a * x + y	a.*(x).+(y)	a.send(:*, x).send(:+, y)
a + x * y	a.+(x.*(y))	a.send(:+, x.send(:*, y))
		(operator precedence preserved)
x[3]	x.[](3)	x.send(:[], 3)
x[3] = 'a'	x.[]=(3,'a')	x.send(:[]=, 3, 'a')
/abc/, %r{abc}	Regexp.new("abc")	Regexp.send(:new, 'abc')
str =~ regex	str.match(regex)	str.send(:match, regex)
regex =~ str	regex.match(str)	regex.send(:match, str)
$1...**$**n (regex capture)	Regexp.last_match(n)	Regexp.send(:last_match,n)

Figure 3.3: The first column is Ruby's syntactic sugar for common operations, the second column shows the explicit method call, and the third column shows how to perform the same method call using Ruby's send, which accepts either a string or a symbol (more idiomatic) for the method name.

method in **ClassName**, whereas **ClassName.method** indicates the class (static) method **method** in **ClassName**. Using this notation, we can say that the expression **3+2** results in calling **Fixnum#+** on the receiver **3**, whereas the expression **"foo"+"bar"** results in calling **String#+** on the receiver **"foo"**.

Similarly, in Java it's common to see explicit casts of a variable to a subclass, such as **Foo x = (Foo)y** where **y** is an instance of a subclass of **Foo**. In Ruby this is meaningless because variables don't have types, and it doesn't matter whether the responding method is in the receiver's class or one of its ancestors.

A method is defined with **def method_name(arg1,arg2)** and ends with **end**; all statements in between are the method definition. Every expression in Ruby has a value—for example, the value of an assignment is its right-hand side, so the value of **x=5** is 5— and if a method doesn't include an explicit **return(blah)**, the value of the last expression in the method is returned. Hence the following trivial method returns 5:

http://pastebin.com/xGYTktUK

```
1  def trivial_method    # no arguments; can also use trivial_method()
2    x = 5
3  end
```

The variable **x** in the example is a local variable; its scope is limited to the block in which it's defined, in this case the method, and is undefined outside that method. In other words, Ruby uses *lexical scoping* for local variables. When we talk about classes in Ruby, we'll see how class and instance variables are alternatives to local variables.

An important Ruby idiom is *poetry mode*: the ability to omit parentheses and curly braces when the parsing is unambiguous. Most commonly, Ruby programmers may omit parentheses around arguments to a method call, and omit curly braces when the *last* argument to a method call is a hash. Hence the following two method calls are equivalent, given a method **link_to** (which we'll meet in Section 4.4) that takes one string argument and one hash argument:

http://pastebin.com/XC0wHvsW

```
1  link_to('Edit', {:controller => 'students', :action => 'edit'})
2  link_to 'Edit',  :controller => 'students', :action => 'edit'
```

Poetry mode is exceedingly common among experienced Rubyists, is used pervasively in

Rails, and provides a welcome elimination of clutter once you get used to it.

Summary

- Everything in Ruby is an object, even primitive types like integers.

- Ruby objects have types, but the variables that refer to them don't.

- Ruby uses lexical scoping for local variables: a variable is defined in the scope in which it's first assigned and in all scopes enclosed inside that one, but reusing the same local variable name in an inner scope temporarily "shadows" the name from the enclosing scope.

- Poetry mode reduces clutter by allowing you to omit parentheses around method arguments and curly braces surrounding a hash, as long as the resulting code is syntactically unambiguous.

■*Elaboration: Number of arguments*

Although parentheses around method arguments are optional both in the method's definition and when calling the method, the *number* of arguments does matter, and an exception is raised if a method is called with the wrong number of arguments. The following code snippet shows two idioms you can use when you need more flexibility. The first is to make the last argument a hash and give it a default value of **{}** (the empty hash). The second is to use a splat (*****), which collects any extra arguments into an array. As with so many Rubyisms, the right choice is whichever results in the most readable code.

http://pastebin.com/K6ev3S7g

```
1  # using 'keyword style' arguments
2  def mymethod(required_arg, args={})
3    do_fancy_stuff if args[:fancy]
4  end
5
6  mymethod "foo",:fancy => true # => args={:fancy => true}
7  mymethod "foo"                # => args={}
8
9  # using * (splat) arguments
10 def mymethod(required_arg, *args)
11   # args is an array of extra args, maybe empty
12 end
13
14 mymethod "foo","bar",:fancy => true # => args=["bar",{:fancy=>true}]
15 mymethod "foo"                      # => args=[]
```

Self-Check 3.3.1. *What is the explicit-**send** equivalent of each of the following expressions:*
a<b, a==b, x[0], x[0]='foo'.
◇ a.send(:<,b), a.send(:==,b), x.send(:[],0), x.send(:[]=,0,'foo') ■

Self-Check 3.3.2. *Suppose method **foo** takes two hash arguments. Explain why we can't use poetry mode to write*
foo :a => 1, :b => 2
◇ Without curly braces, there's no way to tell whether this call is trying to pass a hash with two keys or two hashes of one key each. Therefore poetry mode can only be used when there's a single hash argument and it's the last argument. ■

http://pastebin.com/Y9RC9KgM

```
 1 | class Movie
 2 |   def initialize(title, year)
 3 |     @title = title
 4 |     @year = year
 5 |   end
 6 |   def title
 7 |     @title
 8 |   end
 9 |   def title=(new_title)
10 |     @title = new_title
11 |   end
12 |   def year ; @year ; end
13 |   def year=(new_year) ; @year = new_year ; end
14 |   # How to display movie info
15 |   @@include_year = false
16 |   def Movie.include_year=(new_value)
17 |     @@include_year = new_value
18 |   end
19 |   def full_title
20 |     if @@include_year
21 |       "#{self.title} (#{self.year})"
22 |     else
23 |       self.title
24 |     end
25 |   end
26 | end
27 |
28 | # Example use of the Movie class
29 |
30 | beautiful = Movie.new('Life is Beautiful', '1997')
31 |
32 | # What's the movie's name?
33 | puts "I'm seeing #{beautiful.full_title}"
34 |
35 | # And with the year
36 | Movie.include_year = true
37 | puts "I'm seeing #{beautiful.full_title}"
38 |
39 | # Change the title
40 | beautiful.title = 'La vita e bella'
41 | puts "Ecco, ora si chiama '#{beautiful.title}!'"
```

Figure 3.4: A simple class definition in Ruby. Lines 12 and 13 remind us that it's idiomatic to combine short statements on a single line using semicolons; most Rubyists take advantage of Ruby's conciseness to introduce spaces around the semicolons for readability.

3.4 Classes, Methods, and Inheritance

The excerpt of a class definition for a **Movie** in Figure 3.4 illustrates some basic concepts of defining a class in Ruby. Let's step through it line by line.

Line 1 opens the **Movie** class. As we'll see, unlike in Java, **class Movie** is *not* a declaration but actually a method call that creates an object representing a new class and assigns this object to the constant **Movie**. The subsequent method definitions will occur in the context of this newly-created class.

Line 2 defines the default constructor for the class (the one called when you say **Movie.new**), which *must* be named **initialize**. The inconsistency of naming a method **initialize** but calling it as **new** is an unfortunate idiosyncrasy you'll just have to get used to. (As in Java, you can define additional constructors with other names as well.) This constructor expects two arguments, and in **lines 3–4**, it sets the *instance variables* of the new **Movie** object to those values. The instance variables, such as **@title**, are associated with each instance of an object. The local variables **title** and **year** passed in as arguments are out of scope (undefined) outside the constructor, so if we care about those values we must capture them in instance variables.

Lines 6–8 define a ***getter method*** or ***accessor method*** for the **@title** instance variable. You might wonder why, if **beautiful** were an instance of **Movie**, we couldn't just write **beautiful.@title**. It's because in Ruby, **a.b** always means "Call method **b** on receiver **a**", and **@title** is not the name of any method in the **Movie** class. In fact, it is not a legal name for a method at all, since only instance variable names and class variable names may begin with **@**. In this case, the **title** getter is an instance method of the **Movie** class. That means that any object that is an instance of **Movie** (or of one of **Movie**'s subclasses, if there were any) could respond to this method.

Lines 9–11 define the instance method **title=**, which is distinct from the **title** instance method. Methods whose names end in **=** are ***setter*** or ***mutator*** methods, and just as with the getter, we need this method because we cannot write **beautiful.@title = 'La vita e bella'**. However, as line 40 shows, we *can* write **beautiful.title = 'La vita e bella'**. Beware! If you're used to Java or Python, it's very easy to think of this syntax as *assignment to an attribute*, but it is really just a method call like any other, and in fact could be written as **beautiful.send(:title=, 'La vita e bella')**. And since it is a method call, it has a return value: in the absence of an explicit **return** statement, the value returned by a method is just the value of the last expression evaluated in that method. Since in this case the last expression in the method is the assignment **@title=new_title** and the value of any assignment is its right-hand side, the method happens to return the value of **new_title** that was passed to it.

Unlike Java, which allows attributes as well as getters and setters, Ruby's data hiding or ***encapsulation*** is total: the *only* access to an instance variables or class variables from outside the class is via method calls. This restriction is one reason that Ruby is considered a more "pure" OO language than Java. But since poetry mode allows us to omit parentheses and write **movie.title** instead of **movie.title()**, conciseness need not be sacrificed to achieve this stronger encapsulation.

Lines 12–13 define the getter and setter for **year**, showing that you can use semicolons as well as newlines to separate Ruby statements if you think it looks less cluttered. As we'll soon see, though, Ruby provides a much more concise way to define getters and setters using metaprogramming.

Line 14 is a comment, which in Ruby begins with **#** and extends to the end of the line.

Line 15 defines a ***class variable***, or what Java calls a ***static variable***, that defines whether a movie's year of release is included when its name is printed. Analogously to the setter for **title**, we need one for **include_year=** (lines 16–18), but the presence of **Movie** in the name of the method (**Movie.include_year=**) tells us it's a class method. Notice we haven't defined a getter for the class variable; that means the value of this class variable cannot be inspected at all from outside the class.

Lines 19–25 define the instance method **full_title**, which uses the value of **@@include_year** to decide how to display a movie's full title. Line 21 shows that the syntax **#{}** can be used to interpolate (substitute) the value of an expression into a double-quoted string, as with **#{self.title}** and **#{self.year}**. More precisely, **#{}** evaluates the expression enclosed in the braces and calls **to_s** on the result, asking it to convert itself into a string that can be inserted into the enclosing string. The class **Object** (which is the ancestor of all classes except **BasicObject**) defines a default **to_s**, but most classes override it to produce a prettier representation of themselves.

Java	Ruby
class MyString extends String	class MyString < String
class MyCollection extends Array implements Enumerable	class MyCollection < Array include Enumerable
Static variable: static int anInt = 3	Class variable: @@an_int = 3
Instance variable: this.foo = 1	Instance variable: @foo = 1
Static method: public static int foo(...)	Class method: def self.foo ... end
Instance method: public int foo(...)	Instance method: def foo ... end

Figure 3.5: A summary of some features that translate directly between Ruby and Java.

Summary: Figure 3.5 compares basic OO constructs in Ruby and Java:

- **class Foo** opens a class (new or existing) in order to add or change methods in it. Unlike Java, it is not a declaration but actual code executed immediately, creating a new **Class** object and assigning it to the constant **Foo**.

- **@x** specifies an instance variable and **@@x** specifies a class (static) variable. The namespaces are distinct, so **@x** and **@@x** are different variables.

- A class's instance variables and class variables can be accessed only from within the class. Any access from the "outside world" requires a method call to either a getter or a setter.

- A class method in class **Foo** can be defined using either **def Foo.some_method** or **def self.some_method**.

■ *Elaboration: Using self to define a class method.*

As we'll soon see, the class method definition **def Movie.include_year** can actually appear *anywhere*, even outside the **Movie** class definition, since Ruby allows adding and modifying methods in classes after they've been defined. However, another way to define the class method **include_year** inside the class definition would be **def self.include_year=(...)**. This is because, as we mentioned above, **class Movie** in line 1 is not a declaration but actual code that is executed when this file is loaded, and inside the code block enclosed by **class Movie...end** (lines 2–25), the value of **self** is the new class object created by the **class** keyword. (In fact, **Movie** itself is just a plain old Ruby constant that refers to this class object, as you can verify by doing **c = Movie** and then **c.new('Inception',2010)**.)

■ *Elaboration:* **Why** self.title *in* Movie#full_title?

In lines 19–25, why do we call **self.title** and **self.year** rather than just referring directly to **@title** and **@year**, which would be perfectly legal inside an instance method? The reason is that in the future, we might want to change the way the getters work. For example, when we introduce Rails and ActiveRecord in Section 4.3, we'll see that getters for basic Rails models work by retrieving information from the database, rather than tracking the information using instance variables. Encapsulating instance and class variables using getters and setters hides the implementation of those attributes from the code that uses them, and there's no advantage to be gained by violating that encapsulation inside an instance method, even though it's legal to do so.

Self-Check 3.4.1. *Why is* **movie.@year=1998** *not a substitute for* **movie.year=1998**?
◇ The notation **a.b** always means "call method **b** on receiver **a**", but **@year** is the name of an instance variable, whereas **year=** is the name of an instance method. ■

Self-Check 3.4.2. *Suppose we delete line 12 from Figure 3.4. What would be the result of executing* **Movie.new('Inception',2011).year**?
◇ Ruby would complain that the **year** method is undefined. ■

3.5 All Programming is Metaprogramming

Since defining simple getters and setters for instance variables is so common, we can make the example more Ruby-like by replacing lines 6–11 with the single line **attr_accessor :title** and lines 12–13 with **attr_accessor :year**. **attr_accessor** is not part of the Ruby language—it's a regular method call that defines the getters and setters on the fly. That is, **attr_accessor :foo** defines instance methods **foo** and **foo=** that get and set the value of instance variable **@foo**. The related method **attr_reader** defines only a getter but no setter, and vice versa for **attr_writer**.

This is an example of ***metaprogramming***—creating code at runtime that defines new methods. In fact, in a sense *all* Ruby programming is metaprogramming, since even a class definition is not a declaration as it is in Java but actually code that is executed at runtime. Given that this is true, you might wonder whether you can *modify* a class at runtime. In fact you can, by adding or changing instance methods or class methods, even for Ruby's built-in classes. For example, Figure 3.6 shows a way to do time arithmetic that takes advantage of the **now** method in the **Time** class in the standard Ruby library, which returns the number of seconds since 1/1/1970.

In this example, we *reopened* the **Fixnum** class, a core class that we met earlier, and added six new instance methods to it. Since each of the new methods also returns a fixnum, they can be nicely "chained" to write expressions like **5.minutes.ago**. In fact, Rails includes a more complete version of this feature that does comprehensive time calculations.

Of course, we cannot write **1.minute.ago** since we only defined a method called **minutes**, not **minute**. We could define additional methods with singular names that duplicate the functionality of the methods we already have, but that's not very DRY. Instead, we can take advantage of Ruby's heavy-duty metaprogramming construct **method_missing**. If a method call cannot be found in the receiver's class or any of its ancestor classes, Ruby will then try to call **method_missing** on the receiver, passing it the name and arguments of the nonexistent method. The default implementation of **method_missing** just punts up to the

http://pastebin.com/zxsur5MX

```
 1   #  Note: Time.now returns current time as seconds since epoch
 2   class Fixnum
 3     def seconds  ; self ; end
 4     def minutes  ; self * 60 ; end
 5     def hours    ; self * 60 * 60 ; end
 6     def ago      ; Time.now - self ; end
 7     def from_now ; Time.now + self ; end
 8   end
 9   Time.now
10   # => Mon Nov 07 10:18:10 -0800 2011
11   5.minutes.ago
12   # => Mon Nov 07 10:13:15 -0800 2011
13   5.minutes - 4.minutes
14   # => 60
15   3.hours.from_now
16   # => Mon Nov 07 13:18:15 -0800 2011
```

Figure 3.6: Doing simple time arithmetic by reopening the Fixnum class. Unix was invented in 1970, so its designers chose to represent time as the number of seconds since midnight (GMT) 1/1/1970, sometimes called the beginning of the *epoch*. For convenience, a Ruby Time object responds to arithmetic operator methods by operating on this representation if possible, though internally Ruby can represent any time past or future.

superclass's implementation, but we can override it to implement "singular" versions of the time-calculation methods above:

http://pastebin.com/G0ztHTTP

```
 1   class Fixnum
 2     def method_missing(method_id, *args)
 3       name = method_id.to_s
 4       if name =~ /^(second|minute|hour)$/
 5         self.send(name + 's')
 6       else
 7         super # pass the buck to superclass
 8       end
 9     end
10   end
```

We convert the method ID (which is passed as a symbol) into a string, and use a regular expression to see if the string matches any of the words *hour, minute, second*. If so, we pluralize the name, and send the pluralized method name to **self**, that is, to the object that received the original call. If it doesn't match, what should we do? You might think we should signal an error, but because Ruby has inheritance, we must allow for the possibility that one of our ancestor classes might be able to handle the method call. Calling **super** with no arguments passes the original method call and its original arguments intact up the inheritance chain.

 Try augmenting this example with a **days** method so that you can write **2.days.ago** and **1.day.ago**. Tasteful use of **method_missing** to improve conciseness is part of the Ruby idiom. The Elaboration at the end of Section 3.6 shows how it's used to construct XML documents, and Section 4.3 shows how it enhances the readability of the **find** method in the ActiveRecord part of the Rails framework.

Summary

- **attr_accessor** is an example of metaprogramming: it creates new code at runtime, in this case getters and setters for an instance variable. This style of metaprogramming is extremely common in Ruby.

- When neither a receiver nor any of its ancestor classes can handle a method call, **method_missing** is called on the receiver. **method_missing** can inspect the name of the nonexistent method and its arguments, and can either take action to handle the call or pass the call up to the ancestor, as the default implementation of **method_missing** does.

■ *Elaboration: Pitfalls of dynamic language features*

If your **Bar** class has actually been using an instance variable **@fox** but you accidentally write **attr_accessor :foo** (instead of **attr_accessor :fox**), you will get an error when you write **mybar.fox**. Since Ruby doesn't require you to declare instance variables, **attr_accessor** cannot check whether the named instance variable exists. Therefore, as with all dynamic language features, we must employ care in using it, and cannot "lean on the compiler" as we would in Java. As we will see in Chapter 8, test-driven development (TDD) helps avoid such errors. Furthermore, to the extent that your app is part of a larger Service-Oriented Architecture ecosystem, you *always* have to worry about runtime errors in other services that your app depends on, as we'll see in Chapters 5 and 12.

■ *Elaboration: Variable length argument lists*

A call such as **1.minute** doesn't have any arguments—the only thing that matters is the receiver, **1**. So when the call is redispatched in line 5 of **method_missing**, we don't need to pass any of the arguments that were collected in ***args**. The asterisk is how Ruby deals with variable length argument lists: ***args** will be an array of any arguments passed to the original method, and if no arguments were passed it will be an empty array. It would be correct in any case for line 5 to read **self.send(name+'s', *args)** if we weren't sure what the length of the argument list was.

Self-Check 3.5.1. *In the* **method_missing** *example above, why are* **$** *and* **^** *necessary in the regular expression match in line 4? (Hint: consider what happens if you omit one of them and call* **5.milliseconds** *or* **5.secondary***)*

◇ Without **^** to constrain the match to the beginning of the string, a call like **5.millisecond** would match, which will cause an error when **method_missing** tries to redispatch the call as **5.milliseconds**. Without **$** to constrain the match to the end of the string, a call like **5.secondary** would match, which will cause an error when **method_missing** tries to redispatch the call as **5.secondarys**. ■

Self-Check 3.5.2. *Why should* **method_missing** *always call* **super** *if it can't handle the missing method call itself?*

◇ It's possible that one of your ancestor classes intends to handle the call, but you must explicitly "pass the method call up the chain" with **super** to give the ancestor classes a chance to do so. ■

Self-Check 3.5.3. *In Figure 3.6, is* **Time.now** *a class method or an instance method?*
◇ The fact that its receiver is a class name (**Time**) tells us it's a class method. ∎

3.6 Blocks: Iterators, Functional Idioms, and Closures

Ruby uses the term *block* somewhat differently than other languages do. In Ruby, a block is just a method without a name, or an *anonymous lambda expression* in programming-language terminology. Like a regular named method, it has arguments and can use local variables. Here is a simple example assuming **movies** is an array of **Movie** objects as we defined in the previous examples:

http://pastebin.com/715z16f2

```
1  movies.each do |m|
2    puts "#{m.title} was released in #{m.year}"
3  end
```

The method **each** is an *iterator* available in all Ruby classes that are collection-like. **each** takes one argument—a block—and passes each element of the collection to the block in turn. As you can see, a block is bracketed by **do** and **end**; if the block takes arguments, the argument list is enclosed in |pipe symbols| after the **do**. The block in this example takes one argument: each time through the block, **m** is set to the next element of **movies**.

Unlike named methods, a block can also access any variable accessible to the scope in which the block appears. For example:

http://pastebin.com/vy3sZHEQ

```
1  separator = '=>'
2  movies.each do |m|
3    puts "#{m.title} #{separator} #{m.year}"
4  end
```

In the above code, the value of **separator** is visible inside the block, even though the variable was created and assigned *outside* the block. In contrast, the following would *not* work, because **separator** is not visible within **print_movies**, and therefore not visible to the **each** block:

http://pastebin.com/bdXAcbPc

```
1  def print_movies(movie_list)
2    movie_list.each do |m|
3      puts "#{m.title} #{separator} #{m.rating}"   # === FAILS!! ===
4    end
5  end
6  separator = '=>'
7  print_movies(movies) # FAILS!
```

In programming-language parlance, a Ruby block is a *closure*: whenever the block executes, it can "see" the entire lexical scope available at the place where the block appears in the program text. In other words, it's as if the presence of the block creates an instant snapshot of the scope, which can be reconstituted later whenever the block executes. This fact is exploited by many Rails features that improve DRYness, including view rendering (which we'll see in Section 4.4) and model validations and controller filters (Section 5.1), because they allow separating the definition of *what* is to occur from *when* in time and *where* in the structure of the application it occurs.

The fact that blocks are closures should help explain the following apparent anomaly. If the *first* reference to a local variable is inside a block, that variable is "captured" by the block's scope and is *undefined* after the block exits. So, for example, the following will *not* work, assuming line 2 is the *first* reference to **separator** within this scope:

http://pastebin.com/t8KaAa1y

```
1  movies.each do |m|
2    separator = '=>'  # first assignment is inside a block!
3    puts "#{m.title} #{separator} #{m.rating}"   #  OK
4  end
5  puts "Separator is #{separator}"      # === FAILS!! ===
```

In a lexically-scoped language such as Ruby, variables are visible to the scope within which they're created and to all scopes enclosed by that scope. Because in the above snippet **separator** is *created* within the block's scope, its visibility is limited to that scope.

In summary, **each** is just an instance method on a collection that takes a single argument (a block) and provides elements to that block one at a time. A related use of blocks is operations on collections, a common idiom Ruby borrows from *functional programming*. For example, to double every element in a collection, we could write:

http://pastebin.com/M6pqwJMy

```
1  new_collection = collection.map do |elt|
2    2 * elt
3  end
```

If the parsing is unambiguous, it is idiomatic to use curly braces to delineate a short (one-line) block rather than **do...end**:

http://pastebin.com/nPQHG2yE

```
1  new_collection = collection.map { |elt| 2 * elt }
```

So, no for-loops?
Although Ruby allows **for i in collection, each** allows us to take better advantage of *duck typing*, which we'll see shortly, to improve code reuse.

Ruby has a wide variety of such collection operators; Figure 3.7 lists some of the most useful. With some practice, you will automatically start to express operations on collections in terms of these functional idioms rather than in terms of imperative loops. For example, to return a list of all the words in some file (that is, tokens consisting entirely of word characters and separated by non-word characters) that begin with a vowel, sorted and without duplicates:

http://pastebin.com/dFJjugTf

```
1  # downcase and split are defined in String class
2  words = IO.read("file").
3    split(/\W+/).
4    select { |s|  s =~ /^[aeiou]/i }.
5    map { |s| s.downcase }.
6    uniq.
7    sort
```

(Recall that Ruby allows breaking a single statement across lines for readability as long as it's not ambiguous where the statement ends. The periods at the end of each line make it clear that the statement continues, since a period must be followed by a method call.) In general, if you find yourself writing explicit loops in Ruby, you should reexamine your code to see if these collection idioms wouldn't make it more concise and readable.

Method	#Args	Returns a *new* collection containing...
c.map	1	elements obtained by applying block to each element of **c**
c.select	1	Subset of **c** for which block evaluates to true
c.reject	1	Subset of **c** obtained by removing elements for which block evaluates to true
c.uniq		all elements of **c** with duplicates removed
c.reverse		elements of **c** in reverse order
c.compact		all non-**nil** elements of **c**
c.flatten		elements of **c** and any of its sub-arrays, recursively flattened to contain only non-array elements
c.partition	1	Two collections, the first containing elements of **c** for which the block evaluates to true, and the second containing those for which it evaluates to false
c.sort	2	Elements of **c** sorted according to a block that takes 2 arguments and returns -1 if the first element should be sorted earlier, +1 if the second element should be sorted earlier, and 0 if the two elements can be sorted in either order.
The following methods require the *collection elements* to respond to $<=>$; see Section 3.7.		
c.sort		If **sort** is called *without* a block, the elements are sorted according to how they respond to $<=>$.
c.sort_by	1	Applies the block to each element of **c** and sorts the result. For example, **movies.sort_by { |m| m.title }** sorts **Movie** objects according to how their titles respond to $<=>$.
c.max, c.min		Largest or smallest element in the collection

Figure 3.7: **Some common Ruby methods on collections. For those that expect a block, we show the number of arguments expected by the block; if blank, the method doesn't expect a block. For example, a call to sort, whose block expects 2 arguments, might look like: c.sort { |a,b| a $<=>$ b }. These methods all return a new object rather than modifying the receiver. Some methods also have a *destructive* variant ending in !, for example sort!, that modify their argument in place (and also return the new value). Use destructive methods with extreme care.**

Summary

- Ruby includes aspects of ***functional programming*** such as the ability to operate on entire collections with methods such as **map** and **sort**. It is highly idiomatic to use such methods to manipulate collections rather than iterating over them using for-loops.

- The **each** collection method returns one element of the collection at a time and passes it to a ***block***. Blocks in Ruby can only occur as arguments to methods like **each** that expect a block.

- Blocks are closures: all variables visible to the block's code at the place where the block is defined will also be visible whenever the block executes.

- Most methods that appear to modify a collection, such as **reject**, actually return a new copy with the modifications made. Some have destructive versions whose name ends in **!**, as in **reject!**.

■ *Elaboration: Blocks and metaprogramming in XML Builder*

An elegant example of combining blocks and metaprogramming is the XML Builder[1] class. (As we mentioned briefly in Section 2.3, HTML is closely related to XML.) In the following example, the XML markup shown in lines 1–8 was generated by the Ruby code in lines 9–18. The method calls **name, phone, address**, and so on all use **method_missing** to turn each method call into an XML tag, and blocks are used to indicate tag nesting.
http://pastebin.com/bC02KjiR

```
1  <person type="faculty">
2    <name>Barbara Liskov</name>
3    <contact>
4      <phone location="office">617-253-2008</phone>
5      <email>liskov@csail.mit.edu</email>
6    </contact>
7  </person>
8
9  # Code that generates the above markup:
10 require 'builder'
11 b = Builder::XmlMarkup.new(:indent => 2)
12 b.person :type => 'faculty' do
13   b.name "Barbara Liskov"
14   b.contact do
15     b.phone "617-253-2008", :location => 'office'
16     b.email "liskov@csail.mit.edu"
17   end
18 end
```

Self-Check 3.6.1. *Write one line of Ruby that checks whether a string* **s** *is a palindrome, that is, it reads the same backwards as forwards.* **Hint:** *Use the methods in Figure 3.7, and don't forget that upper vs. lowercase shouldn't matter:* ReDivideR *is a palindrome.*
◇ **s.downcase == s.downcase.reverse**
You might think you could say **s.reverse=~Regexp.new(s)**, but that would fail if **s** happens to contain regexp metacharacters such as **$**. ■

3.7   Mix-ins and Duck Typing

You may be surprised to learn that the collection methods summarized in Figure 3.7 (and several others not in the figure) aren't part of Ruby's **Array** class. In fact, they aren't even part of some superclass from which **Array** and other collection types inherit. Instead, they take advantage of an even more powerful mechanism for reuse, called *mix-ins*.

A mix-in is a collection of related behaviors that can be added to any class, although in some cases the class may have to fulfill a "contract" in order to use the mix-in. This may sound similar to an Interface in Java, but there are two differences. First, a mix-in is easier to reuse: the "contract," if any, is specified in the mix-in's documentation rather than being formally declared as a Java interface would be. Second, unlike a Java interface, which says nothing about *how* a class implements an interface, a mix-in is all about making it easy to reuse an implementation.

A *module* is Ruby's method for packaging together a group of methods as a mix-in. (Modules have other uses too, but mix-ins are the most important.) When a module is included into a class with **include ModuleName**, the instance methods, class methods, and variables in the module become available in the class.

The collection methods in Figure 3.7 are part of a module called **Enumerable** that is part of Ruby's standard library; to mix **Enumerable** into your own class, just say **include Enumerable** inside the class definition.

As its documentation[5] states, **Enumerable** requires the class mixing it in to provide an **each** method, since **Enumerable**'s collection methods are implemented in terms of **each**. Unlike a Java interface, this simple contract is the *only* requirement for mixing in the module; it doesn't matter what class you mix it into as long as that class defines the **each** instance method, and neither the class nor the mix-in have to declare their intentions in advance. For example, the **each** method in Ruby's **Array** class iterates over the array elements, whereas the **each** method in the **IO** class iterates over the lines of a file or other I/O stream. Mix-ins thereby allow reusing whole collections of behaviors across classes that are otherwise unrelated.

The term "duck typing" is a popular description of this capability, because "if something looks like a duck and quacks like a duck, it might as well be a duck." That is, from **Enumerable**'s point of view, if a class has an **each** method, it might as well be a collection, thus allowing **Enumerable** to provide other methods implemented in terms of **each**. Unlike Java's **Interface**, no formal declaration is required for mix-ins; if we invented a new mixin that relied on (say) a class implementing the dereference operator **[]**, we could then mix it into any such class without otherwise modifying the classes themselves. When Ruby programmers say that some class "quacks like an **Array**," they usually mean that it's not necessarily an **Array** nor a descendant of **Array**, but it responds to most of the same methods as **Array** and can therefore be used wherever an **Array** would be used.

Because **Enumerable** can deliver all the methods in Figure 3.7 (and some others) to any class that implements **each**, all Ruby classes that "quack like a collection" mix in **Enumerable** for convenience. The methods **sort** (with no block), **max**, and **min** also require that the *elements* of the collection (not the collection itself) respond to the $<=>$ method, which returns -1, 0, or 1 depending on whether its first argument is less than, equal to, or greater than its second argument. You can still mix in **Enumerable** even if the collection elements don't respond to $<=>$; you just can't use **sort**, **max**, or **min**. In contrast, in Java every collection class that implemented the **Enumerable** interface would have to ensure that its

---

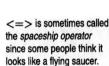

If you use the Emacs editor, you can think of Emacs minor modes (auto-fill, abbreviation support, and so on) as mix-ins that rely on contracts provided by the major mode and use Lisp's dynamic typing to allow mixing them into any major mode.

Watch out! Because Ruby allows adding and defining methods at runtime, **include** cannot check whether the module's contract is fulfilled by the class.

$<=>$ is sometimes called the *spaceship operator* since some people think it looks like a flying saucer.

elements could be compared, whether that functionality was required or not.

In Chapter 8 we will see how the combination of mix-ins, open classes, and **method_missing** allows you to write eminently readable unit tests using the RSpec tool.

Summary

- A *mix-in* is a set of related behaviors that can be added to any class that satisfies the mix-in's contract. For example, **Enumerable** is a set of behaviors on enumerable collections that requires the including class to define the **each** iterator.

- Ruby uses modules to group mix-ins. A module is mixed into a class by putting **include ModuleName** after the **class ClassName** statement.

- A class that implements some set of behaviors characteristic of another class, possibly by using mix-ins, is sometimes said to "quack like" the class it resembles. Ruby's scheme for allowing mix-ins without static type checking is therefore sometimes called *duck typing*.

- Unlike interfaces in Java, mix-ins require no formal declaration. But because Ruby doesn't have static types, it's your responsibility to ensure that the class including the mix-in satisfies the conditions stated in the mix-in's documentation, or you will get a runtime error.

■ *Elaboration: Duck typing in the Time class*

Ruby can represent times arbitrarily far in the past or future, can use timezones, and can handle non-Gregorian calendrical systems. Yet as we saw in Section 3.5, when a **Time** object receives a method call like + that expects an arithmetic argument, it attempts to return a representation of itself compatible with the Unix representation (seconds since the epoch). In other words, a **Time** object is not just a simple integer, but when necessary, it quacks like one.

Self-Check 3.7.1. *Suppose you mix* **Enumerable** *into a class* **Foo** *that does not provide the* **each** *method. What error will be raised when you call* **Foo.new.map { |elt| puts elt }**?
◇ The **map** method in **Enumerable** will attempt to call **each** on its receiver, but since the new **Foo** object doesn't define **each**, Ruby will raise an Undefined Method error. ■

Self-Check 3.7.2. *Which statement is correct and why:* (a) **include 'enumerable'** (b) **include Enumerable**
◇ (b) is correct, since **include** expects the name of a module, which (like a class name) is a constant rather than a string. ■

3.8 Make Your Own Iterators Using Yield

Although Ruby defines **each** for built-in collection classes like **Array**, you can define your own iterators using **each** as well. The idea of making iteration a first-class language feature first appeared in the *CLU* language invented by Barbara Liskov. Ruby's **yield** lets you define

http://pastebin.com/yAYDz8nS

```
1  # return every n'th element in an enumerable
2  module Enumerable
3    def every_nth(count)
4      index = 0
5      self.each do |elt|
6        yield elt if index % count == 0
7        index += 1
8      end
9    end
10 end
11
12 list = (1..10).to_a # make an array from a range
13 list.every_nth(3) { |s| print "#{s}, " }
14 # => 1, 4, 7, 10,
15 list.every_nth(2) { |s| print "#{s}, " }
16 # => 1, 3, 5, 7, 9,
```

Figure 3.8: An example of using Ruby's yield, which is based on a construct introduced in the language CLU. Note that we define every_nth in the Enumerable module, which most collections mix in, as Section 3.7 describes.

your own **each** methods that take a block, providing an elegant way to allow collections to manage their own traversal.

Figure 3.8 shows how this unusual construct works. When a method containing **yield** is called, it starts executing until **yield** is reached; at that point, control is transferred to the block that was passed to the method. If **yield** had any arguments, those arguments become the arguments to the block.

A common use of **yield** is implementing iterators like **each** and **every_nth**. Unlike Java, in which you have to create an iterator by passing it a collection of some type and then repeatedly call **while (iter.hasNext())** and **iter.getNext()**, Ruby iterators allow turning the control structure "inside-out" and letting data structures manage *their own* iteration.

yield also enables reuse in situations where you need to "sandwich" some custom functionality inside of some common functionality. For example, consider an app that creates HTML pages and uses a standard HTML template for most pages that looks like this, where the only difference between different pages is captured by line 8:

Don't confuse this use of the term *yield* with the unrelated usage from operating systems, in which one thread or process is said to *yield* to another by giving up the CPU.

http://pastebin.com/tZ5j3G7J

```
1  <!DOCTYPE html>
2  <html>
3    <head>
4    <title>Report</title>
5    </head>
6    <body>
7      <div id="main">
8        ...user-generated content here...
9      </div>
10   </body>
11 </html>
```

In most languages, we could encapsulate the code that generates the boilerplate in lines 1–7 and 9–11 in methods called **make_header** and **make_footer**, and then require each method that wants to generate a page to do this:

http://pastebin.com/0sTEMcdN

```
1  def one_page
2    page = ''
3    page << make_header()
4    page << "Hello"
5    page << make_footer()
6  end
7  def another_page
8    page = ''
9    page << make_header()
10   page << "World"
11   page << make_footer()
12 end
```

Since this code looks repetitive, we might instead wrap up both calls in a single method:

http://pastebin.com/TsvTN5ZT

```
1  def make_page(contents)
2    page = ''
3    page << make_header()
4    page << contents
5    page << make_footer()
6  end
7  #
8  def one_page
9    make_page("Hello")
10 end
11 def another_page
12   make_page("World")
13 end
```

But in Chapter 2 we learned that useful design patterns arise from the desire to *separate the things that change from those that stay the same.* **yield** provides a better way to encapsulate the common part—the boilerplate "around" the user content—in its own method:

http://pastebin.com/7TbZ12p4

```
1  def make_page
2    page = ''
3    page << make_header()
4    page << yield
5    page << make_footer()
6  end
7  def one_page
8    make_page do
9      "Hello"
10   end
11 end
12 def another_page
13   make_page do
14     "World"
15   end
16 end
```

In this example, when **one_page** calls **make_page**, the **yield** at line 4 returns control to the block at line 9. The block executes, and its return value (in this case, **"Hello"**) is returned to line 4 as the result of the **yield**, and gets appended to **page** (using the « operator), after which **make_page** continues.

We can exploit Ruby's idiom for single-line blocks to boil this down to:

http://pastebin.com/Nqe8MwA5

```
 1 | def make_page
 2 |   make_header << yield << make_footer
 3 | end
 4 |
 5 | def one_page
 6 |   make_page { "Hello" }
 7 | end
 8 | def another_page
 9 |   make_page { "World" }
10 | end
```

As we'll see, **yield** is actually how Rails implements HTML template rendering for views: the common HTML code that goes at the beginning and end of each page is rendered, and then **yield** is used to render the page-specific content in between. In Chapter 11, we'll see how the combination of blocks and the Factory design pattern gives an exceptional degree of conciseness and code beauty in separating the things that change from those that stay the same.

With this brief introduction to Ruby's most distinctive features, we're ready to meet the Rails framework.

Summary

- In the body of a method that takes a block as a parameter, **yield** transfers control to the block and optionally passes it an argument.

- Because the block is a closure, its scope is the one that was in effect when the block was defined, even though the method yielding to the block is executing in a completely different scope.

- Yielding is the general mechanism behind iterators: an iterator is simply a method that traverses some data structure and uses **yield** to pass one element at a time to the iterator's receiver.

Self-Check 3.8.1. *Referring to Figure 3.8, observe that* **every_nth** *uses* **elt** *as an instance variable name in lines 5 and 6. Suppose that in line 13 we used* **elt** *instead of* **s** *as the name of the local variable in our block. What would be the effect of this change, if any, and why?*
◇ There would be no effect. **every_nth** and the block we pass to it execute in different scopes, so there is no "collision" of the local variable name **elt**. ∎

3.9 Fallacies and Pitfalls

 Pitfall: **Writing Java in Ruby.**

It takes some mileage to learn a new language's idioms and how it fundamentally differs from other languages. Common examples for Java programmers new to Ruby include:

- Thinking in terms of casting rather than method calls: **100.0 * 3** doesn't cast 3 to a Float, but calls **Float#***.

- Reading **a.b** as "attribute **b** of object **a**" rather than "call method **b** on object **a**."

- Thinking in terms of classes and traditional static types, rather than duck typing. When calling a method on an object, or doing a mix-in, all that matters is whether the object responds to the method. The object's type or class are irrelevant.

- Writing explicit for-loops rather than using an iterator such as **each** and the collection methods that exploit it via mix-ins such as **Enumerable**. Use functional idioms like **select**, **map**, **any?**, **all?**, and so on.

- Thinking of **attr_accessor** as a declaration of attributes. This shortcut and related ones save you work *if* you want to make an attribute publicly readable or writable. But you don't need to "declare" an attribute in any way at all (the existence of the instance variable is sufficient) and in all likelihood some attributes *shouldn't* be publicly visible. Resist the temptation to use **attr_accessor** as if you were writing attribute declarations in Java.

 Pitfall: **Thinking of symbols and strings as interchangeable.**

While many Rails methods are explicitly constructed to accept either a string or a symbol, the two are not in general interchangeable. A method expecting a string may throw an error if given a symbol, or depending on the method, it may simply fail. For example, **['foo','bar'].include?('foo')** is true, whereas **['foo','bar'].include?(:foo)** is legal but false.

 Pitfall: **Naming a local variable when you meant a local method.**

Suppose class **C** defines a method **x=**. In an instance method of **C**, writing **x=3** will not have the desired effect of calling the **x=** method with the argument 3; rather, it will set a local variable **x** to 3, which is probably not what you wanted. To get the desired effect, write **self.x=3**, which makes the method call explicit.

 Pitfall: **Confusing require with include.**

require loads an arbitrary Ruby file (typically the main file for some gem), whereas **include** mixes in a module. In both cases, Ruby has its own rules for locating the files containing the code; the Ruby documentation describes the use of **$LOAD_PATH**, but you should rarely if ever need to manipulate it directly if you use Rails as your framework and Bundler to manage your gems.

3.10 Concluding Remarks: Idiomatic Language Use

> *Ugly programs are like ugly suspension bridges: they're much more liable to collapse than pretty ones, because the way humans (especially engineer-humans) perceive beauty is intimately related to our ability to process and understand complexity. A language that makes it hard to write elegant code makes it hard to write good code.*
>
> —Eric S. Raymond

If you're coming to Ruby without knowledge of languages such as Lisp or Scheme, the functional programming idioms may be new to you. Unless you're familiar with JavaScript, you probably haven't used closures before. And unless you know **CLU**, Ruby's **yield** may take some getting used to.

There's an old quip among programmers that "you can write Fortran in any language." This comment is perhaps unfair to Fortran—you can write good or bad code in any language—but the intention of the expression is to discourage carrying programming habits from one language into another where they are inappropriate, thereby missing the opportunity to use a mechanism in the new language that might provide a more beautiful solution.

Our advice is therefore to persevere in a new language until you're comfortable with its idioms. Resist the temptation to transliterate your code from other languages without first considering whether there's a more Rubyistic way to code what you need. We'll repeat this advice when we tackle JavaScript in Chapter 6.

Learning to use a new language and making the most of its idioms is a vital skill for software professionals. These are not easy tasks, but we hope that focusing on unique and beautiful features in our exposition of Ruby and JavaScript will evoke intellectual curiosity rather than groans of resignation, and that you will come to appreciate the value of wielding a variety of specialized tools and choosing the most productive one for each new job.

3.11 To Learn More

- Programming Ruby[6] and *The Ruby Programming Language* (Flanagan and Matsumoto 2008), co-authored by Ruby inventor Yukihiro "Matz" Matsumoto, are definitive references for Ruby.

- The online documentation for Ruby[7] gives details on the language, its classes, and its standard libraries. A few of the most useful classes include **IO** (file and network I/O, including CSV files), **Set** (collection operations such as set difference, set intersection, and so on), and **Time** (the standard class for representing times, which we recommend over **Date** even if you're representing only dates without times). These are reference materials, not a tutorial.

- *Learning Ruby* Fitzgerald 2007 takes a more tutorial-style approach to learning the language. The no-cost, Creative Commons-licensed, and quirky Why's (Poignant) Guide to Ruby[8] is an interesting alternative, though some material may be outdated since that document was written for Ruby 1.8.

- *The Ruby Way, Second Edition* is an encyclopedic reference to both Ruby itself and how to use it idiomatically to solve many practical programming problems.

- Many newcomers to Ruby have trouble with **yield**, which has no equivalent in Java, C or C++ (although recent versions of Python and JavaScript do have similar mechanisms). The **coroutines** article on Wikipedia gives good examples of the general coroutine mechanism that **yield** supports. *Ruby Best Practices* Brown 2009 focuses on how to make the best of Ruby's "power tools" like blocks, modules/duck-typing, metaprogramming, etc. If you want to write Ruby like a Rubyist instead of writing Java code in Ruby, this is a great read.

G. T. Brown. *Ruby Best Practices*. O'Reilly Media, 2009. ISBN 0596523009.

M. J. Fitzgerald. *Learning Ruby*. O'Reilly Media, 2007. ISBN 0596529864.

D. Flanagan and Y. Matsumoto. *The Ruby Programming Language*. O'Reilly Media, 2008. ISBN 0596516177.

Notes

[1]`http://validator.w3.org`
[2]`https://api.duckduckgo.com/api`
[3]`http://pastebin.com`
[4]`http://builder.rubyforge.org/`
[5]`http://ruby-doc.org/core-1.9.3/Enumerable.html`
[6]`http://ruby-doc.org/docs/ProgrammingRuby`
[7]`http://ruby-doc.org/`
[8]`http://www.scribd.com/doc/2236084/Whys-Poignant-Guide-to-Ruby`

3.12   Suggested Projects

OO and Classes

Project 3.1. *How many class ancestors does the object* **5** *have? (Hint: use method chaining to follow the superclass chain all the way up to* **BasicObject***)*

Project 3.2. *Given that* **superclass** *returns* **nil** *when called on* **BasicObject** *but a non-***nil** *value otherwise, write a Ruby method that, if passed any object, will print the object's class and its ancestor classes all the way up to* **BasicObject***.*

Project 3.3. *Ben Bitdiddle asks: "If* **i** *is an integer and* **f** *is a floating point number in Ruby, and I write* **i+f***, does* **i** *get converted to a float or does* **f** *get converted to an integer to do the addition?" Explain why Ben's question is ill-formed when applied to Ruby.*

Project 3.4. *Newly enlightened by the answer to Project 3.3 , Ben now observes that writing* **i+=f** *is legal Ruby. His question is: "Is* **+=** *a separate operator in Ruby, or is it purely syntactic sugar for* **i=i+f***?" Devise and carry out an experiment to determine the answer.*

Metaprogramming

Project 3.5. *Building on the example in Section 3.5, take advantage of* **Time***'s duck typing to define a method* **at_beginning_of_year** *that lets you write:*

`http://pastebin.com/NxicVYaP`

```
1 | Time.now.at_beginning_of_year + 1.day
2 | # => 2011-01-02 00:00:00 -0800
```

   Hint 1: The **Time** *documentation[1] will tell you that the* **local** *class method can be used to create a new* **Time** *object with a specified year, month and day.*

   Hint 2: The receiver of **at_beginning_of_year** *in the above code is* **now***, just as it was in the example in Section 3.5. But unlike that example, think carefully about how you'd like* **now** *to quack.*

Project 3.6. *Define a method* **attr_accessor_with_history** *that provides the same functionality as* **attr_accessor** *but also tracks every value the attribute has ever had:*

http://pastebin.com/4ffrvFgC

```
1  class Foo
2    attr_accessor_with_history :bar
3  end
4  f = Foo.new      # => #<Foo:0x127e678>
5  f.bar = 3        # => 3
6  f.bar = :wowzo   # => :wowzo
7  f.bar = 'boo!'   # => 'boo!'
8  f.history(:bar)  # => [3, :wowzo, 'boo!']
```

Mix-ins and Iterators

Project 3.7. *The* **Enumerable** *module includes an iterator* **each_with_index** *that yields each enumerable element along with an index starting from zero (recall that* **Enumerable** *is mixed into Ruby's built-in collection classes by default):*

http://pastebin.com/75zEmrAX

```
1  %w(alice bob carol).each_with_index do |person,index|
2    puts ">> #{person} is number #{index}"
3  end
4  >> alice is number 0
5  >> bob is number 1
6  >> carol is number 2
```

Create an iterator **each_with_custom_index** *in module* **Enumerable** *that lets you determine the starting value and step of the indices:*

http://pastebin.com/wpYexvCW

```
1  %w(alice bob carol).each_with_custom_index(3,2) do |person,index|
2    puts ">> #{person} is number #{index}"
3  end
4  >> alice is number 3
5  >> bob is number 5
6  >> carol is number 7
```

Project 3.8. *Recall that the first two integers in the Fibonacci sequence are 1 and 1, and each successive Fibonacci number is the sum of the previous two. Create a class that returns an iterator for the first n Fibonacci numbers. You should be able to use the class as follows:*

http://pastebin.com/W5nm61P9

```
1  # Fibonacci iterator should be callable like this:
2  f = FibSequence.new(6) # just the first 6 Fibonacci numbers
3  f.each { |s| print(s,':') }   # => 1:1:2:3:5:8:
4  f.reject { |s| s.odd? }       # => [2, 8]
5  f.reject(&:odd?)              # => [2, 8] (a shortcut!)
6  f.map { |x| 2*x }             # => [2, 2, 4, 6, 10, 16]
```

HINT: as long as objects of your class implement **each**, *you can mix in* **Enumerable** *to get* **reject**, **map**, *and so on.*

Project 3.9. *Implement an iterator* **each_with_flattening** *that behaves as follows:*

http://pastebin.com/t79i1ZNu

```
1  [1, [2, 3], 4, [[5, 6], 7]].each_with_flattening { |s| print "#{s}," }
2  >> 1, 2, 3, 4, 5, 6, 7
```

What assumption(s) must your iterator make about its receiver? What assumption(s) must it make about the elements of its receiver?

Project 3.10. *Augment the* **Enumerable** *module with a new iterator,* **each_permuted**, *which returns the elements of a collection in a random order. The iterator may assume that the collection responds to* **each** *but shouldn't make any other assumptions about the elements. Hint: you may want to use the* **rand** *method in the Ruby standard library.*

Project 3.11. *An ordered binary tree is one in which every node has an element value and up to 2 children, each of which is itself an ordered binary tree, and all elements in the left subtree of some node are less than any element in the right subtree of that node.*

Define a **BinaryTree** *collection class that provides the instance methods* << *(insert element),* **empty?** *(returns true if tree has no elements), and* **each** *(the standard iterator that yields each element in turn, in any order you desire).*

Project 3.12. *Augment your ordered binary tree class so that it also provides the following methods, each of which takes a block:* **include?(elt)** *(true if tree includes* **elt***),* **all?** *(true if the given block is true for all elements),* **any?** *(true if the given block is true for any element),* **sort** *(sorts the elements).* **HINT:** *A single line of code suffices to do all this.*

Project 3.13. *Similar to the* **days.ago** *example in Section 3.5, define the appropriate conversions between Euros, US Dollars, and Yen so that you can type the following conversions:*
http://pastebin.com/JhsBT11Z

```
1  # assumes 1 Euro=1.3 US dollars, 1 Yen=0.012 US dollars
2  5.dollars.in(:euros)   # => 6.5
3  (1.euro - 50.yen).in(:dollars)   # => 0.700
```

Project 3.14. *Which of these methods actually cause mutations to happen the way you expect?*
http://pastebin.com/M7dfp9gZ

```
1  def my_swap(a,b)
2    b,a = a,b
3  end
4
5  class Foo
6  attr_accessor :a, :b
7    def my_swap_2()
8      @b,@a = @a,@b
9    end
10 end
11
12 def my_string_replace_1(s)
13   s.gsub( /Hi/, 'Hello')
14 end
15
16 def my_string_replace_2(s)
17   s.gsub!( /Hi/, 'Hello')
18 end
```

Project 3.15. *Extend the* **Time** *class with a* **humanize** *method that prints out an informative phrase describing the time of day to the nearest fifteen-minute division, in twelve-hour mode, and making a special case for midnight:*
http://pastebin.com/4znyp5BZ

```
1  >>  Time.parse("10:47 pm").humanize
2  # => "About a quarter til eleven"
3  >>  Time.parse("10:31 pm").humanize
4  # => "About half past ten"
5  >>  Time.parse("10:07 pm").humanize
6  # => "About ten"
7  >>  Time.parse("23:58").humanize
8  # => "About midnight"
9  >>  Time.parse("00:29").humanize
10 # => "About 12:30"
```

4

SaaS Framework: Introduction to Rails

Charles Antony Richard Hoare (1934–, called "Tony" by almost everyone) received the Turing Award in 1980 for "fundamental contributions to the definition and design of programming languages."

There are two ways of constructing a software design: One way is to make it so simple that there are obviously no deficiencies, *and the other way is to make it so complicated that there are* no obvious deficiencies. *The first method is far more difficult... The price of reliability is the pursuit of the utmost simplicity.*

—Tony Hoare

Concepts

The big ideas in this chapter deal with how Rails simplifies the creation of SaaS apps.

- Rails exposes the client-server, three-tier architecture, and model–view–controller patterns, all of which are common in SaaS apps.

- Rails' ActiveRecord package uses Ruby's metaprogramming and *convention over configuration* to free you from writing any code at all to perform the basic Create, Read, Update and Delete (CRUD) operations on your models, as long as you follow certain conventions about naming classes and variables.

- Rails' ActionView and ActionController packages provide help for creating Web pages, dealing with fill-in forms, and setting up the *routes* that map URIs to controller actions (code in your app).

- A properly-constructed Rails app can be easily adapted to work in a service-oriented architecture, communicating with external services rather than with a human using a browser.

- Debugging SaaS requires understanding the different places something could go wrong during the flow of a SaaS request, and making that information visible to the developer.

All of these Rails facilities are designed to streamline the creation of apps that will work in a Service-Oriented Architecture and exploit proven design patterns for SaaS.

4.1   Rails Basics: From Zero to CRUD

As we saw in Chapter 2, Rails is a SaaS application framework that defines a particular structure for organizing your application's code and provides an interface to a Rails application server such as Rack. The app server waits for a Web browser to contact your app and maps every incoming request (URI and HTTP method) to a particular action in one of your app's controllers. Rails consists of both the framework itself and a new command `rails` that is used to set up and manipulate Rails apps. Three main modules make up the heart of Rails' support for MVC: ActiveRecord for creating models, ActionView for creating views, and ActionController for creating controllers.

Using the explanation of Model–View–Controller in Chapter 2 as a reference framework, we will start from zero and create the Rotten Potatoes app described in Chapter 2 for maintaining a simple database of movie information. We will briefly visit each of the "moving parts" of a basic Rails application with a single model, in the following order:

1. Creating the skeleton of a new app

2. Routing

3. The database and migrations

4. Models and Active Record

5. Controllers, views, forms, and CRUD

-T omits directories for tests that use Ruby's `Test::Unit` framework, since in Chapter 8 we will use the RSpec testing framework instead. `rails --help` shows more options for creating a new app.

Begin by logging into the bookware VM, changing to a convenient directory such as Documents (`cd Documents`), and creating a new, empty Rails app with `rails new myrottenpotatoes -T`. If all goes well, you'll see several messages about files being created, ending with "Your bundle is complete." You can now `cd` to the newly-created `myrottenpotatoes` directory, called the ***app root*** directory for your new app. From now on, unless we say otherwise, all file names will be relative to the app root. Before going further, spend a few minutes examining the contents of the new app directory `myrottenpotatoes`, as described in Figure 4.1, to familiarize yourself with the directory structure common to all Rails apps.

The message "Your bundle is complete" refers to the `Gemfile` that was automatically created for your app. While the Ruby standard library includes a vast collection of useful classes[2], Rubygems is a system for managing external user-contributed Ruby libraries or ***gems***. Bundler, a gem preinstalled with the bookware, looks for a `Gemfile` in the app's root directory that specifies not only what gems your app depends on, but what versions of those gems. It might surprise you that there are already gem names in this file even though you haven't written any app code, but that's because Rails itself is a gem and also depends on several other gems. For example, if you open the `Gemfile` in an editor, you can see that `sqlite3` is listed, because the default Rails development environment expects to use the SQLite3. database

Edit your `Gemfile` by adding the following (anywhere in the file, as long as it's not inside a block beginning with **group**).

Gemfile	list of Ruby gems (libraries) this app uses (Chapter 3)
Rakefile	commands to automate maintenance and deployment (Chapter 12)
app	your application
app/models	model code
app/controllers	controller code
app/views	view templates
app/views/layouts	page templates used by all views in the app (see text)
app/helpers	helper methods to streamline view templates
app/assets	static assets (JavaScript, images, stylesheets)
config	basic configuration information
config/environments	settings for running in development vs. production
config/database.yml	database configuration for development vs. production
config/routes.rb	mappings of URIs to controller actions
db	files describing the database schema
db/development.sqlite3	Data storage for SQLite development database
db/test.sqlite3	Database used for running tests
db/migrate/	Migrations (descriptions of changes to database schema)
doc	generated documentation
lib	additional app code shared among M, V, C
log	log files
public	error pages served by Web server
script	development tools, not part of app
tmp	temporary data maintained at runtime

Figure 4.1: The standard directory structure of a Rails project includes an app directory for the actual application logic with subdirectories for the app's models, views, and controllers, showing how Rails exposes the MVC architectural choice even in the arrangement of project files.

http://pastebin.com/UQTR5UQh

Pastebin is a service for copying-and-pasting book code. (You need to type URI if you're reading the print book; it's a link in ebooks.)

```
1  # use Haml for templates
2  gem 'haml'
3  # use Ruby debugger
4  group :development, :test do
5    gem 'debugger'
6  end
```

This change does two things. First, it specifies that we will use the Haml templating system rather than the built-in `erb`. Second, it specifies that we want to use the interactive debugger **debugger** during development and testing, but not in production.

Once you've made these changes to the `Gemfile`, run `bundle install --without production`, which checks if any gems specified in our `Gemfile` are missing and need to be installed. In this case no installation should be needed, since we've preloaded most gems you need in the bookware VM, so you should see "Your bundle is complete" as before. Bundler creates the file `Gemfile.lock` listing which versions of which Gems are *actually being used* in your development environment; deployment platforms like Heroku use this information to exactly match the gems and versions in your production environment.

Be sure to place both `Gemfile` and `Gemfile.lock` under version control! Appendix A.6 explains the basics if you haven't done this before.

As the margin icon suggests, Bundler is the first of many examples we'll encounter of *automation for repeatability:* rather than manually installing the gems your app needs, listing them in the `Gemfile` and letting Bundler install them automatically ensures that the task can be repeated consistently in a variety of environments, eliminating mistakes in doing such tasks as a possible source of app errors. This is important because when you deploy your app, the information is used to make the deployment environment match your development environment.

Start the app with `rails server` and point a browser to `http://localhost:3000`. Recall from Chapter 2 that a URI that specifies only the hostname and port will fetch the home page. Most Web servers implement the convention that unless the app specifies otherwise, the home page is `index.html`, and indeed the welcome page you should be looking at is stored at `public/index.html`—the generic welcome page for new Rails apps.

Address already in use? If you see this error, you already have an app server listening on the default port of 3000, so find the terminal window where you started it and type Control-C to stop it if necessary.

If you now visit `http://localhost:3000/movies`, you should get a Routing Error from Rails. Indeed, you should verify that *anything* you add to the URI results in this error, and it's because we haven't specified any *routes* mapping URIs to app methods. Try `rake routes` and verify that unlike the result in Chapter 2, it prints nothing since there are no routes in our brand-new app. (You may want to open multiple Terminal windows so that the app can keep running while you try other commands.) More importantly, use an editor to open the file `log/development.log` and observe that the error message is logged there; this is where you look to find detailed error information when something goes wrong. We'll show other problem-finding and debugging techniques in Section 4.5.

To fix this error we need to add some routes. Since our initial goal is to store movie information in a database, we can take advantage of a Rails shortcut that creates RESTful routes for the four basic CRUD actions (Create, Read, Update, Delete) on a model. (Recall that RESTful routes specify self-contained requests of what operation to perform and what entity, or resource, to perform it on.) Edit `config/routes.rb`, which was auto-generated by the `rails new` command and is heavily commented. Replace the contents of the file with the following (the file is mostly comments, so you're not actually deleting much):

http://pastebin.com/JpnwuT56

```
1   Myrottenpotatoes::Application.routes.draw do
2     resources :movies
3     root :to => redirect('/movies')
4   end
```

Very important: In addition, **delete** the file `public/index.html` if it exists. Save the routes.rb file and run `rake routes` again, and observe that because of our change to `routes.rb`, the first line of output says that the URI `GET /movies` will try to call the `index` action of the `movies` controller; this and most of the other routes in the table are the result of the line **resources :movies**, as we'll soon see. The root route `'/'`, RottenPotatoes' "home page," will take us to the main Movie listings page by a mechanism we'll soon see called an *HTTP redirect*.

Using convention over configuration, Rails will expect this controller's actions to be defined in the class **MoviesController**, and if that class isn't defined at application start time, Rails will try to load it from the file `app/controllers/movies_controller.rb`. Sure enough, if you now reload the page `http://localhost:3000/movies` in your browser, you should see a different error: `uninitialized constant MoviesController`. This is good news: a Ruby class name is just a constant that refers to the class object, so Rails is essentially complaining that it can't find the **MoviesController** class, indicating that our route is working correctly! As before, this error message and additional information are captured in the log file `log/development.log`.

Having covered the first two steps in the list—setting up the app skeleton and creating some initial routes—we can move on to setting up the database that will store the models, the "M" of MVC.

> **Symbol or string?** As with many Rails methods, `resources 'movies'` would also work, but idiomatically, a symbol indicates that the value is one of a fixed set of choices rather than an arbitrary string.

Summary: You used the following commands to set up a new Rails app:

- `rails new` sets up the new app; the `rails` command also has subcommands to run the app locally with WEBrick (`rails server`) and other management tasks.

- Rails and the other gems your app depends on (we added the Haml templating system and the Ruby debugger) are listed in the app's `Gemfile`, which Bundler uses to automate the process of creating a consistent environment for your app whether in development or production mode.

- To add routes in `config/routes.rb`, the one-line `resources` method provided by the Rails routing system allowed us to set up a group of related routes for CRUD actions on a RESTful resource.

- The log files in the `log` directory collect error information when something goes wrong.

■ *Elaboration: Automatically reloading the app*

You may have noticed that after changing `routes.rb`, you didn't have to stop and restart the app in order for the changes to take effect. In development mode, Rails reloads all of the app's classes on every new request, so that your changes take effect immediately. In production this would cause serious performance problems, so Rails provides ways to change various app behaviors between development and production mode, as we'll see in Section 4.2.

Route	Example URI and behaviors
get ':controller/:action/:id' or get 'photos/preview/:id'	/photos/preview/3 method: **PhotosController#preview** **params[]**: **{:id=>3}**
get 'photos/preview/:id'	/photos/look/3?color=true Error: no route will match (look doesn't match **preview**)
get 'photos/:action/:id'	/photos/look/3?color=true method: **PhotosController#look** (look matches :**action**) **params[]**: **{:id=>3, :color=>'true'}**
get ':controller/:action/:vol/:num'	/magazines/buy/3/5?newuser=true&discount=2 method: **MagazinesController#buy** **params[]**: **{:vol=>3, :num=>5, :newuser=>'true',** **:discount=>'2'}**

Figure 4.2: As the Elaboration explains, routes can include "wildcard" tokens such as :controller and :action, which determine the controller and action that will be invoked. Any other tokens beginning with :, plus any additional parameters encoded in the URI, will be made available in the params hash.

■ *Elaboration: Non-resource-based routes*

The shortcut **resources :movies** creates RESTful routes for CRUD, but any nontrivial app will have many additional controller actions beyond CRUD. The Rails Routing from the Outside In guide[3] has much more detail, but one way to set up routes is to map components of the URI directly to controller and action names using wildcards, as Figure 4.2 shows.

Self-Check 4.1.1. *Recall the generic Rails welcome page you saw when you first created the app. In the* development.log *file, what is happening when the line* Started GET "assets/rails.png" *is printed? (Hint: recall the steps needed to render a page containing embedded assets, as described in Section 2.3.)*

◇ The browser is requesting the embedded image of the Rails logo for the welcome page. ■

Self-Check 4.1.2. *What are the two steps you must take to have your app use a particular Ruby gem?*

◇ You must add a line to your Gemfile to add a gem and re-run bundle install. ■

4.2 Databases and Migrations

The persistence tier of a Rails app (see Figure 2.7) uses a relational database (RDBMS) by default, for the reasons we discussed in Chapter 2. Amazingly, you don't need to know much about RDBMSs to use Rails, though as your apps become more sophisticated it definitely helps. Just as we use the "lite" Web server WEBrick for development, Rails apps are configured by default to use SQLite3, a "lite" RDBMS, for development. In production you'd use a production-ready database such as MySQL, PostgreSQL or Oracle.

But more important than the "lightweight" aspect is that you wouldn't want to develop or test your app against the production database, as bugs in your code might accidentally damage valuable customer data. So Rails defines three *environments*—production, development, and test—each of which manages its own separate copy of the database, as specified in config/database.yml. The test database is entirely managed by the testing tools and should never be modified manually: it is wiped clean and repopulated at the beginning of every testing run, as we'll see in Chapter 8.

An empty database was created for us by the `rails new` command in the file db/ `development.sqlite3`, as specified in **config/database.yml**. We need to create a table for movie information. We could use the `sqlite3` command-line tool[4] or a SQLite GUI tool to do this manually, but how would we later create the table in our production database when we deploy? Typing the same commands a second time isn't DRY, and the exact commands might be hard to remember. Further, if the production database is something other than SQLite3 (as is almost certainly the case), the specific commands might be different. And in the future, if we add more tables or make other changes to the database, we'll face the same problem.

A better alternative is a ***migration***—a portable script for changing the database schema (layout of tables and columns) in a consistent and repeatable way, just as Bundler uses the Gemfile to identify and install necessary gems (libraries) in a consistent and repeatable way. Changing the schema using migrations is a four-step process:

1. Create a migration describing what changes to make. As with `rails new`, Rails provides a migration ***generator*** that gives you the boilerplate code, plus various helper methods to describe the migration.

2. Apply the migration to the development database. Rails defines a `rake` task for this.

3. Assuming the migration succeeded, update the test database's schema by running `rake db:test:prepare`.

4. Run your tests, and if all is well, apply the migration to the production database and deploy the new code to production. The process for applying migrations in production depends on the deployment environment; Appendix A.8 covers how to do it using Heroku, the cloud computing deployment environment used for the examples in this book.

We'll use the first 3 steps of this process to add a new table that stores each movie's title, rating, description, and release date, to match Chapter 2. Each migration needs a name, and since this migration will create the movies table, we choose the name CreateMovies. Run the command `rails generate migration create_movies`, and if successful, you will find a new file under db/migrate whose name begins with the creation time and date and ends with the name you supplied, for example, `20111201180638_create_movies.rb`. (This naming scheme lets Rails apply migrations in the order they were created, since the file names will sort in date order.) Edit this file to make it look like Figure 4.3. As you can see, migrations illustrate an idiomatic use of blocks: the **ActiveRecord::Migration#create_table** method takes a block of 1 argument and yields to that block an object representing the table being created. The methods **string**, **datetime**, and so on are provided by this table object, and calling them results in creating columns in the newly-created database table; for example, **t.string 'title'** creates a column named `title` that can hold a string, which for most databases means up to 255 characters.

Save the file and type `rake db:migrate` to actually apply the migration and create this table. Note that this housekeeping task also stores the migration number itself in the database, and by default it only applies migrations that haven't already been applied. (Type `rake db:migrate` again to verify that it does nothing the second time.) `rake`

http://pastebin.com/rVw3riS9

```
1  class CreateMovies < ActiveRecord::Migration
2    def up
3      create_table 'movies' do |t|
4        t.string 'title'
5        t.string 'rating'
6        t.text 'description'
7        t.datetime 'release_date'
8        # Add fields that let Rails automatically keep track
9        # of when movies are added or modified:
10       t.timestamps
11     end
12   end
13
14   def down
15     drop_table 'movies' # deletes the whole table and all its data!
16   end
17 end
```

Figure 4.3: A migration that creates a new Movies table, specifying the desired fields and their types. The documentation for the ActiveRecord::Migration class (from which all migrations inherit) is part of the Rails documentation[6], and gives more details and other migration options.

db:rollback will "undo" the last migration by running its **down** method. (Try it. And then run rake db:migrate to re-apply the migration.) However, some migrations, such as those that delete data, can't be "undone"; in these cases, the **down** method should raise an **ActiveRecord::IrreversibleMigration** exception.

Summary

- Rails defines three environments—development, production and test—each with its own copy of the database.

- A migration is a script describing a specific set of changes to the database. As apps evolve and add features, migrations are added to express the database changes required to support those new features.

- Changing a database using a migration takes three steps: create the migration, apply the migration to your development database, and (if applicable) after testing your code apply the migration to your production database.

- The rails generate migration generator fills in the boilerplate for a new migration, and the **ActiveRecord::Migration** class contains helpful methods for defining it.

- rake db:migrate applies only those migrations not already applied to the development database. The method for applying migrations to a production database depends on the deployment environment.

■ *Elaboration: Environments*

Different environments can also override specific app behaviors. For example, production mode might specify optimizations that give better performance but complicate debugging if used in development mode. Test mode may "stub out" external interactions, for example, saving outgoing emails to a file rather than actually sending them. The file `config/environment.rb` specifies general startup instructions for the app, but `config/environments/production.rb` allows setting specific options used only in production mode, and similarly `development.rb` and `test.rb` in the same directory.

Self-Check 4.2.1. *In line 3 of Figure 4.3, how many arguments are we passing to* **create_table***, and of what types?*
◇ Two arguments: the first is a string and the second is a block. We used poetry mode, allowing us to omit parentheses. ■

Self-Check 4.2.2. *In Figure 4.3, the _____ method yields _____ to the block.*
◇ **create_table**; the variable **t** ■

4.3 Models: Active Record Basics

With our **Movies** table ready to go, we've completed the first three steps—app creation, routing, and initial migration—so it's time to write some app code. The database stores the model objects, but as we said in Chapter 2, Rails uses the Active Record design pattern to "connect" models to the database, so that's what we will explore next. Create a file `app/models/movie.rb` containing just these three lines:

http://pastebin.com/1zatve2r

```
1  class Movie < ActiveRecord::Base
2    attr_accessible :title, :rating, :description, :release_date
3  end
```

Thanks to convention over configuration, those three lines in `movie.rb` enable a great deal of behavior. To explore some of it, stop the running application with Control-C and instead run `rails console`, which gives you an interactive Ruby prompt like `irb(main):001.0>` with the Rails framework and all of your application's classes already loaded. Figure 4.4 illustrates some basic ActiveRecord features by creating some movies in our database, searching for them, changing them, and deleting them (CRUD). As we describe the role of each set of lines, you should copy and paste them into the console to execute the code. The URI accompanying the code example will take you to a copy-and-pastable version of the code on Pastebin.

Lines 1–6 (Create) create new movies in the database. **create!** is a method of **ActiveRecord::Base**, from which **Movie** inherits, as do nearly all models in Rails apps. ActiveRecord uses convention over configuration in three ways. First, it uses the name of the class (**Movie**) to determine the name of the database table corresponding to the class (`movies`). Second, it queries the database to find out what columns are in that table (the ones we created in our migration), so that methods like **create!** know which attributes are legal to specify and what types they should be. Third, it gives every **Movie** object attribute getters and setters similar to **attr_accessor**, except that these getters and setters do more than just modify an instance variable. Before going on, type **Movie.all**, which returns a collection of all the objects in the table associated with the **Movie** class.

http://pastebin.com/sGHfp79H

```
1   ####   Create
2   starwars = Movie.create!(:title => 'Star Wars',
3     :release_date => '25/4/1977', :rating => 'PG')
4   # note that numerical dates follow European format: dd/mm/yyyy
5   requiem =  Movie.create!(:title => 'Requiem for a Dream',
6     :release_date => 'Oct 27, 2000', :rating => 'R')
7   #  Creation using separate 'save' method, used when updating existing records
8   field = Movie.new(:title => 'Field of Dreams',
9     :release_date => '21-Apr-89', :rating => 'PG')
10  field.save!
11  field.title = 'New Field of Dreams'
12  ####   Read
13  pg_movies = Movie.where("rating = 'PG'")
14  ancient_movies = Movie.where('release_date < :cutoff and rating = :rating',
15    :cutoff => 'Jan 1, 2000', :rating => 'PG')
16  ####   Another  way to read
17  Movie.find(3)   # exception if key not found; find_by_id returns nil instead
18  ####   Update
19  starwars.update_attributes(:description => 'The best space western EVER',
20    :release_date => '25/5/1977')
21  requiem.rating = 'NC-17'
22  requiem.save!
23  ####   Delete
24  requiem.destroy
25  Movie.where('title = "Requiem for a Dream"')
26  ####   Find returns an enumerable
27  Movie.where('rating = "PG"').each do |mov|
28    mov.destroy
29  end
```

Figure 4.4: Although Model behaviors in MVC are usually called from the controller, these simple examples will help familiarize you with ActiveRecord's basic features before writing the controller.

For the purposes of demonstration, we specified the release date in line 6 using a different format than in line 3. Because Active Record knows from the database schema that **release_date** is a `datetime` column (recall the migration file in Figure 4.3), it will helpfully try to convert whatever value we pass for that attribute into a date.

Recall from Figure 3.1 that methods whose names end in ! are "dangerous." **create!** is dangerous in that if anything goes wrong in creating the object and saving it to the database, an exception will be raised. The non-dangerous version, **create**, returns the newly-created object if all goes well or **nil** if something goes wrong. For interactive use, we prefer **create!** so we don't have to check the return value each time, but in an application it's much more common to use **create** and check the return value.

Lines 7–11 (Save) show that Active Record model objects in memory are independent of the copies in the database, which must be updated explicitly. For example, lines 8–9 create a new **Movie** object *in memory* without saving it to the database. (You can tell by trying **Movie.all** after executing lines 8–9. You won't see *Field of Dreams* among the movies listed.) Line 10 actually persists the object to the database. The distinction is critical: line 11 changes the value of the movie's **title** field, but *only on the in-memory copy*—do **Movie.all** again and you'll see that the database copy hasn't been changed. **save** and **create** both cause the object to be written to the database, but simply changing the attribute values doesn't.

Lines 12–15 (Read) show one way to look up objects in the database. The **where** method is named for the `WHERE` keyword in SQL, the Structured Query Language used by most RDBMSs including SQLite3. You can specify a constraint directly as a string as in line 13, or use keyword substitution as in lines 14–15. Keyword substitution is always preferred

```
 1  # Seed the RottenPotatoes DB with some movies.
 2  more_movies = [
 3    {:title => 'Aladdin', :rating => 'G',
 4      :release_date => '25-Nov-1992'},
 5    {:title => 'When Harry Met Sally', :rating => 'R',
 6      :release_date => '21-Jul-1989'},
 7    {:title => 'The Help', :rating => 'PG-13',
 8      :release_date => '10-Aug-2011'},
 9    {:title => 'Raiders of the Lost Ark', :rating => 'PG',
10      :release_date => '12-Jun-1981'}
11  ]
12
13  more_movies.each do |movie|
14    Movie.create!(movie)
15  end
```

Figure 4.5: Adding initial data to the database is called *seeding*, and is distinct from migrations, which are for managing changes to the schema. Copy this code into db/seeds.rb and run rake db:seed to run it.

because, as we will see in Chapter 12, it allows Rails to thwart *SQL injection* attacks against your app. As with **create!**, the time was correctly converted from a string to a **Time** object and thence to the database's internal representation of time. Since the conditions specified might match multiple objects, **where** always returns an **Enumerable** any of **Enumerable**'s methods, such as those in Figure 3.7.

Line 17 (Read) shows the most primitive way of looking up objects, which is to return a single object corresponding to a given primary key. Recall from Figure 2.11 that every object stored in an RDBMS is assigned a primary key that is devoid of semantics but guaranteed to be unique within that table. When we created our table in the migration, Rails included a numeric primary key by default. Since the primary key for an object is permanent and unique, it often identifies the object in RESTful URIs, as we saw in Section 2.7.

Lines 18–22 (Update) show how to Update an object. As with **create** vs. **save**, we have two choices: use **update_attributes** to update the database immediately, or change the attribute values on the in-memory object and then persist it with **save!** (which, like **create!**, has a "safe" counterpart **save** that returns **nil** rather than raising an exception if something goes wrong).

Lines 23–25 (Delete) show how to Delete an object. The **destroy** method (line 24) deletes the object from the database permanently. You can still inspect the in-memory copy of the object, but trying to modify it, or to call any method on it that would cause a database access, will raise an exception. (After doing the **destroy**, try **requiem.update_attributes(...)** or even **requiem.rating='R'** to prove this.)

Lines 26–29 show that the result of a database read does indeed quack like a collection: we can use **each** to iterate over it and delete each movie in turn.

This whirlwind overview of Active Record barely scratches the surface, but it should clarify how the methods provided by **ActiveRecord::Base** support the basic CRUD actions.

As a last step before continuing, you should *seed* the database with some movies to make the rest of the chapter more interesting, using the code in Figure 4.5. Copy the code into db/seeds.rb and run rake db:seed to run it.

Summary

- Active Record uses convention over configuration to infer database table names from the names of model classes, and to infer the names and types of the columns (attributes) associated with a given kind of model.

- Basic Active Record support focuses on the CRUD actions: create, read, update, delete.

- Model instances can be Created either by calling **new** followed by **save** or by calling **create**, which combines the two.

- Every model instance saved in the database receives an ID number unique within its table called the primary key, whose attribute name (and therefore column name in the table) is **id** and which is never "recycled" (even if the corresponding row is deleted). The combination of table name and **id** uniquely identifies a model stored in the database, and is therefore how objects are usually referenced in RESTful routes.

- Model instances can be Read (looked up) by using **where** to express the matching conditions or **find** to look up the primary key (ID) directly, as might occur if processing a RESTful URI that embeds an object ID.

- Model instances can be Updated with **update_attributes**.

- Model instances can be Deleted with **destroy**, after which the in-memory copy can still be read but not modified or asked to access the database.

■ *Elaboration: Dynamic attribute-based finders*

Until Rails 3, another way to Read from the database was **find_by_***attribute*, for example, **find_by_title('Inception')**, or **find_all_by_rating('PG')**. These methods return an **Enumerable** of all matching elements if the **all** form is used, a single object otherwise, or `nil` if no matches are found. You can even say **find_all_by_release_date_and_rating** and pass two arguments to match the two attributes. ActiveRecord implements these methods by overriding **method_missing** (just as we did in Section 3.5), and in part because of the performance penalty of doing so, these methods are deprecated in Rails 4. We therefore omit them from the main discussion but present them here as an interesting use of **method_missing**.

■ *Elaboration: It quacks like a collection, but it isn't one*

The object returned by ActiveRecord's **all**, **where** and **find**-based methods certainly quacks like a collection, but as we will see in Chapter 11, it's actually a *proxy object* that doesn't even do the query until you force the issue by asking for one of the collection's elements, allowing you to build up complex queries with multiple **where**s without paying the cost of doing the query each time.

■ Elaboration: Overriding convention over configuration

Convention over configuration is great, but there are times you may need to override it. For example, if you're trying to integrate your Rails app with a non-Rails legacy app, the database tables may already have names that don't match the names of your models, or you may want friendlier attribute names than those given by taking the names of the table's columns. All of these defaults can be overridden at the expense of more code, as the ActiveRecord documentation describes. In this book we choose to reap the benefits of conciseness by sticking to the conventions.

Self-Check 4.3.1. *Why are* **where** *and* **find** *class methods rather than instance methods?*

◇ Instance methods operate on one instance of the class, but until we look up one or more objects, we have no instance to operate on. ■

Self-Check 4.3.2. *Do Rails models acquire the methods* **where** *and* **find** *via (a) inheritance or (b) mix-in? (Hint: check the* movie.rb *file.)*

◇ (a) they inherit from **ActiveRecord::Base**. ■

4.4 Controllers and Views

We'll complete our tour by creating some views to support the CRUD actions we just learned about. The RESTful routes we defined previously (rake routes to remind yourself what they are) expect the controller to provide actions for **index**, **show**, **new/create** (recall from Chapter 2 that creating an object requires two interactions with the user), **edit/update** (similarly), and **destroy**. Starting with the two easiest actions, **index** should display a list of all movies, allowing us to click on each one, and **show** should display details for the movie we click on.

For the **index** action, we know from the walk-through examples in Section 4.3 that **Movie.all** returns a collection of all the movies in the Movies table. Thus we need a controller method that sets up this collection and an HTML view that displays it. By convention over configuration, Rails expects the following for a method implementing the Show RESTful action on a Movie resource (note the uses of singular vs. plural and of CamelCase vs. snake_case):

- The model code is in class **Movie**, which inherits from **ActiveRecord::Base** and is defined in app/models/movie.rb

- The controller code is in class **MoviesController**, defined in app/controllers/movies_controller.rb (note that the model's class name is pluralized to form the controller file name.) Your app's controllers all inherit from your app's root controller **ApplicationController** (in app/controllers/application_controller.rb), which in turn inherits from **ActionController::Base**.

- Each instance method of the controller is named using **snake_lower_case** according to the action it handles, so the **show** method would handle the Show action

- The Show view template is in app/views/movies/show.html.haml, with the .haml extension indicating use of the Haml renderer. Other extensions include .xml for a file containing XML Builder code (as we saw in Section 3.6), .erb (which we'll meet shortly) for Rails' built-in Embedded Ruby renderer, and many others.

http://pastebin.com/ZLBvm1iN

```
1 # This file is app/controllers/movies_controller.rb
2 class MoviesController < ApplicationController
3   def index
4     @movies = Movie.all
5   end
6 end
```

http://pastebin.com/dLwJ4ZvH

```
1  -# This file is app/views/movies/index.html.haml
2  %h1 All Movies
3
4  %table#movies
5    %thead
6      %tr
7        %th Movie Title
8        %th Rating
9        %th Release Date
10       %th More Info
11   %tbody
12     - @movies.each do |movie|
13       %tr
14         %td= movie.title
15         %td= movie.rating
16         %td= movie.release_date
17         %td= link_to "More about #{movie.title}", movie_path(movie)
```

Figure 4.6: The controller code and template markup to support the Index RESTful action.

The Rails module that choreographs how views are handled is **ActionView::Base**. Since we've been using the Haml markup for our views (recall we added the Haml gem to our Gemfile dependencies), our view files will have names ending in .html.haml. Therefore, to implement the Index RESTful action, we must define an **index** action in app/controllers/movies_controller.rb and a view template in app/views/movies/index.html.haml. Create these two files using Figure 4.6 (you will need to create the intermediate directory app/views/movies/).

The controller method just retrieves all the movies in the Movies table using the **all** method introduced in the previous section, and assigns it to the **@movies** instance variable. Recall from the tour of a Rails app in Chapter 2 that instance variables defined in controller actions are available to views; line 12 of index.html.haml iterates over the collection **@movies** using **each**. There are three things to notice about this simple template.

First, the columns in the table header (th) just have static text describing the table columns, but the columns in the table body (td) use Haml's = syntax to indicate that the tag content should be evaluated as Ruby code, with the result substituted into the HTML document. In this case, we are using the attribute getters on **Movie** objects supplied by **ActiveRecord**.

Sanitization Haml's = syntax sanitizes[7] the result of evaluating the Ruby code before inserting it into the HTML output, to help thwart cross-site scripting and similar attacks described in Chapter 12.

Second, we've given the table of movies the HTML ID movies. We will use this later for visually styling the page using CSS, as we learned about in Chapter 2.

Third is the call in line 17 to **link_to**, one of many helper methods provided by **ActionView** for creating views. As its documentation[8] states, the first argument is a string that will appear as a link (clickable text) on the page and the second argument is used to create the URI that will become the actual link target. This argument can take several forms; the form we've used takes advantage of the URI helper **movie_path()** (as shown by rake routes for the **show** action), which takes as its argument an instance of a RESTful resource (in this case

Helper method	URI returned	RESTful Route and action	
movies_path	/movies	GET /movies	index
movies_path	/movies	POST /movies	create
new_movie_path	/movies/new	GET /movies/new	new
edit_movie_path(m)	/movies/1/edit	GET /movies/:id/edit	edit
movie_path(m)	/movies/1	GET /movies/:id	show
movie_path(m)	/movies/1	PUT /movies/:id	update
movie_path(m)	/movies/1	DELETE /movies/:id	destroy

Figure 4.7: As described in the documentation for the ActionView::Helpers class, Rails uses metaprogramming to create route helpers based on the name of your ActiveRecord class. m is assumed to be an ActiveRecord Movie object. The RESTful routes are as displayed by the output of rake routes; recall that different routes may have the same URI but different HTTP methods, for example create vs. index.

an instance of **Movie**) and generates the RESTful URI for the Show RESTful route for that object. This behavior is a nice illustration of reflection and metaprogramming in the service of conciseness. As rake routes reminds you, the Show action for a movie is expressed by a URI /movies/:id where :id is the movie's primary key in the Movies table, so that's what the link target created by **link_to** will look like. To verify this, restart the application (rails server in the app's root directory) and visit http://localhost:3000/movies/, the URI corresponding to the index action. If all is well, you should see a list of any movies in the database. If you use your browser's View Source option to look at the generated source, you can see that the links generated by **link_to** have URIs corresponding to the **show** action of each of the movies. (Go ahead and click one, but expect an error since we haven't yet created the controller's **show** method.)

The resources :movies line that we added in Section 4.1 actually creates a whole variety of helper methods for RESTful URIs, summarized in Figure 4.7. As you may have guessed, convention over configuration determines the names of the helper methods, and metaprogramming is used to define them on the fly as the result of calling resources :movies. The creation and use of such helper methods may seem gratuitous until you realize that it is possible to define much more complex and irregular routes beyond the standard RESTful ones we've been using so far, or that you might decide during the development of your application that a different routing scheme makes more sense. The helper methods insulate the views from such changes and let them focus on *what* to display rather than including code for *how* to display it. In fact, if **link_to**'s second argument is a resource for which routes have been set up in routes.rb, **link_to** will automatically generate the RESTful route to show that resource, so line 17 of Figure 4.6 could have been written **link_to "More about #{movie.title}",movie**.

There's one last thing to notice about these views. If you View Source in your browser, you'll see it includes HTML markup that doesn't appear in our Haml template, such as a head element containing links to the assets/application.css stylesheet and a <title> tag. This markup comes from the application template, which "wraps" all views by default. The default file app/views/layouts/application.html.erb created by the rails new command uses Rails' erb templating system, but since we like Haml's conciseness, we recommend deleting that file and replacing it with Figure 4.8, then watch Screencast 4.4.1 to understand how the "wrapping" process works.

http://pastebin.com/a9TbxRmU

```
 1  !!! 5
 2  %html
 3    %head
 4      %title RottenPotatoes!
 5      = stylesheet_link_tag 'application'
 6      = javascript_include_tag 'application'
 7      = csrf_meta_tags
 8
 9    %body
10      #main
11        = yield
```

Figure 4.8: Save this file as `app/views/layouts/application.html.haml` **and delete the existing**
`application.html.erb` **in that directory; this file is its Haml equivalent. Line 6 loads some basic JavaScript support; while
we won't discuss JavaScript programming until Chapter 6, some of Rails' built-in helpers use it transparently. Line 7
introduces protection against** *cross-site request forgery* **attacks described in Chapter 12. We also made the** `title` **element
a bit more human-friendly.**

http://pastebin.com/5hfPskzM

```
 1  # in app/controllers/movies_controller.rb
 2
 3  def show
 4    id = params[:id] # retrieve movie ID from URI route
 5    @movie = Movie.find(id) # look up movie by unique ID
 6    # will render app/views/movies/show.html.haml by default
 7  end
```

**Figure 4.9: An example implementation of the controller method for the Show action. A more robust implementation would
catch and rescue the exception ActiveRecord::RecordNotFound, as we warned in Section 4.3. We'll show how to handle
such cases in Chapter 5.**

Screencast 4.4.1: The Application layout.
`http://vimeo.com/34754667`
The screencast shows that the `app/views/layouts/application.html.haml` template
is used to "wrap" action views by default, using **yield** much like the example in Section 3.8.

On your own, try creating the controller action and view for **show** using a similar process:

1. Use `rake routes` to remind yourself what name you should give to the controller
   method and what parameters will be passed in the URI

2. In the controller method, use the appropriate ActiveRecord method introduced in Section 4.3 to retrieve the appropriate **Movie** object from the database and assign it to an
   instance variable

3. Create a view template in the right location in the `app/views` hierarchy and use Haml
   markup to show the various attributes of the **Movie** object you set up in the controller
   method

4. Exercise your method and view by clicking on one of the movie links on the `index`
   view

Once you're done, you can check yourself against the sample controller method in Figure 4.9 and the sample view in Figure 4.10. Experiment with other values for the arguments
to **link to** and **strftime** to get a sense of how they work.

```
 1  -# in app/views/movies/show.html.haml
 2
 3  %h2 Details about #{@movie.title}
 4
 5  %ul#details
 6    %li
 7      Rating:
 8      = @movie.rating
 9    %li
10      Released on:
11      = @movie.release_date.strftime("%B %d, %Y")
12
13  %h3 Description:
14
15  %p#description= @movie.description
16
17  = link_to 'Back to movie list', movies_path
```

Figure 4.10: An example view to go with Figure 4.9. For future CSS styling, we gave unique ID's to the bullet-list of details (ul) and the one-paragraph description (p). We used the strftime library function[10] to format the date more attractively, and the link_to method with the RESTful helper movies_path (Figure 4.7) to provide a convenient link back to the listings page. In general, you can append _path to any of the RESTful resource helpers in the leftmost column of the rake routes output to call a method that will generate the corresponding RESTful URI.

Since the current "bare-bones" views are ugly, as long as we're going to keep working on this app we might as well have something more attractive to look at. Copy the simple CSS styling below into app/assets/stylesheets/application.css, which is already included by line 5 of the application.html.haml template.

http://pastebin.com/28CD45Cm

```css
/* Simple CSS styling for RottenPotatoes app */
/* Add these lines to app/assets/stylesheets/application.css */

html, body {
  margin: 0;
  padding: 0;
  background: White;
  color: DarkSlateGrey;
  font-family: Tahoma, Verdana, sans-serif;
  font-size: 10pt;
}
div#main {
  margin: 0;
  padding: 0 20px 20px;
}
a {
  background: transparent;
  color: maroon;
  text-decoration: underline;
  font-weight: bold;
}
h1 {
  color: maroon;
  font-size: 150%;
  font-style: italic;
  display: block;
  width: 100%;
  border-bottom: 1px solid DarkSlateGrey;
}
h1.title {
  margin: 0 0 1em;
  padding: 10px;
  background-color: orange;
  color: white;
  border-bottom: 4px solid gold;
  font-size: 2em;
  font-style: normal;
}
table#movies {
  margin: 10px;
  border-collapse: collapse;
  width: 100%;
  border-bottom: 2px solid black;
}
table#movies th {
  border: 2px solid white;
  font-weight: bold;
  background-color: wheat;
}
table#movies th, table#movies td {
  padding: 4px;
  text-align: left;
}
#notice, #warning {
  background: rosybrown;
  margin: 1em 0;
  padding: 4px;
}
form label {
  display: block;
  line-height: 25px;
  font-weight: bold;
  color: maroon;
}
```

> **Summary:**
>
> - The Haml templating language allows you to intersperse HTML tags with Ruby code for your views. The result of evaluating Ruby code can either be discarded or interpolated into the HTML page.
>
> - For conciseness, Haml relies on indentation to reveal HTML element nesting.
>
> - Convention over configuration is used to determine the file names for controllers and views corresponding to a given model. If the RESTful route helpers are used, as in **resources :movies**, convention over configuration also maps RESTful action names to controller action (method) names.
>
> - Rails provides various helper methods that take advantage of the RESTful route URIs, including **link_to** for generating HTML links whose URIs refer to RESTful actions.

■*Elaboration: Optional* `:format` *in routes*

The raw output of `rake routes` includes a token (`.:format`) in most routes, which we omitted for clarity in Figure 2.12. If present, the format specifier allows a route to request resources in an output format other than the default of HTML—for example, `GET /movies.xml` would request the list of all movies as an XML document rather than an HTML page. Although in this simple application we haven't included the code to generate formats other than HTML, this mechanism allows a properly-designed existing application to be easily integrated into a Service-Oriented Architecture—changing just a few lines of code allows all existing controller actions to become part of an external RESTful API.

Self-Check 4.4.1. *In Figure 4.7, why don't the helper methods for the New action* (**new_movie_path**) *and Create action* (**movies_path**) *take an argument, as the Show or Update helpers do?*

◇ Show and Update operate on existing movies, so they take an argument to identify which movie to operate on. New and Create by definition operate on not-yet-existing movies. ■

Self-Check 4.4.2. *In Figure 4.7, why doesn't the helper method for the Index action take an argument? (HINT: The reason is different than the answer to Self-Check 4.4.1.)*

◇ The Index action just shows a list of all the movies, so no argument is needed to distinguish which movie to operate on. ■

Self-Check 4.4.3. *In Figure 4.6, why is there no* **end** *corresponding to the* **do** *in line 12?*
◇ Unlike Ruby itself, Haml relies on indentation to indicate nesting, so the **end** is supplied by Haml when executing the Ruby code in the **do**. ■

4.5 Debugging: When Things Go Wrong

The amazing sophistication of today's software stacks makes it possible to be highly productive, but with so many "moving parts," it also means that things inevitably go wrong, especially when learning new languages and tools. Errors might happen because you mistyped something, because of a change in your environment or configuration, or any number of other reasons. Although we take steps in this book to minimize the pain, such as using Test-Driven Development (Chapter 8) to avoid many problems and providing a VM image with a consistent environment, errors *will* occur. You can react most productively by remembering the acronym **RASP**: Read, Ask, Search, Post.

Read the error message. Ruby's error messages can look disconcertingly long, but a long error message is often your friend because it gives the ***backtrace*** showing not only the method where the error occurred, but also its caller, its caller's caller, and so on. Don't throw up your hands when you see a long error message; use the information to understand both the proximate cause of the error (the problem that "stopped the show") and the possible paths towards the root cause of the error. This will require some understanding of the syntax of the erroneous code, which you might lack if you blindly cut-and-pasted someone else's code with no understanding of how it works or what assumptions it makes. Of course, a syntax error due to cut-and-paste is just as likely to occur when reusing your own code as someone else's, but at least you understand your own code (right?).

A particularly common proximate cause of Ruby errors is "Undefined method **foobar** for **nil:NilClass**", which means "You tried to call method **foobar** on an object whose value is **nil** and whose class is **NilClass**, which doesn't define **foobar**." (**NilClass** is a special class whose only instance is the constant **nil**.)

This often occurs when some computation fails and returns **nil** instead of the object you expected, but you forgot to check for this error and subsequently tried to call a method on what you assumed was a valid object. But if the computation occurred in another method "upstream," the backtrace can help you figure out where.

In SaaS apps using Rails, this confusion can be compounded if the failed computation happens in the controller action but the invalid object is passed as an instance variable and then dereferenced in the view, as in the following excerpts from a controller and view:

http://pastebin.com/vPnA7s4K

```
1  # in controller action:
2  def show
3    @movie = Movie.find_by_id(params[:id]) # what if this movie not in DB?
4    # BUG: we should check @movie for validity here!
5  end
6
7  -# ...later, in the Haml view:
8
9  %h1= @movie.title
10 -# will give "undefined method 'title' for nil:NilClass" if @movie is nil
```

Ask a coworker. If you are programming in pairs, two brains are better than one. If you're in an "open seating" configuration, or have instant messaging enabled, put the message out there.

Search for the error message. You'd be amazed at how often experienced developers deal with an error by using a search engine such as Google to look up key words or key phrases in the error message. You can also search sites like StackOverflow[12], which specialize in helping out developers and allow you to vote for the most helpful answers to particular questions so that they eventually percolate to the top of the answer list.

Post a question on one of those sites if all else fails. Be as specific as possible about what went wrong, what your environment is, and how to reproduce the problem:

- **Vague:** "The sinatra gem doesn't work on my system." There's not enough information here for anyone to help you.

An amusing **perspective** on the perils of blind "shotgun problem solving" is the Jargon File's hacker koan "Tom Knight and the Lisp Machine."[11]

- **Better, but annoying:** "The `sinatra` gem doesn't work on my system. Attached is the 85-line error message." Other developers are just as busy as you and probably won't take the time to extract relevant facts from a long trace.

- **Best:** Look at the actual transcript[13] of this question on StackOverflow. At 6:02pm, the developer provided specific information, such as the name and version of his operating system, the specific commands he successfully ran, and the unexpected error that resulted. Other helpful voices chimed in asking for specific additional information, by 7:10pm, two of the answers had identified the problem.

While it's impressive that he got his answer in just over an hour, it means he also lost an hour of coding time, which is why you should post a question only after you've exhausted the other alternatives. How can you make progress on debugging problems on your own? There are two kinds of problems. In the first kind, an error or exception of some kind stops the app in its tracks. Since Ruby is an interpreted language, syntax errors can cause this (unlike Java, which won't even compile if there are syntax errors). Here are some things to try if the app stops in its tracks.

- Exploit automatic indentation and syntax highlighting. If your text editor insists on indenting a line farther than you want it to be indented, you may have forgotten to close a parenthesis, brace, or **do. . . end** block somewhere upstream, or you may have forgotten to "escape" a special character (for example, a single-quote inside a single-quoted string). If your editor isn't so equipped, you can either write your code on stone tablets, or switch to one of the more productive modern editors suggested in Appendix A.3.

- Look in the log file, usually `log/development.log`, for complete error information including the backtrace. In production apps, this is often your only alternative, as Rails apps are usually configured to display a more user-friendly error page in production mode, rather than the error backtrace you'd see if the error occurred in development mode.

In the second kind of problem, the app runs but produces an incorrect result or behavior. Most developers use a combination of two approaches to debug such problems. The first is to insert *instrumentation*—extra statements to record values of important variables at various points during program execution. There are various places we can instrument a Rails SaaS app—try each of the below to get a feel for how they work:

printf debugging is an old name for this technique, from the C library function that prints a string on the terminal.

- Display a detailed description of an object in a view. For example, try inserting = **debug(@movie)** or = **@movie.inspect** in any view (where the leading = tells Haml to execute the code and insert the result into the view).

- "Stop the show" inside a controller method by raising an exception whose message is a representation of the value you want to inspect, for example, **raise params.inspect** to see the detailed value of the **params** hash inside a controller method. Rails will display the exception message as the Web page resulting from the request.

- Use **logger.debug(** *message***)** to print *message* to the log. **logger** is available in models and controllers and can record messages with a variety of urgencies; compare `config/environments/production.rb` with `development.rb` to see how the default logging level differs in production vs. development environments.

The second way to debug correctness problems is with an interactive debugger. We already installed the debugger gem via our Gemfile; to use the debugger in a Rails app, start the app server using `rails server --debugger`, and insert the statement **debugger** at the point in your code where you want to stop the program. When you hit that statement, the terminal window where you started the server will give you a debugger prompt. In Section 4.7, we'll show how to use the debugger to shed some light on Rails internals.

Summary

- Use a language-aware editor with syntax highlighting and automatic indentation to help find syntax errors.

- Instrument your app by inserting the output of **debug** or **inspect** into views, or by making them the argument of **raise**, which will cause a runtime exception that will display *message* as a Web page.

- To debug using the interactive debugger, make sure your app's Gemfile includes debugger, start the app server with `rails server --debugger`, and place the statement **debugger** at the point in your code where you want to break.

To debug non-Rails apps, insert require 'debugger' at the beginning of your app.

Self-Check 4.5.1. *Why can't you just use* **print** *or* **puts** *to display messages to help debug your SaaS app?*

◇ Unlike command-line apps, SaaS apps aren't attached to a terminal window, so there's no obvious place for the output of a print statement to go. ∎

Self-Check 4.5.2. *Of the three debugging methods described in this section, which ones are appropriate for collecting instrumentation or diagnostic information once your app is deployed and in production?*

◇ Only the **logger** method is appropriate, since the other two methods ("stopping the show" in a controller or inserting diagnostic information into views) would interfere with the usage of real customers if used on a production app. ∎

4.6 Form Submission: New and Create

Our last look at views will deal with a slightly more complex situation: that of submitting a form, such as for creating a new movie or updating an existing one. There are three problems we need to address:

1. How do we display a fill-in form to the user?

2. How is the information filled in by the user actually made available to the controller action, so that it can be used in a **create** or **update** ActiveRecord call?

3. What resource should be returned and displayed as the result of a RESTful request to create or update an item? Unlike when we ask for a list of movies or details about a movie, it's not obvious what to display as the result of a create or update.

Of course, before we go further, we need to give the user a way to get to the fill-in form we're about to create. Since the form will be for creating a new movie, it will correspond to

http://pastebin.com/RPPNrMfK

```
1  %h2 Create New Movie
2
3  = form_tag movies_path, :method => :post do
4
5    = label :movie, :title, 'Title'
6    = text_field :movie, :title
7
8    = label :movie, :rating, 'Rating'
9    = select :movie, :rating, ['G','PG','PG-13','R','NC-17']
10
11   = label :movie, :release_date, 'Released On'
12   = date_select :movie, :release_date
13
14   = submit_tag 'Save Changes'
```

Figure 4.11: **The form the user sees for creating and adding a new movie to RottenPotatoes.**

the RESTful action **new**, and we will follow convention by placing the form in `app/views/movies/new.html.haml`. We can therefore take advantage of the automatically-provided RESTful URI helper **new_movie_path** to create a link to the form. Do this by adding a single line to the end of `index.html.haml`:

http://pastebin.com/XUGTnere

```
1  -# add to end of index.html.haml
2
3  = link_to 'Add new movie', new_movie_path
```

What controller action will be triggered if the user clicks on this link? Since we used the URI helper **new_movie_path**, it will be the **new** controller action. We haven't defined this action yet, but for the moment, since the user is creating a brand-new movie entry, the only thing the action needs to do is cause the corresponding view for the `new` action to be rendered. Recall that by default, every controller method automatically tries to render a template with the corresponding name (in this case `new.html.haml`), so you can just add the following trivial **new** method to `movies_controller.rb`:

http://pastebin.com/FeYh04c6

```
1  def new
2    # default: render 'new' template
3  end
```

Rails makes it easy to describe a fill-in form using form tag helpers[14] available to all views. Put the code in Figure 4.11 into `app/views/movies/new.html.haml` and watch Screencast 4.6.1 for a description of what's going on in it.

Screencast 4.6.1: Views with fill-in forms.

`http://vimeo.com/34754683`

The **form_tag** method for generating a form requires a route to which the form should be submitted—that is, a URI and an HTTP verb. We use the RESTful URI helper and HTTP POST method to generate a route to the **create** action, as `rake routes` reminds us.

As the screencast mentions, not all input field types are supported by the form tag helpers (in this case, the date fields aren't supported), and in some cases you need to generate forms whose fields don't necessarily correspond to the attributes of some ActiveRecord object.

To recap where we are, we created the **new** controller method that will render a view giving the user a form to fill in, placed that view in `new.html.haml`, and arranged to have the form submitted to the **create** controller method. All that remains is to use the information in **params** (the form field values) to actually create the new movie in the database.

Summary

- Rails provides form helpers to generate a fill-in form whose fields are related to the attributes of a particular type of ActiveRecord object.

- When creating a form, you specify the controller action that will receive the form submission by passing **form_tag** the appropriate RESTful URI and HTTP method (as displayed by `rake routes`).

- When the form is submitted, the controller action can inspect **params[]**, which will contain a key for each form field whose value is the user-supplied contents of that field.

Self-Check 4.6.1. *In line 3 of Figure 4.11, what would be the effect of changing* **:method=>:post** *to* **:method=>:get** *and why?*

◇ The form submission would result in listing all movies rather than creating a new movie. The reason is that a route requires both a URI and a method. As Figure 4.7 shows, the **movies_path** helper with the GET method would route to the **index** action, whereas the **movies_path** helper with the POST method routes to the **create** action. ∎

Self-Check 4.6.2. *Given that submitting the form shown in Figure 4.11 will create a new movie, why is the view called* `new.html.haml` *rather than* `create.html.haml`*?*

◇ A RESTful route and its view should name the resource being requested. In this case, the resource requested when the user *loads* this form is the form itself, that is, the ability to create a new movie; hence `new` is an appropriate name for this resource. The resource requested when the user *submits* the form, named by the route specified for form submission on line 3 of the figure, is the actual creation of the new movie. ∎

4.7   Redirection and the Flash

Recall from the examples in Section 4.3 that the **Movie.create!** call takes a hash of attribute names and values to create a new object. As Screencast 4.7.1 shows, the form field names created by the form tag helpers all have names of the form **params['movie']['title']**, **params['movie']['rating']**, and so on. As a result, the value of **params[:movie]** is exactly a hash of movie attribute names and values, which we can pass along directly using **Movie.create!(params[:movie])**.

We must, however, attend to an important detail before this will work. "Mass assignment" of a whole set of attributes is a mechanism that could be used by a malicious attacker to set arbitrary model attributes[15] that shouldn't be changeable by regular users. Section 5.2 describes how Rails can protect against this attack, but prior to version 3.2, the default Rails behavior was *not* to do so. In 2012 security consultant Egor Homakov showed[16] that GitHub had the mass-assignment vulnerability because the developers there hadn't changed the default behavior. The Rails team responded by changing Rails' default behavior to enable protection from mass assignment starting with Rails 3.2. For simplicity in our current example, we'll disable this protection, but in real apps you should use the mechanisms that Section 5.2

n	execute next line
s	execute next statement
f	finish current method call and return
p *expr*	print *expr*, which can be anything that's in scope within the current stack frame
eval *expr*	evaluate *expr*; can be used to set variables that are in scope, as in **eval x=5**
up	go up the call stack, to caller's stack frame
down	go down the call stack, to callee's stack frame
where	display where you are in the call stack
b *file:num*	set a breakpoint at line *num* of *file* (current file if *file:* omitted)
b *method*	set a breakpoint when *method* called
c	continue execution until next breakpoint
q	quit program

Figure 4.12: Command summary of the interactive Ruby debugger.

describes to selectively enable or disable attribute assignment. To temporarily disable this feature in development mode only, find and comment out (place a **#** at the beginning of) the following line in `config/environments/development.rb`:

http://pastebin.com/AU0kFpdq

```
1   config.active_record.mass_assignment_sanitizer = :strict
```

The screencast shows how mass-assignment works in practice, and also shows the helpful technique of using debug breakpoints to provide a detailed look "under the hood" during execution of a controller action.

Screencast 4.7.1: The Create action.

`http://vimeo.com/34754699`

Inside the **create** controller action, we placed a debug breakpoint to inspect what's going on, and used a subset of the debugger commands in Figure 4.12 to inspect the **params** hash. In particular, because our form's field names all looked like **movie[. . .]**, **params['movie']** is itself a hash with the various movie fields, ready for assigning to a new **Movie** object. Like many Rails methods, **params[]** can take either a symbol or a string—in fact **params** is not a regular hash at all, but a **HashWithIndifferentAccess**, a Rails class that quacks like a hash but allows its keys to be accessed as either symbols or strings.

That brings us to the third question posed at the beginning of Section 4.6: what view should we display when the **create** action completes? To be consistent with other actions like **show**, we could create a view `app/views/movies/create.html.haml` containing a nice message informing the user of success, but it seems gratuitous to have a separate view just to do that. What most web apps do instead is return the user to a more useful page—say, the home page, or the list of all movies—but they display a success message as an added element on that page to let the user know that their changes were successfully saved.

Rails makes it easy to implement this behavior. To send the user to a different page, **redirect_to** causes a controller action to end not by rendering a view, but by restarting a whole new request to a different action. Thus, **redirect_to movies_path** is just as if the user suddenly requested the RESTful Index action GET movies (that is, the action corresponding to the helper **movies_path**): the **index** action will run to completion and render its view as usual. In other words, a controller action must finish by either rendering a view or redirecting to another action. Remove the debug breakpoint from the controller action (which you inserted if you modified your code according to Screencast 4.7.1) and modify it to look like the listing below; then test out this behavior by reloading the movie listing page, clicking Add New Movie, and submitting the form.

http://pastebin.com/g5nq88eJ

```
1  # in movies_controller.rb
2  def create
3    @movie = Movie.create!(params[:movie])
4    redirect_to movies_path
5  end
```

Of course, to be user-friendly, we would like to display a message acknowledging that creating a movie succeeded. (We'll soon deal with the case where it fails.) The hitch is that when we call **redirect_to**, it starts a whole new HTTP request; and since HTTP is stateless, all of the variables associated with the **create** request are gone.

To address this common scenario, the **flash[]** is a special method that quacks like a hash, but persists from the current request to the next. (In a moment we'll explore how Rails accomplishes this.) In other words, if we put something into **flash[]** during the current controller action, we can access it during the *subsequent* action. The entire hash is persisted, but by convention, **flash[:notice]** is used for informational messages and **flash[:warning]** is used for messages about things going wrong. Modify the controller action to store a useful message in the **flash**, and try it out:

http://pastebin.com/6DuHAwbN

```
1  # in movies_controller.rb
2  def create
3    @movie = Movie.create!(params[:movie])
4    flash[:notice] = "#{@movie.title} was successfully created."
5    redirect_to movies_path
6  end
```

What happened? Even though creating a new movie appears to work (the new movie shows up in the list of all movies), there's no sign of the helpful message we just created. As you've probably guessed, that's because we didn't actually modify any of the views to display that message!

But which view should we modify? In this example, we chose to redirect the user to the movies listing, so perhaps we should add code to the Index view to display the message. But in the future we might decide to redirect the user someplace else instead, and in any case, the idea of displaying a confirmation message or warning message is so common that it makes sense to factor it out rather than putting it into one specific view.

Recall that app/views/layouts/application.html.haml is the template used to "wrap" all views by default. This is a good candidate for displaying flash messages since any pending messages will be displayed no matter what view is rendered. Make application.html.haml look like Figure 4.13—this requires adding four lines of code between **%body** and **=yield** to display any pending flash messages at the beginning of the page body.

If you do any nontrivial CSS work, you'll want to use a dedicated CSS editor, such as the open-source and cross-platform Amaya[17] or one of many commercial products.

Try styling all **flash** messages to be printed in red text and centered. You'll need to add the appropriate CSS selector(s) in app/assets/stylesheets/application.css to match the HTML elements that display the **flash** in the Application page template. The CSS properties color: red and text-align: center will get these effects, but feel free to experiment with other visual styles, colors, borders, and so on.

http://pastebin.com/4rsZ5qyx

```
1  -# this goes just inside %body:
2  - if flash[:notice]
3    #notice.message= flash[:notice]
4  - elsif flash[:warning]
5    #warning.message= flash[:warning]
```

Figure 4.13: Note the use of CSS for styling the flash messages: each type of message is displayed in a `div` whose unique ID is either `notice` or `warning` depending on the message's type, but that share the common class `message`. This gives us the freedom in our CSS file to either style the two types of messages the same by referring to their class, or style them differently by referring to their IDs. Remarkably, Haml's conciseness allows expressing each `div`'s class and ID attributes *and* the message text to be displayed all on a single line.

Summary

- Although the most common way to finish a controller action is to render the view corresponding to that action, for some actions such as **create** it's more helpful to send the user back to a different view. Using **redirect_to** replaces the default view rendering with a redirection to a different action.

- Although redirection triggers the browser to start a brand-new HTTP request, the **flash** can be used to save a small amount of information that will be made available to that new request, for example, to display useful information to the user regarding the redirect.

- You can DRY out your views by putting markup to display **flash** messages in one of the application's templates, rather than having to replicate it in every view that might need to display such messages.

■ Elaboration: The Session

Actually, the flash is just a special case of the more general facility **session[]**. Like the flash, the session quacks like a hash whose contents persist across requests from the same browser, but unlike the flash, which is automatically erased following the next request, anything you put in the session stays there permanently until you delete it. You can either **session.delete(:key)** to delete individual items just as with a regular hash, or use the **reset_session** method to nuke the whole thing. Keep in mind that the session is based on cookies, so sessions from different users are independent. Also, as we note in Fallacies & Pitfalls, be careful how much you store in the session.

Self-Check 4.7.1. *Why must every controller action either render a view or perform a redirect?*

◇ HTTP is a request-reply protocol, so every action must generate a reply. One kind of reply is a view (Web page) but another kind is a redirect, which instructs the browser to issue a new request to a different URI. ■

Self-Check 4.7.2. *In Figure 4.13, given that we are going to output an HTML tag, why does line 2 begin with - rather than =?*

◇ = directs Haml to evaluate the Ruby expression and substitute it into the view, but we don't want the value of the **if**-expression to be placed in the view—we want the actual HTML tag, which Haml generates from **#notice.message**, plus the result of evaluating **flash[:notice]**,

	Create	Update
Parameters passed to view	none	existing instance of **Movie**
Default form field values	blank	existing movie attributes
Submit button label	"Create Movie" (or "Save Changes")	"Update Movie" (or "Save Changes")
Controller actions	**new** serves form, **create** receives form and modifies database	**edit** serves form, **update** receives form and modifies database
params[]	Attribute values for new movie	Updated attribute values for existing movie

Figure 4.14: The edit/update action pair is very similar to the new/create action pair we've already implemented.

http://pastebin.com/HpVcAmTw

```
1  %h2 Edit Movie
2
3  = form_tag movie_path(@movie), :method => :put do
4
5    = label :movie, :title, 'Title'
6    = text_field :movie, 'title'
7
8    = label :movie, :rating, 'Rating'
9    = select :movie, :rating, ['G','PG','PG-13','R','NC-17']
10
11   = label :movie, :release_date, 'Released On'
12   = date_select :movie, :release_date
13
14   = submit_tag 'Save Changes'
```

Figure 4.15: The Haml markup for the edit view differs from the new view only in line 3.

which is correctly preceded by =. ■

4.8   Finishing CRUD: Edit/Update and Destroy

We can now follow a similar process to add the code for the **update** functionality. Like **create**, this requires two actions—one to display the form with editable information (**edit**) and a second to accept the form submission and apply the updated information (**update**). Of course, we first need to give the user a way to specify the Edit action, so before going further, modify the show.html.haml view so its last two lines match the code below, where line 2 uses the helper **edit_movie_path** to generate a RESTful URI that will trigger the **edit** action for **@movie**.

http://pastebin.com/AKqf6jx2

```
1  -# modify last 2 lines of app/views/movies/show.html.haml to:
2  = link_to 'Edit info', edit_movie_path(@movie)
3  = link_to 'Back to movie list', movies_path
```

Shouldn't we DRY out similar things? In Chapter 5 we'll show a way to take advantage of this similarity to DRY out the views, but for now we'll tolerate a little duplication in order to finish the example.)

In fact, as Figure 4.14 shows, the new/create and edit/update action pairs are similar in many respects.

Use Figure 4.15 to create the edit.html.haml view, which is almost identical to the new view (Figure 4.11)—the only difference is line 3, which specifies the RESTful route for form submission. As rake routes tells us, the **create** action requires an HTTP POST to the

URI /movies, so Figure 4.11 uses **:method=>:post** and the URI helper **movies_path** in the form action. In contrast, the **update** action requires an HTTP PUT to /movies/:id where :id is the primary key of the resource to be updated, so line 3 of Figure 4.15 specifies **:method=>:put** and uses the URI helper **movie_path(@movie)** to construct the URI for editing this specific movie. We could have constructed the URIs manually, using **form_tag "/movies"** in new.html.haml and **form_tag "/movies/#{@movie.id}"** in edit.html.haml, but the URI helpers are more concise, convey intent more clearly, and are independent of the actual URI strings, should those have a reason to change. As we'll see, when your app introduces relationships among different kinds of resources, such as a movie-goer having favorite movies, the RESTful URIs become more complicated and the helpers become correspondingly more concise and easy to read.

Below are the actual controller methods you'll need to add to movies_controller.rb to try out this feature, so go ahead and add them.

http://pastebin.com/UYj53gwM

```
1  # in movies_controller.rb
2
3  def edit
4    @movie = Movie.find params[:id]
5  end
6
7  def update
8    @movie = Movie.find params[:id]
9    @movie.update_attributes!(params[:movie])
10   flash[:notice] = "#{@movie.title} was successfully updated."
11   redirect_to movie_path(@movie)
12 end
```

Try clicking on the Edit link you inserted above to edit an existing movie. Observe that when updating an existing movie, the default filled-in values of the form fields correspond to the movie's current attributes. This is because helpers such as **text_field** in line 6 of the new or edit templates will by default look for an instance variable whose name matches their first argument—in this case, the first argument is **:movie** so the **text_field** helper will look for a variable **@movie**. If it exists and corresponds to an ActiveRecord model, the helper assumes that this form is for editing an existing object, and **@movie**'s current attribute values will be used to populate the form fields. If it doesn't exist or doesn't respond to the attribute method in the second argument (**'title'**), the form fields will be blank. This behavior is a good reason to name your instance variable **@movie** rather than (say) **@my_movie**: you can still get the extra functionality from the helpers, but you'll have to pass extra arguments to them.

The last CRUD action is Delete, which Figure 4.4 shows can be accomplished by calling **destroy** on an ActiveRecord model. As with the Update action, it's common practice to respond to a Delete by destroying the object and then returning the user to some other useful page (such as the Index view) and displaying a confirmation message that the item was deleted, so we already know how to write the controller method—add the following lines to movies_controller.rb:

http://pastebin.com/djpFThe2

```
1  def destroy
2    @movie = Movie.find(params[:id])
3    @movie.destroy
4    flash[:notice] = "Movie '#{@movie.title}' deleted."
5    redirect_to movies_path
6  end
```

(Recall from the explanation accompanying Figure 4.4 that even after destroying an object in the database, the in-memory copy can still be queried for its attributes as long as we don't try to modify it or ask it to persist itself.)

As we did with Edit, we'll provide access to the Delete action from each movie's Show page. What kind of HTML element should we use? `rake routes` tells us the Delete action requires the URI `/movies/:id` with the HTTP verb `DELETE`. This seems similar to Edit, whose URI is similar but uses the `GET` method. Since we've been using the URI helpers to generate routes, we can still use **link_to** in this case, but its behavior is a bit different from what you might expect.

http://pastebin.com/e0CzFW1D

```
1  -# Our Edit link from previous example:
2  = link_to 'Edit info', edit_movie_path(@movie)
3  -# This Delete link will not really be a link, but a form:
4  = link_to 'Delete', movie_path(@movie), :method => :delete
```

If you examine the HTML generated by this code, you'll find that Rails generates a link that includes the unusual attribute `data-method="delete"`. Long before RESTfulness became a prominent SaaS concept, there was already a general guideline that SaaS app requests that used GET should always be "safe"—they should not cause any side effects such as deleting an item or purchasing something, and should be safely repeatable. Indeed, if you try to reload a page that resulted from a POST operation, most browsers will display a warning asking if you really want to resubmit the form. Since deleting something is *not* a "safe" operation, Rails handles deletion using a POST. As the Elaboration at the end of Section 6.5 explains, the unusual HTML generated by **link_to**, when combined with JavaScript, actually results in a form being created and POSTed when the link is clicked—thereby allowing JavaScript-enabled browsers to safely handle the destructive `delete` operation.

> **Search engine crawlers** explore the Web by following GET links. Imagine Google triggering millions of spurious purchases every time it crawled an e-commerce site!

Try modifying the `index` view (list of all movies) so that each table row displaying a movie title also includes an Edit link that brings up the edit form for that movie and a Destroy button that deletes that movie with a confirmation dialog.

Self-Check 4.8.1. *Why does the form in* `new.html.haml` *submit to the* **create** *method rather than the* **new** *method?*

◇ As we saw in Chapter 2, creating a new record requires two interactions. The first one, **new**, loads the form. The second one, **create**, submits the form and causes the actual creation of the new record. ■

Self-Check 4.8.2. *Why does it make no sense to have both a render and a redirect (or two renders, or two redirects) along the same code path in a controller action?*

◇ Render and redirect are two different ways to reply to a request. Each request needs exactly one reply. ■

Summary

- Rails provides various helpers for creating HTML forms that refer to ActiveRecord models. In the controller method that receives the form submission, the keys in the **params** hash are the form fields' name attributes and the corresponding values are the user-selected choices for those fields.

- Creating and updating an object are resources whose visible representation is just the success or failure status of the request. For user friendliness, rather than displaying a web page with just success or failure and requiring the user to click to continue, we can instead **redirect_to** a more useful page such as **index**. Redirection is an alternative way for a controller action to finish, rather than rendering a view.

- For user friendliness, it's typical to modify the application layout to display messages stored in **flash[:notice]** or **flash[:warning]**, which persist until the next request so they can be used with **redirect_to**.

- To specify the URIs required by both form submissions and redirections, we can use RESTFUL URI helpers like **movies_path** and **edit_movie_path** rather than creating the URIs manually.

4.9 Fallacies and Pitfalls

 Pitfall: **Modifying the database manually rather than using migrations, or managing gems manually rather than using Bundler.**

Especially if you've come from other SaaS frameworks, it may be tempting to use the SQLite3 command line or a GUI database console to manually add or change database tables or to install libraries. But if you do this, you'll have no consistent way to reproduce these steps in the future (for example at deployment time) and no way to roll back the changes in an orderly way. Also, since migrations and Gemfiles are just files that become part of your project, you can keep them under version control and see the entire history of your changes.

 Pitfall: **Fat controllers and fat views.**

Because controller actions are the first place in your app's code that are called when a user request arrives, it's remarkably easy for the actions' methods to get fat—putting all kinds of logic in the controller that really belongs in the model. Similarly, it's easy for code to creep into views—most commonly, a view may find itself calling a model method such as **Movie.all**, rather than having the controller method set up a variable such as **@movies=Movie.all** and having the view just use **@movies**. Besides violating MVC, coupling views to models can interfere with caching, which we'll explore in Chapter 5. The view should focus on displaying content and facilitating user input, and the controller should focus on mediating between the view and the model and set up any necessary variables to keep code from leaking into the view.

 Pitfall: **Overstuffing the session[] hash.**

You should minimize what you put in the **session[]** for two reasons. First, with the default Rails configuration, the session is packed into a cookie (Section 2.2.1 and Screencast 2.2.1) at the end of each request and unpacked when the cookie is received with the next request, and the HTTP specification limits cookies to 4 KBytes in size. Second, although you can change Rails' configuration to allow larger session objects by storing them in their own database table instead of a cookie, bulky sessions are a warning that your app's actions aren't very self-contained. That would mean your app isn't very RESTful and may be difficult to use as part of a Service-Oriented Architecture. Although nothing stops you from assigning arbitrary objects to the session, you should keep just the **id**s of necessary objects in the session and keep the objects themselves in model tables in the database.

4.10   Concluding Remarks: Designing for SOA

The introduction to Rails in this chapter may seem to introduce a lot of very general machinery to handle a fairly simple and specific task: implementing a Web-based UI to CRUD actions. However, we will see in Chapter 5 that this solid groundwork will position us to appreciate the more advanced mechanisms that will let you truly DRY out and beautify your Rails apps.

One simple example we can show immediately relates to Service-Oriented Architecture, an important concept introduced in Chapter 1 and to which we'll return often. If we intended RottenPotatoes to be used in an SOA, its RESTful actions might be performed either by a human who expects to see a Web page as a result of the action or by another service that expects (for example) an XML response. To simplify the task of making your app work with SOA, you can return different formats for the same resource using the **respond_to**[18] method of **ActionController** (not to be confused with Ruby's built-in **respond_to?** introduced in Section 3.2). **ActionController::MimeResponds#respond_to** yields an object that can be used to select the format in which to render a response. Here's how the **update** action can be immediately converted into an SOA-friendly RESTful API that updates a movie's attributes and returns an XML representation of the updated object, while preserving the existing user interface for human users:

http://pastebin.com/9ZvvznvJ

```
1  def update
2    @movie = Movie.find params[:id]
3    @movie.update_attributes!(params[:movie])
4    respond_to do |client_wants|
5      client_wants.html {  redirect_to movie_path(@movie)  } # as before
6      client_wants.xml  {  render :xml => @movie.to_xml    }
7    end
8  end
```

Similarly, the only reason **new** requires its own controller action is that the human user needs an opportunity to fill in the values that will be used for **create**. Another *service* would never call the **new** action at all. Nor would it make sense to redirect back to the list of movies after a **create** action: the **create** method could just return an XML representation of the created object, or even the created object's ID.

Thus, as with many tools we will use in this book, the initial learning curve to do a simple task may seem a bit steep, but you will quickly reap the rewards by using this strong foundation to add new functionality and features quickly and concisely.

4.11 To Learn More

- The online documentation for Rails[19] gives details on the language, its classes, and the Rails framework.

- The Ruby Way (Fulton 2006) and The Rails 3 Way (Fernandez 2010) go into great depth on Ruby and Rails advanced features and wizardry.

- *Agile Web Development With Rails, 4th edition* Ruby et al. 2011 is co-authored by David Heinemeier Hansson, the creator of Rails, and is a tutorial-oriented introduction that combines Ruby and Rails, although its emphasis on testing and BDD is less than we would like. You can get it from major retailers or directly from the publisher[20], where you can get a discount for purchasing the print book and (multi-format) ebook together.

- PluralSight[21] publishes high-quality screencasts covering almost every tool and technique in the Rails ecosystem for a very reasonable price (in the authors' opinion). The five-part Introduction to Rails 3[22] screencast is a particularly good complement to the information in this chapter.

- Before writing new code for any functionality that isn't specific to your app, check `rubygems`[23] and `rubyforge`[24] (at least) to see if someone has created a gem that does most of what you need. As we saw in this chapter, using a gem is as easy as adding a line to your `Gemfile` and re-running `bundle install`.

O. Fernandez. *Rails 3 Way, The (2nd Edition) (Addison-Wesley Professional Ruby Series).* Addison-Wesley Professional, 2010. ISBN 0321601661.

H. Fulton. *The Ruby Way, Second Edition: Solutions and Techniques in Ruby Programming (2nd Edition).* Addison-Wesley Professional, 2006. ISBN 0672328844.

S. Ruby, D. Thomas, and D. H. Hansson. *Agile Web Development with Rails 3.2 (Pragmatic Programmers).* Pragmatic Bookshelf, 2011. ISBN 1934356549.

Notes

[1] `http://ruby-doc.org/core-1.9.3/Time.html`
[2] `http://ruby-doc.org/core-1.9.3/`
[3] `http://guides.rubyonrails.org/v3.2.19/routing.html`
[4] `http://www.sqlite.org/cli.html`
[5] `http://api.rubyonrails.org/v3.2.19/`
[6] `http://api.rubyonrails.org/v3.2.19/`
[7] `http://en.wikipedia.org/wiki/HTML_sanitization`
[8] `http://api.rubyonrails.org/v3.2.19/classes/ActionView/Helpers/UrlHelper.html#method-i-link_to`
[9] `http://ruby-doc.org/core-1.9.3/Time.html#method-i-strftime`
[10] `http://ruby-doc.org/core-1.9.3/Time.html#method-i-strftime`
[11] `http://catb.org/jargon/html/koans.html`
[12] `http://stackoverflow.com`
[13] `http://stackoverflow.com/questions/2945228/i-see-gem-in-gem-list-but-have-no-such-file-to-load`
[14] `http://api.rubyonrails.org/v3.2.19/classes/ActionView/Helpers/FormTagHelper.html`

[15]http://guides.rubyonrails.org/v3.2.19/security.html#mass-assignment
[16]http://homakov.blogspot.com/2012/03/how-to.html
[17]http://www.w3.org/Amaya
[18]http://api.rubyonrails.org/v3.2.19/classes/ActionController/MimeResponds.html#method-i-respond_to
[19]http://api.rubyonrails.org/v3.2.19/
[20]http://pragprog.com/book/rails32/agile-web-development-with-rails-3-2
[21]http://pluralsight.com/
[22]http://pluralsight.com/training/courses/TableOfContents/introduction-to-ruby-on-rails-3
[23]http://rubygems.org
[24]http://rubyforge.org

4.12   Suggested Projects

Unless otherwise indicated, these suggested projects are based on the `myrottenpotatoes` app you created in this chapter.

Project 4.1. *Add a default banner to the main application layout that will appear on every page of RottenPotatoes. It should display "RottenPotatoes" in large red letters, but no visual styling information should go into the template itself. (Hint: pick an element type that reflects the role of this banner, assign it a unique ID, and modify the CSS style file to style the element.) Make it so that clicking on the banner always takes you to RP homepage.*

Project 4.2. *Instead of redirecting to the Index action after a successful* **create***, redirect to the* **show** *action for the new movie that was just created. Hint: you can use the* **movie_path** *URI helper but you'll need to supply an argument identifying which movie. To obtain this argument, recall that* **Movie.create** *if successful returns the newly-created object in addition to creating it.*

Project 4.3. *Modify the listing of movies as follows. Each modification task will require making a change at a different layer of abstraction:*

1. *Modify the Index view to include a row number for each row in the movies table. HINT: look up the documentation of the* `each_with_index` *function used in line 11 of the view template.*

2. *Modify the Index view so that hovering a mouse over a row in the movies table causes the row to temporarily assume a yellow background. HINT: look up the* `hover` *pseudo-class supported by CSS.*

3. *Modify the Index controller action to return the movies ordered alphabetically by title, rather than by release date. HINT: Don't try to sort the result of the controller's call to the database. RDBMS's provide ways to specify the order in which a list of results is delivered, and because of Active Record's tight coupling to the underlying RDBMS, the Rails* `ActiveRecord` *library's* `find` *and* `all` *methods provide a way to ask the underlying RDBMS to do this.*

4. *Pretend you didn't have the tight coupling of Active Record, and so you could not assume the underlying storage system can return collection items in any particular order. Modify the Index controller action to return the movies ordered alphabetically by title. HINT: Look up the* `sort` *method in Ruby's* `Enumerable` *module.*

Project 4.4. *What if the user changes his mind before submitting a Create or Update form and decides not to proceed after all? Add a "Cancel" link to the form that just takes the user back to the list of movies.*

Project 4.5. *Modify the "Cancel" link so that if it's clicked as part of a Create flow, the user is taken back to the list of movies, but if clicked as part of an Update flow, the user is taken back to the Show template (view) for the movie he began to edit. Hint: the instance method* **ActiveRecord::Base#new_record?** *returns true if its receiver is a new model object, that is, one that has never been saved in the database. Such objects won't have ID's.*

Project 4.6. *The dropdown menus for Release Date don't allow adding movies released earlier than 2006. Modify it to allow movies as early as 1930. (Hint: check the documentation[1] for the* **date_select** *helper used in the form.)*

Project 4.7. *The* **description** *field of a movie was created as part of the initial migration, but cannot be edited. Make the necessary changes so that the description is visible and editable in the New and Edit views. Hint: you should only need to change two files.*

Project 4.8. *Our current controller methods aren't very robust: if the user manually enters a URI to Show a movie that doesn't exist (for example* /movies/99999*), she will see an ugly exception message. Modify the* **show** *method in the controller so that if the requested movie doesn't exist, the user is redirected to the Index view with a friendly message explaining that no movie with the given ID could be found. (Hint: use* **begin...rescue...end** *to rescue from* **ActiveRecord::RecordNotFound**.*)*

Project 4.9. *Putting it all together exercise: Write and deploy a Rails app that scrapes some information from a Web page using Nokogiri's XPath features, and turns it into an RSS feed using Builder. Verify that you can subscribe to the RSS feed in your browser or RSS news reader.*

5 SaaS Framework: Advanced Rails

Kristen Nygaard (left, 1926–2002) and Ole-Johan Dahl (right, 1931–2002) shared the 2001 Turing Award for inventing fundamental OO concepts including objects, classes, and inheritance, and demonstrating them in Simula, the ancestor of every OO language.

Programming is understanding.

—Kristen Nygaard

Concepts

This chapter covers advanced features of Rails that you can use to make your code more DRY and concise, including how to reuse entire external services such as Twitter to integrate with your apps.

- Rails mechanisms such as controller filters, model lifecycle hooks, and model validations provide a limited form of *aspect-oriented programming*, which allows code about crosscutting concerns to be centralized in a single place and automatically called when needed.

- ActiveRecord **associations** use metaprogramming and reflection to map relationships among resources in your app, such as "belongs to" or "has many", to queries that mirror those relationships in the app's database.

- ActiveRecord **scopes** are composable "filters" you can define on your model data, enabling DRY reuse of model logic.

http://pastebin.com/AY6TjGrp

```
 1  -# in _movie_form.html.haml (the partial)
 2
 3  = label :movie, :title, 'Title'
 4  = text_field :movie, 'title'
 5
 6  = label :movie, :rating, 'Rating'
 7  = select :movie, :rating, Movie.all_ratings
 8
 9  = label :movie, :release_date, 'Released On'
10  = date_select :movie, :release_date
```

http://pastebin.com/F0NzXDqP

```
1  -# new.html.haml using partial
2
3  %h2 Create New Movie
4
5  = form_tag '/movies', :method => :post do
6    = render :partial => 'movie_form'
7    = submit_tag 'Save Changes'
```

http://pastebin.com/J3dz3FjR

```
1  -# edit.html.haml using partial
2
3  %h2 Edit Existing Movie
4
5  = form_tag movie_path(@movie), :method => :put do
6    = render :partial => 'movie_form'
7    = submit_tag 'Update Movie Info'
```

Figure 5.1: A partial (top) that captures the form elements common to both the new and edit templates. The modified new and edit templates both use the partial (line 6 in both snippets), but line 5 is different between the two templates because new and edit submit to different actions. (Use the Pastebin service to copy-and-paste this code.)

5.1   DRYing Out MVC: Partials, Validations and Filters

As Section 6.6 explains, the partial is also the basic unit of view updating for JavaScript-enabled pages.

We'll focus our discussion of DRYness on the three elements of MVC, starting with Views.

A *partial* is Rails' name for a reusable chunk of a view. When similar content must appear in different views, putting that content in a partial and "including" it in the separate files helps DRY out repetition. For example, in Chapter 4, Figure 4.14 noted the similarities between the **new** and **edit** actions, both of whose views display the same form for entering movie information—not very DRY. Figure 5.1 captures this common view code in a partial and shows how to modify the existing new.html.haml and edit.html.haml to use it.

Partials rely heavily on convention over configuration. Their names must begin with an underscore (we used _movie_form.html.haml) which is *absent from* the code that references the partial. If a partial is not in the same directory as the view that uses it, **'layouts/footer'** would cause Rails to look for app/views/layouts/_footer.html.haml. A partial can access all the same instance variables as the view that includes it. A particularly nice use of a partial is to render a table or other collection in which all elements are the same, as Figure 5.2 demonstrates.

Partials are simple and straightforward, but the mechanisms provided by Rails for DRYing out models and controllers are more subtle and sophisticated. It's common in SaaS apps to want to enforce certain validity constraints on a given type of model object or constraints on when certain actions can be performed. For example, when a new movie is added to RottenPotatoes, we may want to check that the title isn't blank, that the release year is a valid

http://pastebin.com/tEALd9RT

```
1    -# A single row of the All Movies table
2    %tr
3      %td= movie.title
4      %td= movie.rating
5      %td= movie.release_date
6      %td= link_to "More about #{movie.title}", movie_path(movie)
```

Figure 5.2: If this partial is saved as `views/movies/_movie.html.haml`**, lines 12–17 of our original** `index.html.haml`
view (Figure 4.6) can be replaced with the single line = render :partial=>'movie', :collection=>@movies. **By**
convention over configuration, the name of the partial without the leading underscore (in this case, movie) **is available as a**
local variable in the partial that is set to each element of @movies **in turn.**

date, and that the rating is one of the allowed ratings. As another example, perhaps we want to allow any user to add new movies, but only allow special "admin" users to delete movies. Both examples involve specifying constraints on entities or actions, and although there might be many places in an app where such constraints should be considered, the DRY philosophy urges us to centralize them in *one* place. Rails provides two analogous facilities for doing this: validations for models and filters for controllers.

Model validations, like migrations, are expressed in a mini-DSL embedded in Ruby, as Figure 5.3 shows. Validation checks are triggered when you call the instance method **valid?** or when you try to save the model to the database (which calls **valid?** before doing so).

Any validation errors are recorded in the **ActiveModel::Errors**[4] object associated with each model; this object is returned by the instance method **errors**. As Figure 5.3 shows, you can inquire about errors on individual attributes (lines 18–20) or use **full_messages** to get all the errors as an array of strings. When writing your own custom validations, as in lines 7–10, you can use **errors.add** to add an error message associated with either a specific invalid attribute of the object or the object in general (by passing **:base** rather than an attribute name).

The example also demonstrates that validations can be conditional. For example, line 6 in Figure 5.3 ensures that the movie's rating is a valid one, *unless* the movie was released before the ratings system went into effect (in the USA, 1 November 1968), in which case we don't need to validate the rating.

We can make use of validation to replace the dangerous **save!** and **update_attributes!** in our controller actions with their safer versions, **save** and **update_attributes**, which fail if validation fails. Figure 5.4 shows how to modify our controller methods to be more idiomatic by taking advantage of this. Modify your **create** and **update** controller actions to match the figure, modify `app/models/movie.rb` to include the validations in Figure 5.3, and then try adding a movie that violates one or more of the validations.

Of course, it would be nice to provide the user an informative message specifying what went wrong and what she should do. This is easy: within a view we *can* get the name of the controller action that called for the view to be rendered, so we can include it in the error message, as line 5 of the following code shows.

Didn't the user choose the rating from a menu? Yes, but the request might be constructed by a malicious user or a *bot*. With SaaS, you can't trust anyone: the server must *always* check its inputs rather than trust them, or risk attack by methods we'll see in Chapter 12.

http://pastebin.com/fNRS4LB6

```
1    -# insert at top of _movie_form.html.haml
2
3    - unless @movie.errors.empty?
4      #warning
5        Errors prevented this movie from being #{controller.action_name}d:
6        %ul
7          - @movie.errors.full_messages.each do |error|
8            %li= error
```

http://pastebin.com/yctJ0riC

```
 1 | class Movie < ActiveRecord::Base
 2 |   def self.all_ratings ; %w[G PG PG-13 R NC-17] ; end #  shortcut: array of
   |       strings
 3 |   validates :title, :presence => true
 4 |   validates :release_date, :presence => true
 5 |   validate :released_1930_or_later # uses custom validator below
 6 |   validates :rating, :inclusion => {:in => Movie.all_ratings},
 7 |     :unless => :grandfathered?
 8 |   def released_1930_or_later
 9 |     errors.add(:release_date, 'must be 1930 or later') if
10 |       release_date && release_date < Date.parse('1 Jan 1930')
11 |   end
12 |   @@grandfathered_date = Date.parse('1 Nov 1968')
13 |   def grandfathered?
14 |     release_date && release_date < @@grandfathered_date
15 |   end
16 | end
17 | # try in console:
18 | m = Movie.new(:title => '', :rating => 'RG', :release_date => '1929-01-01')
19 | # force validation checks to be performed:
20 | m.valid?  # => false
21 | m.errors[:title] # => ["can't be blank"]
22 | m.errors[:rating] # => ["is not included in the list"]
23 | m.errors[:release_date] # => ["must be 1930 or later"]
24 | m.errors.full_messages # => ["Title can't be blank", "Rating is not
25 |   included in the list", "Release date must be 1930 or later"]
```

Figure 5.3: Lines 3–5 use predefined validation behaviors in ActiveModel::Validations::ClassMethods[3]. Lines 6–15 show how you can create your own validation methods, which receive the object to be validated as an argument and add error messages describing any problems. Note that we first validate the presence of release_date, otherwise the comparisons in lines 10 and 14 could fail if release_date is nil.

http://pastebin.com/fauUp1Xn

```
 1 | # replaces the 'create' method in controller:
 2 | def create
 3 |   @movie = Movie.new(params[:movie])
 4 |   if @movie.save
 5 |     flash[:notice] = "#{@movie.title} was successfully created."
 6 |     redirect_to movies_path
 7 |   else
 8 |     render 'new' # note, 'new' template can access @movie's field values!
 9 |   end
10 | end
11 | # replaces the 'update' method in controller:
12 | def update
13 |   @movie = Movie.find params[:id]
14 |   if @movie.update_attributes(params[:movie])
15 |     flash[:notice] = "#{@movie.title} was successfully updated."
16 |     redirect_to movie_path(@movie)
17 |   else
18 |     render 'edit' # note, 'edit' template can access @movie's field values!
19 |   end
20 | end
21 | # note, you will also have to update the 'new' method:
22 | def new
23 |   @movie = Movie.new
24 | end
```

Figure 5.4: If create or update fails, we use an explicit render to re-render the form so the user can fill it in again. Conveniently, @movie will be made available to the view and will hold the values the user entered the first time, so the form will be prepopulated with those values, since (by convention over configuration) the form tag helpers used in _movie_form.html.haml will use @movie to populate the form fields as long as it's a valid Movie object.

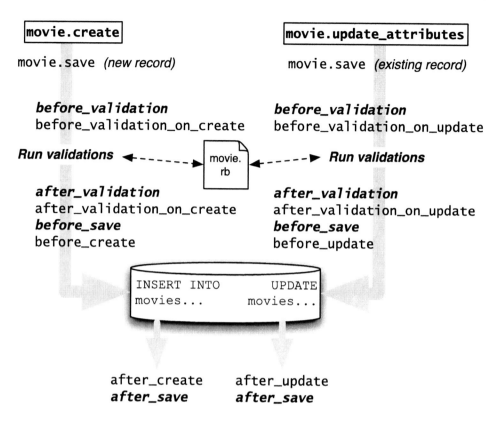

Figure 5.5: The various points at which you can "hook into" the lifecycle of an ActiveRecord model object. All ActiveRecord operations that modify the database (update, create, and so on) all eventually call save, so a before_save callback can intercept every change to the database. See this Rails Guide[6] for additional details and examples.

Screencast 5.1.1 digs deeper and explains how Rails views take advantage of being able to query each model attribute about its validity separately, to give the user better visual feedback about which specific fields caused the problem.

Screencast 5.1.1: How model validations interact with controllers and views.
http://vimeo.com/34754932
The form helpers in our views use the **errors** object to discover which fields caused validation errors and apply the special CSS class field-with-errors to any such fields. By including selectors for that class in app/assets/stylesheets/application.css, we can visually highlight the affected fields for the user's benefit.

In fact, validations are just a special case of a more general mechanism, Active Record lifecycle callbacks[7], which allow you to provide methods that "intercept" a model object at various relevant points in its lifecycle. Figure 5.5 shows what callbacks are available; Figure 5.6 illustrates how to use this mechanism to "canonicalize" (standardize the format of) certain model fields before the model is saved. We will see another use of lifecycle callbacks when we discuss the Observer design pattern in Chapter 11 and caching in Chapter 12.

Analogous to a validation is a controller filter—a method that checks whether certain conditions are true before an action is run, or sets up common conditions that many actions

http://pastebin.com/2zQPLxAZ

```
1   class Movie < ActiveRecord::Base
2     before_save :capitalize_title
3     def capitalize_title
4       self.title = self.title.split(/\s+/).map(&:downcase).
5         map(&:capitalize).join(' ')
6     end
7   end
8   # now try in console:
9   m = Movie.create!(:title => 'STAR  wars', :release_date => '27-5-1977', :
      rating => 'PG')
10  m.title  # => "Star Wars"
```

Figure 5.6: This before_save hook capitalizes each word of a movie title, downcases the rest of the word, and compresses multiple spaces between words to a single space, turning STAR   wars into Star Wars (not necessarily the right behavior for movie titles, but useful for illustration).

http://pastebin.com/3fzBknNQ

```
1   class ApplicationController < ActionController::Base
2     before_filter :set_current_user
3     protected # prevents method from being invoked by a route
4     def set_current_user
5       # we exploit the fact that find_by_id(nil) returns nil
6       @current_user ||= Moviegoer.find_by_id(session[:user_id])
7       redirect_to login_path and return unless @current_user
8     end
9   end
```

Figure 5.7: If there is a logged-in user, the redirect will *not* occur, and the controller instance variable @current_user will be available to the action and views. Otherwise, a redirect will occur to login_path, which is assumed to correspond to a route that takes the user to a login page, about which more in Section 5.2. (and is just like && but has lower precedence, thus ((redirect_to login_path) and (return)) unless...)

rely on. If the conditions are not fulfilled, the filter can choose to "stop the show" by rendering a view template or redirecting to another action. If the filter allows the action to proceed, it will be the action's responsibility to provide a response, as usual.

As an example, an extremely common use of filters is to enforce the requirement that a user be logged in before certain actions can be performed. Assume for the moment that we have verified the identity of some user and stored her primary key (ID) in **session[:user_id]** to remember the fact that she has logged in. Figure 5.7 shows a filter that enforces that a valid user is logged in. In Section 5.2 we will show how to combine the before-filter with the other "moving parts" involved in dealing with logged-in users.

Filters normally apply to all actions in the controller, but **:only** can be used to specify that the filter only guards certain actions, while **:except** can be used to specify that some actions are exempt. Each takes an array of action names. You can define multiple filters: they are run in the order in which they are declared. You can also define after-filters, which run after certain actions are completed, and around-filters, which specify actions to run before and after, as you might do for auditing or timing. Around-filters use **yield** to actually do the controller action:

```
1  # somewhat contrived example of an around-filter
2  around_filter :only => ['withdraw_money', 'transfer_money'] do
3    # log who is trying to move money around
4    start = Time.now
5    yield   # do the action
6    # note how long it took
7    logger.info params
8    logger.info (Time.now - start)
9  end
```

Summary of DRYing out MVC in Rails:

- Partials allow you to reuse chunks of views across different templates, collecting common view elements in a single place.

- Validations let you collect constraints on a model in a single place. Validations are checked anytime the database is about to be modified; failing validation is one of the ways that non-dangerous **save** and **update_attributes** can fail.

- The **errors** field of a model, an **ActiveRecord::Errors** object, records errors that occurred during validation. View form helpers can use this information to apply special CSS styles to fields whose values failed validation, cleanly separating the responsibility for detecting an error from the responsibility for displaying that error to the user.

- Controller filters let you collect conditions affecting many controller actions in a single place by defining a method that always runs before those actions. A filter declared in a controller affects all actions in that controller, and a filter declared in **ApplicationController** affects all actions in all controllers, unless **:only** or **:except** are specified.

■ *Elaboration: Aspect-oriented programming*

Aspect-oriented programming (AOP) is a programming methodology for DRYing out code by separating *crosscutting concerns* such as model validations and controller filters from the main code of the actions to which the concerns apply. In our case, we specify model validations declaratively in one place, rather than invoking them explicitly at each *join point* in the code where we'd want to perform a validity check. A set of join points is collectively called a *pointcut*, and the code to be inserted at each join point (such as a validation in our example) is called *advice*.

Ruby doesn't support full AOP, which would allow you to specify arbitrary pointcuts along with what advice applies to each. But Rails uses Ruby's dynamic language features to define convenient pointcuts such as the AR model lifecycle, which supports validations and other lifecycle callbacks, and join points around controller actions, which support the use of before- and after-filters.

A critique of AOP is that the source code can no longer be read in linear order. For example, when a before-filter prevents a controller action from proceeding, the problem can be hard to track down, especially for someone unfamiliar with Rails who doesn't realize the filter method isn't even being called explicitly but is an advice method triggered by a particular join point. A response to the critique is that if AOP is applied sparingly and tastefully, and all developers understand and agree on the pointcuts, it can improve DRYness and modularity. Validations and filters are the Rails designers' attempt to identify this beneficial middle ground.

Self-Check 5.1.1. *Why didn't the Rails designers choose to trigger validation when you first instantiate one using* **Movie#new**, *rather than waiting until you try to persist the object?*

◇ As you're filling in the attributes of the new object, it might be in a temporarily invalid state, so triggering validation at that time might make it difficult to manipulate the object. Persisting the object tells Rails "I believe this object is ready to be saved." ■

Self-Check 5.1.2. *Why can't we write* **validate released_1930_or_later**, *that is, why must the argument to* **validate** *be either a symbol or a string?*

◇ If the argument is just the "bare" name of the method, Ruby will try to evaluate it at the moment it executes **validate**, which isn't what we want—we want **released_1930_or_later** to be called at the time any validation is to occur. ■

5.2 Single Sign-On and Third-Party Authentication

Authorization refers to whether a principal is allowed to do something. Although separate from authentication, the two are often conflated because many standards handle both.

One way to be more DRY and productive is to avoid implementing functionality that you can instead reuse from other services. One example of this today is *authentication*—the process by which an entity or *principal* proves that it is who it claims to be. In SaaS, end users and servers are two common types of principals that may need to authenticate themselves. Typically, a user proves her identity by supplying a username and password that (presumably) nobody else knows, and a server proves its identity with a *server certificate* (discussed in Chapter 12) whose *provenance* can be verified using cryptography.

In the early days of SaaS, users had to establish separate usernames and passwords for each site. Today, an increasingly common scenario is *single sign-on* (SSO), in which the credentials established for one site (the *provider*) can be used to sign in to other sites that are administratively unrelated to it. Clearly, SSO is central to the usefulness of service-oriented architecture: It would be difficult for services to work together on your behalf if each had its

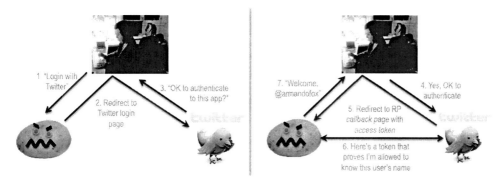

Figure 5.8: Third-party authentication enables SSO by allowing a SaaS app to request that the user authenticate himself via a third-party provider. Once he has done so, the provider sends a token to the requesting app proving that the user authenticated himself correctly and possibly encoding additional privileges the user grants to the requesting app. The flow shown is a simplified version of *OAuth*, an evolving (and mildly controversial) open standard for authentication and authorization used by Twitter, Facebook, Microsoft, Google, Netflix, and many others. Twitter logo and image copyright 2012 Twitter Inc., used for instructional purposes only.

Facebook was an early example of SSO.

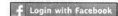

own separate authentication scheme. Given the prevalence and increasing importance of SSO, our view is that new SaaS apps should use it rather than "rolling their own" authentication.

However, SSO presents the dilemma that while you may be happy to use your credentials on site A to login to site B, you usually don't want to reveal those credentials to site B. (Imagine that site A is your financial institution and site B is a foreign company from whom you want to buy something.) Figure 5.8 shows how ***third-party authentication*** solves this problem using RottenPotatoes and Twitter as an example. First, the app requesting authentication (RottenPotatoes) creates a request to an authentication provider on which the user already has an account, in this case Twitter. The request often includes information about what privileges the app wants on the provider, for example, to be able to tweet as this user or learn who the user's followers are.

The SSO process usually begins with a link or button the user must click. That link takes the user to a login page served securely *by the provider*; depending on implementation, the login page may be a popup, an HTML frame or iframe element[8], or a regular page served by the provider's site. The user is then given the chance to login to the provider and decide whether to grant the app the requested privileges. Critically, this interaction takes place entirely between the user and the provider: the requesting app has no access to any part of this interaction. Once authentication succeeds, the provider generates a ***callback*** to the requesting app to give it an ***access token***—a string created using cryptographic techniques that can be passed back to the provider later, allowing the provider to verify that the token could only have been created as the result of a successful login process. At this point, the requesting app is able to do two things:

1. It can believe that the user has proven her identity to the provider, and optionally record the provider's persistent and globally-unique ID or ***guid*** (pronounced GOO-id) for that user, usually provided as part of the access token. For example, Armando Fox's guid on Twitter happens to be 318094297, though this information isn't useful unless accompanied by an access token granting the right to obtain information about that guid.

2. It can use the token to request further information about the user from the provider, de-

http://pastebin.com/V4tw3Ld9

```
1 | rails generate model Moviegoer name:string provider:string uid:string
```

http://pastebin.com/1JaAMKKD

```
 1 | # Edit app/models/moviegoer.rb to look like this:
 2 | class Moviegoer < ActiveRecord::Base
 3 |   attr_accessible :uid, :provider, :name # see text for explanation
 4 |   def self.create_with_omniauth(auth)
 5 |     Moviegoer.create!(
 6 |       :provider => auth["provider"],
 7 |       :uid => auth["uid"],
 8 |       :name => auth["info"]["name"])
 9 |   end
10 | end
```

Figure 5.9: Top (a): **Type this command in a terminal to create a** `moviegoers` **model and migration, and run** `rake` `db:migrate` **to apply the migration. Bottom (b): Then edit the generated** app/models/moviegoer.rb **file to match this code, which the text explains.**

pending on what specific privileges were granted along with successful authentication. For example, a token from Facebook might indicate that the user gave permission for the app to learn who his friends are, but denied permission for the app to post on his Facebook wall.

Happily, adding third-party authentication to Rails apps is straightforward. Of course, before we can enable a user to log in, we need to be able to represent users! So before continuing, create a basic model and migration following the instructions in Figure 5.9.

There are three aspects to managing third-party authentication in Rails. The first is how to actually authenticate the user via a third party. We will use the excellent OmniAuth[9] gem, which abstracts away the entire process in Figure 5.8 by allowing developers to create a *strategy* for each third-party auth provider. A strategy handles all the interactions with the authentication provider (steps 2–4 in Figure 5.8) and ultimately performs an HTTP POST to the URI /auth/*provider*/callback in your app. The data included with the POST indicate the success or failure of the authentication process, and if successful, the access token(s) that your app can use to get additional information about the logged-in user. As of this writing, strategies are available for Facebook, Twitter, Google Apps, and many others, each available as a gem named omniauth-*provider*. We will use Twitter as an example, so add both gem 'omniauth' and gem 'omniauth-twitter' to your Gemfile and run bundle install --without production as usual. You will then need to create a twitter development application and configure the omniauth gem with a twitter provider in **config/initializers/omniauth.rb**. Details in the omniauth-twitter set up instructions[10] on GitHub. Once completed add the code from Figure 5.10(a) to your **config/routes.rb** file, which specify some routes that the OmniAuth strategy will use when it completes the authentication with Twitter.

The second aspect of handling authentication is keeping track of whether the current user has been authenticated. You may have already guessed that this information can be stored in the **session[]**. However, we should keep session management separate from the other concerns of the app, since the session may not be relevant if our app is used in a service-oriented architecture setting. To that end, Figure 5.10(b) shows how we can "create" a session when a user successfully authenticates herself (lines 3–9) and "destroy" it when she logs out (lines 11–15). The "scare quotes" are there because the only thing actually being created or destroyed is the value of **session[:user_id]**, which is set to the primary key of

http://pastebin.com/GUz4rscD

```
1  get    'auth/:provider/callback' => 'sessions#create'
2  post  'logout' => 'sessions#destroy'
3  get    'auth/failure' => 'sessions#failure'
```

http://pastebin.com/eb50EvUx

```
1   class SessionsController < ApplicationController
2     # user shouldn't have to be logged in before logging in!
3     skip_before_filter :set_current_user
4     def create
5       auth=request.env["omniauth.auth"]
6       user=Moviegoer.find_by_provider_and_uid(auth["provider"],auth["uid"]) ||
7         Moviegoer.create_with_omniauth(auth)
8       session[:user_id] = user.id
9       redirect_to movies_path
10    end
11    def destroy
12      session.delete(:user_id)
13      flash[:notice] = 'Logged out successfully.'
14      redirect_to movies_path
15    end
16  end
```

http://pastebin.com/xbMdTJYJ

```
1  #login
2    - if @current_user
3      %p.welcome  Welcome, #{@current_user.name}!
4      = link_to 'Log Out', logout_path
5    - else
6      %p.login= link_to 'Log in with your Twitter account', '/auth/twitter'
```

Figure 5.10: The moving parts in a typical Rails app authentication flow. Top (a): Three routes that follow the OmniAuth gem's convention for mapping the create and destroy actions in a separate **SessionsController**, plus a route that in the future can be used to handle authentication failures (for example, user types wrong Twitter password or denies access to our app). Middle (b): Line 3 skips the before_filter that we added to **ApplicationController** in Figure 5.7. Note that we must delete line 7 in Figure 5.7 since we don't have a login path to redirect to in this example. Upon successful login of a given user, the create action remembers that user's primary key (ID) in the session until the destroy action is called to forget it. Bottom (c): The **@current_user** variable (set in line 6 of **ApplicationController**, Figure 5.7) can be used by a login partial to display an appropriate message. The partial could be included from `application.html.haml` with render :partial=>'sessions/login'.

the logged-in user during the session and **nil** at other times. Figure 5.10(c) shows how this check is abstracted by a **before_filter** in **ApplicationController** (which will be inherited by all controllers) that sets **@current_user** accordingly, so that controller methods or views can just look at **@current_user** without being coupled to the details of how the user was authenticated.

The third aspect is linking our own representation of a user's identity—that is, her primary key in the moviegoers table—with the auth provider's representation, such as the uid in the case of Twitter. Since we may want to expand which auth providers our customers can use in the future, the migration in Figure 5.9(a) that creates the **Moviegoer** model specifies both a uid field and a provider field. What happens the very first time Alice logs into RottenPotatoes with her Twitter ID? The find_by_provider_and_uid query in line 6 of the sessions controller (Figure 5.10(b)) will return **nil**, so **Moviegoer.create_with_omniauth** (Figure 5.9(b), lines 5–10) will be called to create a new record for this user. Note that "Alice as authenticated by Twitter" would therefore be a different user from our point of view than "Alice as authenticated by Facebook," because we have no way of knowing that those represent the same person. That's why some sites that support multiple third-party auth providers give users a way to "link" two accounts to indicate that they identify the same person.

This may seem like a lot of moving parts, but compared to accomplishing the same task without an abstraction such as OmniAuth, this is very clean code: we added fewer than two dozen lines, and by incorporating more OmniAuth strategies, we could support additional third-party auth providers with essentially no new work. Screencast 5.2.1 shows the user experience associated with this code.

Screencast 5.2.1: Logging into RottenPotatoes with Twitter.
http://vimeo.com/41300070
This version of RottenPotatoes, modified to use the OmniAuth gem as described in the text, allows moviegoers to login using their existing Twitter IDs.

However, we have just created a security vulnerability. So far we've exploited the convenience of "mass assignment" from the **params[]** hash to an ActiveRecord object, as when we write **@movie.update_attributes(params[:movie])** in **MoviesController#update**. But what if a malicious attacker crafts a form submission that tries to modify **params[:moviegoer][:uid]** or **params[:moviegoer][:provider]**—fields that should only be modified by the authentication logic—by posting *hidden form fields* named params[moviegoer][uid] and so on? The **attr_accessible** command in line 3 of Figure 5.9(b) is what allows us to mass-assign specific attributes. If we wanted to "protect" sensitive attributes from being mass-assigned from **params** we could use **attr_protected**[11]. The more restrictive **attr_accessible**[12] arranges for *only* the named attributes to be modifiable through mass assignment from **params[]** (or for that matter from any hash). This more restrictive mechanism is recommended because it follows the *principle of least privilege* in computer security, a topic to which we return in Section 12.9 when discussing how to defend customer data.

Summary

- Single sign-on refers to an end-user experience in which a single set of credentials (such as their Google or Facebook username and password) will sign them in to a variety of different services.

- Third-party authentication using standards such as *OAuth* is one way to achieve single-sign on: the requesting app can verify the identity of user via an authentication provider, without the user revealing her credentials to the requesting app.

- The cleanest way to factor out authentication in Rails apps is to abstract the concept of a session. When a user successfully authenticates (perhaps using a framework such as OmniAuth[13]), a session is created by storing the authenticated user's id (primary key) in the **session[]**. When she signs out, the session is destroyed by deleting that information from the **session[]**.

- Use **attr_protected** and **attr_accessible** to identify model attributes that are "sensitive" and should be excluded from mass assignment via a hash, such as user ID information used for session management or authentication.

■*Elaboration: SSO side effects*

In some cases, using SSO enables other features as well; for example, Facebook Connect enables sites to take advantage of Facebook's social network, so that (for example) Bob can see which New York Times articles his friends have been reading once he authenticates himself to the New York Times using Facebook. While these appealing features further strengthen the case for using SSO rather than "rolling your own" authentication, they are separate from the basic concept of SSO, on which this discussion focuses.

Self-Check 5.2.1. *Briefly describe how RottenPotatoes could let you log in with your Twitter ID without you having to reveal your Twitter password to RottenPotatoes.*

◇ RottenPotatoes redirects you to a page hosted by Twitter where you log in as usual. The redirect includes a URL to which Twitter posts back a message confirming that you've authenticated yourself and specifying what actions RottenPotatoes may take on your behalf as a Twitter user. ■

Self-Check 5.2.2. *True or false: If you log in to RottenPotatoes using your Twitter ID, RottenPotatoes becomes capable of tweeting using your Twitter ID.*

◇ False: authentication is separate from permissions. Most third-party authentication providers, including Twitter, allow the requesting app to ask for permission to do specific things, and leave it up to the user to decide whether to allow it. ■

5.3 Associations and Foreign Keys

An *association* is a logical relationship between two types of entities in a software architecture. For example, we might add **Review** and **Moviegoer** classes to RottenPotatoes to allow individual users to write reviews of their favorite movies; we could do this by establishing a one-to-many association from reviews to movies (each review is about exactly one movie)

Figure 5.11: Each end of an association is labeled with its *cardinality*, or the number of entities participating in that "side" of the association, with an asterisk meaning "zero or more". In the figure, each Review belongs to a single Moviegoer and a single Movie, and a Review without a Moviegoer or without a Movie is not allowed. (A cardinality notation of "0..1" rather than "1" would allow "orphaned" reviews.)

id	title	rating
13	Inception	PG-13
41	Star Wars	PG
43	It's Complicated	R

id	movie_id	moviegoer_id	potatoes
21	41	1	5
22	13	2	3
23	13	1	4

id	username
1	alice
2	bob
3	carol

Figure 5.12: In this figure, Alice has given 5 potatoes to Star Wars and 4 potatoes to Inception, Bob has given 3 potatoes to Inception, Carol hasn't provided any reviews, and no one has reviewed It's Complicated. For brevity and clarity, the other fields of the `movies` and `reviews` tables are not shown.

and from reviews to moviegoers (each review is authored by exactly one moviegoer). Figure 5.11 shows these associations using one type of **Unified Modeling Language (UML)** diagram. We will see more examples of UML in Chapter 11.

In Rails parlance, Figure 5.11 shows that:

- A Moviegoer has many Reviews

- A Movie has many Reviews

- A Review belongs to one Moviegoer and to one Movie

In Rails, the "permanent home" for our model objects is the database, so we need a way to represent associations for objects stored there. Fortunately, associations are so common that relational databases provide a special mechanism to support them: **foreign keys**. A foreign key is a column in one table whose job is to reference the primary key of another table to establish an association between the objects represented by those tables. Recall that by default, Rails migrations create tables whose primary key column is called id. Figure 5.12 shows a Moviegoers table to keep track of different users and a Reviews table with foreign key columns `moviegoer_id` and `movie_id`, allowing each review to refer to the primary keys (ids) of the user who authored it and the movie it's about.

For example, to find all reviews for *Star Wars*, we would first form the **Cartesian product** of all the rows of the `movies` and `reviews` tables by concatenating each row of the `movies` table with each possible row of the `reviews` table. This would give us a new table with 9 rows (since there are 3 movies and 3 reviews) and 7 columns (3 from the `movies` table and 4 from the `reviews` table). From this large table, we then select only those rows for which the id from the `movies` table equals the `movie_id` from the `reviews` table, that is, only those movie-review pairs in which the review is about that movie. Finally, we select only those rows for which the movie id (and therefore the review's `movie_id`) are equal to 41, the primary key ID for *Star Wars*. This simple example (called a **join** in relational database parlance) illustrates how complex relationships can be represented and manipulated

http://pastebin.com/W0xJTuc4

```
 1 | # it would be nice if we could do this:
 2 | inception = Movie.find_by_title('Inception')
 3 | alice,bob = Moviegoer.find(alice_id, bob_id)
 4 | # alice likes Inception, bob hates it
 5 | alice_review = Review.new(:potatoes => 5)
 6 | bob_review   = Review.new(:potatoes => 2)
 7 | # a movie has many reviews:
 8 | inception.reviews = [alice_review, bob_review]
 9 | inception.save!
10 | # a moviegoer has many reviews:
11 | alice.reviews << alice_review
12 | bob.reviews << bob_review
13 | # can we find out who wrote each review?
14 | inception.reviews.map { |r| r.moviegoer.name } # => ['alice','bob']
```

Figure 5.13: A straightforward implementation of associations would allow us to refer directly to associated objects, even
though they're stored in different database tables.

using a small set of operations (relational algebra) on a collection of tables with uniform data
layout. In SQL, the Structured Query Language used by substantially all relational databases,
the query would look something like this:

http://pastebin.com/qCTqmark

```
1 | SELECT reviews.*
2 |   FROM movies JOIN reviews ON movies.id=reviews.movie_id
3 |   WHERE movies.id = 41;
```

If we weren't working with a database, though, we'd probably come up with a design
in which each object of a class has "direct references" to its associated objects, rather than
constructing the query plan above. A Moviegoer object would maintain an array of references
to Reviews authored by that moviegoer; a Review object would maintain a reference to the
Moviegoer who wrote it; and so on. Such a design would allow us to write code that looks
like Figure 5.13.

Rails' **ActiveRecord::Associations**[14] module supports exactly this design, as we'll
learn by doing. Apply the code changes in Figure 5.14 as directed in the caption, and you
should then be able to start `rails console` and successfully execute the examples in Figure 5.13.

How does this work? Since everything in Ruby is a method call, we know that Line 8
in Figure 5.13 is really a call to the instance method **reviews=** on a **Movie** object. This
instance method remembers its assigned value (an array of Alice's and Bob's reviews) in
memory. Recall, though, that since a Review is on the "belongs to" side of the association
(Review belongs to a Movie), to associate a review with a movie we must set the `movie_id`
field for that review. *We don't actually have to modify the movies table.* So in this simple
example, **inception.save!** isn't actually updating the movie record for *Inception* at all: it's
setting the `movie_id` field of both Alice's and Bob's reviews to "link" them to *Inception*.
Of course, if we had actually modified any of *Inception*'s attributes, **inception.save!** would
try to persist them; but because **save!** is transactional—that is, it's all-or-nothing—if the
save! fails then *every* aspect of it fails, so neither the changes to *Inception* nor its associated
Reviews would be saved.

Figure 5.15 lists some of the most useful methods added to a **movie** object by virtue of
declaring that it **has_many** reviews. Of particular interest is that since **has_many** implies a
collection of the owned object (Reviews), the **reviews** method quacks like a collection. That
is, you can use all the collection idioms of Figure 3.7 on it—iterate over its elements with

http://pastebin.com/5bwBMzzM

```
1  # Run 'rails generate migration create_reviews' and then
2  #   edit db/migrate/*_create_reviews.rb to look like this:
3  class CreateReviews < ActiveRecord::Migration
4    def up
5      create_table 'reviews' do |t|
6        t.integer    'potatoes'
7        t.text       'comments'
8        t.references 'moviegoer'
9        t.references 'movie'
10     end
11   end
12   def down ; drop_table 'reviews' ; end
13 end
```

http://pastebin.com/0qJQgUwi

```
1  class Review < ActiveRecord::Base
2    belongs_to :movie
3    belongs_to :moviegoer
4    attr_protected :moviegoer_id # see text
5  end
```

http://pastebin.com/NG88vs0V

```
1  # place a copy of the following line anywhere inside the Movie class
2  #  AND inside the Moviegoer class (idiomatically, it should go right
3  #  after 'class Movie' or 'class Moviegoer'):
4    has_many :reviews
```

Figure 5.14: Top (a): Create and apply this migration to create the Reviews table. The new model's foreign keys are related to the existing movies and moviegoers tables by convention over configuration. Middle (b): Put this new Review model in app/models/review.rb. Bottom (c): Make this one-line change to each of the existing files movie.rb and moviegoer.rb.

m.reviews	returns an Enumerable of all owned reviews
m.reviews=[r1,r2]	Replaces the set of owned reviews with the set **r1,r2**, adding or deleting as appropriate, by setting the movie_id field of each of **r1** and **r2** to **m.id** (**m**'s primary key) in the database immediately.
m.reviews<<r1	Adds **r1** to the set of **m**'s reviews by setting **r1**'s movie_id field to **m.id**. The change is written to the database immediately (you don't need to do a separate **save**).
r = m.reviews.build(:potatoes=>5)	Makes **r** a new, *unsaved* **Review** object whose movie_id is preset to indicate that it belongs to **m**. Arguments are the same as for **Review.new**.
r = m.reviews.create(:potatoes=>5)	Like **build** but saves the object immediately (analogous to the difference between **new** and **save**).
Note: if the parent object **m** has never been saved, that is, **m.new_record?** is true, then the child objects aren't saved until the parent is saved.	
m = r.movie	Returns the **Movie** instance associated with this review
r.movie = m	Sets **m** as the movie associated with review **r**

Figure 5.15: A subset of the association methods created by movie has_many :reviews and review belongs_to :movie, assuming m is an existing Movie object and r1,r2 are Review objects. Consult the ActiveRecord::Associations documentation[16] for a full list. Method names of association methods follow convention over configuration based on the name of the associated model.

each, use functional idioms like **sort**, **search** and **map**, and so on, as in lines 8, 11 and 14 of Figure 5.13.

What about the **belongs_to** method calls in `review.rb`? As you might guess, **belongs_to :movie** gives **Review** objects a **movie** instance method that looks up and returns the movie to which this review belongs. Since a review belongs to at most one movie, the method name is singular rather than plural, and returns a single object rather than an enumerable.

> **has_one** is a close relative of **has_many** that singularizes the association method name and operates on a single owned object rather than a collection.

Summary:

- Associations are one-to-one, one-to-many, or many-to-many relationships among application entities.

- Relational databases (RDBMSs) use foreign keys to represent these relationships.

- ActiveRecord's Associations module uses Ruby metaprogramming to create new methods to "traverse" associations by constructing the appropriate database queries. You must still add the necessary foreign key fields yourself with a migration.

■ *Elaboration: Associations in ActiveRecord vs. Data Mapper*

The concept of associations is architectural; the use of foreign keys to represent them is an implementation choice, and the Active Record architectural pattern, which Rails' ActiveRecord library implements, can bridge the two by providing methods for automatic traversal when a relational database is used. But foreign-key-based associations can become so complex that the overhead of managing them limits the scalability of relational databases, which are already the first bottleneck in the 3-tier architecture of Figure 2.7. One way to avoid this pitfall is to use the Data Mapper architectural pattern (see Figure 5.16), in which a Mapper class defines how each model and its associations are represented in the storage system and provides its own code to traverse them. Since DataMapper doesn't rely on foreign key support in the underlying storage system, it can use so-called "NoSQL" storage systems, such as Cassandra[17], MongoDB[18], and CouchDB[19], which omit all but the simplest foreign key support in order to achieve superior horizontal scalability far beyond most RDBMSs. Indeed, you can deploy Ruby-based SaaS apps on Google AppEngine[20] if they use a Google-provided DataMapper library rather than ActiveRecord.

Self-Check 5.3.1. *In Figure 5.14(a), why did we add foreign keys (**references**) only to the* `reviews` *table and not to the* `moviegoers` *or* `movies` *tables?*

◇ Since we need to associate many reviews with a single movie or moviegoer, the foreign keys must be part of the model on the "owned" side of the association, in this case Reviews. ■

Self-Check 5.3.2. *In Figure 5.15, are the association accessors and setters (such as* **m.reviews** *and* **r.movie**) *instance methods or class methods?*

◇ Instance methods, since a collection of reviews is associated with a particular movie, not with movies in general. ■

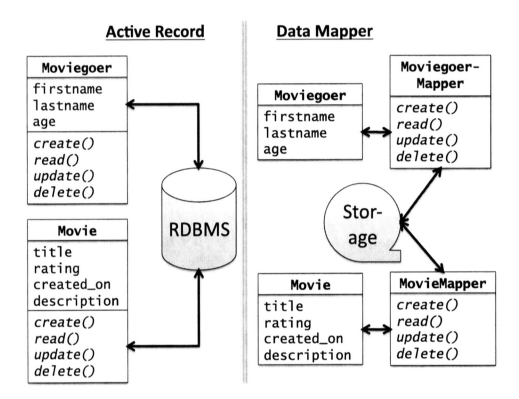

Figure 5.16: In the Active Record design pattern (left), used by Rails, the model object itself knows how it's stored in the persistence tier, and how its relationship to other types of models is represented there. In the Data Mapper pattern (right), used by Google AppEngine, PHP and Sinatra, a separate class isolates model objects from the underlying storage layer. Each approach has pros and cons. This *class diagram* is one form of Unified Modeling Language (UML) diagram, which we'll learn more about in Chapter 11.

http://pastebin.com/3UMDrq1N

```
 1 | # in moviegoer.rb:
 2 | class Moviegoer
 3 |   has_many :reviews
 4 |   has_many :movies, :through => :reviews
 5 |   # ...other moviegoer model code
 6 | end
 7 | alice = Moviegoer.find_by_name('Alice')
 8 | alice_movies = alice.movies
 9 | # MAY work, but a bad idea - see caption:
10 | alice.movies << Movie.find_by_name('Inception') # Don't do this!
```

Figure 5.17: Using through-associations in Rails. As before, the object returned by alice.movies in line 8 quacks like a collection. Note, however, that since the association between a Movie and a Moviegoer occurs *through* a Review belonging to both, the syntax in lines 9 and 10 will cause a Review object to be created to "link" the association, and by default all its attributes will be nil. This is almost certainly not what you want, and if you have validations on the Review object (for example, the number of potatoes must be an integer), the newly-created Review object will fail validation and cause the entire operation to abort.

5.4 Through-Associations

Referring back to Figure 5.11, there are direct associations between Moviegoers and Reviews as well as between Movies and Reviews. But since any given Review is associated with both a Moviegoer and a Movie, we could say that there's an *indirect* association between Moviegoers and Movies. For example, we might ask "What are all the movies Alice has reviewed?" or "Which moviegoers have reviewed *Inception*?" Indeed, line 14 in Figure 5.13 essentially answers the second question.

This kind of indirect association is so common that Rails and other frameworks provide an abstraction to simplify its use. It's sometimes called a *through-association*, since Moviegoers are related to Movies *through* their reviews and vice versa. Figure 5.17 shows how to use the **:through** option to Rails' **has_many** to represent this indirect association. You can similarly add **has_many :moviegoers, :through=>:reviews** to the **Movie** model, and write **movie.moviegoers** to ask which moviegoers are associated with (wrote reviews for) a given movie.

How is a through-association "traversed" in the database? Referring again to Figure 5.12, finding all the movies reviewed by Alice first requires forming the Cartesian product of the *three* tables (movies, reviews, moviegoers), resulting in a table that conceptually has 27 rows and 9 columns in our example. From this table we then select those rows for which the movie's ID matches the review's movie_id *and* the moviegoer's ID matches the review's moviegoer_id. Extending the explanation of Section 5.3, the SQL query might look like this:

http://pastebin.com/uupUEC58

```
 1 | SELECT movies.*
 2 |   FROM movies JOIN reviews ON movies.id = reviews.movie_id
 3 |   JOIN moviegoers ON moviegoers.id = reviews.moviegoer_id
 4 |   WHERE moviegoers.id = 1;
```

For efficiency, the intermediate Cartesian product table is usually not materialized, that is, not explicitly constructed by the database. Indeed, Rails 3 has a sophisticated relational algebra engine that constructs and performs optimized SQL join queries for traversing associations.

The point of these two sections, though, is not just to explain how to use associations, but to help you appreciate the elegant use of duck typing and metaprogramming that makes

http://pastebin.com/BmTg4Fs2

```
1  class Review < ActiveRecord::Base
2    # review is valid only if it's associated with a movie:
3    validates :movie_id, :presence => true
4    # can ALSO require that the referenced movie itself be valid
5    #  in order for the review to be valid:
6    validates_associated :movie
7  end
```

Figure 5.18:   This example validation on an association ensures that a review is only saved if it has been associated with
some movie.

them possible. In Figure 5.14(c) you added **has_many :reviews** to the **Movie** class. The
has_many method performs some metaprogramming to define the new instance method
reviews= that we used in Figure 5.13. As you've no doubt guessed, convention over configuration determines the name of the new method, the table it will use in the database, and
so on. Just like **attr_accessor**, **has_many** is not a declaration, but an actual method call
that does all of this work at runtime, adding a slew of new model instance methods to help
manage the association.

Associations are one of the most feature-rich aspects of Rails, so take a good look at the
full documentation[21] for them. In particular:

- Just like ActiveRecord lifecycle hooks, associations provide additional hooks that can
  be triggered when objects are added to or removed from an association (such as when
  new Reviews are added for a Movie), which are distinct from the lifecycle hooks of
  Movies or Reviews themselves.

- Validations can be declared on associated models, as Figure 5.18 shows.

- Because calling **save** or **save!** on an object that uses associations also affects the
  associated objects, various caveats apply to what happens if any of the saves fails. For
  example, if you have just created a new Movie and two new Reviews to link to it, and
  you now try to save the Movie, any of the three saves could fail if the objects aren't
  valid (among other reasons).

- Additional options to association methods control what happens to "owned"
  objects when an "owning" object is destroyed. For example, **has_many :re-
  views,:dependent=>:destroy** specifies that the reviews belonging to a movie
  should be deleted from the database if the movie is destroyed.

Through-associations summary:

- When two models A and B each have a has-one or has-many relationship to a common third model C, a many-to-many association between A and B can be established
  through C.

- The **:through** option to **has_many** allows you to manipulate either side of a
  through-association just as if it were a direct association. However, if you modify
  a through-association directly, the intermediate model object must be automatically
  created, which is probably not what you intended.

■ *Elaboration: Has and belongs to many*

Given that has_many :through creates "many-to-many" associations between the two outer entities (Movies and Reviews in our running example), could we create such many-to-many relationships directly, without going through an "intermediate" table? ActiveRecord provides another association we don't discuss here, **has_and_belongs_to_many** (HABTM), for pure many-to-many associations in which you don't need to maintain any other information about the relationship besides the fact that it exists. For example, on Facebook, a given user might "like" many wall posts, and a given wall post might be "liked by" many users; thus "like" is a many-to-many relationship between users and wall posts. However, even in that simple example, to keep track of *when* someone liked or unliked a wall post, the concept of a "like" would then need its own model to track these extra attributes. In most cases, therefore, **has_many :through** is more appropriate because it allows the relationship itself (in our example, the movie review) to be represented as a separate model. In Rails, HABTM associations are represented by a *join table* that by convention has no primary key and is created with a special migration syntax.

Self-Check 5.4.1. *Describe in English the steps required to determine all the moviegoers who have reviewed a movie with some given* id *(primary key).*

◇ Find all the reviews whose movie_id field contains the id of the movie of interest. For each review, find the moviegoer whose id matches the review's moviegoer_id field. ■

5.5 RESTful Routes for Associations

How should we RESTfully refer to actions associated with movie reviews? In particular, at least when creating or updating a review, we need a way to link it to a moviegoer and a movie. Presumably the moviegoer will be the **@current_user** we set up in Section 5.2. But what about the movie?

Let's think about this problem from the BDD point of view. Since it only makes sense to create a review when you have a movie in mind, most likely the "Create Review" functionality will be accessible from a button or link on the Show Movie Details page for a particular movie. Therefore, at the moment we display this control, we know what movie the review is going to be associated with. The question is how to get this information to the **new** or **create** method in the **ReviewsController**.

One method we might use is that when the user visits a movie's Detail page, we could use the **session[]**, which persists across requests, to remember the ID of the movie whose details have just been rendered as the "current movie." When **ReviewsController#new** is called, we'd retrieve that ID from the **session[]** and associate it with the review by populating a hidden form field in the review, which in turn will be available to **ReviewsController#create**. However, this approach isn't RESTful, since the movie ID—a critical piece of information for creating a review—is "hidden" in the session.

A more RESTful alternative, which makes the movie ID explicit, is to make the RESTful routes themselves reflect the logical "nesting" of Reviews inside Movies:

http://pastebin.com/r0SdhkJa

```
1   # in routes.rb, change the line 'resources :movies' to:
2   resources :movies do
3     resources :reviews
4   end
```

Helper method	RESTful Route and action	
movie_reviews_path(m)	GET /movies/:movie_id/reviews	index
movie_review_path(m)	POST /movies/:movie_id/reviews	create
new_movie_review_path(m)	GET /movies/:movie_id/reviews/new	new
edit_movie_review_path(m,r)	GET /movies/:movie_id/reviews/:id/edit	edit
movie_review_path(m,r)	GET /movies/:movie_id/reviews/:id	show
movie_review_path(m,r)	PUT /movies/:movie_id/reviews/:id	update
movie_review_path(m,r)	DELETE /movies/:movie_id/reviews/:id	destroy

Figure 5.19: Specifying nested routes in `routes.rb` also provides nested URI helpers, analogous to the simpler ones provided for regular resources. Compare this table with Figure 4.7 in Chapter 4.

Since **Movie** is the "owning" side of the association, it's the outer resource. Just as the original **resources :movies** provided a set of RESTful URI helpers for CRUD actions on movies, this ***nested resource*** route specification provides a set of RESTful URI helpers for CRUD actions on *reviews that are owned by a movie.* Make the above changes to `routes.rb` and try `rake routes`, comparing the output to the simple routes introduced in Chapter 4. Figure 5.19 summarizes the new routes, which are provided *in addition* to the basic RESTful routes on Movies that we've been using all along. Note that via convention over configuration, the URI wildcard **:id** will match the ID of the resource itself—that is, the ID of a review—and Rails chooses the "outer" resource name to make **:movie_id** capture the ID of the "owning"" resource. The ID values will therefore be available in controller actions as **params[:id]** (the review) and **params[:movie_id]** (the movie with which the review will be associated).

Figure 5.20 shows a simplified example of using such nested routes to create the views and actions associated with a new review. Of particular note is the use of a before-filter in **ReviewsController** to ensure that before a review is created, **@current_user** is set (that is, someone is logged in and will "own" the new review) and that the movie captured from the route (Figure 5.19) as **params[:movie_id]** exists in the database. If either condition is not met, the user is redirected to an appropriate page with an error message explaining what happened. If both conditions are met, the controller instance variables **@current_user** and **@movie** become accessible to the controller action and view.

The view uses the **@movie** variable to create a submission path for the form using the **movie_review_path** helper (Figure 5.19 again). When that form is submitted, once again `movie_id` is parsed from the route and checked by the before-filter prior to calling the **create** action. Finally, since in Figure 5.14(b) we declared **moviegoer_id** as a protected attribute, it cannot be assigned to the new review via the mass assignment from **params** (line 23 in the **create** action), so instead we set it by building the review from its other "owner" **@current_user**.

We could link to the page for creating a new review using something like the following on a movie's Details page:

http://pastebin.com/rpJ02W6A

```
1 = link_to 'Add Review', new_movie_review_path(@movie)
```

http://pastebin.com/J5UR6ftj

```
1  class ReviewsController < ApplicationController
2    before_filter :has_moviegoer_and_movie, :only => [:new, :create]
3    protected
4    def has_moviegoer_and_movie
5      unless @current_user
6        flash[:warning] = 'You must be logged in to create a review.'
7        redirect_to '/auth/twitter'
8      end
9      unless (@movie = Movie.find_by_id(params[:movie_id]))
10       flash[:warning] = 'Review must be for an existing movie.'
11       redirect_to movies_path
12     end
13   end
14   public
15   def new
16     @review = @movie.reviews.build
17   end
18   def create
19     # since moviegoer_id is a protected attribute that won't get
20     # assigned by the mass-assignment from params[:review], we set it
21     # by using the << method on the association.  We could also
22     # set it manually with review.moviegoer = @current_user.
23     @current_user.reviews << @movie.reviews.build(params[:review])
24     redirect_to movie_path(@movie)
25   end
26 end
```

http://pastebin.com/5VuxXT4z

```
1  %h1 New Review for #{@movie.title}
2
3  = form_tag movie_reviews_path(@movie) do
4    %label How many potatoes:
5    = select_tag 'review[potatoes]', options_for_select(1..5)
6    = submit_tag 'Create Review'
```

Figure 5.20: Top (a): a controller that manipulates Reviews that are "owned by" both a Movie and a Moviegoer, using before-filters to ensure the "owning" resources are properly identified in the route URI. Bottom (b): A possible Haml view template for creating a new review, that is, app/views/reviews/new.html.haml.

Summary: controller and view support for associations

- The RESTful way to create routes for associations is to capture the IDs of both the resource itself and its associated item(s) in a "nested" route URI.

- When manipulating "owned" resources that have a parent, such as Reviews that are "owned by" a Movie, before-filters can be used to capture and verify the validity of the IDs embedded in the RESTful nested route.

■ *Elaboration: SOA, RESTful association routes, and the session*

RESTful SOA design guidelines suggest that every request be self-contained, so that there is no concept of a session (nor any need for one). In our example, we used nested RESTful resource routes to keep the movie and review IDs together and relied on our authentication framework to set up **@current_user** as the moviegoer who owns the review. For a pure SOA API, we would need to capture the moviegoer ID *and* review ID along with the movie ID. Rails' routing subsystem is flexible enough to allow defining routes with multiple wildcard components for this purpose. In general, this design problem arises whenever you need to create an object with multiple "owners" such as a Review. If not all the owning objects are required in order for the owned object to be valid—for example, if it was possible for a Review to be "anonymous"—another solution would be to separate creation of the review and assigning it to a moviegoer into different RESTful actions.

Self-Check 5.5.1. *Why must we provide values for a review's* **movie_id** *and* **moviegoer_id** *to the* **new** *and* **create** *actions in* **ReviewsController**, *but not to the* **edit** *and* **update** *actions?*

◇ Once the review is created, the stored values of its **movie_id** and **moviegoer_id** fields tell us the associated movie and moviegoer. ■

5.6 Composing Queries With Reusable Scopes

We've said repeatedly that to keep concerns separate in Model–View–Controller, the implementation details of the app's models shouldn't be exposed to controllers, as Figure 5.21 (top) shows. An easy fix would be to create class methods **Movie.with_good_reviews** (perhaps taking one argument to specify the threshold average for "good" reviews) and **Movie.for_kids**, but what if you want to allow the user to filter by *both* attributes—movies for kids with good reviews?

Composable scopes are a powerful feature of ActiveRelation (the "relational algebra" behind ActiveRecord) that help you do this. As Figure 5.22 shows, a named scope is a lambda expression that gets evaluated at runtime. But scopes have two neat features that make them superior to defining explicit methods like **Movie.with_good_reviews**. First, they are *composable*: as lines 15–17 of Figure 5.22 show, the return value from calling a scope is itself an **ActiveRelation** object, to which additional scopes can be applied. This allows chunks of model logic such as these filters to be cleanly reused in different places.

Second, scopes are *evaluated lazily*: the chaining of scopes builds up a relation that can create and execute the corresponding SQL query, but the execution doesn't actually occur until the first matching result is requested. In our example, that happens in the view, in the **each** loop in lines 28–29 of Figure 5.22. Lazy evaluation is a powerful technique from

http://pastebin.com/JyHTtgT5

```
1  # BAD: details of computing review goodness is exposed to controller
2  class MoviesController < ApplicationController
3    def movies_with_good_reviews
4      @movies = Movie.joins(:reviews).group(:movie_id).
5        having('AVG(reviews.potatoes) > 3')
6    end
7    def movies_for_kids
8      @movies = Movie.where('rating in ?', %w(G PG))
9    end
10 end
```

Figure 5.21: Determining what makes a movie "good" or whether a movie is appropriate for kids should really be the Movie model's job, yet in this bad example, those details have been hardwired into two different controller methods. (We used ActiveRecord's group method to group the reviews by movie ID, and then applied SQL's AVERAGE aggregator to retain only those movie IDs whose reviews average more than 3 potatoes.)

http://pastebin.com/JCwE7cNx

```
1  # BETTER: move filter logic into Movie class using composable scopes
2  class Movie < ActiveRecord::Base
3    scope :with_good_reviews, lambda { |threshold|
4      Movie.joins(:reviews).group(:movie_id).
5        having(['AVG(reviews.potatoes) > ?', threshold.to_i])
6    }
7    scope :for_kids, lambda {
8      Movie.where('rating in (?)', %w(G PG))
9    }
10 end
11 # in the controller, a single method can now dispatch:
12 class MoviesController < ApplicationController
13   def movies_with_filters
14     @movies = Movie.with_good_reviews(params[:threshold])
15     @movies = @movies.for_kids         if params[:for_kids]
16     @movies = @movies.with_many_fans    if params[:with_many_fans]
17     @movies = @movies.recently_reviewed if params[:recently_reviewed]
18   end
19   # or even DRYer:
20   def movies_with_filters_2
21     @movies = Movie.with_good_reviews(params[:threshold])
22     %w(for_kids with_many_fans recently_reviewed).each do |filter|
23       @movies = @movies.send(filter) if params[filter]
24     end
25   end
26 end
27 # in the view:
28 - @movies.each do |movie|
29   -# ...code to display the movie here...
```

Figure 5.22: We encapsulate the various filtering criteria using scopes, which can optionally take one or more arguments. Scopes can be composed flexibly at runtime (lines 14–17), for example, in response to the presence of checkboxes named for_kids, with_many_fans, and so on. The alternative implementation movies_with_filters_2 accomplishes the same thing with less code using metaprogramming and extends readily to more scopes.

functional programming that we'll meet again in Chapter 12.

> **Summary of scopes:**
> Scopes let you declaratively specify model logic in a composable way, enabling clean reuse of various chunks of model logic. Because scopes are lazily evaluated—no database query occurs until the first matching result is requested—they can be composed in any order without incurring performance penalties.

Self-Check 5.6.1. *Write a scope expression for movies reviewed within the last n days, where n is a parameter to the scope.*

http://pastebin.com/EG3hcHXi

```
1  class Movie < ActiveRecord::Base
2    scope :recently_reviewed, lambda { |n|
3      Movie.joins(:reviews).where(['reviews.created_at >= ?', n.days.ago]).uniq
4    }
5  end
```

Self-Check 5.6.2. *Why must scope logic be part of a block or lambda-expression? For example, why didn't the designers of Rails use this syntax instead:*

http://pastebin.com/ErKmDCYL

```
1  class Movie < ActiveRecord::Base
2    scope :for_kids, Movie.where('rating in ?', %w(G PG))
3  end
```

◇   With this syntax, the **where** clause would be evaluated immediately (when this code file is loaded) rather than before each query. In other words, only those movies in existence *at the time the file is loaded* (that is, when the application starts up) would be included in the query. ■

5.7 Fallacies and Pitfalls

  Pitfall: **Too many filters or model lifecycle callbacks, or overly complex logic in filters or callbacks.**

Filters and callbacks provide convenient and well-defined places to DRY out duplicated code, but too many of them can make it difficult to follow the app's logic flow. For example, when there are numerous before-filters, after-filters and around-filters that trigger on different sets of controller actions, it can be hard to figure out why a controller action fails to execute as expected or which filter "stopped the show." Things can be even worse if some of the filters are declared not in the controller itself but in a controller from which it inherits, such as **ApplicationController**. Filters and callbacks should be used when you truly want to centralize code that would otherwise be duplicated.

   Pitfall: **Not checking for errors when saving associations.**

Saving an object that has associations implies potentially modifying multiple tables. If any of those modifications fails, perhaps because of validations either on the object or on its associated objects, other parts of the save might silently fail. Be sure to check the return value of **save**, or else use **save!** and rescue any exceptions.

Pitfall: **Nesting resources more than 1 level deep.**

Although it's technically possible to have nested resources multiple levels deep, the routes and actions quickly become cumbersome, which may be a sign that your design isn't properly factored. Perhaps there is an additional entity relationship that needs to be modeled, using a shortcut such as **has_many :through** to represent the final association.

5.8 Concluding Remarks: Languages, Productivity, and Beauty

This chapter showed two examples of using language features to support the productive creation of beautiful and concise code. The first is the use of metaprogramming, closures and higher-order functions to allow model validations and controller filters to be DRYly declared in a single place, yet called from multiple points in the code. Validations and filters are an example of *aspect-oriented programming* (AOP), a methodology that has been criticized because it obfuscates control flow but whose well-circumscribed use can enhance DRYness.

AOP has been compared with the fictitious *COME FROM* programming language construct, which began as a humorous response to Edsger Dijkstra's letter *Go To Statement Considered Harmful* (Dijkstra 1968) promoting structured programming.

The second example is the design choices reflected in the association helper methods. For example, you may have noticed that while the foreign key field for a **Movie** object associated with a review is called movie_id, the association helper methods allow us to reference **review.movie**, allowing our code to focus on the *architectural* association between Movies and Reviews rather than the *implementation detail* of the foreign key names. You could certainly manipulate the **movie_id** or **review_id** fields in the database directly, as Web applications based on less-powerful frameworks are often forced to do, or do so in your Rails app, as in **review.movie_id=some_movie.id**. But besides being harder to read, this code hardwires the assumption that the foreign key field is named movie_id, which may not be true if your models are using advanced Rails features such as polymorphic associations, or if ActiveRecord has been configured to interoperate with a legacy database that follows a different naming convention. In such cases, **review.movie** and **review.movie=** will still work, but referring to **review.movie_id** will fail. Since someday *your* code will be legacy code, help your successors be productive—keep the logical structure of your entities as separate as possible from the database representation.

We might similarly ask, now that we know how associations are stored in the RDBMS, why **movie.save** actually also causes a change to the reviews table when we save a movie after adding a review to it. In fact, calling **save** on the new review object would also work, but having said that a Movie has many Reviews, it just makes more sense to think of saving the Movie when we update which Reviews it has. In other words, it's designed this way in order to make sense to programmers and make the code more beautiful.

All in all, validations, filters, and association helper methods are worth studying as successful examples of tastefully exploiting programming language features to enhance code beauty and productivity.

5.9 To Learn More

- The ActiveRelation part of Rails, which manipulates ActiveRecord associations and generates SQL queries, was completely redesigned for Rails 3 and is amazingly powerful. This guide[22] has many examples beyond those introduced in this chapter that will help you use the database effectively, which as we'll see in Chapter 12 is critical to successful operations.

- The Guides section of the Rails website[23] includes useful guides on a variety of Rails topics including debugging, managing the configuration of your app, and more.

- A concise review of associations basics[24] is in the Guides section of the Rails website.

- *The Rails 3 Way* (Fernandez 2010) is an encyclopedic reference to all aspects of Rails 3, including the extremely powerful mechanisms that support associations.

E. Dijkstra. Go to statement considered harmful. *Communications of the ACM*, 11(3): 147–148, March 1968. URL `https://dl.acm.org/purchase.cfm?id=362947&CFID=100260848&CFTOKEN=27241581`.

O. Fernandez. *Rails 3 Way, The (2nd Edition) (Addison-Wesley Professional Ruby Series)*. Addison-Wesley Professional, 2010. ISBN 0321601661.

Notes

[1] `http://api.rubyonrails.org`
[2] `http://api.rubyonrails.org/v3.2.19/classes/ActiveModel/Validations/ClassMethods.html#method-i-validates`
[3] `http://api.rubyonrails.org/v3.2.19/classes/ActiveModel/Validations/ClassMethods.html#method-i-validates`
[4] `http://api.rubyonrails.org/v3.2.19/classes/ActiveModel/Errors.html`
[5] `http://guides.rubyonrails.org/v3.2.19/active_record_validations_callbacks.html`
[6] `http://guides.rubyonrails.org/v3.2.19/active_record_validations_callbacks.html`
[7] `http://api.rubyonrails.org/v3.2.19/classes/ActiveRecord/Callbacks.html`
[8] `http://en.wikipedia.org/wiki/Iframe#Frames`
[9] `http://www.omniauth.org`
[10] `https://github.com/arunagw/omniauth-twitter`
[11] `http://api.rubyonrails.org/v3.2.19/classes/ActiveModel/MassAssignmentSecurity/ClassMethods.html#method-i-attr_protected`
[12] `http://api.rubyonrails.org/v3.2.19/classes/ActiveModel/MassAssignmentSecurity/ClassMethods.html#method-i-attr_accessible`
[13] `http://www.omniauth.org`
[14] `http://api.rubyonrails.org/v3.2.19/classes/ActiveRecord/Associations/ClassMethods.html`
[15] `http://api.rubyonrails.org/v3.2.19/classes/ActiveRecord/Associations/ClassMethods.html`
[16] `http://api.rubyonrails.org/v3.2.19/classes/ActiveRecord/Associations/ClassMethods.html`
[17] `http://cassandra.apache.org`
[18] `http://mongodb.org`
[19] `http://couchdb.org`
[20] `http://appspot.com`
[21] `http://api.rubyonrails.org/v3.2.19/classes/ActiveRecord/Associations/ClassMethods.html`
[22] `http://guides.rubyonrails.org/v3.2.19/active_record_querying.html`
[23] `http://guides.rubyonrails.org/v3.2.19/`
[24] `http://guides.rubyonrails.org/v3.2.19/association_basics.html`

5.10 Suggested Projects

Filters and authentication:

Project 5.1. *Extend the example in Section 5.2 to allow authentication via Facebook Connect.*

Project 5.2. *Extend your solution to Exercise 5.1 to allow an authenticated user to "link" two accounts. That is, if Alice has previously logged in with Twitter and subsequently logs in with Facebook, she should be able to "link" the two accounts so that in the future, logging in with either one will authenticate her as the same principal.* **Hint:** *Consider creating an additional model* **Identity** *that has a many-to-one relationship to* **Moviegoer**.

Project 5.3. *In the README for the OmniAuth plugin, the author gives the following example code showing how to integrate OmniAuth into a Rails app:*
http://pastebin.com/3shQFuZm

```
1  class SessionsController < ApplicationController
2    def create
3      @user = User.find_or_create_from_auth_hash(auth_hash)
4      self.current_user = @user
5      redirect_to '/'
6    end
7    protected
8    def auth_hash
9      request.env['omniauth.auth']
10   end
11 end
```

The **auth_hash** *method (lines 8–10) has the trivial task of returning whatever OmniAuth returned as the result of trying to authenticate a user. Why do you think the author placed this functionality in its own method rather than just referencing* **request.env['omniauth.auth']** *directly in line 3?*

Associations and RESTful application architecture:

Project 5.4. *Extend the controller code in Figure 5.20 with* **edit** *and* **update** *methods for reviews. Use a controller filter to ensure that a user can only edit or update her own reviews.*

6 SaaS Client Framework: Introduction to JavaScript

Alan Perlis (1922–1990) was the first recipient of the Turing Award (1966), conferred for his influence on advanced programming languages and compilers. In 1958 he helped design ALGOL, which has influenced virtually every imperative programming language including C and Java. To avoid FORTRAN's syntactic and semantic problems, ALGOL was the first language described in terms of a formal grammar, the eponymous **Backus-Naur form** (named for Turing award winner Jim Backus and his colleague Peter Naur).

A language that doesn't affect the way you think about programming is not worth knowing.

—Alan Perlis

Concepts

JavaScript is a dynamic, interpreted scripting language built into modern browsers. This chapter describes its main features, including some that we recommend avoiding because they represent questionable design choices, and how it extends the types of content and applications that can be delivered as SaaS.

- A browser represents a web page as a data structure called the ***Document Object Model*** (DOM). JavaScript code running in the browser can inspect and modify this data structure, causing the browser to redraw the modified page elements.

- When a user interacts with the browser (for example, by typing, clicking, or moving the mouse) or the browser makes progress in an interaction with a server, the browser generates an *event* indicating what happened. Your JavaScript code can take app-specific actions to modify the DOM when such events occur.

- Using ***AJAX***, or Asynchronous JavaScript And XML, JavaScript code can make HTTP requests to a Web server *without* triggering a page reload. The information in the response can then be used to modify page elements in place, giving a richer and often more responsive user experience than traditional Web pages. Rails partials and controller actions can be readily used to handle AJAX interactions.

- Just as we used the highly-productive Rails framework and RSpec TDD tool for server-side SaaS code, here we use the highly-productive ***jQuery*** framework and Jasmine[1] TDD tool to develop client-side code.

- We follow the best practice of "graceful degradation," also referred to as "progressive enhancement": legacy browsers lacking JavaScript support will still provide a good user experience, while JavaScript-enabled browsers will provide an even better experience.

6.1   JavaScript: The Big Picture

Brendan Eich proposed embedding the Scheme language in the browser (Seibel 2009). Although pressure to create a Java-like syntax prevailed, many Scheme ideas survive in JavaScript.

JavaScript, Microsoft JScript, and Adobe ActionScript are dialects of *ECMAScript*, the 1997 standard that codifies the language. We follow standard usage and use "JavaScript" to refer to the language generically.

JavaScript had to "look like Java" only less so—be Java's dumb kid brother or boy-hostage sidekick. Plus, I had to be done in ten days or something worse than JavaScript would have happened.

—Brendan Eich, creator of JavaScript

Despite its name, JavaScript is unrelated to Java: LiveScript, the original name chosen by Netscape Communications Corp., was changed to JavaScript to capitalize on Java's popularity. In fact, as a language JavaScript inherits almost nothing from Java except superficial syntax. It has higher-order functions, which come from the Scheme dialect of Lisp and figure prominently in AJAX programming and in the Jasmine TDD tool. Its dynamic type system is similar to Ruby's and plays a similarly prominent role in how the language is used. If you have a solid grasp of these concepts from Chapters 3 and 8, and are comfortable using CSS selectors as you did in Chapters 2 and 7, learning and using JavaScript productively will be easy.

There are four major uses of JavaScript in today's SaaS ecosystem, which we list in order of "least JavaScript-intensive" to "most JavaScript-intensive":

1. Using JavaScript to enhance the user experience of server-centric SaaS apps that follow the Model–View–Controller architectural pattern. In this case, JavaScript is combined with HTML and CSS to form the "three-legged stool" of client-side SaaS programming. This case is called ***client-side JavaScript*** to clarify that JavaScript is "embedded" in the browser in a way that lets it interact with Web pages. In this scenario, the server typically sends pre-rendered HTML in response to JavaScript requests, and the browser uses these HTML chunks to replace existing page elements.

2. Creating ***single-page applications*** (SPAs) that fit on a single web page, optionally enhanced by connectivity with the server. The user experience is that once the initial page is loaded, no further page reloads or redraws occur, although elements on the page are updated continuously in response to communication with the server. In this scenario, the server appears to the app as one or several Service-Oriented Architecture endpoints that return data encoded in XML or ***JSON*** (JavaScript Object Notation) to the client-side JavaScript code, which parses the data and updates various page elements accordingly.

3. Creating client-side applications such as Google Docs, comparable in complexity to desktop apps and possibly able to operate while disconnected from the Internet. Like all complex software, such apps must be built on some underlying architecture; for example, the Angular[2] framework for JavaScript supports Model–View–Controller.

4. Creating full server-side apps similar to those we've been building using Rails, but using JavaScript frameworks such as Node.js.

In this chapter we focus on cases 1 and 2, keeping the following best practices in mind:

- **Graceful degradation:** In Case 1, a site's user experience should be acceptable even in the absence of JavaScript. (Displaying the message "JavaScript is required for this site" doesn't count.) The more positive-sounding term *progressive enhancement* emphasizes the benefit of adding JavaScript rather than the penalty of omitting it. Why

	Server	**Client**
Language	Ruby	JavaScript
Framework	Rails	jQuery
Client-Server Architecture over HTTP	Controller receives request, interacts with model, renders new page (view)	Controller receives request, interacts with model, and renders a partial or an XML- or JSON-encoded object, which is used by JavaScript code running in browser to modify current page in place
Debugging	Ruby debugger, `rails console`	Firebug, browser's JavaScript console
Testing	RSpec with `rspec-rails`; isolate tests from database using ActiveRecord model fixtures and factories	Jasmine, `jasmine-jquery`; isolate tests from server using HTML and JSON fixtures

Figure 6.1: The correspondence between our exposition of server-side programming with Ruby and Rails and client-side programming with JavaScript continues our focus on productively creating DRY, concise code that is well covered by tests.

should you care about this? One reason is compatibility: according to Microsoft[3], 24% of Chinese Internet users in 2013—over 130 million people—still use Internet Explorer 6, which has serious JavaScript compatibility problems. Another reason is that JavaScript may be disabled for security reasons, especially in enterprise environments where users cannot change their own configuration settings. We refer to all these cases as legacy browsers, and we insist that our app remain usable in the absence of JavaScript. Obviously, this guideline doesn't apply to Case 2, since JavaScript is required for SPAs.

- **Unobtrusive:** JavaScript code should be kept completely separate from page markup. In both cases, this helps separate concerns as we did with Model–View–Controller. In Case 1, it also simplifies supporting legacy browsers.

Figure 6.1 compares our exposition of server-side and client-side programming. Screencast 6.1.1 demonstrates the two JavaScript features we will add to RottenPotatoes in this chapter.

Screencast 6.1.1: Adding JavaScript features to RottenPotatoes.
`http://vimeo.com/45331300`
We will first add a checkbox that allows filtering the RottenPotatoes movie list to exclude films unsuitable for children. This behavior can be implemented entirely in client-side JavaScript using techniques described in Sections 6.4 and 6.5. Next we will change the behavior of the "More info" link for each movie to display the extra info in a "floating" window rather than loading a new page. This will require AJAX, since fetching the movie info requires communicating with the server. Section 6.6 introduces AJAX programming. Both behaviors will be implemented with graceful degradation so that legacy browsers still have a good experience.

JavaScript has a bad reputation that isn't entirely deserved. It began as a language that would allow Web browsers to run simple client-side code to validate form inputs, animate page elements, or communicate with Java applets. Inexperienced programmers began to copy-and-paste simple JavaScript examples to achieve appealing visual effects, albeit with terrible programming practices, giving the language itself a bad reputation. In fact, JavaScript is a powerful and expressive language that incorporates great ideas enabling reuse and DRY-ness, such as closures and higher-order functions, but people without programming experience rarely use these tools properly.

That said, because of JavaScript's turbulent birth, its syntax and semantics have quirks ranging from the idiosyncratic to the regrettable, with almost as many special-case exceptions as there are rules. In addition, there are incompatibilities among different versions of the JavaScript interpreter and across different browsers' JavaScript Application Programming Interface (JSAPI), the browser functionality that lets JavaScript code manipulate the content of the current HTML page. We will avoid compatibility problems in two major ways:

> **quirksmode.org** tells you more about JSAPI browser incompatibilities than you want to know.

1. Restricting ourselves to language features in the ECMAScript 3 standard, which all browsers support

2. Using the powerful jQuery library, rather than individual browsers' JSAPIs, to interact with HTML documents

Section 6.2 introduces the language and how code is connected to Web pages and Section 6.3 describes how its functions work, an understanding of which is the basis of writing clean and unobtrusive JavaScript code. Section 6.4 introduces jQuery[4], which overlays the separate browsers' incompatible JSAPIs with a single API that works across all browsers, and Section 6.5 describes how jQuery's features make it easy to program interactions between page elements and JavaScript code.

> **jQuery** can be viewed as an enhanced Adapter (Section 11.6) to the various browsers' JSAPIs.

Section 6.6 introduces AJAX programming. In 1998, Internet Explorer 5 introduced a new mechanism that allowed JavaScript code to communicate with a SaaS server *after* a page had been loaded, and use information from the server to update the page "in place" without the user having to reload a new page. Other browsers quickly copied the technology. Developer Jesse James Garrett coined[5] the term **AJAX**, for Asynchronous JavaScript And XML, to describe how the combination of this technology to power impressive "Web 2.0" apps like Google Maps.

> Ironically, modern AJAX programming involves much less XML than originally, as we'll see.

Testing client-side JavaScript is challenging because browsers will fail silently when an error occurs rather than displaying JavaScript error messages to unsuspecting users. Fortunately, the Jasmine TDD framework will help you test your code, as Section 6.7 describes.

Finally, Section 6.8 describes the mechanisms for both developing and testing browser-based single-page apps (SPAs), which are becoming increasingly popular.

Summary of JavaScript background:

- JavaScript resembles Java in name and syntax only; despite nontrivial flaws, it embodies great ideas found in Scheme and Ruby.

- We focus on client-side JavaScript, that is, on using the language to enhance the user experience of pages delivered by a server-centric SaaS app. We strive for graceful degradation (user experience without JavaScript should be usable, if impoverished) and unobtrusiveness (JavaScript code should be completely separate from page markup).

Self-Check 6.1.1. *True or false: one early advantage of JavaScript for form validation (preventing a user from submitting a form with invalid data) was the ability to remove validation code from the server and move it to the client instead.*

◇ False; there is no guarantee the submission actually came from that page (anyone with a command line tool can construct an HTTP request), and even if it did, the user might be working with a legacy browser. As we point out repeatedly in SaaS, the server cannot trust anyone and must always validate its inputs. ∎

6.2 Client-Side JavaScript for Ruby Programmers

Stop me if you think you've heard this before.

—variously attributed

Despite its name and syntax, JavaScript has more in common with Ruby than with Java:

- Almost everything is an object. The basic JavaScript object looks like a Ruby hash, except that its keys (property names) must be strings.

- Typing is dynamic: variables don't have types, but the objects they refer to do.

- Classes and types matter even less than they do in Ruby—in fact, despite the syntactic appearance of much JavaScript code in the wild, JavaScript has no classes, although there are coding conventions that are used to achieve some of the effects of having classes.

- Functions are closures that carry their environment around with them, allowing them to execute properly at a different place and time than where they were defined. Just as anonymous blocks (**do. . . end**) are ubiquitous in Ruby, anonymous functions (**function() {. . . }**) are ubiquitous in JavaScript.

- JavaScript is interpreted and includes metaprogramming and introspection facilities.

Figure 6.2 shows JavaScript's basic syntax and constructs, which should look familiar to Java and Ruby programmers. The Fallacies & Pitfalls section describes several JavaScript pitfalls associated with the figure; read them carefully after you've finished this chapter, or you may find yourself banging your head against one of JavaScript's unfortunate misfeatures or a JavaScript mechanism that looks and works almost but not quite like its Ruby counterpart. For example, whereas Ruby uses **nil** to mean both "undefined" (a variable that has never been given a value) and "empty" (a value that is always false), JavaScript's **null** is distinct from its **undefined**, which is what you get as the "value" of a variable that has never been initialized.

As the first row of Figure 6.2 shows, JavaScript's fundamental type is the **object**, an unordered collection of key/value pairs, or as they are called in JavaScript, *properties* or *slots*. The name of a property can be any string, including the empty string. The value of a property can be any JavaScript expression, including another object; it cannot be **undefined**.

JavaScript allows you to express *object literals* by specifying their properties and values directly, as Figure 6.3 shows. This simple object-literal syntax is the basis of *JSON*, or JavaScript Object Notation, which despite its name is a language-independent way to represent data that can be exchanged between SaaS services or between a SaaS client and server. In fact, lines 2–11 in the figure (minus the trailing semicolon on line 11) are a legal JSON

Objects	movie={title: 'The Godfather', 'releaseInfo': {'year': 1972, rating: 'PG'}}
	Quotes optional around property name if it's a legal variable name; objects can be nested. Access an object's properties with **movie.title**, or **movie['title']** if property name isn't a legal variable name or isn't known until runtime.
	for (*var* **in** *obj*) {...} iterates over *obj*'s property names in arbitrary order.
Types	**typeof** *x* returns a string representation of *x*'s primitive type: one of **"object"**, **"string"**, **"array"**, **"number"**, **"boolean"**, **"function"**, **"undefined"**. *All numbers are doubles.*
Strings &Regexps	**"string"**, **'also a string'**, **'joining'+'strings'**
	'mad, mad world'.split(/[,]+/) == ["mad","mad","world"]
	'mad, mad world'.slice(3,8)==", mad" ; 'mad, mad world'.slice(-3)=="rld"
	'mad'.indexOf('d')==2, 'mad'.charAt(2)=='d', 'mad'.charCodeAt(4)==100
	'mad'.replace(/(\w)$/,'$1$1er')=="madder"
	/*regexp*/.**exec**(*string*) if no match returns **null**, if match returns array whose zeroth element is whole string matched and additional elements are parenthesized capture groups. *string*.**match**(/*regexp*/) does the same, *unless* the **/g** regexp modifier is present. /*regexp*/.**test**(*string*) (faster) returns **true** or **false** but no capture groups.
	Alternate constructor: **new RegExp('[Hh]e(l+)o')**
Arrays	**var a = [1, {two: 2}, 'three'] ; a[1] == {two: 2}**
	Zero-based, grow dynamically; objects whose keys are numbers (see Fallacies & Pitfalls)
	arr.sort(function (a,b) {...}) Function returns -1,0 or 1 for **a<b,a==b,a>b**
Numbers	**+ - / %**, also **+=**, etc., **++ --**, **Math.pow**(*num,exp*)
	Math.round(n), **Math.ceil(n)**, **Math.floor(n)** round their argument to nearest, higher, or lower integer respectively
	Math.random() returns a random number in (0,1)
Conversions	'catch'+22=='catch22', '4'+'11'=='411'
	parseInt('4oneone')==4, parseInt('four11')==NaN
	parseInt('0101',10)==101, parseInt('0101',2)==5, parseInt('0101')==65
	(numbers beginning with **0** are parsed in octal by default, unless radix is specified)
	parseFloat('1.1b23')==1.1, parseFloat('1.1e3')==1100
Booleans	**false**, **null**, **undefined** (undefined value, different from **null**), 0, the empty string '', and **NaN** (not-a-number) are *falsy* (Boolean false); **true** and all other values are ***truthy***.
Naming	**localVar, local_var, ConstructorFunction, GLOBAL**
	All are conventions; JavaScript has no specific capitalization rules. **var** keyword scopes variable to the function in which it appears, otherwise it becomes a global (technically, a property of the global object, as Section 6.3 describes). Variables don't have types, but the objects they refer to do.
Control flow	**while()**, **for(;;)**, **if...else if...else**, **?:** (ternary operator), **switch/case**, **try-catch/throw**, **return**, **break**
	Statements separated by semicolons; interpreter tries to auto-insert "missing" ones, but this is perilous (see Fallacies & Pitfalls)

Figure 6.2: Analogous to Figure 3.1, this table summarizes basic constructs of JavaScript. See the text for important pitfalls. Whereas Ruby uses nil as both an explicit null value and the value returned for nonexistent instance variables, JavaScript distinguishes undefined, which is returned for undeclared or unassigned variables, from the special value null and Boolean false. However, all three are "falsy"—they evaluate to false in a conditional.

http://pastebin.com/gaR9tA4k

```
1   var potatoReview =
2   {
3     "potatoes": 5,
4     "reviewer": "armandofox",
5     "movie": {
6       "title": "Casablanca",
7       "description": "Casablanca is a classic and iconic film starring ...",
8       "rating": "PG",
9       "release_date":  "1942-11-26T07:00:00Z"
10    }
11  };
12  potatoReview['potatoes']  // => 5
13  potatoReview['movie'].title    // => "Casablanca"
14  potatoReview.movie.title      // => "Casablanca"
15  potatoReview['movie']['title'] // => "Casablanca"
16  potatoReview['blah']          // => undefined
```

Figure 6.3: JavaScript notation for object literals, that is, objects you specify by enumerating their properties and values explicitly. If the property name is a legal JavaScript variable name, quotes can be omitted or the idiomatic dot-notation shortcut (lines 13–14) can be used, although quotes are always required around all strings when an object is expressed in JSON format. Since objects can contain other objects, hierarchical data structures can be built (line 5) and traversed (lines 13–15).

representation. Officially, each property value in a JSON object can be a Number, Unicode String, Boolean (true or false are the only possible values), null (empty value), or a nested Object recursively defined. Unlike full JavaScript, though, in the JSON representation of an object all strings *must* be quoted, so the example in the top row of Figure 6.2 would need quotes around the word **title** to comply with JSON syntax. Figure 6.4 summarizes a variety of tools for checking the syntax and style of both JavaScript code and JavaScript-related data structures and protocols that we'll meet in the rest of this chapter.

JSON.org defines JSON's precise syntax and lists parsing libraries available for other languages.

The fact that a JavaScript object can have function-valued properties is used by well-engineered libraries to collect all their functions and variables into a single ***namespace***. For example, as we'll see in Section 6.4, jQuery defines a single global variable **jQuery** through which all features of the jQuery library are accessed, rather than littering the global namespace with the many objects in the library. We will follow a similar practice by defining a small number of global variables to encapsulate all our JavaScript code.

The term *client-side JavaScript* refers specifically to JavaScript code that is associated with HTML pages and therefore runs in the browser. Each page in your app that wants to use JavaScript functions or variables must include the necessary JavaScript code itself. The recommended and unobtrusive way to do this is using a **script** tag referencing the file containing the code, as Figure 6.5 shows. The Rails view helper **javascript_include_tag 'application'**, which generates the above tag, can be placed in your app/views/layouts/ application.html.haml or other layout template that is part of every page served by your app. If you then place your code in one or more separate .js files in app/assets/ javascripts, when you deploy to production Rails will do the following steps automatically:

1. Concatenate the contents of all JavaScript files in this directory;

2. Compress the result by removing whitespace and performing other simple transformations (the uglifier gem);

3. Place the result in a single large file in the public subdirectory that will be served directly by the presentation tier with no Rails intervention;

Name	Tool type	Description
JSLint	Web-based	Copy and paste your code into the form at `jslint.com` to check it for errors and stylistic pitfalls according to the guidelines in Doug Crockford's *JavaScript: The Good Parts*. Also checks for legal but unsafe constructions; some developers find it overly pedantic.
JavaScript Lint	Command-line	Matthias Miller's command-line tool, preinstalled in bookware VM, reports errors and warnings based on the same JavaScript interpreter used by the Firefox browser. To run it, type `jsl -process` *file*`.js`
Closure	Command-line	Google's source-to-source compiler[6] translates JavaScript to better JavaScript, removing dead code and minifying as it goes, and giving errors and warnings. Its associated Linter tool goes even further and enforces Google's JavaScript style guidelines. Not preinstalled in bookware VM; requires Java.
YUI	Command-line	Yahoo's YUI Compressor[7] minifies JavaScript and CSS more aggressively than some other tools and looks for stylistic problems in the process. Not preinstalled in bookware VM; requires Java.
JSONlint	Web-based	This tool at jsonlint.com[8] checks your JSON data structures for syntax errors.

Figure 6.4: A variety of tools for debugging your JavaScript code and associated data structures and server interactions. One challenge is that just as with the C language, there are many competing coding guidelines for JavaScript—Google's, Yahoo's, the Node.js project's, and others—and different tools check and enforce different coding styles.

http://pastebin.com/7SztJxcj

```
1   <script src="/public/javascripts/application.js"></script>
```

http://pastebin.com/KBnYjPhc

```
1   <html>
2     <head><title>Update Address</title></head>
3     <body>
4       <!-- BAD: embedding scripts directly in page, esp. in body -->
5       <script>
6       <!-- // BAD: "hide" script body in HTML comment
7           // (modern browsers may not see script at all)
8         function checkValid() {    // BAD: checkValid is global
9           if !(fieldsValid(getElementById('addr'))) {
10            // BAD: > and < may confuse browser's HTML parser
11            alert('>>> Please fix errors & resubmit. <<<');
12          }
13        // BAD: "hide" end of HTML comment (1.3) in JS comment: -->
14      </script>
15      <!-- BAD: using HTML attributes for JS event handlers -->
16      <form onsubmit="return checkValid()" id="addr" action="/update">
17        <input onchange="RP.filter_adult" type="checkbox"/>
18        <!-- BAD: URL using 'javascript:' -->
19        <a href="javascript:back()">Go Back</a>
20      </form>
21    </body>
22  </html>
```

Figure 6.5: Top: The unobtrusive and recommended way to load JavaScript code in your HTML view(s). Bottom: Three obtrusive ways to embed JavaScript into HTML pages, all deprecated because they mix JavaScript code with HTML markup. Sadly, all are common in the "street JavaScript" found on poorly-engineered sites, yet all are easily avoided by using the script src= method and by using the unobtrusive techniques described in the rest of this chapter for connecting JavaScript code to HTML elements.

4. Adjust the URLs emitted by **javascript_include_tag** so that the user's browser loads not only your own JavaScript files but also the jQuery library.

This automatic behavior, supported by modern production environments including Heroku, is called the ***asset pipeline***. Described more fully in this guide[9], the asset pipeline also allows us to use languages like CoffeeScript, as we'll see later. You might think it wasteful for the user's browser to load a single enormous JavaScript file, especially if only a few pages in your app use JavaScript and any given page only uses a small subset of your JavaScript code. But the user's browser only loads the large file once and then caches it until you redeploy your app with changed .js files. Also, in development mode, the asset pipeline skips the "precompilation" process and just loads each of the JavaScript files separately, since they're likely to be changing frequently while you're developing.

Minifying is a term used to describe the compression transformations, which reduce the size of the jQuery 1.7.2 library from 247 KiB to 32 KiB.

Summary of Client-Side JavaScript and HTML:

- Like Ruby, JavaScript is interpreted and dynamically typed. The basic object type is a hash with keys that are strings and values of arbitrary type, including other hashes.

- The fundamental JavaScript data type is an object, which is an unordered collection of property names and values, similar to a hash. Since objects can nest, they can represent hierarchical data structures. JavaScript's simple object-literal notation is the inspiration for the JSON data interchange format.

- The preferred unobtrusive way to associate JavaScript with an HTML page is to include in the HTML document's `head` element a `script` tag whose `src` attribute gives the URL of the script itself, so that the JavaScript code can be kept separate from HTML markup. The Rails helper **javascript_include_tag** generates the correct URL that takes advantage of Rails' asset pipeline.

■ *Elaboration: JSON, XML, or YAML for structured data?*

You've now seen at least three different ways to represent structured data: XML (Section 8.1), YAML (Sections 4.2 and 8.5), and JSON (lines 2–11 of Figure 6.3. These three standards, and ***many others***, address the problem of data ***serialization*** (also called ***marshalling*** or ***deflating***)—translating a program's internal data structures into a representation that can be "resurrected" later. Deserialization (unmarshalling, inflating) is often performed by a different program, possibly written in a different language or at the other end of a network connection, so the serialization format must be portable. As we'll see in Section 6.8, JSON is becoming the most popular serialization format between SaaS clients and servers; in fact, Ruby 1.9 added an alternate hash notation **{foo: 'bar'}**, equivalent to **{:foo=>'bar'}**, to mimic JSON.

Self-Check 6.2.1. *In Ruby, when a method call takes no arguments, the empty parentheses following the method call are optional. Why wouldn't this work in JavaScript?*
◇ Because JavaScript functions are first-class objects, a function name without parentheses would be an expression whose value is the function itself, rather than a call to the function.

■

6.3   Functions and Constructors

In Chapter 3 we mentioned that object-orientation and class inheritance are distinct language design concepts, although many people mistakenly conflate them because popular languages like Java use both. JavaScript is object-oriented, but lacks classes. Nonetheless, it has some mechanisms that look and act similarly to those in languages with classes. Unfortunately, the questionable design of these mechanisms leads to a lot of confusion for newcomers to JavaScript, especially regarding the behavior of the keyword **this**. We will concern ourselves with three common uses of **this**. In this section we introduce the first two of these uses, and an associated pitfall. In Section 6.5 we introduce the third use.

Try these examples in Firebug[10] or your browser's built-in JavaScript console; there's no standardized interactive JavaScript interpreter analogous to Ruby's `irb`.

Lines 1–8 of Figure 6.6 show a function called **Movie**. This syntax for defining functions may be unfamiliar, whereas the alternate syntax in lines 9–11 looks comfortably familiar. Nonetheless, we will use the first syntax for two reasons. First, unlike Ruby, functions in JavaScript are true *first-class objects*—you can pass them around, assign them to variables, and so on. The syntax in line 1 makes it clear that **Movie** is simply a variable whose value happens to be a function. Second, although it's not obvious, the variable **Movie** in line 9 is being declared in JavaScript's global namespace—hardly beautiful. In general we want to minimize clutter in the global namespace, so we will usually create one or a few objects named by global variables associated with our app, and all of our JavaScript functions will be the values of properties of those objects.

If we call the **Movie** function using JavaScript's **new** keyword (line 13), the value of **this** in the function body will be a new JavaScript object that will eventually be returned by the function, similar to Ruby's **self** inside an **initialize** constructor method. In this case, the returned object will have properties **title**, **year**, **rating**, and **full_title**, the last of which is a property whose value is a function. If line 14 looks like a function call to you, then you've been hanging around Ruby too long; since functions are first-class objects in JavaScript, this line just returns the value of **full_title**, which is the function itself, not the result of calling it! To actually call it, we need to use parentheses, as in line 15. When we make that call, within the body of **full_title**, **this** will refer to the object whose property the function is, in this case **pianist**.

Remember, though, that while these examples look just like calling a class's constructor and calling an instance method in Ruby, JavaScript has no concept of classes or instance methods. In fact, there is nothing about a particular JavaScript function that makes it a constructor; instead, it's the use of **new** when calling the function that makes it a constructor, causing it to create and return a new object. The reason this works is because of JavaScript's *prototype inheritance* mechanism, which we don't discuss further (but see the Elaboration below to learn more). Nonetheless, forgetting this subtle distinction may confuse you when you expect class-like behaviors and don't get them.

However, a JavaScript misfeature can trip us up here. It is (unfortunately) perfectly legal to call **Movie** as a plain old function *without* using the **new** keyword, as in line 17. If you do this, JavaScript's behavior is completely different in two horrible, horrible ways. First, in the body of **Movie**, **this** will not refer to a brand-new object but instead to the *global object,* which defines various special constants such as **Infinity**, **NaN**, and **null**, and supplies various other parts of the JavaScript environment. When JavaScript is run in a browser, the global object happens to be a data structure representing the browser window. Therefore, lines 2–5 will be creating and setting new properties of this object—clearly not what we intended, but unfortunately, when **this** is used in a scope where it would otherwise be undefined, it refers

http://pastebin.com/4nBsjb0t

```
 1  var Movie = function(title,year,rating) {
 2    this.title = title;
 3    this.year = year;
 4    this.rating = rating;
 5    this.full_title = function() { // "instance method"
 6      return(this.title + ' (' + this.year + ')');
 7    };
 8  };
 9  function Movie(title,year,rating) {  // this syntax may look familiar...
10    // ...
11  }
12  // using 'new' makes Movie the new objects' prototype:
13  pianist = new Movie('The Pianist', 2002, 'R');
14  pianist.full_title;    // => function() {...}
15  pianist.full_title(); // => "The Pianist (2002)"
16  // BAD: without 'new', 'this' is bound to global object in Movie call!!
17  juno = Movie('Juno', 2007, 'PG-13'); // DON'T DO THIS!!
18  juno;                  // undefined
19  juno.title;            // error: 'undefined' has no properties
20  juno.full_title();     // error: 'undefined' has no properties
```

Figure 6.6: Since functions are first-class objects, it is fine for an object to have a property whose value is a function, as full_title is. We will make extensive use of this characteristic. Note the pitfall in lines 14–18.

to the global object, a serious design defect in the language. (See Fallacies and Pitfalls and To Learn More if you want to learn about the reasons for this odd behavior, a discussion of which is beyond the scope of this introduction to the language.)

Second, since **Movie** doesn't explicitly return anything, its return value (and therefore the value of **juno**) will be **undefined**. Whereas a Ruby function returns the value of the last expression in the function by default, a JavaScript function returns **undefined** unless it has an explicit **return** statement. (The **return** in line 6 belongs to the **full_title** function, not to **Movie** itself.) Hence, lines 19–20 give errors because we're trying to reference a property (**title**) on something that isn't even an object.

You can avoid this pitfall by rigorously following the widespread JavaScript convention that a function's name should be capitalized if and only if the function is intended to be called as a constructor using **new**. Functions that are not "constructor-like" should be given names beginning with lowercase letters.

Summary: Functions and Constructors

- JavaScript functions are first-class objects: they can be assigned to variables, passed to other functions, or returned from functions.

- Although JavaScript doesn't have classes, one way of managing namespaces in an orderly way in JavaScript is to store functions as object properties, allowing a single object (hash) to collect a set of related functions as a class would.

- If the **new** keyword is used to call a function, **this** in the function body will refer to a new object whose property values can be initialized in the "constructor." This mechanism is similar to creating new instances of a class, though JavaScript lacks classes.

- However, if a function is called *without* the **new** keyword, **this** in the function body will refer to the global object, which is almost never what you wanted, and the function will return **undefined**. To avoid this pitfall, capitalize the names of constructor-like functions intended to be called with **new**, but don't capitalize the names of any other functions.

■ *Elaboration: Prototypal inheritance*

Every JavaScript object inherits from exactly one prototype object—new strings inherit from **String.prototype**, new arrays from **Array.prototype**, and so on, up to **Object** (the empty object). If you look up a property on an object that doesn't have that property, its prototype is checked, then its prototype's prototype, and so on until one of the prototypes responds with the property or **undefined** is returned. Given this background, the effect of calling a function using the **new** keyword is to create a new object whose prototype is the same as the function's prototype.

Prototypes come from Self, a language originally designed at the legendary Xerox PARC and which heavily influenced **NewtonScript**, the programming language for the ill-fated Apple Newton "handheld." Proper use of prototypal inheritance affords an effective kind of implementation reuse that is different from what classes provide. Unfortunately, as Crockford notes in *JavaScript: The Good Parts* Crockford 2008, JavaScript's implementation of prototypal inheritance is halfhearted and uses a confusing syntax, perhaps in an effort to resemble "classical" languages with class inheritance.

Self-Check 6.3.1. *What is the difference between evaluating* **square.area** *and* **square.area()** *in the following JavaScript code?*

http://pastebin.com/CfuHynff

```
1  var square = {
2    side: 3,
3    area: function() {
4      return this.side*this.side;
5    }
6  };
```

◇ **square.area()** is a function call that in this case will return 9, whereas **square.area** is an unapplied function object. ■

Self-Check 6.3.2. *Given the code in Self-Check 6.3.1, explain why it's is incorrect to write* **s=new square**.

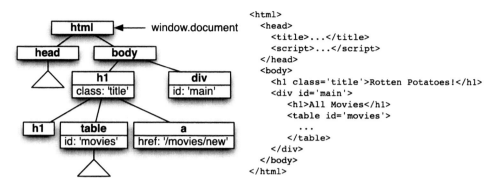

```
<html>
  <head>
    <title>...</title>
    <script>...</script>
  </head>
  <body>
    <h1 class='title'>Rotten Potatoes!</h1>
    <div id='main'>
        <h1>All Movies</h1>
        <table id='movies'>
          ...
        </table>
    </div>
  </body>
</html>
```

Figure 6.7: A simplified view of the DOM tree corresponding to the RottenPotatoes "list of movies" page with skeletal HTML markup. An open triangle indicates places where we've elided the rest of the subtree for brevity. this.document is set to point to the DOM tree's root when a page is loaded.

◇ **square** is just an object, not a function, so it cannot be called as a constructor (or at all). ∎

6.4 The Document Object Model and jQuery

The World Wide Web Consortium Document Object Model (W3C DOM)[11] is "a platform- and language-neutral interface that will allow programs and scripts to dynamically access and update the content, structure and style of documents"—in other words, a standard representation of an HTML, XML, or XHTML document consisting of a hierarchy of elements. A DOM element is recursively defined in that one of its properties is an array of child elements, as Figure 6.7 shows. Hence a DOM node representing the <html> element of an HTML page is sufficient to represent the whole page, since every element on a well-formed page is a descendant of <html>. Other DOM element properties correspond to the HTML element's attributes (**href**, **src**, and so on). When a browser loads a page, the HTML of the page is parsed into a DOM tree similar to Figure 6.7.

> **DOM** technically refers to the standard itself, but developers often use it to mean the specific DOM tree corresponding to the current page.

How does JavaScript get access to the DOM? When JavaScript is embedded in a browser, the global object, named by the global variable **window**, defines additional browser-specific properties and functions, collectively called the JSAPI. Whenever a new page is loaded, a new global **window** object is created that shares no data with the global objects of other visible pages. One of the properties of the global object is **window.document**, which is the root element of the current document's DOM tree and also defines some functions to query, traverse, and modify the DOM; one of the most common is **getElementById**, which you may have run across while perusing others' JavaScript code.

However, to avoid compatibility problems stemming from different browsers' implementations of the JSAPI, we will bypass these native JSAPI functions entirely in favor of jQuery's more powerful "wrappers" around them. jQuery also adds additional features and behaviors absent from the native JSAPIs, such as animations and better support for CSS and AJAX (Section 6.6). jQuery defines a global function **jQuery()** (aliased as **$()**) that, when passed a CSS selector (examples of which we saw in Figure 2.5), returns all of the current page's DOM elements matching that selector. For example, **jQuery('#movies')** or **$('#movies')** would return the single element whose ID is movies, if one exists on the page; **$('h1.title')** would return all the h1 elements whose CSS class is title. A more general version of this

> The **jquery-rails** gem documentation[12] explains how to manually add jQuery to your app if using a Rails version earlier than 3.1.

The call **jQuery.noConflict()** "undefines" the **$** alias, in case your app uses the browser's built-in **$** (usually an alias for **document.-getElementById**) or loads another JavaScript library such as Prototype[13] that also tries to define **$**.

functionality is **.find(***selector***)**, which only searches the DOM subtree rooted at the target. To illustrate the distinction, **$('p span')** finds *any* span element that is contained inside a p element, whereas if **elt** already refers to a *particular* p element, then **elt.find('span')** only finds span elements that are descendants of **elt**.

Whether you use **$()** or **find**, the return value is a node set (collection of one or more elements) matching the selector, or **null** if there were no matches. Each element is "wrapped" in jQuery's DOM element representation, giving it abilities beyond the browser's built-in JSAPI. From now on, we will refer to such elements as "jQuery-wrapped" elements, to distinguish them from the representation that would be returned by the browser's native JSAPI. In particular, you can do various things with jQuery-wrapped elements in the node set, as Figure 6.8 shows:

- To change an element's visual appearance, define CSS classes that create the desired appearances, and use jQuery to add or remove CSS class(es) from the element at runtime.

- To change an element's content, use jQuery functions that set the element's HTML or plain text content.

- To animate an element (show/hide, fade in/out, and so on), invoke a jQuery function on that element that manipulates the DOM to achieve the desired effect.

Note, however, that even when a node set includes multiple matching elements, it is not a JavaScript array and you cannot treat it like one: you cannot write **$('tr')[0]** to select the first row of a table, even if you first call jQuery's **toArray()** function on the node set. Instead, following the Iterator design pattern, jQuery provides an **each** iterator defined on the collection that returns one element at a time while hiding the details of how the elements are stored in the collection, just as **Array#each** does in Ruby.

Screencast 6.4.1 shows some simple examples of these behaviors from the browser's JavaScript console. We will use these to implement the features of Screencast 6.1.1.

Screencast 6.4.1: Manipulating the DOM with jQuery.
`http://vimeo.com/46694004`
jQuery makes it easy to manipulate the DOM from JavaScript and provides a built-in library of useful visual effects. These simple examples show that JavaScript can not only read element and content information on the page, but also modify the elements, causing the browser to redraw them. This behavior is the key to client-side JavaScript.

Finally, as we will see, the **jQuery()** or **$()** function is **overloaded**: its behavior depends on the number and types of arguments with which it's called. In this section we introduced just one of its four behaviors, namely for selecting elements in the DOM; we will soon see the others.

Property or function, example	Value/description
$(*dom-element***)** **$(this)**	Returns a set of jQuery-wrapped DOM element(s) specified by the argument, which can be a CSS3 selector (such as **'span.center'** or **'#main'**), the element object returned by the browser's **getElementById** function, or in an event handler, the element that received the event, named by **this**. The return value of this function is suitable as the target for any of the below calls. (Recall that the term *target* is used in JavaScript the way *receiver* is used in Ruby.)
is(*cond***)**	Test if the element is **':checked'**, **':selected'**, **':enabled'**, **':disabled'**. Note that these strings were chosen to resemble Ruby symbols, though JavaScript doesn't have symbols.
addClass(), **removeClass()**, **hasClass()**	Shortcuts for manipulating the `class` attribute: add or remove the specified CSS class (a string) from the element, or test whether the given class is currently associated with the element.
insertBefore(), **insertAfter()**	Insert the target element(s) before or after the argument. That is, **newElt.insertBefore(existingElt)** inserts **newElt** just before **existingElt**, which must exist.
remove()	Remove the target element(s) from the DOM.
replaceWith(*new***)**	Replace the target element(s) with the *new* element(s) provided.
clone()	Return a complete copy of the target element, recursively cloning its descendants.
html(), **text()**	Return (with no argument) or set (with one argument) the element's complete HTML content or plain-text content. If the element has other elements nested inside it, you can replace its HTML with nested elements but don't have to, but replacing its text will obliterate the nested elements.
val()	Return (with no argument) or set (with one argument) the current value of the element. For text boxes, value is the current string contents; for buttons, the button's label; for select menus, the text of the currently selected value.
attr(*attr,[newval]***)** **$('img').attr('src',** **'http://imgur.com/xyz')**	Return or (with second argument) set the value of the given attribute on the element.
hide(*duration,callback***)**, **show()**, **toggle()** **slideUp()**, **slideDown()**, **slideToggle()** **fadeOut()**, **fadeIn()**, **fadeTo(***duration,target,callback***)**	Hide or show elements selected by the target. Optional *duration* is one of **'fast'**, **'slow'**, or the integer number of milliseconds that the animation should last. Optional *callback* is a function to call when animation completes. Other sets of animations with same arguments include **slideDown/slideUp/slideToggle** and **fadeOut/fadeIn**. For **fadeTo**, second argument is target opacity, from 0.0 (transparent) to 1.0 (opaque).
evt(***func***) **$('li').click(function() {** **$(this).hide();** **});**	Set *func* as the handler for event *evt* on the element(s) selected by the target. *func* can be an anonymous function or a named function. See Figure 6.9 for some of the most important event types.

Figure 6.8: Some attributes and functions defined on jQuery's enhanced DOM element objects; they should be called with the appropriate element or collection of elements as the target of the call (like receiver in Ruby). Functions that only make sense applied to a single element, such as attr, apply to the first element when used on a collection of elements. Functions that can both read and modify element properties act as getters when the final (or only) argument is absent, and setters when it's present. Unless otherwise noted, all functions return their target, so calls can be chained, as in *elt*.insertBefore(...).hide(). See the jQuery documentation[15] for more features beyond this subset.

Summary of the DOM and jQuery:

- The World Wide Web Consortium Document Object Model (W3C DOM) is a language-independent representation of the hierarchy of elements that constitute an HTML document.

- All JavaScript-enabled browsers provide JavaScript language bindings to access and traverse the DOM. This set of functionality, together with JavaScript access to other browser features, is collectively called the JavaScript Application Programming Interface or JSAPI.

- The powerful jQuery library provides a uniform adapter to browsers' differing JS-APIs and adds many enhanced functions such as CSS-based DOM traversal, animation, and other special effects.

Self-Check 6.4.1. *Why is* **this.document**, *when it appears outside the scope of any function, equivalent to* **window.document**?
◇ Outside of any function, the value of **this** is the global object. When JavaScript runs in a Web browser, the global object is the window object. ■

Self-Check 6.4.2. *True or false: even after the user closes a window in her Web browser, the JavaScript code associated with that window can still access and traverse the HTML document the window had been displaying.*
◇ False. Each new HTML document gets its own global object and DOM, which are destroyed when the document's window is closed. ■

6.5   Events and Callbacks

So far all of our DOM manipulation has been by typing JavaScript commands directly. As you've no doubt guessed, much more interesting behaviors are possible when DOM manipulation can be triggered by user actions. As part of the JSAPI for the DOM, browsers allow attaching JavaScript *event handlers* to the user interface: when the user performs a certain UI action, such as clicking a button or moving the mouse into or out of a particular HTML element, you can designate a JavaScript function that will be called and have the opportunity to react. This capability makes the page behave more like a desktop UI in which individual elements respond visually to user interactions, and less like a static page in which any interaction causes a whole new page to be loaded and displayed.

The less precise term Dynamic HTML was sometimes used in the past to refer to the effects of combining JavaScript-based DOM manipulation and CSS.

Figure 6.9 summarizes the most important events defined by the browser's native JSAPI and improved upon by jQuery. While some are triggered by user actions on DOM elements, others relate to the operation of the browser itself or to "pseudo-UI" events such as form submission, which may occur via clicking a Submit button, pressing the Enter key (in some browsers), or another JavaScript callback causing the form to be submitted. To attach a behavior to an event, simply provide a JavaScript function that will be called when the event *fires*. We say that this function, called a *callback* or *event handler*, is *bound* to that event on that DOM element. Although events are automatically triggered by the browser, you can also trigger them yourself: for example, **e.trigger('click')** triggers the **click** event handler for element **e**. As we will see in Section 6.7, this ability is useful when testing: you can simulate

Events on arbitrary elements	**click**, **dblclick**, **mousedown/mouseup**, **mouseenter/mouseleave**, **keypress** (**event.which** gives the ASCII code of the key pressed) **focus/blur** (element gains/loses focus), **focusin/focusout** (parent gains/loses focus)
Events on user-editable controls (forms, checkboxes, radio buttons, text boxes, text fields, menus)	**change** fires when any control's state or content is changed. **select** (user selects text; string **event.which** is selected text) **submit** fires when the user attempts to submit the form by any means.

Figure 6.9: **A few of the JavaScript events defined by the jQuery API. Set a handler for an event with** *element*.on(*'evt'*, *func*) **or as a shortcut,** *element.evt(func)*. **Hence, $('h1').on('click', function() {...}) is equivalent to $('h1').click(function() {...}). The callback** *func* **will be passed an argument (which you're free to ignore) whose value is the jQuery Event object describing the event that was triggered. Remember that on and its shortcuts will bind the callback to** *all* **elements matching the selector, so be sure the selector you pass is unambiguous, for example by identifying an element by its ID.**

user interaction and check that the correct changes are applied to the DOM in response to a UI event.

Browsers define built-in behavior for some events and elements: for example, clicking on a link visits the linked page. If such an element also has a programmer-supplied **click** handler, the handler runs first; if the handler returns a truthy value (Figure 6.2), the built-in behavior runs next, but if the handler returns a falsy value, the built-in behavior is suppressed. What if an element has *no* handler for a user-initiated event, as is the case for images? In that case, its parent element in the DOM tree is given the chance to respond to the event handler. For example, if you click on an img element inside a div and the img has no click handler, then the div will receive the click event. This process continues until some element handles the event or it "bubbles" all the way up to the top-level **window**, which may or may not have a built-in response depending on the event.

Our discussion of events and event handlers motivates the third common use of JavaScript's **this** keyword (recall that Section 6.3 introduced the first two uses). When an event is handled, in the body of the event handler function, jQuery will arrange for **this** to refer to the element to which the handler is attached (which may not be the element that originally received the event, if the event "bubbled up" from a descendant). However, if you were programming *without* jQuery, the value of **this** in an event handler is the global object (**document.window**), and you have to examine the event's data structure (usually passed as the final argument to the handler) to identify the element that handled the event. Since handling events is such a common idiom, and most of the time an event handler wants to inspect or manipulate the state of the element on which the event was triggered, jQuery is written to explicitly set **this** to that DOM element.

Putting all these pieces together, Figure 6.10 shows the client-side JavaScript to implement a checkbox that, when checked, will hide any movies with ratings other than G or PG. Our general strategy for JavaScript can be summarized as:

1. Identify the DOM elements we want to operate on, and make sure there is a convenient and unambiguous way of selecting them using **$()**.

2. Create the necessary JavaScript functions to manipulate the elements as needed. For this simple example we can just write them down, but as we'll see in Section 6.7, for AJAX or more complex functions we will use TDD (Chapter 8) to develop the code.

3. Define a setup function that binds the appropriate JavaScript functions to the elements

http://pastebin.com/s9tPrqjZ

```
 1  var MovieListFilter = {
 2    filter_adult: function () {
 3      // 'this' is *unwrapped* element that received event (checkbox)
 4      if ($(this).is(':checked')) {
 5        $('tr.adult').hide();
 6      } else {
 7        $('tr.adult').show();
 8      };
 9    },
10    setup: function() {
11      // construct checkbox with label
12      var labelAndCheckbox =
13        $('<label for="filter">Only movies suitable for children</label>' +
14          '<input type="checkbox" id="filter"/>' );
15      labelAndCheckbox.insertBefore('#movies');
16      $('#filter').change(MovieListFilter.filter_adult);
17    }
18  }
19  $(MovieListFilter.setup); // run setup function when document ready
```

Figure 6.10: Using jQuery to add a "filter movies" checkbox to RottenPotatoes' list of movies page; put this code in app/assets/javascripts/movie_list_filter.js. The text walks through the example in detail, and additional figures in the rest of the chapter generalize the techniques shown here. Our examples use jQuery's DOM manipulation features rather than the browser's built-in ones because the jQuery API is more consistent across different browsers than the official W3C DOM specification.

and performs any other necessary DOM manipulation.

4. Arrange to call the setup function once the document is loaded.

For Step 1, we will modify our existing Rails movie list view to attach the CSS class adult to any table rows for movies rated other than G or PG. All we have to do is change line 13 of the Index template (Figure 4.6) as follows, thereby allowing us to write **$('tr.adult')** to select those rows:

http://pastebin.com/JM9NP8sP

```
 1    %tr{:class => ('adult' unless movie.rating =~ /^G|PG$/)}
```

For Step 2, we provide the function **filter_adult**, which we will arrange to be called whenever the checkbox is checked or unchecked. As lines 4–8 of Figure 6.10 show, if the checkbox is checked, the adult movie rows are hidden; if unchecked, they are revealed. Recall from Figure 6.8 that **:checked** is one of jQuery's built-in behaviors for checking the state of an element. Remember also that jQuery selectors such as **$('tr.adult')** generally return a collection of matching elements, and actions like **hide()** are applied to the whole collection.

Why does line 4 refer to **$(this)** rather than just **this**? The mechanism by which user interactions are dispatched to JavaScript functions is part of the browser's JSAPI, so the value of **this** is the *browser's* representation of the checkbox (the element that handled the event). In order to use the more powerful jQuery features such as **is(':checked')**, we have to "wrap" the native element as a jQuery element by calling **$** on it in order to give it these special powers. The first row of Figure 6.12 shows this usage of **$**.

<input> outside <form>? Yes—it's legal in HTML 4 and later, as long as you manage all the input's behaviors yourself, as we're doing.

For Step 3, we provide the **setup** function, which does two things. First, it creates a label and a checkbox (lines 12–14), using the **$** mechanism shown in the second row of Figure 6.12, and inserts them just before the movies table (line 15). Again, by creating a jQuery element we are able to call **insertBefore** on it, which is not part of the browser's built-in JSAPI. Most jQuery functions such as **insertBefore** return the target object itself, allowing "chaining" of function calls as we've seen in Ruby.

var m = new Movie();	(Figure 6.6, line 13) In the body of the **Movie** function, **this** will be bound to a new object that will be returned from the function, so you can use **this.title** (for example) to set its properties. The new object's prototype will be the same as the function's prototype.
pianist.full_title();	(Figure 6.6, line 15) When **full_title** executes, **this** will be bound to the object that "owns" the function, in this case **pianist**.
$('#filter').change(MovieListFilter.filter_adult);	(Figure 6.10, line 16) When **filter_adult** is called to handle a **change** event, **this** will refer to the element on which the handler was bound, in this case one of the element(s) matching the CSS selector **#filter**.

Figure 6.11: The three common uses of this introduced in Sections 6.3 and 6.5. See Fallacies and Pitfalls for more on the use and misuse of this.

Second, the setup function binds the **filter_adult** function to the checkbox's **change** handler. You might have expected to bind to the checkbox's **click** handler, but **change** is more robust because it's an example of a "pseudo-UI" event: it fires whether the checkbox was changed by a mouse click, a keypress (for browsers that have keyboard navigation turned on, such as for users with disabilities that prevent use of a mouse), or even by other JavaScript code. The **submit** event on forms is similar: it's better to bind to that event than to bind to the **click** handler on the form-submit button, in case the user submits the form by hitting the Enter key.

Why didn't we just add the label and checkbox to the Rails view template? The reason is our design guideline of graceful degradation: by using JavaScript to create the checkbox, legacy browsers will not render the checkbox at all. If the checkbox was part of the view template, users of legacy browsers would still see the checkbox, but nothing would happen when they clicked on it.

Why does line 16 refer to **MovieListFilter.filter_adult**? Couldn't it just refer to **filter_adult**? No, because that would imply that **filter_adult** is a variable name visible in the scope of the **setup** function, but in fact it's not a variable name at all—it's just a function-valued property of the object **MovieListFilter**, which *is* a (global) variable. It is good JavaScript practice to create one or a few global objects to "encapsulate" your functions as properties, rather than writing a bunch of functions and polluting the global namespace with their names.

The last step is Step 4, which is to arrange for the **setup** function to be called. For historical reasons, JavaScript code associated with a page can begin executing *before* the entire page has been loaded and the DOM fully parsed. This feature was more important for responsiveness when browsers and Internet connections were slower. Nonetheless, we usually want to wait until the page is finished loading and the entire DOM has been parsed, or else we might be trying to bind callbacks on elements that don't exist yet! Line 19 does this, adding **MovieListFilter.filter_adult** to the list of functions to be executed once the page is finished loading, as the last row of Figure 6.12 shows. Since you can call **$()** multiple times to run multiple setup functions, you can keep each file's setup function together with that file's functionality, as we've done here. To run this example place all the code from Figure 6.12 in **app/assets/javascripts/movie_list_filter.js**.

This was a dense example, but it illustrates the basic jQuery functionality you'll need for many UI enhancements. The figures and tables in this section generalize the techniques introduced in the example, so it's worth spending some time perusing them. In particular, Figure 6.12 summarizes the four different ways to use jQuery's **$**, all of which we've now seen.

Uses of $() or jQuery() with example	Value/side effects, line number in Figure 6.10
$(*sel*) $('.mov span')	return collection of jQuery-wrapped elements selected by CSS3 selector *sel* (line 16)
$(*elt*) $(this), $(document), $(document.getElementById('main'))	When an element is returned by a JSAPI call such as **getElementById** or supplied to an event-handler callback, use this function to create a jQuery-wrapped version of the element, on which you can call the operations in Figure 6.8 (line 4)

$(*HTML[, attribs]*)
$('\<p\>\<b\>bold\</b\>words\</p\>'),
$('\<img/\>', {
  src: '/rp.gif',
  click: handleImgClick })
	Returns a new jQuery-wrapped HTML element corresponding to the passed text, which must contain at least one HTML tag with angle brackets (otherwise jQuery will think you're passing a CSS selector and calling it as in the previous table row). If a JavaScript object is passed for *attribs*, it is used to construct the element's attributes. (Lines 13–14) The new element is not automatically inserted into the document; Figure 6.8 shows some methods for doing that, one of which is used in line 15.

$(*func*) $(function () {...});	Run the provided function once the document has finished loading and the DOM is ready to be manipulated. This is a shortcut for **$(document).ready(***func***)**, which is itself a jQuery wrapper around the **onLoad()** handler of the browser's built-in JSAPI. (line 19)

Figure 6.12: **The four ways to invoke the overloaded function jQuery() or $() and the effects of each. All four are demonstrated in Figure 6.10.**

Summary of jQuery's DOM and event handlers:

- You can set or override how various HTML elements react to user input by binding JavaScript handlers or **callbacks** to specific events on specific elements. jQuery allows you to bind both "physical" user events such as mouse clicks and "logical" pseudo-events such as form submission. Figure 6.9 summarizes a subset of jQuery events.

- Inside an event handler, jQuery causes **this** to be bound to the *browser's* DOM representation of the element that handled the event. We usually "wrap" the element to get **$(this)**, a "jQuery-wrapped" element that supports enhanced jQuery operations, such as **$(this).is(':checked')**.

- One of jQuery's advanced features is the ability to apply transformations such as **show()** and **hide()** to a collection of elements (for example, a group of elements named by a single CSS selector) as well as a single element.

- For both DRYness and graceful degradation, the binding of event handlers to elements should occur in a setup function that is called when the document is loaded and ready; that way, legacy non-JavaScript browsers will not run the function at all. Passing a function to **$()** adds it to the list of setup functions that will be run once the document is finished loading.

http://pastebin.com/AqHkMHRk

```
1   // from file jquery_ujs.js in jquery-rails 3.0.4 gem
2   // (Line numbers may differ if you have a different gem version)
3   // line 23:
4     $.rails = rails = {
5       // Link elements bound by jquery-ujs
6       linkClickSelector: 'a[data-confirm], a[data-method], a[data-remote], a[
             data-disable-with]',
7   // line 160:
8       handleMethod: function(link) {
9           // ...code elided...
10          form = $('<form method="post" action="' + href + '"></form>'),
11          metadata_input = '<input name="_method" value="' + method + '" type="
                hidden" />';
12        // ...code elided...
13        form.hide().append(metadata_input).appendTo('body');
14        form.submit();
15      }
```

Figure 6.13:   When `jquery_ujs` is loaded, `<a>` elements having any of the attributes `data-confirm`, `data-method`, `data-remote`, or `data-disable-with` are bound to a handler handleMethod that executes when the link is clicked. If the link has a `data-method` attribute, the handler constructs an ephemeral `<form>` passing the value of `data-method` as the hidden `_method` attribute, hides the form (so it doesn't appear on the page when constructed), and submits it. In Rails 2 and earlier, the link _ to helper generated inline (obtrusive) JavaScript; Rails 3 changed the behavior to more beautiful unobtrusive JavaScript.

■ *Elaboration: Custom events*

Most of jQuery's events are based on the built-in events recognized by browsers, but you can also define your own custom events and use **trigger** to trigger them. For example, you might enclose menus for month and day in a single outer element such as a `div` and then define a custom **update** event on the `div` that checks that the month and day are compatible. You could isolate the checking code in a separate event handler for **update**, and use **trigger** to call it from within the **change** handlers for the individual month and day menus. This is one way that custom handlers help DRY out your JavaScript code.

■ *Elaboration: JavaScript and Rails view helpers*

In Section 4.8 we used the Rails **link _ to** helper with **:method=>:delete** to create a clickable link that would trigger the `delete` controller method. We noted that the unusual HTML generated by the helper looked something like this:

http://pastebin.com/nRgdBDwU

```
1   <a href="/movies/1" data-method="delete" rel="nofollow">Delete</a>
```

Rails' conventional way to handle a delete operation is using an HTTP POST operation that submits a form with the additional argument `_method="delete"`, since most browsers cannot issue HTTP DELETE requests directly. Given the knowledge you've gained in this section, Figure 6.13 shows how **link _ to** actually works by annotating code excerpts from the file `jquery_ujs.js`, which is part of the `jquery-rails` gem that every Rails app uses by default. Since Web crawlers don't usually execute JavaScript, the attribute `rel="nofollow"` is a *request* to the crawler or other client not to follow the link, but there's no guarantee the client will respect this request. That's why it's important that your routes only allow the "destructive" controller actions to be called with non-GET methods.

Self-Check 6.5.1. *Explain why calling* **$**(selector) *is equivalent to calling* **$**(window.document).find(selector).

◇ **document** is a property of the browser's built-in global object (**window**) that refers to the browser's representation of the root of the DOM. Wrapping the document element using **$** gives it access to jQuery functions such as **find**, which locates all elements matching the selector that are in the subtree of its target; in this case, the target is the DOM root, so it will find any matching elements in the entire document. ■

Self-Check 6.5.2. *In Self-Check 6.5.1, why did we need to write* **$(document).find** *rather than* **document.find***?*
◇ **document**, also known as **window.document**, is the browser's native representation of the **document** object. Since **find** is a jQuery function, we need to "wrap" **document** to give it special jQuery powers. ■

Self-Check 6.5.3. *What would happen if we omitted the last line of Figure 6.10, which arranges to call the* **setup** *function?*
◇ The browser would behave like a legacy browser without JavaScript. The checkbox wouldn't be drawn (since that happens in the **setup** function) and even if it were, nothing would happen when it was clicked, since the **setup** function binds our JavaScript handler for the checkbox's **change** event. ■

6.6 AJAX: Asynchronous JavaScript And XML

In 1998, Microsoft added a new function to the JavaScript global object defined by Internet Explorer 5. **XmlHttpRequest** (usually shortened to XHR) allowed JavaScript code to initiate HTTP requests to a server *without* loading a new page and use the server's response to modify the DOM of the current page. This new function, key to AJAX apps, allowed creating a rich interactive UI that more closely resembled a desktop application, as Google Maps powerfully demonstrated. Happily, you already know all the ingredients needed for "AJAX on Rails" programming:

1. Create a controller action or modify an existing one (Section 4.4) to handle the AJAX requests made by your JavaScript code. Rather than rendering an entire view, the action will render a partial (Section 5.1) to generate a chunk of HTML for insertion into the page.

2. Construct your RESTful URI in JavaScript and use XHR to send the HTTP request to a server. As you may have guessed, jQuery has helpful shortcuts for many common cases, so we will use jQuery's higher-level and more powerful functions rather than calling XHR directly.

3. Because JavaScript is by definition *single-threaded*—it can only work on one task at a time until that task completes—the browser's UI would be "frozen" while JavaScript awaited a response from the server. Therefore XHR instead returns immediately and lets you provide an event handler callback (as you did for browser-only programming in Section 6.5) that will be triggered when the server responds or an error occurs.

4. When the response arrives at the browser, your callback is passed the response content. It can use jQuery's **replaceWith()** to replace an existing element entirely, **text()** or **html()** to update an element's content in place, or an animation such as **hide()** to hide

http://pastebin.com/mcmdUnqA

```
1  %p= movie.description
2
3  = link_to 'Edit Movie', edit_movie_path(movie)
4  = link_to 'Close', '', {:id => 'closeLink'}
```

http://pastebin.com/ck2q1ZxJ

```
1  class MoviesController < ApplicationController
2    def show
3      id = params[:id] # retrieve movie ID from URI route
4      @movie = Movie.find(id) # look up movie by unique ID
5      render(:partial => 'movie', :object => @movie) if request.xhr?
6      # will render app/views/movies/show.<extension> by default
7    end
8  end
```

Figure 6.14: (a) Top: a simple partial that will be rendered and returned to the AJAX request. We give the "Close" link a unique element ID so we can conveniently bind a handler to it that will hide the popup. (b) Bottom: The controller action that renders the partial, obtained by a simple change to Figure 4.9: if the request is an AJAX request, line 5 performs a render and immediate return. The :object option makes @movie available to the partial as a local variable whose name matches the partial's name, in this case movie. If xhr? is not true, the controller method will perform the default rendering action, which is to render the show.html.haml view as usual.

or show elements, as Figure 6.8 showed. Because JavaScript functions are closures (like Ruby blocks), the callback has access to all the variables visible at the time the XHR call was made, even though it executes at a later time and in a different environment.

Let's illustrate how each step works for the AJAX feature shown in Screencast 6.1.1, in which movie details appear in a floating window rather than loading a separate page. Step 1 requires us to identify or create a new controller action that will handle the request. We will just use our existing **MoviesController#show** action, so we don't need to define a new route. This design decision is defensible since the AJAX version of the action performs the same function as the original version, namely the RESTful "show" action. We will modify the **show** action so that if it's responding to an AJAX request, it will render the simple partial in Figure 6.14(a) rather than an entire view. You could also define separate controller actions exclusively for AJAX, but that might be non-DRY if they duplicate the work of existing actions.

How does our controller action know whether **show** was called from JavaScript code or by a regular user-initiated HTTP request? Fortunately, every major JavaScript library and most browsers set an HTTP header X-Requested-With: XMLHttpRequest on all AJAX HTTP requests. The Rails helper method **xhr?**, defined on the controller instance's **request** object representing the incoming HTTP request, checks for the presence of this header. Figure 6.14(b) shows the controller action that will render the partial.

Moving on to step 2, how should our JavaScript code construct and fire off the XHR request? As the screencast showed, we want the floating window to appear when we click on the link that has the movie name. As Section 6.5 explained, we can "hijack" the built-in behavior of an element by attaching an explicit JavaScript **click** handler to it. Of course, for graceful degradation, we should only hijack the link behavior if JavaScript is available. So following the same strategy as the example in Section 6.5, our **setup** function (lines 2–8 of Figure 6.15) binds the handler and creates a hidden div to display the floating window. Legacy browsers won't run that function and will just get the default behavior of clicking on the link.

HiJax is sometimes humorously used to describe this technique.

http://pastebin.com/zZPKvmVW

```
1   var MoviePopup = {
2     setup: function() {
3       // add hidden 'div' to end of page to display popup:
4       var popupDiv = $('<div id="movieInfo"></div>');
5       popupDiv.hide().appendTo($('body'));
6       $(document).on('click', '#movies a', MoviePopup.getMovieInfo);
7     }
8     ,getMovieInfo: function() {
9       $.ajax({type: 'GET',
10              url: $(this).attr('href'),
11              timeout: 5000,
12              success: MoviePopup.showMovieInfo,
13              error: function(xhrObj, textStatus, exception) { alert('Error!');
                     }
14              // 'success' and 'error' functions will be passed 3 args
15             });
16      return(false);
17     }
18     ,showMovieInfo: function(data, requestStatus, xhrObject) {
19       // center a floater 1/2 as wide and 1/4 as tall as screen
20       var oneFourth = Math.ceil($(window).width() / 4);
21       $('#movieInfo').
22         css({'left': oneFourth,  'width': 2*oneFourth, 'top': 250}).
23         html(data).
24         show();
25       // make the Close link in the hidden element work
26       $('#closeLink').click(MoviePopup.hideMovieInfo);
27       return(false);  // prevent default link action
28     }
29     ,hideMovieInfo: function() {
30       $('#movieInfo').hide();
31       return(false);
32     }
33   };
34   $(MoviePopup.setup);
```

Figure 6.15: The ajax function constructs and sends an XHR request with the given characteristics. type specifies the HTTP verb to use, url is the URL or URI for the request, timeout is the number of milliseconds to wait for a response before declaring failure, success specifies a function to call with the returned data, and error specifies a function to call if a timeout or other error occurs. Many more options to the ajax function are available, in particular for more robust error handling.

http://pastebin.com/vWwDrYEc

```
1   #movieInfo {
2     padding: 2ex;
3     position: absolute;
4     border: 2px double grey;
5     background: wheat;
6   }
```

Figure 6.16: Adding this code to `app/assets/stylesheets/application.css` specifies that the "floating" window should be positioned at absolute coordinates rather than relative to its enclosing element, but as the text explains, we don't know until runtime what those coordinates should be, so we use jQuery to dynamically modify #movieInfo's CSS style properties when we are ready to display the floating window.

The actual click handler **getMovieInfo** must fire off the XHR request and provide a callback function that will be called with the returned data. For this we use jQuery's **ajax** function, which takes an object whose properties specify the characteristics of the AJAX request, as lines 10–15 of Figure 6.15 show. Our example shows a subset of the properties you can specify in this object; one important property we don't show is **data**, which can be either a string of arguments to append to the URI (as in Figure 2.3) or a JavaScript object, in which case the object's properties and their values will be serialized into a string that can be appended to the URI. As always, such arguments would then appear in the **params[]** hash available to our Rails controller actions.

> Of course, **$.ajax** is just an alias for **jQuery.ajax**.

Screencast 6.6.1 uses the Firebug interactive debugger as well as the Rails debugger to step through the rest of the code in Figure 6.15. Getting the URI that is the target of the XHR request is easy: since the link we're hijacking already links to the RESTful URI for showing movie details, we can query its `href` attribute, as line 11 shows. Lines 13–14 remind us that function-valued properties can specify either a named function, as **success** does, or an anonymous function, as **error** does. To keep the example simple, our error behavior is rudimentary: no matter what kind of error happens, including a timeout of 5000 ms (5 seconds), we just display an alert box. In case of success, we specify **showMovieInfo** as the callback.

Screencast 6.6.1: Interactively single-stepping through AJAX.
`http://vimeo.com/47064979`
AJAX debugging requires a combination of a JavaScript debugger such as Firebug and a server-side debugger such as `debugger`, which you met in Chapter 4. Be aware that Firefox's "Information" views (such as we used in Screencast 2.3.2 work by modifying the DOM itself to show the popups and tooltips, so if you're "testing things out" using the JavaScript console, you may get unexpected results if these features are active. *Note:* The JavaScript code in the screencast uses the name **RP** rather than **MoviePopup** to name the global variable that stores the JavaScript functions related to this example, but other than that difference, the code is the same.

Some interesting CSS trickery happens in lines 20 and 23 of Figure 6.15. Since our goal is to "float" the popup window, we can use CSS to specify its positioning as `absolute` by adding the markup in Figure 6.16. But without knowing the size of the browser window, we don't know how large the floating window should be or where to place it. **showMovieInfo** computes the dimensions and coordinates of a floating `div` half as high and one-fourth as tall as the browser window itself (line 20). It replaces the HTML contents of the `div` with the data returned from the server (line 22), centers the element horizontally over the main window and 250 pixels from the top edge (line 23), and finally shows the `div`, which up until now has been hidden (line 24).

There's one last thing to do: the floated div has a "Close" link that should make it disappear, so line 26 binds a very simple **click** handler to it. Finally, **showMovieInfo** returns **false** (line 27). Why? Because the handler was called as the result of clicking on a link (<a>) element, we need to return **false** to suppress the default behavior associated with that action, namely following the link. (For the same reason, the "Close" link's **click** handler returns **false** in line 31.)

With so many different functions to call for even a simple example, it can be hard to trace the flow of control when debugging. While you can always use **console.log(**_string_**)** to write messages to your browser's JavaScript console window, it's easy to forget to remove these in production, and as Chapter 8 describes, such "`printf` debugging" can be slow, inefficient and frustrating. In Section 6.7 we'll introduce a better way by creating tests with Jasmine.

Lastly, there is one caveat we need to mention which could arise when you use JavaScript to dynamically create new elements at runtime, although it didn't arise in this particular example. We know that **$('.myClass').on('click',**_func_**)** will bind _func_ as the click handler for all current elements that match CSS class `myClass`. But if you then use JavaScript to create new elements matching `myClass` _after_ the initial page load and initial call to **on**, those elements won't have the handler bound to them, because **on** can only bind handlers to already-existing elements.

A common solution to this problem is to take advantage of a jQuery mechanism that allows an ancestor element to delegate event handling to a descendant, by using **on**'s polymorphism: **$('body').on('click','.myClass',**_func_**)** binds the HTML body element (which always exists) to the `click` event, but _delegates_ the event to any descendant matching the selector `.myClass`. Since the delegation check is done each time an event is processed, new elements matching `.myClass` will "automagically" have _func_ bound as their click handler when created.

Summary of AJAX:

- To create an AJAX interaction, figure out what what elements will acquire new behaviors, what new elements may need to be constructed to support the interaction or display responses, and so on.

- An AJAX interaction will usually involve three pieces of code: the handler that initiates the request, the callback that receives the response, and the code in the **document.ready** function (setup function) to bind the handler. It's more readable to do each in a separate named function rather than providing anonymous functions.

- Just as we did in the example of Section 6.5, for graceful degradation, any page elements used _only_ in AJAX interactions should be constructed in your setup function(s), rather than being included on the HTML page itself.

- Both interactive debuggers such as Firebug or the JavaScript consoles in Google Chrome and Safari and "`printf` debugging" using **console.log()** can help you find JavaScript problems, but a better way is through testing, which we show how to do in Section 6.7.

■ *Elaboration: Event-driven programming*

The programming model in which operations specify a completion callback rather than wait-ing for completion to occur is called **event-driven programming**. As you might conclude from the number of handlers and callbacks in this simple example, event-driven programs are considered harder to write and debug than **task-parallel** programs such as Rails apps, in which separate machinery in the app server effectively creates multiple copies of our app to handle multiple simultaneous users. Of course, behind the scenes, the operating system is switching among those tasks just as programmers do manually in JavaScript: when one user's "copy" of the app is blocked waiting for a response from the database, for example, another user's copy is allowed to make progress, and the first copy gets "called back" when the database response arrives. In this sense, event-driven and task-parallel programming are duals, and emerging standards such as WebWorkers[16] enable task parallelism in JavaScript by allowing different copies of a JavaScript program to run simultaneously on different operat-ing system threads. However, JavaScript itself lacks concurrency abstractions such as Java's **synchronized** and inter-thread communication, so concurrency must be managed explicitly by the application.

Self-Check 6.6.1. *In line 13 of Figure 6.15, why did we write* **MoviePopup.showMovieInfo** *instead of* **MoviePopup.showMovieInfo()***?*

◇ The former is the actual function, which is what **ajax** expects as its **success** property, whereas the latter is a *call* to the function. ■

Self-Check 6.6.2. *In line 33 of Figure 6.15, why did we write* **$(MoviePopup.setup)** *rather than* **$('MoviePopup.setup')** *or* **$(MoviePopup.setup())***?*

◇ We need to pass the actual function to **$()**, not its name or the result of calling it. ■

Self-Check 6.6.3. *Continuing Self-Check 6.6.2, if we had accidentally called* **$('MoviePopup.setup')***, would the result be a syntax error or legal but unintended behavior?*

◇ Recall that **$()** is overloaded, and when called with a string, it tries to interpret the string as HTML markup if it contains any angle brackets or a CSS selector otherwise. The latter applies in this case, so it would return an empty collection, since there are no elements whose tag is MoviePopup and whose CSS class is setup. ■

6.7 Testing JavaScript and AJAX

Even our simple AJAX example has many moving parts. In this section we show how to test it using Jasmine, an open-source JavaScript TDD framework developed by Pivotal Labs. Jasmine is designed to mimic RSpec and support the same TDD practices RSpec supports. The rest of this section assumes you've read Chapter 8 or are otherwise proficient with TDD and RSpec; as Figure 6.17 shows, we will reuse all those TDD concepts in Jasmine.

To start using Jasmine, add **gem 'jasmine'** to your Gemfile and run bundle as usual, then run the commands in Figure 6.18 from your app's root directory. For esoteric reasons, we can't run a completely empty Jasmine test suite, so create the file spec/javascripts/sanity_check_spec.js containing the following code:

http://pastebin.com/gD120Ena

```
1  describe('Jasmine sanity check', function() {
2    it('works', function() {  expect(true).toBe(true); });
3  });
```

What	RSpec/Ruby	Jasmine/JavaScript
Libraries	`rspec, rspec-rails` gems	`jasmine` gem, `jasmine-jquery` add-on
Setup	`rails generate rspec:install`	`rails generate jasmine:install`
Test files	`spec/models/, spec/ controllers/, spec/helpers`	`spec/javascripts/`
Naming conventions	`spec/models/movie_spec.rb` contains tests for `app/models/movie.rb`	`spec/javascripts/movie_popup_spec.js` contains tests for `app/assets/javascripts/ movie_popup.js`; `spec/javascripts/ moviePopupSpec.js` contains tests for `app/ assets/javascripts/moviePopup.js`
Configuration file	`.rspec`	`spec/javascripts/support/jasmine.yml`
Run all tests	`rake spec`	`rake jasmine`, then visit `http://localhost:8888`; or `rake jasmine:ci` to run once using Selenium/Webdriver and capture the output; or use `jasmine-headless-webkit`[17] to run from command line with no browser

Figure 6.17: Comparison of setting up and using Jasmine and RSpec. All paths are relative to the app root and all commands should be run from the app root. As you can see, the main difference is the use of `lower_snake_case` for filenames and method names in Ruby, versus `lowerCamelCase` in JavaScript.

http://pastebin.com/YPssaaXU

```
1  rails generate jasmine:install
2  mkdir spec/javascripts/fixtures
3  curl https://raw.githubusercontent.com/velesin/jasmine-jquery/master/lib/
       jasmine-jquery.js > spec/javascripts/helpers/jasmine-jquery.js
4  git add spec/javascripts
```

Figure 6.18: Creating the Jasmine-related directories in your app. Line 1 creates a `spec/javascripts` directory where our tests will go, with subdirectories `support` and `helper` analogous to RSpec's setup (Section 8.2). Line 2 adds a subdirectory for fixtures (Section 8.5). Line 3 installs an add-on to Jasmine that provides extra support for testing jQuery-based code and for using fixtures. Line 4 adds these new JavaScript TDD files to your project.

To run tests, type `rake jasmine`, and once it's running browse to `http://localhost:8888` to see the test results. From now on, when we change any code in `app/assets/javascripts` or tests in `spec/javascripts`, just reload the browser page to rerun all the tests.

Testing AJAX code must address two problems, and if you have read about TDD in Chapter 8, you're already familiar with the solutions to both. First, just as we did in Section 8.6, we must be able to "stub out the Internet" by intercepting AJAX calls, so that we can return "canned" AJAX responses and test our JavaScript code in isolation from the server. We will solve this problem using stubs. Second, our JavaScript code expects to find certain elements on the rendered page, but as we just saw, when running Jasmine tests the browser is viewing the Jasmine reporting page rather than our app. Happily, we can use fixtures to test JavaScript code that relies on the presence of certain DOM elements on the page, just as we used them in Section 8.5 to test Rails app code that relies on the presence of certain items in the database.

Figure 6.19 gives an overview of Jasmine for RSpec users. We will walk through five happy-path Jasmine specs for the popup-window functionality developed in Section 6.6. While these tests are hardly exhaustive even for the happy path, our goal is to illustrate Jasmine testing techniques generally and the use of Jasmine stubs and fixtures in AJAX testing specifically.

The basic structure of Jasmine test cases is immediately evident in Figure 6.21: like RSpec, Jasmine uses **it** to specify a single example and nestable **describe** blocks to group related sets of examples. Just as in RSpec, **describe** and **it** take a block of code as an argument, but whereas in Ruby code blocks are delimited by **do. . . end**, in JavaScript they are anonymous functions (functions without a name) of zero arguments. The punctuation sequence **})**; is so prevalent because **describe** and **it** are JavaScript functions of two arguments, the second of which is a function of no arguments.

The **describe('setup')** examples check that the **MoviePopup.setup** function correctly creates the `#movieInfo` container but keeps it hidden from display. **toExist** and **toBeHidden** are expectation matchers provided by the Jasmine-jQuery add-on. Since Jasmine loads all your JavaScript files before running any examples, the call to **setup** (line 34 of Figure 6.15) occurs before our tests run; hence it's reasonable to test whether that function did its work.

The **describe('AJAX call to server')** examples are more interesting because they use stubs and fixtures to isolate our client-side AJAX code from the server with which it communicates. Figure 6.20 summarizes the stubs and fixtures available in Jasmine and Jasmine-jQuery. Like RSpec, Jasmine allows us to run test setup and teardown code using **beforeEach** and **afterEach**. In this set of examples, our setup code loads the HTML fixture shown in Figure 6.22, to mimic the environment the **getMovieInfo** handler would see if it was called after movie list was displayed. The fixtures functionality is provided by Jasmine-jQuery; each fixture is loaded inside of `div#jasmine-fixtures`, which is inside of `div#jasmine_content` on the main Jasmine page, and all the fixtures are cleared out after each spec to preserve test independence.

The first example (line 12 of Figure 6.21) checks that the AJAX call uses the correct movie URL derived from the table. To do this, it uses Jasmine's **spyOn** to stub out the **$.ajax** function. Like RSpec's **stub**, this call *replaces* any existing function of the same name, so when we manually **trigger** the click action on the (only) a element in the `#movies` table, if all is working well we should expect our spy function to have been called. Because in JavaScript it's common for functions to be the values of object properties, **spyOn** takes two

Self-checking?
`rake jasmine:ci` runs the Jasmine suite just once using Webdriver and collects the output, and the (faster) `jasmine-headlesswebkit`[18] or the Jasmine-Rails[19] gem run tests without the overhead of running a browser. Either method would work in an automated continuous integration (CI) environment (Section 12.3) where there's no human watching the test results on the browser page.

Structure of test cases

- **it("does something", function() {...})**
  Specifies a single test (spec) by giving a descriptive name and a function that performs the test.

- **describe("behaviors", function(){...})**
  Collects a related set of specs; the function body consists of calls to **it**, **beforeEach**, and **afterEach**. **describe**s can be nested.

- **beforeEach** and **afterEach**
  Setup/teardown functions that are run before each **it** block within the same **describe** block. As with RSpec, if **describe**s are nested, all **beforeEach** are run from the outside in, and all **afterEach** from the inside out.

Expectations

An expectation in a spec takes the form **expect(*object*).*expectation*** or **expect(*object*).not.*expectation***
Commonly used expectations built into Jasmine:

- **toEqual(*val*), toBeTruthy(), toBeFalsy()**
  Test for equality using ==, or that an expression evaluates to Boolean true or false.

Commonly used expectations provided by the Jasmine jQuery add-on—in this case, the argument of **expect** should be a jQuery-wrapped element or set of elements:

- **toBeSelected(), toBeChecked(), toBeDisabled(), toHaveValue(stringValue)**
  Expectations on input elements in forms.

- **toBeVisible(), toBeHidden()**
  Hidden is true if the element has zero width and height, if it is a form input with `type="hidden"`, or if the element or one of its ancestors has the CSS property `display: none`.

- **toExist(), toHaveClass(*class*), toHaveId(*id*), toHaveAttr(*attrName,attrValue*)**
  Tests various attributes and characteristics of an element.

- **toHaveText(*stringOrRegexp*), toContainText(*string*)**
  Tests if the element's text exactly matches the given string or regexp, or contains the given substring.

Figure 6.19: A partial summary of a *small subset* of commonly used features in Jasmine and Jasmine-jQuery, following the structure of Figures 8.17 and 8.18 and extracted from the complete Jasmine documentation[22] and Jasmine jQuery add-on[23] documentation.

Stubs (Spies)

- **spyOn(***obj***, 'func')**
  Creates and returns a spy (mock) of an existing function, which must be a function-valued property of *obj* named by `func`. The spy *replaces* the existing function.

- **calls** is a property of a spy that tracks calls that have been made to it, and the array **args[]** of the arguments of each call.

The following modifiers can be called on a spy to control its behavior:

- **and.returnValue(***value***)**

- **and.throwError(exception)**

- **and.callThrough()**

- **and.callFake(***func***)**

  func must be a function of zero arguments, though it has access to the arguments with which the spy was called via *spy*.**calls.mostRecent().args[]**, and can call other functions using these arguments.

Fixtures and factories (requires `jasmine-jquery`)

- **sandbox({class: 'myClass', id: 'myId'})**
  Creates an empty `div` with the given HTML attributes, if any; default is an empty `div` with no CSS class and an ID of `sandbox`. An alternative way to create the argument to **setFixtures** that avoids putting literal HTML strings into your test code.

- **loadFixtures("***file***.html")**
  Load HTML content from in `spec/javascripts/fixtures/`*file*`.html` and put it inside a `div` with ID `jasmine-fixtures`, which is cleaned out between test cases.

- **setFixtures(***HTMLcontent***)**
  Create a fixture directly instead of loading it from a file. *HTMLcontent* can be a literal string of HTML such as **<p class="foo">text</p>** or a jQuery-wrapped element such as **$('<p class="foo">text</p>')**.

- **getJSONFixture("***file***.json")**
  Returns the JSON object in `spec/javascripts/fixtures/`*file*`.json`. Useful for storing mock data to simulate the result of an AJAX call without having to put literal JSON objects into your test code.

Figure 6.20: Continuation of Figure 6.19 describing stubs (*spies* in Jasmine) and fixtures.

http://pastebin.com/zhQw7uUd

```
1  describe('MoviePopup', function() {
2    describe('setup', function() {
3      it('adds popup Div to main page', function() {
4        expect($('#movieInfo')).toExist();
5      });
6      it('hides the popup Div', function() {
7        expect($('#movieInfo')).toBeHidden();
8      });
9    });
10   describe('clicking on movie link', function() {
11     beforeEach(function() { loadFixtures('movie_row.html'); });
12     it('calls correct URL', function() {
13       spyOn($, 'ajax');
14       $('#movies a').trigger('click');
15       expect($.ajax.calls.mostRecent().args[0]['url']).toEqual('/movies/1');
16     });
17     describe('when successful server call', function() {
18       beforeEach(function() {
19         var htmlResponse = readFixtures('movie_info.html');
20         spyOn($, 'ajax').and.callFake(function(ajaxArgs) {
21           ajaxArgs.success(htmlResponse, '200');
22         });
23         $('#movies a').trigger('click');
24       });
25       it('makes #movieInfo visible', function() {
26         expect($('#movieInfo')).toBeVisible();
27       });
28       it('places movie title in #movieInfo', function() {
29         expect($('#movieInfo').text()).toContain('Casablanca');
30       });
31     });
32   });
33 });
```

Figure 6.21: Five happy-path Jasmine specs for the AJAX code developed in Section 6.6. Lines 2–9 check whether the MoviePopup.setup function correctly sets up the floating div that will be used to display movie info. Lines 10–32 check the behavior of the AJAX code without actually calling the RottenPotatoes server by stubbing around the AJAX call.

http://pastebin.com/1PdEwxnQ

```
1  <table id="movies">
2    <tbody>
3      <tr class="adult">
4        <td>Casablanca</td>
5        <td>PG</td>
6        <td><a href="/movies/1">More about Casablanca</a></td>
7      </tr>
8    </tbody>
9  </table>
```

Figure 6.22: This HTML fixture mimics a row of the #movies table generated by the RottenPotatoes list-of-movies view (Figure 4.6); it goes in spec/javascripts/fixtures/movie_row.html. You can generate such fixtures by copy-and-pasting HTML code from "View Source" in the browser, or for source that was generated dynamically by JavaScript (such as the "Hide adult movies" checkbox), by inspecting $('#movieInfo').html() in the JavaScript console. Fallacies and Pitfalls describes a way to prevent such fixtures from getting out of sync if you change your app's views.

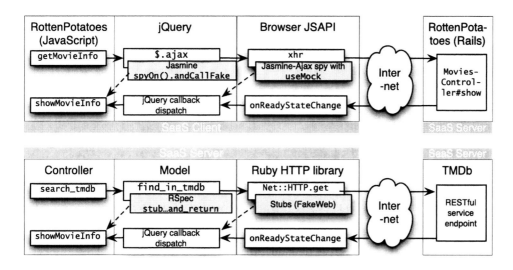

Figure 6.23: Top: Normally, our **getMovieInfo** function calls jQuery's ajax, which calls xhr in the browser's JSAPI, which sends the request to the server. The server's reply triggers callback logic in the browser's JSAPI, which calls an internal jQuery method that eventually calls our **showMovieInfo** callback. If we stub the ajax function, we can cause showMovieInfo to be called immediately; we can also stub "farther away" by stubbing xhr (using the Jasmine-Ajax plugin), causing the jQuery internal dispatcher to be called immediately. Bottom: Graphical representation of the discussion accompanying Figure 8.16 in Section 8.6.

http://pastebin.com/pnTj5S5c

```
1  <p>Casablanca is a classic and iconic film starring
2     Humphrey Bogart and Ingrid Bergman.</p>
3  <a href="" id="closeLink">Close</a>
```

Figure 6.24: This HTML fixture mimics the ajax response from the movies controller show action; it goes in spec/javascripts/fixtures/movie_info.html.

arguments, an object (**$**) and the name of the function-valued property of that object on which to spy (**'ajax'**).

Line 15 looks complex, but it's straightforward. Each Jasmine spy remembers the arguments passed to it in each of its calls, e.g. **calls.mostRecent()**, and as you recall from the explanation in Section 6.6, a *real* call to the AJAX function takes a single object (lines 9–15 of Figure 6.15) whose **url** property is the URL to which the AJAX call should go. Line 15 of the spec is simply checking the value of this URL. In effect, it's testing whether **$(this).attr('href')** is the correct JavaScript code to extract the AJAX URL from the table.

Figure 6.23 shows the similarity between the challenges of stubbing the Internet for testing AJAX and stubbing the Internet for testing code in a Service-Oriented Architecture (Section 8.6). As you can see, in both scenarios, the decision of where to stub depends on how much of the stack we want to exercise in our tests.

Line 19 reads in a fixture that will take the place of the ajax response from the movies controller show action, see Figure 6.24. In lines 20–22 we see the use fo the **callFake** function to not only intercept an AJAX call, but also to fake a successful response using the fixture. This and the triggering of the AJAX call (line 23) is repeated for each of the following two tests which check that both the **#movieInfo** popup is visible (line 26) and that it contains text from the movie description (line 29).

http://pastebin.com/9rsFCnwE

```
1  describe('element sanitizer', function() {
2    it('removes IMG tags from evil HTML', function() {
3      setFixtures(sandbox({class: 'myTestClass'}));
4      $('.myTestClass').text("Evil HTML! <img src='http://evil.com/xss'>");
5      $('.myTestClass').sanitize();
6      expect($('.myTestClass').text()).not.toContain('<img');
7    });
8  });
```

Figure 6.25: Jasmine-jQuery's sandbox method creates a new HTML `div` with the given attributes; its `id` defaults to `sandbox` **if not given. Lines 4–5 use the sandbox-created element. The sandbox can be used to temporarily contain elements constructed in a factory-like way without "polluting" the test code with HTML markup.**

This concise introduction, along with the summary tables in this section, should get you started using BDD for your JavaScript code. The best sources of complete documentation for these tools are the Jasmine documentation[24] and the Jasmine jQuery add-on[25] documentation.

Summary of Jasmine BDD for JavaScript:

- Like RSpec, Jasmine specs are anonymous functions accompanied by a descriptive string. They are introduced by the Jasmine function **it**, can be grouped with (nested) **describe** blocks that have associated **beforeEach** and **afterEach** (test setup and teardown) calls.

- **spyOn** can be used to stub an existing method by replacing it with a spy. The spy's behavior can be controlled with functions like **and.callThrough**, **and.returnValue**, and so on, as Figure 6.20 shows.

- Jasmine-jQuery's HTML fixtures can provide both the "before" content for triggering an AJAX request and the "after" content for testing the results of a successful or failed AJAX request.

■ *Elaboration: Why no Jasmine specs for client-side-only code?*

We didn't include specs for the client-side-only example in Section 6.5 for the same reason we didn't write view specs in Chapter 8: a widespread practice is to test client-side view behaviors with integration or acceptance level tests, such as Cucumber scenarios using Webdriver (Section 7.6).

■ *Elaboration: Testing client-side form validation*

A common JavaScript use case is to validate entries in a form as the user types, before the form can be submitted. You can test such self-validating forms by creating an HTML fixture representing a form or part of a form, using *element*.**val()** to set the value of one or more form inputs, and triggering *element*.**blur()** to cause the element to lose focus, simulating the user's pressing the Tab key or using the mouse to navigate to a different form field. You can then either check that the other form fields were properly updated with the new value (by inspecting their *element*.**val()**) or spy on the validation function with **.and.callThrough()** to ensure that it is called as result of blur.

■ *Elaboration: Fixtures or factories?*

As Section 8.5 explains, in Rails apps it's often preferable to use a factory to create necessary test doubles "in place" rather than specifying fixtures. So why do we describe the use of fixtures rather than factories for AJAX testing? One reason is that the tradeoff is different in JavaScript. In the Rails app, fixtures are loaded into the database before tests are run, and various ActiveRecord methods such as **find** may behave differently when different fixtures are present; therefore fixtures may break test Independence. Factories are an appealing alternative in Rails because gems such as FactoryGirl make it easy to instantiate test doubles "just in time" in each test that needs them. In Jasmine, to substitute an HTML "factory" for HTML fixtures, we would use **$("")** to create inline HTML elements, but many developers view this as undesirable because mixing HTML markup with JavaScript test code makes the latter hard to read. Jasmine-jQuery provides some simple support for using factories without excessively polluting your test code with HTML markup, as Figure 6.25 shows, but in general we see that fixtures for AJAX testing avoid some of the pitfalls of fixtures for Rails testing. They do, however, introduce a pitfall of their own—the possibility of getting "out of sync" with the app's views. See Fallacies and Pitfalls for a discussion of this pitfall and its solution.

Self-Check 6.7.1. *Jasmine-jQuery also supports* **toContain** *and* **toContainText** *to check if a string of text or HTML occurs within an element. In line 7 of Figure 6.21, why would it be* incorrect *to substitute* **.not.toContain('<div id="movieInfo"></div>')** *for* **toBe-Hidden()***?*

◇ A hidden element is not visible, but it still contains the text or HTML associated with the element. Hence **toContain**-style matchers can be used to test the *content* of an element but not its *visibility*. In addition, there are many ways for an element to be hidden—its CSS could include `display:none`, it could have zero width and height, or its ancestor could be hidden—and the **toBeHidden()** matcher checks all of these. ■

Self-Check 6.7.2. *Like RSpec, Jasmine supports* **and.returnValue()** *for returning a canned value from a stub. In Figure 6.21, why why did we have to write* **and.callFake** *to pass* **ajaxArgs** *to a function as the result of stubbing* **ajax**, *rather than simply writing* **and.returnValue(ajaxArgs)***?*

◇ Remember that AJAX calls are asynchronous. It's *not* the case that the **$.ajax** call returns data from the server: normally, it returns immediately, and sometime later, your callback is called with the data from from the server. **and.callFake** simulates this behavior. ■

6.8 Single-Page Apps and JSON APIs

Google Maps was an early example of the emerging category called client-side single-page apps (SPAs). In a SPA, after the initial page load from the server, all interaction appears to the user to occur without any page reloads. While we won't develop a full SPA in this section, we will show the techniques necessary to do so.

So far, we have concentrated on using JavaScript to enhance server-centric SaaS apps; since HTML has long been the *lingua franca* of content served by those apps, rendering a partial and using JavaScript to insert the "ready-made" partial into the DOM was a sensible way to proceed. But with SPAs, it's more common for client-side code to request some "raw" data from the server, and use that data to construct or modify DOM elements. How can a Rails app return raw data rather than HTML markup to JavaScript client code?

```
1  Review.first.to_json
2  #  =>  "{\"created_at\":\"2012-10-01T20:44:42Z\",  \"id\":1,  \"movie_id\":1,
3     \"moviegoer_id\":2,\"potatoes\":3,\"updated_at\":\"2013-07-28T18:01:35Z\"}"
```

Figure 6.26: Rails' built-in to_json can serialize simple ActiveRecord objects by calling itself recursively on each attribute of the model. As you can see, it doesn't traverse associations—the review's movie_id and moviegoer_id are serialized to integers, not to the Movie and Moviegoer objects to which the integer foreign keys refer. You can effect more sophisticated serialization by overriding to_json in your ActiveRecord models.

One simple mechanism is for the controller action to use **render :text** to return a plain string. But if we need to send structured data to the client, we face the same problem that we solved using a relational database in Section 2.6—how to "freeze-dry" the data so that its structure can be "reconstituted" correctly at the client, that is, how to **serialize** and subsequently **deserialize** the data.

In the early days of SPAs, XML seemed a promising choice for a serialization format. The X in AJAX stands for XML, and Section 8.1 shows a simple example of data returned from a server in XML format. But although XML looks simple, the full XML specification has many quirks that make a fully compliant parser complex and challenging to write. While most major browsers have XML parsers built in, their JSAPIs are incompatible, and jQuery doesn't provide any façade for them as it does for DOM manipulation. Even lightweight XML parsers such as Sax-JS[26] add about 1300 LOC to your JavaScript app, and don't provide convenient access to the DOM.

An appealing alternative is therefore JSON, the JavaScript Object Notation that we met in Figure 6.3. It's much simpler than XML but sufficient for representing many apps' data structures, and has become so popular that many RESTful APIs can serve either JSON or XML: you specify which one you want either by calling a different endpoint (URL) for each format or by passing a parameter in the REST API call. Since the JSON format is a proper subset of JavaScript's built-in object notation, we could in principle just write **var e=eval(j)** to deserialize a JSON-encoded string **j** into a "live" JavaScript object **e**. In practice, modern browsers' JSAPIs include a function **JSON.parse** which is not only much faster than **eval** but also safer: whereas **eval** will evaluate arbitrary (untrusted and possibly evil) JavaScript code, **JSON.parse** will raise an error if asked to parse anything other than valid JSON data structures. (JSONLint, listed in Figure 6.4, validates the syntax of JSON expressions.)

To use JSON in our client-side code, we must address three questions:

1. How do we get the server app to generate JSON in response to AJAX requests, rather than rendering HTML view templates or partials?

2. How does the client specify that it expects a JSON response, and how does it use the JSON response data to modify the DOM?

3. When testing AJAX requests that expect JSON responses, how can we use fixtures to "stub out the server" and test these behaviors in isolation, as we did in Section 6.7?

The first question is easy. If you have control over the server code, your Rails controller actions can emit JSON rather than XML or a Haml template by using **render :json=>**object, which sends a JSON representation of an object back to the client as the single response from the controller action. Like rendering a template, you are only allowed a single call to **render** *http://pastebin.com/6cUbpbfY*

```
 1   var MoviePopupJson = {
 2     // 'setup' function omitted for brevity
 3     getMovieInfo: function() {
 4       $.ajax({type: 'GET',
 5               dataType: 'json',
 6               url: $(this).attr('href'),
 7               success: MoviePopupJson.showMovieInfo
 8               // 'timeout' and 'error' functions omitted for brevity
 9              });
10       return(false);
11     }
12     ,showMovieInfo: function(jsonData, requestStatus, xhrObject) {
13       // center a floater 1/2 as wide and 1/4 as tall as screen
14       var oneFourth = Math.ceil($(window).width() / 4);
15       $('#movieInfo').
16         css({'left': oneFourth,  'width': 2*oneFourth, 'top': 250}).
17         html($('<p>' + jsonData.description + '</p>'),
18              $('<a id="closeLink" href="#"></a>')).
19         show();
20       // make the Close link in the hidden element work
21       $('#closeLink').click(MoviePopupJson.hideMovieInfo);
22       return(false);  // prevent default link action
23     }
24     // hideMovieInfo omitted for brevity
25   };
```

Figure 6.27: **This version of MoviePopup expects a JSON rather than HTML response (line 5), so the success function uses the returned JSON data structure to create new HTML elements inside the popup** div **(lines 17–19; observe that jQuery DOM-manipulation functions such as append can take multiple arguments of distinct pieces of HTML to create). The functions omitted for brevity are the same as in Figure 6.15.**

per action, so all the response data for a given controller action must be packed into a single JSON object.

render :json works by calling **to_json** on *object* to create the string to send back to the client. The default implementation of **to_json** can serialize simple ActiveRecord objects, as Figure 6.26 shows.

To make an AJAX call that expects a JSON-encoded response, we just ensure that the argument object passed to **$.ajax** includes a **dataType** property whose value is the string json, as Figure 6.27 shows. The presence of this property tells jQuery to automatically call **JSON.parse** on the returned data, so you don't have to do so yourself.

How can we test this code without calling the server every time? Happily, Jasmine-jQuery's fixture mechanism allows us to specify JSON fixtures as well as HTML fixtures, as Figure 6.28 shows.

Of course, we must also arrange for the server to return a JSON object, as discussed above.

http://pastebin.com/sq6FASzh

```
1  describe('MoviePopupJson', function() {
2    describe('successful AJAX call', function() {
3      beforeEach(function() {
4        loadFixtures('movie_row.html');
5        var jsonResponse = getJSONFixture('movie_info.json');
6        spyOn($, 'ajax').and.callFake(function(ajaxArgs) {
7          ajaxArgs.success(jsonResponse, '200');
8        });
9        $('#movies a').trigger('click');
10     });
11     // 'it' clauses are same as in movie_popup_spec.js
12   });
13 });
```

Figure 6.28: Jasmine-jQuery expects to find fixture files containing `.json` **data in** `spec/javascripts/fixtures/json`.
After executing line 5, jsonResponse will contain the actual JavaScript object (not the raw JSON string!) that will get passed to the success handler.

Summary of Single-Page Apps:

- Whereas JavaScript-enhanced traditional SaaS apps will typically render complete chunks of HTML (for example, using partials) that the client will simply "plug into" the current HTML page, SPAs will usually receive structured data from one or more services and use that data to synthesize new content or modify existing content on the page.

- JSON's simplicity and its natural fit with JavaScript are rapidly making it the preferred format for interchanging structured data in SPAs. Rails can serialize simple ActiveRecord models to JSON with **render :json=>** *object*, but you can override ActiveRecord's **to_json** method to serialize arbitrarily complex data structures.

- Setting the **dataType** property to `"json"` in an **$.ajax** call tells jQuery to automatically deserialize the server's response data into a JSON object.

- A spy that returns a JSON fixture can be used to simulate a server's response in testing a SPA, allowing Jasmine tests to be isolated from the remote server(s) the SPA relies on.

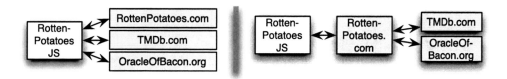

Figure 6.29: Architecture of in-browser SPAs that retrieve assets from multiple distinct services. Left: If the JavaScript code was served from RottenPotatoes.com, the default *same-origin policy* that browsers implement for JavaScript will forbid the code from making AJAX calls to servers in other domains. The *cross-origin resource sharing* (CORS) specification relaxes this restriction but is only supported by very recent browsers. Right: in the traditional SPA architecture, a single server serves the JavaScript code and interacts with other remote services. This arrangement respects the same-origin policy and also allows the main server to do additional work on behalf of the client if needed.

■ *Elaboration: Other ways to stub out the Internet for AJAX*

Section 8.6 discusses how stubbing the Internet to isolate tests from external services can be done either "near the client" or "far from the client." In Section 6.7 we stubbed "near the client" by stubbing **$.ajax** and forcing it to immediately call the **success** function rather than allowing it to proceed with the external HTTP request. This technique is similar to how we stubbed **find_in_tmdb** in Section 8.6 to return a value immediately rather than allowing it to make a real HTTP request. An alternative, which would more thoroughly exercise the code that handles the actual AJAX server responses, is to stub at the network level, just as FakeWeb does for Rails apps. Just as FakeWeb lets you provide "canned" XML or HTML responses based on the arguments of an XHR call, jasmine-ajax[27], a Jasmine extension from Pivotal Labs, lets you provide "canned" XML, HTML or JSON responses to AJAX XHR calls that are used instead of allowing the XHR call to proceed. You can then spy on the handler functions **success, failure, timeout,** and so on passed to **$.ajax** to make sure the correct handler is called depending on the server's response.

Self-Check 6.8.1. *In Figure 6.28 showing the use of a JSON fixture, why do we* also *still need the HTML fixture to be loaded in line 4?*

◇ Line 9 tries to trigger the click handler for an element matching #movies a, and if we don't load the HTML fixture representing a row of the movies table, no such element will exist. (Indeed, the **MoviePopupJson.setup** function tries to bind a click handler on this element, so that would also fail.) This is an example of using both an HTML fixture to simulate the user clicking on a page element and a JSON fixture to simulate a successful response from the server in response to that click. ■

■ *Elaboration: Same-origin policy*

You can also arrange for your SPA to communicate with a RESTful server façade (Section 11.6), as Figure 6.29 shows. You might do this if your SPA relies on content from multiple sites: for security, JavaScript browser apps are bound by a *same origin policy*, which says that a JavaScript app can only make AJAX requests to the same origin (scheme, host name, and port number, as described in Section 2.2) from which the app itself was served.

6.9   Fallacies and Pitfalls

 Fallacy: **AJAX will surely improve my app's responsiveness because more action happens right in the browser.**

In a carefully-engineered app, AJAX may well have the *potential* to improve responsiveness of certain interactions. However, many factors in using AJAX also work against this goal. Your JavaScript code must be fetched from the server, as must any libraries or frameworks on which it relies, such as jQuery, before any AJAX action can take place; on platforms such as mobile phones, this may incur an up-front latency that negates any later savings. Wide variation in JavaScript performance across different browser types and devices, Internet connection speeds spanning a range from 1 Mbps (smart phones) to 1000 Mbps (high-speed wired networks), and other factors beyond your control, all conspire to make overall AJAX performance effects difficult to predict; in some cases, AJAX may slow things down. Like all powerful tools, AJAX should be used with a solid understanding of precisely how and why it will improve responsiveness, rather than added on in the vague hope that it will somehow help because the app feels slow. The techniques in Chapter 12 will help you identify and resolve some common performance problems.

 Pitfall: **Creating a site that fails without JavaScript rather than being enhanced by it.**

For reasons of accessibility by people with disabilities, security, and cross-browser compatibility, a well-designed site should work *better* if JavaScript is available, but *acceptably* otherwise. For example, GitHub's pages for browsing code repos work well without JavaScript but work more smoothly and quickly with JavaScript. Try the site both ways for a great example of progressive enhancement. Tests also run faster without JavaScript: having a site for which JavaScript is optional means you can do the majority of your integration testing in the faster "headless browser" mode of Cucumber and Capybara.

 Pitfall: **Silent JavaScript failures in production code.**

When an unexpected exception occurs in your Rails code, you know it right away, as we've already seen: your app displays an ugly error page, or if you've been careful, a service like Hoptoad immediately contacts you to report the error, as we describe in Chapter 12). But JavaScript problems manifest as silent failures—the user clicks a control or loads a page, and nothing happens. These problems are especially pernicious because if they occur while an AJAX request is in progress, the **success** callback will never get called. So be warned: jQuery provides shortcuts for common uses of **$.ajax()** such as **$.get(url,data,callback)**, **$.post(url,data,callback)**, **$.load(url_and_selector)**, and **$.getJSON(url,data,callback)**, but all of these fail silently if anything goes wrong, whereas **$.ajax()** allows you to specify additional callbacks to be called in case of errors.

 Pitfall: **Silent JavaScript failures in tests.**

The "silent failure" pitfall also arises when using Jasmine: if there are syntax errors in any of your JavaScript files or specs, when you reload the browser page that runs your Jasmine specs, you may see a blank page with no hint as to where the errors are. We suggest using Doug Crockford's JSLint[28] tool, which not only finds syntax errors but also points out bad habits and the use of JavaScript mechanisms that Crockford and others consider misfeatures.

Similarly, you may accidentally load HTML fixtures that result in illegal HTML. For example, you might accidentally create a fixture containing an element whose ID duplicates an existing element, or a fixture containing improperly-nested elements or HTML syntax errors. Since fixtures are loaded into an actual page when tests are run, the results of an ill-formed page may be unpredictable or result in silent failures.

 Pitfall: **Providing only expensive server operations and relying on JavaScript to do the rest.**

If JavaScript is so powerful, why not write substantially all of the app logic in it, using the server as just a thin API to a database? For one thing, as we'll see in Chapter 12, successful scaling requires *reducing* the load on the database, and unless the APIs exposed to your JavaScript client code are carefully thought out, there's a risk of making needlessly complex database queries so that client-side JavaScript code can pick out the data it needs for each view. Second, whereas you have nearly complete control of performance (and therefore of the user experience) on the server side, you have nearly none on the client side. Because of wide variation in browser types, Internet connection speeds, and other factors beyond your control, JavaScript performance on each user's browser is largely out of your hands, making it difficult to provide consistent performance for the user experience.

 Pitfall: **Allowing HTML or JavaScript fixtures to get out of sync with the app code or each other.**

A risk of using HTML fixtures to test your AJAX functionality is that the fixtures are based on the HTML generated by your app, and if you change the app's view templates without also changing the fixtures, you may be running tests against HTML that doesn't match the true output of your app.

One solution is automation: this workflow from Pivotal Labs[29] uses RSpec (Chapter 8) to automatically create fixtures from your app's views for use in Jasmine tests. This solution also avoids another subtle problem: tests that operate on a small fixture but fail on the full-page DOM. For example, two event handlers that try to respond to the same event will probably do the wrong thing in production, but if they are only tested one at a time using separate fixtures, the unit tests will not catch this problem. Running specs using full-page "fixtures" rather than fixtures for different snippets of a page would solve this, and Pivotal's automated workflow does this in an elegant way.

 Pitfall: **Incorrect use of this in JavaScript functions.**

The value of **this** in the body of a JavaScript function is the source of much grief and confusion for programmers new to the language. In particular, after seeing a couple of examples, new programmers don't realize that the value of **this** for a particular function is not dependent on how that function is written, but on how it is called, so different calls to the same function can result in different bindings for **this**. A complete discussion of why **this** works as it does is beyond the scope of this introduction, but the To Learn More section offers some pointers for those interested in delving deeper, which will take you into the realm of how JavaScript is influenced by its ancestors Scheme and Self.

Until you understand the issue more deeply, you can make your own code safe by following the common cases we outlined, which Figure 6.11 summarizes.

⚠️   *Pitfall:* **JavaScript—the bad parts.**

> *The ++ operator was invented by [Ken] Thompson for pointer arithmetic. We now know that pointer arithmetic is bad, and we don't do it anymore; it's been implicated in buffer-overrun attacks and other evil stuff. The last popular language to include the ++ operator is C++, a language so bad it was named after this operator.*
>
> —Douglas Crockford, *Programming and Your Brain*, keynote at USENIX WebApps'12 conference

The entrepreneurial boom in which JavaScript was born was a time of ridiculous schedule pressures: LiveScript was designed, implemented, and released in a product in 10 days. As a result, the language has some widely-regarded misfeatures and pitfalls that some have compared to "gotchas" in the C language, so we urge you to use Doug Crockford's JSLint[30] tool to warn you of both potential pitfalls and opportunities to beautify your JavaScript code. This tool is preinstalled in the virtual machine image supplied with the bookware; you can run it by typing `jsl -process` *filename* at the command line. It has myriad options, which you can read about on the JSLint website[31].

Some specific pitfalls to avoid include the following:

1. The interpreter helpfully tries to insert semicolons it believes you forgot, but sometimes its guesses are wrong and result in drastic and unexpected changes in code behavior, such as the following example:

http://pastebin.com/AZk8Q4uK

```
1  // good: returns new object
2  return {
3    ok: true;
4  };
5  // bad: returns undefined, because JavaScript
6  //  inserts "missing semicolon" after return
7  return
8  {
9    ok: true;
10 };
```

One good workaround is to adopt a consistent coding style designed to make "punctuation errors" quickly visible, such as the coding style recommended for Node.js package developers[32].

2. Despite a syntax that suggests block scope—for example, the body of a for-loop inside a function gets its own set of curly braces inside which additional **var** declarations can appear—*all* variables declared with **var** in a function are visible *everywhere* throughout that function, including to any nested functions. Hence, in a common construction such as **for (var m in movieList)**, the scope of **m** is the entire function in which the for-loop appears, not just the body of the for-loop itself. The same is true for variables declared with **var** inside the loop body. This behavior, called *function scope*, was invented in Algol 60. Keeping functions short (remember SOFA from Section 9.5?) helps avoid the pitfall of block vs. function scope.

3. An **Array** is really just a object whose keys are nonnegative integers. In some JavaScript implementations, retrieving an item from a linear array is marginally faster than retrieving an item from a hash, but not enough to matter in most cases. The pitfall

is that if you try to index an array with a number that is negative or not an integer, a string-valued key will be created. That is, **a[2.1]** becomes **a["2.1"]**.

4. The comparison operators == and != perform type conversions automatically, so **'5'==5.0** is true. The operators === and !== perform comparisons without doing any conversions. This is potentially confusing because Ruby also has a === ("three-qual") operator that does something quite different.

5. Equality for arrays and hashes is based on identity and not value, so **[1,2,3]==[1,2,3]** is false. Unlike Ruby, in which the **Array** class can define its own == operator, in JavaScript you must work around these built-in behaviors, because == is part of the language.

6. Strings are immutable, so methods like **toUpperCase()** always return a new object. Hence write **s=s.toUpperCase()** if you want to replace the value of an existing variable.

7. If you call a function with more arguments than its definition specifies, the extra arguments are ignored; if you call it with fewer, the unassigned arguments are **undefined**. In either case, the array **arguments[]** (within the function's scope) gives access to all arguments that were actually passed.

8. String literals behave differently from strings created with **new String** if you try to create new properties on them, as the code excerpt below shows. The reason is that JavaScript creates a temporary "wrapper object" around **fake** to respond to **fake.newprop=1**, performs the assignment, then immediately destroys the wrapper object, leaving the "real" **fake** without any **newprop** property. You can set extra properties on strings if you create them explicitly with **new**. But better yet, don't set properties on built-in types: define your own prototype object and use composition rather than inheritance (Chapter 11) to make a string one of its properties, then set the other properties as you see fit. (This restriction applies equally to numbers and Booleans for the same reasons, but it doesn't apply to arrays because, as we mentioned earlier, they are just a special case of hashes.)

http://pastebin.com/LWxdsn3F

```
1  real = new String("foo");
2  fake = "foo";
3  real.newprop = 1;
4  real.newprop       // => 1
5  fake.newprop = 1; // BAD: silently fails since 'fake' isn't true object
6  fake.newprop       // => undefined
```

6.10 Concluding Remarks: JavaScript Past, Present and Future

JavaScript's privileged position as the client-side language of the Web has focused a lot of energy on it. Since most smart phones and tablets can now run JavaScript, source-portable mobile device apps can be created using HTML, CSS and JavaScript, rather than creating separate versions for different mobile platforms such as iOS and Android. Frameworks like PhoneGap[33] make JavaScript a productive path to creating mobile apps, especially when combined with flexible UI frameworks such as jQuery Mobile[34] or Sencha Touch. Indeed, today the main reason *not* to use JavaScript for mobile apps is insufficient performance, but because of increased reliance on JavaScript for both "Web 2.0" sites and complex SPAs such as Google Docs, developers have been focusing on both performance and productivity in JavaScript.

Performance. Just-in-time compilation (JIT) techniques and other advanced language engineering features are being brought to bear on the language, closing the performance gap with other interpreted and even some compiled languages. Over half a dozen *JavaScript engine* implementations and one compiler (Google's Closure) are available as of this writing, most of them open source, and vendors such as Microsoft, Apple, Google, and others compete on the performance of their browsers' JavaScript interpreters. Evaluating the performance of interpreted languages is tricky, since results depend on the implementation of the interpreter as well as the specific application, but benchmarks of the Box2D physics engine[35] found the JavaScript version to be 5x slower than the Java version and 10–12x slower than the C version, and found performance differences of up to a factor of three using different JavaScript interpreters. Still, JavaScript is now fast enough that in May 2011, Hewlett-Packard used it to rewrite large parts of its Palm webOS operating system. We can expect this trend to continue, because JavaScript is one of the first languages to receive attention when new hardware becomes available that could be useful for user-facing apps: for example, WebCL proposes JavaScript bindings for the OpenCL language used for programming Graphics Processing Units (GPUs).

Productivity. We saw over and over again in studying Ruby and Rails that productivity goes hand in hand with conciseness. JavaScript's syntax is hardly concise and often awkward—in part because JavaScript was always functional at heart (recall that its creator originally wanted to use Scheme as the browser scripting language) but burdened by a marketing-driven requirement to resemble the imperative language Java. CoffeeScript[36], first released in 2010, tries to restore some syntactic conciseness and beauty befitting JavaScript's better nature. A source-to-source translator compiles CoffeeScript (`.coffee`) files into `.js` files containing regular JavaScript, which are served to the browser. The Rails asset pipeline, which Section A.8 discusses further, automates this compilation so you don't need to manually generate the `.js` files or include them in your source tree. Since CoffeeScript compiles to JavaScript, it can't do anything that JavaScript doesn't already do, but it provides more concise syntactic notation for many common constructs. As an example, Figure 6.30 shows the much less noisy CoffeeScript version of the Jasmine spec in Figure 6.21.

Unfortunately, after a few years "in the wild," CoffeeScript's design has been criticized for fundamental design problems that limit its usefulness in large projects. Two major objections are its scoping of all outer variables as global[37] and a sensitivity to whitespace that results in ambiguous interpretations of source code[38], violating the "Principle of Least Surprise" that is one of the cornerstones of Ruby's design. Time will tell whether CoffeeScript will largely displace JavaScript or remain a "niche language" used only in smaller projects.

Tools for SPA developers creating JSON-centric apps are improving as well. For example, Yahoo's open-source Mojito[39] framework allows the same JavaScript code to render HTML from JSON on either the client or a Node-based server. However, there is a potential huge downside to apps taking this route: their content will be neither indexable nor searchable by search engines, without which the Web loses a great deal of its utility. There are technological solutions to this problem, but at the moment there is little discussion about them.

In addition to that disadvantage, JavaScript's single-threaded execution model, which some feel hampers productivity because it requires event-driven programming, seems un-

http://pastebin.com/gEyt3RUd

```
 1  describe 'MoviePopup', ->
 2    describe 'setup', ->
 3      it 'adds popup Div to main page', -> expect $('#movieInfo').toExist
 4      it 'hides the popup Div', -> expect $('#movieInfo').toBeHidden
 5    describe 'AJAX call to server', ->
 6      beforeEach -> loadFixtures('movie_row.html')
 7      it 'calls correct URL', ->
 8        spyOn $, 'ajax'
 9        $('#movies a').trigger 'click'
10        expect($.ajax.mostRecentCall.args[0]['url']).toEqual '/movies/1'
11      describe 'when successful', ->
12        beforeEach ->
13          @htmlResponse = readFixtures 'movie_info.html'
14          spyOn($, 'ajax').andCallFake (ajaxArgs) ->
15            ajaxArgs.success(htmlResponse, '200')
16          $('#movies a').trigger 'click'
17        it 'makes #movieInfo visible', -> expect $('#movieInfo').toBeVisible
18        it 'places movie title in #movieInfo', ->
19          expect($('#movieInfo').text).toContain 'Casablanca'
```

Figure 6.30: The CoffeeScript version of Figure 6.21. Among other differences, CoffeeScript provides the *Haskell*-like concise syntax -> for functions, uses Haml-like indentation rather than braces to indicate structure, and allows Ruby-like omission of most parentheses as well as borrowing the @ instance-variable notation to refer to properties of this. Some find the resulting code easier to read, as it has $1/3$ fewer lines and a lot less punctuation than the plain JavaScript version.

likely to change anytime soon. Some bemoan the adoption of JavaScript-based server-side frameworks such as Node, a JavaScript library that provides event-driven versions of the same POSIX (Unix-like) operating system facilities used by task-parallel code. Rails core committer Yehuda Katz summarized the opinions of many experienced programmers: when things happen in a deterministic order, such as server-side code handling a controller action in a SaaS app, a sequential and blocking model is easier to program; when things happen in an unpredictable order, such as reacting to external stimuli like user-initiated user interface events, the asynchronous model makes more sense. Your authors firmly believe that the future of software is "cloud+client" apps, and our view is that it's more important to choose the right language or framework for each job than to obsess about whether a single language or framework will become dominant for both the client and cloud parts of the app.

Finally, whereas in the early days of the Web it was common for pages to be hand-authored in HTML and CSS (perhaps using WYSIWYG authoring tools), today the vast majority of HTML is generated by frameworks like Rails. In a similar way, developments such as CoffeeScript suggest that while JavaScript will remain the *lingua franca* of browser programming, it may increasingly become a target language rather than the one in which most people code directly.

6.11 To Learn More

We covered only a small part of the language-independent DOM representation using its JavaScript API. The DOM representation itself has a rich set of data structures and traversal methods, and APIs are available for all major languages, such as the dom4j[40] library for Java and the Nokogiri[41] gem for Ruby.

Here are additional useful resources for mastering JavaScript and jQuery:

- A great presentation by Google JavaScript guru Miško Hevery: *How JavaScript works: introduction to JavaScript and Browser DOM*[42]

- Yehuda Katz[43] is an active core committer to both Rails and jQuery, among other high-profile projects. His programmer-oriented blog posts discuss tips and techniques ranging from the practical to the esoteric for both Ruby and JavaScript. In particular, he has a nice post on the subtle difference between Ruby blocks and JavaScript anonymous functions[44] and another on why **this** works the way it does in JavaScript functions[45].

- jQuery is an extremely powerful library whose potential we barely tapped. *jQuery: Novice to Ninja* (Castledine and Sharkie 2012) is an excellent reference with many examples that go far beyond our introduction.

- *JavaScript: The Good Parts* (Crockford 2008), by the creator of the JSLint[46] tool, is a highly opinionated, intellectually rigorous exposition of JavaScript, focusing uncompromisingly on the disciplined use of its good features while candidly exposing the pitfalls of its design flaws. This book is "must" reading if you plan to write entire JavaScript apps comparable to Google Docs.

- The ProgrammableWeb[47] site lists hundreds of service APIs, both RESTful and non-RESTful and serving both XML and JSON data, that you may find useful for SPAs and mashups. Some are completely open and require no authentication; others require a developer key which may be free or non-free.

E. Castledine and C. Sharkie. *jQuery: Novice to Ninja, 2nd Edition - New Kicks and Tricks*. SitePoint Books, 2012.

D. Crockford. *JavaScript: The Good Parts*. O'Reilly Media, 2008.

P. Seibel. *Coders at Work: Reflections on the Craft of Programming*. Apress, 2009. ISBN 1430219483.

Notes

[1] http://pivotal.github.com/jasmine
[2] http://angularjs.org
[3] http://www.ie6countdown.com
[4] http://jquery.org
[5] http://www.adaptivepath.com/ideas/ajax-new-approach-web-applications
[6] http://developers.google.com/closure
[7] http://yui.github.io/yuicompressor
[8] http://jsonlint.com
[9] http://guides.rubyonrails.org/v3.2.19/asset_pipeline.html
[10] http://getfirebug.org
[11] http://www.w3.org/DOM
[12] https://github.com/rails/jquery-rails
[13] http://prototypejs.org
[14] http://api.jquery.com
[15] http://api.jquery.com
[16] http://en.wikipedia.org/wiki/Web_Workers
[17] http://johnbintz.github.com/jasmine-headless-webkit/
[18] http://johnbintz.github.com/jasmine-headless-webkit/
[19] https://github.com/searls/jasmine-rails
[20] http://pivotal.github.com/jasmine
[21] http://github.com/velesin/jasmine-jquery
[22] http://pivotal.github.com/jasmine

[23]http://github.com/velesin/jasmine-jquery
[24]http://pivotal.github.com/jasmine
[25]http://github.com/velesin/jasmine-jquery
[26]http://github.com/isaacs/sax-js
[27]https://github.com/pivotal/jasmine-ajax
[28]http://jslint.com
[29]http://pivotallabs.com/javascriptspecs-bind-reality/
[30]http://jslint.com
[31]http://jslint.com
[32]https://npmjs.org/doc/coding-style.html
[33]http://phonegap.com
[34]http://jquerymobile.org
[35]http://blog.j15r.com/2011/12/for-those-unfamiliar-with-it-box2d-is.html
[36]http://coffeescript.org
[37]https://donatstudios.com/CoffeeScript-Madness
[38]http://ruoyusun.com/2013/03/17/my-take-on-coffeescript.html
[39]http://developer.yahoo.com/blogs/ydn/posts/2012/04/
[40]http://dom4j.sourceforge.net
[41]http://nokogiri.org
[42]http://misko.hevery.com/2010/07/14/how-javascript-works/
[43]http://yehudakatz.com
[44]http://yehudakatz.com/2012/01/10/javascript-needs-blocks/
[45]http://yehudakatz.com/2011/08/11/understanding-javascript-function-invocation-and-this
[46]http://jslint.com
[47]http://programmableweb.com

6.12 Suggested Projects

Project 6.1. *A disadvantage of prototype inheritance is that all object attributes (properties) are public. (Recall that in Ruby,* no *attributes are public: getter and setter methods, defined either explicitly or using* **attr_accessor***, are the only way to access attributes from outside the class.) However, we can take advantage of closures to get private attributes. Create a simple constructor for User objects that accepts a username and password, and provides a* **checkPassword** *method tells whether a supplied password is correct but disallows inspecting the actual password. This "accessors only" idiom is used throughout jQuery. (Hint: the constructor should return an object one of whose properties is a function that exploits JavaScript closures to "remember" the password initially supplied to the constructor. The returned object should* not *have a property that holds the password.)*

Project 6.2. *In the example used in Section 6.5, suppose you couldn't modify the server code to add the* adult *CSS class to rows in the* movies *table. How might you identify the rows to be hidden using only client-side JavaScript?*

Project 6.3. *Write JavaScript to create cascading menus for day, month, and year that allow the entry of valid dates only. For example, if February is selected as the month, the Day menu should only go from 1–28, unless the Year menu indicates a leap year, in which case the Day menu should go from 1–29, and so on.*

As a bonus, wrap your JavaScript in a Rails helper that results in date menus with the same menu names and option tags as the Rails' built-in helpers, making your JavaScript menus a drop-in replacement. **Note:** *it's important that the menus also work in non-JavaScript-enabled browsers; in that case, the menus should statically display 1–31 for the days of the month.*

Project 6.4. *Create the AJAX code necessary to create cascading menus based on a* **has_many** *association. That is, given Rails models A and B where A* **has_many** *Bs, the first menu in the pair should list the A choices, and when one is selected, retrieve the corresponding B choices and populate the B menu.*

Project 6.5. *Augment the validation functionality in ActiveModel (which we met in Chapter 5) to automatically generate JavaScript code that validates form inputs before the form is submitted. For example, given RottenPotatoes'* **Movie** *model asserts that a movie must have a nonblank title, JavaScript code should prevent the "Add New Movie" form from being submitted if the validation is not met, displays a helpful message to the user, and highlights the field(s) that had validation problems. Handle at least the built-in validations such as nonblank, minimum/maximum string lengths, numerical values with range constraints, and for bonus points, validations based on regular expressions.*

Project 6.6. *Following the approach of the jQuery example in Section 6.5, use JavaScript to implement a set of checkboxes for the list of movies page, one for each rating (G, PG, and so on), which when checked allow movies with that rating to stay in the list. When the page first loads, all should be checked; unchecking any of them should hide the movies with that rating.*

Project 6.7. *Extend the example of Section 6.6 so that if the user repeatedly expands and collapses the same row in the movies table, a request to the server for that movie's info is only made the first time. In other words, implement client-side JavaScript caching for the movie info retrieved on each AJAX call.*

Project 6.8. *If you visit* `twitter.com` *and the page takes more than a few seconds to load, a popup appears apologizing for the delay and suggesting you try reloading the page. Explain how you would implement this behavior using JavaScript.* **Hint:** *Remember that JavaScript code can begin executing as soon as it's loaded, whereas the* **document.ready** *function won't run until the document has been completely loaded and parsed.*

Project 6.9. *Use the JSON and jQuery techniques in this chapter to use BDD to develop the following single-page app (SPA) counterpart to RottenPotatoes, which we call LocalPotatoes. When the user enters her US postal code (called "zip code" in the US), LocalPotatoes uses the RSS feed (Really Simple Syndication) provided free by the Fandango[1] movie fan site to retrieve the names and locations of nearby movie theaters and the titles of movies playing there. This data is returned in XML, so you'll need to do some minimal XML parsing in your JavaScript code to extract the theater names and movie names. A list of theaters is displayed on the client page; when the user clicks on a theater name, the Google Maps JavaScript API[2] is used to center the map on that theater's location, and the movies showing at that theater are listed in the Movies box. Clicking on the name of a movie looks up information about it using the free Open Movie Database API[3], which can return basic results in either JSON or XML, and displays the movie's promotional artwork and overall rating by Internet Movie Database[4] users.*

Project 6.10. *Consider a site that sells a small fixed number of items, and the user just indicates how many of each item she wants by choosing a quantity from a dropdown menu next to each item name. Write unobtrusive JavaScript code that watches these dropdown menus, and every time any of them changes, updates a Total field with the total value of the order by multiplying each quantity by the appropriate item price and then summing over the results. The total field should be read-only (i.e. not user-changeable).*

Your Order

Widgets	$25.00	1 ÷	$25.00
Foobars	$16.00	3 ÷	$48.00
Veems	$3.00	9 ÷	$27.00
Total			**$100.00**

Figure 6.31: A simple shopping cart with dropdown menus to select how many of each item to purchase.

Project 6.11. *Figure 6.21 only tests the happy path spec (***describe('when successful')***) using AJAX stubbing. Add specs for the sad paths* **when server error** *and* **when timeout***.*

Part II

Software Development: Agile vs. Plan-and-Document

Niklaus Wirth (1934–) received the Turing Award in 1984 for developing a sequence of innovative programming languages, including Algol-W, Euler, Modula, and Pascal.

7 Requirements: Behavior-Driven Design and User Stories

Clearly, programming courses should teach methods of design and construction, and the selected examples should be such that a gradual development *can be nicely demonstrated.*

—Niklaus Wirth, "Program Development by Stepwise Refinement," *CACM* 14(5), May 1971

Concepts

The big concepts of this chapter are requirements elicitation, cost estimation, project scheduling, and monitoring progress.

The version of these concepts for the Agile lifecycle, which follows *Behavior-Driven Development* (*BDD*), are:

- *User stories* to elicit functional requirements.

- *Low-fidelity (Lo-Fi)* user interfaces and *storyboards* to elicit UI requirements.

- **Points** to turn user stories into cost estimates.

- *Velocity* to measure and estimate schedule.

- Using the tool *Cucumber* to transform user stories into acceptance tests.

- Using the tool *Pivotal Tracker* to track project progress, to calculate velocity, and to estimate time to milestones.

For the Plan and Document lifecycle, you will become familiar with the same concepts in a quite different format:

- Requirements elicitation via **interviewing**, *scenarios*, and *use cases*, requirements documentation via a *Software Requirements Specification* (*SRS*), and requirement fulfillment using *requirements traceability*.

- Cost estimation based on project manager experience or formulas such as *CO-COMO*, scheduling and monitoring progress using *PERT charts*, and change management using *version control systems* for documentation and schedule as well as the code.

- *Risk analysis* and management to increase chances of project being successful.

Both lifecycles illustrate the difference between *functional* versus *non-functional requirements* and **explicit** versus **implicit requirements**.

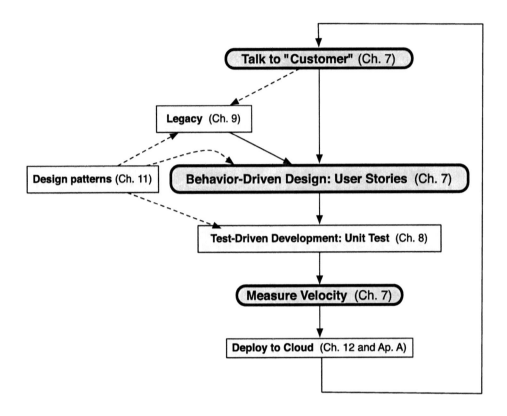

Figure 7.1: An iteration of the Agile software lifecycle and its relationship to the chapters in this book. This chapter emphasizes talking to customers as part of Behavior-Driven Design.

7.1   Introduction to Behavior-Driven Design and User Stories

Behavior-Driven Design is Test-Driven Development done correctly.

—Anonymous

Software projects fail because they don't do what customers want; or because they are late; or because they are over budget; or because they are hard to maintain and evolve; or all of the above.

The Agile lifecycle was invented to attack these problems for many common types of software. Figure 7.1 shows one iteration of the Agile lifecycle from Chapter 1, highlighting the portion covered in this chapter. As we saw in Chapter 1, the Agile lifecycle involves:

Agile stakeholders include users, customers, developers, maintenance programmers, operators, project management, ...

- Working closely and continuously with stakeholders to develop requirements and tests.

- Maintaining a working prototype while deploying new features typically every two weeks—called an *iteration*—and checking in with stakeholders to decide what to add next and to validate that the current system is what they really want. Having a working prototype and prioritizing features reduces the chances of a project being late or over budget, or perhaps increasing the likelihood that the stakeholders are satisfied with the current system once the budget is exhausted!

Unlike a plan-and-document lifecycle in Chapter 1, Agile development does not switch phases (and people) over time from development mode to maintenance mode. With Agile, you are basically in maintenance mode as soon as you've implemented the first set of features. This approach helps make the project easier to maintain and evolve.

We start the Agile lifecycle with ***Behavior-Driven Design (BDD)***. BDD asks questions about the behavior of an application *before and during development* so that the stakeholders are less likely to miscommunicate. Requirements are written down as in plan-and-document, but unlike plan-and-document, requirements are continuously refined to ensure the resulting software meets the stakeholders' desires. That is, using the terms from Chapter 1, the goal of BDD requirements is ***validation*** (build the right thing), not just ***verification*** (build the thing right).

The BDD version of requirements is ***user stories***, which describe how the application is expected to be used. They are lightweight versions of requirements that are better suited to Agile. User stories help stakeholders plan and prioritize development. Thus, like plan-and-document, you start with requirements, but in BDD user stories take the place of design documents in plan-and-document.

By concentrating on the *behavior* of the application versus the *implementation* of application, it is easier to reduce misunderstandings between stakeholders. As we shall see in the next chapter, BDD is closely tied to Test-Driven Development (TDD), which *does* test implementation. In practice they work together hand-in-hand, but for pedagogical reasons we introduce them sequentially.

User stories came from the Human Computer Interface (HCI) community. They developed them using 3-inch by 5-inch index cards or "3-by-5 cards," or in countries where metric paper sizes are used, A7 cards of 74 mm by 105 mm. (We'll see other examples of paper and pencil technology from the HCI community shortly.) These cards contain one to three sentences written in everyday nontechnical language written jointly by the customers and developers. The rationale is that paper cards are nonthreatening and easy to rearrange, thereby enhancing brainstorming and prioritizing. The general guidelines for the user stories themselves is that they must be testable, be small enough to implement in one iteration, and have business value. Section 7.3 gives more detailed guidance for good user stories.

Note that individual developers working by themselves without customer interaction don't need these 3-by-5 cards, but this "lone wolf" developer doesn't match the Agile philosophy of working closely and continuously with the customer.

We will use the RottenPotatoes app from Chapters 2 and 4 as the running example in this chapter and the next one. We start with the stakeholders, which are simple for this simple app:

- The operators of RottenPotatoes, and

- The movie fans who are end-users of RottenPotatoes.

We'll introduce a new feature in Section 7.8, but to help understand all the moving parts, we'll start with a user story for an existing feature of RottenPotatoes so that we can understand the relationship of all the components in a simpler setting. The user story we picked is to add movies to the RottenPotatoes database:

http://pastebin.com/BpmHu0Nq

```
1 | Feature: Add a movie to RottenPotatoes
2 |   As a movie fan
3 |   So that I can share a movie with other movie fans
4 |   I want to add a movie to RottenPotatoes database
```

Pastebin is a service for copying-and-pasting book code. (You need to type the URI into a browser if you're reading the print book; it's a link in ebooks.)

This user story format was developed by the startup company Connextra and is named after them; sadly, this startup is no longer with us. The format is:

http://pastebin.com/We7vY0eg

```
1  Feature name
2    As a [kind of stakeholder],
3    So that [I can achieve some goal],
4    I want to [do some task]
```

This format identifies the stakeholder since different stakeholders may describe the desired behavior differently. For example, users may want to link to information sources to make it easier to find the information while operators may want links to trailers so that they can get an income stream from the advertisers. All three clauses have to be present in the Connextra format, but they are not always in this order.

Summary of BDD and User Stories

- BDD emphasizes working with stakeholders to define the behavior of the system being developed. Stakeholders include nearly everyone: customers, developers, managers, operators, ...

- *User stories*, a device borrowed from the HCI community, make it easy for nontechnical stakeholders to help create requirements.

- *3x5 cards*, each with a user story of one to three sentences, are an easy and nonthreatening technology that lets *all* stakeholders brainstorm and prioritize features.

- The Connextra format of user stories captures the stakeholder, the stakeholder's goal for the user story, and the task at hand.

Self-Check 7.1.1. *True or False: User stories on 3x5 cards in BDD play the same role as design requirements in plan-and-document.*

◇ True. ■

■*Elaboration: User Stories and Case Analysis*

User stories represent a lightweight approach to *use-case analysis*, a term traditionally used in software engineering to describe a similar process. A full use case analysis would include the use case name; actor(s); goals of the action; summary of the use case; preconditions (state of the world before the action); steps occurring in the scenario (both the actions performed by the user and the system's responses); related use cases; and postconditions (state of the world after the action). A *use case diagram* is a type of UML diagram (see Chapter 11) with stick figures standing in for the actors, and can be used to generalize or extend use cases or to include a use case by reference. For example, if we have a use case for "user logs in" and another use case for "logged-in user views her account summary", the latter could include the former by reference, since a precondition to the second use case is that the user has logged in.

7.2 Points, Velocity, and Pivotal Tracker

One way to measure the productivity of a team would be simply to count the number of user stories completed per iteration, and then calculate the average number of stories per week. The average would then be used to decide how many stories to try to implement each iteration.

The problem with this measure is that some stories are much harder than others, leading to mispredictions. The simple solution is to rate each user story in advance on a simple integer scale. We recommend starting with a three-point scale: 1 for straightforward stories, 2 for medium stories, and 3 for very complex stories. (As you get experience with rating and completing stories, you can use a wider range.) The average is now of the number of **points** per iteration a team completes, which is called **velocity**. The **backlog** is the name of the collection of stories that have not yet been completed in this iteration.

> **Fibonacci scale** With more experience, the Fibonacci scale is commonly used: 1, 2, 3, 5, and 8. (Each new number is sum of previous two.) However, at places like Pivotal Labs, 8 is extremely rare.

Note that velocity measures work rate based on the team's self-evaluation. As long as the team rates user stories consistently, it doesn't matter whether the team is completing 5 points or 10 points per iteration. The purpose of velocity is to give all stakeholders an idea how many iterations it will take a team to add the desired set of features, which helps set reasonable expectations and reduces chances of disappointment.

Pivotal Tracker is a service that tracks user stories and velocity.

Figure 7.2 shows Tracker's UI. You start by entering user stories, which requires filling in the difficulty rating. You then prioritize the stories by placing them either into the Current panel or into the Backlog panel. The order of the stories within each panel defines their relative priority. When stories are completed, they are placed into a Done panel and Tracker suggests stories from the backlog in priority order. Another category is the Icebox panel, which contains unprioritized stories. They can stay "on ice" indefinitely, but when you're ready to start working on them, just drag them to the Current or Backlog panels.

> **Tracker Intro** Pivotal Labs has produced an excellent 3-minute video intro[5] to using Tracker.

Tracker also allows the insertion of markers of Release points in the prioritized lists of user stories. As it calculates velocity based on points completed, it also supplies the current estimate of when these software releases will actually occur. This approach is in sharp contrast to management by schedule, where a manager picks a release date and the team is expected to work hard to meet the deadline.

Another Pivotal feature that is not really a story is a *Spike*. A spike is a short investigation into a technique or problem that the teams wants explored before sitting down to do serious coding. An example would be a "spike" on recommendation algorithms. After a spike is done, the spike code must be thrown away. The spike let you know what approach you want to follow, and now you should write it correctly.

Tracker recently added a new concept to combine a collection of related user stories into a group called an *Epic*. Epics have their own panel and their own progress bar in Tracker, and can be ordered independently of the user stories in the backlog. The idea is to give software engineers the big picture of where the application is in the development process with regard to big features.

Developers do not decide when the user stories are completed. The developer pushes the Deliver button, which sends it to the Product Owner—exactly the same role as in the Scrum organization. The Product Owner tries out the user story and then either hits the Accept button that marks user story as done or hits the Reject button, which marks the story as needing to be Restarted by the developer.

Teams need a virtual commons in which to share information, and Tracker allows you to

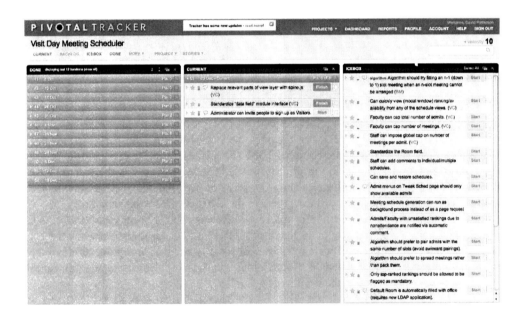

Figure 7.2: Screen image of the UI of the Pivotal Tracker service.

attach documents to user stories, which seems a perfect place for Lo-Fi sketches and design documents. Here are other good cyberspace locales your team could use to communicate and share information such as meeting notes, software architecture, and so on:

- Every GitHub repository (see Section A.7) offers a Wiki, which allows team members to jointly edit a document and add files.

- Google Docs[6] allows joint creation and viewing of drawings, presentations, spread-sheets, and text documents.

- Campfire[7] is a web-based service for password-protected online chat rooms.

Summary: To help the team manage each iteration and to predict how long the team will take to implement new features, the team assigns points to rate difficulty of user stories and tracks the team's **velocity**, or average points per iteration. Pivotal Tracker provides a service that helps prioritize and keep track of user stories and their status, calculates velocity, and predicts software development time based on the team's history.

Self-Check 7.2.1. *True or False: When comparing two teams, the one with the higher velocity is more productive.*

◇ False: Since each team assigns points to user stories, you cannot use velocity to compare different teams. However, you could look over time for a given team to see if there were iterations that were significantly less or more productive. ∎

Self-Check 7.2.2. *True or False: When you don't know how to approach a given user story, just give it 3 points.*

◇ False: A user story should not be so complex that you don't have an approach to implementing it. If they are, you should go back to your stakeholders to refactor the user story into a set of simpler tasks that you do know how to approach. ∎

7.3 SMART User Stories

What makes a good user story versus a bad one? The SMART acronym offers concrete and (hopefully) memorable guidelines: Specific, Measurable, Achievable, Relevant, and Time-boxed.

- *Specific.* Here are examples of a vague feature paired with a specific version:

  http://pastebin.com/vnUt6KLF

  ```
  1  Feature: User can search for a movie (vague)
  2  Feature: User can search for a movie by title (specific)
  ```

- *Measurable.* Adding Measurable to Specific means that each story should be testable, which implies that there are known expected results for some good inputs. An example of a pair of an unmeasurable versus measurable feature is

  http://pastebin.com/rbLcwD2f

  ```
  1  Feature:  RottenPotatoes should have good response time (unmeasurable)
  2  Feature:  When adding a movie, 99% of Add Movie pages
  3           should appear within 3 seconds (measurable)
  ```

Only the second case can be tested to see if the system fulfills the requirement.

- *Achievable.* Ideally, you implement the user story in one Agile iteration. If you are getting less than one story per iteration, then they are too big and you need to subdivide these stories into smaller ones. As mentioned above, the tool **Pivotal Tracker** measures **Velocity**, which is the rate of completing stories of varying difficulty.

- *Relevant.* A user story must have business value to one or more stakeholders. To drill down to the real business value, one technique is to keep asking "Why." Using as an example a ticket-selling app for a regional theater, suppose the proposal is to add a Facebook linking feature. Here are the "Five Whys" in action with their recursive questions and answers:

  1. Why add the Facebook feature? As box office manager, I think more people will go with friends and enjoy the show more.
  2. Why does it matter if they enjoy the show more? I think we will sell more tickets.
  3. Why do you want to sell more tickets? Because then the theater makes more money.
  4. Why does theater want to make more money? We want to make more money so that we don't go out of business.
  5. Why does it matter that theater is in business next year? If not, I have no job.

  (We're pretty sure the business value is now apparent to at least one stakeholder!)

- *Timeboxed.* Timeboxing means that you stop developing a story once you've exceeded the time budget. Either you give up, divide the user story into smaller ones, or reschedule what is left according to a new estimate. If dividing looks like it won't help, then you go back to the customers to find the highest value part of the story that you can do quickly.

  The reason for a time budget per user story is that it is extremely easy to underestimate the length of a software project. Without careful accounting of each iteration, the whole project could be late, and thus fail. Learning to budget a software project is a critical skill, and exceeding a story budget and then refactoring it is one way to acquire that skill.

One important concept expands upon the R of SMART. The **minimum viable product** (MVP) is a subset of the full set of features that when completed has business value in the real world. Not only are the stories Relevant, but the combination of all of them makes the software product viable in the marketplace. Obviously, you can't start selling the product if it's not viable, so it makes sense to give priority to the stories that will let the product be shipped. The Epic or a Release point of Pivotal Tracker can help identify the stories of the MVP.

Summary of SMART User Stories

- The **SMART** acronym captures the desirable features of a good user story: Specific, Measurable, Achievable, Relevant, and Timeboxed.

- The **Five Whys** are a technique to help you drill down to uncover the real business relevance of a user story.

Self-Check 7.3.1. *Which SMART guideline(s) does the feature below violate?*
http://pastebin.com/TuyS5mpC

```
1 | Feature: RottenPotatoes should have a good User Interface
```

◊ It is not Specific, not Measurable, not Achievable (within 1 iteration), and not Timeboxed. While business Relevant, this feature goes just one for five. ∎

Self-Check 7.3.2. *Rewrite this feature to make it SMART.*
http://pastebin.com/cdV6mjBb

```
1 | Feature: I want to see a sorted list of movies sold.
```

◊ Here is one SMART revision of this user story:
http://pastebin.com/pZMPJqPq

```
1 | Feature: As a customer, I want to see the top 10 movies sold,
2 |          listed by price, so that I can buy the cheapest ones first.
```

∎

Given user stories as the work product from eliciting requirements of customers, we can introduce a metric and tool to measure productivity.

7.4 Lo-Fi User Interface Sketches and Storyboards

We usually need to specify a user interface (UI) when adding a new feature since many SaaS applications interact with end users. Thus, part of the BDD task is often to propose a UI to match the user stories. If a user story says a user needs to login, then we need a mockup of a page that has the login. Alas, building software prototypes of user interfaces can intimidate stakeholders from suggesting improvements—just the opposite of the effect we need at this early point of the design.

What we want is the UI equivalent of 3x5 cards; engaging to the nontechnical stakeholder and encouraging trial and error, which means it must be easy to change or even discard. Just as the HCI community advocates 3x5 cards for user stories, they recommend using kindergarten tools for UI mockups: crayons, construction paper, and scissors. They call this low-tech approach to user interfaces **Lo-Fi UI** and the paper prototypes *sketches*. For example, Figure 7.3 shows a Lo-Fi sketch of the UI for adding a movie to RottenPotatoes.

Ideally, you make sketches for all the user stories that involve a UI. It may seem tedious, but eventually you are going to have to specify all the UI details when using HTML to make the real UI, and it's a lot easier to get it right with pencil and paper than with code.

Lo-Fi sketches show what the UI looks like at one instant in time. However, we also need to show how the sketches work together as a user interacts with a page. Filmmakers face a similar challenge with scenes of a movie. Their solution, which they call **storyboarding**, is to go through the entire film as if it was a comic book, with drawings for every scene. Instead of a linear sequence of images like in a movie, the storyboard for a UI is typically a tree or graph of screens driven by different user choices.

To make a storyboard, you must think about all the user interactions with a web app:

- Pages or sections of pages,

- Forms and buttons, and

- Popups.

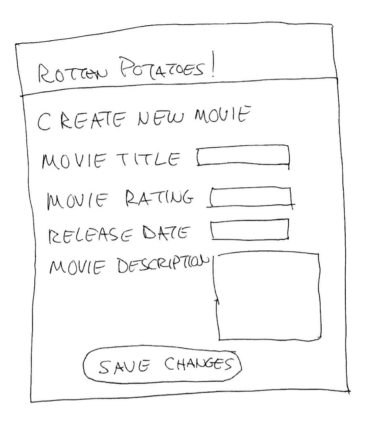

Figure 7.3: Window that appears when adding a movie to RottenPotatoes.

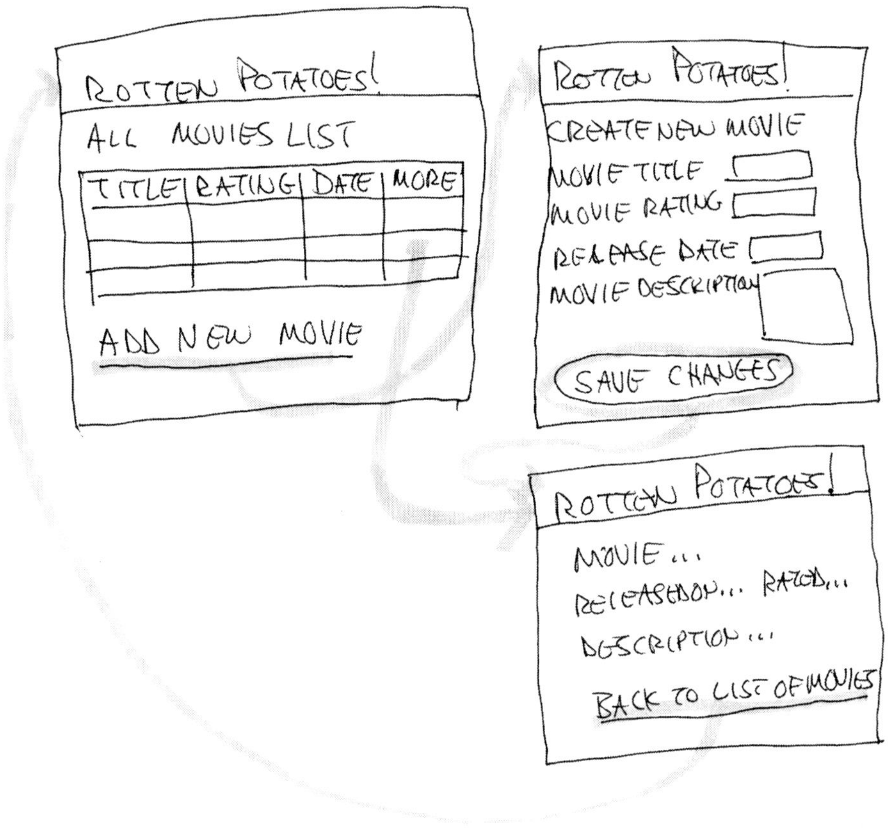

Figure 7.4: Storyboard of images for adding a movie to RottenPotatoes.

Figure 7.4 shows a sequence of Lo-Fi sketches with indications of what the user clicks to cause the transitions between sketches. After drawing the sketches and storyboards, you are ready to write HTML. Chapter 2 showed how Haml markup becomes HTML, and how the **class** and **id** attributes of HTML elements can be used to attach styling information to them via Cascading Style Sheets (CSS). The key to the Lo-Fi approach is to get a good overall structure from your sketches, and do minimal CSS (if any) to get the view to look more or less like your sketch. Remember that the common parts of the page layout—banners, structural `divs`, and so on—can go into `views/layouts/application.html.haml`.

Start the process by looking at the Lo-Fi UI sketches and split them into "blocks" of the layout. Use CSS `divs` for obvious layout sections. There is no need to make it pretty until after you have everything working. Adding CSS styling, images, and so on is the fun part, but make it look good *after* it works.

Since the example in Section 7.6 involved existing functionality, there is no need to modify the Haml or CSS. The next section adds a new feature to RottenPotatoes and thus needs Haml changes.

Summary: Borrowing from the HCI community once again, ***Lo-Fi sketches*** are low cost ways to explore the user interface of a user story. Paper and pencil makes them easy to change or discard, which once again can involve all stakeholders. ***Storyboards*** capture the interaction between different pages depending on what the user does. It is much less effort to experiment in this low cost medium before using Haml and CSS to create the pages you want in HTML.

Self-Check 7.4.1. *True or False: The purpose of the Lo-Fi UI and storyboards is to debug the UI before you program it.*

◇ True. ∎

7.5   Agile Cost Estimation

Given that the Agile Manifesto values customer collaboration over contract negotiation, it is unsurprising that it does *not* follow the plan-and-document approach of making a cost estimate and schedule for a given set of features as part of bid to win a contract, as we shall see in Section 7.10). This section describes the process at Pivotal Labs, which relies upon Agile development (Burkes 2012).

Pivotal Labs is a software consultancy that teaches clients the Agile lifecycle while collaborating with them to develop a specific software product.

Because Pivotal does Agile, Pivotal never commits to delivering features X, Y, and Z by date D. Pivotal commits to providing a certain amount of resources to work in the most efficient way possible up to date D. Along the way, Pivotal needs the client to work with the project team to define priorities, and let Tracker's velocity guide the decisions as to which features actually make it into the release on date D.

A potential client first gets in contact with the Agile team. If it looks like a good fit for the Agile team, they first do a 30 to 60 minute phone call telling potential clients what an engagement looks like, how it's different from other "outsourcing" agencies, what type of time commitment it will require on the customer's part, and so on. This first call makes clear that the Agile team works on a time and materials basis, not on a fixed bid basis, as is usually the case with plan-and-document processes. The Agile team gets them to describe at a high level what they want developed, what their current development process looks like, what their current staffing is, and so on.

If the clients are comfortable with what they heard, and the Agile team thinks it still sounds like a good fit, the clients visit for what Pivotal calls a "scoping." A scoping is a roughly 90 minute conversation with a potential client, preferably in person. The Agile team asks the client to bring the person responsible for the product, a lead developer if they have one, a designer if they have one, any existing designs for what they want built, and so on. Basically, the client representatives bring whatever they think can clarify exactly what they want done. the Agile team brings two engineers to the scoping.

During the scoping, the Agile team asks the client to describe what they want done in detail, and they ask a series of questions designed to identify unknowns, risks, external integrations, and so forth. Essentially, the Agile team wants to identify anything that would add uncertainty to the estimate that the Agile team will deliver. If the Agile team gets a client with a very clear definition of what they want to build, a finished design, no external integrations, and so on, the Agile team can produce a fairly tightly-scoped estimate, such as "20 to 22 weeks." On the other hand, if they don't have clear product definition, lots of external integrations, or other uncertainty, the Agile team's estimate will have a greater range, such as "18 to 26 weeks." If you use pair programming (see Section 10.2), as Pivotal Labs does, the cost estimates would be in "pair weeks."

After the client leaves the scoping, the Pivot engineers involved will stay behind for another 15 to 30 minutes, and agree on an estimate in terms of weeks. They deliver their findings, which include the estimate, identification of risks, and so on, to the sales staff, who then turn that into a proposal email to the client.

Because the Agile team does time and materials only, it's easy to turn estimated weeks into an estimated range of expense.

Summary: Following the Agile Manifesto's emphasis on customer cooperation over contracts, an Agile team's notion of "cost estimation" is therefore more about advising the client on what team size can provide the maximum efficiency, following Brooks's Law that there is a point of diminishing returns on team size (see Section 7.11). The Agile team's goal in the scoping process is to identify that point, then ramp the team up to that size over time. Agile companies bid costs for time and materials based on short discussions with external customers. As we shall see in Section 7.10, this approach is in sharp contrast with companies that follow plan-and-document processes, which promise customers a set of features for an agreed upon cost by an agreed upon date.

Self-Check 7.5.1. *True or False: As practitioners of Agile Development, Pivotal Labs does not use contracts.*

◇ False. Pivotal certainly offers customers a contract that they sign, but it is primarily a promise to pay Pivotal for its best effort over to make the customer happy for a limited range of time. ■

With the already helpful role of user stories for measuring progress behind us, we introduce a tool that lets user stories play yet another important role.

7.6 Introducing Cucumber and Capybara

Remarkably enough, the tool **Cucumber** turns customer-understandable user stories into **acceptance tests**, which ensure the customer is satisfied, and **integration tests**, which

http://pastebin.com/CSCVp9M3

```
 1  Feature: User can manually add movie
 2
 3  Scenario: Add a movie
 4    Given I am on the RottenPotatoes home page
 5    When I follow "Add new movie"
 6    Then I should be on the Create New Movie page
 7    When I fill in "Title" with "Men In Black"
 8    And I select "PG-13" from "Rating"
 9    And I press "Save Changes"
10    Then I should be on the RottenPotatoes home page
11    And I should see "Men In Black"
```

Figure 7.5: A Cucumber scenario associated with the adding a movie feature for RottenPotatoes.

ensure that the interfaces between modules have consistent assumptions and communicate correctly. (Chapter 1 describes types of testing). The key is that Cucumber meets halfway between the customer and the developer: user stories don't look like code, so they are clear to the customer and can be used to reach agreement, but they also aren't completely freeform. This section explains how Cucumber accomplishes this minor miracle.

In the Cucumber context we will use the term *user story* to refer to a single *feature* with one or more *scenarios* that show different ways a feature is used. The keywords **Feature** and **Scenario** identify the respective components. Each scenario is in turn composed of a sequence of 3 to 8 *steps*.

Figure 7.5 is an example user story, showing a feature with one scenario of adding the movie *Men In Black*; the scenario has eight steps. (We show just a single scenario in this example, but features usually have many scenarios.) Although stilted writing, this format that Cucumber can act upon is still easy for the nontechnical customer to understand and help develop, which is a founding principle of Agile and BDD.

Cucumber keywords Given, When, Then, And, and **But** have different names just for benefit of human readers, but they are all aliases to the same method. Thus, you don't have to remember the syntax for many different keywords.

Each step of a scenario starts with its own keyword. Steps that start with **Given** usually set up some preconditions, such as navigating to a page. Steps that start with **When** typically use one of Cucumber's built-in web steps to simulate the user pressing a button, for example. Steps that start with **Then** will usually check to see if some condition is true. The conjunction **And** allows more complicated versions of **Given**, **When**, or **Then** phrases. The only other keyword you see in this format is **But**.

A separate set of files defines the Ruby code that tests these steps. These are called *step definitions*. Generally, many steps can use a single step definition.

How does Cucumber match the steps of the scenarios with the *step definitions* that perform these tests? The trick is that Cucumber uses regular expressions or *regexes* (Chapter 3) to match the English phrases in the steps of the scenarios to the step definitions of the testing harness.

For example, below is a string from a step definition in the scenario for RottenPotatoes:

http://pastebin.com/hwkkP8Mr

```
 1  Given /^(?:|I )am on (.+)$/
```

This regex can match the text "I am on the RottenPotatoes home page" on line 4 of Figure 7.5. The regex also captures the string after the phrase "am on " until the end of the line ("the RottenPotatoes home page"). The body of the step definition contains Ruby code that tests the step, likely using captured strings such as the one above.

Thus, a way to think of the relationship between step definitions and steps is that step definitions are like method definitions, and the steps of the scenarios are like method calls.

We then need a tool that will act as a user and pretend to use the feature under different scenarios. In the Rails world, this tool is called *Capybara*, and Cucumber integrates seamlessly with it. Capybara "pretends to be a user" by taking actions in a simulated web browser, for example, clicking on a link or button. Capybara can interact with the app to receive pages, parse the HTML, and submit forms as a user would.

Summary of Cucumber Introduction

- Cucumber combines a *feature* that you want to add with a set of *scenarios*. We call this combination a *user story*.

- The steps of the scenarios use the keyword **Given** to identify the current state, **When** to identify the action, and **Then** to identify the consequence of the action.

- The scenario steps also use the keywords **And** and **But** to act as conjunctions to make more complex descriptions of state, action, and consequences.

- *Cucumber* matches *steps* to *step definitions* using *regular expressions*.

- *Capybara* puts the SaaS application through its paces by simulating a user and browser performing the steps of the scenarios.

- By storing *features* in files along with different *scenarios* of feature use composed of many *steps*, and storing Ruby code in separate files containing *step definitions* that tests each type of step, the Rails tools *Cucumber* and *Capybara* automatically test the behavior of the SaaS app.

Self-Check 7.6.1. *True or False: Cucumber matches scenario steps to step definitions using regexes and Capybara pretends to be a user that interacts with the SaaS application according to these scenarios.*

◇ True. ∎

■ *Elaboration: Stubbing the web*

The way we use Cucumber and Capybara in this chapter doesn't allow us to test JavaScript code, which is covered in Chapter 6. With appropriate options, Cucumber can control Webdriver, which actually fires up a *real* browser and "remote controls" it to make it do what the stories say, including all JavaScript code. For this chapter, we will stick to using Capybara's "headless browser simulator" mode, which is much faster and is appropriate for testing everything except JavaScript. Figure 7.16 towards the end of the chapter shows the relationship among these tools.

7.7 Running Cucumber and Capybara

A major benefit of user stories in Cucumber is *Red-Yellow-Green analysis*. Once a user story is written, we can try to run it immediately. In the beginning, steps may initially be highlighted either in Red (for failing) or Yellow (not yet implemented). Our goal is to take each step and go from Yellow or Red to Green (for passing), by incrementally adding what's

Cucumbers are green
The test-passing green color
of the cucumber plant gives
this tool its name.

needed to make it pass. In some cases, this is really easy. In the next chapter, we similarly try to go from Red to Green at the level of *unit tests*. Recall that unit tests are for individual methods whereas Cucumber scenarios test entire paths through the app and thus can be acceptance tests or integration tests.

Like other useful tools we've seen, Cucumber is supplied as a Ruby gem, so the first thing we need to do is declare that our app depends on this gem and use Bundler to install it. Building on the `myrottenpotatoes` app you started in Chapter 4, add the following lines to `Gemfile`; we've indicated that Cucumber and its related gems are only needed in the `test` environment and not the `production` and `development` environments (Section 4.2 introduced the three environments in which Rails apps can run).

http://pastebin.com/s8EB8Mhs

```
1  # add to end of Gemfile
2  group :test do
3    gem 'cucumber-rails', :require => false
4    gem 'cucumber-rails-training-wheels' # some pre-fabbed step definitions
5    gem 'database_cleaner' # to clear Cucumber's test database between runs
6    gem 'capybara'         # lets Cucumber pretend to be a web browser
7    gem 'launchy'          # a useful debugging aid for user stories
8  end
```

Once you've modified `Gemfile`, run `bundle install --without production`. If all goes well, you'll eventually see "Your bundle is complete."

We now have to set up the directories and "boilerplate" files that Cucumber and Capybara need. Like Rails itself, Cucumber comes with a *generator* that does this for you. In the app's root directory, run the following two commands (if they ask whether it's OK to overwrite certain files such as `cucumber.rake`, you can safely say yes):

```
rails generate cucumber:install capybara
rails generate cucumber_rails_training_wheels:install
```

Running these two generators gives you commonly used step definitions as a starting point, such as interactions with a web browser. For this app, you will find them in `myrottenpotatoes/features/step_definitions/web_steps.rb`. In addition to these predefined steps, you'll need to create new step definitions to match the unique functionality of your app. You will probably want to learn the most common predefined step definitions and use them when you write your features so that you can write fewer step definitions.

Before trying to run Cucumber, there's one more step we must take: you must initialize the test database by running `rake db:test:prepare`. You need to do this before the first time you run tests or whenever the database schema is changed. Section 4.2 provides a more detailed description.

At this point, you're ready to start using Cucumber. You add the features themselves in the `features` directory as files with a `.feature` file extension. Copy the user story in Figure 7.5 and paste it into a file called `AddMovie.feature` in the directory `features`. To see how scenarios and the step definitions interact and how they change color like maple trees in New England when the seasons change, type

```
cucumber features/AddMovie.feature
```

Watch the screencast to see what to do next.

http://pastebin.com/RbPqfg1g

```
1 | # add to paths.rb, just after "when /^the home\s?page$/
2 | # '/'"
3 |
4 | when /^the RottenPotatoes home page/
5 |   '/movies'
6 | when /^the Create New Movie page/
7 |   '/movies/new'
```

Figure 7.6: The code we need to add to features/support/paths.rb in order to make the AddMovie scenario pass. Note that the first line on both paths.rb and websteps.rb is an instruction to 'DELETE THIS FILE', which is something that you should do once you have become familiar with the basics of cucumber and capybara. The files paths.rb and websteps.rb are part of the cucumber rails training wheels gem, and are useful when you are just getting started with cucumber, but ultimately need to be removed for serious use. Please continue to use them for the time being.

Screencast 7.7.1: Cucumber Part I.

`http://vimeo.com/34754747`

The screencast shows how Cucumber checks to see whether the tests work by coloring the step definitions. Failing steps are red, unimplemented steps are yellow, and passing steps are green. (Steps after a failed red step are blue, indicating that they have not yet been tried.) The first step on line 4 is red, so Cucumber skips the rest. It fails because there is no path in paths.rb that matches "the RottenPotatoes home page", as the Cucumber error message explains. The message even suggests how to fix the failure by adding such a path to `paths.rb`. See Figure 7.6. This new path turns this first step as green as a cucumber, but now the third step on line 6 is red. As the error message explains, it fails because no path matches "Create New Movie page", and we fix it again by adding the path to paths.rb. All steps now are as cool as a cucumber, and the AddMovie scenario passes.

Summary: To add features as part of BDD, we need to define acceptance criteria first. Cucumber enables both capturing requirements as user stories and getting integration and acceptance tests out of that story. Moreover, we get automatically runnable tests so that we'll have regression tests to help maintain the code as we evolve it further. (We'll see this approach again in Chapter 9 with a much larger application than RottenPotatoes.)

Self-Check 7.7.1. *Cucumber colors steps green that pass the test. What is the difference between steps colored yellow and red?*

◇ Yellow steps have not yet been implemented while red steps have been implemented but fail the test. ∎

7.8 Enhancing RottenPotatoes

As a second example of user stories and Lo-Fi UIs, suppose we want to search The Open Movie Database (TMDb) to find information about a movie we are interested in adding to RottenPotatoes. As we'll see in Chapter 8, TMDb has an API (application programming interface) designed to allow its information to be accessed in a Service-Oriented Architecture.

In this chapter, we use Cucumber to develop two scenarios and the corresponding Lo-Fi UI sketches to show how we would like RottenPotatoes to integrate with TMDb, and we'll get one of the scenarios to go green by temporarily "faking out" some of the code. In Chapter 8, we'll write the code needed to get the other scenario to go green. Getting the first couple of scenarios working can seem tedious, because you usually have to add a lot of infrastructure, but it goes much faster after that, and in fact you will even be able to re-use your step definitions to create higher-level "declarative" steps, as we will see in Section 7.9.

The storyboard in Figure 7.7 shows how we envision the feature working. The home page of RottenPotatoes, which lists all movies, will be augmented with a search box where we can type some title keywords of a movie and a "Search" button that will search TMDb for a movie whose title contains those keywords. If the search does match—the so-called "happy path" of execution—the first movie that matches will be used to "pre-populate" the fields in the Add New Movie page that we already developed in Chapter 4. (In a real app, you'd want to create a separate page showing all matches and letting the user pick one, but we're deliberately keeping the example simple.) If the search doesn't match any movies—the "sad path"—we should be returned to the home page with a message informing us of this fact.

Normally you'd complete the happy path first, and when you reach a failing or pending step that requires writing *new* code, you do so via Test Driven Development (TDD). We'll do that in Chapter 8 by writing code that really calls TMDb and integrating it back into this scenario. For now, we'll start with the sad path to illustrate Cucumber features and the BDD process. Figure 7.8 shows the sad path scenario for the new feature; create a file `features/search_tmdb.feature` containing this code. When we run the feature with `cucumber features/search_tmdb.feature`, the second step *Then I should see "Search TMDb for a movie"* should fail (red), because we haven't yet added this text to the home page `app/views/movies/index.html.haml`. So, our first task is to get this step to go green by making that change.

Technically, a "pure" BDD approach could be to get this step to pass just by adding the text *Search TMDb for a movie* anywhere in that view, and then re-running the scenario. But of course we know that the very next step *When I fill in "Search Terms" with "Movie That Does Not Exist"* will also fail, because we haven't added a form field called "Search Terms" to the view either. So in the interest of efficiency, modify `index.html.haml` by adding the lines in Figure 7.9, which we now explain.

Line 3 is the text that allows *Then I should see "Search TMDb for a movie"* to pass. The remaining lines create the fill-in form; we introduced these in Chapter 4, so some of this markup should be familiar. Two things are worth noting. First, as with any user interaction in a view, we need a controller action that will handle that interaction. In this case, the interaction is submitting the form with search keywords. Line 5 says that when the form is submitted, the controller action **search_tmdb** will receive the form submission. That code doesn't exist yet, so we had to choose a descriptive name for the action.

Doing it over and over? rake cucumber runs all your features, or more precisely, those selected by the *default profile* in Cucumber's configuration file cucumber.yml.[8] In the next chapter we'll meet a tool called autotest that automates re-running tests when you make changes to files.

The second thing to note is the use of the HTML `label` tag. Figure 2.14 in Chapter 2 tells us that lines 7 and 8 will expand to the following HTML markup:

http://pastebin.com/itVarUq5

```
1  <label for='search_terms'>Search Terms</label>
2  <input id="search_terms" name="search_terms" type="text" />
```

The key is that the `for` attribute of the `label` tag matches the `id` attribute of the `input` tag, which was determined by the first argument to the **text_field_tag** helper called in line 8 of Figure 7.9. This correspondence allows Cucumber to determine what form field is being referenced by the name "Search Terms" in line 11 of Figure 7.8: *When I fill in "Search Terms"*....

As you may recall from Section 4.1, we have to make sure there is a route to this new controller action. The top part of the Figure 7.10 shows the line you must add to `config/`

Figure 7.7: Storyboard of UI for searching The Movie Database.

http://pastebin.com/qTYS5tLs

```
1   Feature: User can add movie by searching for it in The Movie Database (TMDb)
2
3     As a movie fan
4     So that I can add new movies without manual tedium
5     I want to add movies by looking up their details in TMDb
6
7   Scenario: Try to add nonexistent movie (sad path)
8
9     Given I am on the RottenPotatoes home page
10    Then I should see "Search TMDb for a movie"
11    When I fill in "Search Terms" with "Movie That Does Not Exist"
12    And I press "Search TMDb"
13    Then I should be on the RottenPotatoes home page
14    And I should see "'Movie That Does Not Exist' was not found in TMDb."
```

Figure 7.8: A sad path scenario associated with adding a feature to search The Movie Database.

http://pastebin.com/QtUf0qsB

```
1   -# add to end of app/views/movies/index.html.haml:
2
3   %h1 Search TMDb for a movie
4
5   = form_tag :action => 'search_tmdb' do
6
7     %label{:for => 'search_terms'} Search Terms
8     = text_field_tag 'search_terms'
9     = submit_tag 'Search TMDb'
```

Figure 7.9: The Haml code for the Search TMDb page.

routes.rb to add a form submission (POST) route to that action.

However, even with the new route, this step still will fail with an exception: even though we have a button with the name "Search TMDb", the **form_tag** specifies that **MoviesController#search_tmdb** is the controller action that should receive the form, yet no such method exists in movies_controller.rb. Figure 7.1 says that we should now use Test-Driven Development (TDD) techniques to create that method. But since TDD is the topic of the next chapter, we're going to cheat a bit in order to get the scenario running. Since this is the "sad path" scenario where no movies are found, we will temporarily create a controller method that *always* behaves as if nothing was found, so we can finish testing the sad path. Also, The bottom part of Figure 7.10 shows the code you should add to app/controllers/ movies_controller.rb to create the "fake" hardwired **search_tmdb** action.

If you're new to BDD, this step might surprise you. Why would we deliberately create a fake controller method that doesn't actually call TMDb, but just pretends the search failed? In this case, the answer is that it lets us finish the rest of the scenario, making sure that our HTML views match the Lo-Fi sketches and that the sequence of views matches the story-boards. Indeed, once you make the changes in Figure 7.10, the entire sad path should pass. Screencast 7.8.1 summarizes what we've done so far.

http://pastebin.com/tdxgK77Z

```
1  # add to routes.rb, just before or just after 'resources :movies' :
2
3  # Route that posts 'Search TMDb' form
4  post '/movies/search_tmdb'
```

http://pastebin.com/cGmgFyEZ

```
1  # add to movies_controller.rb, anywhere inside
2  #   'class MoviesController < ApplicationController':
3
4  def search_tmdb
5    # hardwire to simulate failure
6    flash[:warning] = "'#{params[:search_terms]}' was not found in TMDb."
7    redirect_to movies_path
8  end
```

Figure 7.10: (Top) A route that triggers this mechanism when a form is POSTed. (Bottom) This "fake" controller method always behaves as if no matches were found. It retrieves the keywords typed by the user from the params hash (as we saw in Chapter 4), stores a message in the flash[], and redirects the user back to the list of movies. Recall from Chapter 4 that we added code to app/views/layouts/application.html.haml to display the contents of the flash on every view.

Screencast 7.8.1: Cucumber Part II.

`http://vimeo.com/34754766`

In this screencast, we do a sad path to illustrate features of Cucumber because it is able to use existing code. The first step on line 5 of Figure 7.8 passes but the step on line 6 fails because we haven't modified index.html.haml to include the name of the new page or to include a form for typing in a movie to search for. We fix this by adding this form to index.html.haml, using the same Rails methods described in Sections 4.4 and 4.6 of Chapter 4. There is no route that would match an incoming URI. To keep things simple, we will set up a route just for that action in config/routes.rb, again using techniques discussed in Section 4.1 of Chapter 4. When creating a form, we have to specify which controller action will receive it; we chose the name search_tmdb for controller action. (We'll implement this method in the next chapter). Once we have updated index.html.haml, created the route in config/routes.rb, and named the controller action, Cucumber colors all the steps green.

What about the happy path, when we search for an existing movie? Observe that the first two actions on that path—going to the Rotten Potatoes home page and making sure there is a search form there, corresponding to lines 9 and 10 of Figure 7.8—are the same as for the sad path. That should ring a Pavlovian bell in your head asking how you can DRY out the repetition.

Figure 7.11 shows the answer. The Cucumber Background command shows the steps that should be run before any other scenarios of a feature are run, which letâĂŹs us DRY-out the happy and sad path scenarios. Modify features/search_tmdb.feature to match the figure and once again run cucumber features/search_tmdb.feature. Unsurprisingly, the step at line 23 will fail, because we have hardwired the controller method to pretend there is never a match in TMDb, resulting in a redirect back the home page rather than to the Search Results page. At this point, we could change the controller method to hardwire success and make the happy path green, but besides the fact that this would cause the sad path to go red, in the next chapter we will see a better way. In particular, we'll develop the *real* controller action using Test-Driven Development (TDD) techniques that "cheat" to set up the inputs and the state of the world to test particular conditions in isolation. Once you learn both BDD

http://pastebin.com/7nQQ6zwg

```
 1  Feature: User can add movie by searching for it in The Movie Database (TMDb)
 2
 3    As a movie fan
 4    So that I can add new movies without manual tedium
 5    I want to add movies by looking up their details in TMDb
 6
 7  Background: Start from the Search form on the home page
 8
 9    Given I am on the RottenPotatoes home page
10    Then I should see "Search TMDb for a movie"
11
12  Scenario: Try to add nonexistent movie (sad path)
13
14    When I fill in "Search Terms" with "Movie That Does Not Exist"
15    And I press "Search TMDb"
16    Then I should be on the RottenPotatoes home page
17    And I should see "'Movie That Does Not Exist' was not found in TMDb."
18
19  Scenario: Try to add existing movie (happy path)
20
21    When I fill in "Search Terms" with "Inception"
22    And I press "Search TMDb"
23    Then I should be on the "Search Results" page
24    And I should not see "not found"
25    And I should see "Inception"
```

Figure 7.11: DRYing out the common steps between the happy and sad paths using the Background keyword, which groups steps that should be performed before *each* scenario in a feature file.

and TDD, you'll see that you commonly iterate between these two levels as part of normal software development.

Summary:

- Adding a new feature for a SaaS app normally means you specify a UI for the feature, write new step definitions, and perhaps even write new methods before Cucumber can successfully color steps green.

- Usually, you'd write and complete scenarios for the happy path(s) first; we began with the sad path only because it allowed us to better illustrate some Cucumber features.

- The **Background** keyword can be used to DRY out common steps across related scenarios in a single feature file.

- Usually, system-level tests such as Cucumber scenarios shouldn't "cheat" by hardwiring fake behavior in methods. BDD and Cucumber are about behavior, not implementation, so we would instead use other techniques such as TDD (which the next chapter describes) to write the actual methods to make all scenarios pass.

Self-Check 7.8.1. *True or False: You need to implement all the code being tested before Cucumber will say that the test passes.*

◇ False. A sad path can pass without having the code written need to make a happy path pass. ∎

7.9 Explicit vs. Implicit and Imperative vs. Declarative Scenarios

Now that we have seen user stories and Cucumber in action, we are ready to cover two important testing topics that involve contrasting perspectives.

The first is ***explicit versus implicit requirements.*** A large part of the formal specification in plan-and-document is requirements, which in BDD are user stories developed by the stakeholders. Using the terminology from Chapter 1, they typically correspond to acceptance tests. Implicit requirements are the logical consequence of explicit requirements, and typically correspond to what Chapter 1 calls integration tests. An example of an implicit requirement in RottenPotatoes might be that by default movies should be listed in chronological order by release date.

The good news is that you can use Cucumber to kill two birds with one stone—create acceptance tests *and* integration tests—if you write user stories for both explicit and implicit requirements. (The next chapter shows how to use another tool for unit testing.)

The second contrasting perspective is ***imperative versus declarative scenarios.*** The example scenario in Figure 7.5 above is imperative, in that you are specifying a logical sequence of user actions: filling in a form, clicking on buttons, and so on. Imperative scenarios tend to have complicated **When** statements with lots of **And** steps. While such scenarios are useful in ensuring that the details of the UI match the customer's expectations, it quickly becomes tedious and non-DRY to write most scenarios this way.

To see why, suppose we want to write a feature that specifies that movies should appear in alphabetical order on the list of movies page. For example, "Zorro" should appear after "Apocalypse Now", even if "Zorro" was added first. It would be the height of tedium to express this scenario naively, because it mostly repeats lines from our existing "add movie" scenario—not very DRY:

http://pastebin.com/qR9UTSsP

```
1   Feature: movies should appear in alphabetical order, not added order
2
3   Scenario: view movie list after adding 2 movies (imperative and non-DRY)
4
5     Given I am on the RottenPotatoes home page
6     When I follow "Add new movie"
7     Then I should be on the Create New Movie page
8     When I fill in "Title" with "Zorro"
9     And I select "PG" from "Rating"
10    And I press "Save Changes"
11    Then I should be on the RottenPotatoes home page
12    When I follow "Add new movie"
13    Then I should be on the Create New Movie page
14    When I fill in "Title" with "Apocalypse Now"
15    And I select "R" from "Rating"
16    And I press "Save Changes"
17    Then I should be on the RottenPotatoes home page
18    Then I should see "Apocalypse Now" before "Zorro" on the RottenPotatoes home
         page sorted by title
```

Cucumber is supposed to be about *behavior* rather than implementation—focusing on *what* is being done—yet in this poorly-written scenario, only line 18 mentions the behavior of interest!

An alternative approach is to think of using the step definitions to make a ***domain language*** (which is different from a formal ***Domain Specific Language (DSL)***) for your application. A domain language is informal but uses terms and concepts specific to your application, rather than generic terms and concepts related to the implementation of the user interface. Steps written in a domain language are typically more declarative than imperative

http://pastebin.com/h7e2xtZu

```
1   Given /I have added "(.*)" with rating "(.*)"/ do |title, rating|
2     steps %Q{
3       Given I am on the Create New Movie page
4       When  I fill in "Title" with "#{title}"
5       And   I select "#{rating}" from "Rating"
6       And   I press "Save Changes"
7     }
8   end
9
10  Then /I should see "(.*)" before "(.*)" on (.*)/ do |string1, string2, path|
11    step "I am on #{path}"
12    regexp = /#{string1}.*#{string2}/m #   /m means match across newlines
13    page.body.should =~ regexp
14  end
```

Figure 7.12: Adding this code to `movie_steps.rb` creates new step definitions matching lines 5 and 6 of the declarative scenario by reusing your existing steps. steps (line 2) reuses a sequence of steps and step (line 11) reuses a single step. Recall from Figure 3.1 that %Q is an alternative syntax for double-quoting a string, and that Given, When, Then and so on are synonyms provided for readability. (We will learn about should, which appears in line 13, in the next chapter.)

in that they describe the state of the world rather than the sequence of steps to get to that state and they are less dependent on the details of the user interface.

A declarative version of the above scenario might look like this:

http://pastebin.com/355SUaaT

```
1   Feature: movies should appear in alphabetical order, not added order
2
3   Scenario: view movie list after adding movie (declarative and DRY)
4
5     Given I have added "Zorro" with rating "PG-13"
6     And   I have added "Apocalypse Now" with rating "R"
7     Then  I should see "Apocalypse Now" before "Zorro" on the RottenPotatoes
          home page sorted by title
```

The declarative version is obviously shorter, easier to maintain, and easier to understand since the text describes the state of the app in a natural form: "I am on the RottenPotatoes home page sorted by title."

The good news is that, as Figure 7.12 shows, you can *reuse* your existing imperative steps to implement such scenarios. This is a very powerful form of reuse, and as your app evolves, you will find yourself reusing steps from your first few imperative scenarios to create more concise and descriptive declarative scenarios. Declarative, domain-language-oriented scenarios focus the attention on the feature being described rather than the low-level steps you need to set up and perform the test.

Summary:

- We can use Cucumber for both acceptance and integration testing if we write user stories for both explicit and implicit requirements. Declarative scenarios are simpler, less verbose, and more maintainable than imperative scenarios.

- As you get more experienced, the vast majority of your user stories should be in a domain language that you have created for your app via your step definitions, and the stories should worry less about user interface details. The exception is for the specific stories where there is business value (customer need) in expressing the details of the user interface.

■ *Elaboration: The BDD ecosystem*

There is enormous momentum, especially in the Ruby community where testable, beautiful, and self-documenting code is highly valued, to document and promote best practices for BDD. Good scenarios serve as both documentation of the app designers' intent and executable acceptance and integration tests; they therefore deserve the same attention to beauty as the code itself. For example, this free screencast from RailsCasts[9] describes *scenario outlines*, a way to DRY out a repetitive set of happy or sad paths whose expected outcomes differ based on how a form is filled in, similar to the contrast between our happy and sad paths above. The Cucumber wiki[10] is a good place to start, but as with all programming, you'll learn BDD best by doing it often, making mistakes, and revising and beautifying your code and scenarios as you learn from your mistakes.

Self-Check 7.9.1. *True or False: Explicit requirements are usually defined with imperative scenarios and implicit requirements are usually defined with declarative scenarios.*
◇ False. These are two independent classifications; both requirements can use either type of scenarios. ■

7.10 The Plan-And-Document Perspective

> *As is well known to software engineers (but not to the general public), by far the largest class of [software] problems arises from errors made in the eliciting, recording, and analysis of requirements.*

> —Daniel Jackson, Martyn Thomas, and Lynette Millett (Editors), *Software for Dependable Systems: Sufficient Evidence?*, 2007

Recall that the hope for plan-and-document methods is to make software engineering as predictable in budget and schedule as civil engineering. Remarkably, user stories, points, and velocity correspond to *seven* major tasks of the plan-and-document methodologies. They include:

1. Requirements Elicitation

2. Requirements Documentation

3. Cost Estimation

4. Scheduling and Monitoring Progress

These are done up front for the Waterfall model and at the beginning of each major iteration for the Spiral and RUP models. As requirements change over time, these items above imply other tasks:

5. Change Management for Requirements, Cost, and Schedule

6. Ensuring Implementation Matches Requirement Features

Finally, since accuracy of the budget estimate and the schedule is vital to the success of the plan-and-document process, there is another task not found in BDD:

7. Risk Analysis and Management

The hope is that by imagining all the risks to the budget and schedule in advance, the project can make plans to avoid or overcome them.

As we shall see in Chapter 10, the plan-and-document processes assume that each project has a manager. While the whole team may participate in requirements elicitation and risk analysis and help document them, it is up to the project manager to estimate costs, make and maintain the schedule, and decide which risks to address and how to overcome or avoid them.

Advice for project managers comes from all corners, from practitioners who offer guidelines and rules of thumb based on their experience to researchers who have measured many projects to come up with formulas for estimating budget and schedule. There are also tools to help. Despite this helpful advice and tools, the project statistics from Chapter 1 (Johnson 1995, 2009)—that 40% to 50% exceed the budget and schedule by factors of 1.7 to 3.0 and that 20% to 30% of projects are cancelled or abandoned—document the difficulty of accurate making accurate budgets and schedules.

We now give quick overviews of these seven tasks so that you can be familiar with what is done in plan-and-document processes to give you a head start if you need to use them in the future. These overviews help explain the inspiration for the Agile Manifesto. If you are unclear on how to successfully perform these tasks, it may be due more to their inherent difficulties rather than to brevity.

1. Requirements Elicitation. Like User Stories, requirement elicitation involves participation by all stakeholders, using one of several techniques. The first is ***interviewing***, where stakeholders answer predefined questions or just have informal discussions. Note that one goal is to understand the social and organization environment to see how tasks are *really* done versus the official story. Another technique is to cooperatively create ***scenarios***, which can start with an initial assumption of the state of the system, show the flow of the system for a happy case and a sad case, list what else is going on in the system, and then the state of the system at the end of the scenario. Related to scenarios and user stories, a third technique is to create ***use cases***, which are lists of steps between a person and a system to achieve a goal (see the elaboration in Section 7.1).

In addition to ***functional requirements*** such as those listed above, ***non-functional requirements*** include performance goals, dependability goals, and so on.

2. Requirements Documentation. Once elicited, the next step is to document the requirements in a ***Software Requirements Specification*** (***SRS***). Figure 7.13 gives an outline for an SRS based on IEEE Standard 830-1998. A SRS for a patient management system[11] is 14 pages long, but they are often hundreds of pages.

Part of the process is to check the SRS for:

Table of Contents
1. Introduction
  1.1 Purpose
  1.2 Scope
  1.3 Definitions, acronyms, and abbreviations
  1.4 References
  1.5 Overview
2. Overall description
  2.1 Product perspective
  2.2 Product functions
  2.3 User characteristics
  2.4 Constraints
  2.5 Assumptions and dependencies
3. Specific requirements
  3.1 External interface requirements
    3.1.1 User interfaces
    3.1.2 Hardware interfaces
    3.1.3 Software interfaces
    3.1.4 Communication interfaces
  3.2 System features
    3.2.1 System feature 1
      3.2.1.1 Introduction/purpose of feature
      3.2.1.2 Stimulus/response sequence
      3.2.1.3 Associated function requirements
        3.2.1.3.1 Functional requirement 1
        . . .
        3.2.1.3.n Functional requirement n
    3.2.2 System feature 2
    . . .
    3.2.m System feature m
  3.3 Performance requirements
  3.4 Design constraints
  3.5 Software system attributes
  3.6 Other requirements

Figure 7.13: A table of contents for the IEEE Standard 830-1998 recommended practice for Software Requirements Specifications. We show Section 3 organized by feature, but the standard offers many others ways to organize Section 3: by mode, user class, object, stimulus, functional hierarchy, or even mixing multiple organizations.

- Validity–are all these requirements really necessary?

- Consistency–do requirements conflict?

- Completeness–are all requirements and constraints included?

- Feasibility–can the requirements really be implemented?

Techniques to test for these four characteristics include having stakeholders—developers, customers, testers, and so on—proof-read the document, trying to build a prototype that includes the basic features, and generating test cases that check the requirements.

A project may find it useful to have two types of SRS: a high-level SRS that is for management and marketing and a detailed SRS for the project development team. The former is presumably a subset of the latter. For example, the high-level SRS might leave out the functional requirements that correspond to 3.2.1.3 in Figure 7.13.

■ *Elaboration: Formal specification languages*

Formal specification languages such as Alloy or Z allow the project manager to write executable requirements, which makes it easier to validate the implementation. Not surprisingly, the cost is both a more difficult document to write and usually a much longer requirements document to read. The advantage is both precision in the specification and the potential to automatically generate tests cases or even use formal methods for verification of correctness (see Section 8.9).

---

3. Cost Estimation. The project manager then decomposes the SRS into the tasks to implement it, and then estimates the number of weeks to complete each task. The advice is to decompose no finer than one week. Just as a user story with more than seven points should be divided into smaller user stories, any task with an estimate of more than eight weeks should be further divided into smaller tasks.

The total effort is traditionally measured in person-months, perhaps in homage to Brooks's classic software engineering book *The Mythical Man-Month* (Brooks 1995). Managers use salaries and overhead rates to convert person-months into an actual budget.

The cost estimate is likely done twice: once to bid a contract, and once again after the contract is won. The second estimate is done after the software architecture is designed, so that the tasks as well as the effort per task can be more easily and accurately identified.

The project manager surely wants the second estimate to be no larger than the first, since that is what the customer will pay. One suggestion is to add a safety margin by multiplying your original estimate by 1.3 to 1.5 to try to handle estimation inaccuracy or unforeseen events. Another is to make three estimates: a best case, expected case, and worst case, and then use that information to make your best guess.

The two approaches to estimating are experiential or quantitative. The first assumes the project managers have significant experience either at the company or in the industry, and they rely on that experience to make accurate estimates. It certainly increases confidence when the project is similar to tasks that the organization has already successfully completed.

The quantitative or algorithmic approach is to estimate the programming effort of the tasks in a technical measure such as lines of code (LOC), and then divide by a productivity measure like LOC per person-month to yield person-months per task. The project manager can get help from others to get estimates on LOC, and like velocity, can look at the historical record of the organization's productivity to calculate person-months.

Since cost estimates for software projects have such a dismal record, there has been considerable effort on improving the quantitative approach by collecting information about completed projects and finding models that predict the outcomes (Boehm and Valerdi 2008). The next step in sophistication follows this formula:

$$\text{Effort} = \text{Organizational Factors} \times \text{Code Size}^{\text{Size Penalty}} \times \text{Product Factors} \qquad (7.1)$$

where Organizational Factors include practices for this type of product, Code Size is measured as before, Size Penalty reflects that effort is not linear in code size, and Product Factors include experience of development team with this type of product, dependability requirements, platform difficulty, and so on. Example constants from real projects are 2.94 for Organizational Factors; Size Penalty between 1.10 and 1.24; and Product Factors between 0.9 and 1.4.

> **Constructive Cost Model (COCOMO)** is the basis of this 1981 formula. Its 1995 successor is called COCOMO II.

While these estimates are quantitative, they certainly depend on the project manager's subjective picks for Code Size, Size Penalty, and Product Factors.

The successor to the COCOMO formula above asks the project manager to pick many more parameters. COCOMO II adds three more formulas to adjust estimates for 1) developing prototypes, 2) accounting for the amount of code reuse, and 3) a post-detailed-architecture estimate. This last formula expands Size Penalty by adding a normalized product of 5 independent factors and replaces Product Factors by a product of 17 independent factors.

The British Computer Society Survey of more than 1000 projects mentioned in Chapter 1 found that 92% of project managers made their estimates using experience instead of formulas (Taylor 2000).

As no more than 20% to 30% of projects are meet their budget and schedule, what happens to the rest? Another 20% to 30% of the projects are indeed cancelled or abandoned, but the remaining 40% to 50% are still valuable to the customer even if late. Customers and providers typically then negotiate a new contract to deliver the product with a limited set of missing features by a near-term date.

■ *Elaboration: Function points*

Function points are an alternative measure to LOC that can lead to estimates that are more accurate. They are based on the function inputs, outputs, external queries, input files, output files, and the complexity of each. The corresponding productivity measure is then function points per person-month.

---

4. Scheduling and Monitoring Progress. Given the SRS has been broken into tasks whose effort has been estimated, the next step is to use a scheduling tool that shows which tasks can be performed in parallel and which have dependencies so they must be performed sequentially. The format is typically a box and arrow diagram such as a *PERT chart*. Figure 7.14 gives an example. Such tools can identify the *critical path*, which determines the minimum time for project. The project manager that places the graph in a table with rows associated with the people on the project, and then assigns people to tasks.

> **PERT** stands for Program Evaluation and Review Technique, which was invented by the US Navy in the 1950s for its nuclear submarine program.

Once again, this process is typically done twice, once when bidding the contract, and once after the contract is won and the detailed architecture design is complete. Safety margins are again used to ensure that the first schedule, which is when the customer expects the product to be released, is not longer than the second version.

Similar to calculating velocity, the project manager can see if the project is behind by comparing the predicted expenditures and time for tasks to the actual expenditures and

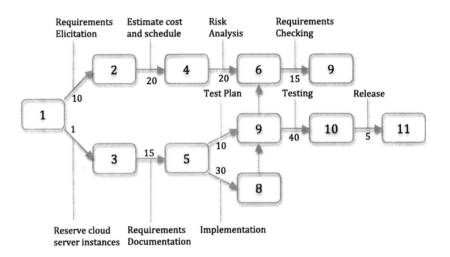

Figure 7.14: Numbered nodes represent milestones and labeled lines represent tasks, with arrowheads representing dependencies. Diverging lines from a node represent concurrent tasks. The numbers on the other side of lines represent the time allocated for the task. Dotted lines indicate dependencies that need no resources, so they have no time allocated for the task.

progress to date. A way to make project status clear to all stakeholders is to add interme-diate milestones to the schedule, which lets everyone see if the project is on schedule and on budget.

5. Change Management for Requirements, Cost, and Schedule. As stated many times in this book, customers are likely to ask for changes to the requirements as the project evolves for many reasons, including a better understanding of what is wanted after trying a prototype, changing market conditions for the project, and so on. The challenge for the project man-ager is keep the requirement documents, the schedule, and cost predictions up-to-date as the project changes. Thus, version control systems are needed for evolving documents as well as for programs, so the norm should be checking in the revised documentation along with the revised code.

Requirements Creep is the term developers use to describe the dreaded increase in requirements over time.

6. Ensuring Implementation Matches Requirement Features. The Agile process con-solidates these many major tasks into three tightly coupled ones: User Stories, acceptance tests in Cucumber, and the code that comes from BDD/TDD process. Thus, there is little confusion in the relationship between particular stories, tests, and code.

However, plan-and-document methodologies involve many more mechanisms without tight integration. Thus, we need tools that allow the project manager to check to see if the implementation matches the requirements. The relationship between features in requirements and what is implemented is called *requirements traceability*. Tools that implement trace-ability essentially offer cross-references between a portion of the design, the portion of the code that implements the feature, code reviews that checked it, and the tests that validate it.

If there is both a high-level SRS and a detailed SRS, *forward traceability* refers to the traditional path from requirements to implementation, while *backwards traceability* is the mapping from a detailed requirement back to a high-level requirement.

7. Risk Analysis and Management. In an effort to improve the accuracy of cost estima-tion and scheduling, plan-and-document methodologies have borrowed risk analysis from the business school. The philosophy is that by taking the time up front to identify potential risks to the budget and schedule, a project can either do extra work to reduce the changes of risks or change the plan to avoid risks. Ideally, risk identification and management occurs over the first third of a project. It does not bode well if they are identified late in the development cycle.

Risks are classified as technical, organizational, or business. An example of a technical risk might be that the relational database chosen cannot scale to the workload the project needs. An organizational risk might be that many members of the team are unfamiliar with J2EE, which the project depends upon. A business risk could be that by the time to project is complete, the product is not competitive in the market.

Example of actions to overcome the above risks would be to acquire a more scalable database, send team members to a J2EE workshop, and do competitive survey of existing products, including their current features and plans for improvements.

The approach to identify risks is to ask everyone for their worst-case scenarios. The project manager puts them into a "risk table," assigns probability of each happening as a percentage between 0 and 100, and the impact on a numeric scale of 1 to 4, representing negligible, marginal, critical, and catastrophic. You can then sort the risk table by the product of the probability and impact of each risk.

There are many more potential risks than projects can afford to address, so the advice is to address the top 20% of the risks, in the hope that they represent 80% of the potential risks to the budget and schedule. Trying to address all potential risks could lead to an effort that is

Tasks	In Plan and Document	In Agile
Requirements Documentation	Software Requirements Specification such as IEEE Standard 830-1998	User stories, Cucumber, Points, Velocity
Requirements Elicitation	Interviews, Scenarios, Use Cases	
Change Management for Requirements, Schedule, and Budget	Version Control for Documentation and Code	
Ensuring Requirements Features	Traceability to link features to tests, reviews, and code	
Scheduling and Monitoring	Early in project, contracted delivery date based on cost estimation, using PERT charts. Milestones to monitor progress	
Cost Estimation	Early in project, contracted cost based on manager experience or estimates of task size combined with productivity metrics	Evaluate to pick range of effort for time and materials contract
Risk Management	Early in project, identify risks to budget and schedule, and take actions to overcome or avoid them	

Figure 7.15: The relationship between the requirements related tasks of Plan-and-Document versus Agile methodologies.

larger than the original software project! Risk reduction is a major reason for iteration in both the Spiral and RUP models. Iterations and prototypes should reduce risks associated with a project.

Section 7.5 mentions asking the customers about risks for the project as part of the cost estimation in Agile, but the difference is that it used to decide the range of the cost estimate rather than becoming a significant part of the project itself.

Summary The hope of the original efforts in software engineering was to make software development as predictable in quality, cost, and schedule as building a bridge. Perhaps because less than a sixth of software projects are completed on time and on budget with full funtionality, the plan-and-document process has many steps to try to achieve this difficult goal. Agile does not try to predict cost and schedule at the start of the project, instead relying on working with customers on frequent iterations and agreeing on a range of time for the best effort to achieve the customer's goals. Rating user stories on difficulty and recording the points actually completed per iteration increases the chances of more realistic estimates. Figure 7.15 shows the resulting different tasks given the differing perspectives of these two philosophies.

Self-Check 7.10.1. *Name three plan-and-document techniques that help with requirements elicitation.*
◇ Interviewing, Scenarios, and Use Cases. ∎

7.11 Fallacies and Pitfalls

 Fallacy: **If a software project is falling behind schedule, you can catch up by adding more people to the project.**

The main theme of Fred Brooks's classic book, *The Mythical Man-Month*, is that not only does adding people not help, it makes it worse. The reason is twofold: it takes a while for new people to learn about the project, and as the size of the project grows, the amount of communication increases, which can reduce the time available for people to get their work done. His summary, which some call Brooks's Law, is

> *Adding manpower to a late software project makes it later.*

—Fred Brooks, Jr.

 Pitfall: **Customers who confuse mock-ups with completed features.**

As a developer, this pitfall may seem ridiculous to you. But nontechnical customers sometimes have difficulty distinguishing a highly polished digital mock-up from a working feature! The solution is simple: use paper-and-pencil techniques such as hand-drawn sketches and storyboards to reach agreement with the customer—there can be no doubt that such Lo-Fi mockups represent *proposed* rather than implemented functionality.

 Pitfall: **Adding cool features that do not make the product more successful.**

Agile development was inspired in part by the frustration of software developers building what they thought was cool code that customers dropped. The temptation is strong to add a feature that you think would be great, but it can also be disappointing when your work is discarded. User stories help all stakeholders prioritize development and reduce chances of wasted effort on features that only developers love.

 Pitfall: **Sketches without storyboards.**

Sketches are static; interactions with a SaaS app occur as a sequence of actions over time. You and the customer must agree not only on the general content of the Lo-Fi UI sketches, but on what happens when they interact with the page. "Animating" the Lo-Fi sketches—"OK, you clicked on that button, here's what you see; is that what you expected?"—goes a long way towards ironing out misunderstandings *before* the stories are turned into tests and code.

 Pitfall: **Using Cucumber solely as a test-automation tool rather than as a common middle ground for all stakeholders.**

If you look at `web_steps.rb`, you'll quickly notice that low-level, imperative Cucumber steps such as "When I press Cancel" are merely a thin wrapper around Capybara's "headless browser" API, and you might wonder (as some of the authors' students have) why you should use Cucumber at all. But Cucumber's real value is in creating documentation that nontechnical stakeholders and developers can agree on *and* that serves as the basis for automating acceptance and integration tests, which is why the Cucumber features and steps for a mature app should evolve towards a "mini-language" appropriate for that app. For example, an app for scheduling vacations for hospital nurses would have scenarios that make heavy use of domain-specific terms such as *shift, seniority, holiday, overtime,* and so on, rather than focusing on the low-level interactions between the user and each view.

 Pitfall: **Trying to predict what you need before you need it.**

Part of the magic of Behavior-Driven Design (and Test-Driven Development in the next chapter) is that you write the tests *before* you write the code you need, and then you write code needed to pass the tests. This top-down approach again makes it more likely for your efforts to be useful, which is harder to do when you're predicting what you think you'll need. This observation has also been called the YAGNI principle—You Ain't Gonna Need It.

 Pitfall: **Careless use of negative expectations.**

Beware of overusing *Then I should not see. . . .* Because it tests a negative condition, you might not be able to tell if the output is what you intended—you can only tell what the output *isn't*. Many, many outputs don't match, so that is not likely to be a good test. For example, if you were testing for the *absence* of "Welcome, Dave!" but you accidentally wrote **Then I should not see "Greetings, Dave!"**, the scenario will pass even if the app incorrectly emits "Welcome, Dave!". Always include positive expectations such as *Then I should see. . .* to check results.

 Pitfall: **Careless use of positive expectations.**

Even if you use positive expectations such as *Then I should see. . .* , what if the string you're looking for occurs multiple times on the page? For example, if the logged-in user's name is Emma and your scenario is checking whether Jane Austen's book *Emma* was correctly added to the shopping cart, a scenario step *Then I should see "Emma"* might pass even if the cart isn't working. To avoid this pitfall, use Capybara's **within** helper, which constrains the scope of matchers such as *I should see* to the element(s) matching a given CSS selector, as in `Then I should see "Emma" within "div#shopping_cart"`, and use unambiguous HTML `id` or `class` attributes for page elements you want to name in your scenarios. The Capybara documentation[12] lists all the matchers and helpers.

 Pitfall: **Delivering a story as "done" when only the happy path is tested.**

As should be clear by now, a story is only a candidate for delivery when both the happy path and the most important sad paths have been tested. Of course, as Chapter 8 describes, there are many more ways for something to work incorrectly than to work correctly, and sad-path tests are not intended to be a substitute for finer-grained test coverage. But from the user's point of view, correct app behavior when the user accidentally does the wrong thing is just as important as correct behavior when she does the right thing.

7.12 Concluding Remarks: Pros and Cons of BDD

> *In software, we rarely have meaningful requirements. Even if we do, the only measure of success that matters is whether our solution solves the customer's shifting idea of what their problem is.*
>
> —Jeff Atwood, *Is Software Development Like Manufacturing?*, 2006

Figure 7.16 shows the relationship of the testing tools introduced in this chapter to the testing tools in the following chapters. Cucumber allows writing user stories as features, scenarios, and steps and matches these steps to step definitions using regular expressions. The step definitions invoke methods in Cucumber and Capybara. We need Capybara because we are writing a SaaS application, and testing requires a tool to act as the user and web

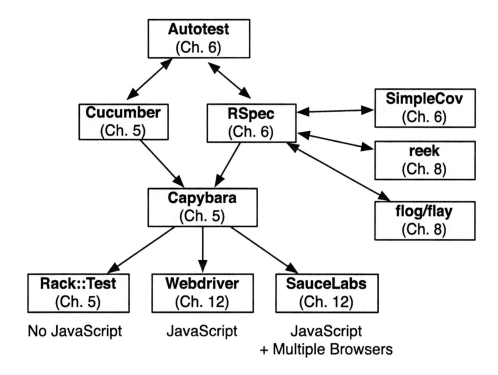

Figure 7.16: The relationship of Cucumber, RSpec, Capybara, and the many other testing tools and services described in this book. This chapter uses Rack::Test, since our application does not yet use JavaScript. If it did, we'd have to use the slower but more complete Webdriver. Chapter 12 shows how we can replace Webdriver with the service from SauceLabs to test your app with many browsers instead of just one.

browser. If the app was not for SaaS, then we could invoke the methods that test the app directly in Cucumber.

The advantage of user stories and BDD is creating a common language shared by all stakeholders, especially the nontechnical customers. BDD is perfect for projects where the requirements are poorly understood or rapidly changing, which is often the case. User stories also make it easy to break projects into small increments or iterations, which makes it easier to estimate how much work remains. The use of 3x5 cards and paper mockups of user interfaces keeps the nontechnical customers involved in the design and prioritization of features, which increases the chances of the software meeting the customer's needs. Iterations drive the refinement of this software development process. Moreover, BDD and Cucumber naturally leads to writing tests *before* coding, shifting the validation and development effort from debugging to testing.

Comparing user stories, Cucumber, points, and velocity to the plan-and-document processes makes it clear that BDD plays many important roles in the Agile process:

1. Requirement elicitation

2. Requirement documentation

3. Acceptance tests

Google places these posters inside restrooms to remind developers of the importance of testing. Used with permission.

4. Traceability between features and implementation

5. Scheduling and monitoring of project progress

The downside of user stories and BDD is that it may be difficult or too expensive to have continuous contact with the customer throughout the development process, as some customers may not want to participate. This approach may also not scale to very large software development projects or to safety critical applications. Perhaps plan-and-document is a better match in both situations.

Another potential downside of BDD is that the project could satisfy customers but not result in a good software architecture, which is an important foundation for maintaining the code. Chapter 11 discusses design patterns, which should be part of your software development toolkit. Recognizing which pattern matches the circumstances and refactoring code when necessary (see Chapter 9) reduces the chances of BDD producing poor software architectures.

All this being said, there is enormous momentum in the Ruby community (which places high value on testable, beautiful and self-documenting code) to document and promote best practices for specifying behavior both as a way to document the intent of the app's developers and to provide executable acceptance tests. The Cucumber wiki[13] is a good place to start.

BDD may not seem initially the natural way to develop software; the strong temptation is to just start hacking code. However, once you have learned BDD and had success at it, for most developers there is no going back. Your authors remind you that good tools, while sometimes intimidating to learn, repay the effort many times over in the long run. Whenever possible in the future, we believe you'll follow the BDD path to writing beautiful code.

7.13 To Learn More

- The Cucumber wiki[14] has links to documentation, tutorials, examples, screencasts, best practices, and lots more on Cucumber.

- *The Cucumber Book* (Wynne and Hellesøy 2012), co-authored by the tool's creator and one of its earliest adopters, includes detailed information and examples using Cucumber, excellent discussions of best practices for BDD, and additional Cucumber uses such as testing RESTful service automation.

- Ben Mabey[15] (a core Cucumber developer) and Jonas Nicklas[16], among others, have written eloquently about the benefits of declarative vs. imperative Cucumber scenarios. In fact, the main author of Cucumber, Aslak Hellesøy, deliberately removed[17] **web_steps.rb** (which we met in Section 7.7) from Cucumber in October 2011, which is why we had to separately install the `cucumber_rails_training_wheels` gem to get it for our examples.

ACM IEEE-Computer Society Joint Task Force. Computer science curricula 2013, Ironman Draft (version 1.0). Technical report, February 2013. URL http://ai.stanford.edu/users/sahami/CS2013/.

B. W. Boehm and R. Valerdi. Achievements and challenges in COCOMO-based software resource estimation. *IEEE Software*, 25(5):74–83, Sept 2008.

F. P. Brooks. *The Mythical Man-Month*. Addison-Wesley, Reading, MA, Anniversary edition, 1995. ISBN 0201835959.

D. Burkes. Personal communication, December 2012.

J. Johnson. The CHAOS report. Technical report, The Standish Group, Boston, Massachusetts, 1995. URL `http://blog.standishgroup.com/`.

J. Johnson. The CHAOS report. Technical report, The Standish Group, Boston, Massachusetts, 2009. URL `http://blog.standishgroup.com/`.

A. Taylor. IT projects sink or swim. *BCS Review*, Jan. 2000. URL `http://archive.bcs.org/bulletin/jan00/article1.htm`.

M. Wynne and A. Hellesøy. *The Cucumber Book: Behaviour-Driven Development for Testers and Developers*. Pragmatic Bookshelf, 2012. ISBN 1934356808.

Notes

[1] `http://http://www.fandango.com/rss/moviefeed`
[2] `https://developers.google.com/maps/documentation/javascript/tutorial`
[3] `http://www.omdbapi.com`
[4] `http://imdb.com`
[5] `http://www.youtube.com/watch?v=mTYcHg51sWY`
[6] `http://docs.google.com`
[7] `http://campfirenow.com`
[8] `https://github.com/cucumber/cucumber/wiki/cucumber.yml`
[9] `http://railscasts.com/episodes/159-more-on-cucumber`
[10] `http://cukes.info`
[11] `http://www.cs.st-andrews.ac.uk/~ifs/Books/SE9/CaseStudies/MHCPMS/SupportingDocs/MHCPMSCaseStudy.pdf`
[12] `http://rubydoc.info/github/jnicklas/capybara/`
[13] `http://cukes.info`
[14] `http://cukes.info`
[15] `http://benmabey.com/2008/05/19/imperative-vs-declarative-scenarios-in-user-stories.html`
[16] `http://elabs.se/blog/15-you-re-cuking-it-wrong`
[17] `http://aslakhellesoy.com/post/11055981222/the-training-wheels-came-off`

7.14 Suggested Projects

Project 7.1. *Create step definitions that would allow you to write the following steps in a RottenPotatoes scenario:*
`http://pastebin.com/tni5pA8w`

```
1 | Given the movie "Inception" exists
2 | And it has 5 reviews
3 | And its average review score is 3.5
```

Hint: *Instance variables in Cucumber step definitions are associated with the scenario, not with the step.*

Project 7.2. *Suppose in RottenPotatoes, instead of dials to pick the rating and pick the release date, the choice was instead fill in the blank form. First, make the appropriate changes to the scenario in Figure 7.5. List the step definitions from* `features/cucumber/web_steps.rb` *that Cucumber would now invoke in testing these new steps.*

Project 7.3. *Add a sad path scenario to the feature in Figure 7.5 of what happens when a user leaves the title field empty.*

Project 7.4. *Write down a list of background steps that will populate the RottenPotatoes site with a few movies.*

Project 7.5. *Create a lo-fi mockup showing the current behavior of the RottenPotatoes app.*

Project 7.6. *Come up with a feature that you would like to add to RottenPotatoes, and draw a storyboards showing how it would be implemented and used.*

Project 7.7. *Create a list of steps such as those in Figure 7.12 that would be used to implement the step:*

http://pastebin.com/6RvBzD4f

```
1|  When / I delete the movie: "(.*)"/ do |title|
```

Project 7.8. *Use Cucumber and Mechanize to create integration tests or acceptance tests for an existing SaaS application that has no testing harness.*

Project 7.9. *Create a Cucumber step definition that allows you to check for multiple instances of a string on a page, such as* `Then I should see "Hurrah" 3 times`. *Hint: Consider what happens if you try to split the page text into chunks separated by the string to be matched.*

Project 7.10. *Enhance your step definition from the previous exercise so that matches can be scoped to a CSS selector, as in* `Then I should see "Hurrah" 3 times within "div#congratulations"`.

Project 7.11. *Transform two paragraphs of the patient management system[1] found online and turn them into User Stories in the Connextra format. Are they all SMART? Which ones are function and which are non-functional?*

Project 7.12. *Transform the RottenPotatoes user stories into a Software Requirements Specification document. Where any hard to express in an SRS?*

Project 7.13. *Use an ad hoc method to estimate software development effort (e.g., time) from a Plan-and-Document process and compare to actual effort required that is tracked using a tool like Pivotal Tracker. Note: The margin icon identifies projects from the ACM/IEEE 2013 Software Engineering standard (ACM IEEE-Computer Society Joint Task Force 2013).*

Project 7.14. *Describe the fundamental challenges of and common techniques used for requirements elicitation.*

Project 7.15. *Differentiate between forward and backward tracing and explain their roles in the requirements validation process.*

Project 7.16. *List several examples of software risks.*

Project 7.17. *Describe different categories of risk in software systems.*

Project 7.18. *Describe the impact of risk in a Plan-and-Document lifecycle.*

8 Software Testing: Test-Driven Development

Donald Knuth (1938–) one of the most illustrious computer scientists, received the Turing Award in 1974 for major contributions to the analysis of algorithms and the design of programming languages, and in particular for his contributions to his multi-volume *The Art of Computer Programming*. Many consider this series the definitive reference on analysis of algorithms; "bounty checks" from Knuth for finding errors in his books are among the most prized trophies among computer scientists. Knuth also invented the widely-used TEX typesetting system, with which this book was prepared.

One of the most important lessons, perhaps, is the fact that SOFTWARE IS HARD. . . . TEX and METAFONT proved to be much more difficult than all the other things I had done (like proving theorems or writing books). The creation of good software demands a significantly higher standard of accuracy than those other things do, and it requires a longer attention span than other intellectual tasks.

—Donald Knuth, Keynote address to 11th World Computer Congress, 1989

Concepts

The big concepts of this chapter are test creation, test coverage, and levels of testing.

The five principles for creating good tests are Fast, Independent, Repeatable, Self-checking, and Timely (FIRST). To help keep tests Fast and Independent from the behavior of other classes, use **mock objects** and **stubs**. They are examples of **seams**, which change program behavior during test without changing the source code itself.

Testing in the Agile lifecycle, which follows **Test-Driven Development** (**TDD**), follows these steps:

- Starting from the acceptance and integration tests derived from **User stories**, write failing **unit tests** that test the nonexistent code you wish you had. We will use the RSpec tool to do this.

- Write just enough code to pass one test and look for opportunities to **refactor** the code before continuing with the next test. Since failed tests are reported in red and passing results are green, the sequence is called **Red–Green–Refactor**.

- Use **mocks** and **stubs** in your tests to isolate the behavior of the code you're testing from the behavior of other classes or methods on which it depends.

- Various **code coverage** metrics help you determine which parts of your code need more testing.

For the Plan and Document lifecycle, you use some of the same concepts in a quite different order and even with different people:

- The program manager assigns programming tasks based on the SRS, so **unit testing** starts after coding. **Quality-Assurance** (**QA**) testers take over from the developers to perform the higher level tests.

- **Top-down**, **Bottom-up**, and **Sandwich** are options on how to combine the resulting code to perform **integration testing**. The testing plan and results are documented, such as by following IEEE Standard 829-2008.

- After integration testing, the QA team performs a **systems test** before releasing it to the customer. Testing stops when a specified level of coverage is reached, such as "95% statement coverage."

- An alternative to testing, used for small critical software, is **formal methods**. They use formal specifications of correct program behavior that are automatically verified by theorem provers or by exhaustive state search, both of which can go beyond what conventional testing can do.

Their approaches to testing are some of the starkest differences between Agile and Plan-and-Document lifecycles: when test writing starts, the order that levels of tests are written, and even who does the testing.

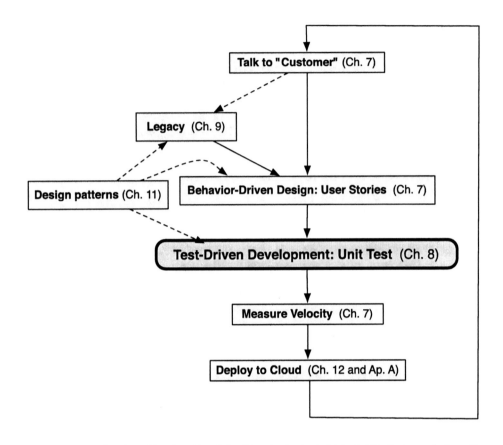

Figure 8.1: The Agile software lifecycle and its relationship to the chapters in this book. This chapter emphasizes unit testing as part of Test-Driven Development.

8.1 Background: A RESTful API and a Ruby Gem

Method or function?
Following the terminology of OOP (object-oriented programming), we use *method* to mean a named piece of code that implements a behavior associated with a class, whether it's more like a function that returns a value or more like a procedure that causes side effects. Additional historical terms for such a piece of code include *function, routine, subroutine,* and *subprogram.*

Chapter 1 introduced the Agile lifecycle and distinguished two aspects of software assurance: validation ("Did you build the right thing?") and verification ("Did you build the thing right?"). In this chapter, we focus on verification—building the thing right—via software testing as part of the Agile lifecycle. Figure 8.1 highlights the portion of the Agile lifecycle covered in this chapter.

Although testing is only one technique used for verification, we focus on it because its role is often misunderstood, and as a result it doesn't get as much attention as other parts of the software lifecycle. In addition, as we will see, approaching software construction from a test-centric perspective often improves the software's readability and maintainability. In other words, *testable code tends to be good code, and vice versa.*

In Chapter 7 we began working on a new feature for RottenPotatoes to enable information about a movie to be imported automatically from The Open Movie Database[2], or TMDb for short. In this chapter, we'll develop the necessary methods to complete this feature.

Like many SaaS applications, TMDb is designed to be part of a Service-Oriented Architecture: it has an *API* (application programming interface) that allows external applications, not just human Web surfers, to use its functionality. As Screencast 8.1.1 shows, TMDb's API is RESTful, allowing each request made by an external application to be entirely self-contained, as described in Chapter 2.

Screencast 8.1.1: Using the TMDb API.
`http://vimeo.com/83460540`
TMDb's API is accessed by constructing a RESTful URI for the appropriate function, such as "search for movies matching a keyword" or "retrieve detailed information about a specific movie". To prevent abuse and track each user of the API separately, each developer must first obtain their own *API key* by requesting one via the TMDb website. Request URI's that do not include a valid API key are not honored, returning an error instead. For request URI's containing a valid API key, TMDb returns a JSON object as the result of the request encoded by the URI. This flow—construct a RESTful URI that includes an API key, receive a JSON response—is a common pattern for interacting with external services.

Usually, calling such an API from RottenPotatoes would require us to use the **URI** class in the Ruby standard library to construct the request URI containing our API key, use the **Net::HTTP** class to issue the request to `api.themoviedb.org`, and parse the resulting JSON object (perhaps using the `json` gem). But sometimes we can be more productive by standing on the shoulders of others, as we can in this case. The gem `themoviedb` is a user-contributed Ruby "wrapper" around TMDb's RESTful API, mentioned on the TMDb API documentation pages. Screencast 8.1.2 shows how to use it.

Screencast 8.1.2: Simplified use of the TMDb API with the `themoviedb` gem.
`http://vimeo.com/84683958`
Not every RESTful API has a corresponding Ruby library, but for those that do, such as TMDb, the library can hide the API details behind a few simple Ruby methods. Ahmet Abdi's `themoviedb` gem conveniently constructs the correct RESTful URIs, performs the remote service calls, and parses the JSON results into Ruby objects representing movies, playlists, and so on. But as this screencast shows, we must be careful in how we detect and handle errors interacting with the remote service.

Summary: TMDb (The Movie Database) has a service-oriented API that can be accessed by sending HTTP requests with properly-constructed HTTP URIs and returns an HTTP response whose body is a JSON object containing the response data. Conveniently, the work of creating the appropriate requests and parsing the JSON responses is handled by an open-source Ruby gem, which we can use instead of dealing directly with URIs and JSON.

■ *Elaboration: RESTful APIs and Developer Keys*

Most RESTful APIs require a developer key; some provide it free, others make you pay. For example, a free Google API key[3] allows you to use various Google services such as maps and geocoding. In some cases, like TMDb, you simply embed the key in the URL of each call, using SSL to transmit requests securely (Section 12.9) so malicious users cannot snoop on the key. However, API endpoints that access user-specific data often require more sophisticated third-party authentication, usually using a scheme such as OAuth, which is introduced in Section 5.2.

Self-Check 8.1.1. *True or false: in order to use the TMDb API from another language such as Java, we would need a Java library equivalent to* themoviedb *gem.*

◇ False: the API consists of a set of HTTP requests and JSON responses, so as long as we can transmit and receive bytes over TCP/IP and have the ability to parse strings (the JSON responses), we can use the APIs without a special library. ∎

8.2   FIRST, TDD, and Red–Green–Refactor

Developers "tossing their code over the wall" to **Quality Assurance (QA)** is not typical for SaaS applications, as are the days of QA engineers manually exercising the software and filing bug reports. Indeed, the idea that quality assurance is the responsibility of a separate group rather than the result of a good process is considered antiquated for SaaS apps. Today's SaaS developers bear far more responsibility for testing their own code and participating in reviews; the responsibilities of QA have largely shifted to improving the testing tools infrastructure, helping developers make their code more testable, and verifying that customer-reported bugs are reproducible, as we'll discuss further in Chapter 10. As we shall see, the Agile lifecycle also expects the QA team to be the developers.

Testing today is also far more automated. Automated testing doesn't mean that tests are created automatically for you, but that the tests are self-checking: the test code itself can determine whether the code being tested works or not, without requiring a human to manually check test output or interact with the software. A high degree of automation is key to supporting the five principles for creating good tests, which are summarized by the acronym FIRST: **F**ast, **I**ndependent, **R**epeatable, **S**elf-checking, and **T**imely.

- **F**ast: it should be easy and quick to run the subset of test cases relevant to your current coding task, to avoid interfering with your train of thought. We will use a Ruby tool called Autotest to help with this.

- **I**ndependent: No test should rely on preconditions created by other tests, so that we can prioritize running only a subset of tests that cover recent code changes.

- **R**epeatable: test behavior should not depend on external factors such as today's date or on "magic constants" that will break the tests if their values change, as occurred with many 1960s programs when the year 2000 arrived[4].

Y2K bug in action This photo was taken on Jan. 3, 2000. (Wikimedia Commons)

- **S**elf-checking: each test should be able to determine on its own whether it passed or failed, rather than relying on humans to check its output.

- **T**imely: tests should be created or updated at the same time as the code being tested. As we'll see, with test-driven development the tests are written *immediately before* the code.

Test-driven development (TDD) advocates the use of tests to *drive* the development of code. When TDD is used to create new code, as we do in this chapter, it is sometimes referred to as *test-first development* since the tests come into existence before any of the code being tested. When TDD is used to extend or modify legacy code, as we'll do in Chapter 9, new tests may be created for code that already exists. As we explore TDD in this chapter, we'll show how the Ruby tools support TDD and FIRST. Although TDD may feel strange when you first try it, it tends to result in code that is well tested, more modular, and easier to read than most code developed. While TDD is obviously not the only way to achieve those goals, it is difficult to end up with seriously deficient code if TDD is used correctly.

We will write tests using RSpec, a **domain-specific language** (DSL) for testing Ruby code. A DSL is a small programming language designed to ease tackling problems within a single area (domain) at the expense of generality. You've already seen examples of *external* (standalone) DSLs, such as HTML for describing Web pages. RSpec is an *internal* or *embedded* DSL: RSpec code is just Ruby code, but takes advantage of Ruby's features and syntax so as to make up a "mini-language" focused on the job of testing. Regular expressions are another example of an internal DSL embedded in Ruby.

> **Note:** These examples and instructions are for RSpec versions *earlier than 3.0*. A future version of the book will update these instructions for RSpec 3.0 and later.

RSpec can also be used for integration tests, but we prefer Cucumber since it facilitates dialogue with the customer and automates acceptance as well as integration tests.

RSpec's facilities help us capture *expectations* of how our code should behave. Such tests are executable specifications or "specs" written in Ruby, hence the name RSpec. How can we capture expectations in tests before there is any code to be tested? The surprising answer is that we write a test that exercises the *code we wish we had*, which forces us to think not only about what the code will do, but how it will be used by its callers and collaborators (other pieces of code that have to work with it). We did this in Chapter 7 in the Cucumber scenario step *And I click "Search TMDb"*: when we modified the List Movies view (`views/movies/ index.html.haml`) to include a "Search TMDb" button, we picked the name **search_tmdb** for the not-yet-existing controller method that would respond to the click. Of course, since no method **MoviesController#search_tmdb** existed, the Cucumber step failed (showing red) when you tried to actually run the scenario. In the rest of this chapter we will use TDD to develop the **search_tmdb** method.

Bar#foo is idiomatic Ruby notation denoting the *instance* method **foo** of class **Bar**. The notation **Bar.foo** denotes the *class* method **foo**.

In the MVC architecture, the controller's job is to respond to a user interaction, call the appropriate model method(s) to retrieve or manipulate any necessary data, and generate an appropriate view. We might therefore describe the *desired* behavior of our as-yet-nonexistent controller method as follows:

- It should call a model method to perform the TMDb search, passing it the search terms typed by the user.

- It should select the Search Results HTML view (in Rails parlance, the Search Results *template*) for rendering.

- It should make the TMDb search results available to that template.

Note that none of the methods or templates in this list of desiderata actually exists yet! That is the essence of TDD: write a concrete and concise list of the desired behaviors (the spec), and use it to drive the creation of the methods and templates.

Figure 8.2 shows how we would express these requirements in RSpec. As in Chapter 3, we encourage you learn by doing. Before creating this file, you need to set up RottenPotatoes to use RSpec for testing, which requires four steps:

You can see what they are in `spec/spec_helper.rb`.

1. In the **group :test** block in the Gemfile, add **gem 'rspec-rails'**

http://pastebin.com/2BXbVMN8

```
1   require 'spec_helper'
2
3   describe MoviesController do
4     describe 'searching TMDb' do
5       it 'should call the model method that performs TMDb search'
6       it 'should select the Search Results template for rendering'
7       it 'should make the TMDb search results available to that template'
8     end
9   end
```

Figure 8.2: Skeleton of RSpec examples for MoviesController#search_tmdb. By convention over configuration, the
specs for app/controllers/movies_controller.rb are expected to be in
spec/controllers/movies_controller_spec.rb, and so on. (Use Pastebin to copy-and-paste this code.)

2. Since our app will be using and relying on themoviedb gem as well, add **gem 'the-moviedb'** outside of any **group** block (since the gem will be used in the production, development, and testing environments)

3. As always when modifying the Gemfile, run bundle install --without production

4. In the app root directory of RottenPotatoes, run rails generate rspec:install to set up the files and directories RSpec needs. This step also creates a default spec/spec_helper.rb file that sets up some helper methods we will use in all the examples.

You're now ready to create the file spec/controllers/movies_controller_-spec.rb as shown in Figure 8.2. Line 1 loads some helper methods that will be used by all RSpec tests; in general, for Rails apps this will be the first line of any specfile. Line 3 says that the following specs **describe** the behavior of the **MoviesController** class. Because this class has several methods, line 4 says that this first set of specs describes the behavior of the method that searches TMDb. As you can see, **describe** can be followed by either a class name or a descriptive documentation string.

The next three lines are placeholders for *examples*, the RSpec term for a short piece of code that tests *one* specific behavior of the **search_tmdb** method. We haven't written any test code yet, but the next screencast shows that we can not only execute these test skeletons with the rspec command, but more importantly, automate running them with the autotest tool. While the command rake spec is one way to run the complete set of all tests, the automation of autotest helps productivity since we don't have to shift our attention between writing code and running tests. It also makes running tests Faster since it is smart about focusing only on tests that are still failing or for which the code has changed recently, rather than re-running the entire test suite every time. To use autotest, inside the **group :test** section of your Gemfile add the line **gem autotest-rails**, and run bundle as usual to make sure the gem is installed. Then in the root directory of your app, just type autotest to start it. For the rest of the chapter, we'll assume that autotest is running and that whenever you add tests or application code you will get immediate feedback from RSpec. In the next section we'll create our first tests using TDD.

Screencast 8.2.1: Executing the empty test skeletons and automating execution with `autotest`.

`http://vimeo.com/34754856`

When we run the `RSpec` command, examples (**it** clauses) containing no code are displayed in yellow as "pending". You can also explicitly mark an example using **pending** and provide a description of why it's pending. Rather than manually running **spec** each time we add or change some code, we can use the `autotest` command, which automatically reruns the appropriate specs whenever you change a specfile or code file.

Summary

- Good tests should be **F**ast, **I**ndependent, **R**epeatable, **S**elf-checking, and **T**imely (FIRST).

- RSpec is a domain-specific language embedded in Ruby for writing tests. Convention over configuration determines where the specfile corresponding to a given class file should reside.

- Within a specfile, a single *example*, introduced by the **it** method, tests a single behavior of a method. **describe** groups examples hierarchically according to the set of behaviors they test.

Self-Check 8.2.1. *A single RSpec test case or* example *is introduced by the keyword* ____. *A group of related examples is introduced by the keyword* ____, *which can be nested to organize examples hierarchically.*

◇ **it**; **describe** ∎

Self-Check 8.2.2. *Since RSpec matches tests to classes using convention over configuration, we would put the tests for* `app/models/movie.rb` *in the file* ____.

◇ `spec/models/movie_spec.rb` ∎

8.3 Seams, Doubles, and the Code You Wish You Had

Figure 8.3 captures the basic TDD method. You might think we've violated the TDD methodology by writing down three test cases in Figure 8.2 before completing the code for any of those cases, but in practice, there's nothing wrong with creating **it** blocks for tests you know you will want to write. Now, though, it's time to get down to business and start working on the tests.

The first example (test case) in Figure 8.2 states that the **search_tmdb** method should call a model method to perform the TMDb search, passing the keywords typed by the user to that method. In Chapter 7, we modified the **index** view of RottenPotatoes by adding an HTML form whose submission would be handled by **MoviesController#search_tmdb**; the form contained a single text field called **search_terms** for the user to fill in. Our test case will therefore need to emulate what happens when the user types something into the **search_terms** field and submits the form. As we know, in a Rails app the **params** hash is automatically populated with the data submitted in a form so that the controller method can

---

Debugging and autotest To use the interactive debugger introduced in Chapter 4 with `autotest`, add **require 'debugger'** to `spec/spec_helper.rb` and insert **debugger** calls wherever you want the action to stop.

1. Before you write any new code, write a test for *one* aspect of the behavior it *should* have. Since the code being tested doesn't exist yet, writing the test forces you to think about how you *wish* the code would behave and interact with its collaborators if it did exist. We call this "exercising the code you wish you had."

2. **Red** step: Run the test, and verify that it fails because you haven't yet implemented the code necessary to make it pass.

3. **Green** step: Write the *simplest possible* code that causes *this* test to pass without breaking any existing tests.

4. **Refactor** step: Look for opportunities to *refactor* either your code or your tests—changing the code's structure to eliminate redundancy, repetition, or other ugliness that may have arisen as a result of adding the new code. The tests ensure that your refactoring doesn't introduce bugs.

5. Repeat until all behaviors necessary to pass a scenario step are complete.

Figure 8.3: The Test-Driven Development (TDD) loop is also known as Red–Green–Refactor because of its skeleton in steps 2–4. The last step assumes you are developing code in order to complete a scenario, such as the one you started in Chapter 7.

http://pastebin.com/6tJvd0hx

```
 1   require 'spec_helper'
 2
 3   describe MoviesController do
 4     describe 'searching TMDb' do
 5       it 'should call the model method that performs TMDb search' do
 6         post :search_tmdb, {:search_terms => 'hardware'}
 7       end
 8       it 'should select the Search Results template for rendering'
 9       it 'should make the TMDb search results available to that template'
10     end
11   end
```

Figure 8.4: Filling out the first spec. Whereas a "bare" it (line 8) serves as a placeholder for a yet-to-be-written example, an it accompanied by a do. . . end block (lines 5–7) is an actual test case.

examine it. Happily, RSpec provides a **post** method that simulates posting a form to a controller action: the first argument is the action name (controller method) that will receive the post, and the second argument is a hash that will become the **params** seen by the controller action. We can now write the first line of our first spec, as Figure 8.4 shows. As the next screencast shows, though, we must overcome a couple of hurdles just to get to the Red phase of Red–Green–Refactor.

Screencast 8.3.1: Developing the first example requires adding an empty controller method and creating an empty view.
`http://vimeo.com/34754876`
To get past RSpec's errors, we first have to create an empty controller method and its corresponding route, so that the action (form submission by the user) would have somewhere to go. Then we need to create an empty view so that the controller action has something to render. That one line of test code drove us to ensure that our new controller method and the view it will ultimately render have the correct names and have a matching route.

At this point RSpec reports Green for our first example, but that's not really accurate because the example itself is incomplete: we haven't actually checked whether **search_tmdb** calls a model method to search TMDb, as the spec requires. (We did this deliberately in order to illustrate some of the mechanics necessary to get your first specs running. Usually, since

http://pastebin.com/fyyXrYJD

```
1  require 'spec_helper'
2
3  describe MoviesController do
4    describe 'searching TMDb' do
5      it 'should call the model method that performs TMDb search' do
6        fake_results = [mock('movie1'), mock('movie2')]
7        Movie.should_receive(:find_in_tmdb).with('hardware').
8          and_return(fake_results)
9        post :search_tmdb, {:search_terms => 'hardware'}
10     end
11     it 'should select the Search Results template for rendering'
12     it 'should make the TMDb search results available to that template'
13   end
14 end
```

Figure 8.5: Completing the example by asserting that the controller method will call the code we wish we had in the Movie model. Lines 5–10 in this listing replace lines 5–7 in Figure 8.4.

each spec tends to be short, you'd complete a spec before re-running your tests.)

How should we check that **search_tmdb** calls a model method, since no model method exists yet? Again, we will write a test for the behavior of the *code we wish we had*, as directed in step 1 of Figure 8.3. Let's pretend we have a model method that does just what we want. In this case, we'd probably want to pass the method a string and get back a collection of **Movie** objects based on TMDb search results matching that string. *If* that method existed, our controller method might therefore call it like this:

http://pastebin.com/ACNefdqY

```
1  @movies = Movie.find_in_tmdb(params[:search_terms])
```

> The code we wish we had will be a class method, since finding movies in TMDb is a behavior related to movies in general and not to a particular instance of a **Movie**.

Figure 8.5 shows the code for a test case that asserts such a call will occur. In this case, the code we are testing—the *subject code*—is **search_tmdb**. However, part of the behavior we're testing appears to depend on **find_in_tmdb**. Since **find_in_tmdb** is code we don't yet have, the goal of lines 6–8 is to "fake" the behavior it would exhibit if we did have it. Line 6 uses RSpec's **mock** method to create an array of two "test double" **Movie** objects. In particular, whereas a real **Movie** object would respond to methods like **title** and **rating**, the test double would raise an exception if you called any methods on it. Given this fact, why would we use doubles at all? The reason is to isolate these specs from the behavior of the **Movie** class, which might have bugs of its own. Mocks are like puppets whose behavior we completely control, allowing us to isolate unit tests from their collaborator classes and keep tests Independent (the I in FIRST).

Returning to Figure 8.5, lines 6–7 express the *expectation* that the **Movie** class should receive a call to the method **find_in_tmdb** and that method should receive the single argument **'hardware'**. RSpec will open the **Movie** class and define a class method called **find_in_tmdb** whose only purpose is to track whether it gets called, and if so, whether the right arguments are passed. Critically, *if a method with the same name already existed in the* **Movie** *class, it would be temporarily "overwritten"* by this *method stub*. That's why in our case it doesn't matter that we haven't written the "real" **find_in_tmdb**: it wouldn't get called anyway!

> In fact, an alias for **mock** is **double**. For clarity, use **mock** when you're going to ask the fake object to do things, and **double** when you just need a stand-in.

The use of **should_receive** to temporarily replace a "real" method for testing purposes is an example of using a *seam*: "a place where you can alter behavior in your program without editing in that place." (Feathers 2004) In this case, **should_receive** creates a seam by overriding a method in place, without us having to edit the file containing the original method (although in this case, the original method doesn't even exist yet). Seams are also important when it comes to adding new code to your application, but in the rest of this chapter we will see many more examples of seams in testing. Seams are useful in testing because they let us break dependencies between a piece of code we want to test and its collaborators, allowing the collaborators to behave differently under test than they would in real life.

Line 8 (which is just a continuation of line 7) specifies that **find_in_tmdb** should return the collection of doubles we set up in line 6. This completes the illusion of "the code we wish we had": we're calling a method that doesn't yet exist, and supplying the result we wish it would give if it existed! If we omit **with**, RSpec will still check that **find_in_tmdb** gets called, but won't check if the arguments are what we expected. If we omit **and_return**, the fake method call will return **nil** rather than a value chosen by us. In any case, after each example is run, RSpec performs a *teardown* step that restores the classes to their original condition, so if we wanted to perform these same fake-outs in other examples, we'd need to specify them in each one (though we'll soon see a way to DRY out such repetition). This automatic teardown is another important part of keeping tests Independent.

> Technically, in this case it would be OK to omit **and_return**, since this example isn't checking the return value, but we included it for illustrative purposes.

This new version of the test fails because we established an expectation that **search_tmdb** would call **find_in_tmdb**, but the **search_tmdb** isn't even written yet. Therefore the last step is to go from Red to Green by adding just enough code to **search_tmdb** to pass this test. We say the test *drives* the creation of the code, because adding to the test results in a failure that must be addressed by adding new code in the model. Since the only thing this particular example is testing is the method call to **find_in_tmdb**, it suffices to add to **search_tmdb** the single line of code we had in mind as "the code we wished we had":

http://pastebin.com/vWt9uxGQ

```
1  @movies = Movie.find_in_tmdb(params[:search_terms])
```

If TDD is new to you, this has been a lot to absorb, especially when testing an app using a powerful framework such as Rails. Don't worry—now that you have been exposed to the main concepts, the next round of specs will go faster. It takes a bit of faith to jump into this system, but we have found that the reward is well worth it. Read the summary below and consider having a sandwich and reviewing the concepts in this section before moving on.

Summary

- The TDD cycle of Red–Green–Refactor begins with writing a test that fails because the *subject code* it's testing doesn't exist yet (Red) and then adding the minimum code necessary to pass just that one example (Green).

- Seams let you change the behavior of your application in a particular place without editing in that place. Typical test setup often establishes seams by using **mock** or its alias **double** to create test double objects, or by using **should_receive...and_return** to *stub* (replace and control the return value of) collaborator methods. Mocks and stubs are seams that help with testability by isolating the behavior of the code being tested from the behavior of its collaborators.

- Each example sets up preconditions, executes the subject code, and asserts something about the results. Assertions such as **should, should_not, should_receive**, and **with** make tests Self-checking, eliminating the need for a human programmer to inspect test results.

- After each test, an automatic teardown destroys the mocks and stubs and unsets any expectations, so that tests remain Independent.

■ *Elaboration: Seams in other languages*

In non-object-oriented languages such as C, seams are hard to create. Since all method calls are resolved at link time, usually the developer creates a library containing the "fake" (test double) version of a desired method, and carefully controls library link order to ensure the test-double version is used. Similarly, since C data structures are accessed by reading directly from memory rather than calling accessor methods, data structure seams (mocks) are usually created by using preprocessor directives such as **#ifdef TESTING** to compile the code differently for testing vs. production use.

In statically-typed OO languages like Java, since method calls are resolved at runtime, one way to create seams is to create a subclass of the class under test and override certain methods when compiling against the test harness. Mocking objects is also possible, though the mock object must satisfy the compiler's expectations for a fully-implemented "real" object, even if the mock is doing only a small part of the work that a real object would. The JMock website[5] shows some examples of inserting testing seams in Java.

In dynamic OO languages like Ruby that let you modify classes at runtime, we can create a seam almost anywhere and anytime. RSpec exploits this ability in allowing us to create just the specific mocks and stubs needed by each test, which makes tests easy to write.

Self-Check 8.3.1. *In Figure 8.5, why must the* **should_receive** *expectation in line 7 come* before *the* **post** *action in line 9?*

◇ The expectation needs to set up a test double for **find_in_tmdb** that can be monitored to make sure it was called. Since the **post** action is eventually going to result in calling **find_in_tmdb**, the double must be set up before the **post** occurs, otherwise the real **find_in_tmdb** would be called. (In this case, **find_in_tmdb** doesn't even exist yet, so the test would fail for that reason.) ■

http://pastebin.com/T5rakACv

```
 1 require 'spec_helper'
 2
 3 describe MoviesController do
 4   describe 'searching TMDb' do
 5     it 'should call the model method that performs TMDb search' do
 6       fake_results = [mock('movie1'), mock('movie2')]
 7       Movie.should_receive(:find_in_tmdb).with('hardware').
 8         and_return(fake_results)
 9       post :search_tmdb, {:search_terms => 'hardware'}
10     end
11     it 'should select the Search Results template for rendering' do
12       fake_results = [mock('Movie'), mock('Movie')]
13       Movie.stub(:find_in_tmdb).and_return(fake_results)
14       post :search_tmdb, {:search_terms => 'hardware'}
15       response.should render_template('search_tmdb')
16     end
17     it 'should make the TMDb search results available to that template'
18   end
19 end
```

Figure 8.6:   **Filling out the second example. Lines 11–16 replace line 11 from Figure 8.5.**

8.4   Expectations, Mocks, Stubs, and Example Setup & Teardown

Returning to our original specfile skeleton from the listing in Figure 8.2, line 6 says that **search_tmdb** should select the "Search Results" view for rendering. Of course, that view doesn't exist yet, but as in the first example we wrote above, that needn't stop us.

Is this really necessary? Since the default view is determined by convention over configuration, all we're really doing here is testing Rails' built-in functionality. But if we were rendering one view if the action succeeded but a different view for displaying an error, examples like this would verify that the correct view was selected.

Since we know from Chapter 3 that the default behavior of the method **Movies-Controller#search_tmdb** is to attempt to render the view app/views/movies/search_tmdb.html.haml (which we created in Chapter 7), our spec just needs to verify that the controller action will indeed try to render that view template. To do this we will use the **response** method of RSpec: once we have done a **get** or **post** action in a controller spec, the object returned by the **response** method will contain the app server's response to that action, and we can assert an expectation that the response *would have rendered* a particular view. This happens in line 15 of Figure 8.6, which illustrates another kind of RSpec assertion: *object*.**should** *match-condition*. In this example, *match-condition* is supplied by **render_template()**, so the assertion is satisfied if the object (in this case the response from the controller action) attempted to render a particular view. We will see the use of **should** with other *match-conditions*. The negative assertion **should_not** can be used to specify that the *match-condition* should not be true.

There are two things to notice about Figure 8.6. First, since each of the two examples (lines 5–10 and 11–16) are self-contained and Independent, we have to create the test doubles and perform the **post** command separately in each. Second, whereas the first example uses **should_receive**, the second example uses **stub**, which creates a test double for a method but *doesn't* establish an expectation that that method will necessarily be called. The double springs into action *if* the method is called, but it's not an error if the method is never called. Make the changes so that your specfile looks like Figure 8.6; autotest should still be running and report that this second example passes.

In this simple example, you could argue that we're splitting hairs by using **should_-receive** in one example and **stub** in another, but the goal is to illustrate that *each example should test a single behavior.* This second example is *only* checking that the correct view is selected for rendering. It's *not* checking that the appropriate model method gets called—

```
1  require 'spec_helper'
2
3  describe MoviesController do
4    describe 'searching TMDb' do
5      before :each do
6        @fake_results = [mock('movie1'), mock('movie2')]
7      end
8      it 'should call the model method that performs TMDb search' do
9        Movie.should_receive(:find_in_tmdb).with('hardware').
10         and_return(@fake_results)
11       post :search_tmdb, {:search_terms => 'hardware'}
12     end
13     it 'should select the Search Results template for rendering' do
14       Movie.stub(:find_in_tmdb).and_return(@fake_results)
15       post :search_tmdb, {:search_terms => 'hardware'}
16       response.should render_template('search_tmdb')
17     end
18     it 'should make the TMDb search results available to that template'
19   end
20 end
```

Figure 8.7: DRYing out the controller examples using a before block (lines 5–7).

that's the job of the first example. In fact, even if the method **Movie.find_in_tmdb** actually *was* implemented already, we'd still stub it out in these examples, because examples should isolate the behaviors under test from the behaviors of other classes with which the subject code collaborates.

Before we write another example, we consider the Refactor step of Red–Green–Refactor. Given that lines 6 and 12 are identical, Figure 8.7 shows one way to DRY them out by *factoring out* common setup code into a **before(:each)** block. As the name implies, this code is executed before *each* of the examples within the **describe** example group, similar to the **Background** section of a Cucumber feature, whose steps are performed before each scenario. There is also **before(:all)**, which runs setup code just once for a whole group of tests; but you risk making your tests dependent on each other by using it, since it's easy for hard-to-debug dependencies to creep in that are only exposed when tests are run in a different order or when only a subset of tests are run.

While the concept of factoring out common setup into a **before** block is straightforward, we had to make one syntactic change to make it work, because of the way RSpec is implemented. Specifically, we had to change **fake_results** into an instance variable **@fake_results**, because local variables occurring inside each test case's **do...end** block disappear once that test case finishes running. In contrast, instance variables of an example group are visible to all examples in that group. Since we are setting the value in the **before :each** block, every test case will see the same initial value of **@fake_results**.

There's just one example left to write, to check that the TMDb search results will be made available to the response view. Recall that in Chapter 7, we created views/movies/ search_tmdb.html.haml under the assumption that **@movies** would be set up by the controller action to contain the list of matching movies from TMDb. That's why in **MoviesController#search_tmdb** we assigned the result of calling **find_in_tmdb** to the instance variable **@movies**. (Recall that instance variables set in a controller action are available to the view.)

The RSpec **assigns()** method keeps track of what instance variables were assigned in the controller method. Hence **assigns(:movies)** returns whatever value (if any) was assigned to

Instance variable of what? @fake_results is an instance variable not of the class under test (**MoviesController**), but of the **Test::Spec::-ExampleGroup** object that represents a group of test cases.

http://pastebin.com/LJiz2q2q

```
 1 | require 'spec_helper'
 2 |
 3 | describe MoviesController do
 4 |   describe 'searching TMDb' do
 5 |     before :each do
 6 |       @fake_results = [mock('movie1'), mock('movie2')]
 7 |     end
 8 |     it 'should call the model method that performs TMDb search' do
 9 |       Movie.should_receive(:find_in_tmdb).with('hardware').
10 |         and_return(@fake_results)
11 |       post :search_tmdb, {:search_terms => 'hardware'}
12 |     end
13 |     it 'should select the Search Results template for rendering' do
14 |       Movie.stub(:find_in_tmdb).and_return(@fake_results)
15 |       post :search_tmdb, {:search_terms => 'hardware'}
16 |       response.should render_template('search_tmdb')
17 |     end
18 |     it 'should make the TMDb search results available to that template' do
19 |       Movie.stub(:find_in_tmdb).and_return(@fake_results)
20 |       post :search_tmdb, {:search_terms => 'hardware'}
21 |       assigns(:movies).should == @fake_results
22 |     end
23 |   end
24 | end
```

Figure 8.8: Asserting that @movie is set up correctly by search_tmdb. Lines 18–22 in this listing replace line 18 in Figure 8.7.

@movies in **search_tmdb**, and our spec just has to verify that the controller action correctly sets up this variable. In our case, we've already arranged to return our doubles as the result of the faked-out method call, so the correct behavior for **search_tmdb** would be to set **@movies** to this value, as line 21 of Figure 8.8 asserts.

■ *Elaboration: More than we need?*

Strictly speaking, for the purposes of this example the stubbed **find_in_tmdb** could have returned any value at all, such as the string "I am a movie", because the *only* behavior tested by this example is whether the correct instance variable is being set up and made available to the view. In particular, this example doesn't care what the *value* of that variable is, or whether **find_in_tmdb** is returning something sensible. But since we already had doubles set up, it was easy enough to use them in this example.

Our last task in Red–Green–Refactor is the Refactor step.   The second and third examples are identical except for the last line in each one (lines 16 and 21). To DRY them out, Figure 8.9 starts a separate nested example group with **describe**, grouping the common behaviors of the last two examples into their own **before** block. We chose the description string `after valid search` to name this **describe** block because the examples in this subgroup all assume that a valid call to **find_in_tmdb** has occurred. (That assumption itself is tested by the first example.)

When example groups are nested, any **before** blocks associated with the outer nesting are executed prior to those associated with the inner nesting. So, for example, considering the test case in lines 18–20 of Figure 8.9, the setup code in lines 5–7 is run first, followed by the setup code in lines 14–17, and finally the example itself (lines 18–20).

Our next task will be to use TDD to create the model method **find_in_tmdb** that we've so far been stubbing out. Since this method is supposed to call the actual TMDb service,

```
1   require 'spec_helper'
2
3   describe MoviesController do
4     describe 'searching TMDb' do
5       before :each do
6         @fake_results = [mock('movie1'), mock('movie2')]
7       end
8       it 'should call the model method that performs TMDb search' do
9         Movie.should_receive(:find_in_tmdb).with('hardware').
10          and_return(@fake_results)
11        post :search_tmdb, {:search_terms => 'hardware'}
12      end
13      describe 'after valid search' do
14        before :each do
15          Movie.stub(:find_in_tmdb).and_return(@fake_results)
16          post :search_tmdb, {:search_terms => 'hardware'}
17        end
18        it 'should select the Search Results template for rendering' do
19          response.should render_template('search_tmdb')
20        end
21        it 'should make the TMDb search results available to that template' do
22          assigns(:movies).should == @fake_results
23        end
24      end
25    end
26  end
```

Figure 8.9: Completed and refactored spec for search_tmdb. The nested group starting at line 13 allows DRYing out the duplication between lines 14–15 and 19–20 in Figure 8.8.

we will again need to use stubbing, this time to avoid having our examples depend on the behavior of a remote Internet service.

Summary

- An example of the Refactor step of Red–Green–Refactor is to move common setup code into a **before** block, thus DRYing out your specs.

- Like **should_receive**, stubbing with **stub** creates a "test double" method for use in tests, but unlike **should_receive**, **stub** doesn't require that the method actually be called.

- **assigns()** allows a controller test to inspect the values of instance variables set by a controller action.

Self-Check 8.4.1. *Specify whether each of the following RSpec constructs is used to (a) create a seam, (b) determine the behavior of a seam, (c) neither: (1)* **assigns()**; *(2)* **should_receive**; *(3)* **stub**; *(4)* **and_return**.

◇ (1) c, (2) a, (3) a, (4) b ∎

Self-Check 8.4.2. *Why is it usually preferable to use* **before(:each)** *rather than* **before(:all)**?

◇ Code in a **before(:each)** block is run before each spec in that block, setting up identical preconditions for all those specs and thereby keeping them Independent. ∎

8.5   Fixtures and Factories

Mocks and stubs are appropriate when you need a stand-in with a small amount of functionality to express a test case. But suppose you were testing a new method **Movie#name_with_rating** that you know will examine the **title** and **rating** attributes of a **Movie** object. You could create a mock that knows all that information, and pass that mock:

http://pastebin.com/mTMdUt2i

```
1  fake_movie = mock('Movie')
2  fake_movie.stub(:title).and_return('Casablanca')
3  fake_movie.stub(:rating).and_return('PG')
4  fake_movie.name_with_rating.should == 'Casablanca (PG)'
```

But there are two reasons not to use a mock here. First, this mock object needs almost as much functionality as a real **Movie** object, so you're probably better off using a real object. Second, since the instance method being tested is part of the **Movie** class itself, it makes sense to use a real object since this isn't a case of isolating the test code from collaborator classes.

You have two choices for where to get a real **Movie** object to use in such tests. One choice is to set up one or more *fixtures*—a fixed state used as a baseline for one or more tests. The term *fixture* comes from the manufacturing world: a test fixture is a device that holds or supports the item under test. Since all state in Rails SaaS apps is kept in the database, a fixture file defines a set of objects that is automatically loaded into the test database before tests are run, so you can use those objects in your tests without first setting them up. Like setup and teardown of mocks and stubs, the test database is erased and reloaded with the fixtures before *each spec*, keeping tests Independent. Rails looks for fixtures in a file containing **YAML** (Yet Another Markup Language) objects. As Figure 8.10 shows, YAML is a very simpleminded way of representing hierarchies of objects with attributes, similar to XML, which we saw at the beginning of the chapter. The fixtures for the **Movie** model are loaded from `spec/fixtures/movies.yml`, and are available to your specs via their symbolic names, as Figure 8.10 shows.

Strictly speaking, it's not erased, but each spec is run inside a *database transaction* that is rolled back when the spec finishes.

But unless used carefully, fixtures can interfere with tests being Independent, as every test now depends implicitly on the fixture state, so changing the fixtures might change the behavior of tests. In addition, although each individual test probably relies on only one or two fixtures, the union of fixtures required by all tests can become unwieldy. For this reason, many programmers prefer to use a *factory*—a framework designed to allow quick creation of full-featured objects (rather than mocks) at testing time. For example, the popular FactoryGirl[6] tool for Rails lets you define a factory for Movie objects and create just the objects you need quickly for each test, selectively overriding only certain attributes, as Figure 8.11 shows. (FactoryGirl is part of the bookware.) In our simple app, using a factory doesn't confer much benefit over just calling **Movie.new** to create a new Movie directly. But in more complicated apps in which object creation and initialization involve many steps—for example, objects that have many attributes that must be initialized at creation time—a factory helps DRY out your test preconditions (**before** blocks) and streamline your test code.

Before adding more functionality, let's dig a bit more deeply into how RSpec works. RSpec's **should** is a great example of the use of Ruby language features to improve readability and blur the line between tests and documentation. The following screencast explains in a bit more detail how an expression such as **value.should == 5** is actually handled.

http://pastebin.com/LViW2uA8

```
1   # spec/fixtures/movies.yml
2   milk_movie:
3     id: 1
4     title: Milk
5     rating: R
6     release_date: 2008-11-26
7
8   documentary_movie:
9     id: 2
10    title: Food, Inc.
11    release_date: 2008-09-07
```

http://pastebin.com/n6hkM1Cw

```
1   # spec/models/movie_spec.rb:
2
3   require 'spec_helper.rb'
4
5   describe Movie do
6     fixtures :movies
7     it 'should include rating and year in full name' do
8       movie = movies(:milk_movie)
9       movie.name_with_rating.should == 'Milk (R)'
10    end
11  end
```

Figure 8.10: Fixtures declared in YAML files (top) are automatically loaded into the test database before each spec is executed (bottom).

http://pastebin.com/60Th29d1

```
1   # spec/factories/movie.rb
2
3   FactoryGirl.define do
4     factory :movie do
5       title 'A Fake Title' # default values
6       rating 'PG'
7       release_date { 10.years.ago }
8     end
9   end
```

http://pastebin.com/DVpJAWgr

```
1   # in spec/models/movie_spec.rb
2   describe Movie do
3     it 'should include rating and year in full name' do
4       # 'build' creates but doesn't save object; 'create' also saves it
5       movie = FactoryGirl.build(:movie, :title => 'Milk', :rating => 'R')
6       movie.name_with_rating.should == 'Milk (R)'
7     end
8   end
9   # More concise: uses Alternative RSpec2 'subject' syntax', and mixes in
10  # FactoryGirl methods in spec_helper.rb (see FactoryGirl README)
11  describe Movie do
12    subject { build :movie, :title => 'Milk', :rating => 'R' }
13    its(:name_with_rating) { should == 'Milk (R)' }
14  end
```

Figure 8.11: Using factories rather than fixtures preserves Independence among tests. Frameworks such as FactoryGirl (gem 'factory_girl_rails' in Gemfile) make this easy by streamlining the creation of real (not mock) objects.

Screencast 8.5.1: How Ruby's dynamic language features make specs more readable.
`http://vimeo.com/34754890`
RSpec mixes a module containing the **should** method into the **Object** class. **should** expects to be passed a *matcher* that can be evaluated to the condition being asserted. RSpec methods such as **be** can be used to construct such a matcher; because of Ruby's flexible syntax and optional parentheses, an assertion such as **value.should be** $<$ **5** can be understood by fully parenthesizing and de-sugaring it to **value.should(be.<(5))**. In addition, RSpec uses Ruby's **method_missing** feature (described in Chapter 3) to detect matchers beginning with **be_** or **be_a_**, allowing you to create assertions such as **cheater.should be_disqualified**. *(Note: The spec shown at the beginning of this Beta Edition screencast doesn't correspond to the example being developed in this section. However, this doesn't affect the main point of the screencast, which is to illustrate in detail how **should** works in RSpec.)*

(Further Note: you may need the command **require 'rspec/expectations'** *to get the examples in this screencast to work.)*

Summary

- When a test needs to operate on a real object rather than a mock, the real object can be created on the fly by a factory or preloaded as a fixture. But beware that fixtures can create subtle interdependencies between tests, breaking Independence.

- Tests are a form of internal documentation. RSpec exploits Ruby language features to let you write exceptionally readable test code. Like application code, test code is there for humans, not for the computer, so taking the time to make your tests readable not only deepens your understanding of them but also documents your thoughts more effectively for those who will work with the code after you've moved on.

■ *Elaboration: New expectation syntax*

As of RSpec version 2.11, a new and somewhat different expectation syntax is also supported. For example, rather than writing `foo.should==5`, we can now write `expect(foo).to eq(5)`. This article[7] describes both the rationale for the change and the reason we cannot write `expect(foo).to==5`; both arguments are subtle. While the "classic" `should` syntax is still supported, the new `expect`-style syntax more closely resembles how expectations for JavaScript tests are written in Jasmine (Section 6.7). Figure 8.19 shows a partial list of correspondences between the "classic" and new syntaxes, based on the complete RSpec documentation[8].

Self-Check 8.5.1. *Suppose a test suite contains a test that adds a model object to a table and then expects to find a certain number of model objects in the table as a result. Explain how the use of fixtures may affect the Independence of the tests in this suite, and how the use of Factories can remedy this problem.*

◇ If the fixtures file is ever changed so that the number of items initially populating that table changes, this test may suddenly start failing because its assumptions about the initial state of the table no longer hold. In contrast, a factory can be used to quickly create only those objects needed for each test or example group on demand, so no test needs to depend on any global "initial state" of the database. ■

http://pastebin.com/TVmi7Zxu

```
1  require 'spec_helper'
2
3  describe Movie do
4    describe 'searching Tmdb by keyword' do
5      it 'should call Tmdb with title keywords' do
6        Tmdb::Movie.should_receive(:find).with('Inception')
7        Movie.find_in_tmdb('Inception')
8      end
9    end
10 end
```

http://pastebin.com/XvaAGUUQ

```
1  class Movie < ActiveRecord::Base
2
3    def self.find_in_tmdb(string)
4      Tmdb::Movie.find(string)
5    end
6
7    # rest of file elided for brevity
8  end
```

Figure 8.12: (Top) the happy path spec for using the TMDb gem; (bottom) Initial happy path implementation driven by happy path spec.

8.6 Implicit Requirements and Stubbing the Internet

We've now created two of the three parts of the new "Search TMDb" feature: we created the view in Chapter 7 and we used TDD to drive the creation of the controller action in the previous sections. All that remains to finish the user story we started in Chapter 7 is the model method **find_in_tmdb**, which actually uses Service-Oriented Architecture technology to communicate with TMDb. Using TDD to drive its implementation will go quickly now that we know the basics.

By convention over configuration, specs for the **Movie** model go in spec/models/ movie_spec.rb. Figure 8.12 shows the happy path for calling **find_in_tmdb**, which describes what happens when everything works correctly. (Complete specs must also cover the sad paths, as we'll soon see.) Inside the overall **describe Movie**, we've added a nested **describe** block for the keyword-search function. Our first spec says that when **find_in_tmdb** is called with a string parameter, it should pass that string parameter to the TMDb gem's **Tmdb::Movie.find** class method. This spec should immediately fail because we haven't defined **find_in_tmdb** yet, so we are at the Red stage already. Of course, at this stage, **find_in_tmdb** is trivial, so the bottom of Figure 8.12 shows its initial implementation that gets us from Red to Green.

Why doesn't the controller method **search_tmdb** just call **Tmdb::Movie.find** directly, rather than passing an argument to the seemingly "intermediate" method **find_in_tmdb**? There are two reasons. First, if the TMDb gem's API changes, perhaps to accommodate a change to the TMDb service API itself, we can insulate the controller from those changes because all the knowledge of how to use the gem to communicate with the service is encapsulated inside the **Movie** model class. This indirection is an example of separating things that change from those that stay the same, a key underlying idea in the use of design patterns, which was introduced briefly in Section 2.1 and is elaborated at length in Chapter 11. The second and more important reason is that this spec is subtly incomplete: **find_in_tmdb** has additional jobs to do. Our test cases have been based on the *explicit requirement* de-

Where's the gem? Don't we need to **require 'themoviedb'** somewhere in the model definition or the specs? For a non-Rails app, yes, but Rails automatically **requires** any gems you specify in the Gemfile.

http://pastebin.com/cPXrpyMT

```
1  require 'spec_helper'
2
3  describe Movie do
4    describe 'searching Tmdb by keyword' do
5      it 'should call Tmdb with title keywords given valid API key' do
6        Tmdb::Movie.should_receive(:find).with('Inception')
7        Movie.find_in_tmdb('Inception')
8      end
9      it 'should raise an InvalidKeyError with invalid API key' do
10       lambda { Movie.find_in_tmdb('Inception') }.
11         should raise_error(Movie::InvalidKeyError)
12     end
13   end
14 end
```

Figure 8.13: The code we wish we had would raise a very specific exception to signal a missing API key (line 11), but this spec fails because find_in_tmdb has no logic to check for an error in the service call and raise this exception.

scribed in the user story of Chapter 7: when the user types in the name of a movie and clicks *Search TMDb*, she should see a page showing matching results. But Screencast 8.1.2 showed that if a valid API key does not accompany a request, an exception is raised that isn't very communicative to the programmer about the real source of the error. Our strategy will be to catch this exception and raise our own **InvalidKeyError** when the invalid-key problem occurs, sometimes called "wrapping" an exception. In this way, if the gem's error behavior changes in the future, we can make the changes here in the model, and the caller (in this case **search_tmdb**) need only worry about handling **InvalidKeyError**.

> In previous editions of this book, the gem API, service API, and error behavior without a valid API key were all different, yet the only changes needed to this example were encapsulated in the model!

This leads to a new ***implicit requirement*** that we discovered while experimenting with the gem:

- It should raise an "invalid key" exception if an invalid key is provided.

The revised spec in Figure 8.13 expresses this implicit requirement as a new spec. Note that we renamed our first spec to indicate that it applies to the case when the API key is valid, and added a new spec to cover the case when the API key is invalid.

But now we have two dilemmas. The first dilemma is that this spec would actually call the real TMDb service every time it was executed, making the spec neither **F**ast (each call takes a few seconds to complete) nor **R**epeatable (the test will behave differently if TMDb is down or your computer is not connected to the Internet). Even if you only ran tests while connected to the Internet, it is very bad etiquette to have your tests constantly contacting a production service.

We can fix this by introducing a seam that isolates the caller from the callee. We know from Screencast 8.1.2 that when an invalid key is used, **Tmdb::Movie.find** raises a **NoMethodError**, and we can then inspect **Tmdb::Api.response** to verify that the HTTP response **code** is 401, which means "Unauthorized." We can mimic that behavior with a stub that "fakes" the behavior that happens when the gem makes a service call with a bad API key. Figure 8.14 shows this spec. Notice that we had to "wrap" the call to **find_in_tmdb** in line 12 in a **lambda**. We *expect* the call to raise an exception, but if a spec actually raises an exception, it stops the testing run! So in order to make the spec **S**elf-checking, we invoke **should** on the callable **lambda** object, which will cause the lambda to be executed in a "controlled environment" where RSpec can catch any exceptions and match them to our expectation.

http://pastebin.com/cjcEZd4Y

```
1   require 'spec_helper'
2
3   describe Movie do
4     describe 'searching Tmdb by keyword' do
5       it 'should call Tmdb with title keywords given valid API key' do
6         Tmdb::Movie.should_receive(:find).with('Inception')
7         Movie.find_in_tmdb('Inception')
8       end
9       it 'should raise an InvalidKeyError with no API key' do
10        Tmdb::Movie.stub(:find).and_raise(NoMethodError)
11        Tmdb::Api.stub(:response).and_return({'code' => 401})
12        lambda { Movie.find_in_tmdb('Inception') }.
13          should raise_error(Movie::InvalidKeyError)
14      end
15    end
16  end
```

Figure 8.14: The stubs in lines 10–11 mimic the behavior we observed in Screencast 8.1.2 when an invalid API key is supplied.

http://pastebin.com/1GRqdr91

```
1   class Movie < ActiveRecord::Base
2
3     class Movie::InvalidKeyError < StandardError ; end
4
5     def self.find_in_tmdb(string)
6       begin
7         Tmdb::Movie.find(string)
8       rescue NoMethodError => tmdb_gem_exception
9         if Tmdb::Api.response['code'] == 401
10          raise Movie::InvalidKeyError, 'Invalid API key'
11        else
12          raise tmdb_gem_exception
13        end
14      end
15    end
16
17    # rest of file elided for brevity
18  end
```

Figure 8.15: Adding code to find_in_tmdb to catch the exception, including a definition of our own new exception type (line 3). If the API response code is 401, we know the problem was an invalid key, but if it's something else, we don't know what the problem is, so to be safe we just re-raise the original exception.

This spec fails for the right reason, that is, because we haven't added code to **find_in_tmdb** to check for an exception in the gem. Figure 8.15 shows the new code added to **find_in_tmdb** to make the spec pass. Notice that if a **NoMethodError** occurs but the API response code cannot be verified to be 401 (lines 9–13 of Figure 8.15), we just re-raise the original exception since in this case we don't know what's wrong (and there's nothing in themoviedb gem documentation to tell us). Similarly, if some exception other than **NoMethodError** occurs, we won't catch it, and the caller will have to deal with it.

But now we can see the second dilemma in Figure 8.14: we have two passing specs that clearly test behavior under *different* conditions—valid API key vs. invalid API key—yet there is nothing in the test code that tells us that! This error is a common antipattern when writing tests that involve using another API, whether for a remote service or for another class. Since our tests never call the "real" remote TMDb service, what we really want is to group our tests into two different sets, based on whether we are simulating successful calls with a valid API key or failed calls due to an invalid API key.

http://pastebin.com/CT0XWNrH

```
 1  require 'spec_helper'
 2
 3  describe Movie do
 4    describe 'searching Tmdb by keyword' do
 5      context 'with valid API key' do
 6        it 'should call Tmdb with title keywords' do
 7          Tmdb::Movie.should_receive(:find).with('Inception')
 8          Movie.find_in_tmdb('Inception')
 9        end
10      end
11      context 'with invalid API key' do
12        before :each do
13          Tmdb::Movie.stub(:find).and_raise(NoMethodError)
14          Tmdb::Api.stub(:response).and_return({'code' => 401})
15        end
16        it 'should raise an InvalidKeyError with no API key' do
17          lambda { Movie.find_in_tmdb('Inception') }.
18            should raise_error(Movie::InvalidKeyError)
19        end
20      end
21    end
22  end
```

Figure 8.16: The specs are now clearly grouped according to the different circumstances (valid API key or not) under which find_in_tmdb is tested. An added benefit of this grouping is that we can DRY out the setup of the stubs that simulate the invalid-key scenario by putting them into a before block that applies to all specs in that group.

Figure 8.16 shows how to do this in RSpec. **context** is just a synonym for **describe**, and besides letting us group the specs according to their purpose, we can also use **before** blocks to setup the stubs that will simulate calls with a bad API key. Any future specs for testing other cases involving a bad API key can now just go into this **context** block.

Figure 8.16 raises a more general question: where should we stub external methods when testing using an external service? We chose to stub **find_in_tmdb** and mimic the results of the gem's calls to TMDb, but a more robust integration testing approach would instead stub "closer to the remote service." In particular, we could create fixtures—files containing the content returned by actual calls to the service, such as the JSON objects in Screencast 8.1.1— and arrange to intercept calls to the remote service and return the contents of those fixture files instead. The FakeWeb[9] gem does exactly this: it stubs out the entire Web except for particular URIs that return a canned response when accessed from a Ruby program. (You can think of FakeWeb as **stub...with...and_return** for the whole Web.) There's even a companion gem VCR[10] that automates getting a response from the real service, saving the response data in a fixture file, and then "replaying" the fixture when your tests cause the remote service to be "called" by intercepting low-level calls in the Ruby HTTP library.

VCR (for *Videocassette Recorder*) was an analog-tape video-recording device popular in the 1980s but made obsolete by DVDs in the early 2000s. The vcr gem even uses the term "cassette" to refer to the stored server responses that are replayed during tests.

From an integration-testing standpoint, FakeWeb is the most realistic way to test interactions with a remote service, because the stubbed behavior is "farthest away"—we are stubbing as late as possible in the flow of the request. Therefore, when creating Cucumber scenarios to test external service integration, FakeWeb is usually the appropriate choice. From a unit testing point of view (as we've adopted in this chapter) it's less compelling, since we are concerned with the correct behavior of specific class methods, and we don't mind stubbing "close by" in order to observe those behaviors in a controlled environment.

Summary

- Sometimes explicit requirements lead to additional implicit requirements—additional constraints that are not "visible" like the explicit requirements but must still be satisfied for the explicit requirement to be met. Implicit requirements are just as important as explicit ones and should be tested with the same rigor.

- If we need to check that the subject code raises an exception, we can do so by making a lambda-expression the receiver of an expectation like **should** or **should_not** and using the matcher **raise_error**.

- To create **F**ast and **R**epeatable specs for code that communicates with an external service, we use stubs to mimic the service's behavior. **context** blocks can group specs that test different behaviors of the remote service, using **before** blocks to set up necessary stubs or other preconditions to simulate each behavior.

- The question of "where to stub" an external service depends on what the purpose of the tests is. Stubbing "far away" using FakeWeb is more realistic and appropriate for functional or integration tests; stubbing "close by" in a gem or library that communicates with the remote service is often adequate for low-level unit tests.

■ *Elaboration: Declared vs. undeclared exceptions*

In statically-typed languages such as Java, the compiler enforces that a method must declare any exceptions it might throw. If the callee wants to add a new type of exception, the callee's method signature changes, requiring the callee and all callers to be recompiled. This approach doesn't extend well to SaaS apps, which may communicate with other services like TMDb whose evolution and behavior are not under the caller's control. As we've seen, we must rely on the remote service's API documentation to tell us what could go wrong, as well as capture and handle other undocumented failure modes. Thus, while Ruby doesn't require declared exceptions as Java does, Ruby apps still need to understand and handle exceptional behaviors arising from interactions with another API, especially when that API calls a remote service.

Self-Check 8.6.1. *Given that failing to initialize a valid API key causes* themoviedb *gem to raise an exception, why doesn't line 7 of Figure 8.13 raise an exception?*
◇ Line 6 replaces the **Tmdb::Movie.find** call with a stub, preventing the "real" method from executing and raising an exception. ■

Self-Check 8.6.2. *Considering line 10 of Figure 8.13, suppose we didn't wrap the call to* **find_in_tmdb** *in a lambda-expression. What would happen and why?*
◇ If **find_in_tmdb** correctly raises the exception, the spec will fail because the exception will stop the run. If **find_in_tmdb** incorrectly fails to raise an exception, the spec will fail because the assertion **should raise_error** expects one. Therefore the test would always fail whether **find_in_tmdb** was correct or not. ■

Self-Check 8.6.3. *Name two likely violations of FIRST that arise when unit tests actually call an external service as part of testing.*
◇ The test may no longer be Fast, since it takes much longer to call an external service than to compute locally. The test may no longer be Repeatable, since circumstances beyond our

control could affect its outcome, such as the temporary unavailability of the external service.

∎

8.7 Coverage Concepts and Unit vs. Integration Tests

How much testing is enough? A poor but unfortunately widely-given answer is "As much as you can do before the shipping deadline." A very coarse-grained alternative is the **code-to-test ratio**, the number of non-comment lines of code divided by number of lines of tests of all types. In production systems, this ratio is usually less than 1, that is, there are more lines of test than lines of app code. The command `rake stats` issued in the root directory of a Rails app computes this ratio based on the number of lines of RSpec tests and Cucumber scenarios.

A more precise way to approach the question is in terms of **code coverage**. Since the goal of testing is to exercise the subject code in at least the same ways it would be exercised in production, what fraction of those possibilities is actually exercised by the test suite? Surprisingly, measuring coverage is not as straightforward as you might suspect. Here is a simple fragment of code and the definitions of several commonly-used coverage terms as they apply to the example.

- S0 or Method coverage: Is every method executed at least once by the test suite? Satisfying S0 requires calling **foo** and **bar** at least once each.

  > Sometimes written with a subscript, S_0.

- S1 or Call coverage or Entry/Exit coverage: Has each method been called from every place it could be called? Satisfying S1 requires calling **bar** from both line 4 and line 6.

- C0 or Statement coverage: Is every statement of the source code executed at least once by the test suite, counting both branches of a conditional as a single statement? In addition to calling **bar**, satisfying C0 would require calling **foo** at least once with **x** true (otherwise the statement in line 4 will never be executed), and at least once with **y** false.

- C1 or Branch coverage: Has each branch been taken in each direction at least once? Satisfying C1 would require calling **foo** with both false and true values of **x** and with values of **y** and **z** such that **y && z** in line 4 evaluates once to true and once to false. A more stringent condition, **decision coverage**, requires that each *subexpression* that independently affects a conditional expression be evaluated to true and false. In this example, a test would additionally have to separately set **y** and **z** so that the condition **y && z** fails once for **y** being false and once for **z** being false.

- C2 or Path coverage: Has every possible route through the code been executed? In this simple example, where **x,y,z** are treated as booleans, there are 8 possible paths.

- Modified Condition/Decision Coverage (MCDC) combines a subset of the above levels: Every point of entry and exit in the program has been invoked at least once, every decision in the program has taken all possible outcomes at least once, and each condition in a decision has been shown to independently affect that decision's outcome.

Achieving C0 coverage is relatively straightforward, and a goal of 100% C0 coverage is not unreasonable. Achieving C1 coverage is more difficult since test cases must be constructed more carefully to ensure each branch is taken at least once in each direction. C2

Structure of test cases:

- before(:each) do... end
  Set up preconditions executed before each spec (use **before(:all)** to do just once, at your own risk)

- it 'should do something' do... end
  A single example (test case) for one behavior

- describe 'collection of behaviors' do... end
  Groups a set of related examples

Mocks and stubs:

- m=mock('movie')
  Creates a mock object with no predefined methods

- m.stub(:rating).and_return('R')
  Replaces the existing **rating** method on **m**, or defines a new **rating** method if none exists, that returns the canned response **'R'**

- m=mock('movie', :rating=>'R')
  Shortcut that combines the 2 previous examples

- Movie.stub(:find).and_return(@fake_movie)
  Forces **@fake_movie** to be returned *if* **Movie.find** is called, but doesn't require that it be called

Useful methods and objects for controller specs: Your specs must be in the spec/controllers subdirectory for these methods to be available.

- post '/movies/create',
  {:title=>'Milk', :rating=>'R'}
  Causes a POST request to /movies/create and passes the given hash as the value of **params**. **get, put, delete** also available.

- response.should render_template('show')
  Checks that the controller action renders the **show** template for this controller's model

- response.should redirect_to(:controller => 'movies', :action => 'new')
  Checks that the controller action redirects to **MoviesController#new** rather than rendering a view

Figure 8.17: Some of the most useful RSpec methods introduced in this chapter. See the full RSpec documentation[12] for details and additional methods not listed here.

Assertions on method calls: can also negate, e.g. **should_not_receive**

- **Movie.should_receive(:find).exactly(2).times**
  Stubs **Movie.find** and ensures it's called exactly twice (omit **exactly** if you don't care how many calls; **at_least()** and **at_most()** also available

- **Movie.should_receive(:find).with('Milk','R')**
  Checks that **Movie.find** is called with exactly 2 arguments having these values

- **Movie.should_receive(:find).with(anything())**
  Checks that **Movie.find** is called with 1 argument whose value isn't checked

- **Movie.should_receive(:find).**
  with(hash_including :title=>'Milk')
  Checks that **Movie.find** is called with 1 argument that must be a hash (or something that quacks like one) that includes the key **:title** with the value **'Milk'**

- **Movie.should_receive(:find).with(no_args())**
  Checks that **Movie.find** is called with zero arguments

Matchers

- **greeting.should == 'bonjour'**
  Compares its argument for equality with receiver of assertion

- **value.should be >= 7**
  Compares its argument with the given value; syntactic sugar for **value.should(be.>=(7))**

- **result.should be_remarkable**
  Calls **remarkable?** (note question mark) on **result**

Figure 8.18: Continuation of summary of useful RSpec methods introduced in this chapter.

Classic RSpec syntax	New expectation syntax (RSpec $\geq$ 2.11)
expr.**should ==** *value*	**expect(***expr***).to eq(***value***)**
expr.**should_not ==** *value*	**expect(***expr***).not_to eq(***value***)**
expr.**should be_close(***value,delta***)**	**expect(***expr***).to** **be_within(***delta***).of(***value***)**
expr.**should be >10**	**expect(***expr***).to be >10**
expr.**should_not be_nil**	**expect(***expr***).not_to be_nil**
"string".should_not match(/*regexp***/)**	**expect("string").not_to match(/***regexp***/)**
[1,2,3].should =~[2,1,3]	**expect([1,2,3]).to match_array([2,1,3])**
response.**should render_template(***tmpl***)**	**expect(***response***).to render_template(***tmpl***)**
lambda { *code* }.should *expectation*	**expect { *code* }.to** *expectation*

Figure 8.19: A partial mapping from the "classic" and new syntaxes for RSpec expectations. For the negative expectation examples, you can infer the corresponding positive expectation by removing the word not.

```
 1   class MyClass
 2     def foo(x,y,z)
 3       if x
 4         if (y && z) then bar(0) end
 5       else
 6         bar(1)
 7       end
 8     end
 9     def bar(x) ; @w = x ; end
10   end
```

Figure 8.20: A simple code example to illustrate basic coverage concepts.

coverage is most difficult of all, and not all testing experts agree on the additional value of achieving 100% path coverage. Therefore, code coverage statistics are most valuable to the extent that they highlight undertested or untested parts of the code and show the overall comprehensiveness of your test suite. The next screencast shows how to use the SimpleCov[13] Ruby gem (included in the bookware) to quickly check the C0 coverage of your RSpec tests.

Screencast 8.7.1: Using SimpleCov to check C0 coverage.
http://vimeo.com/34754907
The SimpleCov tool, provided as a Ruby gem, measures and displays the C0 coverage of your specs. You can zoom in on each file and see which specific lines were covered by your tests.

This chapter, and the above discussion of coverage, have focused on unit tests. Chapter 7 explained how user stories could become automated acceptance tests; those are ***integration tests*** or ***system tests*** because each test (that is, each scenario) exercises a lot of code in many different parts of the application, rather than relying on fake objects such as mocks and stubs to isolate classes from their collaborators. Integration tests are important, but insufficient. Their resolution is poor: if an integration test fails, it is harder to pinpoint the cause since the test touches many parts of the code. Their coverage tends to be poor because even though a single scenario touches many classes, it executes only a few code paths in each class. For the same reason, integration tests also tend to take longer to run. On the other hand, while unit tests run quickly and can isolate the subject code with great precision (improving both coverage resolution and error localization), because they rely on fake objects to isolate the subject code, they may mask problems that would only arise in integration tests.

Somewhere in between these levels are ***functional tests***, which exercise a well-defined subset of the code. They rely on mocks and stubs to isolate a set of cooperating classes rather than a single class or method. For example, controller specs such as Figure 8.9 use **get** and **post** methods to submit URIs to the app, which means they rely on the routing subsystem to work correctly in routing those calls to the appropriate controller methods. (To see this for yourself, temporarily remove the line **resources :movies** from `config/routes.rb` and try re-running the controller specs.) However, the controller specs are still isolated from the database by stubbing out the model method **find_in_tmdb** that would normally communicate with the database.

In other words, high assurance requires both good coverage and a mix of all three kinds of tests. Figure 8.21 summarizes the relative strengths and weaknesses of different types of

	Unit	**Functional**	**Integration/System**
What is tested	One method/class	Several methods/classes	Large chunks of system
Rails example	Model specs	Controller specs	Cucumber scenarios
Preferred tool	RSpec	RSpec	Cucumber
Running time	Very fast	Fast	Slow
Error localization	Excellent	Moderate	Poor
Coverage	Excellent	Moderate	Poor
Use of mocks & stubs	Heavy	Moderate	Little/none

Figure 8.21: Summary of the differences among unit tests, functional tests, and integration or whole-system tests.

tests.

Summary

- Static and dynamic measures of coverage, including code-to-test ratio (reported by `rake stats`), C0 coverage (reported by SimpleCov), and C1–C2 coverage, measure the extent to which your test suite exercises different paths in your code.

- Unit, functional, and integration tests differ in terms of their running time, resolution (ability to localize errors), ability to exercise a variety of code paths, and ability to "sanity-check" the whole application. All three are vital to software assurance.

Self-Check 8.7.1. *Why does high test coverage not necessarily imply a well-tested application?*

◇ Coverage says nothing about the quality of the tests. However, low coverage certainly implies a poorly-tested application. ■

Self-Check 8.7.2. *What is the difference between C0 code coverage and code-to-test ratio?*

◇ C0 coverage is a *dynamic* measurement of what fraction of all statements are executed by a test suite. Code-to-test ratio is a *static* measurement comparing the total number of lines of code to the total number of lines of tests. ■

Self-Check 8.7.3. *Why is it usually a bad idea to make extensive use of* **mock** *or* **stub** *in Cucumber scenarios such as those described in Chapter 7?*

◇ Cucumber is a tool for full-system testing and acceptance testing. Such testing is specifically intended to exercise the entire system, rather than "faking" certain parts of it as we have done using seams in this chapter. (However, if the "full system" includes interacting with outside services we don't control, such as the interaction with TMDb in this example, we do need a way to "fake" their behavior for testing. That topic is the subject of Exercise 8.3.) ■

8.8 Other Testing Approaches and Terminology

The field of software testing is as broad and long-lived as software engineering and has its own literature. Its range of techniques includes formalisms for proving things about coverage, empirical techniques for selecting which tests to create, and directed-random testing. Depending on an organization's "testing culture," you may hear different terminology than we've used in this chapter. Ammann and Offutt's *Introduction to Software Testing* (Ammann and Offutt 2008) is one of the best comprehensive references on the subject. Their approach is to divide a piece of code into **basic blocks**, each of which executes from the beginning to the end with no possibility of branching, and then join these basic blocks into a graph in which conditionals in the code result in graph nodes with multiple out-edges. We can then think of testing as "covering the graph": each test case tracks which nodes in the graph it visits, and the fraction of all nodes visited at the end of the test suite is the test coverage. Ammann and Offutt go on to analyze various structural aspects of software from which such graphs can be extracted, and present systematic automated techniques for achieving and measuring coverage of those graphs.

One insight that emerges from this approach is that the levels of testing described in the previous section refer to **control flow coverage**, since they are only concerned with whether specific parts of the code are executed or not. Another important coverage criterion is **define–use coverage** or **DU-coverage**: given a variable **x** in some program, if we consider every place that **x** is assigned a value and every place that the value of **x** is used, DU-coverage asks what fraction of all *pairs* of define and use sites are exercised by a test suite. This condition is weaker than all-paths coverage but can find errors that control-flow coverage alone would miss.

Another testing term distinguishes **black-box tests**, whose design is based solely on the software's external specifications, from **white-box tests** (also called **glass-box tests**), whose design reflects knowledge about the software's implementation that is not implied by external specifications. For example, the external specification of a hash table might just state that when we store a key/value pair and later read that key, we should get back the stored value. A black-box test would specify a random set of key/value pairs to test this behavior, whereas a white-box test might exploit knowledge about the hash function to construct worst-case test data that results in many hash collisions. Similarly, white-box tests might focus on boundary values—parameter values likely to exercise different parts of the code. In our TMDb example, we saw that `themoviedb` gem raises an unusual exception when an invalid key is supplied, so that code path needs to be tested separately. Conversely, we can test the "nonblank but invalid" codepath with *any* representative nonblank invalid key—we won't learn anything new by testing with several different nonblank invalid keys.

Mutation testing, invented by Ammann and Offutt, is a test-automation technique in which small but syntactically legal changes are automatically made to the program's source code, such as replacing **a+b** with **a-b** or replacing **if (c)** with **if (!c)**. Most such changes should cause at least one test to fail, so a mutation that causes *no* test to fail indicates either a lack of test coverage or a very strange program. The Ruby gem `mutant` performs mutation testing in conjunction with RSpec, but as of the publication date of this edition, the `mutant-rails` gem that integrates it seamlessly with Rails is not yet working. Given the importance of testing in the Ruby community, this will likely change soon.

Fuzz testing consists of throwing random data at your application and seeing what breaks. About 1/4 of common Unix utilities can be made to crash by fuzz testing, and Microsoft estimates that 20–25% of their bugs are found this way. *Dumb fuzzing* generates completely random data, while *smart fuzzing* includes knowledge about the app's structure. For example, smart fuzzing for a Rails app might include randomizing the variables and values occurring in form postings or in URIs embedded in page views, creating URIs that are syntactically valid but might expose a bug. Smart fuzzing for SaaS can also include attacks such as cross-site scripting or SQL injection, which we'll discuss in Chapter 12. Tarantula[14] (a fuzzy spider that crawls your site) is a Ruby gem for fuzz-testing Rails applications.

> **Summary of other testing approaches:** We can think of testing as "covering a graph" of possible software behaviors. The graph can represent control flow (basic block coverage), variable assignment and
> usage (DU-coverage), a space of random inputs (fuzz testing), or a space of possible tests with respect to specific errors in the code (mutation testing). The different approaches are complementary and tend to catch different types of bugs.

Self-Check 8.8.1. *The Microsoft Zune music player had an infamous bug that caused all Zunes to "lock up" on December 31, 2008. Later analysis showed that the bug would be triggered on the last day of any leap year. What kinds of tests—black-box vs. glass-box (see Section 1.8), mutation, or fuzz—would have been likely to catch this bug?*

◇ A glass-box test for the special code paths used for leap years would have been effective. Fuzz testing might have been effective: since the bug occurs roughly once in every 1460 days, a few thousand fuzz tests would likely have found it. ∎

8.9 The Plan-And-Document Perspective

The project manager takes the Software Requirements Specification from the requirements planning phase and divides it into the individual program units. Developers then write the code for each unit, and then perform unit tests to make sure they work. In many organizations, quality assurance staff performs the rest of the higher-level tests, such as module, integration, system, and acceptance tests.

There are three options on how to integrate the units and perform integration tests:

1. **Top-down integration** starts with the top of tree structure showing the dependency among all the units. The advantage of top-down is that you quickly get some of the high level functions working, such as the user interface, which allows stakeholders to offer feedback for the app in time to make changes. The downside is that you have to create many stubs to get the app to limp along in this nascent form.

2. **Bottom-up integration** starts at the bottom of the dependency tree and works up. There is no need for stubs, as you can integrate all the pieces you need for a module. Alas, you don't get an idea how the app will look until you get all the code written and integrated.

3. **Sandwich integration**, not surprisingly, tries to get the best of both worlds by integrating from both ends simultaneously. Thus, you try to reduce the number of stubs by selectively integrating some units bottom-up and try to get the user interface operational sooner by selectively integrating some units top-down.

The next step for the QA testers after integration tests is the system test, as the full app should work. This is the last step before showing it to customers for them to try out. Note that system tests both non-functional requirements, such as performance, as well as functional requirements of features found in the SRS.

One question for plan-and-document is how to decide when testing is complete. Typically, an organization will enforce a standard level of testing coverage before a product is ready for the customer. Examples might be statement coverage (all statements executed at least once), or all user input opportunities are tested with both good input and problematic input.

In the plan and document process, the final test is for the customers to try the product in their environment to decide whether they will accept the product or not. That is, the aim is validation, not just verification. In Agile development, the customer is involved in trying prototypes of the app early in the process, so there is no separate system test before running the acceptance tests.

As you should expect from the plan-and-document process, documentation plays an important role in testing. Figure 8.22 gives an outline for test plan based on IEEE Standard 829-2008.

While testing is fundamental to software engineering, quoting another Turing Award winner:

> *Program testing can be used to show the presence of bugs, but never to show their absence!*

—Edsger W. Dijkstra

Thus, there has been a great deal of research investigating approaches to verification beyond testing. Collectively, these techniques are known as **formal methods**. The general strategy is to start with a formal specification and prove that the behavior of the code follows the behavior of that spec. These are mathematical proofs, either done by a person or done by a computer. The two options are **automatic theorem proving** or **model checking**. Theorem proving uses a set of inference rules and a set of logical axioms to produce proofs from scratch. Model checking verifies selected properties by exhaustive search of all possible states that a system could enter during execution.

Because formal methods are so computationally intensive, they tend to be used only when the cost to repair errors is very high, the features are very hard to test, and the item being verified is not too large. Examples include vital parts of hardware like network protocols or safety critical software systems like medical equipment. For formal methods to actually work, the size of the design must be limited: the largest formally verified software to date is an operating system kernel that is less than 10,000 lines of code, and its verification cost about $500 per line of code (Klein et al. 2010).

Hence, formal methods are *not* good matches to high-function software that changes frequently, as is generally the case for Software as a Service.

Edsger W. Dijkstra (1930–2002) received the 1972 Turing Award for fundamental contributions to developing programming languages.

To put the cost of formal methods in perspective, NASA spent $35M per year to maintain 420,000 lines of code[15] for the space shuttle, or about $80 per line of code per year.

Master Test Plan Outline
1. Introduction
1.1. Document identifier
1.2. Scope
1.3. References
1.4. System overview and key features
1.5. Test overview
1.5.1 Organization
1.5.2 Master test schedule
1.5.3 Integrity level schema
1.5.4 Resources summary
1.5.5 Responsibilities
1.5.6 Tools, techniques, methods, and metrics

2. Details of the Master Test Plan
2.1. Test processes including definition of test levels
2.1.1 Process: Management
2.1.1.1 Activity: Management of test effort
2.1.2 Process: Acquisition
2.1.2.1 Activity: Acquisition support test
2.1.3 Process: Supply
2.1.3.1 Activity: Planning test
2.1.4 Process: Development
2.1.4.1 Activity: Concept
2.1.4.2 Activity: Requirements
2.1.4.3 Activity: Design
2.1.4.4 Activity: Implementation
2.1.4.5 Activity: Test
2.1.4.6 Activity: Installation/checkout
2.1.5 Process: Operation
2.1.5.1 Activity: Operational test
2.1.6 Process: Maintenance
2.1.6.1 Activity: Maintenance test
2.2. Test documentation requirements
2.3. Test administration requirements
2.4. Test reporting requirements

3. General
3.1. Glossary
3.2. Document change procedures and history

Figure 8.22: Outline of Master Test Plan Documentation that follows the IEEE Standard 829-2008.

Tasks	In Plan and Document	In Agile
Test Plan and Documentation	Software Test Documentation such as IEEE Standard 829-2008	User stories
Order of Coding and Testing	1. Code units 2. Unit test 3. Module test 4. Integration test 5. System test 6. Acceptance test	1. Acceptance test 2. Integration test 3. Module test 4. Unit test 5. Code units
Testers	Developers for unit tests; QA testers for module, integration, system, and acceptance tests	Developers
When Testing Stops	Company policy (e.g., statement coverage, happy and sad user inputs)	All tests pass (green)

Figure 8.23: The relationship between the testing tasks of Plan-and-Document versus Agile methodologies.

Summary: Testing and formal methods reduce the risks of errors in designs.

- Unlike BDD/TDD, the plan-and-document process starts with writing code before you write the tests.

- Developers then perform unit tests.

- Especially in large projects, different people perform the higher-level tests. The integration tests options of putting the units together are top-down, bottom-up, or sandwich.

- Testers do a separate system test to ensure the product passes both functional and non-functional requirements before exposing it to customers for the final acceptance test.

- *Formal methods* rely on formal specifications and automated proofs or exhaustive state search to verify more than what testing can do, but they are so expensive to perform that today they are only applicable to small, stable, critical portions of hardware or software.

- Figure 8.23 shows the resulting different tests tasks for plan-and-document versus Agile processes.

Self-Check 8.9.1. *Compare and contrast integration strategies including top-down, bottom-up, and sandwich integration.*

◇ Top-down needs stubs to perform the tests, but it lets stakeholders get a feeling for how the app works. Bottom-up does not need stubs, but needs potentially everything written before stakeholders see it work. Sandwich integration works from both ends to try to get both benefits. ∎

8.10   Fallacies and Pitfalls

 Fallacy: **100% test coverage with all tests passing means no bugs.**

There are many reasons this statement can be false. Complete test coverage says nothing about the quality of the individual tests. As well, some bugs may require passing a certain value as a method argument (for example, to trigger a divide-by-zero error), and control flow testing often cannot reveal such a bug. There may be bugs in the interaction between your app and an external service such as TMDb; stubbing out the service so you can perform local testing might mask such bugs.

 Pitfall: **Dogmatically insisting on 100% test coverage all passing (green) before you ship.**

As we saw above, 100% test coverage is not only difficult to achieve at levels higher than C1, but gives no guarantees of bug-freedom even if you do achieve it. Test coverage is a useful tool for estimating the overall comprehensiveness of your test suite, but high confidence requires a variety of testing methods—integration as well as unit, fuzzing as well as hand-constructing test cases, define-use coverage as well as control-flow coverage, mutation testing to expose additional holes in the test strategy, and so on. Indeed, in Chapter 12 we will discuss operational issues such as security and performance, which call for additional testing strategies beyond the correctness-oriented ones described in this chapter.

 Fallacy: **You don't need much test code to be confident in the application.**

While insisting on 100% coverage may be counterproductive, so is going to the other extreme. The ***code-to-test ratio*** in production systems (lines of noncomment code divided by lines of tests of all types) is usually less than 1, that is, there are more lines of test than lines of app code. As an extreme example, the SQLite database included with Rails contains over 1200 times as much test code as application code[16] because of the wide variety of ways in which it can be used and the wide variety of different kinds of systems on which it must work properly! While there is controversy over how useful a measure the code-to-test ratio is, given the high productivity of Ruby and its superior facilities for DRYing out your test code, a `rake stats` ratio between 0.2 and 0.5 is a reasonable target.

 Pitfall: **Relying too heavily on just one kind of test (unit, functional, integration).**

Even 100% unit test coverage tells you nothing about interactions among classes. You still need to create tests to exercise the interactions between classes (functional or module testing) and to exercise complete paths through the application that touch many classes and change state in many places (integration testing). Conversely, integration tests touch only a tiny fraction of all possible application paths, and therefore exercise only a few behaviors in each method, so they are not a substitute for good unit test coverage to get assurance that your lower-level code is working correctly. A common rule of thumb used at Google and elsewhere (Whittaker et al. 2012) is "70–20–10": 70% short and focused unit tests, 20% functional tests that touch multiple classes, 10% full-stack or integration tests.

 Pitfall: **Undertested integration points due to over-stubbing.**

Mocking and stubbing confer many benefits, but they can also hide potential problems at integration points—places where one class or module interacts with another. Suppose **Movie** has some interactions with another class **Moviegoer**, but for the purposes of unit testing **Movie**, all calls to **Moviegoer** methods are stubbed out, and vice versa. Because stubs are written to "fake" the behavior of the collaborating class(es), we no longer know if **Movie** "knows how to talk to" **Moviegoer** correctly. Good coverage with functional and integration tests, which don't stub out all calls across class boundaries, avoids this pitfall.

 Pitfall: **Writing tests after the code rather than before.**

Thinking about "the code we wish we had" from the perspective of a test for that code tends to result in code that is testable. This seems like an obvious tautology until you try writing the code first without testability in mind, only to discover that surprisingly often you end up with mock trainwrecks (see next pitfall) when you do try to write the test.

In addition, in the traditional Waterfall lifecycle described in Chapter 1, testing comes after code development, but with SaaS that can be in "public beta" for months, no one would suggest that testing should only begin after the beta period. Writing the tests first, whether for fixing bugs or creating new features, eliminates this pitfall.

 Pitfall: **Mock Trainwrecks.**

Mocks exist to help isolate your tests from their collaborators, but what about the collaborators' collaborators? Suppose our **Movie** object has a **pics** attribute that returns a list of images associated with the movie, each of which is a **Picture** object that has a **format** attribute. You're trying to mock a **Movie** object for use in a test, but you realize that the method to which you're passing the **Movie** object is going to expect to call methods on its **pics**, so you find yourself doing something like this:

http://pastebin.com/N3UdnZq1

```
1 movie = mock('Movie', :pics => [mock('Picture', :format => 'gif')])
2 Movie.count_pics(movie).should == 1
```

This is called a *mock trainwreck*, and it's a sign that the method under test (**count_pics**) has excessive knowledge of the innards of a **Picture**. In the Chapters 9 and 11 we'll encounter a set of additional guidelines to help you detect and resolve such **code smells**.

 Pitfall: **Inadvertently creating dependencies regarding the order in which specs are run, for example by using before(:all).**

If you specify actions to be performed only once for a whole group of test cases, you may introduce dependencies among those test cases without noticing. For example, if a **before :all** block sets a variable and test example A changes the variable's value, test example B could come to rely on that change if A is usually run before B. Then B's behavior in the future might suddenly be different if B is run first, which might happen because autotest prioritizes running tests related to recently-changed code. Therefore it's best to use **before :each** and **after :each** whenever possible.

 Pitfall: **Forgetting to re-prep the test database when the schema changes.**

Remember that tests run against a separate copy of the database, not the database used in development (Section 4.2). Therefore, whenever you modify the schema by applying a migration, you must also run `rake db:test:prepare` to apply those changes to the test database; otherwise your tests may fail because the test code doesn't match the schema.

8.11   Concluding Remarks: TDD vs. Conventional Debugging

In this chapter we've used RSpec to develop a method using TDD with unit tests. Although TDD may feel strange at first, most people who try it quickly realize that they already use the unit-testing techniques it calls for, but in a different workflow. Often, a typical developer will write some code, assume it probably works, test it by running the whole application, and hit a bug. As an MIT programmer lamented at the first software engineering conference in 1968: "We build systems like the Wright brothers built airplanes—build the whole thing, push it off a cliff, let it crash, and start over again."

Once a bug has been hit, if inspecting the code doesn't reveal the problem, the typical developer would next try inserting print statements around the suspect area to print out the values of relevant variables or indicate which path of a conditional was followed. The TDD developer would instead write assertions using **should** or **expect**.

If the bug still can't be found, the typical developer might isolate part of the code by carefully setting up conditions to skip over method calls he doesn't care about or change variable values to force the code to go down the suspected buggy path. For example, he might do this by setting a breakpoint using a debugger and manually inspecting or manipulating variable values before continuing past the breakpoint. In contrast, the TDD developer would isolate the suspect code path using stubs and mocks to control what happens when certain methods are called and which direction conditionals will go.

By now, the typical developer is absolutely convinced that he'll certainly find the bug and won't have to repeat this tedious manual process, though this usually turns out to be wrong. The TDD developer has isolated each behavior in its own spec, so repeating the process just means re-running the spec, which can even happen automatically using `autotest`.

In other words: If we write the code first and have to fix bugs, we end up using the same techniques required in TDD, but less efficiently and more manually, hence less productively.

But if we use TDD, bugs can be spotted immediately as the code is written. If our code works the first time, using TDD still gives us a regression test to catch bugs that might creep into this part of the code in the future.

8.12   To Learn More

- *How Google Tests Software* (Whittaker et al. 2012) is a rare glimpse into how Google has scaled up and adapted the techniques described in this chapter to instill a culture of testing that is widely admired by its competitors.

- The online RSpec documentation[17] gives complete details and additional features used in advanced testing scenarios.

- *The RSpec Book* (Chelimsky et al. 2010) is the definitive published reference to RSpec and includes examples of features, mechanisms and best practices that go far beyond this introduction.

P. Ammann and J. Offutt. *Introduction to Software Testing*. Cambridge University Press, 2008. ISBN 0521880386.

D. Chelimsky, D. Astels, B. Helmkamp, D. North, Z. Dennis, and A. Hellesøy. *The RSpec Book: Behaviour Driven Development with Rspec, Cucumber, and Friends (The Facets of Ruby Series)*. Pragmatic Bookshelf, 2010. ISBN 1934356379.

M. Feathers. *Working Effectively with Legacy Code.* Prentice Hall, 2004. ISBN 9780131177055.

G. Klein, K. Elphinstone, G. Heiser, J. Andronick, D. Cock, P. Derrin, D. Elkaduwe, K. Engelhardt, R. Kolanski, M. Norrish, T. Sewell, H. Tuch, and S. Winwood. seL4: Formal verification of an OS kernel. *Communications of the ACM (CACM)*, 53(6):107–115, June 2010.

J. A. Whittaker, J. Arbon, and J. Carollo. *How Google Tests Software*. Addison-Wesley Professional, 2012. ISBN 0321803027.

Notes

[1] http://www.cs.st-andrews.ac.uk/~ifs/Books/SE9/CaseStudies/MHCPMS/SupportingDocs/MHCPMSCaseStudy.pdf
[2] http://themoviedb.org
[3] https://code.google.com/apis/console
[4] http://en.wikipedia.org/wiki/Y2k
[5] http://jmock.org/getting-started.html
[6] https://github.com/thoughtbot/factory_girl_rails
[7] http://myronmars.to/n/dev-blog/2012/06/rspecs-new-expectation-syntax
[8] http://rubydoc.info/gems/rspec-expectations/frames
[9] http://fakeweb.rubyforge.org
[10] http://github.com/vcr
[11] http://rspec.info
[12] http://rspec.info
[13] https://github.com/colszowka/simplecov
[14] https://github.com/relevance/tarantula
[15] http://www.fastcompany.com/magazine/06/writestuff.html
[16] http://www.sqlite.org/testing.html
[17] http://rspec.info

8.13   Suggested Projects

Project 8.1. *(Discussion) Describe the role that formal methods can play in the development of complex software and compare their use as validation and verification techniques with testing.*

Project 8.2. *Compare and contrast integration strategies including top-down, bottom-up, and sandwich integration.*

Project 8.3. *Complete the happy path of the Cucumber scenario started in Chapter 7 for retrieving movie info from TMDb. To keep the scenario Independent of the real TMDb service, you'll need to download and use the FakeWeb gem to "stub out" calls to the TMDb service.*

Project 8.4. *Write specs and code to test the implicit requirement that an empty collection is returned when a request is made with a valid API key but no results match in TMDb.*

Project 8.5. *In Section 8.3, we stubbed the method* **find_in_tmdb** *both to isolate the testing of the controller from other classes and because the method did not yet exist. How would such stubbing be handled in Java?*

Project 8.6. *Based on the specfile below, to what method(s) must instances of* **Foo** *respond in order for the tests to pass?*

http://pastebin.com/CugB7gup

```
 1  require 'foo'
 2  describe Foo do
 3    describe "a new foo" do
 4      before :each do ; @foo = Foo.new ; end
 5      it "should be a pain in the butt" do
 6        @foo.should be_a_pain_in_the_butt
 7      end
 8      it "should be awesome" do
 9        @foo.should be_awesome
10      end
11      it "should not be nil" do
12        @foo.should_not  be_nil
13      end
14      it "should not be the empty string" do
15        @foo.should_not == ""
16      end
17    end
18  end
```

Project 8.7. *In Chapter 7, we created a "Find in TMDb" button on the index page of Rot-tenPotatoes that would post to* **search_tmdb***, but we never wrote a spec that verifies that the button routes to the correct action. Write this spec using RSpec's* **route_to** *assertion matcher and add it to the controller spec. (Hint: since this route doesn't correspond to a basic CRUD action, you won't be able to use the built-in RESTful URI helpers to specify the route, but you can use the* **:controller** *and* **:action** *arguments to* **route_to** *to specify the action explicitly.)*

Project 8.8. *Increase the C0 coverage of* `movies_controller.rb` *to 100% by creating additional specs in* `movies_controller_spec.rb`.

Project 8.9. *In 1999, the $165 million Mars Climate Orbiter spacecraft burned up while entering the Martian atmosphere because one team working on thruster software had ex-pressed thrust in metric (SI) units while another team working on a different part of the thruster software had expressed them in Imperial units. What kind(s) of correctness tests— unit, functional, or integration—would have been necessary to catch this bug?*

Project 8.10. *Ruby Rod has just filled in his username and password and is about to click the Login button on Ben Bitdiddle's Rails app. The desired result, if his login arguments are correct, would be a page displaying a "Welcome, Ruby Rod."*

Consider each of the steps that occurs as a result of this interaction. For each one, determine whether it could be tested by:

- *a unit test for a model*

- *a functional test for a controller/view pair*

- *a functional test for a route*

- *a headless-browser-based full-stack test (Cucumber + Capybara in headless mode)*

- a remote-control-browser-based full-stack test (Cucumber + Capybara using Web-driver)

1. Rod clicks the Login button

2. A URL is generated as a result of the button click

3. The URL is received by the server hosting Ben's app

4. The URL is converted into a route

5. A controller method is called according to the route

6. The username and password are verified

7. The 'welcome' view is selected for rendering

8. Rod's name is interpolated into the text of the welcome view

9. The welcome view is rendered in Rod's browser

Project 8.11. *In the San Francisco Bay Area, public transportation users can purchase a card called Clipper that serves as a common fare medium across transit agencies that currently have their own media. Among other things, it's supposed to do calculations of discounts when transferring between agencies, since many agencies have such agreements. But when it was first deployed, there were software bugs that sometimes resulted in computing these discounts incorrectly. Here is a scenario similar to one that really happened in 2011[1]. Two of the rules for computing interagency discounts are:*

1. *A Muni bus ticket costs $2, and is valid for 90 minutes to transfer to* any *bus.*

2. *A BART train ticket costs $1.75.*

Consider the following boundary condition scenario.

1. *A rider starts her trip on Muni, paying $2.00.*

2. *She transfers from Muni to BART, paying an additional $1.75 to ride BART.*

3. *When she exits BART less than 90 minutes later, she transfers to another Muni bus. She should not be charged anything, because her original Muni fare is valid for 90 minutes on any bus. But in fact she is charged $2.00—a new Muni fare.*

If step 3 had occurred more than 90 minutes after step 1, it would have been correct to charge her $2.00. Use TDD and RSpec to develop a testing strategy that would check the behavior of both cases.

Software Maintenance: Enhancing Legacy Software Using Refactoring and Agile Methods

Butler Lampson

(1943–) was the intellectual leader of the legendary Xerox Palo Alto Research Center (Xerox PARC), which during its heyday in the 1970s invented graphical user interfaces, object-oriented programming, laser printing, and Ethernet. Three PARC researchers eventually won Turing Awards for their work there. Lampson received the 1994 Turing Award for contributions to the development and implementation of distributed personal computing environments: workstations, networks, operating systems, programming systems, displays, security, and document publishing.

There probably isn't a "best" way to build the system, or even any major part of it; much more important is to avoid choosing a terrible way, and to have clear division of responsibilities among the parts.

—Butler Lampson, *Hints for Computer System Design,* 1983

Concepts

Like a shark that must keep moving to live, software must change to remain viable. The big concepts in this chapter are that Agile development is a good approach to both maintain software and to enhance legacy code, and that *refactoring* is necessary on all development processes to keep code maintainable.

When writing code, **software metrics** and **code smells** can identify code that is hard to read. Transforming the code by *refactoring* should improve software metrics and eliminate code smells. Methods should be Short, do One thing, have Few arguments, and maintain a single level of Abstraction (SOFA).

To enhance legacy code using the Agile lifecycle :

- Understand the code at the **change points**, where you can plausibly make changes. Reading and enhancing comments is one way to understand the code.

- Explore how it works from all stakeholders' perspective, which involves reading tests, design documents, and inspecting code.

- Write *characterization tests* to beef up test coverage *before* making changes to the code.

For the Plan and Document lifecycle:

- A **maintenance manager** runs the project during maintenance and estimates cost of *change requests*.

- Using cost-benefit analysis, a **Change Control Committee** triages change requests.

- Like Agile, maintenance relies on *regression testing* to ensure new releases work well and *refactoring* to make the code easier to maintain.

Surprisingly, the Agile process matches many needs of the maintenance phase of Plan-and-Development lifecycle.

Agile and Plan-and-Document processes have the same maintenance goals and many of the same techniques, but Agile suggests getting there by constant incremental refactoring rather than recoding all up front.

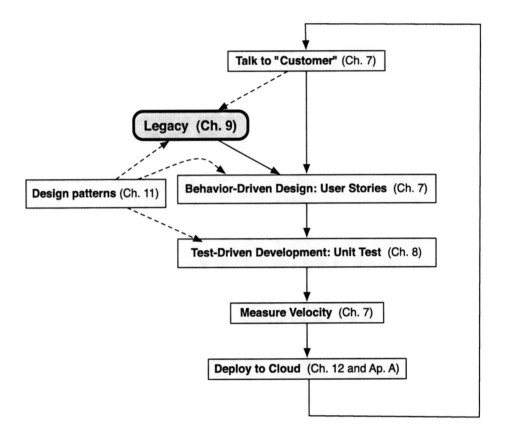

Figure 9.1: The Agile software lifecycle and its relationship to the chapters in this book. This chapter covers how Agile techniques can be helpful when enhancing legacy apps.

9.1 What Makes Code "Legacy" and How Can Agile Help?

1. Continuing Change: [software] systems must be continually adapted or they become progressively less satisfactory

—Lehman's first law of software evolution

As Chapter 1 explained, ***legacy code*** stays in use because it *still meets a customer need*, even though its design or implementation may be outdated or poorly understood. In this chapter we will show how to apply Agile techniques to enhance and modify legacy code. Figure 9.1 highlights this topic in the context of the overall Agile lifecycle.

Maintainability is the ease with which a product can be improved. In software engineering, maintenance consists of four categories (Lientz et al. 1978):

- Corrective maintenance: repairing defects and bugs

- Perfective maintenance: expanding the software's functionality to meet new customer requirements

Highly-readable unit, functional and integration tests (Chapter 8)	Git commit log messages (Chapter 10)
Lo-fi UI mockups and Cucumber-style user stories (Chapter 7)	Comments and RDoc-style documentation embedded in the code (Section 9.4)
Photos of whiteboard sketches about the application architecture, class relationships, etc. (Section 9.2)	Archived email, wiki/blog, notes, or video recordings of code and design reviews, for example in Campfire[2] or Basecamp[3] (Chapter 10)

Figure 9.2: While up-to-date formal design documents are valuable, Agile suggests we should place relatively more value on documentation that is "closer to" the working code.

- Adaptive maintenance: coping with a changing operational environment even if no new functionality is added; for example, adapting to changes in the production hosting environment

- Preventive maintenance: improving the software's structure to increase future maintainability.

Practicing these kinds of maintenance on legacy code is a skill learned by doing: we will provide a variety of techniques you can use, but there is no substitute for mileage. That said, a key component of all these maintenance activities is **refactoring**, a process that changes the structure of code (hopefully improving it) without changing the code's functionality. The message of this chapter is that *continuous refactoring improves maintainability.* Therefore, a large part of this chapter will focus on refactoring.

Any piece of software, however well-designed, can eventually evolve beyond what its original design can accommodate. This process leads to maintainability challenges, one of which is the challenge of working with legacy code. Some developers use the term "legacy" when the resulting code is poorly understood because the original designers are long gone and the software has accumulated many **patches** not explained by any current design documents. A more jaded view, shared by some experienced practitioners (Glass 2002), is that such documents wouldn't be very useful anyway. Once development starts, necessary design changes cause the system to drift away from the original design documents, which don't get updated. In such cases developers must rely on *informal* design documents such as those that Figure 9.2 lists.

How can we enhance legacy software without good documentation? As Michael Feathers writes in *Working Effectively With Legacy Code* (Feathers 2004), there are two ways to make changes to existing software: *Edit and Pray* or *Cover and Modify*. The first method is sadly all too common: familiarize yourself with some small part of the software where you have to make your changes, edit the code, poke around manually to see if you broke anything (though it's hard to be certain), then deploy and pray for the best.

In contrast, *Cover and Modify* calls for creating tests (if they don't already exist) that cover the code you're going to modify and using them as a "safety net" to detect unintended behavioral changes caused by your modifications, just as regression tests detect failures in code that used to work. The cover and modify point of view leads to Feathers's more precise definition of "legacy code", which we will use: *code that lacks sufficient tests to modify with confidence, regardless of who wrote it and when.* In other words, code that you wrote three months ago on a different project and must now revisit and modify might as well be legacy code.

Happily, the Agile techniques we've already learned for developing new software can also help with legacy code . Indeed, the task of understanding and evolving legacy software can be seen as an example of "embracing change" over longer timescales. If we inherit well-structured software with thorough tests, we can use BDD and TDD to drive addition of functionality in small but confident steps. If we inherit poorly-structured or undertested code, we need to "bootstrap" ourselves into the desired situation in four steps:

1. Identify the **change points**, or places where you will need to make changes in the legacy system. Section 9.2 describes some exploration techniques that can help, and introduces one type of Unified Modeling Language (UML) diagram for representing the relationships among the main classes in an application.

2. If necessary, add **characterization tests** that capture how the code works now, to establish a baseline "ground truth" before making any changes. Section 9.3 explains how to do this using tools you're already familiar with.

3. Determine whether the change points require **refactoring** to make the existing code more testable or accommodate the required changes, for example, by breaking dependencies that make the code hard to test. Section 9.6 introduces a few of the most widely-used techniques from the many catalogs of refactorings that have evolved as part of the Agile movement.

4. Once the code around the change points is well factored and well covered by tests, make the required changes, using your newly-created tests as regressions and adding tests for your new code as in Chapters 7 and 8.

Summary of how Agile can help legacy code:

- Maintainability is the ease with which software can be enhanced, adapted to a changing operating environment, repaired, or improved to facilitate future maintenance. A key part of software maintenance is refactoring, a central part of the Agile process that improves the structure of software to make it more maintainable. Continuous refactoring therefore improves software maintainability.

- Working with legacy code begins with exploration to understand the code base, and in particular to understand the code at the **change points** where we expect to make changes.

- Without good test coverage, we lack confidence that refactoring or enhancing the code will preserve its existing behavior. Therefore, we adopt Feathers's definition— "Legacy code is code without tests"—and create characterization tests where necessary to beef up test coverage before refactoring or enhancing legacy code.

■ *Elaboration: Embedded documentation*

RDoc is a documentation system that looks for specially formatted comments in Ruby code and generates programmer documentation from them. It is similar to and inspired by JavaDoc. RDoc syntax is easily learned by example and from the Ruby Programming wikibook[4]. The default HTML output from RDoc can be seen, for example, in the Rails documentation[5]. Consider adding RDoc documentation as you explore and understand legacy code; running `rdoc .` (that's a dot) in the root directory of a Rails app generates RDoc documentation from every `.rb` file in the current directory, `rdoc -help` shows other options, and `rake -T doc` in a Rails app directory lists other documentation-related Rake tasks.

Self-Check 9.1.1. *Why do many software engineers believe that when modifying legacy code, good test coverage is more important than detailed design documents or well-structured code?*

◇ Without tests, you cannot be confident that your changes to the legacy code preserve its existing behaviors. ■

9.2 Exploring a Legacy Codebase

If you've chosen the right data structures and organized things well, the algorithms will almost always be self-evident. Data structures, not algorithms, are central to programming.

—Rob Pike

The goal of exploration is to understand the app from both the customers' and the developers' point of view. The specific techniques you use may depend on your immediate aims:

- You're brand new to the project and need to understand the app's overall architecture, documenting as you go so others don't have to repeat your discovery process.

- You need to understand just the moving parts that would be affected by a specific change you've been asked to make.

- You're looking for areas that need beautification because you're in the process of porting or otherwise updating a legacy codebase.

Just as we explored SaaS architecture in Chapter 2 using height as an analogy, we can follow some "outside-in" steps to understand the structure of a legacy app at various levels:

1. Check out a scratch branch to run the app in a development environment

2. Learn and replicate the user stories, working with other stakeholders if necessary

3. Examine the database schema and the relationships among the most important classes

4. Skim all the code to quantify code quality and test coverage

Since operating on the live app could endanger customer data or the user experience, the first step is to get the application running in a development or staging environment in which perturbing its operation causes no inconvenience to users. Create a ***scratch branch*** of the

```
1   # on production computer:
2   RAILS_ENV=production rake db:schema:dump
3   RAILS_ENV=production rake db:fixtures:extract
4   # copy db/schema.rb and test/fixtures/*.yml to development computer
5   # then, on development computer:
6   rake db:create          # uses RAILS_ENV=development by default
7   rake db:schema:load
8   rake db:fixtures:load
```

**Figure 9.3: You can create an empty development database that has the same schema as the production database and then
populate it with fixtures. Although Chapter 8 cautions against the abuse of fixtures, in this case we are using them to
replicate known behavior from the production environment in your development environment.**

repo that you never intend to check back in and can therefore be used for experimentation.
Create a development database if there isn't an existing one used for development. An easy
way to do this is to clone the production database if it isn't too large, thereby sidestepping
numerous pitfalls:

- The app may have relationships such as has-many or belongs-to that are reflected in the
  table rows. Without knowing the details of these relationships, you might create an invalid subset of data. Using RottenPotatoes as an example, you might inadvertently end
  up with a **review** whose `movie_id` and `moviegoer_id` refer to nonexistent movies or
  moviegoers.

- Cloning the database eliminates possible differences in behavior between production
  and development resulting from differences in database implementations, difference in
  how certain data types such as dates are represented in different databases, and so on.

- Cloning gives you realistic valid data to work with in development.

If you can't clone the production database, or you have successfully cloned it but it's
too unwieldy to use in development all the time, you can create a development database by
extracting fixture data from the real database[6] using the steps in Figure 9.3.

Once the app is running in development, have one or two experienced customers demonstrate how they use the app, indicating during the demo what changes they have in mind
(Nierstrasz et al. 2009). Ask them to talk through the demo as they go; although their comments will often be in terms of the user experience ("Now I'm adding Mona as an admin
user"), if the app was created using BDD, the comments may reflect examples of the original
user stories and therefore the app's architecture. Ask frequent questions during the demo,
and if the maintainers of the app are available, have them observe the demo as well. In Section 9.3 we will see how these demos can form the basis of "ground truth" tests to underpin
your changes.

Once you have an idea of how the app works, take a look at the database schema; Fred
Brooks, Rob Pike, and others have all acknowledged the importance of understanding the data
structures as a key to understanding the app logic. You can use an interactive database GUI
to explore the schema, but you might find it more efficient to run `rake db:schema:dump`,
which creates a file `db/schema.rb` containing the database schema in the migrations DSL
introduced in Section 4.2. The goal is to match up the schema with the app's overall architecture.

Figure 9.4 shows a simplified Unified Modeling Language (UML) class diagram generated by the `railroady` gem that captures the relationships among the most important classes

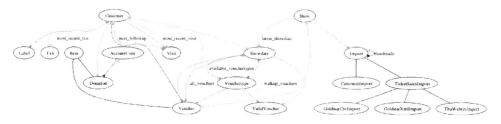

Figure 9.4: This simplified Unified Modeling Language (UML) class diagram, produced automatically by the `railroady` gem, shows the models in a Rails app that manages ticket sales, donations, and performance attendance for a small theater. Edges with arrowheads or circles show relationships between classes: a Customer has many Visits and Vouchers (open circle to arrowhead), has one most_recent_visit (solid circle to arrowhead), and a has and belongs to many Labels (arrowhead to arrowhead). Plain edges show inheritance: Donation and Voucher are subclasses of Item. (All of the important classes here inherit from ActiveRecord::Base, but `railroady` draws only the app's classes.) We will see other types of UML diagrams in Chapter 11.

and the most important attributes of those classes. While the diagram may look overwhelming initially, since not all classes play an equally important structural role, you can identify "highly connected" classes that are probably central to the application's functions. For example, in Figure 9.4, the **Customer** and **Voucher** classes are connected to each other and to many other classes. You can then identify the tables corresponding to these classes in the database schema.

Having familiarized yourself with the app's architecture, most important data structures, and major classes, you are ready to look at the code. The goal of inspecting the code is to get a sense of its overall quality, test coverage, and other statistics that serve as a proxy for how painful it may be to understand and modify. Therefore, before diving into any specific file, run `rake stats` to get the total number of lines of code and lines of tests for each file; this information can tell you which classes are most complex and therefore probably most important (highest LOC), best tested (best code-to-test ratio), simple "helper" classes (low LOC), and so on, deepening the understanding you bootstrapped from the class diagram and database schema. (Later in this chapter we'll show how to evaluate code with some additional quality metrics to give you a heads up of where the hairiest efforts might be.) If test suites exist, run them; assuming most tests pass, read the tests to help understand the original developers' intentions. Then spend one hour (Nierstrasz et al. 2009) inspecting the code in the most important classes as well as those you believe you'll need to modify (the *change points*), which by now you should be getting a good sense of.

Summary of legacy code exploration:

- The goal of exploration is to understand how the app works from multiple stakeholders' points of view, including the customer requesting the changes and the designers and developers who created the original code.

- Exploration can be aided by reading tests, reading design documents if available, inspecting the code, and drawing or generating UML class diagrams to identify relationships among important entities (classes) in the app.

- Once you have successfully seen the app demonstrated in production, the next steps are to get it running in development by either cloning or fixturing the database and to get the test suite running in development.

■ *Elaboration: Class–Responsibility–Collaborator (CRC) cards*

CRC cards (Figure 9.5) were proposed in 1989[7] as a way to help with object-oriented design. Each card identifies one class, its responsibilities, and collaborator classes with which it interacts to complete tasks. As this external screencast[8] shows, a team designing new code selects a user story (Section 7.1). For each story step, the team identifies or creates the CRC card(s) for the classes that participate in that step and confirms that the classes have the necessary Responsibilities and Collaborators to complete the step. If not, the collection of classes or responsibilities may be incomplete, or the division of responsibilities among classes may need to be changed. When exploring legacy code, you can create CRC cards to document the classes you find while following the flow from the controller action that handles a user story step through the models and views involved in the other story steps.

Self-Check 9.2.1. *What are some reasons it is important to get the app running in development even if you don't plan to make any code changes right away?*

◇ A few reasons include:

1. For SaaS, the existing tests may need access to a test database, which may not be accessible in production.

2. Part of your exploration might involve the use of an interactive debugger or other tools that could slow down execution, which would be disruptive on the live site.

3. For part of your exploration you might want to modify data in the database, which you can't do with live customer data.

■

9.3 Establishing Ground Truth With Characterization Tests

If there are no tests (or too few tests) covering the parts of the code affected by your planned changes, you'll need to create some tests. How do you do this given limited understanding of how the code works now? One way to start is to establish a baseline for "ground truth" by creating ***characterization tests***: tests written after the fact that capture and describe the

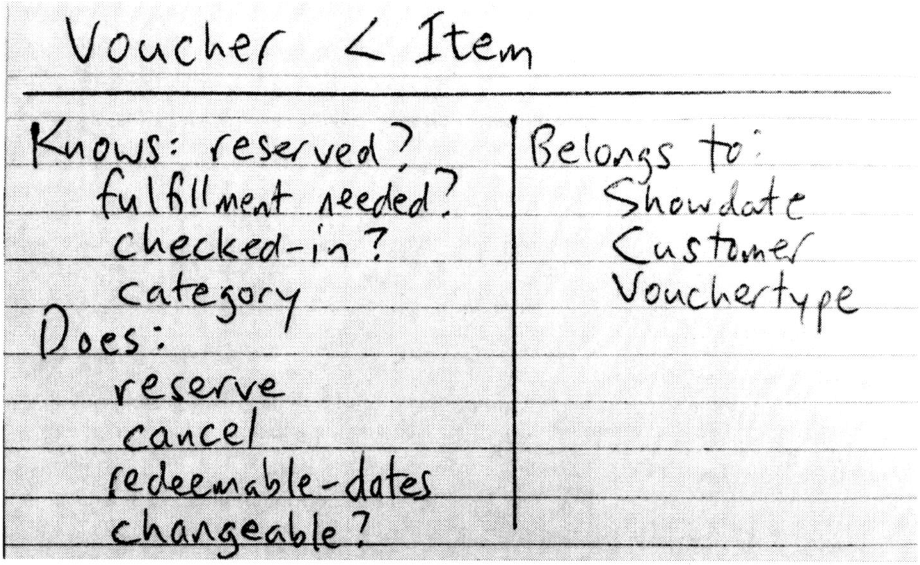

Figure 9.5: A 3-by-5 inch (or A7 size) Class–Responsibility–Collaborator (CRC) card representing the Voucher class from Figure 9.4. The left column represents Voucher's responsibilities—things it knows (instance variables) or does (instance methods). Since Ruby instance variables are always accessed through instance methods, we can determine responsibilities by searching the class file `voucher.rb` for instance methods and calls to attr_accessor. The right column represents Voucher's collaborator classes; for Rails apps we can determine many of these by looking for has_many and belongs_to in `voucher.rb`.

http://pastebin.com/fvDf8t31

```
 1 | # WARNING! This code has a bug! See text!
 2 | class TimeSetter
 3 |   def self.convert(d)
 4 |     y = 1980
 5 |     while (d > 365) do
 6 |       if (y % 400 == 0 ||
 7 |           (y % 4 == 0 && y % 100 != 0))
 8 |         if (d > 366)
 9 |           d -= 366
10 |           y += 1
11 |         end
12 |       else
13 |         d -= 365
14 |         y += 1
15 |       end
16 |     end
17 |     return y
18 |   end
19 | end
```

Figure 9.6: This method is hard to understand, hard to test, and therefore, by Feathers's definition of legacy code, hard to modify. In fact, it contains a bug—this example is a simplified version of a bug in the Microsoft Zune music player that caused any Zune booted on December 31, 2008, to freeze permanently, and for which the only resolution was to wait until the first minute of January 1, 2009, before rebooting. Screencast 9.3.1 shows the bug and fix.

actual, current behavior of a piece of software, even if that behavior has bugs. By creating a **R**epeatable automatic test (see Section 8.2) that mimics what the code does right now, you can ensure that those behaviors stay the same as you modify and enhance the code, like a high-level regression test.

It's often easiest to start with an integration-level characterization test such as a Cucumber scenario, since these make the fewest assumptions about how the app works and focus only on the user experience. Indeed, while good scenarios ultimately make use of a "domain language" rather than describing detailed user interactions in imperative steps (Section 7.9), at this point it's fine to start with imperative scenarios, since the goal is to increase coverage and provide ground truth from which to create more detailed tests. Once you have some green integration tests, you can turn your attention to unit- or functional-level tests, just as TDD follows BDD in the outside-in Agile cycle.

Whereas integration-level characterization tests just capture behaviors that we observe without requiring us to understand *how* those behaviors happen, a unit-level characterization test seems to require us to understand the implementation. For example, consider the code in Figure 9.6. As we'll discuss in detail in the next section, it has many problems, not least of which is that it contains a bug. The method **convert** calculates the current year given a starting year (in this case 1980) and the number of days elapsed since January 1 of that year. If 0 days have elapsed, then it is January 1, 1980; if 365 days have elapsed, it is December 31, 1980, since 1980 was a leap year; if 366 days have elapsed, it is January 1, 1981; and so on. How would we create unit tests for **convert** without understanding the method's logic in detail?

Feathers describes a useful technique for "reverse engineering" specs from a piece of code we don't yet understand: create a spec with an assertion that we know will probably fail, run the spec, and use the information in the error message to change the spec to match actual behavior. Screencast 9.3.1 shows how we do this for **convert**, resulting in the specs in Figure 9.7 and even finding a bug in the process!

```
1   require 'simplecov'
2   SimpleCov.start
3   require './time_setter'
4   describe TimeSetter do
5     { 365 => 1980, 366 => 1981, 900 => 1982 }.each_pair do |arg,result|
6       it "#{arg} days puts us in #{result}" do
7         TimeSetter.convert(arg).should == result
8       end
9     end
10  end
```

Figure 9.7: This simple spec, resulting from the reverse-engineering technique shown in Screencast 9.3.1, achieves 100% C0 coverage and helps us find a bug in Figure 9.6.

Screencast 9.3.1: Creating characterization specs for TimeSetter.
`http://vimeo.com/47043669`
We create specs that assert incorrect results, then fix them based on the actual test behavior. Our goal is to capture the current behavior as completely as possible so that we'll immediately know if code changes break the current behavior, so we aim for 100% C0 coverage (even though that's no guarantee of bug-freedom!), which is challenging because the code as presented has no seams. Our effort results in finding a bug that crippled thousands of Microsoft Zune players on December 31, 2008.

Summary of characterization tests:

- To Cover and Modify when we lack tests, we first create characterization tests that capture how the code works now.

- Integration-level characterization tests, such as Cucumber scenarios, are often easier to start with since they only capture externally visible app behavior.

- To create unit- and functional-level characterization tests for code we don't fully understand, we can write a spec that asserts an incorrect result, fix the assertion based on the error message, and repeat until we have sufficient coverage.

Self-Check 9.3.1. *State whether each of the following is a goal of unit and functional testing, a goal of characterization testing, or both:a*

   i Improve coverage

  ii Test boundary conditions and corner cases

 iii Document intent and behavior of app code

 iv Prevent regressions (reintroduction of earlier bugs)

◇ (i) and (iii) are goals of unit, functional, and characterization testing. (ii) and (iv) are goals of unit and functional testing, but non-goals of characterization testing. ∎

http://pastebin.com/c7FTpZxQ

```
1   # Add one to i.
2   i += 1
3
4   # Lock to protect against concurrent access.
5   mutex = SpinLock.new
6
7   # This method swaps the panels.
8   def swap_panels(panel_1, panel_2)
9     # ...
10  end
```

Figure 9.8: **Examples of bad comments, which state the obvious. You'd be surprised how often comments just mimic code even in otherwise well-written apps. (These examples and the advice on comments comes from John Ousterhout).**

http://pastebin.com/7PthRNCW

```
1   # Good Comment:
2   # Scan the array to see if the symbol exists
3
4   # Much better than:
5   # Loop through every array index, get the
6   # third value of the list in the content to
7   # determine if it has the symbol we are looking
8   # for. Set the result to the symbol if we
9   # find it.
```

Figure 9.9: **Example of comments that raises the level of abstraction compared to comments that describe how you implement it. (These examples and the advice on comments comes from John Ousterhout).**

■ *Elaboration: What about specs that should pass, but don't?*

If the test suite is out-of-date, some tests may be failing red. Rather than trying to fix the tests before you understand the code, mark them as "pending" (for example, using RSpec's **pending** method) with a comment that reminds you to come back to them later to find out why they fail. Stick to the current task of preserving existing functionality while improving coverage, and don't get distracted trying to fix bugs along the way.

9.4 Comments

Not only does legacy code often lack tests and good documentation, but its comments are often missing or inconsistent with the code. Thus far, we have not offered advice on how to write good comments, as we assume you already know how to write good code in this book. We now offer a brief sermon on comments, so that once you write successful characterization tests you can capture what you've learned by adding comments to the legacy code.

Ideally, you write comments as you code; if you come back later you will have forgotten the design ideas, so the comments will just mimic the code. Alas, this mistake is common with legacy code.

Comments should describe things that aren't obvious from the code. This advice is a double-edged sword, as it means

- *Don't* just repeat what's obvious from the code. Figure 9.8 gives examples of bad comments.

- *Do* think about what's not obvious at both the low level and the high level. Figure 9.9 gives a better example.

Obvious refers to someone who will come along later and read your code, not the original coder. Examples of what is not obvious include the units for variables, code invariants, and subtle problems that required a particular implementation. It is particularly important to document the design issues that went through your mind while you were writing the code, explaining *why* the code is written this way. In this case you are trying to document what went through another programmer's mind; once you figure it out, be sure to write it down before you forget!

In general, comments should raise the level of abstraction from the code. The programmer's goal is to write classes and other code that hides complexity; that is, to make the code easier to use than to make it easier to write. Abstraction may not be obvious from implementation; comments should capture the abstraction. For example, what do I need to know to invoke a method? I shouldn't have to read the code of a method before calling it.

One reason we are excited about the material in this book is that virtually every other software engineering sermons in this book are paired with a tool that makes it easy for you to stay on the true path and for others to check to see if you have strayed. Alas, such is not the case for this sermon on comments. The only enforcement mechanism beyond self-discipline is inspection, which Section 10.7 describes.

Summary of comments:

- Comments are best written at the same time as the code, not as an afterthought.

- Comments should not repeat what is obvious from the code. For example, explain *why* the code is written this way.

- Comments should raise the level of abstraction from the code.

Self-Check 9.4.1. *True or False: One reason legacy code is long lasting is because it typically has good comments.*
◇ False. We wish it were true. Comments are often missing or inconsistent with the code, which is one reason it is called legacy code rather than beautiful code. ∎

9.5 Metrics, Code Smells, and SOFA

> *7. Declining Quality - The quality of [software] systems will appear to be declining unless they are rigorously maintained and adapted to operational environment changes.*
>
> —Lehman's seventh law of software evolution

A key theme of this book is that engineering software is about creating not just working code, but *beautiful* working code. This chapter should make clear why we believe this: beautiful code is easier and less expensive to maintain. Given that software can live much longer than hardware, even engineers whose aesthetic sensibilities aren't moved by the idea of beautiful code can appreciate the practical economic advantage of reducing lifetime maintenance costs.

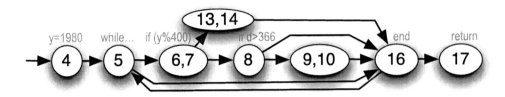

Figure 9.10: **The node numbers in this control flow graph correspond to line numbers in Figure 9.6. Cyclomatic complexity is $E - N + 2P$ where E is the number of edges, N the number of nodes, and P the number of connected components. convert scores a cyclomatic complexity of 4 as measured by `saikuro` and an ABC score (Assignments, Branches, Conditionals) of 23 as measured by `flog`. Figure 9.11 puts these scores in context.**

How can you tell when code is less than beautiful, and how do you improve it? We've all seen examples of code that's less than beautiful, even if we can't always pin down the specific problems. We can identify problems in two ways: quantitatively using **software metrics** and qualitatively using **code smells**. Both are useful and tell us different things about the code, and we apply both to the ugly code in Figure 9.6.

Software metrics are quantitative measurements of code complexity, which is often an estimate of the difficulty of thoroughly testing a piece of code. Dozens of metrics exist, and opinion varies widely on their usefulness, effectiveness, and "normal range" of values.

Most metrics are based on the **control flow graph** of the program, in which each graph node represents a **basic block** (a set of statements that are always executed together), and an edge from node A to node B means that there is some code path in which B's basic block is executed immediately after A's.

Figure 9.10 shows the control flow graph corresponding to Figure 9.6, which we can use to compute two widely-used indicators of method-level complexity:

1. **Cyclomatic complexity** measures the number of linearly-independent paths through a piece of code.

2. **ABC score** is a weighted sum of the number of **A**ssignments, **B**ranches and **C**onditionals in a piece of code.

These analyses are usually performed on source code and were originally developed for statically-typed languages. In dynamic languages, the analyses are complicated by metaprogramming and other mechanisms that may cause changes to the control flow graph at runtime. Nonetheless, they are useful first-order metrics, and as you might expect, the Ruby community has developed tools to measure them. `saikuro` computes a simplified version of cyclomatic complexity and `flog` computes a variant of the ABC score that is weighted in a way appropriate for Ruby idioms. Both of these and more are included in the `metric_fu` gem (part of the courseware). Running `rake metrics` on a Rails app computes various metrics including these, and highlights parts of the code in which multiple metrics are outside their recommended ranges. In addition, CodeClimate[9] provides many of these metrics as a service: by creating an account there and linking your GitHub repository to it, you can view a "report card" of your code metrics anytime, and the report is automatically updated when you push new code to GitHub. Figure 9.11 summarizes useful metrics we've seen so far that speak to testability and therefore to code beauty.

The second way to spot code problems is by looking for **code smells**, which are structural characteristics of source code not readily captured by metrics. Like real smells, code

Metric	Tool	Target score	Book Reference
Code-to-test ratio	`rake stats`	$\leq 1:2$	Section 8.7
C0 coverage	SimpleCov	$\geq 90\%$	Section 8.7
ABC score	`flog` (`rake metrics`)	< 20/method	Section 9.5
Cyclomatic	`saikuro` (`rake metrics`)	< 10/method	Section 9.5

Figure 9.11: A summary of useful metrics we've seen so far that highlight the connection between beauty and testability, including Ruby tools that compute them and suggested "normal" ranges. (The recommended value for cyclomatic complexity comes from NIST, the U.S. National Institute of Standards and Technologies.) The `metric_fu` gem includes `flog`, `saikuro`, and additional tools for computing metrics we'll meet in Chapter 11.

Name	Symptom	Possible refactorings
Shotgun Surgery	Making a small change to a class or method results in lots of little changes rippling to other classes or methods.	Use Move Method or Move Field to bring all the data or behaviors into a single place.
Data Clump	The same three or four data items seem to often be passed as arguments together or manipulated together.	Use Extract Class or Preserve Whole Object to create a class that groups the data together, and pass around instances of that class.
Inappropriate Intimacy	One class exploits too much knowledge about the implementation (methods or attributes) of another.	Use Move Method or Move Field if the methods really need to be somewhere else, use Extract Class if there is true overlap between two classes, or introduce a Delegate to hide the implementation.
Repetitive Boilerplate	You have bits of code that are the same or nearly the same in various different places (non-DRY).	Use Extract Method to pull redundant code into its own method that the repetitive places can call. In Ruby, you can even use **yield** to extract the "enclosing" code and having it yield back to the nonrepetitive code.

Figure 9.12: Four whimsically-named code smells from Fowler's list of 22, along with the refactorings (some of which we'll meet in the next section) that might remedy the smell if applied. Refer to Fowler's book for the refactorings mentioned in the table but not introduced in this book.

smells call our attention to places that *may* be problematic. Martin Fowler's classic book on refactoring (Fowler et al. 1999) lists 22 code smells, four of which we show in Figure 9.12, and Robert C. Martin's *Clean Code* (Martin 2008) has one of the more comprehensive catalogs with an amazing 63 code smells, of which three are specific to Java, nine are about testing, and the remainder are more general.

Design smells (see Chapter 11) tell us when something's wrong in the way classes interact, rather than within the methods of a specific class.

Four particular smells that appear in Martin's *Clean Code* are worth emphasizing, because they are symptoms of other problems that you can often fix by simple refactorings. These four are identified by the acronym **SOFA**, which states that a well-written method should:

- be **S**hort, so that its main purpose is quickly grasped;

- do only **O**ne thing, so testing can focus on thoroughly exercising that one thing;

- take **F**ew arguments, so that all-important combinations of argument values can be tested;

- maintain a consistent level of **A**bstraction, so that it doesn't jump back and forth between saying *what to do* and saying *how to do it*.

Figure 9.6 violates at least the first and last of these, and exhibits other smells as well, as we can see by running `reek` on it:

What	Guideline	Example
Variable or class name	Noun phrase	PopularMovie, top_movies
Method with side effects	Verb phrase	pay_for_order, charge_credit_card!
Method that returns a value	Noun phrase	movie.producers, actor_list
Boolean variable or method	Adjective phrase	already_rated?, @is_oscar_winner

Figure 9.13: variable-naming guidelines based on simple English, excerpted from Green and Ledgard 2011. Given that disk space is free and modern editors have auto-completion that saves you retyping the full name, your colleagues will thank you for writing @is_oscar_winner instead of OsWin.

http://pastebin.com/xP9B1iEy

```
1  start with Year = 1980
2  while (days remaining > 365)
3    if Year is a leap year
4      then if possible, peel off 366 days and advance Year by 1
5    else
6      peel off 365 days and advance Year by 1
7  return Year
```

Figure 9.14: The computation of the current year given the number of days since the beginning of a start year (1980) is much more clear when written in pseudocode. Notice that *what the method does* is quick to grasp, even though each step would have to be broken down into more detail when turned into code. We will refactor the Ruby code to match the clarity and conciseness of this pseudocode.

http://pastebin.com/ybbRJHG0

```
1  time_setter.rb -- 5 warnings:
2    TimeSetter#self.convert calls (y + 1) twice (Duplication)
3    TimeSetter#self.convert has approx 6 statements (LongMethod)
4    TimeSetter#self.convert has the parameter name 'd' (UncommunicativeName)
5    TimeSetter#self.convert has the variable name 'd' (UncommunicativeName)
6    TimeSetter#self.convert has the variable name 'y' (UncommunicativeName)
```

Not DRY (line 2). Admittedly this is only a minor duplication, but as with any smell, it's worth asking ourselves why the code turned out that way.

Uncommunicative names (lines 4–6). Variable **y** appears to be an integer (lines 6, 7, 10, 14) and is related to another variable **d**—what could those be? For that matter, what does the class **TimeSetter** set the time to, and what is being converted to what in **convert**? Four decades ago, memory was precious and so variable names were kept short to allow more space for code. Today, there's no excuse for poor variable names; Figure 9.13 provides suggestions.

Too long (line 3). More lines of code per method means more places for bugs to hide, more paths to test, and more mocking and stubbing during testing. However, excessive length is really a symptom that emerges from more specific problems—in this case, failure to stick to a single level of Abstraction. As Figure 9.14 shows, **convert** really consists of a small number of high-level steps, each of which could be divided into sub-steps. But in the code, there is no way to tell where the boundaries of steps or sub-steps would be, making the method harder to understand. Indeed, the nested conditional in lines 6–8 makes it hard for a programmer to mentally "walk through" the code, and complicates testing since you have to select sets of test cases that exercise each possible code path.

The ancient wisdom that a method shouldn't exceed one screenful of code was based on text-only terminals with 24 lines of 80 characters. A modern 22-inch monitor shows 10 times that much, so guidelines like SOFA are more reliable today.

As a result of these deficiencies, you probably had to work hard to figure out what this relatively simple method does. (You might blame this on a lack of comments in the code, but once the above smells are fixed, there will be hardly any need for them.) Astute readers usually note the constants 1980, 365, and 366, and infer that the method has something to do with leap years and that 1980 is special. In fact, **convert** calculates the current year given a starting year of 1980 and the number of days elapsed since January 1 of that year, as Figure 9.14 shows using simple pseudocode. In Section 9.5, we will make the Ruby code as transparent as the pseudocode by *refactoring* it—applying transformations that improve its structure without changing its behavior.

Summary

- Software metrics provide a quantitative measure of code quality. While opinion varies on which metrics are most useful and what their "normal" values should be (especially in dynamic languages such as Ruby), metrics such as cyclomatic complexity and ABC score can be used to guide your search toward code that is in particular need of attention, just as low C0 coverage identifies undertested code.

- Code smells provide qualitative but specific descriptions of problems that make code hard to read. Depending on which catalog you use, over 60 specific code smells have been identified.

- The acronym SOFA names four desirable properties of a method: it should be **S**hort, do **O**ne thing, have **F**ew arguments, and maintain a single level of **A**bstraction.

Self-Check 9.5.1. *Give an example of a dynamic language feature in Ruby that could distort metrics such as cyclomatic complexity or ABC score.*

◇ Any metaprogramming mechanism could do this. A trivial example is **s="if (d>=366)/...]"; eval s**, since the evaluation of the string would cause a conditional to be executed even though there's no conditional in the code itself, which contains only an assignment to a variable and a call to the **eval** method. A subtler example is a method such as **before_filter** (Section 5.1), which essentially adds a new method to a list of methods to be called before a controller action. ■

Self-Check 9.5.2. *Which SOFA guideline—be Short, do One thing, have Few arguments, stick to a single level of Abstraction—do you think is most important from a unit-testability point of view?*

◇ Few arguments implies fewer ways that code paths in the method can depend on the arguments, making testing more tractable. Short methods are certainly easier to test, but this property usually follows when the other three are observed. ■

9.6 Method-Level Refactoring: Replacing Dependencies With Seams

> *2. Increasing Complexity - As [a software] system evolves, its complexity increases unless work is done to maintain or reduce it.*
>
> —Lehman's second law of software evolution

With the characterization specs developed in Section 9.3, we have a solid foundation on which to base our refactoring to repair the problems identified in Section 9.5. The term *refactoring* refers not only to a general process, but also to an instance of a specific code transformation. Thus, just as with code smells, we speak of a catalog of refactorings, and

Name (Chapter)	Problem	Solution
Extract method (6)	You have a code fragment that can be grouped together.	Turn the fragment into a method whose name explains the purpose of the method.
Decompose Conditional (9)	You have a complicated conditional (if-then-else) statement.	Extract methods from the condition, "then" part, and "else" part(s).
Replace Method with Method Object (6)	You have a long method that uses local variables in such a way that you cannot apply Extract Method.	Turn the method into its own object so that all the local variables become instance variables on that object. You can then decompose the method into other methods on the same object.
Replace Magic Number with Symbolic Constant (8)	You have a literal number with a particular meaning.	Create a constant, name it after the meaning, and replace the number with it.

Figure 9.15: **Four example refactorings, with parentheses around the chapter in which each appears in Fowler's book. Each refactoring has a name, a problem that it solves, and an overview of the code transformation(s) that solve the problem. Fowler's book also includes detailed mechanics for each refactoring, as Figure 9.16 shows.**

there are many such catalogs to choose from. We prefer Fowler's catalog, so the examples in this chapter follow Fowler's terminology and are cross-referenced to Chapters 6, 8, 9, and 10 of his book *Refactoring: Ruby Edition* (Fields et al. 2009). While the correspondence between code smells and refactorings is not perfect, in general each of those chapters describes a group of method-level refactorings that address specific code smells or problems, and further chapters describe refactorings that affect multiple classes, which we'll learn about in Chapter 11.

Each refactoring consists of a descriptive name and a step-by-step process for transforming the code via small incremental steps, testing after each step. Most refactorings will cause at least temporary test failures, since unit tests usually depend on implementation, which is exactly what refactoring changes. A key goal of the refactoring process is to minimize the amount of time that tests are failing (red); the idea is that each refactoring step is small enough that adjusting the tests to pass before moving on to the next step is not difficult. If you find that getting from red back to green is harder than expected, you must determine if your understanding of the code was incomplete, or if you have really broken something while refactoring.

Getting started with refactoring can seem overwhelming: without knowing what refactorings exist, it may be hard to decide how to improve a piece of code. Until you have some experience improving pieces of code, it may be hard to understand the explanations of the refactorings or the motivations for when to use them. Don't be discouraged by this apparent chicken-and-egg problem; like TDD and BDD, what seems overwhelming at first can quickly become familiar.

As a start, Figure 9.15 shows four of Fowler's refactorings that we will apply to our code. In his book, each refactoring is accompanied by an example and an extremely detailed list of mechanical steps for performing the refactoring, in some cases referring to other refactorings that may be necessary in order to apply this one. For example, Figure 9.16 shows the first few steps for applying the Extract Method refactoring. With these examples in mind, we can refactor Figure 9.6.

Long method is the most obvious code smell in Figure 9.6, but that's just an overall

1. Create a new method, and name it after the intention of the method (name it by what it does, not by how it does it). If the code you want to extract is very simple, such as a single message or function call, you should extract it if the name of the new method reveals the intention of the code in a better way. If you can't come up with a more meaningful name, don't extract the code.

2. Copy the extracted code from the source method into the new target method.

3. Scan the extracted code for references to any variables that are local in scope to the source method. These are local variables and parameters to the method.

4. See whether any temporary variables are used only within this extracted code. If so, declare them in the target method as temporary variables.

5. Look to see whether any of these local-scope variables are modified by the extracted code. If one variable is modified, see whether you can treat the extracted code as a query and assign the result to the variable concerned. If this is awkward, or if there is more than one such variable, you can't extract the method as it stands. You may need to use *Split Temporary Variable* and try again. You can eliminate temporary variables with *Replace Temp with Query* (see the discussion in the examples).

6. Pass into the target method as parameters local-scope variables that are read from the extracted method.

7. ...

Figure 9.16: Fowler's detailed steps for the Extract Method refactoring. In his book, each refactoring is described as a step-by-step code transformation process that may refer to other refactorings.

symptom to which various specific problems contribute. The high ABC score (23) of **convert** suggests one place to start focusing our attention: the condition of the **if** in lines 6–7 is difficult to understand, and the conditional is nested two-deep. As Figure 9.15 suggests, a hard-to-read conditional expression can be improved by applying the very common refactoring *Decompose Conditional*, which in turn relies on *Extract Method*. We move some code into a new method with a descriptive name, as Figure 9.17 shows. Note that in addition to making the conditional more readable, the separate definition of **leap_year?** makes the leap year calculation separately testable and provides a seam at line 6 where we could stub the method to simplify testing of **convert**, similar to the example in the Elaboration at the end of Section 8.6. In general, when a method mixes code that says *what to do* with code that says *how to do it*, this may be a warning to check whether you need to use Extract Method in order to maintain a consistent level of Abstraction.

The conditional is also nested two-deep, making it hard to understand and increasing **convert**'s ABC score. The *Decompose Conditional* refactoring also breaks up the complex condition by replacing each arm of the conditional with an extracted method. Notice, though, that the two arms of the conditional correspond to lines 4 and 6 of the pseudocode in Figure 9.14, both of which have the *side effects* of changing the values of **d** and **y** (hence our use of **!** in the names of the extracted methods). In order for those side effects to be visible to **convert**, we must turn the local variables into class variables throughout **TimeSetter**, giving them more descriptive names **@@year** and **@@days_remaining** while we're at it. Finally, since **@@year** is now a class variable, we no longer need to pass it as an explicit argument to **leap_year?**. Figure 9.18 shows the result.

As long as we're cleaning up, the code in Figure 9.18 also fixes two minor code smells. The first is uncommunicative variable names: **convert** doesn't describe very well what this method does, and the parameter name **d** is not useful. The other is the use of "magic number" literal constants such as 1980 in line 4; we apply *Replace Magic Number with Symbolic Constant* (Fowler chapter 8) to replace it with the more descriptive constant name **START-**

http://pastebin.com/N90nw3bu

```
 1  # NOTE: line 7 fixes bug in original version
 2  class TimeSetter
 3    def self.convert(d)
 4      y = 1980
 5      while (d > 365) do
 6        if leap_year?(y)
 7          if (d >= 366)
 8            d -= 366
 9            y += 1
10          end
11        else
12          d -= 365
13          y += 1
14        end
15      end
16      return y
17    end
18    private
19    def self.leap_year?(year)
20      year % 400 == 0 ||
21        (year % 4 == 0 && year % 100 != 0)
22    end
23  end
```

Figure 9.17: Applying the Extract Method refactoring to lines 3–4 of Figure 9.6 makes the conditional's purpose immediately clear (line 6) by replacing the condition with a well-named method (lines 19–22), which we declare private to keep the class's implementation details well encapsulated. For even more transparency, we could apply Extract Method again to leap_year? by extracting methods every_400_years? and every_4_years_except_centuries?. Note: Line 7 reflects the bug fix described in Screencast 9.3.1.

http://pastebin.com/gdT1DzjG

```
 1  # NOTE: line 7 fixes bug in original version
 2  class TimeSetter
 3    ORIGIN_YEAR = 1980
 4    def self.calculate_current_year(days_since_origin)
 5      @@year = ORIGIN_YEAR
 6      @@days_remaining = days_since_origin
 7      while (@@days_remaining > 365) do
 8        if leap_year?
 9          peel_off_leap_year!
10        else
11          peel_off_regular_year!
12        end
13      end
14      return @@year
15    end
16    private
17    def self.peel_off_leap_year!
18      if (@@days_remaining >= 366)
19        @@days_remaining -= 366 ; @@year += 1
20      end
21    end
22    def self.peel_off_regular_year!
23      @@days_remaining -= 365 ; @@year += 1
24    end
25    def self.leap_year?
26      @@year % 400 == 0 ||
27        (@@year % 4 == 0 && @@year % 100 != 0)
28    end
29  end
```

Figure 9.18: We decompose the conditional in line 7 by replacing each branch with an extracted method. Note that while the total number of lines of code has increased, convert itself has become Shorter, and its steps now correspond closely to the pseudocode in Figure 9.14, sticking to a single level of Abstraction while delegating details to the extracted helper methods.

```
1  # An example call would now be:
2  #   year = TimeSetter.new(367).calculate_current_year
3  # rather than:
4  #   year = TimeSetter.calculate_current_year(367)
5  class TimeSetter
6    ORIGIN_YEAR = 1980
7    def initialize(days_since_origin)
8      @year = ORIGIN_YEAR
9      @days_remaining = days_since_origin
10   end
11   def calculate_current_year
12     while (@days_remaining > 365) do
13       if leap_year?
14         peel_off_leap_year!
15       else
16         peel_off_regular_year!
17       end
18     end
19     return @year
20   end
21   private
22   def peel_off_leap_year!
23     if (@days_remaining >= 366)
24       @days_remaining -= 366 ; @year += 1
25     end
26   end
27   def peel_off_regular_year!
28     @days_remaining -= 365 ; @year += 1
29   end
30   def leap_year?
31     @year % 400 == 0 ||
32       (@year % 4 == 0 && @year % 100 != 0)
33   end
34 end
```

Figure 9.19: If we use Fowler's recommended refactoring, the code is cleaner because we now use instance variables rather than class variables to track side effects, but it changes the way calculate_current_year is called because it's now an instance method. This would break existing code and tests, and so might be deferred until later in the refactoring process.

ING_YEAR. What about the other constants such as 365 and 366? In this example, they're probably familiar enough to most programmers to leave as-is, but if you saw 351 rather than 365, and if line 26 (in **leap_year?**) used the constant 19 rather than 4, you might not recognize the leap year calculation for the ***Hebrew calendar***. Remember that refactoring only improves the code for human readers; the computer doesn't care. So in such cases use your judgment as to how much refactoring is enough.

In our case, re-running flog on the refactored code in Figure 9.18 brings the ABC score for the newly-renamed **calculate_current_year** from 23.0 down to 6.6, which is well below the suggested NIST threshold of 10.0. Also, reek now reports only two smells. The first is "low cohesion" for the helper methods **peel_off_leap_year** and **peel_off_regular_year**; this is a design smell, and we will discuss what it means in Chapter 11. The second smell is declaration of class variables inside a method. When we applied Decompose Conditional and Extract Method, we turned local variables into class variables **@@year** and **@@days_remaining** so that the newly-extracted methods could successfully modify those variables' values. Our solution is effective, but clumsier than *Replace Method with Method Object* (Fowler chapter 6). In that refactoring, the original method **convert** is turned into an object *instance* (rather than a class) whose instance variables capture the object's state; the helper methods then operate on the instance variables.

Figure 9.19 shows the result of applying such a refactoring, but there is an important caveat. So far, none of our refactorings have caused our characterization specs to fail, since the specs were just calling **TimeSetter.convert**. But applying *Replace Method With Method Object* changes the calling interface to **convert** in a way that makes tests fail. If we were working with real legacy code, we would have to find every site that calls **convert**, change it to use the new calling interface, and change any failing tests accordingly. In a real project, we'd want to avoid changes that needlessly break the calling interface, so we'd need to consider carefully whether the readability gained by applying this refactoring would outweigh the risk of introducing this breaking change.

Summary of refactoring:

- A refactoring is a particular transformation of a piece of code, including a name, description of when to use the refactoring and what it does, and detailed sequence of mechanical steps to apply the refactoring. Effective refactorings should improve software metrics, eliminate code smells, or both.

- Although most refactorings will inevitably cause some existing tests to fail (if not, the code in question is probably undertested), a key goal of the refactoring process is to minimize the amount of time until those tests are modified and once again passing green.

- Sometimes applying a refactoring may result in recursively having to apply simpler refactorings first, as *Decompose Conditional* may require applying *Extract Method*.

■ Elaboration: Refactoring and language choice

Some refactorings compensate for programming language features that may encourage bad code. For example, one suggested refactoring for adding seams is *Encapsulate Field*, in which direct access to an object's instance variables is replaced by calls to getter and setter methods. This makes sense in Java, but as we've seen, getter and setter methods provide the *only* access to a Ruby object's instance variables from outside the object. (The refactoring still makes sense inside the object's own methods, as the Elaboration at the end of Section 3.4 suggests.) Similarly, the *Generalize Type* refactoring suggests creating more general types to improve code sharing, but Ruby's mixins and duck typing make such sharing easy. As we'll see in Chapter 11, it's also the case that some design patterns are simply unnecessary in Ruby because the problem they solve doesn't arise in dynamic languages.

Self-Check 9.6.1. *Which is* not *a goal of method-level refactoring: (a) reducing code complexity, (b) eliminating code smells, (c) eliminating bugs, (d) improving testability?*
◇ (c). While debugging is important, the goal of refactoring is to *preserve* the code's current behavior while changing its structure. ■

9.7 The Plan-And-Document Perspective

One reason for the term *lifecycle* from Chapter 1 is that a software product enters a maintenance phase after development completes. Roughly two-thirds of the costs are in maintenance versus one-third in development. One reason that companies charge roughly 10% of the price of software for annual maintenance is to pay the team that does the maintenance.

Organizations following Plan-And-Document processes typically have different teams for development and maintenance, with developers being redistributed onto new projects once the project is released. Thus, we now have a ***maintenance manager*** who takes over the roles of the project manager during development, and we have ***maintenance software engineers*** working on the team that make the changes to the code. Sadly, maintenance engineering has an unglamorous reputation, so it is typically performed by either the newest or least accomplished managers and engineers in an organization. Many organizations use different people for Quality Assessment to do the testing and for user documentation.

For software products developed using Plan-And-Document processes, the environment for maintenance is very different from the environment for development:

- *Working software*—A working software product is in the field during this whole phase, and new releases must not interfere with existing features.

- *Customer collaboration*—Rather than trying to meet a specification that is part of a negotiated contract, the goal for this phase is to work with customers to improve the product for the next release.

- *Responding to change*—Based on use of the product, customers send a stream of ***change requests***, which can be new features as well as bug fixes. One challenge of the maintenance phase is prioritizing whether to implement a change request and in which release should it appear.

> **Change requests** are called ***maintenance requests*** in IEEE standards.

Regression testing plays a much bigger role in maintenance to avoid breaking old features when developing new ones. Refactoring also plays a much bigger role, as you may need to refactor to implement a change request or simply to make the code more maintainable. There is less incentive for the extra cost and time to make the product easier to maintain in Plan-And-Document processes initially if the company developing the software is not the one that maintains it, which is one reason refactoring plays a smaller role during development.

As mentioned above, ***change management*** is based on change requests made by customers and other stakeholders to fix bugs or to improve functionality (see Section 10.7). They typically fill out ***change request forms***, which are tracked using a ticket tracking system so that each request is responded to and resolved. A key tool for change management is a version control system, which tracks all modifications to all objects, as we describe in Sections 10.4 and 10.5.

The prior paragraphs should sound familiar, for we are describing Agile development; in fact, the three bullets are copied from the Agile Manifesto (see Section 1.3). Thus, *maintenance is essentially an Agile process.* Change requests are like user stories; the triaging of change requests is similar to the assignment of points and using Pivotal Tracker to decide how to prioritize stories; and new releases of the software product act as Agile iterations of the working prototype. Plan-and-document maintenance even follows the same strategy of breaking a large change request into many smaller ones to make them easier to assess and implement, just as we do with user stories assigned more than eight points (see Section 7.2). Hence, if the same team is developing and maintaining the software, nothing changes after the first release of the product when using the Agile lifecycle.

Although one paper reports successfully using an Agile process to maintain software developed using Plan-And-Document processes (Poole and Huisman 2001), normally an or-

Tasks	In Plan and Document	In Agile
Customer change request	Change request forms	User story on 3x5 cards in Connextra format
Change request cost/time estimate	By Maintenance Manager	Points by Development Team
Triage of change requests	Change Control Board	Development team with customer participation
Roles	Maintenance Manager	N.A.
	Maintenance SW Engineers QA team Documentation teams Customer support group	Development team

Figure 9.20: The relationship between the maintenance related tasks of Plan-and-Document versus Agile methodologies.

ganization that follows Plan-And-Document for development also follows it for maintenance. As we saw in earlier chapters, this process expects a strong project manager who makes the cost estimate, develops the schedule, reduces risks to the project, and formulates a careful plan for all the pieces of the project. This plan is reflected in many documents, which we saw in Figures 7.13 and 8.22 and will see in the next chapter in Figures 10.9, 10.10, and 10.11. Thus, the impact of change in Plan-And-Document processes is not just the cost to change the code, but also to change the documentation and testing plan. Given the many more objects of Plan-And-Document, it takes more effort to synchronize to keep them all consistent when a change is made.

A *change control board* examines all significant requests to decide if the changes should be included in the next version of the system. This group needs estimates of the cost of a change to decide whether or not to approve the change request. The maintenance manager must estimate the effort and time to implement each change, much as the project manager did for the project initially (see Section 7.10). The group also asks the QA team for the cost of testing, including running all the regression tests and developing new ones (if needed) for a change. The documentation group also estimates the cost to change the documentation. Finally, the customer support group checks whether there is a workaround to decide if the change is urgent or not. Besides cost, the group considers the increased value of the product after the change when deciding what to do.

To help keep track what must be done in Plan-And-Document processes, you will not be surprised to learn that IEEE offers standards to help. Figure 9.21 shows the outline of a maintenance plan from the IEEE Maintenance Standard 1219-1998.

Ideally, changes can all be scheduled to keep the code, documents, and plans all in synchronization with an upcoming release. Alas, some changes are so urgent that everything else is dropped to try to get the new version to the customer as fast as possible. For example:

- The software product crashes.

- A security hole has been identified that makes the data collected by the product particularly vulnerable.

- New releases of the underlying operating system or libraries force changes to the product for it to continue to function.

Table of Contents
1. Introduction
2. References
3. Definitions
4. Software Maintenance Overview
4.1 Organization
4.2 Scheduling Priorities
4.3 Resource Summary
4.4 Responsibilities
4.5 Tools, Techniques, and Methods
5. Software Maintenance Process
5.1 Problem/modification identification/classification, and prioritization
5.2 Analysis
5.3 Design
5.4 Implementation
5.5 System Testing
5.6 Acceptance Testing
5.7 Delivery
6. Software Maintenance Reporting Requirements
7. Software Maintenance Administrative Requirements
7.1 Anomaly Resolution and Reporting
7.2 Deviation Policy
7.3 Control Procedures
7.4 Standards, Practices, and Conventions
7.5 Performance Tracking
7.6 Quality Control of Plan
8. Software Maintenance Documentation Requirements

Figure 9.21: Maintenance plan outline from the IEEE 1219-1998 Standard for Maintenance in Systems and Software Engineering.

- A competitor brings out product or feature that if not matched will dramatically affect the business of the customer.

- New laws are passed that affect the product.

Backfilling is the term maintenance engineers use to describe getting code back in synch after emergencies.

While the assumption is that the team will update the documentation and plans as soon as the emergency is over, in practice emergencies can be so frequent that the maintenance team can't keep everything in synch. Such a buildup is called a ***technical debt***. Such procrastination can lead to code that is increasingly difficult to maintain, which in turn leads to an increasing need to refactor the code as the code's "viscosity" makes it more and more difficult to add functionality cleanly. While refactoring is a natural part of Agile, it less likely for the Change Control Committee to approve changes that require refactoring, as these changes are much more expensive. That is–as the name is intended to indicate–if you don't repay your technical debt, it grows: the "uglier" the code gets, the more error-prone and time-consuming it is to refactor!

In addition to estimating the cost of each potential change for the Change Control Board, an organization's management may ask what will be the annual cost of maintenance of a project. The maintenance manager may base this estimate on software metrics, just as the project manager may use metrics to estimate the cost to develop a project (see Section 7.10). The metrics are different for maintenance, as they are measuring the maintenance process. Examples of metrics that may indicate increased difficulty of maintenance include the average time to analyze or implement a change request and increases in the number of change requests made or approved.

At some point in the lifecycle of a software product, the question arises whether it is time for it to be replaced. An alternative that is related to refactoring is called ***reengineering***. Like refactoring, the idea is to keep functionality the same but to make the code much easier to maintain. Examples include:

- Changing the database schema.

- Using a reverse engineering tool to improve documentation.

- Using a structural analysis tool to identify and simplify complex control structures.

- Using a language translation tool to change code from a procedure-oriented language like C or COBOL to an object-oriented language like C++ or Java.

The hope is that reengineering will be much less expensive and much more likely to succeed than reimplementing the software product from scratch.

Summary: The insight from this section is that you can think of Agile as a maintenance process, in that change is the norm, you are in continuous contact with the customer, and that new iterations of the product are routinely deployed to the customer as new releases. Hence, regression testing and refactoring are standard in the Agile process just as they are the maintenance phase of Plan-and-Document. In Plan-and-Document processes:

- *Maintenance managers* play the role of project managers: they interface with the customer and upper management, make the cost and schedule estimates, documents the maintenance plan, and manage the *maintenance software engineers*.

- Customers and other stakeholders issue *change requests*, which a *Change Control Committee* triages based on the benefit of the change and cost estimates from the maintenance manager, the documentation team, and the QA team.

- *Regression testing* plays a bigger role in maintenance to ensure that new features do not interfere with old ones.

- *Refactoring* plays a bigger role as well, in part because there is often less refactoring in Plan-and-Document processes during product development than in Agile development.

- An alternative to starting over when the code becomes increasingly difficult to maintain is to *reengineer* the code to lower the cost of having a much more maintainable system.

One argument for Agile development is therefore as follows: if two-thirds of the cost of product are in the maintenance phase, why not use the same maintenance-compatible software development process for the whole lifecycle?

Self-Check 9.7.1. *True or False: The cost of maintenance usually exceeds the cost of development.*
◇ True. ∎

Self-Check 9.7.2. *True or False: Refactoring and reengineering are synonyms.*
◇ False: While related terms, reengineering often relies on automatic tools and occurs as software ages and maintainability becomes more difficult, yet refactoring is a continuous process of code improvement that happens during both development and maintenance. ∎

Self-Check 9.7.3. *Match the Plan-and-Document maintenance terms on the left to the Agile terms on the right:*

Change request	*Iteration*
Change request cost estimate	*Icebox, Active columns in Pivotal Tracker*
Change request triage	*Points*
Release	*User story*

◇ Change request ⟺ User story; Change request cost estimate ⟺ Points; Release ⟺ Iteration; and Change request triage ⟺ Icebox, Active columns in Pivotal Tracker. ∎

9.8   Fallacies and Pitfalls

 Pitfall: **Conflating refactoring with enhancement.**

When you're refactoring or creating additional tests (such as characterization tests) in preparation to improve legacy code, there is a great temptation to fix "little things" along the way: methods that look just a little messy, instance variables that look obsolete, dead code that looks like it's never reached from anywhere, "really simple" features that look like you could quickly add while doing other tasks. *Resist these temptations!* First, the reason to establish ground-truth tests ahead of time is to bootstrap yourself into a position from which you can make changes with confidence that you're not breaking anything. Trying to make such "improvements" in the absence of good test coverage invites disaster. Second, as we've said before and will repeat again, programmers are optimists: tasks that look trivial to fix may sidetrack you for a long time from your primary task of refactoring, or worse, may get the code base into an unstable state from which you must backtrack in order to continue refactoring. The solution is simple: when you're refactoring or laying groundwork, focus obsessively on completing those steps *before* trying to enhance the code.

 Fallacy: **It'll be faster to start from a clean slate than to fix this design.**

Putting aside the practical consideration that management will probably wisely forbid you from doing this anyway, there are many reasons why this belief is almost always wrong. First, if you haven't taken the time to understand a system, you are in no position to estimate how hard it will be to redesign, and probably will underestimate the effort vastly, given programmers' incurable optimism. Second, however ugly it may be, the current system *works*; a main tenet of doing short Agile iterations is "always have working code," and by starting over you are immediately throwing that away. Third, if you use Agile methods in your redesign, you'll have to develop user stories and scenarios to drive the work, which means you'll need to prioritize them and write up quite a few of them to make sure you've captured at least the functionality of the current system. It would probably be faster to use the techniques in this chapter to write scenarios for just those parts of the system to be improved and drive new code from there, rather than doing a complete rewrite.

Does this mean you should *never* wipe the slate clean? No. As Rob Mee of Pivotal Labs points out, a time may come when the current codebase is such a poor reflection of the original design intent that it becomes a liability, and starting over may well be the best thing to do. (Sometimes this results from not refactoring in a timely way!) But in all but the most trivial systems, this should be regarded as the "nuclear option" when all other paths have been carefully considered and determined to be inferior ways to meet the customer's needs.

 Pitfall: **Rigid adherence to metrics or "allergic" avoidance of code smells.**

In Chapter 8 we warned that correctness cannot be assured by relying on a single type of test (unit, functional, integration/acceptance) or by relying exclusively on quantitative code coverage as a measure of test thoroughness. Similarly, code quality cannot be assured by any single code metric or by avoiding any specific code smells. Hence the `metric_fu` gem inspects your code for multiple metrics and smells so you can identify "hot spots" where multiple problems with the same piece of code call for refactoring.

9.9 Concluding Remarks: Continuous Refactoring

> *A ship in port is safe, but that's not what ships are built for.*
>
> —Grace Murray Hopper

As we said in the opening of the chapter, modifying legacy code is not a task to be undertaken lightly, and the techniques required must be honed by experience. The first time is always the hardest. But fundamental skills such as refactoring help with both legacy code and new code, and as we saw, there is a deep connection among legacy code, refactoring, and testability and test coverage. We took code that was neither good nor testable—it scored poorly on complexity metrics and code smells, and isolating behaviors for unit testing was awkward—and refactored it into code that has much better metric scores, is easier to read and understand, and is easier to test. In short, we showed that *good methods are testable and testable methods are good.* We used refactoring to beautify existing code, but the same techniques can be used when performing the enhancements themselves. For example, if we need to add functionality to an existing method, rather than simply adding a bunch of lines of code and risk violating one or more SOFA guidelines, we can apply Extract Method to place the functionality in a new method that we call from the existing method. As you can see, this technique has the nice benefit that we already know how to develop new methods using TDD!

This observation explains why TDD leads naturally to good and testable code—it's hard for a method not to be testable if the test is written first—and illustrates the rationale behind the "refactor" step of Red–Green–Refactor. If you are refactoring constantly as you code, each individual change is likely to be small and minimally intrusive on your time and concentration, and your code will tend to be beautiful. When you extract smaller methods from larger ones, you are identifying collaborators, describing the purpose of code by choosing good names, and inserting seams that help testability. When you rename a variable more descriptively, you are documenting design intent.

But if you continue to encrust your code with new functionality *without* refactoring as you go, when refactoring finally does become necessary (and it will), it will be more painful and require the kind of significant scaffolding described in Sections 9.2 and 9.3. In short, refactoring will suddenly change from a background activity that takes incremental extra time to a foreground activity that commands your focus and concentration at the expense of adding customer value.

Since programmers are optimists, we often think "That won't happen to me; I wrote this code, so I know it well enough that refactoring won't be so painful." But in fact, your code becomes legacy code the moment it's deployed and you move on to focusing on another part of the code. Unless you have a time-travel device and can talk to your former self, you might not be able to divine what you were thinking when you wrote the original code, so the code's clarity must speak for itself.

This Agile view of continuous refactoring should not surprise you: just as with development, testing, or requirements gathering, refactoring is not a one-time "phase" but an ongoing process. In Chapter 12 we will see that the view of continuous vs. phased also holds for deployment and operations.

It may be a surprise that the fundamental characteristics of Agile make it an excellent match to the needs of software maintenance. In fact, we can think of Agile as not having a development phase at all, but being in maintenance mode from the very start of its lifecycle!

Category	Refactorings		
Composing Methods	*Extract method* *Replace method with method object* Remove parameter assignments	Replace temp with method Inline temp Substitute algorithm	Introduce explaining variable Split temp variable
Organizing Data	self-encapsulate field replace array/hash with Object	replace data value with object *Replace magic number with symbolic constant*	change value to reference
Simplifying Conditionals	*Decompose Conditional* Replace Conditional with Polymorphism Consolidate Duplicate Conditional Fragments	Consolidate Conditional Replace Type Code with Polymorphism Remove Control Flag	Introduce Assertion Replace Nested Conditional with Guard Clauses Introduce Null Object
Simplifying Method Calls	Rename Method Replace Parameter with Explicit Methods	Add Parameter Preserve Whole Object	Separate Query from Modifier Replace Error Code with Exception

Figure 9.22: Several more of Fowler's refactorings, with the ones introduced in this chapter in italics.

Duplicated Code Divergent Change	Temporary Field Feature Envy	Large Class Primitive Obsession	Long Parameter List Metaprogramming Madness
Data Class	Lazy Class	Speculative Generality	Parallel Inheritance Hierarchies
Refused Bequest Too Many Comments	Message Chains Case Statements	Middle Man Alternative Classes with Different Interfaces	Incomplete Library Class

Figure 9.23: Several of Fowler's and Martin's code smells, with the ones introduced in this chapter in italics.

9.10 To Learn More

Working with legacy code isn't exclusively about refactoring, but as we've seen, refactoring is a major part of the effort. The best way to get better at refactoring is to do it a lot. Initially, we recommend you browse through Fowler's refactoring book just to get an overview of the many refactorings that have been cataloged. We recommend the Ruby-specific version (Fields et al. 2009), since not all smells or refactorings that arise in statically-typed languages occur in Ruby; versions are available for other popular languages, including Java. We introduced only a few in this chapter; Figure 9.22 lists more. As you become more experienced, you'll recognize refactoring opportunities without consulting the catalog each time.

Code smells came out of the Agile movement. Again, we introduced only a few from a more extensive catalog; Figure 9.23 lists more. We also introduced some simple software metrics; over four decades of software engineering, many others have been produced to capture code quality, and many analytical and empirical studies have been done on the costs and benefits of software maintenance. Robert Glass (Glass 2002) has produced a pithy collection of *Facts & Fallacies of Software Engineering*, informed by both experience and the scholarly literature and focusing in particular on the perceived vs. actual costs and benefits of maintenance activities.

M. Feathers. *Working Effectively with Legacy Code*. Prentice Hall, 2004. ISBN 9780131177055.

J. Fields, S. Harvie, M. Fowler, and K. Beck. *Refactoring: Ruby Edition*. Addison-Wesley Professional, 2009. ISBN 0321603508.

M. Fowler, K. Beck, J. Brant, W. Opdyke, and D. Roberts. *Refactoring: Improving the Design of Existing Code*. Addison-Wesley Professional, 1999. ISBN 0201485672.

R. L. Glass. *Facts and Fallacies of Software Engineering*. Addison-Wesley Professional, 2002. ISBN 0321117425.

R. Green and H. Ledgard. Coding guidelines: Finding the art in the science. *Communications of the ACM*, 54(12):57–63, Dec 2011.

B. P. Lientz, E. B. Swanson, and G. E. Tompkins. Characteristics of application software maintenance. *Communications of the ACM*, 21(6):466–471, 1978.

R. C. Martin. *Clean Code: A Handbook of Agile Software Craftsmanship*. Prentice Hall, 2008. ISBN 9780132350884.

O. Nierstrasz, S. Ducasse, and S. Demeyer. *Object-Oriented Reengineering Patterns*. Square Bracket Associates, 2009. ISBN 395233412X.

C. Poole and J. W. Huisman. Using extreme programming in a maintenance environment. *Software, IEEE*, 18(6):42–50, 2001.

Notes

[1] http://www.akit.org/2011/06/clipper-could-be-overcharging-you-for.html
[2] http://campfirenow.com
[3] http://basecamphq.com
[4] http://en.wikibooks.org/wiki/Ruby_Programming/RubyDoc
[5] http://api.rubyonrails.org
[6] http://paulschreiber.com/blog/2010/06/15/rake-task-extracting-database-contents/
[7] http://c2.com/doc/oopsla89/paper.html
[8] https://vimeo.com/24668095
[9] http://codeclimate.org

9.11   Suggested Projects

Project 9.1. *You're tasked with designing a RESTful API for a hypothetical legacy enrollment system (Berkeley's is called TeleBears). An outside-in description of the system (that is, without examining its database schema) is as follows:*

- *A course has a department, course number, and title, for example, "Computer Science, 169, Software Engineering".*

- *An offering of a course specifies additional information:*

  - *the semester (Fall, Spring or Summer) and year that the course is taught,*

  - *the building and room number,*

  - *the day(s) and time(s) of lectures each week,*

– the day(s) and time(s) of small-section meetings each week (not all courses have
these),

– the instructor,

– the limit on how many students may enroll.

Each offering has a unique ID called the control number.

Sketch a UML diagram describing the design of such a system, and a set of RESTful routes
(in the form of either a simplified routes.rb file or a table similar to that in Figure 5.19) to
support at least the following operations:

• Search for course offerings by any combination of department name, instructor name
(partial match OK), semester being offered

• Get meeting times for a course offering (lecture sections, recitation sections, etc., each
with unique timeslot-ID, day and time)

• Enroll a student in a course offering

Project 9.2. *Given your design for Project 9.1, estimate the impact of a change request that
would allow multiple simultaneous "sections" of a course to be taught in the same semester.
The change may affect the schema, class interactions, how searches are handled, and so on.*

Project 9.3. *Select an existing external Web service that has a relatively straightforward
user interface, and use Cucumber to create some integration-level characterization tests for
it. You can use the mechanize gem to allow Cucumber to run against a remote site.*

Project 9.4. *Identify a working legacy software system that you will inspect. For suggestions,
you could use the list of open-source Rails projects at Open Source Rails[1], or you could select
one of two projects created by students who have used this book: ResearchMatch[2], which
helps match students with research opportunities at their university, and VisitDay[3], which
helps organize meetings between students and faculty members.*

*Pick one of these projects, clone or fork the repo, and get the application running in
a development environment. This will probably require creating a development database,
setting up config/development.rb to match, and creating the database schema from db/
schema.rb.*

Project 9.5. *Continuing Project 9.4, try to get the test suites running in development. Once
the tests are running, use SimpleCov to evaluate the test coverage. (Hint: as described in
Chapter 8, you can add SimpleCov in the RSpec configuration file spec/spec_helper.rb.)*

Project 9.6. *Continuing Project 9.4, gather some metrics on code quality and code smells.
You can use the tools described in this chapter such as reek and metric_fu, or you can try
using CodeClimate[4], which offers code review as a service.*

Project 9.7. *Continuing Project 9.4, pick one subsystem (for example, the model, view and controller associated with one type of resource) of the app and conduct a design review. Identify one weakness in the current design, and remove it through refactoring. Make sure you have test coverage in place to ensure that your refactoring doesn't change existing functionality.*

Project 9.8. *Continuing Project 9.4, conduct a detailed code inspection and review of one nontrivial source file. Identify one or more code smells in the file and remove them by refactoring. Make sure you have test coverage in place to ensure that your refactoring doesn't change existing functionality.*

Fred Brooks, Jr.
(1931–) is the author of the classic software engineering book *The Mythical Man-Month*, based on his years leading the IBM OS/360 operating system effort after managing the System/360 project and reporting directly to IBM Chairman T.J. Watson Jr. The System/360 was the first family of computers that had an instruction-set-compatible architecture across a product family, so many have argued that it is the first system to which the term "computer architecture" could be meaningfully applied. Brooks received the 1999 Turing Award for landmark contributions to computer architecture, operating systems, and software engineering.

There are no winners on a losing team, and no losers on a winning team.

—Fred Brooks, quoting North Carolina basketball coach Dean Smith, 1990

Concepts

The big concepts of this chapter are team size and organization and configuration management to keep track of the artifacts that a team builds.

The version of these concepts for the Agile lifecycle is:

- *"Two-pizza"* teams are four to nine people in size.

- Self-organizing teams follow the **Scrum** model, which relies on one teammate to act as the **Product Owner**, who represents the customer, and one to act as the **ScrumMaster**, who acts as a buffer between the team and external distractions. These roles rotate between the team members over time.

- *Pair programming* is a way to increase communication among members of the team and to improve code quality by having two sets of eyeballs examining it when the tests and the code are being developed.

- Good *version control* practices, supported by tools such as *Git*, address code management challenges of a project that includes four to nine software engineers.

For the Plan and Document lifecycle, you will become familiar with the same concepts from a different perspective:

- The *project manager* writes the contract, interfaces with the customer and upper management, recruits and manages the development team, resolves conflicts, and documents the plans for managing configurations and the project itself.

- While group sizes are similar to Agile, large teams can be created by combining groups into a hierarchy under the project manager, with each group having its own leader.

- **Inspections** let outsiders give feedback on the current design and future plans and check to see if good practices are being followed.

- *Configuration management* includes *version control* of software components during development, **system building** of a coherent working program from those components, *release management* to ship new versions of products, and *change management* while maintaining a shipped product.

Programming is now primarily a team sport no matter what the lifecycle, and this chapter covers techniques that can help teams succeed.

10.1   It Takes a Team: Two-Pizza and Scrum

The Six Phases of a Project:

1. *Enthusiasm*

2. *Disillusionment*

3. *Panic*

4. *Search for the Guilty*

5. *Punishment of the Innocent*

6. *Praise for non-participants*

—Dutch Holland(Holland 2004)

As we've said many times in this book, the Agile lifecycle uses iterations of typically one to two weeks that start and end with a working prototype. Each iteration implements some user stories, which act as acceptance tests or integration tests. The stakeholders examine the product after the iteration to see if this is what everyone wants, and then prioritize the remaining user stories.

The days of the hero programmer are now past. Whereas once a brilliant individual could create breakthrough software, the rising bar on functionality and quality means software development now is primarily a team sport. Hence, success today means that not only do you have great design and coding skills, but that you work well with others and can help make your team succeed. As the opening quote from Fred Brooks states, you cannot win if your team loses, and you cannot fail if your team wins.

Jeff Bezos, the CEO of Amazon who received his college degree in computer science, coined the two-pizza characterization of team size.

Hence, the first step of a software development project is to form and organize a team. As to its size, "two-pizza" teams—the group that can be fed by two pizzas in a meeting— typically develop SaaS projects. Our discussions with senior software engineers suggest the typical team size range varies by company, but the inclusive range of the typical ranges is from four to nine people.

While there are many ways to organize a two-pizza software development, a popular one today is ***Scrum*** (Schwaber and Beedle 2001). Its frequent short meetings—15 minutes every day at the same place and time—inspire the name, when each team member answers three questions:

A scrum is held on every minor infraction in rugby. The game stops to bring the players together for a quick "meeting" in order to restart the game.

1. What have you done since yesterday?

2. What are you planning to do today?

3. Are there any impediments or stumbling blocks?

The benefit of these daily scrums is that by understanding what each team member was doing, the team can identify work that would help others make progress that is more rapid.

When combined with the weekly or biweekly iteration model of Agile to collect the feedback from all the stakeholders, the Scrum organization makes it more likely that the rapid progress will be towards what the customers want. Rather than use the Agile term iteration, Scrum uses the term ***sprint***.

A Scrum has three main roles:

1. **Team**—A two-pizza size team that delivers the software.

2. **ScrumMaster**—A team member who acts as buffer between the Team and external distractions, keeps the team focused on the task at hand, enforces team rules, and removes impediments that prevent the team from making progress. One example is enforcing **coding standards**, which are style guidelines that improve the consistency and readability of the code.

3. **Product Owner**—A team member (not the ScrumMaster) who represents the voice of the customer and prioritizes user stories.

Coding standards or **style sheets** are available for Rails[5], Python[6], JavaScript[7], C++[8], and most other programming languages.

Scrum relies on self-organization, and team members often rotate through different roles. For example, we recommend that each member rotate through the Product Owner role, changing on every iteration or sprint.

In any group working together, conflicts can occur around which technical direction the group should go. Depending in part on the personalities of the members of the team, they may not be able to quickly reach agreement. One approach to resolving conflicts is to start with a list on all the items on which the sides agree, as opposed to starting with the list of disagreements. This technique can make the sides see that perhaps they are closer together than they thought. Another approach is for each side to articulate the other's arguments. This technique makes sure both sides understand what the arguments are, even if they don't agree with some of them. This step can reduce confusion about terms or assumptions, which may be the real cause of the conflict.

Summary: SaaS is a good match to two-pizza teams and Scrum, a self-organized small team that meets daily. Two team members take on the additional roles of ScrumMaster, who removes impediments and keeps the team focused, and Product Owner, who speaks for the customer. It can be helpful to follow structured strategies to resolve conflicts when they occur.

■ *Elaboration: Coding standards*

are style guidelines that everyone on the team is expected to follow. The goal is to improve the consistency and readability of the code. For example, here is one for Rails[9], and Google offers them for Python[10], JavaScript[11], and several other languages.

Self-Check 10.1.1. *True or False: Scrum is at its best when it is difficult to plan ahead.*
◇ True: Scrum relies more on real-time feedback than on the traditional management approach of central planning with command and control. ■

Given a team organization, we are now ready to start programming.

10.2 Pair Programming

Q: At Google, you share an office, and you even code together.
Sanjay: We usually sit, and one of us is typing and the other is looking on, and we're chatting all the time about ideas, going back and forth.

—Interview with Jeff Dean and Sanjay Ghemawat, creators of MapReduce (Hoffmann 2013)

Figure 10.1: Sarah Mei and JR Boyens at Pivotal Labs engaged in pair programming. Sarah is driving and JR is observing. Although two keyboards are visible, only Sarah is coding; the computer in front of JR is for documentation and other relevant information such as Pivotal Tracker, as you can see in the right-hand photo. All the pairing stations (visible in the background) are identical and don't have email or other software installed; other computers away from the pairing stations are provided for checking email. Photo by Tonia Fox, courtesy of Pivotal Labs.

The name Extreme Programming (XP), which is the variant of the Agile lifecycle we follow in this book, suggests a break from the way software was developed in the past. One new option in this brave new software world is **pair programming**. The goal is improved software quality by having more than one person developing the same code. As the name suggests, two software developers share one computer. Each takes on a different role:

- The **driver** enters the code and thinks tactically about how to complete the current task, explaining his or her thoughts out loud as appropriate while typing.

- The **observer** or **navigator**—following the automobile analogy more closely—reviews each line of code as it is typed in, and acts as a safety net for the driver. The observer is also thinking strategically about future problems that will need to be addressed, and makes suggestions to the driver.

Dilbert on Pair Programming The comic strip Dilbert comments humorously on pair programming in these two[12] strips[13].

Normally a pair will take alternate driving and observing as they perform tasks. Figure 10.1, shows engineers at Pivotal Labs—makers of Pivotal Tracker—who spend most of the day doing pair programming.(Moore 2011)

Pair programming is cooperative, and should involve a lot of talking. It focuses effort to the task at hand, and two people working together increases the likelihood of following good development practices. If one partner is silent or checking email, then it's not pair programming, just two people sitting near each other.

Pair programming has the side effect of transferring knowledge between the pair, including programming idioms, tool tricks, company processes, customer desires, and so on. Thus, to widen the knowledge base, some teams purposely swap partners per task so that eventually everyone is paired together. For example, **promiscuous pairing** of a team of four leads to six different pairings.

The studies of pair programming versus solo programming support the claim of reduced development time and improvement in software quality. For example, (Cockburn and Williams 2001) found a 20% to 40% decrease in time and that the initial code failed to 15% of the tests instead of 30% by solo programmers. However, it took about 15% more hours collectively for the pair of programmers to complete the tasks versus the solo programmers. The majority of professional programmers, testers, and managers with 10 years of experience at Microsoft reported that pair programming worked well for them and produced higher-quality.(Begel and Nagappan 2008) A study of pair programming studies concludes that pair programming is quicker when programming task complexity is low—perhaps one point tasks on the Tracker scale—and yields code solutions of higher quality when task complexity is high, or three points on our Tracker scale. In both cases, it took more effort than do solo programmers.(Hannay et al. 2009)

The experience at Pivotal Labs suggests that these studies may not factor in the negative impact on productivity of the distractions of our increasingly interconnected modern world: email, Twitter, Facebook, and so on. Pair programming forces both programmers to pay attention to the task at hand for hours at a time. Indeed, new employees at Pivotal Labs go home exhausted since they were not used to concentrating for such long stretches.

Even if pair programming takes more effort, one way to leverage the productivity gains from Agile and Rails is to "spend" it on pair programming. Having two heads develop the code can reduce the time to market for new software or improve quality of end product. We recommend you try pair programming to see if you like it, which some developers love.

Summary: When it's time to start coding, one approach is pair programming, which promises in higher quality and shorter development time but perhaps higher programming costs due to two people doing the work. The pair splits into a driver and an observer, with the former working tactically to complete the task at hand and the latter thinking strategically about future challenges and making suggestions to the driver.

Self-Check 10.2.1. *True or False: Research suggests that pair programming is quicker and less expensive than solo programming.*

◇ False: While there have not been careful experiments that would satisfy human subject experts, and it is not clear whether they account for the lack of distractions when pair programming, the current consensus of researchers is that pair programming is more expensive—more programmer hours per tasks—than solo programming. ∎

Self-Check 10.2.2. *True or False: A pair will eventually figure out who is the best driver and who is the best observer, and then stick primarily to those roles.*

◇ False: An effective pair will alternate between the two roles, as it's more beneficial (and more fun) for the individuals to both drive and observe. ∎

For a team to work together on a common code base with many revisions and interdependent pieces, you need tools to help manage the effort.

10.3 Agile Design and Code Reviews?

Section 10.7 describes the use of design reviews or code reviews to improve quality of the software product. Most companies using Agile methods do not perform design or code reviews.

For example, the conventional wisdom at Pivotal Labs is that pair programming makes such reviews superfluous, as the code is continuously being reviewed during development. At GitHub, formal code reviews are replaced by ***pull requests***, in which a developer requests that her latest code changes be integrated into the main codebase, as we describe in the next section. All developers on the team see each such request and determine how it might

http://pastebin.com/ZNhAt2RR

```
1   Roses are red,
2   Violets are blue.
3   <<<<<<< HEAD:poem.txt
4   I love GitHub,
5   =======
6   ProjectLocker rocks,
7   >>>>>>> 77976da35a11db4580b80ae27e8d65caf5208086:poem.txt
8   and so do you.
```

Figure 10.2: When Bob tries to merge Amy's changes, Git inserts conflict markers in poem.txt to show a merge conflict. Line 3 marks the beginning of the conflicted region with <<<; everything until === (line 5) shows the contents of the file in HEAD (the latest commit in Bob's local repo) and everything thereafter until the end-of-conflict marker >>>(line 7) shows Amy's changes (the file as it appears in Amy's conflicting commit, whose commit-ID is on line 7). Lines 1,2 and 8 were either unaffected or merged automatically by Git.

affect their own code. If anyone has a concern, an online discussion coalesces around the pull request, perhaps facilitated by tools such as Campfire or GitHub Issue tracking (see Section 10.6), which might result in changes to the code in question before the pull request is completed. Since many pull requests occur each day, these "mini-reviews" are occurring continuously, so there is no need for special meetings.

10.4 Version Control for the Two-Pizza Team: Merge Conflicts

There is a really interesting group of people in the United States and around the world who do social coding now. The most interesting stuff is not what they do on Twitter, it's what they do on GitHub.

—Al Gore, former US Vice President, 2013

This section and the next one assume familiarity with basic version control practices in Git. Section A.6 summarizes the basics and Section 10.10 suggests in-depth resources.

Good version control practices are even more critical for a team than for individuals. How is the repository managed? What happens if team members accidentally make conflicting changes to a set of files? Which lines in a given file were changed when, and by whom were they changed? How does one developer work on a new feature without introducing problems into stable code? When software is developed by a team rather than an individual, version control can be used to address these questions using *merging* and *branching*. Both tasks involve combining changes made by many developers into a single code base, a task that sometimes requires manual resolution of conflicting changes.

Many earlier VCSs such as Subversion supported *only* the shared-repository model of development, and the "one true repo" was often called the *master*, a term that means something quite different in Git.

Small teams working on a common set of features commonly use a *shared-repository* model for managing the repo: one particular copy of the repo (the *origin*) is designated as authoritative, and all developers agree to push their changes to the origin and periodically pull from the origin to get others' changes. Famously, Git itself doesn't care which copy is authoritative—any developer can *pull* changes from or *push* changes to any other developer's copy of that repo if the repo's permissions are configured to allow it—but for small teams, it's convenient (and conventional) for the origin repo to reside in the cloud, for example on GitHub or ProjectLocker. Team members *clone* the repo onto their development machines, do their work, make their commits, and push the commits to origin.

We already know that git push and git pull can be used to back up your copy of the repo to the cloud, but in the context of a team, these operations acquire additional important meanings: if Amy commits her changes to her repo, those changes aren't visible to her teammate Bob until she does a push and Bob does a pull. This raises the possibility of a *merge conflict* scenario:

1. Amy and Bob each have a current copy of the origin repo.

2. Amy makes and commits a set of changes to file A.

3. Amy makes and commits a separate set of changes to file B.

4. Amy pushes her commits to origin.

5. Bob makes and commits his own changes to file A, but doesn't touch file B.

6. Bob tries to push his commits, but is prevented from doing so because additional commits have occurred in the origin repo since Bob last pulled. Bob must bring his copy of the repo up-to-date with respect to the origin before he can push his changes.

Note that the presence of additional commits doesn't necessarily mean that conflicting changes were made—in particular, Bob is unaffected by Amy's commit to file B (step 3). In our example, though, steps 2 and 5 *do* represent conflicting changes to the same file. When Bob performs `git pull`, Git will try to **merge** Bob's and Amy's changes to file A. If Amy and Bob had edited different parts of file A, Git would automatically incorporate both sets of changes into file A and commit the merged file in Bob's repo. However, if Amy and Bob edited parts of file A that are within a few lines of each other, as in Figure 10.2, Git will conclude that there is no safe way to automatically create a version of the file that reflects both sets of changes, and it will leave a conflicted *and uncommitted* version of the file in Bob's repo, which Bob must manually edit and commit.

> `git pull` actually combines the separate commands `git fetch`, which copies new commits from the origin, and `git merge`, which tries to reconcile them with the local repo.

In either case, once Bob has committed file A, he can now push his changes, after which the origin repo successfully reflects both Amy's and Bob's changes. The next time Amy pulls, she will get the merge of her changes and Bob's.

This example shows an important rule of thumb: *always commit before merging* (and therefore before pulling, which implicitly performs a merge). Committing ensures that you have a stable snapshot of your own work before attempting to merge changes made by others. Git warns you if you try to merge or pull with uncommitted files, and even provides mechanisms to recover from this scenario if you choose to proceed anyway (see Figure 10.3); but your life will be easier if you *commit early and often,* making it easier to undo or recover from mistakes.

> Git's advanced features like *rebasing* and *commit squashing* can merge many small commits into a few larger ones to keep the publicly-visible change history clean.

Since working in a team means that multiple developers are changing the contents of files, Figure 10.4 lists some useful Git commands to help keep track of who did what and when. Figure 10.5 shows some convenient notational alternatives to the cumbersome 40-digit Git commit-IDs.

- `git reset --hard ORIG_HEAD`
  Revert your repo to last committed state just before the merge.

- `git reset --hard HEAD`
  Revert your repo to last committed state.

- `git checkout` *commit* `--` *[file]*
  Restore a file, or if omitted the whole repo, to its state at *commit* (see Figure 10.5 for ways to refer to a commit besides its 40-digit SHA-1 hash). Can be used to recover files that were previously deleted using `git rm`.

- `git revert` *commit*
  Reverts the changes introduced by *commit*. If that commit was the result of a merge, effectively undoes the merge, and leaves the current branch in the state it was in before the merge. Git tries to back out just the changes introduced by that commit without disturbing other changes since that commit, but if the commit happened a long time ago, manual conflict resolution may be required.

Figure 10.3: When a merge goes awry, these commands can help you recover by undoing all or part of the merge.

`git blame` *[file]*	Annotate each line of a file to show who changed it last and when.
`git diff` *[file]*	Show differences between current working version of *file* and last committed version.
`git diff` *branch [file]*	Show differences between current version of *file* and the way it appears in the most recent commit on *branch* (see Section 10.5).
`git log` *[ref..ref] [files]*	Show log entries affecting all *files* between the two commits specified by the *ref*s (which must be separated by exactly two dots), or if omitted, entire log history affecting those files.
`git log --since="`*date*`"` *files*	Show the log entries affecting all *files* since the given date (examples: `"25-Dec-2011"`, `"2 weeks ago"`).

Figure 10.4: Git commands to help track who changed what file and when. Many commands accept the option `--oneline` to produce a compact representation of their reports. If an optional *[file]* argument is omitted, default is "all tracked files." Note that all these commands have *many* more options, which you can see with `git help` *command*.

`HEAD`	the most recently committed version on the current branch.
`HEAD~`	the prior commit on the current branch (`HEAD~`*n* refers to the *n*'th previous commit).
`ORIG_HEAD`	When a merge is performed, `HEAD` is updated to the newly-merged version, and `ORIG_HEAD` refers to the commit state before the merge. Useful if you want to use `git diff` to see how each file changed as a result of the merge.
`1dfb2c~2`	2 commits prior to the commit whose ID has `1dfb2c` as a unique prefix.
`"`*branch*`@{`*date*`}"`	The last commit prior to *date* (see Figure 10.4 for date format) on *branch*, where `HEAD` refers to the current branch.

Figure 10.5: Convenient ways to refer to certain commits in Git commands, rather than using a full 40-digit commit-ID or a unique prefix of one. `git rev-parse` *expr* resolves any of the above expressions into a full commit-ID.

Summary of merge management for small teams:

1. Small teams typically use a "shared-repo" model, in which pushes and pulls use a single authoritative copy of the repo. In Git, the authoritative copy is referred to as the `origin` repo and is often stored in the cloud on GitHub or on an internal company server.

2. Before you start changing files, *commit* your own changes locally and then *merge* the changes made by others while you were away. In Git, the easiest way to merge changes from the origin repo is `git pull`.

3. If changes cannot be automatically merged, you must manually edit the conflicted file by looking for the *conflict markers* in the merged file, and then commit and push the fixed version. With Git, a conflict is considered resolved when the conflicted file is re-committed.

■ *Elaboration: Remote collaboration: fork-and-pull for public repos*

Git was designed to support very-large-scale projects with many developers, such as the Linux kernel. The ***fork-and-pull*** management model allows subgroups to work on independent and possibly divergent sets of changes without interfering with each others' efforts. A remote subgroup can fork your repo[14], which creates their own copy of it on GitHub to receive their pushes. When they are ready to contribute stable code back to your repo, the subgroup creates a pull request[15] asking you to merge selected commits from their forked repo back into your origin repo. Pull requests therefore allow selective merging of two repos that otherwise remain separate.

Self-Check 10.4.1. *True or false: If you attempt* `git push` *and it fails with a message such as "Non-fast-forward (error): failed to push some refs," this means some file contains a merge conflict between your repo's version and the origin repo's version.*
◇ False. It just means that your copy of the repo is missing some commits that are present in the origin copy, and until you merge in those missing commits, you won't be allowed to push your own commits. Merging in these missing commits *may* lead to a merge conflict, but frequently does not. ■

10.5 Using Branches Effectively

Besides taking snapshots of your work and backing it up, version control also lets you manage multiple versions of a project's code base simultaneously, for example, to allow part of the team to work on an experimental new feature without disrupting working code, or to fix a bug in a previously-released version of the code that some customers are still using.

Branches are designed for such situations. Rather than thinking of commits as just a sequence of snapshots, we should instead think of a *graph* of commits: a branch is started by creating a logical copy of the code tree as it exists at some particular commit. Unlike a real tree branch, a repo branch not only diverges from the "trunk" but can also be merged back into it.

From that point on, the new branch and the one from which it was split are separate: commits to one branch don't affect the other, though depending on project needs, commits

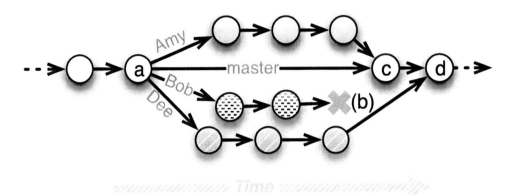

Figure 10.6: **Each circle represents a commit. Amy, Bob and Dee each start branches based on the same commit (a) to work on different RottenPotatoes features. After several commits, Bob decides his feature won't work out, so he deletes his branch (b); meanwhile Amy completes her tests and code and merges her feature branch back into the master branch, creating the merge-commit (c). Finally, Dee completes her feature, but since the master branch has changed due to Amy's merge-commit (c), Dee has to do some manual conflict resolution to complete her merge-commit (d).**

in either may be merged back into the other. Indeed, branches can even be split off from other branches, but overly complex branching structures offer few benefits and are difficult to maintain.

We highlight two common branch management strategies that can be used together or separately, both of which strive to ensure that the master branch always contains a stable working version of the code. Figure 10.6 shows a ***feature branch***, which allows a developer or sub-team to make the changes necessary to implement a particular feature without affecting the master branch until the changes are complete and tested. If the feature is merged into the master and a decision is made later to remove it (perhaps it failed to deliver the expected customer value), the specific commits related to the merge of the feature branch can sometimes be undone, as long as there haven't been many changes to the master that depend on the new feature.

Flickr developers now use[16] a repository with no feature branches at all—commits always go to the master branch!

Figure 10.7 shows how ***release branches*** are used to fix problems found in a specific release. They are widely used for delivering non-SaaS products such as libraries or gems whose releases are far enough apart that the master branch may diverge substantially from the most recent release branch. For example, the Linux kernel, for which developers check in thousands of lines of code per day, uses release branches to designate stable and long-lived releases of the kernel. Release branches often receive multiple merges from the development or master branch and contribute multiple merges to it. Release branches are less common in delivering SaaS because of the trend toward continuous integration/continuous deployment (Section 1.8): if you deploy several times per week, the deployed version won't have time to get out of sync with the master branch, so you might as well deploy directly from the master branch. We discuss continuous deployment further in Chapter 12.

GitFlow[17], a branch management strategy that captures many best practices, may be useful for larger projects with long-lived branches.

Figure 10.8 shows some commands for manipulating Git branches. Newly-created Git repos start out with a single branch called `master`. At any given time, the ***current branch*** is whichever one you're working on in your copy of the repo. Since in general each copy of the repo contains all the branches, you can quickly switch back and forth between branches in the same repo (but see Screencast 10.5.1 for an important caveat about doing so).

When multiple branches are present, how do you specify which one should receive pushes

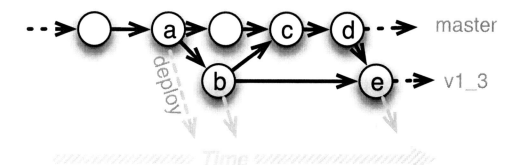

Figure 10.7: (a) A new release branch is created to "snapshot" version 1.3 of RottenPotatoes. A bug is found in the release and the fix is committed in the release branch (b); the app is redeployed from the release branch. The commit(s) containing the fix are merged into the master branch (c), but the code in the master has evolved sufficiently from the code in the release that manual adjustments to the bug fix need to be made. Meanwhile, the dev team working on master finds a critical security flaw and fixes it with one commit (d). The specific commit containing the security fix can be merged into the release branch (e) using `git cherry-pick`, since we don't want to apply any other master branch changes to the release branch except for this fix.

or pulls? As Figure 10.8 shows, the `git push` and `git pull` commands we've been using so far are actually abbreviated special cases—these commands handle pushes and pulls using branches as well.

Screencast 10.5.1: Using Branches with Git.
`http://vimeo.com/41257323`
This screencast shows how to create and manage a new branch in Git (for example, to develop a new feature), how to merge the branch's changes back into the trunk from which it was split, and how to undo the merge of the branch if something goes wrong (for example, if it turns out the feature had bugs and needs to be backed out). It also emphasizes an important caveat and shows why you should always commit your changes in the current branch before switching to a different branch.

Summary of branching:

- Branches allow variation in a code base. For example, feature branches support the development of new features without destabilizing working code, and release branches allow fixing bugs in previous releases whose code has diverged from the main line of development.

- Merging changes from one branch into another (for example, from a feature branch back into the `master` branch) may result in conflict merges for certain files, so always commit before you merge and before switching to a different branch to work on.

- With Agile + SaaS, feature branches are usually short-lived and release branches uncommon.

- `git branch`
  List existing branches in repo, indicating current branch witn *. If you're using `sh` or a `bash`-derived shell on a Unix-like system, placing the following in `~/.profile` will make the shell prompt display the current Git branch when you're in a Git repo directory:

  http://pastebin.com/KP0suYyx

  ```
  1 | export PS1="[`git branch --no-color 2>/dev/null | \
  2 |   sed -e '/^[^*]/d' -e 's/* \(.*\)/\1/'`]% "
  ```

- `git checkout` *name*
  Switch to existing branch *name*.

- `git branch` *name*
  If branch *name* exists, switch to it; otherwise create a new branch called *name* without switching to it. The shortcut `git checkout -b` *name [commit-id]* creates and switches to a new branch based on *commit-id*, which defaults to most recent commit in the current branch.

- `git push` *[repo] [branch]*
  Push the changes (commits) on *branch* to remote repository *repo*. (The first time you do this for a given branch, it creates that branch on the remote *repo*.) With no arguments, pushes the current local branch to the current branch's remote, or the remote called `origin` by default.

- `git pull` *[repo] [branch]*
  Fetches and merges commits from branch *branch* on the remote *repo* into your local repo's **current** branch *(even if the current branch's name doesn't match the branch name you're pulling from—beware!)*. To fetch a remote branch `foo` for which you have no corresponding local branch, first use `git checkout -b foo` to create a local branch by that name and switch to it, then `git pull origin foo`. With no arguments, *repo* and *branch* default to the values of `git config branch.`*currentbranch*`.remote` and `git config branch.`*currentbranch*`.merge` respectively, which are automatically set up by certain Git commands and can be changed with `git branch --track`. If you setup a new repo in the usual way, *repo* defaults to `origin` and *branch* defaults to `master`.

- `git remote show` *[repo]*
  If *repo* omitted, show a list of existing remote repos. If *repo* is the name of an existing remote repo, shows branches located at *repo* and which of your local branches are set up to track them. Also shows which local branches are not up-to-date with respect to *repo*.

- `git merge` *branch*
  Merge all changes from *branch* into the current branch.

- `git cherry-pick` *commits*
  Rather than merging all changes (commits) from a given branch, apply *only* the changes introduced by each of the named *commits* to the current branch.

- `git checkout` *branch file1 file2...*
  For each file, merge the differences in *branch*'s version of that file into the current branch's version of that file.

Figure 10.8: Common Git commands for handling branches and merging. Branch management involves merging; Figure 10.3 tells how to undo merges gone awry.

■ *Elaboration: Long-lived Branches and Rebasing*

While you're working on a feature branch, its commits will diverge from the trunk; if you work on it for too long, the "big merge" when you're done may be very painful with many conflicts. The pain can be mitigated by frequent *rebasing*, an operation in which you incrementally merge some recent changes from another branch, then tell Git to rearrange things to look as if your branch had originated from a later commit. While rebasing is useful for long-lived branches such as release branches or long-lived experimental branches, if you're breaking down your user stories into manageable sizes (Section 7.2) and doing frequent deployments (Section 12.3), rebasing should rarely be necessary in agile SaaS development.

Self-Check 10.5.1. *Describe a scenario in which merges could go in both directions—changes in a feature branch merged back into the master branch, and changes in the master branch merged into a feature branch. (In Git, this is called a* **crisscross merge**.*)*

◇ Diana starts a new branch to work on a feature. Before she completes the feature, an important bug is fixed and the fix is merged into the master branch. Because the bug is in a part of the code that interacts with Diana's feature, she merges the fix from master into her own feature branch. Finally, when she finishes the feature, her feature branch is merged back into master. ■

10.6 Reporting and Fixing Bugs: The Five R's

Inevitably, bugs happen. If you're lucky, they are found before the software is in production, but production bugs happen too. Everyone on the team must agree on processes for managing the phases of the bug's lifecycle:

1. **R**eporting a bug

2. **R**eproducing the problem, or else **R**eclassifying it as "not a bug" or "won't be fixed"

3. creating a **R**egression test that demonstrates the bug

4. **R**epairing the bug

5. **R**eleasing the repaired code

Any stakeholder may find and **r**eport a bug in server-side or client-side SaaS code. A member of the development or QA team must then **r**eproduce the bug, documenting the environment and steps necessary to trigger it. This process may result in **r**eclassifying the bug as "not a bug" for various reasons:

- This is not a bug but a request to make an enhancement or change a behavior that is working as designed

- This bug is in a part of the code that is being undeployed or is otherwise no longer supported

- This bug occurs only with an unsupported user environment, such as a very old browser lacking necessary features for this SaaS app

- This bug is already fixed in the latest version (uncommon in SaaS, whose users are always using the latest version)

Once the bug is confirmed as genuine and reproducible, it's entered into a bug management system. A plethora of such systems exists, but the needs of many small to medium teams can be met by a tool you're already using: Pivotal Tracker allows marking a story as a Bug rather than a Feature, which assigns the story zero points but otherwise allows it to be tracked to completion just like a regular user story. An advantage of this tool is that Tracker manages the bug's lifecycle for you, so existing processes for delivering user stories can be readily adapted to fixing bugs. For example, fixing the bug must be prioritized relative to other work; in a waterfall process, this may mean prioritization relative to other outstanding bugs while in the maintenance phase, but in an agile process it usually means prioritization relative to developing new features from user stories. Using Tracker, the Product Manager can move the bug story above or below other stories based on the bug's severity and impact on the customer. For example, bugs that may cause data loss in production will get prioritized very high.

"Severity 1" bugs at Amazon.com require the responsible engineers to initiate a conference call within 15 minutes of learning of the bug—a stricter responsiveness requirement than for on-call physicians! (Bodík et al. 2006)

The next step is repair, which always begins with *first* creating the *simplest possible* automated test that fails in the presence of the bug, and *then* changing the code to make the test(s) pass green. This should sound familiar to you by now as a TDD practitioner, but this practice is true even in non-TDD environments: *no bug can be closed out without a test.* Depending on the bug, unit tests, functional tests, integration tests, or a combination of these may be required. *Simplest* means that the tests depend on as few preconditions as possible, tightly circumscribing the bug. For example, simplifying an RSpec unit test would mean minimizing the setup preceding the test action or in the **before** block, and simplifying a Cucumber scenario would mean minimizing the number of **Given** or **Background** steps. These tests usually get added to the regular regression suite to ensure the bug doesn't recur undetected. A complex bug may require multiple commits to fix; a common policy in BDD+TDD projects is that commits with failing or missing tests shouldn't be merged to the main development branch until the tests pass green.

Many bug tracking systems can automatically cross-reference bug reports with the commit-IDs that contain the associated fixes and regression tests. For example, using GitHub's service hooks[18], a commit can be annotated with the story ID of the corresponding bug or feature in Tracker, and when that commit is pushed to GitHub, the story is automatically marked as Delivered. Depending on team protocol and the bug management system in use, the bug may be "closed out" either immediately by noting which release will contain the fix or after the release actually occurs.

As we will see in Chapter 12, in most agile teams releases are very frequent, shortening the bug lifecycle.

Summary: the 5 R's of bug fixing

- A bug must be reported, reproduced, demonstrated in a regression test, and repaired, all before the bug fix can be released.

- No bug can be closed out without an automated test demonstrating that we really understand the bug's cause.

- Bugs that are really enhancement requests or occur only in obsolete versions of the code or in unsupported environments may be reclassified to indicate they're not going to be fixed.

Self-Check 10.6.1. *Why do you think "bug fix" stories are worth zero points in Tracker even though they follow the same lifecycle as regular user stories?*

◇ A team's velocity would be artificially inflated by fixing bugs, since they'd get points for implementing the feature in the first place and then more points for actually getting the implementation right. ∎

Self-Check 10.6.2. *True or false: a bug that is triggered by interacting with another service (for example, authentication via Twitter) cannot be captured in a regression test because the necessary conditions would require us to control Twitter's behavior.*

◇ False: integration-level mocking and stubbing, for example using the FakeWeb gem[19] or the techniques described in Section 8.6, can almost always be used to mimic the external conditions necessary to reproduce the bug in an automated test. ∎

Self-Check 10.6.3. *True or false: a bug in which the browser renders the wrong content or layout due to JavaScript problems might be reproducible manually by a human being, but it cannot be captured in an automated regression test.*

◇ False: tools such as Jasmine and Webdriver (Section 6.7) can be used to develop such tests. ∎

10.7 The Plan-And-Document Perspective

In Plan-And-Document processes, project management starts with the project manager. Project managers are the bosses of the projects:

- They write the contract to win the project from the customer.

- They recruit the development team from existing employees and new hires.

- They typically write team members' performance reviews, which shape salary increases.

- From a Scrum perspective (Section 10.1), they act as Product Owner—the primary customer contact—*and* they act as ScrumMaster, as they are the interface to upper management and they procure resources for the team.

- As we saw in Section 7.10, project managers also estimate costs, make and maintain the schedule, and decide which risks to address and how to overcome or avoid them.

- As you would expect for Plan-And-Document processes, project managers must document their project management plan. Figure 10.9 gives an outline of Project Management Plans from the corresponding IEEE standard.

As a result of all the these responsibilities, project managers receive much of the blame if projects have problems. Quoting a textbook author from his introduction to project management:

> *However, if a post mortem were to be conducted for every [problematic] project, it is very likely that a consistent theme would be encountered: project management was weak.*

> — Pressman 2010

We cover four major tasks for project managers to increase their chances of being successful:

1. Project overview	5.2 Project work plans
1.1 Project summary	5.2.1 Work activities
1.1.1 Purpose, scope and objectives	5.2.2 Schedule allocation
1.1.2 Assumptions and constraints	5.2.3 Resource allocation
1.1.3 Project deliverables	5.2.4 Budget allocation
1.1.4 Schedule and budget summary	5.2.5 Procurement plan
1.2 Evolution of the plan	6. Project assessment and control
2. References	6.1 Requirements management plan
3. Definitions	6.2 Scope change control plan
4. Project context	6.3 Schedule control plan
4.1 Process model	6.4 Budget control plan
4.2 Process improvement plan	6.5 Quality assurance plan
4.3 Infrastructure plan	6.6 Subcontractor management plan
4.4 Methods, tools and techniques	6.7 Project closeout plan
4.5 Product acceptance plan	7. Product delivery
4.6 Project organization	8. Supporting process plans
4.6.1 External interfaces	8.1 Project supervision and work environment
4.6.2 Internal interfaces	8.2 Decision management
4.6.3 Authorities and responsibilities	8.3 Risk management
5. Project planning	8.4 Configuration management
5.1 Project initiation	8.5 Information management
5.1.1 Estimation plan	8.5.1 Documentation
5.1.2 Staffing plan	8.5.2 Communication and publicity
5.1.3 Resource acquisition plan	8.6 Quality assurance
5.1.4 Project staff training plan	8.7 Measurement
	8.8 Reviews and audits
	8.9 Verification and validation

Figure 10.9: Format of a project management plan from the IEEE 16326-2009 ISO/IEC/IEEE Systems and Software Engineering–Life Cycle Processes–Project Management standard.

1. Team size, roles, space, communication

2. Managing people and conflicts

3. Inspections and metrics

4. Configuration management

1. Team size, roles, space, and communication. The Plan-and-Document processes can scale to larger sizes, where group leaders report to the project manager. However, each subgroup typically stays the size of the two-pizza teams we saw in Section 10.1. Size recommendations are three to seven people (Braude and Berstein 2011) to no more than ten (Sommerville 2010). Fred Brooks gave us the reason in Chapter 7: the more people you add to a team increases the number of people who can work in parallel, but it also increases the amount of time each person must spend communicating. These team sizes are reasonable considering the fraction of time spent communicating.

Given we know the size of the team, members of a subgroup in Plan-and-Document processes can be given different roles in which they are expected to lead. For example (Pressman 2010):

• Configuration management leader

• Quality assurance leader

• Requirements management leader

• Design leader

• Implementation leader

One surprising result is that the type of space for the team to work in affects project management. One study found that collocating the team in open space could double productivity.(Teasley et al. 2000) The reasons include that team members had easy access to each other for both coordination of their work and for learning, and they could post their work artifacts on the walls so that all could see. Another study of teams in open space concludes:

One of the main drivers of success was the fact that the team members were at hand, ready to have a spontaneous meeting, advise on a problem, teach/learn something new, etc. We know from earlier work that the gains from being at hand drops off significantly when people are first out of sight, and then most severely when they are more than 30 meters apart.

— Allen and Henn 2006

While the team relies on email and texting for communicating and shares information in wikis and the like, there is also typically a weekly meeting to help coordinate the project. Recall that the goal is to minimize the time spent communicating unnecessarily, so it is important that the meetings be effective. Below is our digest of advice from the many guidelines found on the Web on how to have efficient meetings. We use the acronym SAMOSAS as a memory device; surely bringing a plate of them will make for an effective meeting!

Samosas are a popular stuffed deep-fried snack from India.

• **S**tart and stop meeting on time.

• **A**genda created in advance of meeting; if there is no agenda, then cancel the meeting.

- Minutes must be recorded so everyone can recall results afterwards; the first agenda item is finding a note taker.

- One speaker at a time; no interruptions when another is speaking.

- Send material in advance, since people read much faster than speakers talk.

- Action items at end of meeting, so people know what they should do as a result of the meeting.

- Set the date and time of the next meeting.

2. Managing people and conflicts. Thousands of books have been written on how to management people, but the two most useful ones that we have found are *The One Minute Manager* and *How to Win Friends and Influence People*.(Blanchard and Johnson 1982; Carnegie 1998) What we like about the first book is that it offers short quick advice. Be clear about the goals of what you want done and how well it should be done, but leave it up to the team member how to do it to encourage creativity. When meeting with individuals to review progress, start with the good things to help build their confidence and to give them time to learn the tasks at hand. At the same time, you need to be honest with them about what is not going well, and what they need to do to fix it. What we like about the second book is that it helps teach the art of persuasion, to get people to do what you think should be done without ordering them to do it. These skills also help persuade people you *cannot* command: your customers and your management.

Both books are helpful when it comes to resolving conflicts within a team. Conflicts are not necessarily bad, in that it can be better to have the conflict than to let the project crash and burn. Intel Corporation labels this attitude *constructive confrontation*. If you have a strong opinion that a person is proposing the wrong thing technically, you are obligated to bring it up, even to your bosses. The Intel culture is speak up even if you disagree with the highest ranked people in the room.

If conflict continues, given that Plan-and-Document processes have a project manager, that person can make the final decision. One reason the US made it to the moon in the 1960s is that a leader of NASA, Wernher von Braun, had a knack for quickly resolving conflicts on close decisions. His view was that picking an option arbitrarily but quickly was frequently better, since the choice was roughly 50-50, so that the project could move ahead rather than take the time to carefully collect all the evidence to see which choice was slightly better.

However, once a decision is made, the teams needs to embrace it and move ahead. The Intel motto for this resolution is *disagree and commit*: "I disagree, but I am going to help even if I don't agree."

3. Inspections and metrics. Inspections like ***design reviews*** and ***code reviews*** allow feedback on the system even before everything is working. The idea is that once you have a design and initial implementation plan, you are ready for feedback from developers beyond your team. Design and code reviews follow the Waterfall lifecycle in that each phase is completed in sequence before going on to the next phase, or at least for the phases of a single iteration in Spiral or RUP development.

A design review is a meeting where the authors of program present its design with the goal of improving software quality by benefiting from the experience of the people attending the meeting. A code review is held once the design has been implemented. This peer-oriented feedback also helps with knowledge exchange within the organization and offers coaching that can help the careers of the presenters.

Shalloway suggests that formal design code reviews are often too late in the process to make a big impact on the result.(Shalloway 2002) He recommends to instead have earlier, smaller meetings that he calls "approach reviews." The idea is to have a few senior developers assist the team in coming up with an approach to solve the problem. The group brainstorms about different approaches to help find a good one.

If you plan to do a formal design review, Shalloway suggests that you first hold a "mini-design review" after the approach has been selected and the design is nearing completion. It involves the same people as before, but the purpose is to prepare for the formal review.

The formal review itself should start with a high-level description of what the customers want. Then give the architecture of the software, showing the APIs of the components. It will be important to highlight the design patterns used at different levels of abstraction (see Chapter 11). You should expect to explain *why* you made the decisions, and whether you considered plausible alternatives. Depending on the amount of time and the interests of those at the meeting, the final phase would be to go through the code of the implemented methods. At all these phases, you can get more value from the review if you have a concrete list of questions or issues that you would like to hear about.

One advantage of code reviews is that they encourage people outside your team to look at your comments as well as your code. As we don't have a tool that can enforce the advice from Chapter 9 about making sure the comments raise the level of abstraction, the only enforcing mechanism is the code review.

In addition to reviewing the code and the comments, inspections can give feedback on every part of the project in Plan-and-Document processes: the project plan, schedule, requirements, testing plan, and so on. This feedback helps with **verification and validation** of the whole project, to ensure that it is on a good course. There is even an IEEE standard on how to document the verification and validation plan for the project, which Figure 10.10 shows.

Like the algorithmic models for cost estimation (see Section 7.10), some researchers have advocated that software metrics could replace inspections or reviews to assess project quality and progress. The idea is to collect metrics across many projects in organization over time, establish a baseline for new projects, and then see how the project is doing compared to baseline. This quote captures the argument for metrics:

> *Without metrics, it is difficult to know how a project is executing and the quality level of the software.*
>
> — Braude and Berstein 2011

Below are sample metrics that can be automatically collected:

- Code size, measured in thousands of lines of code (**KLOC**) or in function points (Section 7.10).

- Effort, measured in person months spent on project.

- Project milestones planned versus fulfilled.

- Number of test cases completed.

- Defect discovery rate, measured in defects discovered via testing per month.

1. Purpose	5.4 Hardware V&V Processes, Activities and Tasks
2. Referenced documents	5.4.1 Hardware Concept
3. Definitions	5.4.2 Hardware Requirements
4. V&V overview	5.4.3 Hardware Design
4.1 Organization	5.4.4 Hardware Fabrication
4.2 Master schedule	5.4.5 Hardware Integration Test
4.3 Integrity level scheme	5.4.6 Hardware Qualification Test
4.4 Resources summary	5.4.7 Hardware Acceptance Test
4.5 Responsibilities	5.4.8 Hardware Transition
4.6 Tools, techniques, and methods	5.4.9 Hardware Operation
5. V&V processes	5.4.10 Hardware Maintenance
5.1 Common V&V Processes, Activities and Tasks	5.4.11 Hardware Disposal
5.2 System V&V Processes, Activities and Tasks	6. V&V reporting requirements
5.2.1 Acquisition Support	6.1 Task reports
5.2.2 Supply Planning	6.2 Anomaly reports
5.2.3 Project Planning	6.3 V&V final report
5.2.4 Configuration Management	6.4 Special studies reports (optional)
5.2.5 Stakeholder Requirements Definition	6.5 Other reports (optional)
5.2.6 Requirements Analysis	7. V&V administrative requirements
5.2.7 Architectural Design	7.1 Anomaly resolution and reporting
5.2.8 Implementation	7.2 Task iteration policy
5.2.9 Integration	7.3 Deviation policy
5.2.10 Transition	7.4 Control procedures
5.2.11 Operation	7.5 Standards, practices, and conventions
5.2.12 Maintenance	8. V&V test documentation requirements
5.2.13 Disposal	
5.3 Software V&V Processes, Activities and Tasks	
5.3.1 Software Concept	
5.3.2 Software Requirements	
5.3.3 Software Design	
5.3.4 Software Construction	
5.3.5 Software Integration Test	
5.3.6 Software Qualification Test	
5.3.7 Software Acceptance Test	
5.3.8 Software Installation and Checkout (Transition)	
5.3.9 Software Operation	
5.3.10 Software Maintenance	
5.3.11 Software Disposal	

Figure 10.10: Outline of a plan for System and Software Verification and Validation from the IEEE 1012-2012 Standard.

- Defect repair rate, measured in defects fixed per month.

Other metrics can be derived from these so as to normalize the numbers to help compare results from different projects: KLOC per person month, defects per KLOC, and so on.

The problem with this approach is that there is little evidence of correlation between these metrics that we can automatically collect and project outcomes. Ideally, the metrics would correlate and we could have much finer grain understanding than comes from the occasional and time consuming inspections. This quote captures the argument de-emphasizing metrics:

> *However, we are still quite a long way from this ideal situation, and there are no signs that automated quality assessment will become a reality in the foreseeable future*

> — Sommerville 2010

4. Configuration management. Configuration management includes four varieties of changes, three of which we have seen before. The first is ***version management***, which we saw above in Sections 10.4 and 10.5. This variety keeps track of versions of components as they are changed. The second, ***system building***, is closely related to the first. Tools like make assemble the compatible versions of components into an executable program for the target system. The third variety is ***release management,*** which we cover in Chapter 12. The last is ***change management***, which comes from change requests made by customers and other stakeholders to fix bugs or to improve functionality (see Section 9.7).

As you surely expect by now, IEEE has a standard for Configuration Management. Figure 10.11 shows its table of contents.

Table of Contents
1. Overview
1.1 Scope
1.2 Purpose
2. Definitions, acronyms, and abbreviations
2.1 Definitions
2.2 Acronyms and abbreviations
3. Tailoring
4. Audience
5. The configuration management process
6. CM planning lower-level process
6.1 Purpose
6.2 Activities and tasks
7. CM management lower-level process
7.1 Purpose
7.2 Activities and tasks
8. Configuration identification lower-level process
8.1 Purpose
8.2 Activities and tasks
9. Configuration change control lower-level process
9.1 Purpose
9.2 Activities and Tasks
10. Configuration status accounting lower-level process
10.1 Purpose
10.2 Activities and tasks
11. CM configuration auditing lower-level process
11.1 Purpose
11.2 Activities and Tasks
12. Interface control lower-level process
12.1 Purpose
12.2 Activities and Tasks
13. Supplier configuration item control lower-level process
13.1 Purpose
13.2 Activities and Tasks
14. Release management lower-level process
14.1 Purpose
14.2 Activities and tasks

Figure 10.11: A table of contents for the IEEE 828-2012 Standard for Configuration Management in Systems and Software Engineering.

> **Summary:** In Plan-and-Document processes:
>
> - Project managers are in charge: they write the contract, recruit the team, and inter-face with the customer and upper management.
>
> - The project manager documents the project plan and configuration plan, along with the verification and validation plan that ensures that other plans are followed!
>
> - To limit time spent communicating, groups are three to ten people. They can be composed into hierarchies to form larger teams reporting to the project manager, with each group having its own leader.
>
> - Guidelines for managing people include giving them clear goals but empowering them, and starting with the positive in reviews but being honest about shortcomings and how to overcome them.
>
> - While conflicts need to be resolved, they can be helpful in finding the best path forward for a project.
>
> - Inspections like design reviews and code reviews let outsiders give feedback on the current design and future plans, which lets the team benefit from the experience of others. They are also a good way to check if good practices are being followed and if the plans and documents are sensible.
>
> - Configuration management is a broad category that includes change management while maintaining a product, version control of software components, system build-ing of a coherent working program from those components, and release management to ship the product to customers.

Self-Check 10.7.1. *Compare the size of teams in Plan-and-Document processes versus Agile processes.*

◇ Plan-and-Document processes can form hierarchies of subgroups to create a much larger project, but each subgroup is basically the same size as a "two-pizza" team for Agile. ■

Self-Check 10.7.2. *True or False: Design reviews are meetings intended to improve the quality of the software product using the wisdom of the attendees, but they also result in technical information exchange and can be highly educational for junior members of the organization, whether presenters or just attendees.*

◇ True. ■

10.8 Fallacies and Pitfalls

 Pitfall: **Always watching the master while pair programming.**

If one member of the pair has much more experience, the temptation is to let the more senior member do all the driving, with the more junior member becoming essentially the permanent observer. This relationship is not healthy, and will likely lead to disengagement by the junior member.

Pitfall: **Dividing work based on the software stack rather than on features.**

It's less common than it used to be to divide the team into a front-end specialist, back-end specialist, customer liaison, and so forth, but it still happens. Your authors and others believe that better results come from having each team member deliver *all* aspects of a chosen feature or story—Cucumber scenarios, RSpec tests, views, controller actions, model logic, and so on. Especially when combined with pair programming, having each developer maintain a "full stack" view of the product spreads architectural knowledge around the team.

 Pitfall: **Accidentally stomping on changes after merging or switching branches.**

If you do a pull or merge, or if you switch to a different branch, some files may suddenly have different contents on disk. If any such files are already loaded into your editor, the versions being edited will be *out of date*, and even worse, if you now save those files, you will either overwrite merged changes or save a file that isn't in the branch you think it is. The solution is simple: *before* you pull, merge or switch branches, make sure you commit all current changes; *after* you pull, merge or switch branches, reload any files in your editor that may be affected—or to be really safe, just quit your editor before you commit. Be careful too about the potentially destructive behavior of certain Git commands such as `git reset`, as described in "Gitster" Scott Chacon's informative and detailed blog post[20].

 Pitfall: **Letting your copy of the repo get too far out of sync with the origin (authoritative) copy.**

It's best not to let your copy of the repo diverge too far from the origin, or merges (Section 10.5) will be painful. You should always `git pull` before starting to work, and `git push` as soon as your locally-committed changes are stable enough to inflict on your teammates. If you're working on a long-lived feature branch that is at risk of getting out of sync with the master, see the documentation for `git rebase` to periodically "re-sync" your branch without merging it back into master until it's ready.

 Fallacy: **It's fine to make simple changes on the master branch.**

Programmers are optimists. When we set out to change our code, we always think it will be a one-line change. Then it turns into a five-line change; then we realize the change affects another file, which has to be changed as well; then it turns out we need to add or change existing tests that relied on the old code; and so on. For this reason, *always* create a feature branch when starting new work. Branching with Git is nearly instantaneous, and if the change truly does turn out to be small, you can delete the branch after merging to avoid having it clutter your branch namespace.

 Fallacy: **Since each subteam is working on its own branch, we don't need to communicate regularly or merge frequently.**

Branches are a great way for different team members to work on different features simultaneously, but without frequent merges and clear communication of who's working on what, you risk an increased likelihood of merge conflicts and accidental loss of work when one developer "resolves" a merge conflict by deleting another developer's changes.

10.9 Concluding Remarks: Teams, Collaboration, and Four Decades of Version Control

The first 90% of the code accounts for the first 10% of the development time. The remaining 10% of the code accounts for the other 90% of the development time.

—Tom Cargill, quoted in *Programming Pearls*, 1985

The history of version control systems mirrors the movement towards distributed collaboration among "teams of teams," with two-pizza teams emerging as a popular unit of cohesiveness. From about 1970–1985, the original Unix **Source Code Control System** (SCCS) and its longer-lived descendant **Revision Control System** (RCS) allowed only one developer at a time to "lock" a particular file for editing—others could only read but not edit the file until the first developer checked the file back in, releasing the lock. SCCS and RCS also required all developers to use the same (then timeshared) computer, whose file system held the repo. In a project with many files, this locking mechanism quickly became a bottleneck, so in 1986 the **Concurrent Versions System** (CVS) finally allowed simultaneous editing of the same file with automatic merging, and allowed the master repo to be on a different computer than the developer's copy, facilitating distributed development. **Subversion**, introduced in 2001, had much better support for branches, allowing developers to independently work on different versions of a project, but still assumed all developers working on a particular code tree would push their changes to a single "master" copy of the repo. Git completed the decentralization by allowing any copy of a repo to push or pull from any other, enabling completely decentralized "teams of teams," and by making branching and merging much quicker and easier than its predecessors. Today, distributed collaboration is the norm: rather than a large distributed team, fork-and-pull allows a large number of agile two-pizza teams to make independent progress, and the use of Git to support such efforts has become ubiquitous. This new two-pizza team size makes it easier for a team to stay organized than the giant programming teams possible in Plan-and-Document.

Despite these improvements, software projects are still infamous for being late and over budget. The techniques in this chapter can help an agile team avoid those pitfalls. Checking in with all stakeholders on each iteration guides your team into spending its resources most effectively and is more likely to result in software that makes customers happy within the time and cost budget. The Scrum team organization fits well with Agile lifecycle and the challenges of developing SaaS. Disciplined use of version control allows developers to make progress on many fronts simultaneously without interfering with each others' work, and also allows disciplined and systematic management of the bug lifecycle.

The Plan-and-Document processes rely on the project manager to make the time and cost estimates, assess risks, and to run the project so that it delivers the product on time and on budget with the required functionality. This more autocratic approach is in contrast with the egalitarian approach of Scrum, where the ScrumMaster and Product Owner roles rotate between the members of the Agile team. Everything is documented in Plan-and-Document lifecycles, including the project management plan, the configuration management plan, and the plan on how to verify and validate that the project is following the plans. Inspections from developers outside the team give feedback on the plans and the code, and help assess the project's progress.

Once a project is completed in any lifecycle, it is important to take the time to think about on what you learned on this project before leaping head first into your next one. Reflect on what went well, what didn't go well, and what you would do differently. It is not a sin to make a mistake, as long as you learn from it; the sin is making the same mistake repeatedly.

10.10 To Learn More

- You can find very detailed descriptions of Git's powerful features in *Version Control With Git* (Loeliger 2009), which takes a more tutorial approach, and in the free Git Community Book[21], which is also useful as a thorough reference on Git. For detailed help on a specific command, use `git help` *command*, for example, `git help branch`; but be aware that these explanations are for reference, not tutorial.

- Many medium-sized projects that don't use Pivotal Tracker, or whose bug-management needs go somewhat beyond what Tracker provides, rely on the Issues feature built into every GitHub repo. The Issues system allows each team to create appropriate "labels" for different bug types and priorities and create their own "bug lifecycle" process. Large projects with wide software distribution use considerably more sophisticated (and complex) bug tracking systems such as the open-source Bugzilla[22].

ACM IEEE-Computer Society Joint Task Force. Computer science curricula 2013, Ironman Draft (version 1.0). Technical report, February 2013. URL http://ai.stanford.edu/users/sahami/CS2013/.

T. J. Allen and G. Henn. *The Organization and Architecture of Innovation: Managing the Flow of Technology*. Butterworth-heinemann, 2006.

A. Begel and N. Nagappan. Pair programming: What's in it for me? In *Proceedings of the Second ACM-IEEE international symposium on Empirical software engineering and measurement*, pages 120–128, Kaiserslautern, Germany, October 2008.

K. H. Blanchard and S. Johnson. *The One Minute Manager*. William Morrow, Cambridge, MA, 1982.

P. Bodík, A. Fox, M. I. Jordan, D. Patterson, A. Banerjee, R. Jagannathan, T. Su, S. Tenginakai, B. Turner, and J. Ingalls. Advanced tools for operators at Amazon.com. In *First Workshop on Hot Topics in Autonomic Computing (HotAC'06)*, Dublin, Ireland, June 2006.

E. Braude and M. Berstein. *Software Engineering:Modern Approaches, Second Edition*. John Wiley and Sons, 2011. ISBN 9780471692089.

D. Carnegie. *How to Win Friends and Influence People*. Pocket, 1998.

A. Cockburn and L. Williams. The costs and benefits of pair programming. *Extreme Programming Examined*, pages 223–248, 2001.

J. Hannay, T. Dyba, E. Arisholm, and D. Sjoberg. The effectiveness of pair programming: A meta-analysis. *Information and Software Technology*, 51(7):1110–1122, July 2009.

L. Hoffmann. Q&a: Big challenge. *Communications of the ACM (CACM)*, 56(9):112–ff, Sept. 2013.

D. Holland. *Red Zone Management.* WinHope Press, 2004. ISBN 0967140188.

J. Loeliger. *Version Control with Git: Powerful Tools and Techniques for Collaborative Software Development.* O'Reilly Media, 2009. ISBN 0596520123.

J. Moore. ipad 2 as a remote presence device? *Pivotal Blabs,* 2011. URL `http://pivotallabs.com/blabs/categories/pair-programming`.

R. Pressman. *Software Engineering: A Practitioner's Approach, Seventh Edition.* McGraw Hill, 2010. ISBN 0073375977.

K. Schwaber and M. Beedle. *Agile Software Development with Scrum (Series in Agile Software Development).* Prentice Hall, 2001. ISBN 0130676349.

A. Shalloway. *Agile Design and Code Reviews.* 2002. URL `http://www.netobjectives.com/download/designreviews.pdf`.

I. Sommerville. *Software Engineering, Ninth Edition.* Addison-Wesley, 2010. ISBN 0137035152.

S. Teasley, L. Covi, M. S.Krishnan, and J. S. Olson. How does radical collocation help a team succeed? In *Proceedings of the 2000 ACM conference on Computer supported cooperative work,* pages 339–346, Philadelphia, Pennsylvania, December 2000.

Notes

[1] `http://www.opensourcerails.com/`
[2] `http://github.com/ucberkeley/researchmatch`
[3] `http://github.com/vinsonchuong/meetinglibs`
[4] `http://codeclimate.com`
[5] `https://github.com/bbatsov/rails-style-guide`
[6] `http://google-styleguide.googlecode.com/svn/trunk/pyguide.html`
[7] `http://google-styleguide.googlecode.com/svn/trunk/javascriptguide.xml`
[8] `http://google-styleguide.googlecode.com/svn/trunk/cppguide.xml`
[9] `https://github.com/bbatsov/rails-style-guide`
[10] `http://google-styleguide.googlecode.com/svn/trunk/pyguide.html`
[11] `http://google-styleguide.googlecode.com/svn/trunk/javascriptguide.xml`
[12] `http://dilbert.com/strips/comic/2003-01-09/`
[13] `http://dilbert.com/strips/comic/2003-01-11/`
[14] `http://help.github.com/fork-a-repo/`
[15] `http://help.github.com/send-pull-requests/`
[16] `http://code.flickr.com/blog/2009/12/02/flipping-out/`
[17] `http://nvie.com/posts/a-successful-git-branching-model/`
[18] `http://github.com/`
[19] `http://fakeweb.rubyforge.org`
[20] `http://progit.org/2011/07/11/reset.html`
[21] `http://book.git-scm.com`
[22] `http://mozilla.org`

10.11   Suggested Projects

Project 10.1. *Select several exercises from the book, assign points to them and then measure your velocity as you work through them.*

Project 10.2. *Think about a website that you frequently visit, or a web app that you often use; list some user stories that would guide you to create a similar application from the ground up.*

Project 10.3. *(Discussion) Think about the last project you worked on in a group. How many of the ideas and practices discussed in the chapter did you and your group use? Of those that were used, which did you find the most useful? Which unused methods do you think would have been the most helpful?*

Project 10.4. *(Discussion) A suggested project in Chapter 1 was to make a list of the Top 10 most important applications. Given such a list, which would best be developed and maintained using a two-pizza sized team with a Scrum organization? Which ones would not? List your reasons for each choice.*

Project 10.5. *(Discussion) Why do you think did Pivotal added Epics to Tracker? What was the problem that they were solving with this new feature?*

Project 10.6. *(Discussion) Find a nearby programming colleague to try pair programming for a few days. Several of the suggested projects in the early chapters are good candidates for pair programming. How hard was it to find a place where you could sit side-by-side? Do you find it forces you both the concentrate more to create higher quality code, in part setting distractions aside, or does it seem less productive since essentially only one person is doing any work?*

Project 10.7. *With a programming partner, come up with a simple website or application that you could build. Ideally, it should be no more complicated than RottenPotatoes! Using the methods and tools described in this chapter–pair programming, velocity, version control–work on and complete your project. Which of the tools or methods were the most helpful?*

Project 10.8. *(Discussion) Next time you go to a meeting, keep track how many of SAMOSA guidelines are being violated. If there are several, suggest as an experiment that you try following SAMOSA. What did you notice about the differences between the two meetings? Did SAMOSA help or hurt the meeting?*

Project 10.9. *Undertake, as part of a team activity, an inspection of a medium-size code segment. Note: The margin icon identifies projects from the ACM/IEEE 2013 Software Engineering standard (ACM IEEE-Computer Society Joint Task Force 2013).*

Project 10.10. *(Discussion) Subversion (svn) was a popular version control system developed by CollabNet five years before Linus Torvalds created git. What were the problems with svn that Torvalds was trying to solve with git? How well did he succeed? What do you think are the pros and cons of svn versus git?*

Project 10.11. *Describe the difference between centralized and distributed software configuration management.*

Project 10.12. *Identify configuration items and use a source code control tool like GitHub in a small team-based project.*

Project 10.13. *Create and follow an agenda for a team meeting.*

Project 10.14. *Select and use a defined coding standard in a small software project.*

Project 10.15. *Identify and justify necessary roles in a software development team for a Plan-and-Document process.*

Project 10.16. *List the sources, hazards, and potential benefits of team conflict.*

Project 10.17. *Apply a conflict resolution strategy in a team setting.*

Project 10.18. *Following a Plan-and-Document lifecycle, prepare a project plan for a software project that includes estimates of size and effort, a schedule, resource allocation, configuration control, change management, and project risk identification and management.*

Project 10.19. *Demonstrate your capability to select and use software tools–including Cucumber, RPSEC, Pivotal Tracker–in support of the development of a software product described in Exercise 10.18.*

11 Design Patterns for SaaS Classes

William Kahan (1933–) received the 1989 Turing Award for his fundamental contributions to numerical analysis. Kahan dedicated himself to "making the world safe for numerical computations."

Things are genuinely simple when you can think correctly about what's going on without having a lot of extraneous or confusing thoughts to impede you. Think of Einstein's maxim, "Everything should be made as simple as possible, but no simpler."

—"A Conversation with William Kahan," *Dr. Dobbs' Journal*, 1997

Concepts

The big concept of this chapter is that *design patterns* can improve the quality of the classes. A design pattern captures proven solutions to problems by separating the things that change from those that don't.

Five object-oriented design principles identified by the acronym SOLID describe sound design of interactions among classes. An *antipattern* indicates poor class design, which a *design smell* can identify. Thus, using design smells to detect violations to the **SOLID principles** for good class design is analogous to using *code smells* to detect violations of the **SOFA principles** for good method design (Section 9.7).

The five letters of the SOLID acronym stand for:

1. **Single Responsibility Principle**: a class should have one and only one responsibility; that is, only one reason to change. The **Lack of Cohesion Of Methods** metric indicates the antipattern of too large a class.

2. **Open/Closed Principle**: a class should be open for extension, but closed against modification. The **Case Statement** design smell suggests a violation.

3. **Liskov Substitution Principle**: a method designed to work on an object of type T should also work on an object of any subtype of T. That is, all of T's subtypes should preserve T's "contract." The **refused bequest** design smell often indicates a violation.

4. **Dependency Injection Principle**: if two classes depend on each other but their implementations may change, it would be better for them to both depend on a separate abstract interface which is "injected" between them.

5. **Demeter Principle**: a method can call other methods in its own class, and methods on the classes of its own instance variables; everything else is taboo. A design smell that indicates a violation is **inappropriate intimacy**.

For Agile, *refactoring* is the vehicle for improving the design of classes and methods; in some cases refactoring may allow you to apply an appropriate *design pattern*. In contrast, for the Plan-and-Document lifecycles:

- The early design phase makes it easier to select a good initial software architecture and class designs.

- The specification is broken into problems and then into subproblems, where developers try to use patterns to solve them.

- As design precedes coding, *design reviews* can offer early feedback.

- One concern is whether the design must change once coding begins.

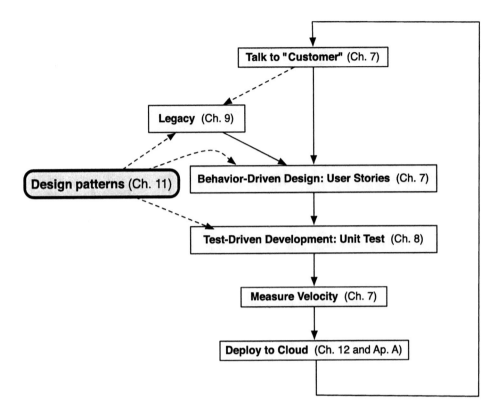

Figure 11.1: The Agile software lifecycle and its relationship to the chapters in this book. This chapter covers design patterns, which influence BDD and TDD for new apps *and* for enhancing legacy code.

11.1 Patterns, Antipatterns, and SOLID Class Architecture

In Chapter 2, we introduced the idea of a design pattern: a reusable structure, behavior, strategy, or technique that captures a proven solution to a collection of similar problems by *separating the things that change from those that stay the same*. Patterns play a major role in helping us achieve our goal throughout this book: producing code that is not only correct (TDD) and meets a customer need (BDD), but is also concise, readable, DRY, and generally beautiful. Figure 11.1 highlights the role of design patterns in the Agile lifecycle as covered in this chapter.

While we have already seen architectural patterns such as Client–Server and structural patterns such as Model–View–Controller, this chapter examines design patterns that apply to classes and class architecture. As Figure 11.2 shows, we will follow a similar approach as we did in Chapter 9. Rather than simply listing a catalog of design patterns, we'll motivate their use by starting from some guidelines about what makes a class architecture good or bad, identifying smells and metrics that indicate possible problem spots, and showing how some of these problems can be fixed by refactoring—both within classes and by moving code across classes—to eliminate the problems. In some cases, we can refactor to make the code match an existing and proven design pattern. In other cases, the refactoring doesn't necessarily result

Chapter 9	Chapter 11
Code smells warn of problems in methods of a class	Design smells warn of problems in relationships among classes
Many catalogs of code smells and refactorings; we use Fowler's as definitive	Many catalogs of design smells and design patterns; we use Ruby-specific versions of the Gang of Four (GoF) design patterns as definitive
ABC, Cyclomatic Complexity metrics complement code smells with quantitative warnings	LCOM (Lack of Cohesion of Methods) metric complements design smells with quantitative warnings
Refactoring by extracting methods and moving code within a class	Refactoring by extracting classes and moving code between classes
SOFA guidelines for good methods (**S**hort, do **O**ne thing, **F**ew arguments, single **A**bstraction level)	SOLID guidelines for good class architecture (**S**ingle responsibility, **O**pen/Closed, **L**iskov substitution, dependency **I**njection, **D**emeter)
Some code smells don't apply in Ruby	Some design smells don't apply in Ruby or SaaS

Figure 11.2: The parallels between the warning symptoms and remedies introduced for individual classes and methods in Chapter 9 and those introduced for inter-class relationships in this chapter. For reasons explained in the text, whereas most books use the I in SOLID for Interface Segregation (a smell that doesn't arise in Ruby) and D for injecting Dependencies, we instead use I for Injecting dependencies and D for the Demeter principle, which arises frequently in Ruby.

in major structural changes to the class architecture.

As with method-level refactoring, application of design patterns is best learned by doing, and the number of design patterns exceeds what we can cover in one chapter of one book. Indeed, there are entire books just on design patterns, including the seminal *Design Patterns: Elements of Reusable Object-Oriented Software* (Gamma et al. 1994), whose authors became known as the "Gang of Four" or GoF, and their catalog known as the "***GoF design patterns***." The 23 GoF design patterns are divided into Creational, Structural, and Behavioral design patterns, as Figure 11.3 shows. As with Fowler's original book on refactoring, the GoF design patterns book gave rise to other books with examples tailored to specific languages including Ruby (Olsen 2007).

The GoF authors cite two overarching principles of good object-oriented design that inform most of the patterns:

Since the GoF design patterns evolved in the context of statically typed languages, some of them address problems that don't arise in Ruby. For example, patterns that eliminate type signature changes that would trigger recompilation are rarely used in Ruby, which isn't compiled and doesn't use types to enforce contracts.

- Prefer Composition and Delegation over Inheritance.

- Program to an Interface, not an Implementation.

We will learn what these catch-phrases mean as we explore some specific design patterns.

In an ideal world, all programmers would use design patterns tastefully, continuously refactoring their code as Chapter 9 suggests, and all code would be beautiful. Needless to say, this is not always the case. An *antipattern* is a piece of code that seems to want to be expressed in terms of a well-known design pattern, but isn't—often because the original (good) code has evolved to fill new needs without refactoring along the way. ***Design smells***, similar to the code smells we saw in Chapter 9, are warning signs that your code may be headed towards an antipattern. In contrast to code smells, which typically apply to methods within a class, design smells apply to relationships between classes and how responsibilities are divided among them. Therefore, whereas refactoring a method involves moving code around *within* a class, refactoring a design involves moving code *between* classes, creating new classes or modules (perhaps by extracting commonality from existing ones), or removing classes that aren't pulling their weight.

Creational patterns
***Abstract Factory*, Factory Method**: Provide an interface for creating families of related or dependent objects without specifying their concrete classes **Singleton:** Ensure a class has only one instance, and provide a global point of access to it. **Prototype:** Specify the kinds of objects to create using a prototypical instance, and create new objects by copying this prototype. As we'll see in Chapter 6, prototype-based inheritance is part of the JavaScript language. **Builder:** Separate the construction of a complex object from its representation allowing the same construction process to create various representations
Structural patterns
Adapter, Proxy, Façade*, Bridge**: Convert the programming interface of a class into another (sometimes simpler) interface that clients expect, or decouple an abstraction's interface from its implementation, for dependency injection or performance ***Decorator: Attach additional responsibilities to an object dynamically, keeping the same interface. Helps with "Prefer composition or delegation over inheritance." **Composite**: Provide operations that work on both an individual object and a collection of that type of object **Flyweight:** Use sharing to support large numbers of similar objects efficiently
Behavioral patterns
Template Method, Strategy: Uniformly encapsulate multiple varying strategies for same task ***Observer:*** One or more entities need to be notified when something happens to an object ***Iterator, Visitor:*** Separate traversal of a data structure from operations performed on each element of the data structure ***Null Object:*** (Doesn't appear in GoF catalog) Provide an object with defined neutral behaviors that can be safely called, to take the place of conditionals guarding method calls **State:** Encapsulate an object whose behaviors (methods) differ depending on which of a small number of internal states the object is in **Chain of Responsibility:** Avoid coupling the sender of a request to its receiver by giving more than one object a chance to handle the request, passing request up the chain until someone handles it **Mediator:** Define an object that encapsulates how a set of objects interact without those objects having to refer to each other explicitly, allowing decoupling **Interpreter:** Define a representation for a language along with an interpreter that executes the representation **Command:** Encapsulate an operation request as an object, thereby letting you parameterize clients with different requests, queue or log requests, and support undoable operations

Figure 11.3: The 23 *GoF design patterns* spanning three categories, with italics showing a subset we'll encounter as we illustrate and fix SOLID violations and with closely-related patterns grouped into a single entry, as with Abstract Factory and Factory Method. Whenever we introduce a design pattern, we'll explain the pattern's goal, show a Unified Modeling Language representation (introduced in the next section) of the class architecture before and after refactoring to that pattern, and when possible, give an example of how the pattern is used "in the wild" in Rails itself or in a Ruby gem.

Principle	Meaning	Warning smells	Refactoring fix
Single Responsibility	A class should have one and only one reason to change	Large class, poor LCOM (Lack of Cohesion Of Methods) score, data clumps	Extract class, move methods
Open/Closed	Classes should be open for extension but closed for modification	Conditional complexity, **case**-based dispatcher	Use Strategy or Template Method, possibly combined with Abstract Factory pattern; use Decorator to avoid explosion of subclasses
Liskov Substitution	Substituting a subclass for a class should preserve correct program behavior	Refused bequest: subclass destructively overrides an inherited method	Replace inheritance with delegation
Injection of Dependencies	Collaborating classes whose implementation may vary at runtime should depend on an intermediate "injected" dependency	Unit tests that require *ad hoc* stubbing to create seams; constructors that hardwire a call to another class's constructor, rather than allowing runtime determination of *which* other class to use	Inject a dependency on a shared interface to isolate the classes; use Adapter, Façade, or Proxy patterns as needed to make the interface uniform across variants
Demeter Principle	Speak only to your friends; treat your friends' friends as strangers	Inappropriate intimacy, feature envy, mock trainwrecks (Section 8.10)	Delegate behaviors and call the delegate methods instead

Figure 11.4: The SOLID design guidelines and some smells that may suggest your code violates one or more of them. We diverge a little bit from standard usage of SOLID: we use I for Injecting dependencies and D for the Demeter principle, whereas most books use I for Interface Segregation (which doesn't apply in Ruby) and D for injecting Dependencies.

Similar to SOFA in Chapter 9, the mnemonic SOLID (credited to Robert C. Martin) stands for a set of five design principles that clean code should respect. As in Chapter 9, design smells and quantitative metrics can tell us when we're in danger of violating one or more SOLID guidelines; the fix is often a refactoring that eliminates the problem by bringing the code in line with one or more design patterns.

Figure 11.4 shows the SOLID mnemonics and what they tell us about good composition of classes. In our discussion of selected design patterns, we'll see violations of each one of these guidelines, and show how refactoring the bad code (in some cases, with the goal of applying a design pattern) can fix the violation. In general, the SOLID principles strive for a class architecture that avoids various problems that thwart productivity:

"Uncle Bob" Martin, an American software engineer and consultant[1] since 1970, is a founder of Agile/XP and a leading member of the *Software Craftsmanship* movement, which encourages programmers to see themselves as creative professionals learning a disciplined craft in an apprenticeship model.

1. Viscosity: it's easier to fix a problem using a quick hack, even though you know that's not the right thing to do.

2. Immobility: it's hard to be DRY and because the functionality you want to reuse is wired into the app in a way that makes extraction difficult.

3. Needless repetition: possibly as a consequence of immobility, the app has similar functionality duplicated in multiple places. As a result, a change in one part of the app often ripples to many other parts of the app, so that a small change in functionality requires a lot of little changes to code and tests, a process sometimes called *shotgun surgery*.

4. Needless complexity: the app's design reflects generality that was inserted before it was needed.

As with refactoring and legacy code, seeking out design smells and addressing them by refactoring with judicious use of design patterns is a skill learned by doing. Therefore, rather than presenting "laundry lists" of design smells, refactorings, and design patterns, we focus our discussion around the SOLID principles and give a few representative examples of the overall process of identifying design smells and assessing the alternatives for addressing them. As you tackle your own applications, perusing the more detailed resources listed in Section 11.11 is essential.

Summary of patterns, antipatterns and SOLID:

- Good code should accommodate evolutionary change gracefully. Design patterns are proven solutions to common problems that thwart this goal. They work by providing a clean way to separate the things that may change or evolve from those that stay the same and a clean way to accommodate those changes.

- Just as with individual methods, refactoring is the process of improving the structure of a class architecture to make the code more maintainable and evolvable by moving code across classes as well as refactoring within the class. In some cases, these refactorings lead us to one of the 23 "Gang of Four" (GoF) design patterns.

- Just as with individual methods, design smells and metrics can serve as early warnings of an *antipattern*—a piece of code that would be better structured if it followed a design pattern.

■ *Elaboration: Other types of patterns*

As we've emphasized since the beginning of this book, judicious use of patterns pervades good software engineering. To complement class-level design patterns, others have developed catalogs of architectural patterns for enterprise applications[2] (we met some in Chapter 2), parallel programming patterns[3], computational patterns (to support specific algorithm families such as graph algorithms, linear algebra, circuits, grids, and so on), *Concurrency patterns*, and user interface patterns[4].

Grady Booch (1955–), internationally recognized for his work in software engineering and collaborative development environments, developed UML with Ivar Jacobson and James Rumbaugh.

Self-Check 11.1.1. *True or false: one measure of the quality of a piece of software is the degree to which it uses design patterns.*

◇ False: while design patterns provide proven solutions to some common problems, code that doesn't exhibit such problems may not need those patterns, but that doesn't make it poor code. The GoF authors specifically warn against measuring code quality in terms of design pattern usage. ■

11.2 Just Enough UML

The **Unified Modeling Language** or UML is not a textual language, but a set of graphical notation techniques to "specify, visualize, modify, construct, and document the artifacts of an object-oriented software-intensive system under development[5]." UML evolved from 1995 to the present through the unification of previously-distinct modeling language standards and diagram types, which Figure 11.5 lists.

Structure diagrams	
Class	Describes the structure of a system by showing the system's classes, their attributes, and the relationships among the classes.
Component	Describes how a software system is split up into components and shows the dependencies among these components.
Composite structure	Describes the internal structure of a class and the collaborations that this structure makes possible.
Deployment	Describes the hardware used in system implementations and the execution environments and artifacts deployed on the hardware.
Object	Shows a complete or partial view of the structure of an example modeled system at a specific time.
Package	Describes how a system is split up into logical groupings by showing the dependencies among these groupings.
Profile	Describes reusable domain-specific "stereotype" objects from which specific object types can be derived for use in a particular application.
Interaction diagrams	
Communication	Shows the interactions between objects or parts in terms of sequenced messages. They represent a combination of information taken from Class, Sequence, and Use Case Diagrams describing both the static structure and dynamic behavior of a system.
Interaction overview	Provides an overview in which the nodes represent communication diagrams.
Sequence	Shows how objects communicate with each other in terms of a sequence of messages. Also indicates the lifespans of objects relative to those messages.
Timing diagrams	A specific type of interaction diagram where the focus is on timing constraints.
Behavior diagrams	
Activity	Describes the business and operational step-by-step workflows of components in a system. An activity diagram shows the overall flow of control.
State machine	Describes the states and state transitions of the system.
Use Case	Describes the functionality provided by a system in terms of actors, their goals represented as use cases, and any dependencies among those use cases.

Figure 11.5: The fourteen types of diagrams defined by UML 2.2 for describing a software system. These descriptions are based on the excellent Wikipedia summary of UML[7], which also shows an example of each diagram type. Use case diagrams are similar to Agile user stories, but lack the level of detail that allows tools like Cucumber to bridge the gap between user stories and integration/acceptance tests.

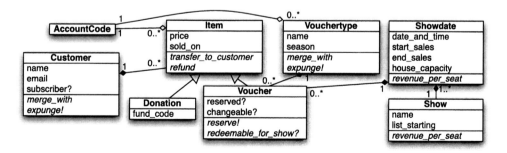

Figure 11.6: This UML *class diagram* shows a subset of the classes in the theater-ticketing app consistent with Figures 9.4 and 9.5. Each box represents a class with its most important methods and attributes (responsibilities). Inheritance is represented by an arrow. Classes with associations are connected by lines whose endpoints are annotated with a multiplicity and optionally a diamond—open for aggregations, filled for compositions, absent otherwise.

While this book focuses on more lightweight Agile modeling—indeed, UML-based modeling has been criticized as being too "bloated" and heavyweight—some types of UML diagrams are widely used even in Agile modeling. Figure 11.6 shows a UML *class diagram*, which depicts each actual class in the app, its most important class and instance variables and methods, and its relationship to other classes, such as has-many or belongs-to associations. Each end of the line connecting two associated classes is annotated with the minimum and maximum number of instances that can participate in that "side" of the association, called the association's *multiplicity*, using the symbol ***** for "unlimited". For example, a multiplicity **1..*** means "one or more", **0..*** means "zero or more", and **1** means "exactly one." UML distinguishes two kinds of "owning" (has-one or has-many) associations. In an *aggregation*, the owned objects survive destruction of the owning object. For example, *Course has many Students* is an aggregation because the students happily don't get destroyed when the course is over! In a *composition*, the owned objects are usually destroyed when the owning object is destroyed. For example, *Movie has many Reviews* is a composition since deleting a Movie should cause all of its reviews to be deleted.

Class diagrams are popular even among software engineers who don't use the other parts of UML. With this introduction to UML in hand, we can use class diagrams to illustrate "before and after" class architecture when we improve code using the SOLID guidelines and design patterns.

Summary of Unified Modeling Language (UML):

- UML comprises a family of diagram types to illustrate various aspects of a software design and implementation.

- UML class diagrams are widely used even by engineers who don't use other UML features. They show a class's name, its most important public and private methods and attributes, and its relationship to other classes.

■ *Elaboration: When to use UML?*

While heavyweight, UML is useful for modeling very large applications divided into subsystems being worked on by widely-distributed teams. Also, since UML notation is language-neutral, it can be helpful for coordinating international teams. Because of UML's maturity, many tools support its use; the challenge is keeping the diagrams "in sync" with the code and the design, which is why most such tools try to go in both directions, synthesizing code skeletons from UML and extracting UML diagrams from code. One such tool useful for learning UML is UMPLE[8], a domain-specific language developed at the University of Ottawa for expressing class relationships. The Try Umple[9] web site can generate UML class diagrams from UMPLE code, generate UMPLE code from diagrams you draw yourself, or generate executable code in various programming languages corresponding to your UMPLE code or UML diagrams. It's a great tool for exploring UML and class diagrams, but we don't recommend using the Ruby code it generates, which is non-DRY and somewhat non-idiomatic.

Self-Check 11.2.1. *In a UML class diagram depicting the relationship "University has many Departments," what multiplicities would be allowable on each side of the association?*

◇ The University side has multiplicity **1**, because a Department must belong to exactly one

LCOM variant	Scores	Interpretation
Revised Henderson-Sellers LCOM	0 (best) to 1 (worst)	0 means all instance methods access all instance variables. 1 means any given instance variable is used by only one instance method, that is, the instance methods are fairly independent of each other.
LCOM-4	1 (best) to n (worst)	Estimates number of responsibilities in your class as number of connected components in a graph in related methods' nodes are connected by an edge. A score $n > 1$ suggests that up to $n - 1$ responsibilities could be extracted into their own classes.

Figure 11.7: The "recommended" lack of cohesion of methods (LCOM) score depends heavily on which LCOM variant is used. The table shows two of the most widely-used variants.

University. The Department side has multiplicity **1..***, because one or more Departments can belong to a University. ∎

Self-Check 11.2.2. *Should the relationship "University has many Departments" be modeled as an aggregation or a composition?*

◇ It should be a composition, since departments wouldn't survive the closing of a university. ∎

11.3 Single Responsibility Principle

The *Single Responsibility Principle* (SRP) of SOLID states that a class should have one and only one responsibility—that is, only one reason to change. For example, in Section 5.2, when we added single sign-on to RottenPotatoes, we created a new **SessionsController** to handle the sign-on interaction. An alternate strategy would be to augment **MoviegoersController**, since sign-on is an action associated with moviegoers. Indeed, before the single sign-on approach described in Chapter 5, this was the recommended way to implementing password-based authentication in earlier versions of Rails. But such a scheme would require changing the **Moviegoer** model and controller whenever we wanted to change the authentication strategy, even though the "essence" of a Moviegoer doesn't really depend on how he or she signs in. In MVC, each controller should specialize in dealing with one resource; an authenticated user session is a distinct resource from the user himself, and deserves its own RESTful actions and model methods. As a rule of thumb, if you cannot describe the responsibility of a class in 25 words or less, it may have more than one responsibility, and the new ones should be split out into their own classes.

In statically typed compiled languages, the cost of violating SRP is obvious: any change to a class requires recompilation and may also trigger recompilation or relinking of other classes that depend on it. Because we don't pay this price in interpreted dynamic languages, it's easy to let classes get too large and violate SRP. One tip-off is lack of *cohesion*, which is the degree to which the elements of a single logical entity, in this case a class, are related. Two methods are related if they access the same subset of instance or class variables or if one calls the other. The *LCOM* metric, for *Lack of Cohesion Of Methods*, measures cohesion for a class: in particular, it warns you if the class consists of multiple "clusters" in which methods within a cluster are related, but methods in one cluster aren't strongly related to methods in other clusters. Figure 11.7 shows two of the most commonly used variants of the LCOM metric.

The *Data Clumps* design smell is one warning sign that a good class is evolving toward the "multiple responsibilities" antipattern. A Data Clump is a group of variables or values that

In Section 9.6, after successfully refactoring **convert**, reek reported "low cohesion" in the **TimeSetter** class because we used class variables rather than instance variables for maintaining what was actually instance state, as that section described.

http://pastebin.com/hi5175Wr

```
1  class Moviegoer
2    attr_accessor :name, :street, :phone_number, :zipcode
3    validates :phone_number, # ...
4    validates :zipcode, # ...
5    def format_phone_number ; ... ; end
6    def verify_zipcode ; ... ; end
7    def format_address(street, phone_number, zipcode) # data clump
8      # do formatting, calling format_phone_number and verify_zipcode
9    end
10 end
11 # After applying Extract Class:
12 class Moviegoer
13   attr_accessor :name
14   has_one :address
15 end
16 class Address
17   belongs_to :moviegoer
18   attr_accessor :phone_number, :zipcode
19   validates :phone_number, # ...
20   validates :zipcode, # ...
21   def format_address ; ... ; end # no arguments - operates on 'self'
22   private # no need to expose these now:
23   def format_phone_number ; ... ; end
24   def verify_zipcode ; ... ; end
25 end
```

Figure 11.8:   To perform Extract Class, we identify the group of methods that shares a responsibility distinct from that of the rest of the class, move those methods into a new class, make the "traveling together" data items on which they operate into instance variables of the class, and arrange to pass an instance of the class around rather than the individual items.

are always passed together as arguments to a method or returned together as a set of results from a method. This "traveling together" is a sign that the values might really need their own class. Another symptom is that something that used to be a "simple" data value acquires new behaviors. For example, suppose a **Moviegoer** has attributes **phone_number** and **zipcode**, and you want to add the ability to check the zip code for accuracy or canonicalize the formatting of the phone number. If you add these methods to **Moviegoer**, they will reduce its cohesion because they form a "clique" of methods that only deal with specific instance variables. The alternative is to use the *Extract Class* refactoring to put these methods into a new **Address** class, as Figure 11.8 shows.

Summary of Single Responsibility Principle:

- A class should have one and only one reason to change, that is, one responsibility.

- A poor LCOM (Lack of Cohesion Of Methods) score and the Data Clump design smell are both warnings of possible SRP violations. The Extract Class refactoring can help remove and encapsulate additional responsibilities in a separate class.

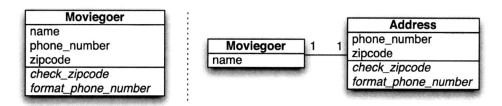

Figure 11.9: UML class diagrams before (left) and after (right) extracting the Address class from Moviegoer.

■ *Elaboration: Interface Segregation Principle*

Related to SRP is the *Interface Segregation Principle* (ISP, and the original **I** in SOLID), which states that if a class's API is used by multiple quite different types of clients, the API probably should be segregated into subsets useful to each type of clients. For example, the **Movie** class might provide both movie metadata (MPAA rating, release date, and so on) and an interface for searching TMDb, but it's unlikely that a client using one of those two sets of services would care about the other. The problem solved by ISP arises in compiled languages in which changes to an interface require recompiling the class, thereby triggering recompilation or relinking of classes that use that interface. While documenting separate interfaces for distinct sets of functionality is good style, ISP rarely arises in Ruby since there are no compiled classes, so we won't discuss it further.

Self-Check 11.3.1. *Draw the UML class diagrams showing class architecture before and after the refactoring in Figure 11.8.*
◇ Figure 11.9 shows the UML diagrams. ■

11.4 Open/Closed Principle

The *Open/Closed Principle* (OCP) of SOLID states that classes should be "open for extension, but closed against modification." That is, it should be possible to extend the behavior of classes without modifying existing code on which other classes or apps depend.

While adding subclasses that inherit from a base class is one way to extend existing classes, it's often not enough by itself. Figure 11.10 shows why the presence of **case**-based dispatching logic—one variant of the *Case Statement* design smell—suggests a possible OCP violation.

Depending on the specific case, various design patterns can help. One problem that the smelly code in Figure 11.10 is trying to solve is that the desired subclass of **Formatter** isn't known until runtime, when it is stored in the **@format** instance variable. The *abstract factory pattern* provides a common interface for instantiating an object whose subclass may not be known until runtime. Ruby's duck typing and metaprogramming enable a particularly elegant implementation of this pattern, as Figure 11.11 shows. (In statically-typed languages, to "work around" the type system, we have to create a factory method for each subclass and have them all implement a common interface—hence the name of the pattern.)

Another approach is to take advantage of the *Strategy pattern* or *Template Method pattern*. Both support the case in which there is a general approach to doing a task but many possible variants. The difference between the two is the level at which commonality

http://pastebin.com/xxHCeLzV

```
 1  class Report
 2    def output
 3      formatter =
 4        case @format
 5        when :html
 6          HtmlFormatter.new(self)
 7        when :pdf
 8          PdfFormatter.new(self)
 9          # ...etc
10        end
11    end
12  end
```

Figure 11.10: The Report class depends on a base class Formatter with subclasses HtmlFormatter and PdfFormatter. Because of the explicit dispatch on the report format, adding a new type of report output requires modifying Report#output, and probably requires changing other methods of Report that have similar logic—so-called *shotgun surgery*.

http://pastebin.com/HZsLHVcc

```
 1  class Report
 2    def output
 3      formatter_class =
 4        begin
 5          @format.to_s.classify.constantize
 6        rescue NameError
 7          # ...handle 'invalid formatter type'
 8        end
 9      formatter = formatter_class.send(:new, self)
10      # etc
11    end
12  end
```

Figure 11.11: Ruby's metaprogramming and duck typing enable an elegant implementation of the abstract factory pattern. classify is provided by Rails to convert snake_case to UpperCamelCase. constantize is syntactic sugar provided by Rails that calls the Ruby introspection method Object#const_get on the receiver. We also handle the case of an invalid value of the formatter class, which the bad code doesn't.

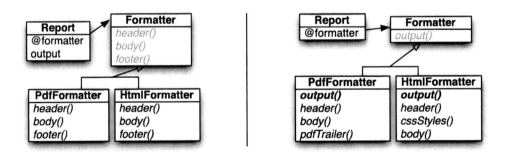

Figure 11.12: In Template Method (left), the extension points are header, body, and footer, since the Report#output method calls @formatter.header, @formatter.body, and so on, each of which delegates to a specialized counterpart in the appropriate subclass. (Light gray type indicates methods that just delegate to a subclass.) In Strategy (right), the extension point is the output method itself, which delegates the entire task to a subclass. Delegation is such a common ingredient of composition that some people refer to it as the *delegation pattern*.

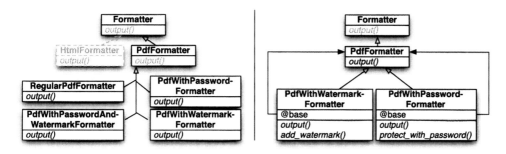

Figure 11.13: (Left) The multiplication of subclasses resulting from trying to solve the Formatter problem using inheritance shows why your class designs should "prefer composition over inheritance." (Right) A more elegant solution uses the Decorator design pattern.

is captured. With Template Method, although the implementation of each step may differ, the set of steps is the same for all variants; hence it is usually implemented using inheritance. With Strategy, the overall task is the same, but the set of steps may be different in each variant; hence it is usually implemented using composition. Figure 11.12 shows how either pattern could be applied to the report formatter. If every kind of formatter followed the same high-level steps—for example, generate the header, generate the report body, and then generate the footer—we could use Template Method. On the other hand, if the steps themselves were quite different, it would make more sense to use Strategy.

An example of the Strategy pattern in the wild is OmniAuth (Section 5.2): many apps need third-party authentication, and the steps are quite different depending on the auth provider, but the API to all of them is the same. Indeed, OmniAuth even refers to its plug-ins as "strategies."

A different kind of OCP violation arises when we want to *add* behaviors to an existing class and discover that we cannot do so without modifying it. For example, PDF files can be generated with or without password protection and with or without a "Draft" watermark across the background. Both features amount to "tacking on" some extra behavior to what **PdfFormatter** already does. If you've done a lot of object-oriented programming, your first thought might therefore be to solve the problem using inheritance, as the UML diagram in Figure 11.13 (left) shows, but there are four permutations of features so you'd end up with four subclasses with duplication across them—hardly DRY. Fortunately, the ***decorator pattern*** can help: we "decorate" a class or method by wrapping it in an enhanced version that has the same API, allowing us to compose multiple decorations as needed. Figure 11.14 shows the code corresponding to the more elegant decorator-based design of the PDF formatter shown in Figure 11.13 (right).

In the wild, the ActiveSupport module of Rails provides method-level decoration via **alias_method_chain**, which is very useful in conjunction with Ruby's open classes, as Figure 11.15 shows. A more interesting example of Decorator in the wild is the Rack application server we've been using since Chapter 2. The heart of Rack is a "middleware" module that receives an HTTP request and returns a three-element array consisting of an HTTP response code, HTTP headers, and a response body. A Rack-based application specifies a "stack" of middleware components that all requests traverse: to add a behavior to an HTTP request (for example, to intercept certain requests as OmniAuth does to initiate an authentication flow), we decorate the basic HTTP request behavior. Additional decorators add support for SSL (Secure Sockets Layer), measuring app performance, and some types of

Python's "decorators"[10] are, unfortunately, completely unrelated to the Decorator design pattern.

http://pastebin.com/u8aYdwEL

```
1  class PdfFormatter
2    def initialize ; ... ; end
3    def output ; ... ; end
4  end
5  class PdfWithPasswordFormatter < PdfFormatter
6    def initialize(base) ; @base = base ; end
7    def protect_with_password(original_output) ; ... ; end
8    def output ; protect_with_password @base.output ; end
9  end
10 class PdfWithWatermarkFormatter < PdfFormatter
11   def initialize(base) ; @base = base ; end
12   def add_watermark(original_output) ; ... ; end
13   def output ; add_watermark @base.output ; end
14   end
15 end
16 # If we just want a plain PDF
17 formatter = PdfFormatter.new
18 # If we want a "draft" watermark
19 formatter = PdfWithWatermarkFormatter.new(PdfFormatter.new)
20 # Both password protection and watermark
21 formatter = PdfWithWatermarkFormatter.new(
22   PdfWithPasswordFormatter.new(PdfFormatter.new))
```

Figure 11.14: To apply Decorator to a class, we "wrap" class by creating a subclass (to follow the Liskov Substitution Principle, as we'll learn in Section 11.5). The subclass delegates to the original method or class for functionality that isn't changed, and implements the extra methods that extend the functionality. We can then easily "build up" just the version of PdfFormatter we need by "stacking" decorators.

http://pastebin.com/rdyrjyAN

```
1  # reopen Mailer class and decorate its send_email method.
2  class Mailer
3    alias_method_chain :send_email, :cc
4    def send_email_with_cc(recipient,body) # this is our new method
5      send_email_without_cc(recipient,body) # will call original method
6      copy_sender(body)
7    end
8  end
9  # now we have two methods:
10 send_email(...)              # calls send_email_with_cc
11 send_email_with_cc(...)      # same thing
12 send_email_without_cc(...) # call (renamed) original method
```

Figure 11.15: To decorate an existing method Mailer#send_email, we reopen its class and use alias_method_chain to decorate it. Without changing any classes that call send_email, all calls now use the decorated version that sends email and copies the sender.

HTTP caching.

Summary of Open/Closed Principle:

- To make a class open for extension but closed against modification, we need mechanisms that enable specific **extension points** at places we think extensions might be needed in the future. The *Case Statement* design smell is one symptom of a possible OCP violation.

- If the extension point takes the form of a task with varying implementations for the steps, the Strategy and Template Method patterns may apply. Both are often used in conjunction with the Abstract Factory pattern, since the variant to create may not be known until runtime.

- If the extension point takes the form of selecting different subsets of features that "add on" to existing class behaviors, the Decorator pattern may apply. The Rack application server is designed this way.

■ *Elaboration: Closed against what?*

"Open for extension but closed for modification" presupposes that you know in advance what the useful extension points will be, so you can leave the class open for the "most likely" changes and strategically close it against changes that might break its dependents. In our example, since we already had more than one way to do something (format a report), it seemed reasonable to allow additional formatters to be added later, but you don't always know in advance what extension points you'll want. Make your best guess, and deal with change as it comes.

Self-Check 11.4.1. *Here are two statements about delegation:*

1. *A subclass delegates a behavior to an ancestor class*

2. *A class delegates a behavior to a descendant class*

Looking at the examples of the Template Method, Strategy, and Decorator patterns (Figures 11.12 and 11.13), which statement best describes how each pattern uses delegation?

◇ In Template Method and Strategy, the ancestor class provides the "basic game plan" which is customized by delegating specific behaviors to different subclasses. In Decorator, each subclass provides special functionality of its own, but delegates back to the ancestor class for the "basic" functionality. ■

11.5 Liskov Substitution Principle

The **Liskov Substitution Principle** (LSP) is named for Turing Award winner Barbara Liskov, who did seminal work on subtypes that heavily influenced object-oriented programming. Informally, LSP states that a method designed to work on an object of type T should also work on an object of any subtype of T. That is, all of T's subtypes should preserve T's "contract."

http://pastebin.com/hr0DqtWt

```ruby
 1  class Rectangle
 2    attr_accessor :width, :height, :top_left_corner
 3    def new(width,height,top_left) ... ; end
 4    def area ... ; end
 5    def perimeter ... ; end
 6  end
 7  # A square is just a special case of rectangle...right?
 8  class Square < Rectangle
 9    # ooops...a square has to have width and height equal
10    attr_reader :width, :height, :side
11    def width=(w)  ; @width = @height = w ; end
12    def height=(w) ; @width = @height = w ; end
13    def side=(w)   ; @width = @height = w ; end
14  end
15  # But is a Square really a kind of Rectangle?
16  class Rectangle
17    def make_twice_as_wide_as_high(dim)
18      self.width = 2*dim
19      self.height = dim              # doesn't work!
20    end
21  end
```

Figure 11.16: Behaviorally, rectangles have some capabilities that squares don't have—for example, the ability to set the lengths of their sides independently, as in Rectangle#make_twice_as_wide_as_high.

This may seem like common sense, but it's subtly easy to get wrong. Consider the code in Figure 11.16, which suffers from an LSP violation. You might think a **Square** is just a special case of **Rectangle** and should therefore inherit from it. But *behaviorally,* a square is *not* like a rectangle when it comes to setting the length of a side! When you spot this problem, you might be tempted to override **Rectangle#make_twice_as_wide_as_high** within **Square**, perhaps raising an exception since this method doesn't make sense to call on a **Square**. But that would be a *refused bequest*—a design smell that often indicates an LSP violation. The symptom is that a subclass either destructively overrides a behavior inherited from its superclass or forces changes to the superclass to avoid the problem (which itself should indicate a possible OCP violation). The problem is that inheritance is all about implementation sharing, but if a subclass won't take advantage of its parent's implementations, it might not deserve to be a subclass at all.

The fix, therefore, is to again use composition and delegation rather than inheritance, as Figure 11.17 shows. Happily, because of Ruby's duck typing, this use of composition and delegation still allows us to pass an instance of **Square** to most places where a **Rectangle** would be expected, even though it's no longer a subclass; a statically-typed language would have to introduce an explicit interface capturing the operations common to both **Square** and **Rectangle**.

http://pastebin.com/1hJ4bYsM

```
1  # LSP-compliant solution: replace inheritance with delegation
2  # Ruby's duck typing still lets you use a square in most places where
3  #  rectangle would be used - but no longer a subclass in LSP sense.
4  class Square
5    attr_accessor :rect
6    def initialize(side, top_left)
7      @rect = Rectangle.new(side, side, top_left)
8    end
9    def area       ; rect.area      ; end
10   def perimeter ; rect.perimeter ; end
11   # A more concise way to delegate, if using ActiveSupport (see text):
12   #  delegate :area, :perimeter, :to => :rectangle
13   def side=(s) ; rect.width = rect.height = s ; end
14 end
```

Figure 11.17: As with some OCP violations, the problem arises from a misuse of inheritance. As Figure 11.17 shows, preferring composition and delegation to inheritance fixes the problem. Line 12 shows a concise syntax for delegation available to apps using ActiveSupport (and all Rails apps do); similar functionality for non-Rails Ruby apps is provided by the Forwardable module in Ruby's standard library.

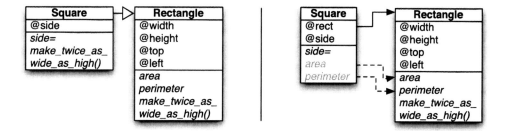

Figure 11.18: Left: The UML class diagram representing the original LSP-violating code in Figure 11.16, which destructively overrides Rectangle#make_twice_as_wide_as_high. Right: the class diagram for the refactored LSP-compliant code in Figure 11.17.

Summary of the Liskov Substitution Principle:

- LSP states that a method that operates on objects of some class should also work correctly on objects of any subclass of that class. When a subclass differs behaviorally from one of its parents, an LSP violation can arise.

- The *refused bequest* design smell, in which a subclass destructively overrides a parent behavior or forces changes to the parent class so that the behavior is not inherited—often signals an LSP violation.

- Many LSP violations can be fixed by using composition of classes rather than inheritance, achieving reuse through delegation rather than through subclassing.

Self-Check 11.5.1. *Why is* **Forwardable** *in the Ruby standard library provided as a module rather than a class?*

◇ Modules allow the delegation mechanisms to be mixed in to any class that wants to use them, which would be awkward if **Forwardable** were a class. That is, **Forwardable** is itself an example of preferring composition to inheritance! ■

11.6 Dependency Injection Principle

The dependency injection principle (DIP), sometimes also called dependency inversion, states that if two classes depend on each other but their implementations may change, it would be better for them to both depend on a separate abstract interface that is "injected" between them.

Suppose RottenPotatoes now adds email marketing—interested moviegoers can receive emails with discounts on their favorite movies. RottenPotatoes integrates with the external email marketing service MailerMonkey to do this job:

http://pastebin.com/ZdhcYb7w

```
1  class EmailList
2    attr_reader :mailer
3    delegate :send_email, :to => :mailer
4    def initialize
5      @mailer = MailerMonkey.new
6    end
7  end
8  # in RottenPotatoes EmailListController:
9  def advertise_discount_for_movie
10   moviegoers = Moviegoer.interested_in params[:movie_id]
11   EmailList.new.send_email_to moviegoers
12 end
```

Suppose the feature is so successful that you decide to extend the mechanism so that moviegoers who are on the Amiko social network can opt to have these emails forwarded to their Amiko friends as well, using the new **Amiko** gem that wraps Amiko's RESTful API for friend lists, posting on walls, messaging, and so on. There are two problems, however.

First, **EmailList#initialize** has a hardcoded dependency on **MailerMonkey**, but now we will sometimes need to use **Amiko** instead. This runtime variation is the problem solved by dependency injection—since we won't know until runtime which type of mailer we'll need, we modify **EmailList#initialize** so we can "inject" the correct value at runtime:

http://pastebin.com/8PHBpm5k

```
1  class EmailList
2    attr_reader :mailer
3    delegate :send_email, :to => :mailer
4    def initialize(mailer_type)
5      @mailer = mailer_type.new
6    end
7  end
8  # in RottenPotatoes EmailListController:
9  def advertise_discount_for_movie
10   moviegoers = Moviegoer.interested_in params[:movie_id]
11   mailer = if Config.has_amiko? then Amiko else MailerMonkey end
12   EmailList.new(mailer).send_email_to moviegoers
13 end
```

You can think of DIP as injecting an additional seam between two classes, and indeed, in statically compiled languages DIP helps with testability. This benefit is less apparent in Ruby, since as we've seen we can create seams almost anywhere we want at runtime using mocking or stubbing in conjunction with Ruby's dynamic language features.

The second problem is that **Amiko** exposes a different and more complex API than the simple **send_email** method provided by **MailerMonkey** (to which **Email-List#send_email** delegates in line 3), yet our controller method is already set up to call **send_email** on the mailer object. The *Adapter pattern* can help us here: it's designed to convert an existing API into one that's compatible with an existing caller. In this case, we can define a new class **AmikoAdapter** that converts the more complex **Amiko** API into the simpler one that our controller expects, by providing the same **send_email** method that **MailerMonkey** provides:

http://pastebin.com/Eimsw8ZF

```
1  class AmikoAdapter
2    def initialize ; @amiko = Amiko.new(...) ; end
3    def send_email
4      @amiko.authenticate(...)
5      @amiko.send_message(...)
6    end
7  end
8  # Change the controller method to use the adapter:
9  def advertise_discount_for_movie
10   moviegoers = Moviegoer.interested_in params[:movie_id]
11   mailer = if Config.has_amiko? then AmikoAdapter else MailerMonkey end
12   EmailList.new(mailer).send_email_to moviegoers
13 end
```

ActiveRecord has been criticized for configuring the database at startup from `database.yml` rather than using DIP. Presumably the designers judged that the database wouldn't change while the app was running. While DIP-induced seams also help with stubbing and mocking, Chapter 8 shows that Ruby's open classes and metaprogramming let you insert test seams wherever needed.

When the Adapter pattern not only converts an existing API but also simplifies it—for example, the **Amiko** gem also provides many other Amiko functions unrelated to email, but **AmikoAdapter** only "adapts" the email-specific part of that API—it is sometimes called the *Façade pattern*.

Lastly, even in cases where the email strategy is known when the app starts up, what if we want to disable email sending altogether from time to time? Figure 11.19 (top) shows a naive approach: we have moved the logic for determining which emailer to use into a new **Config** class, but we still have to "condition out" the email-sending logic in the controller method if email is disabled. But if there are other places in the app where a similar check must be performed, the same condition logic would have to be replicated there (shotgun surgery). A better alternative is the *Null Object pattern*, in which we create a "dummy" object that has all the same behaviors as a real object but doesn't do anything when those behaviors are called. Figure 11.19 (bottom) applies the Null Object pattern to this example, avoiding the proliferation of conditionals throughout the code.

Figure 11.20 shows the UML class diagrams corresponding to the various versions of our

http://pastebin.com/js6C67mJ

```
1   class Config
2     def self.email_enabled? ; ... ; end
3     def self.emailer ; if has_amiko? then Amiko else MailerMonkey end ; end
4   end
5   def advertise_discount_for_movie
6     if Config.email_enabled?
7       moviegoers = Moviegoer.interested_in(params[:movie_id])
8       EmailList.new(Config.emailer).send_email_to(moviegoers)
9     end
10  end
```

http://pastebin.com/avRQAgZc

```
1   class Config
2     def self.emailer
3       if email_disabled? then NullMailer else
4         if has_amiko? then AmikoAdapter else MailerMonkey end
5       end
6     end
7   end
8   class NullMailer
9     def initialize ; end
10    def send_email ; true ; end
11  end
12  def advertise_discount_for_movie
13    moviegoers = Moviegoer.interested_in(params[:movie_id])
14    EmailList.new(Config.emailer).send_email_to(moviegoers)
15    end
16  end
```

Figure 11.19: Top: a naive way to disable a behavior is to "condition it out" wherever it occurs. Bottom: the Null Object pattern eliminates the conditionals by providing "dummy" methods that are safe to call but don't do anything.

DIP example.

An interesting relative of the Adapter and Façade patterns is the ***Proxy pattern***, in which one object "stands in" for another that has the same API. The client talks to the proxy instead of the original object; the proxy may forward some requests directly to the original object (that is, delegate them) but may take other actions on different requests, perhaps for reasons of performance or efficiency.

A classic example of this pattern is ActiveRecord associations (Section 5.3). Recall that under the relationship *Movie has many Reviews*, we could write **r=@movie.reviews**. What kind of object is **r**? Although we've seen that we can treat **r** as an enumerable collection, it's actually a proxy object that responds to all the collection methods (**length**, <<, and so on), but without querying the database except when it has to. Another example of a use for the proxy pattern would be for sending email while disconnected from the Internet. If the real Internet-based email service is accessed via a **send_email** method, a proxy object could provide a **send_email** method that just stores an email on the local disk until the next time the computer is connected to the Internet. This proxy shields the client (email GUI) from having to change its behavior when the user isn't connected.

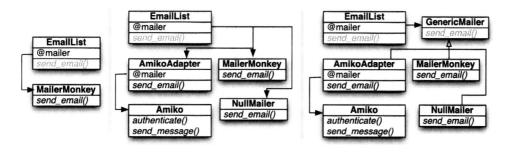

Figure 11.20: Left: Without dependency injection, EmailList depends directly on MailerMonkey. Center: With dependency injection, @mailer can be set at runtime to use any of MailerMonkey, NullMailer (which implements the Null Object pattern to disable email), or AmikoAdapter (which implements the Adapter/Façade pattern over Amiko), all of which have the same API. Right: In statically typed languages, the abstract superclass GenericMailer formalizes the fact that all three mailers have compatible APIs, but in Ruby this superclass is often omitted if it consists entirely of abstract methods (as is the case here), since abstract methods and classes aren't part of the language.

Summary of Dependency Injection:

- Dependency injection inserts a seam between two classes by passing in (injecting) a dependency whose value may not be known until runtime, rather than hardwiring a dependency into the source code.

- Because dependency injection is often used to vary which of a collection of implementations is used at runtime, it's often seen together with the Adapter pattern, in which a class converts one API into another that a client expects to use.

- Variations on Adapter include Façade, in which the API is not only adapted but also simplified, and Proxy, in which the API is exactly imitated but the behaviors changed to accommodate different usage conditions without the client (caller of the API) having to change its behavior.

- The Null Object pattern is another mechanism for replacing unwieldy conditionals with safe "neutral" behaviors as a way of disabling a feature.

■ *Elaboration: Did injecting a dependency violate the Open/Closed Principle?*

You might wonder whether our "fix" to add a second type of mailer service violates OCP, because adding support for a third mailer would then require modifying **advertise_discount_- for_movie**. If you had reason to believe you might indeed need to add additional mailers later, you could combine this with the Abstract Factory pattern introduced in Section 11.4. This scenario is an example of making a judgment call about whether the possibility of handling additional mailers is an extension point you want to leave open, or a change you feel the app wouldn't accommodate well and should therefore be strategically closed against.

Self-Check 11.6.1. *Why does proper use of DIP have higher impact in statically typed languages?*

◇ In such languages, you cannot create a runtime seam to override a "hardwired" behavior as you can in dynamic languages like Ruby, so the seam must be provided in advance by injecting the dependency. ■

http://pastebin.com/iaNeSeCJ

```
1   # This example is adapted from Dan Manges's blog, dcmanges.com
2   class Wallet ; attr_accessor :credit_balance ; end
3   class Moviegoer
4     attr_accessor :wallet
5     def initialize
6       # ...setup wallet attribute with correct credit balance
7     end
8   end
9   class MovieTheater
10    def collect_money(moviegoer, amount)
11      # VIOLATION OF DEMETER (see text)
12      if moviegoer.wallet.credit_balance < amount
13        raise InsufficientFundsError
14      else
15        moviegoer.wallet.credit_balance -= due_amount
16        @collected_amount += due_amount
17      end
18    end
19  end
20  # Imagine testing the above code:
21  describe MovieTheater do
22    describe "collecting money" do
23      it "should raise error if moviegoer can't pay" do
24        # "Mock trainwreck" is a warning of a Demeter violation
25        wallet = mock('wallet', :credit_balance => 5.00)
26        moviegoer = mock('moviegoer', :wallet => wallet)
27        lambda { @theater.collect_money(moviegoer, 10.00) }.
28          should raise_error(...)
29      end
30    end
31  end
```

Figure 11.21:   Line 12 contains a Demeter violation: while it's reasonable for MovieTheater to know about Moviegoer, it also knows about the implementation of Wallet, since it "reaches through" the wallet attribute to manipulate the wallet's credit_balance. Also, we're handling the problem of "not enough cash" in MovieTheater, even though logically it seems to belong in Wallet.

11.7   Demeter Principle

The name comes from the Demeter Project on adaptive and aspect-oriented programming, which in turn is named for the Greek goddess of agriculture to signify a "from the ground up" approach to programming.

The Demeter Principle or **Law of Demeter** states informally: "Talk to your friends—don't get intimate with strangers." Specifically, a method can call other methods in its own class, and methods on the classes of its own instance variables; everything else is taboo. Demeter isn't originally part of the SOLID guidelines, as Figure 11.4 explains, but we include it here since it is highly applicable to Ruby and SaaS, and we opportunistically hijack the **D** in SOLID to represent it.

The Demeter Principle is easily illustrated by example. Suppose RottenPotatoes has made deals with movie theaters so that moviegoers can buy movie tickets directly via RottenPotatoes by maintaining a credit balance (for example, by receiving movie theater gift cards).

Figure 11.21 shows an implementation of this behavior that contains a Demeter Principle violation. A problem arises if we ever change the implementation of **Wallet**—for example, if we change **credit_balance** to **cash_balance**, or add **points_balance** to allow moviegoers to accumulate PotatoPoints by becoming top reviewers. All of a sudden, the **MovieTheater** class, which is "twice removed" from **Wallet**, would have to change.

Two design smells can tip us off to possible Demeter violations. One is *inappropriate intimacy*: the **collect_money** method manipulates the **credit_balance** attribute of **Wallet** directly, even though managing that attribute is the **Wallet** class's responsibility. (When the same kind of inappropriate intimacy occurs repeatedly throughout a class, it's sometimes

http://pastebin.com/QtxWkUy6

```
 1  # Better: delegate credit_balance so MovieTheater only accesses Moviegoer
 2  class Moviegoer
 3    def credit_balance
 4      self.wallet.credit_balance   # delegation
 5    end
 6  end
 7  class MovieTheater
 8    def collect_money(moviegoer,amount)
 9      if moviegoer.credit_balance >= amount
10        moviegoer.credit_balance -= due_amount
11        @collected_amount += due_amount
12      else
13        raise InsufficientFundsError
14      end
15    end
16  end
```

http://pastebin.com/rgB4LnMk

```
 1  class Wallet
 2    attr_reader :credit_balance # no longer attr_accessor!
 3    def withdraw(amount)
 4      raise InsufficientFundsError if amount > @credit_balance
 5      @credit_balance -= amount
 6      amount
 7    end
 8  end
 9  class Moviegoer
10    # behavior delegation
11    def pay(amount)
12      wallet.withdraw(amount)
13    end
14  end
15  class MovieTheater
16    def collect_money(moviegoer, amount)
17      @collected_amount += moviegoer.pay(amount)
18    end
19  end
```

Figure 11.22: (Top) If Moviegoer delegates credit_balance to its wallet, MovieTheater no longer has to know about the implementation of Wallet. However, it may still be undesirable that the payment *behavior* (subtract payment from credit balance) is exposed to MovieTheater when it should really be the responsibility of Moviegoer or Wallet only. (Bottom) Delegating the behavior of payment, rather than the attributes through which it's accomplished, solves the problem and eliminates the Demeter violation.

called **feature envy**, because **Moviegoer** "wishes it had access to" the features managed by **Wallet**.) Another smell that arises in tests is the ***mock trainwreck***, which occurs in lines 25–27 of Figure 11.21: to test code that violates Demeter, we find ourselves setting up a "chain" of mocks that will be used when we call the method under test.

Once again, delegation comes to the rescue. A simple improvement comes from delegating the **credit_balance** attribute, as Figure 11.22 (top) shows. But the best delegation is that in Figure 11.22 (bottom), since now the behavior of payment is entirely encapsulated within **Wallet**, as is the decision of when to raise an error for failed payments.

Inappropriate intimacy and Demeter violations can arise in any situation where you feel you are "reaching through" an interface to get some task done, thereby exposing yourself to dependency on implementation details of a class that should really be none of your business. Three design patterns address common scenarios that could otherwise lead to Demeter violations. One is the Visitor pattern, in which a data structure is traversed and you provide a callback method to execute for each member of the data structure, allowing you to "visit" each element while remaining ignorant of the way the data structure is organized. Indeed, the

http://pastebin.com/zznALkdt

```
1  class EmailList
2    observe Review
3    def after_create(review)
4      moviegoers = review.moviegoers # from has_many :through, remember?
5      self.email(moviegoers, "A new review for #{review.movie} is up.")
6    end
7    observe Moviegoer
8    def after_create(moviegoer)
9      self.email([moviegoer], "Welcome, #{moviegoer.name}!")
10   end
11   def self.email ; ... ; end
12 end
```

Figure 11.23: An email list subsystem observes other models so it can generate email in response to certain events. The Observer pattern is an ideal fit since it collects all the concerns about when to send email in one place.

"data structure" could even be materialized lazily as you visit the different nodes, rather than existing statically all at once. An example of this pattern in the wild is the Nokogiri[11] gem, which supports traversal of HTML and XML documents organized as a tree: in addition to searching for a specific element in a document, you can have Nokogiri traverse the document and call a visitor method you provide at each document node.

A simple special case of Visitor is the *Iterator pattern*, which is so pervasive in Ruby (you use it anytime you use **each**) that many Rubyists hardly think of it as a pattern. Iterator separates the implementation of traversing a collection from the behavior you want to apply to each collection element. Without iterators, the behavior would have to "reach into" the collection, thereby knowing inappropriately intimate details of how the collection is organized.

Observer was first implemented in the MVC framework of *Smalltalk*, from which Ruby inherits its object model.

The last design pattern that can help with some cases of Demeter violations is the *Observer pattern*, which is used when one class (the observer) wants to be kept aware of what another class is doing (the subject) without knowing the details of the subject's implementation. The Observer design pattern provides a canonical way for the subject to maintain a list of its observers and notify them automatically of any state changes in which they have indicated interest, using a narrow interface to separate the concept of observation from the specifics of what each observer does with the information.

While the Ruby standard library includes a mixin[12] called **Observable**, Rails' ActiveSupport provides a more concise Observer that lets you observe any model's ActiveRecord lifecycle hooks (**after_save** and so on), introduced in Section 5.1. Figure 11.23 shows how easy it is to add an **EmailList** class to RottenPotatoes that "subscribes" to two kinds of state changes:

1. When a new review is added, it emails all moviegoers who have already reviewed that same movie.

2. When a new moviegoer signs up, it sends her a "Welcome" email.

In addition to ActiveRecord lifecycle hooks, Rails caching, which we will encounter in Chapter 12, is another example of the Observer pattern in the wild: the cache for each type of ActiveRecord model observes the model instance in order to know when model instances become stale and should be removed from the cache. The observer doesn't have to know the implementation details of the observed class—it just gets called at the right time, like Iterator and Visitor.

To close out this section, it's worth pointing out an example that looks like it violates Demeter, but really doesn't. It's common in Rails views (say, for a **Review**) to see code such as:

http://pastebin.com/s9X4Eiq3

```
1  %p Review of:   #{@review.movie.title}
2  %p Written by:  #{@review.moviegoer.name}
```

Aren't these Demeter violations? It's a judgment call: strictly speaking, a **review** shouldn't know the implementation details of **movie**, but it's hard to argue that creating delegate methods **Review#movie_title** and **Review#moviegoer_name** would enhance readability in this case. The general opinion in the Rails community is that it's acceptable for views whose purpose is to display object relationships to also expose those relationships in the view code, so examples like this are usually allowed to stand.

Summary of Demeter Principle:

- The Demeter Principle states that a class shouldn't be aware of the details of collaborator classes from which it is further away than "once removed." That is, you can access instance methods in your own class and in the classes corresponding to your nearest collaborators, but not on *their* collaborators.

- The Inappropriate Intimacy design smell, which sometimes manifests as a Mock Trainwreck in unit tests, may signal a Demeter violation. If a class shows many instances of Inappropriate Intimacy with another class, it is sometimes said to have Feature Envy with respect to the other class.

- Delegation is the key mechanism for resolving these violations.

- Design patterns cover some common manipulations of classes without violating Demeter, including Iterator and Visitor (separating traversal of an aggregate from behavior) and Observer (separating notification of "interesting" events from the details of the class being observed).

■ *Elaboration: Observers, Visitors, Iterators, and Mixins*

Because of duck typing and mixins, Ruby can express many design patterns with far less code than statically-typed languages, as the Wikipedia entries for *Observer*, *Iterator* and *Visitor* clearly demonstrate by using Java-based examples. In contrast to Ruby's internal iterators based on **each**, statically-typed languages usually provide external iterators and visitors in which you set up the iterator over a collection and ask the iterator explicitly whether the collection has any more elements, sometimes requiring various contortions to work around the type system. Similarly, Observer usually requires modifying the subject class(es) so that they can implement an **Observable** interface, but Ruby's open classes allow us to skip that step, as Figure 11.23 showed: from the programmer's point of view, all of the logic is in the observing class, not the subjects.

Self-Check 11.7.1. *Ben Bitdiddle is a purist about Demeter violations, and he objects to the expression* **@movie.reviews.average_rating** *in the movie details view, which shows a movie's average review score. How would you placate Ben and fix this Demeter violation?*

http://pastebin.com/z5zdp8MY

```
1  # naive way:
2  class Movie
3    has_many :reviews
4    def average_rating
5      self.reviews.average_rating # delegate to Review#average_rating
6    end
7  end
8  # Rails shortcut:
9  class Movie
10   has_many :reviews
11   delegate :average_rating, :to => :review
12 end
```

Self-Check 11.7.2. *Notwithstanding that "delegation is the key mechanism" for resolving Demeter violations, why should you be concerned if you find yourself delegating many methods from class A to class B just to resolve Demeter violations present in class C?*

◇ You might ask yourself whether there should be a direct relationship between class C and class B, or whether class A has "feature envy" for class B, indicating that the division of responsibilities between A and B might need to be reengineered. ∎

11.8   The Plan-And-Document Perspective

A strength of Plan-and-Document is that careful upfront planning can result in a product with a good software architecture that uses design patterns well. This preplanning is reflected in the alternative catch phrase for these processes of **Big Design Up Front**, as Chapter 1 mentions.

A Plan-and-Document development team starts with the **Software Requirements Specification** (**SRS**) (see Section 7.10), which the team breaks into a series of problems. For each one, the team looks for one or more architecture patterns that might solve the problem. The team then goes down to the next level of subproblems, and looks for design patterns that match them. The philosophy is to learn from the experience of others captured as patterns so as to avoid repeating the mistakes of your predecessors. Another way to get feedback from more experienced engineers is to hold a **design review** (see Section 10.7). Note that design reviews can be done before any code is written in Plan-and-Document processes.

Thus, compared to Agile, there is considerably more effort in starting with a good design in Plan-and-Document. As Martin Fowler points out in his article *Is Design Dead?*[13], a frequent critique of Agile is that it encourages developers to jump in and start coding without any design, and rely too much on refactoring to fix things later. As the critics sometimes say, you can build a doghouse by slapping stuff together and planning as you go, but you can't build a skyscraper that way.

Agile supporters counter that Plan-and-Document methods are just as bad: by disallowing any code until the design is complete, it's impossible to be confident that the design will be implementable or that it really captures the customer's needs. This critique especially holds when the architects/designers will not be writing the code or may be out of touch with current coding practices and tools. As a result, say Agile proponents, when coding starts, the design will have to change anyway.

Both sides have a point, but the critique can be phrased in a more nuanced way as "How much design makes sense up front?" For example, Agile developers plan for persistent storage as part of their SaaS apps, even though the first BDD and TDD tests they write will not touch the database. A more subtle example is horizontal scaling. As we alluded to in Chapter 2, and will discuss more fully in Chapter 12, designers of successful SaaS *must* think about horizontal scalability early on. Even though it may be months before scalability matters, design decisions early in the project can cripple scalability, and it may be difficult to change them without major rewriting and refactoring.

A possible solution to the conundrum is captured by a rule of thumb in Fowler's article. If you have previously done a project that has some design constraint or element, it's OK to plan for it in a new project that is similar, because your previous experience will likely lead to reasonable design decisions this time.

> **Summary:** Plan-and-Document processes have an explicit design phase that is a natural fit to the use of design patterns in the software development process. One potential drawback is uncertainty as to whether the initial architecture and design patterns will need to change as the code is written and as the system evolves. In contrast, the Agile process relies on refactoring to incorporate design patterns as the code evolves, although experienced developers may lay plans for software architectures and design patterns that they expect to need based on previous, similar projects.

Self-Check 11.8.1. *True or False: Agile design is an oxymoron.*

◇ False. Although there is no separate design phase in Agile development, the refactoring that is the norm in Agile can incorporate design patterns. ∎

11.9 Fallacies and Pitfalls

 Pitfall: **Over-reliance or under-reliance on patterns.**

As with every tool and methodology we've seen, slavishly following design patterns is a pitfall: they can help point the way when your problem could take advantage of a proven solution, but they cannot by themselves ensure beautiful code. In fact, the GoF authors specifically warn *against* trying to evaluate the soundness of a design based on the number of patterns it uses. In addition, if you apply design patterns too early in your design cycle, you may try to implement a pattern in its full generality even though you may not need that generality for solving the current problem. That will complicate your design because most design patterns call for *more* classes, methods, and levels of indirection than the same code would require without this level of generality. In contrast, if you apply design patterns too late, you risk falling into antipatterns and extensive refactoring.

What to do? Develop taste and judgment through learning by doing. You will make some mistakes as you go, but your judgment on how to deliver working and maintainable code will quickly improve.

 Pitfall: **Over-reliance on UML or other diagrams.**

A diagram's purpose is communication of intent. Reading UML diagrams is not necessarily easier than reading user stories or well-factored TDD tests. Create a diagram when it helps to clarify a class architecture; don't rely on them as a crutch.

 Fallacy: **SOLID principles aren't needed in dynamic languages.**

As we saw in this chapter, some of the problems addressed by SOLID don't really arise in dynamically-typed languages like Ruby. Nonetheless, the SOLID guidelines still represent good design; in static languages, there is simply a much more tangible up-front cost to ignoring them. In dynamic languages, while the opportunity exists to use dynamic features to make your code more elegant and DRY without the extra machinery required by some of the SOLID guidelines, the corresponding risk is that it's easier to fall into sloth and end up with ugly antipattern code.

 Pitfall: **Lots of private methods in a class.**

You may have already discovered that methods declared **private** are hard to test, because by definition they can only be called from within an instance method of that class—meaning they cannot be called directly from an RSpec test. Although you can use a hack to temporarily make the method public (**MyClass.send(:public,:some_private_method)**), private methods complex enough to need their own tests should be considered a smell: the methods themselves may be too long, violating the **S**hort guideline of SOFA, and the class containing these methods may be violating the *Single Responsibility Principle*. In this case, consider extracting a collaborator class whose methods are public (and therefore easy to test and easy to shorten by refactoring) but are only called from the original class, thereby improving maintainability and testability.

 Pitfall: **Using initialize to implement factory patterns.**

In Section 11.4, we showed an example of Abstract Factory pattern in which the correct subclass constructor is called directly. Another common scenario is one in which you have a class **A** with subclasses **A1** and **A2**, and you want calls to **A**'s constructor to return a new object of the correct subclass. You usually cannot put the factory logic into the **initialize** method of **A**, because that method must by definition return an instance of class **A**. Instead, give the factory method a different name such as **create**, make it a class method, and call it from **A**'s constructor:

http://pastebin.com/Xv7iY4kd

```
1  class A
2    def self.create(subclass, *args) # subclass must be either 'A1' or 'A2'
3      return Object.const_get(subclass).send(:new, *args)
4    end
5  end
```

11.10 Concluding Remarks: Frameworks Capture Design Patterns

The process of preparing programs for a digital computer is especially attractive, not only because it can be economically and scientifically rewarding, but also because it can be an aesthetic experience much like composing poetry or music.

—Donald Knuth

The original 23 design patterns from the Gang of Four have been expanded dramatically since their book appeared. There are numerous repositories of design patterns (Cunningham 2013; Noble and Johnson 2013), with some tailored to specific problem areas such as user interfaces (Griffiths 2013; Toxboe 2013).

A problem for novice developers is that even if you read the Gang of Four book or study these repositories, it is hard to know which pattern to apply. If you don't have previous experience with a given design pattern, and you try to design for it in an anticipatory manner, you're more likely to get it wrong, so you should instead wait to add it later when and if it's really needed.

The good news is that frameworks like Rails encapsulate others' design experience to provide abstractions and design constraints that have been proven through reuse. For example, it may not occur to you to design your app's actions around REST, but it turns out that doing so results in a design that is more consistent with the scalability success stories of the Web. While the Gang of Four went out of their way to differentiate design patterns from frameworks to try to make it clear what design patterns are—more abstract, narrower in focus, and not targeted to a problem domain—today frameworks are a great way for a novice to get started with design patterns. By examining the patterns in a framework that are instantiated as code, you can gain experience on how to create your own code based on design patterns.

11.11 To Learn More

Design Patterns (Gamma et al. 1994) is the classic Gang of Four text on design patterns. While canonical, it's a bit slower reading than some other sources, and the examples are heavily oriented to C++. *Design Patterns in Ruby* (Olsen 2007) treats a subset of the GoF patterns in detail showing Ruby examples. It also discusses patterns made unnecessary by Ruby language features. *Clean Code* (Martin 2008) has a more thorough exposition of both the SOFA and SOLID guidelines that motivate the use of design patterns.

Rather than presenting a "laundry list" of patterns, we tried to motivate a subset of patterns by showing the design smells they fix. *Rails Antipatterns* (Pytel and Saleh 2010) gives great examples of how real-life code that starts with a good design can become cluttered over time, and how to beautify and streamline it by refactoring, often using one or more of the appropriate design patterns. Figure 11.24 shows a few examples of those refactorings, largely drawn from Martin Fowler's online catalog of refactorings[14] and comprehensive book (Fields et al. 2009).

Finally, M.V. Mäntylä and C. Lassenius have created an online taxonomy[15] of code and design smells grouped into descriptively-named categories such as "The Bloaters", "The Change Preventers", and so on, summarizing their 2006 journal article[16] on this topic.

ACM IEEE-Computer Society Joint Task Force. Computer science curricula 2013, Ironman Draft (version 1.0). Technical report, February 2013. URL `http://ai.stanford.edu/users/sahami/CS2013/`.

W. Cunningham. Portland pattern repository, 2013. URL `http://c2.com/ppr/`.

J. Fields, S. Harvie, M. Fowler, and K. Beck. *Refactoring: Ruby Edition*. Addison-Wesley Professional, 2009. ISBN 0321603508.

E. Gamma, R. Helm, R. Johnson, and J. M. Vlissides. *Design Patterns: Elements of Reusable Object-Oriented Software*. Addison-Wesley Professional, 1994. ISBN 0201633612.

R. Griffiths. HCI design patterns, 2013. URL `http://www.hcipatterns.org/patterns`.

Smell	Description	Fix
Comment deodorant, inappropriate name	Obfuscated variable or method names make lots of comments necessary	Reduce need for comments throug names and (as necessary) by add smells within the offending code
Lazy class, data class	A class does too little, for example, providing nothing but getters and setters for some object but no other logic	Merge methods that encapsulate th into another class
Duplicated code, combinatorial explosion	Nearly the same code repeated with subtle changes in multiple methods, in same class	Extract common parts using DRY like blocks and **yield** (Section 3.8 helper methods (Section 9.6), using Strategy design pattern (Section 11
Parallel inheritance hierarchy	Nearly the same code repeated with subtle changes in different classes that inherit from different ancestors; for example, numerous pieces of code using slightly different combinations of data or behavior	Extract commonality into its own c egate to that class (Section 11.7). I different ancestors need the functio tracting it into a module that can be

Figure 11.24: Some smells are relatively easily fixed by a local modification. These are excerpted from Fowler's *Refactoring, Ruby Edition* (Fields et al. 2009).

R. C. Martin. *Clean Code: A Handbook of Agile Software Craftsmanship*. Prentice Hall, 2008. ISBN 9780132350884.

J. Noble and R. Johnson. Design patterns library, 2013. URL `http://hillside.net/patterns`.

R. Olsen. *Design Patterns in Ruby*. Addison-Wesley Professional, 2007. ISBN 9780321490452.

C. Pytel and T. Saleh. *Rails AntiPatterns: Best Practice Ruby on Rails Refactoring (Addison-Wesley Professional Ruby Series)*. Addison-Wesley Professional, 2010. ISBN 9780321604811.

A. Toxboe. UI patterns, 2013. URL `http://ui-patterns.com/`.

Notes

[1] `http://butunclebob.com`
[2] `http://martinfowler.com/eaaCatalog`
[3] `http://www.cs.uiuc.edu/homes/snir/PPP/`
[4] `http://ui-patterns.com`
[5] `http://foldoc.org/index.cgi?query=UML&action=Search`
[6] `http://en.wikipedia.org/wiki/Unified_Modeling_Language`
[7] `http://en.wikipedia.org/wiki/Unified_Modeling_Language`
[8] `http://cruise.site.uottawa.ca/umple/`
[9] `http://try.umple.org`
[10] `http://en.wikipedia.org/wiki/Python_syntax_and_semantics#Decorators`
[11] `http://nokogiri.org`
[12] `http://www.ruby-doc.org/stdlib-1.9.3/libdoc/observer/rdoc/Observable.html`
[13] `http://www.martinfowler.com/articles/designDead.html`
[14] `http://martinfowler.com/refactoring/catalog`
[15] `http://www.soberit.hut.fi/mmantyla/BadCodeSmellsTaxonomy.htm`
[16] `http://www.soberit.hut.fi/~mmantyla/ESE_2006.pdf`

11.12 Suggested Projects

Project 11.1. *Describe a design that would allow adding a feature to RottenPotatoes wherein customers could buy movie ticket vouchers online. To keep it simple, assume the customer buys a voucher for a ticket to a particular movie via RottenPotatoes, and that voucher can be exchanged at any movie theater showing that movie. (This way RottenPotatoes doesn't have to know about specific movie theaters.) Assume you don't know in advance which payment service will be used for processing credit card charges, but that it will have a RESTful API of some kind. After creating user stories and lo-fi mockups for the new feature, your design will need to address at least the following:*

- *Determining how to model the resources and relationships among them (associations) to support the new feature*

- *Determining how to encapsulate interaction with the payment service, even though you don't yet know which service will be used*

For the following projects, you will need to identify a working legacy software system that you will inspect. For suggestions, you could use the list of open-source Rails projects at Open Source Rails[1], or you could select one of two projects created by students who have used this book: ResearchMatch[2], which helps match students with research opportunities at their university, and VisitDay[3], which helps organize meetings between students and faculty members.

Project 11.2. *Describe one or more design patterns that could be applicable to the design of the software system. Note: The margin icon identifies projects from the ACM/IEEE 2013 Software Engineering standard (ACM IEEE-Computer Society Joint Task Force 2013).*

Project 11.3. *For a simple system suitable for a given user story, discuss and select an appropriate design paradigm.*

Project 11.4. *Apply simple examples of patterns in the software design.*

Project 11.5. *Discuss and select an appropriate software architecture suitable for a given user story in this system. Does the system's implementation of that user story reflect your own architectural recommendation?*

Project 11.6. *Analyze the software design from the perspective of a significant internal quality attribute such as maintainability and lack of viscosity.*

12 Non-functional Requirements for SaaS: Performance, Releases, Reliability, and Practical Security

**Barbara Liskov
(1939–),** one of the first women in the USA to receive a Ph.D. in computer science (in 1968), received the 2008 Turing Award for foundational innovations in programming language design. Her inventions include abstract data types and iterators, both of which are central to Ruby.

You never need optimal performance, you need good-enough performance ...Programmers are far too hung up with performance.

—Barbara Liskov, 2011

Concepts

The big concept of this chapter is how to avoid the following headaches when your app is deployed: crashes, becoming unresponsive if it experiences a surge in popularity, or compromising customer data. Such non-functional characteristics can be more important than functional features since such headaches can drive users away.

In the Agile lifecycle:

- The difficult **performance** challenge for a SaaS app is *latency*, which can be helped by **overprovisioning** in limited cases. The *Apdex* metric is a standard measure to see if an app is meeting its *Service Level Objective* (*SLO*).

- You increase the chances of meeting the SLO by keeping your app running on a *Platform as a Service*, which manages much of the administration and scaling for you.

- The backend database is often the reason an app has to abandon the PaaS solution, but you can stay on the database longer by using *caching*, by creating indices, and by avoiding unnecessary and expensive database queries.

- **Releases** are more challenging in SaaS since you normally need to deploy new versions without first taking down old ones. **Feature flags** make it easier to quickly deploy and remove new features should the need arise.

- **Security** can be enhanced by following the *principles of least privilege* and *fail-safe defaults*, which limit access to assets on a "need-to-know" basis, and the **principle of psychological acceptability**, which states that the user interface must not be more difficult with protection features than without them.

- *Defensive programming* anticipates flaws before they appear and can lead to systems that are both more reliable and more secure.

For Plan-and-Document lifecycles:

- Performance is just a possible non-functional requirement.

- Releases are less frequent, larger events than in Agile.

- The *Mean Time to Failure* is a holistic measure, including errors by the hardware, the software, and the operators. Reducing *Mean Time to Repair* can be just as effective as trying to increase MTTF, and it is easier to measure than MTTF.

- Security can be enhanced by making the system robust against software flaws that leave it open to attacks, such as *buffer overflows*, *arithmetic overflows*, and *data races*.

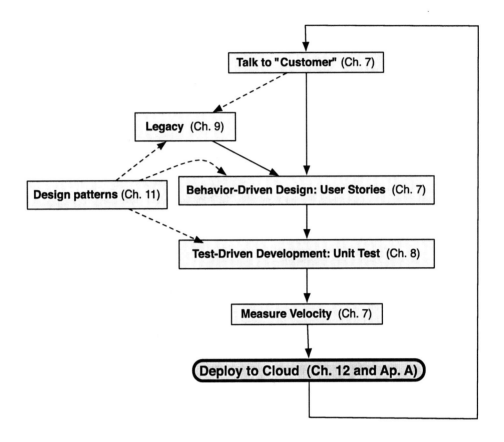

Figure 12.1: The Agile software lifecycle and its relationship to the chapters in this book. This chapter covers deploying the app into the cloud so that the customer can evaluate this Agile iteration.

12.1 From Development to Deployment

Users are a terrible thing. Systems would be infinitely more stable without them.

—Michael Nygard, *Release It!* (Nygard 2007)

The moment a SaaS app is deployed, its behavior changes because it has actual users. If it is a public-facing app, it is open to malicious attacks as well as accidental success, but even private apps such as internal billing systems must be *designed for deployability and monitorability* in order to ensure smooth deployment and operations. Fortunately, as Figure 12.1 reminds us, deployment is part of every iteration in the Agile lifecycle—indeed, many Agile SaaS companies deploy several times *per day*—so you will quickly become practiced in "routine" deployments.

SaaS deployment is much easier than it used to be. Just a few years ago, SaaS developers had to learn quite a bit about system administration in order to manage their own production servers. For small sites they were typically hosted on shared Internet Service Providers ("managed-hosting ISP"), on virtual machines running on shared hardware (Virtual Private Server or VPS), or on one or more dedicated computers physically located at the

ISP's datacenter ("hosting service"). Today, the horizontal scaling enabled by cloud computing (Section 2.4) has given rise to companies like Heroku that provide a ***Platform as a Service*** (PaaS): a curated software stack ready for you to deploy your app, with much of the administration and scaling responsibility managed for you, making deployment much more developer-friendly. PaaS providers may either run their own datacenters or, increasingly, rely on lower-level Infrastructure as a Service (IaaS) providers such as the Amazon public cloud, as Heroku does. Other emerging PaaS's are CloudFoundry, a PaaS software layer that can be deployed on either a company's existing servers or a public cloud, and Microsoft Azure, a set of managed services based on Windows Server and running in Microsoft's cloud.

For early-stage and many mature SaaS apps, PaaS is now the preferred way to deploy: basic scaling issues and performance tuning are handled for you by professional SaaS administrators who are more experienced at operations than most developers. Of course, when a site becomes large enough or popular enough, its technical needs may outgrow what PaaS can provide, or economics may suggest bringing operations "in-house", which as we will see is a major undertaking. Therefore one goal of this chapter is to help your app stay within the PaaS-friendly usage tier for as long as possible. Indeed, if your app is internally-facing, so that its maximum user base is bounded and it runs in a more protected and less hostile environment than public-facing apps, you may have the good fortune to stay in that tier indefinitely.

As we will see, a key to managing the growth of your app is controlling the demands placed on the database, which is harder to scale horizontally. One insight of this chapter is that the performance and security problems you face are the same for both small- and large-scale SaaS apps, but the solutions differ because PaaS providers can be very helpful in solving some of the problems, saving you the work of a custom-built solution.

Notwithstanding the title of this chapter, the terms **performance** and **security** are often overused and ill defined. Here is a more focused list of key operational criteria we will address.

- Responsiveness: How long do most users wait before the app delivers a useful response? (Section 12.2)

- Release management: how can you deploy or upgrade your app "in place" without reducing availability and responsiveness? (Sections 12.3 and 12.4)

- Availability: what percentage of the time is your app correctly serving requests? (Section 12.5)

- Scalability: as the number of users increases, either gradually and permanently or as a one-time surge of popularity, can your app maintain its steady-state availability and responsiveness without increasing the operational cost per user? Chapter 2 noted that three-tier SaaS apps on cloud computing have excellent *potential* horizontal scalability, but good design alone doesn't guarantee that your app will scale (though poor design guarantees that it won't). Caching (Section 12.7) and avoiding abuse of the database (Section 12.8) can help.

- Privacy: is important customer data accessible only to authorized parties, such as the data's owner and perhaps the app's administrators?

- Authentication: can the app ensure that a given user is who he or she claims to be, by verifying a password or using third-party authentication such as Facebook Connect or

OpenID in such a way that an impostor cannot successfully impersonate another user without having obtained the user's credentials?

- Data integrity: can the app prevent customer data from being tampered with, or at least detect when tampering has occurred or data may have been compromised?

The first three items in the above list might be collectively referred to as *performance stability*, while the last three collectively make up *security*, which we discuss in Section 12.9.

Summary

- High availability and responsiveness, release management without downtime, and scalability without increasing per-user costs are three key *performance stability* concerns of SaaS apps, and defending your customers' data is the app's key security concern.

- Good PaaS providers can provide infrastructure mechanisms to automatically handle some of the details of maintaining performance stability and security, but as a developer you must also address these concerns in various aspects of your app's design and implementation, using mechanisms we will discuss in this chapter.

- Compared to shrink-wrapped software, SaaS developer-operators are typically much more involved with deploying, releasing, and upgrading their apps and monitoring them for problems with performance or security.

Self-Check 12.1.1. *Which aspects of application scalability are* not *automatically handled for you in a PaaS environment?*

⋄ If your app "outgrows" the capacity of the largest database offered by the PaaS provider, you will need to manually build a solution to split it into multiple distinct databases. This task is highly app-specific so PaaS providers cannot provide a generic mechanism to do it. ∎

12.2   Quantifying Responsiveness

Performance is a feature.

—Jeff Atwood, co-founder of StackOverflow

Speed is a feature.

—Adam De Boor, Gmail software engineer, Google

Responsiveness is the perceived delay between when a user takes an action such as clicking on a link and when the user perceives a response, such as new content appearing on the page. Technically, responsiveness has two components: **latency**, the initial delay to start receiving new content, and **throughput**, the time it takes for all the content to be delivered. As recently as the mid-1990s, many home users connected to the Internet using telephone modems that took 100 ms (milliseconds) to deliver the first packet of information. They could sustain at most 56 Kbps (56×10^3 bits per second) while transferring the rest, so a Web page or image 50 KBytes in size or 400 Kbits could take more than eight seconds to deliver. However, today's home customers increasingly use broadband connections whose throughput is 1–20 Mbps, so responsiveness for Web pages is dominated by latency rather than throughput.

Since responsiveness has such a large effect on user behavior, SaaS operators carefully monitor the responsiveness of their sites. Of course, in practice, not every user interaction with the site takes the same amount of time, so evaluating performance requires appropriately characterizing a distribution of response times. Consider a site on which 8 out of 10 requests complete in 100 ms, 1 out of 10 completes in 250 ms, and the remaining 1 out of 10 completes in 850 ms. If the user satisfaction threshold T for this site is 200 ms, it is true that the *average* response time of $(8(100)+1(250)+1(850))/10 = 190$ms is below the satisfaction threshold. But on the other hand, 20% of requests (and therefore, up to 20% of users) are receiving unsatisfactory service. Two definitions are used to measure latency in a way that makes it impossible to ignore the bad experience of even a small number of users:

- A **service level objective** (SLO) usually takes the form of a quantitative statement about the quantiles of the latency distribution over a time window of a given width. For example, "95% of requests within any 5-minute window should have a latency below 100 ms." In statistical terms, the 95th quantile of the latency distribution must not exceed 100 ms.

  SLA vs. SLO: A *service level agreement* (SLA) is a contract between a service provider and its customers that provides for customer consideration if the SLO is not met.

- The **Apdex** score (Application Performance Index) is an open standard[4] that computes a simplified SLO as a number between 0 and 1 inclusive representing the fraction of satisfied users. Given a user satisfaction threshold latency T selected by the application operator, a request is *satisfactory* if it completes within time T, *tolerable* if it takes longer than T but less than $4T$, and *unsatisfactory* otherwise. The Apdex score is then (Satisfactory +0.5(Tolerable)) / (Number of samples). In the example above, the Apdex score would be $(8 + 0.5(1))/10 = 0.85$.

Of course, the total response time perceived by the users includes many factors beyond your SaaS app's control. It includes DNS lookup, time to set up the TCP connection and send the HTTP request to the server, and Internet-induced latency in receiving a response containing enough content that the browser can start to draw something (so-called "time to glass," a term that will soon seem as quaint as "counterclockwise"). Especially when using curated PaaS, SaaS developer/operators have the most control over the code paths in their own apps: routing and dispatch, controller actions, model methods, and database access. We will therefore focus on measuring and improving responsiveness in those components.

Google believes[5] that this fact puts them under even more pressure to be responsive, so that getting a response from any Google service is no slower than contacting the service to begin with.

For small sites, a perfectly reasonable way to mitigate latency is to **overprovision** (provide excess resources relative to steady-state) at one or more tiers, as Section 2.4 suggested for the presentation and logic tiers. A few years ago, overprovisioning meant purchasing additional hardware that might sit idle, but pay-as-you-go cloud computing lets you "rent" the extra servers for pennies per hour only when needed. Indeed, companies like RightScale[6] offer just this service on top of Amazon EC2.

As we will see, a key insight that helps us is that *the same problems that push us out of the "PaaS-friendly" tier are the ones that will hinder scalability of our post-PaaS solutions*, so understanding what kinds of problems they are and how to solve them will serve you well in either situation.

What are the thresholds for user satisfaction on responsiveness? A classic 1968 study from the human-computer interaction literature (Miller 1968) found three interesting thresholds: if a computer system responds to a user action within 100 ms, it's perceived as instantaneous; within 1 second, the user will still perceive a cause-and-effect connection between their action and the response, but will perceive the system as sluggish; and after about 8 seconds, the user's attention drifts away from the task while waiting for a response. Surprisingly, more than thirty years later, a scholarly study in 2000 (Bhatti et al. 2000) and another by independent firm Zona Research in 2001 affirmed the "eight second rule." While many believe that a faster Internet and faster computers have raised users' expectations, the eight-second rule is still used as a general guideline. New Relic, whose monitoring service we introduce later, reported in March 2012 that the average page load for all pages they monitor worldwide is 5.3 seconds and the average Apdex score is 0.86.

Summary

- Responsiveness measures how "snappy" an interactive app feels to users. Given today's high-speed Internet connections and fast computers, responsiveness is dominated by latency. Service Level Objectives (SLOs) quantify responsiveness goals with statements such as "99% of requests within any 5-minute window should have a latency below 100 ms."

- The Apdex score is a simple SLO measure between 0.0 and 1.0 in which a site gets "full credit" for requests that complete within a site-specific latency threshold T, "half credit" for requests that complete within $4T$, and no credit for requests taking longer than that.

- The problems that threaten availability and responsiveness are the same whether we use PaaS or not, but it's worth trying to stay within the PaaS tier because it provides machinery to help mitigate those problems.

Self-Check 12.2.1. *True or False: From the perspective of responsiveness, faster is better.*
◇ False. Faster than 100 ms is not perceptible to people, and people abandon sites only when responsiveness is slows to 8 seconds or worse. ∎

12.3 Continuous Integration and Continuous Deployment

As we discussed in Section 1.2, prior to SaaS, software releases were major and infrequent milestones after which product maintenance responsibility passed largely to the Quality Assurance or Customer Service department. In contrast, Many Agile companies deploy new versions frequently (sometimes several times *per day*) and the developers stay close to operations and to customer needs.

In Agile development, making deployment a *non*-event requires complete automation, so that typing one command triggers all the actions to deploy a new version of the software, including cleanly aborting the deploy without modifying the released version if anything goes wrong. As with iteration-based TDD and BDD, by deploying frequently you become good at it, and by automating deployment you ensure that it's done consistently every time. As you've seen, Heroku provides support for deployment automation, though automation tools such as Capistrano[7] help automate Rails deployments in non-PaaS environments.

Of course, deployment can only be successful if the app is well tested and stable in development. Although we've already focused heavily on testing in this book, two things change in deployment. First, behavioral or performance differences between the deployed and development versions of your app may arise from differences between the development and production environments or differences between users' browsers (especially for JavaScript-intensive apps). Second, deployment also requires testing the app in ways it was *never* meant to be used—users submitting nonsensical input, browsers disabling cookies or JavaScript, miscreants trying to turn your site into a distributor of **malware** (as we describe further in Section 12.9)—and ensuring that it survives those conditions without compromising customer data or responsiveness.

A key technology in improving assurance for deployed code is **continuous integration** (CI), in which every change pushed to the code base triggers a set of integration tests to make sure nothing has broken. The idea is similar to how we used `autotest` in Chapter 8, except that the complete integration test suite may include tests that a developer might not normally run on his own, such as:

With compiled languages such as Java, CI usually means building the app and then testing it.

- Browser compatibility: correct behavior across different browsers that have differences in CSS or JavaScript implementations

- Version compatibility: correct behavior on different versions of the Ruby interpreter (Ruby 1.9, JRuby, and so on), the Rack application server, or for software that may be hosted in a variety of environments, different versions of Ruby gems

- Service-oriented architecture integration: correct behavior when external services on which the app depends behave in unexpected ways (very slow connection, return a flood of garbage information, and so on)

- Stress: performance and stress tests such as those described in Section 12.6

- Hardening: testing for protection against malicious attacks such as those described in Section 12.9

CI systems are typically integrated into the overall development process rather than simply running tests passively. For example, Salesforce's CI system runs 150,000+ tests in parallel across many machines, and if any test fails, it performs binary searches across checkins to pinpoint the culprit and automatically opens a bug report for the developer responsible for that checkin (Hansma 2011). Travis[8], an open-source hosted CI system for Ruby apps, runs integration tests whenever it is notified of a new code push via GitHub's **post-receive URI** repo; it then uses OAuth (which we met in Section 5.2) to check out the code runs `rake test`, another demonstration of using `rake` tasks for automation. SauceLabs[9] provides hosted CI focused on cross-browser testing: your app's Webdriver-based Cucumber scenarios are run against a variety of browsers and operating systems, with each test run captured as a screencast so you can visually inspect what the browser looked like for tests that failed.

Although deployment is a non-event, there is still a role for release milestones: they reassure the customer that new work is being deployed. For example, a customer-requested feature may require multiple commits to implement, each of which may include a deployment, but the overall feature remains "hidden" in the user interface until all changes are completed. "Turning on" the feature would be a useful release milestone. For this reason, many continuous-deployment workflows assign distinct and often whimsical labels to specific release points (such as "Bamboo" and "Cedar" for Heroku's software stacks), but just use the Git commit-id to identify deployments that don't include customer-visible changes.

Summary of Continuous Integration (CI):

- CI consists of running a set of integration tests prior to deployment that are usually more extensive than what a single developer would run on his own.

- CI relies heavily on automation. Workflows can be constructed that automatically trigger CI when commits are pushed to a specific repo or branch.

- Continuous deployment (automatic deployment to production when all CI tests pass) may result in several deployments per day, many of which include changes not visible to the customer that "build towards" a feature that will be unveiled at a Release milestone.

■ *Elaboration: Staging*

Many companies maintain an additional environment besides development and production called the *staging site*. The staging site is usually identical to production except that it is usually smaller in scale, uses a separate database with test data (possibly extracted from real customer data), and is closed to outside users. The rationale is that stress testing and integration testing a staging version is the closest possible experience to the production site. Another use is to test out migrations on a database that closely resembles the production database before deploying the migrations to production. Rails and its associated tools support staging by defining an additional `staging:` environment in `config/environments/staging.rb` and `config/database.yml`.

Self-Check 12.3.1. *Given the prevalence of continuous deployment in Agile software companies, how would you characterize the difference between a deployment and a release?*

◇ A release typically contains new features visible to the customer, whereas a deploy might contain new code that builds toward those features incrementally. ■

12.4   Releases and Feature Flags

As we know from Chapter 4, app changes sometimes require migrations to change the database schema. The challenge arises when the new code does not work with the old schema and vice-versa. To make the example concrete, suppose RottenPotatoes currently has a `moviegoers` table with a `name` column, but we want to change the schema to have separate `first_name` and `last_name` columns instead. If we change the schema before changing the code, the app will break because methods that expect to find the `name` column will fail. If we change the code before changing the schema, the app will break because the new methods will look for `first_name` and `last_name` columns that don't exist yet.

We could try to solve this problem by deploying the code and migration ***atomically***: take the service offline, apply the migration in Figure 12.2 to perform the schema change and copy the data into the new column, and bring the service back online. This approach is the simplest

http://pastebin.com/T32gfwVL

```
1  class ChangeNameToFirstAndLast < ActiveRecord::Migration
2    def up
3      add_column 'moviegoers', 'first_name', :string
4      add_column 'moviegoers', 'last_name', :string
5      Moviegoer.all.each do |m|
6        m.update_attributes(:first => $1, :last => $2) if
7          m.name =~ /^(.*)\s+(.*)$/
8      end
9      remove_column 'moviegoers', 'name'
10   end
11 end
```

Figure 12.2: A migration that changes the schema and modifies the data to accommodate the change. In Section 12.4 we explain why there is no down-migration method. (Use Pastebin to copy-and-paste this code.)

http://pastebin.com/NsarhWSE

```
1  class SplitName1 < ActiveRecord::Migration
2    def up
3      add_column 'moviegoers', 'first_name', :string
4      add_column 'moviegoers', 'last_name', :string
5      add_column 'moviegoers', 'migrated', :boolean
6      add_index 'moviegoers', 'migrated'
7    end
8  end
```

Figure 12.3: A partial migration that only adds columns but doesn't change or remove any. Section 12.8 explains why the index (line 6) is a good idea.

http://pastebin.com/5B8KcNze

```
1  class Moviegoer < ActiveRecord::Base
2    # here's version n+1, using Setler gem for feature flag:
3    scope :old_schema, where :migrated => false
4    scope :new_schema, where :migrated => true
5    def self.find_matching_names(string)
6      if Featureflags.new_name_schema
7        Moviegoer.new_schema.where('last_name LIKE :s OR first_name LIKE :s',
8          :s => "%#{string}%") +
9          Moviegoer.old_schema.where('name like ?', "%#{string}%")
10     else # use only old schema
11       Moviegoer.where('name like ?', "%#{string}%")
12     end
13   end
14   # automatically update records to new schema when they are saved
15   before_save :update_schema, :unless => lambda { |m| m.migrated? }
16   def update_schema
17     if name =~ /^(.*)\s+(.*)$/
18       self.first_name = $1
19       self.last_name = $2
20     end
21     self.migrated = true
22   end
23 end
```

Figure 12.4: Feature-flag wrapping for a model method that finds moviegoers by matching a string against their first or last names. Lines 15–22 install a before-save callback that will automatically update a record to the new schema whenever it's saved, so normal usage of the app will cause the records to be migrated piecemeal.

solution, but may cause unacceptable unavailability: a complex migration on a database of hundreds of thousands of rows can take tens of minutes or even hours to run.

The second option is to split the change across multiple deployments using a *feature flag*—a configuration variable whose value can be changed *while the app is running* to control which code paths in the app are executed. Notice that each step below is nondestructive: as we did with refactoring in Chapter 9, if something goes wrong at a given step the app is still left in a working intermediate state.

1. Create a migration that makes *only* those changes to the schema that *add* new tables or columns, including a column indicating whether the current record has been migrated to the new schema or not, as in Figure 12.3.

2. Create version $n+1$ of the app in which every code path affected by the schema change is split into two code paths, of which one or the other is executed based on the value of a *feature flag*. Critical to this step is that correct code will be executed regardless of the feature flag's value at any time, so the feature flag's value can be changed without stopping and restarting the app; typically this is done by storing the feature flag in a special database table. Figure 12.4 shows an example.

3. Deploy version $n+1$, which may require pushing the code to multiple servers, a process that can take several minutes.

4. Once deployment is complete (all servers have been updated to version $n + 1$ of the code), while the app is running set the feature flag's value to True. In the example in Figure 12.4, each record will be migrated to the new schema the next time it's modified for any reason. If you wanted to speed things up, you could also run a low-traffic background job that opportunistically migrates a few records at a time to minimize the additional load on the app, or migrates many records at a time during hours when the app is lightly loaded, if any. If something goes wrong at this step, turn off the feature flag; the code will revert to the behavior of version n, since the new schema is a proper superset of the old schema and the **before_save** callback is nondestructive (that is, it correctly updates the user's name in both the old and new schemata).

5. If all goes well, once all records have been migrated, deploy code version $n + 2$, in which the feature flag is removed and only the code path associated with the new schema remains.

6. Finally, apply a new migration that removes the old `name` column and the temporary `migrated` column (and therefore the index on that column).

What about a schema change that modifies a column's name or format rather than adding or removing columns? The strategy is the same: add a new column, remove the old column, and if necessary rename the new column, using feature flags during each transition so that every deployed version of the code works with both versions of the schema.

When we introduced migrations in Chapter 4, we noted that a migration can include both an **up** and a **down** method, yet the example in Figure 12.3 has no **down** method. Shouldn't we include one in case the upgrade goes awry? Surprisingly, no. Down-migrations are useful during development, but risky in production. Because they are rarely used, they are usually less-than-thoroughly tested, and in the inevitable panic following the discovery that something has gone awry, it is difficult to be confident that they will really work without causing even more damage.

Even if you are confident that the down-migration works correctly, other developers may have pushed irreversible migrations after the one you're trying to down-migrate. And at some point you yourself will need to create an irreversible migration, and you will need a way to recover from problems when applying it. Feature flags can help: if something is going wrong, revert the value of the feature flag so that the code reverts to its previous behavior, then take your time debugging the problem.

Summary

- To perform a complex upgrade that changes both the app code and the schema, use a feature flag whose value can be changed while the app is running. Start with a migration and code push that include both the old and new versions, and when this intermediate version is running, change the feature flag's value to enable the new code paths that use the new schema.

- Once all data has been incrementally migrated as a result of changing the feature flag's value, you can deploy a new migration and code push that eliminate the old code paths and old schema. On the other hand, if anything goes wrong during the rollout, you can change the feature flag's value back in order to continue using the old schema and code until you determine what went wrong.

- Deployed apps always move forward: if something goes wrong, fix it with another up-migration that undoes the damage rather than trying to apply a down-migration that hasn't been tested in production and may make things worse if applied.

■ *Elaboration: Other uses for feature flags*

Besides handling destructive migrations, feature flags have other uses as well:

- Preflight checking: roll out a feature to a small percentage of users only, in order to make sure the feature doesn't break anything or have a negative effect on overall site performance.

- A/B testing: roll out two different versions of a feature to two different sets of users to see which version most improves user retention, purchases, and so on.

- Complex feature: sometimes the complete functionality associated with a feature may require multiple incremental deployment cycles such as the one described above. In this case, a separate feature flag can be used to keep the feature hidden from the user interface until 100% of the new feature code has been deployed.

The rollout[10] gem supports the use of feature flags for all these cases.

Self-Check 12.4.1. *Which of the following are appropriate places to store the value of a simple Boolean feature flag and why: (a) a YAML file in the app's* `config` *directory, (b) a column in an existing database table, (c) a separate database table?*

◇ The point of a feature flag is to allow its value to be changed at runtime without modifying the app. Therefore (a) is a poor choice because a YAML file cannot be changed without touching the production servers while the app is running. ∎

12.5   Quantifying Availability

The best performance improvement is the transition from the nonworking state to the working state.

—John Ousterhout, designer of *magic* and Tcl/Tk

As we learned in Chapter 1, **availability** refers to the fraction of time your site is available and working correctly. For example, Google Apps guarantees[11] its enterprise customers a minimum of "three nines" or 99.9% availability, though Nygard wryly notes (Nygard 2007) that less-disciplined sites provide closer to "two eights" (88.0%).

Overprovisioning not only helps with latency, as mentioned above, but it also lets you deal gracefully with server crashes: temporarily losing one server degrades performance by $1/n$, so an easy solution is to overprovision by deploying $n + 1$ servers. However, at large scale, systematic overprovisioning is infeasible: services using 1,000 computers cannot readily afford to keep 200 additional servers turned on just for overprovisioning.

One way to improve the reliability of software is to make it more robust. **Defensive programming** is a philosophy that tries to anticipate potential software flaws and write code to handle them. Here are three examples:

- *Check input values.* A common cause of problems is for the user to input values that the developer doesn't expect. Checking that the input is in a reasonable range for individual values, that it is not too big for a series of data, and that the collection of inputs are logically consistent can reduce the chances of outages.

- *Check input data type.* Another mistake users can make is to enter an unexpected type of data in response to a query. Making sure the user enters a valid type of data increases the chances of success for the app.

- *Catch exceptions.* Modern programming languages offer the ability to execute code when exceptions occur, such as arithmetic overflow. Offering code that can catch any exception increases the chances of the app continuing to run well even when unexpected events occur.

Another availability challenge is a bug that lead to outages but only appears after a long time or under heavy load. A classic example is a resource leak: a long-running process eventually runs out of a resource, such as memory, because it cannot reclaim 100% of the unused resource due to either an application bug or the inherent design of a language or framework. **Software rejuvenation** is a long-established way to alleviate a resource leak: the Apache web server runs a number of identical worker processes, and when a given worker process has "aged" enough, that process stops accepting requests and dies, to be replaced by a fresh worker. Since only one worker ($1/n$ of total capacity) is "rejuvenated" at a time, this process is sometimes called **rolling reboot**, and most PaaS platforms employ some variant of it. Another example is running out of session storage when sessions are stored in a database table, which is why Rails' default behavior is to serialize each user's session object into a cookie stored at the user's browser, although this limits each user's session object to 4KiB in size.

Summary

- Availability measures the percentage of time over a specified window that your app is correctly responding to user requests. Availability is usually measured in "nines" with the gold standard of 99.999% ("five nines", corresponding to five minutes of downtime per year) set by the US telephone network and rarely matched by SaaS apps.

- *Defense programming* improves availability by adding code that handles potential flaws before they are known.

- *Software rejuvenation* improves availability by restarting members of an identical set of processes on a rotating schedule to neutralize resource leaks.

Self-Check 12.5.1. *For a SaaS app to scale to large numbers of users, it must maintain its* ____ *and* ____ *as the number of users increases, without increasing the* ____.
◇ Availability; responsiveness; cost per user ■

12.6 Monitoring and Finding Bottlenecks

If you're not monitoring it, it's probably broken.

—variously attributed

Given the importance of responsiveness and availability, how can we measure them, and if they're unsatisfactory, how can we identify what parts of our app need attention? *Monitoring* consists of collecting app performance data for analysis and visualization. In the case of SaaS, application performance monitoring (APM) refers to monitoring the Key Performance Indicators (KPIs) that *directly impact business value*. KPIs are by nature app-specific—for example, an e-tailer's KPIs might include responsiveness of adding an item to a shopping cart and percentage of user searches in which the user selects an item that is in the top 5 search results.

SaaS apps can be monitored internally or externally. Internal or passive monitoring works by instrumenting your app, adding data collection code to the app itself, the environment in which it runs, or both. Before cloud computing and the prominence of SaaS and highly-productive frameworks, such monitoring required installing programs that collected metrics periodically, inserting instrumentation into the source code of your app, or both. Today, the combination of hosted PaaS, Ruby's dynamic language features, and well-factored frameworks such as Rails allows internal monitoring without modifying your app's source code or installing software. For example, New Relic[12] unobtrusively collects instrumentation about your app's controller actions, database queries, and so on. Because the data is sent back to New Relic's SaaS site where you can view and analyze it, this architecture is sometimes called RPM for Remote Performance Monitoring. The free level of New Relic RPM is available as a Heroku add-on or a standalone gem you can deploy in your own non-PaaS production environment.

Internal monitoring can also occur during development, when it is often called *profiling*. New Relic and other monitoring solutions can be installed in development mode as well. How much profiling should you do? If you've followed best practices in writing and testing

What is monitored	Focus	Example tool
What is my site's availability and average response time, as seen by users around the world?	business-level	Pingdom[13], SiteScope[14]
What pages (views) in my app are most popular and what paths do customers follow through the app?	business-level	Google Analytics[15]
What controller actions or database queries are slowest?	app-level	New Relic[16], Scout[17]
What unexpected exceptions or errors did customers experience and what were they doing at the moment the error occurred?	app-level	Exceptional[18], AirBrake[19]
What is the health and resource usage of the OS-level processes that support my app (Apache web server, MySQL DB server, and so on)?	infrastructure/ process-level	god[20], *monit*

Figure 12.5: Different types of monitoring and example tools that provide them for Rails SaaS apps. All except the last row (process-level health monitoring) are delivered as SaaS and offer a free service tier that provides basic monitoring.

your app, it may be most productive to just deploy and see how the app behaves under load, especially given the unavoidable differences between the development and production environments, such as the lack of real user activity and the use of a development-only database such as SQLite3 rather than a highly tuned production database such as PostgreSQL. After all, with agile development, it's easy to deploy incremental fixes such as implementing basic caching (Section 12.7) and fixing abuses of the database (Sections 12.8).

A second kind of monitoring is external monitoring (sometimes called probing or active monitoring), in which a separate site makes live requests to your app to check availability and response time. Why would you need external monitoring given the detailed information available from internal monitoring that has access to your code? Internal monitoring may be unable to reveal that your app is sluggish or down altogether, especially if the problem is due to factors other than your app's code—for example, performance problems in the presentation tier or other parts of the software stack beyond your app's boundaries. External monitoring, like an integration test, is a true end-to-end test of a limited subset of your app's code paths as seen by actual users "from the outside." Figure 12.5 distinguishes different types of monitoring and some tools to perform them, many delivered as SaaS.

Once a monitoring tool has identified the slowest or most expensive requests, *stress testing* or *longevity testing* on a staging server can quantify the level of demand at which those requests become bottlenecks. The free and widely-used command line tool *httperf*, maintained by Hewlett-Packard Laboratories[21], can simulate a specified number of users requesting simple sequences of URIs from an app and recording metrics about the response times. Whereas tools like Cucumber let you write expressive scenarios and check arbitrarily complex conditions, httperf can only follow simple sequences of URIs and only checks whether a successful HTTP response was received from the server. In a typical stress test, the test engineer will set up several computers running httperf against the staging site and gradually increase the number of simulated users until some resource becomes the bottleneck.

Summary

- As with testing, no single type of monitoring will alert you of all problems: use a combination of internal and external (end-to-end) monitoring.

- Hosted monitoring such as Pingdom and PaaS-integrated monitoring such as New Relic greatly simplify monitoring compared to the early days of SaaS.

- Stress testing and longevity testing can reveal the bottlenecks in your SaaS app and frequently expose bugs that would otherwise remain hidden.

Self-Check 12.6.1. *Which of the following key performance indicators (KPIs) would be relevant for Application Performance Monitoring: CPU utilization of a particular computer; completion time of slow database queries; view rendering time of 5 slowest views.*
◇ Query completion times and view rendering times are relevant because they have a direct impact on responsiveness, which is generally a Key Performance Indicator tied to business value delivered to the customer. CPU utilization, while useful to know, does not directly tell us about the customer experience. ■

12.7 Improving Rendering and Database Performance With Caching

There are only two hard things in computer science: cache invalidation and naming things.

—Phil Karlton, attributed by Martin Fowler, who can't find the exact reference

The idea behind caching is simple: information that hasn't changed since the last time it was requested can simply be regurgitated rather than recomputed. In SaaS, caching can help two kinds of computation. First, if information needed from the database to complete an action hasn't changed, we can avoid querying the database at all. Second, if the information underlying a particular view or view fragment hasn't changed, we can avoid re-rendering the view (recall that rendering is the process of transforming Haml with embedded Ruby code and variables into HTML). In any caching scenario, we must address two issues:

1. **Naming:** how do we specify that the result of some computation should be cached for later reuse, and name it in a way that ensures it will be used only when that exact same computation is called for?

2. **Expiration:** How do we detect when the cached version is out of date (stale) because the information on which it depends has changed, and how do we remove it from the cache? The variant of this problem that arises in microprocessor design is often referred to as *cache invalidation.*

Figure 12.6 shows how caching can be used at each tier in the 3-tier SaaS architecture and what Rails entities are cached at each level. The simplest thing we could do is cache the entire HTML page resulting from rendering a particular controller action. For example, the **MoviesController#show** action and its corresponding view depend only on the attributes of the particular movie being displayed (the **@movie** variable in the controller method and Haml template). Figure 12.7 shows how to cache the entire HTML page for a movie, so that

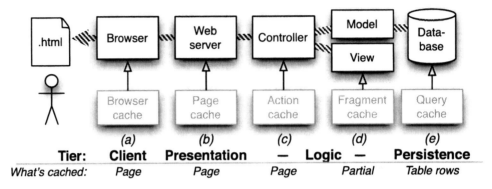

	(a)	(b)	(c)	(d)	(e)
Tier:	**Client**	**Presentation**	**— Logic —**		**Persistence**
What's cached:	*Page*	*Page*	*Page*	*Partial*	*Table rows*

Figure 12.6: The goal of multiple levels of caching is to satisfy each HTTP request as close to the user as possible. (a) A Web browser that has previously visited a page can reuse the copy in its local cache after verifying with the server that the page hasn't changed. (b) Otherwise, the Web server may be able to serve it from the page cache, bypassing Rails altogether. (c) Otherwise, if the page is generated by an action protected by a before-filter, Rails may be able to serve it from the action cache without querying the database or rendering any templates. (d) Otherwise, some of the fragments comprised by the view templates may be in the fragment cache. (e) As a last resort, the database's query cache serves the results of recent queries whose results haven't changed, such as Movie.all.

future requests to that page neither access the database nor re-run the Haml renderer, as in Figure 12.6(b).

Of course, this is unsuitable for controller actions protected by before-filters, such as pages that require the user to be logged in and therefore require executing the controller filter. In such cases, changing **caches_page** to **caches_action** will still execute any filters but allow Rails to deliver a cached page without consulting the database or re-rendering views, as in Figure 12.6(c). Figure 12.9 shows the benefits of page and action caching for this simple example. Note that in Rails page caching, the name of the cached object *ignores* embedded parameters in URIs such as /movies?ratings=PG+G, so parameters that affect how the page would be displayed should instead be part of the RESTful route, as in /movies/ratings/PG+G.

An in-between case involves action caching in which the main page content doesn't change, but the layout does. For example, your app/views/layouts/application.html.haml may include a message such as "Welcome, Alice" containing the name of the logged-in user. To allow action caching to work properly in this case, passing **:layout=>false** to **caches_action** will result in the layout getting fully re-rendered but the action (content part of the page) taking advantage of the action cache. Keep in mind that since the controller action won't be run, any such dynamic content appearing in the layout must be set up in a before-filter.

Page-level caching isn't useful for pages whose content changes dynamically. For example, the list of movies page (**MoviesController#index** action) changes when new movies are added or when the user filters the list by MPAA rating. But we can still benefit from caching by observing that the index page consists largely of a collection of table rows, each of which depends only on the attributes of one specific movie, as Figure 5.2 in Section 5.1 shows. Figure 12.8 shows how adding a single line to the partial of Figure 5.2 caches the rendered HTML fragment corresponding to each movie.

A convenient shortcut provided by Rails is that if the argument to **cache** is an ActiveRecord object whose table includes an updated_at or updated_on column, the cache will auto-expire a fragment if its table row has been updated since the fragment was first cached.

http://pastebin.com/7PycU0MK

```
1  class MoviesController < ApplicationController
2    caches_page :show
3    cache_sweeper :movie_sweeper
4    def show
5      @movie = Movie.find(params[:id])
6    end
7  end
```

http://pastebin.com/UzJHx6As

```
1   class MovieSweeper < ActionController::Caching::Sweeper
2     observe Movie
3     # if a movie is created or deleted, movie list becomes invalid
4     #   and rendered partials become invalid
5     def after_save(movie)    ; invalidate ; end
6     def after_destroy(movie) ; invalidate ; end
7     private
8     def invalidate
9       expire_action :action => ['index', 'show']
10      expire_fragment 'movie'
11    end
12  end
```

Figure 12.7: (Top) Line 2 specifies that Rails should cache the result of the show action. Action caching is implemented as a before-filter that checks whether a cached version should be used and an around-filter that captures and caches the rendered output, making it an example of the Decorator design pattern (Section 11.4). (Bottom) This "sweeper," referenced by line 3 of the controller, uses the Observer design pattern (Section 11.7) to add ActiveRecord lifecycle hooks (Section 5.1) to expire any objects that might become stale as a result of updating a particular movie.

http://pastebin.com/XxPdsdQf

```
1  -# A single row of the All Movies table
2   - cache(movie) do
3     %tr
4       %td= movie.title
5       %td= movie.rating
6       %td= movie.release_date
7       %td= link_to "More about #{movie.title}", movie_path(movie)
```

Figure 12.8: Compared to Figure 5.2 in Section 5.1, only line 2 has been added. Rails will generate a name for the cached fragment based on the pluralized resource name and primary key, for example, movies/23.

Nonetheless, for clarity, line 10 of the sweeper in Figure 12.7 shows how to explicitly expire a fragment whose name matches the argument of **cache** whenever the underlying **movie** object is saved or destroyed.

Unlike action caching, which avoids running the controller action at all, checking the fragment cache occurs *after* the controller action has run. Given this fact, you may already be wondering how fragment caching helps reduce the load on the database. For example, suppose we add a partial to the list of movies page to display the **@top_5** movies based on average review scores, and we add a line to the **index** controller action to set up the variable:

http://pastebin.com/3Ba360Vt

```
1  -# a cacheable partial for top movies
2  - cache('top_moviegoers') do
3      %ul#topmovies
4        - @top_5.each do |movie|
5          %li= moviegoer.name
```

http://pastebin.com/x88niV53

```
1  class MoviegoersController < ApplicationController
2    def index
3      @movies = Movie.all
4      @top_5 = Movie.joins(:reviews).group('movie_id').
5        order("AVG(potatoes) DESC").limit(5)
6    end
7  end
```

Action caching is now less useful, because the **index** view may change when a new movie is added *or* when a review is added (which might change what the top 5 reviewed movies are). If the controller action is run before the fragment cache is checked, aren't we negating the benefit of caching, since setting **@top_5** in lines 4–5 of the controller method causes a database query?

Surprisingly, no. In fact, lines 4–5 *don't* cause a query to happen: they construct an object that *can* do the query if it's ever asked for the result! This is called *lazy evaluation*, an enormously powerful programming-language technique that comes from the *lambda calculus* underlying functional programming. Lazy evaluation is used in Rails' ActiveRelation (ARel) subsystem, which is used by ActiveRecord. The actual database query doesn't happen until **each** is called in line 5 of of the Haml template, because that's the first time the ActiveRelation object is asked to produce a value. But since that line is inside the **cache** block starting on line 2, if the fragment cache hits, the line will never be executed and therefore the database will never be queried. Of course, you must still include logic in your cache sweeper to correctly expire the top-5-movies fragment when a new review is added.

In summary, both page- and fragment-level caching reward our ability to separate things that change (non-cacheable units) from those that stay the same (cacheable units). In page or action caching, split controller actions protected by before-filters into an "unprotected" action that can use page caching and a filtered action that can use action caching. (In an extreme case, you can even enlist a *content delivery network* (CDN) such as Amazon CloudFront to replicate the page at hundreds of servers around the world.) In fragment caching, use partials to isolate each noncacheable entity, such as a single model instance, into its own partial that can be fragment-cached.

Earlier versions of Rails lacked lazy query evaluation, so controller actions had to explicitly check the fragment cache to avoid needless queries—very non-DRY.

No cache	Action cache	Speedup vs. no cache	Page cache	Speedup vs. no cache	Speedup vs. action cache
449 ms	57 ms	**8x**	21ms	**21x**	**3x**

Figure 12.9: For a PostgreSQL shared database on Heroku containing 1K movies and over 100 reviews per movie, the table shows the time in milliseconds to retrieve a list of the first 100 reviews sorted by creation date, with and without page and action caching. The numbers are from the log files visible with `heroku logs`.

Summary of caching:

To maximize the benefits of caching, separate cacheable from non-cacheable units: controller actions can be split into cacheable and non-cacheable versions depending on whether a before-filter must be run, and partials can be used to break up views into cacheable fragments.

■ *Elaboration: Where are cached objects stored?*

In development, cached objects are generally stored in the local file system. On Heroku, the Memcachier addon stores cached content in the in-memory database `memcached` (pronounced *mem-cash-dee*; the suffix *-d* reflects the Unix convention for naming ***daemon*** processes that run constantly in the background). Rails cache stores must implement a common API so that different stores can be used in different environments—a great example of Dependency Injection, which we encountered in Section 11.6.

Self-Check 12.7.1. *We mentioned that passing* :**layout**=>**false** *to* **caches_action** *provides most of the benefit of action caching even when the page layout contains dynamic elements such as the logged-in user's name. Why doesn't the* **caches_page** *method also allow this option?*

◇ Since page caching is handled by the presentation tier, not the logic tier, a hit in the page cache means that Rails is bypassed entirely. The presentation tier has a copy of the whole page, but only the logic tier knows what part of the page came from the layout and what part came from rendering the action. ■

12.8 Avoiding Abusive Database Queries

As we saw in Section 2.4, the database will ultimately limit horizontal scaling—not because you run out of space to store tables, but more likely because a single computer can no longer sustain the necessary number of queries per second while remaining responsive. When that happens, you will need to turn to techniques such as sharding and replication, which are beyond the scope of this book (but see To Learn More for some suggestions).

Even on a single computer, database performance tuning is enormously complicated. The widely-used open source database MySQL has dozens of configuration parameters, and most database administrators (DBAs) will tell you that at least half a dozen of these are "critical" to getting good performance. Therefore, we focus on how to keep your database usage within the limit that will allow it to be hosted by a PaaS provider: Heroku, Amazon Web Services, Microsoft Azure, and others all offer hosted relational databases managed by professional DBAs responsible for baseline tuning. Many useful SaaS apps can be built at this scale—for example, all of Pivotal Tracker[22] fits in a database on a single computer.

One way to relieve pressure on your database is to avoid needlessly expensive queries.

http://pastebin.com/kN8Fdz2H

```
 1  # assumes class Moviegoer with has_many :movies, :through => :reviews
 2
 3  # in controller method:
 4  @fans = Moviegoer.where("zip = ?", code) # table scan if no index!
 5
 6  # in view:
 7  - @fans.each do |fan|
 8    - fan.movies.each do |movie|
 9      // BAD: each time thru this loop causes a new database query!
10      %p= movie.title
11
12  # better: eager loading of the association in controller.
13  # Rails automatically traverses the through-association between
14  # Moviegoers and Movies through Reviews
15  @fans = Moviegoer.where("zip = ?", code).includes(:movies)
16  # GOOD: preloading movies reviewed by fans avoids N queries in view.
17
18  # BAD: preload association but don't use it in view:
19  - @fans.each do |fan|
20    %p= @fan.name
21    // BAD: we never used the :movies that were preloaded!
```

Figure 12.10:   The query in the controller action (line 4) accesses the database once to retrieve rows of @fans, but each pass through the loop in lines 8–10 causes another separate database access, resulting in $n+1$ accesses for a fan who has reviewed n movies. Line 15, in contrast, performs a single *eager load* query that also retrieves all the movies, which is nearly as fast as line 4 since most of the overhead of small queries is in performing the database access.

http://pastebin.com/zrGFXsbt

```
 1  class AddEmailIndexToMoviegoers < ActiveRecord::Migration
 2    def up
 3      add_index 'moviegoers', 'email', :unique => true
 4      # :unique is optional - see text for important warning!
 5      add_index 'moviegoers', 'zip'
 6    end
 7  end
```

Figure 12.11:   Adding an index on a column speeds up queries that match on that column. The index is even faster if you specify :unique, which is a promise you make that no two rows will have the same value for the indexed attribute; to avoid errors in case of a duplicate value, use this in conjunction with a uniqueness validation as described in Section 5.1).

Two common mistakes for less-experienced SaaS authors arise in the presence of associations:

1. The *n+1 queries* problem occurs when traversing an association performs more queries than necessary.

2. The *table scan* problem occurs when your tables lack the proper **indices** to speed up certain queries.

Lines 1–17 of Figure 12.10 illustrate the so-called n+1 queries problem when traversing associations, and also show why the problem is more likely to arise when code creeps into your views: there would be no way for the view to know the damage it was causing. Of course, just as bad is eager loading of information you won't use, as in lines 18–21 of Figure 12.10. The bullet[23] gem helps detect both problems.

Another database abuse to avoid is queries that result in a **full table scan**. Consider line 4 of Figure 12.10: in the worst case, the database would have to examine every row of the moviegoers table to find a match on the email column, so the query will run more and more

# of reviews:	2000	20,000	200,000		200,000
Read 100, no indices	0.94	1.33	5.28	Create 1K, no indices	9.69
Read 100, FK indices	0.57	0.63	0.65	Create 1K, all indices	11.30
Performance	166%	212%	808%	Performance	−17%

Figure 12.12: For a PostgreSQL shared database on Heroku containing 1K movies, 1K moviegoers, and 2K to 200K reviews, this table shows the benefits and penalties of indexing. The first part compares the time in seconds to read 100 reviews with no indices vs. with foreign key (FK) indices on `movie_id` and `moviegoer_id` in the `reviews` table. The second part compares the time to create 1,000 reviews in the absence of indices and in the presence of indices over *every possible pair* of `reviews` columns, showing that even in this pathological case, the penalty for using indices is slight.

slowly as the table grows, taking time $O(n)$ for a table with n rows. The solution is to add a ***database index*** on the `moviegoers.email` column, as Figure 12.11 shows. An index is a separate data structure maintained by the database that uses ***hashing*** techniques over the column values to allow constant-time access to any row when that column is used as the constraint. You can have more than one index on a given table and even have indices based on the values of multiple columns. Besides obvious attributes named explicitly in **where** queries, ***foreign keys*** (the subject of the association) should usually be indexed. For example, in the example in Figure 12.10, the **moviegoer_id** field in the `reviews` table would need an index in order to speed up the query implied by **fan.movies**.

Of course, indices aren't free: each index takes up space proportional to the number of table rows, and since every index on a table must be updated when table rows are added or modified, updates to heavily-indexed tables may be slowed down. However, because of the read-mostly behavior of typical SaaS apps and their relatively simple queries compared to other database-backed systems such as Online Transaction Processing (OLTP), your app will likely run into many other bottlenecks before indices begin to limit its performance. Figure 12.12 shows an example of the dramatic performance improvement provided by indices.

Summary of avoiding abusive queries:

- The $n + 1$ queries problem, in which traversing a 1-to-n association results in $n + 1$ short queries rather than a single large query, can be avoided by judicious use of eager loading.

- Full-table scans in queries can be avoided by judicious use of database indices, but each index takes up space and slows down update performance. A good starting point is to create indices for all foreign key columns and all columns referenced in the **where** clause of frequent queries.

■ *Elaboration: SQL EXPLAIN*

Many SQL databases, including MySQL and PostgreSQL (but not SQLite), support an `EXPLAIN` command that describes the *query plan*: which tables will be accessed to perform a query and which of those tables have indices that will speed up the query. Unfortunately, the output format of `EXPLAIN` is database-specific. Starting with Rails 3.2, EXPLAIN is automatically run[24] on queries that take longer than a developer-specified threshold in development mode, and the query plan is written to `development.log`. The query_reviewer[25] gem, which currently works only with MySQL, runs `EXPLAIN` on all queries generated by ActiveRecord and inserts the results into a `div` at the top of every page view in development mode.

Self-Check 12.8.1. *An index on a database table usually speeds up _____ at the expense of _____ and _____.*

◇ Query performance at the expense of space and table-update performance ■

12.9 Security: Defending Customer Data in Your App

My response was "Congratulations, Ron, that should work."

—Len Adleman, reacting to Ron Rivest's encryption proposal, 1977

As security is its own field in computing, there is no shortage of material to review or topics to study. Perhaps as a result, security experts have boiled down their advice into principles that developers can follow. Here are three:

- The *principle of least privilege* states that a user or software component should be given no more privilege—that is, no further access information and resources—than what is necessary to perform its assigned task. This is analogous to the "need-to-know" principle for classified information. One example of this principle in the Rails world is that the Unix processes corresponding to your Rails app, your database, and the Web server (presentation tier) should run with low privilege and in an environment where they cannot even create new files in the file system. Good PaaS providers, including Heroku, offer a deployment environment configured in just this way.

- The *principle of fail-safe defaults* states that unless a user or software component is given explicit access to an object, it should be denied access to the object. That is, the default should be denial of access. Proper use of **attr_accessible** as described in Section 5.2 follows this principle.

- The *principle of psychological acceptability* states that the protection mechanism should not make the app harder to use than if there were no protection. That is, the user interface needs to be easy to use so that the security mechanisms are routinely followed.

The rest of this section covers five specific security vulnerabilities that are particularly relevant for SaaS applications: protecting data using encryption, cross-site request forgery, SQL injection and cross-site scripting, prohibiting calls to private controller methods, and self-denial-of-service.

Protecting Data Using Encryption. Since competent PaaS providers make it their business to stay abreast of security-related issues in the infrastructure itself, developers who use

Ronald Rivest (1947–), Adi Shamir (1952–), and Leonard Adleman (1945–) received the 2002 Turing Award for making public-key cryptography useful in practice. In the eponymous RSA algorithm, the security properties of keypairs are based on the difficulty of factoring large integers and performing modular exponentiation, that is, determining m such that $C = m^E \bmod N$.

PaaS can focus primarily on attacks that can be thwarted by good coding practices. Data-related attacks on SaaS attempt to compromise one or more of the three basic elements of security: privacy, authenticity, and data integrity. The goal of **Transport Layer Security** (TLS) and its predecessor Secure Sockets Layer (SSL) is to **encrypt** all HTTP traffic by transforming it using cryptographic techniques driven by a *secret* (such as a password) known only to the two communicating parties. Running HTTP over such a secure connection is called HTTPS.

Establishing a shared secret with a site you've never visited before is a challenging problem whose practical solution, **public key cryptography**, is credited to Ron Rivest, Adi Shamir and Len Adleman (hence **RSA**). A *principal* or communicating entity generates a *keypair* consisting of two matched parts, one of which is made public (accessible to everyone in the world) and the other of which is kept secret.

A keypair has two important properties:

1. A message encrypted using the private key can only be decrypted using the public key, and vice-versa.

2. The private key cannot be deduced from the public key, and vice-versa.

Property 1 provides the foundation of SSL: if you receive a message that is decryptable with Bob's public key, only someone possessing Bob's private key could have created it. A variation is the digital signature: to attest to a message, Bob generates a one-way digest of the message (a short "fingerprint" that would change if the message were altered) and encrypts the digest using his private key as a way of attesting "I, Bob, vouch for the information in the message represented by this digest."

To offer SSL-secured access to his site `rottenpotatoes.com`, Bob generates a keypair consisting of a public part KU and a private part KP. He proves his identity using conventional means such as government-issued IDs to a **certificate authority** (CA) such as VeriSign. The CA then uses its own private key CP to sign an **SSL certificate** that states, in effect, "`rottenpotatoes.com` has public key KU." Bob installs the certificate on his server and enables his SaaS stack to accept SSL connections—usually trivial in a PaaS environment. Finally, he enables SSL in his Rails app by adding **force_ssl**[26] to any controller to force all its actions to use SSL, or using the **:only** or **:except** filter options to limit which actions are affected.

The CA's public key CU is built into most Web browsers, so when Alice's browser first connects to `https://rottenpotatoes.com` and requests the certificate, it can verify the CA's signature and obtain Bob's public key KU from the certificate. Alice's browser then chooses a random string as the secret, encrypts it using KU, and sends it to `rottenpotatoes.com`, which alone can decrypt it using KP. This shared secret is then used to encrypt HTTP traffic using much faster **symmetric-key cryptography** for the duration of the session. At this point, any content sent via HTTPS is reasonably secure from eavesdroppers, and Alice's browser believes the server it's talking to is the genuine RottenPotatoes server, since only a server possessing KP could have completed the key exchange step.

It's important to recognize that this is the limit of what SSL can do. In particular, the server knows nothing about Alice's identity, and no guarantees can be made about Alice's data other than its privacy during transmission to RottenPotatoes.

Cross-site request forgery. A CSRF attack (sometimes pronounced "sea-surf") involves tricking the user's browser into visiting a different web site for which the user has a valid cookie, and performing an illicit action on that site as the user. For example, suppose Alice

Section A.5 introduces the `ssh` (Secure Shell) tools included with the bookware.

Alice and Bob are the *archetypal principals* who appear in security scenarios, along with eavesdropper Eve, malicious Mallory, and other colorful characters.

force_ssl is implemented as a before-filter that causes an immediate redirect from `http://site/action` to `https://site/action`.

http://pastebin.com/h1spRdpd

```
1  class MoviesController
2    def search
3      movies = Movie.where("name = '#{params[:title]}'") # UNSAFE!
4      # movies = Movie.where("name = ?", params[:title])   # safe
5    end
6  end
```

Figure 12.13: Code that is vulnerable to a SQL injection attack. Uncommenting line 4 and deleting line 3 would thwart the attack using a *prepared statement*, which lets ActiveRecord "sanitize" malicious input before inserting it in the query.

params[:title]	SQL statement
Aladdin	SELECT "movies".* FROM "movies" WHERE (title='Aladdin')
'); DROP TABLE "movies"; --	SELECT "movies".* FROM "movies" WHERE (title=''); DROP TABLE "movies"; --

Figure 12.14: If Mallory enters the text in the second row of the table as a movie title, line 3 of Figure 12.13 becomes a dangerous SQL statement that deletes the whole table. (The final --, the SQL comment character, avoids executing any SQL code that might have come after DROP TABLE.) SQL injection was often successful against early frameworks such as PHP, in which queries were hand-coded by programmers.

has recently logged into her MyBank.com account, so her browser now has a valid cookie for MyBank.com showing that she is logged in. Now Alice visits a chat forum where malicious Mallory has posted a message with the following embedded "image":

http://pastebin.com/rtzYtTmj

```
1  <p>Here's a risque picture of me:
2    <img src="http://mybank.com/transfer/mallory/5000">
3  </p>
```

When Alice views the blog post, or if she receives an email with this link embedded in it, her browser will try to "fetch" the image from this RESTful URI, which happens to transfer $5000 into Mallory's account. Alice will see a "broken image" icon without realizing the damage. CSRF is often combined with Cross-site Scripting (see below) to perform more sophisticated attacks.

There are two steps to thwarting such attacks. The first is to ensure that RESTful actions performed using the GET HTTP method have no side effects. An action such as bank withdrawal or completing a purchase should be handled by a POST. This makes it harder for the attacker to deliver the "payload" using embedded asset tags like IMG, which browsers *always* handle using GET. The second step is to insert a randomly-generated string based on the current session into every page view and arrange to include its value as a hidden form field on every form. This string will look different for Alice than it will for Bob, since their sessions are distinct. When a form is submitted without the correct random string, the submission is rejected. Rails automates this defense: all you need to do is render **csrf_meta_tags** in every such view and add **protect_from_forgery** to any controller that might handle a form submission. Indeed, when you use rails new to generate a new app, these defenses are included in app/views/layouts/application.html.haml and app/controllers/application_controller.rb respectively.

SQL injection and cross-site scripting. Both of these attacks exploit SaaS apps that handle attacker-provided content unsafely. In ***SQL injection***, Mallory enters form data that she hopes will be interpolated directly into a SQL query statement executed by the app. Figure 12.14 shows an example and its defense—using prepared statements. In ***cross-site scripting***, Mallory prepares a fragment of JavaScript code that performs a harmful action;

http://pastebin.com/rxwYGwB6

```
1 | <h2><%= movie.title %></h2>
2 | <p>Released on <%= movie.release_date %>. Rated <%= movie.rating %>.</p>
```

http://pastebin.com/ytYnC2h6

```
1 | <h2><script>alert("Danger!");</script></h2>
2 | <p>Released on 1992-11-25 00:00:00 UTC. Rated G.</p>
```

http://pastebin.com/QN5KcdTy

```
1 | <h2>&lt;script&gt;alert("Danger!");&lt;/script&gt;</h2>
2 | <p> Released on 1992-11-25 00:00:00 UTC. Rated G.</p>
```

Figure 12.15: Top: a fragment of a view template using Rails' built-in eRB renderer rather than Haml. Middle: Mallory manually enters a new movie whose "title" is the string <script>alert("Danger!");</script>. When this movie's Show action is rendered, the "title" will be inserted directly into the HTML view, causing the JavaScript code to be executed when Alice's browser renders the page. Bottom: The defense is to "sanitize" any input that will be interpolated into HTML. Happily, Haml's = operator does this automatically, resulting in impotent code where the angle brackets have been properly escaped for HTML.

her goal is to get RottenPotatoes to render that fragment as part of a displayed HTML page, triggering execution of the script. Figure 12.15 shows a benign example and the defense; real examples often include JavaScript code that steals Alice's valid cookie and transmits it to Mallory, who can now "hijack" Alice's session by passing Alice's cookie as her own. Worse, even if the XSS attack only succeeds in reading the page content from another site and not the cookie, the page content might contain the CSRF-prevention token generated by `csrf_meta_tags` corresponding to Alice's session, so XSS is often used to enable CSRF.

Prohibiting calls to private controller methods. It's not unusual for controllers to include "sensitive" helper methods that aren't intended to be called by end-user actions, but only from inside an action. Use **protected** for any controller method that isn't the target of a user-initiated action and check `rake routes` to make sure no routes include wildcards that could match a nonpublic controller action.

Self-denial-of-service. A malicious denial-of-service attack seeks to keep a server busy doing useless work, preventing access by legitimate users. You can inadvertently leave yourself open to these attacks if you allow arbitrary users to perform actions that result in a lot of work for the server, such as allowing the upload of a large file or generating an expensive report. (Uploading files also carries other risks, so you should "outsource" that responsibility to other services, such as the Progstr-Filer Heroku addon[28].) A defense is to use a separate background task such as a Heroku worker[29] to offload long-running jobs from the main app server.

A final warning about security is in order. The "arms race" between SaaS developers and evildoers is ongoing, so even a carefully maintained site isn't 100% safe. In addition to defending against attacks on customer data, you should *also* be careful about handling sensitive data. Don't store passwords in cleartext; store them encrypted, or better yet, rely on third-party authentication as described in Section 5.2, to avoid embarrassing[30] incidents[31] of[32] password[33] theft.[34] Don't even *think* of storing credit card numbers, even encrypted. The Payment Card Industry association imposes an audit burden costing tens of thousands of dollars per year to any site that does this (to prevent credit[35] card[36] fraud[37]), and the burden is only slightly less severe if your code ever manipulates a credit card number even if you don't store it. Instead, offload this responsibility to sites like PayPal[38] or Stripe[39] that specialize in meeting these heavy burdens.

Security firm Symantec reported[27] that XSS accounted for over 80% of security vulnerabilities in 2007.

JavaScript is the language of choice for XSS, but any technology that mixes code into HTML pages is vulnerable, including ActiveX, VBScript, and Flash.

When Amazon put 1000 Xbox 360 units on sale for just $100 rather than the list price of $399, during the first 5 minutes the site was brought to its knees by millions of users clicking "Reload" to get the deal.

Attack	Rails Defenses
Eavesdropping	Install SSL certificate and use **force_ssl** in controllers (optional: **:only=>** or **:except=>** specific actions) to encrypt traffic using SSL
Cross-site request forgery (CSRF)	Render **csrf_meta_tags** in all views (for example, by including it in main layout) and specify **protect_from_-forgery** in **ApplicationController**
Cross-site scripting (XSS)	Use Haml's = to sanitize HTML during rendering
SQL injection	Use prepared queries with placeholders, rather than interpolating strings directly into queries
Mass assignment of sensitive attributes	Use **attr_protected** or **attr_-accessible** to protect sensitive attributes from user assignment (Section 5.2)
Executing protected actions	Use **before_filter** to guard sensitive public methods in controllers; declare nonpublic controller methods as **private** or **protected**
Self-denial-of-service, pathologically slow clients	Use separate background workers to perform long-running tasks, rather than tying up the app server

Figure 12.16: Some common attacks against SaaS apps and the Rails mechanisms that defend against them.

> **Summary of defending customer data:**
>
> - Following the principles of **least privilege**, **fail-safe defaults**, and **psychological acceptability** can lead to more secure systems.
>
> - SSL and TLS keep data private as it travels over an HTTP connection, but provide no other privacy guarantees. They also assure the browser of the server's identity (unless the Certificate Authority that originally certified the server's identity has been compromised), but not vice-versa.
>
> - Developers who deploy on a well-curated PaaS should focus primarily on attacks that can be thwarted by good coding practices. Figure 12.16 summarizes some common attacks on SaaS apps and the Rails mechanisms that thwart them.
>
> - In addition to deploying app-level defenses, particularly sensitive customer data should either be stored in encrypted form or not at all, by outsourcing its handling to specialized services.

Self-Check 12.9.1. *True or false: If a site has a valid SSL certificate, Cross-Site Request Forgery (CSRF) and SQL Injection attacks are harder to mount against it.*
◇ False. The security of the HTTP channel is irrelevant to both attacks. CSRF relies only on a site erroneously accepting a request that has a valid cookie but originated elsewhere. SQL injection relies only on the SaaS server code unsafely interpolating user-entered strings into a SQL query. ∎

Self-Check 12.9.2. *Why can't CSRF attacks be thwarted by checking the Referer: header of an HTTP request?*
◇ The header can be trivially forged. ∎

12.10 The Plan-And-Document Perspective

Non-functional requirements can be more important than adding new features, as violations can cause loss of millions of dollars, millions of users, or both. For example, sales for Amazon.com in the fourth quarter of 2012 was $23.3B, so the loss of income due to Amazon being down just one hour would average $10M. That same year a break-in of the Nebraska Student Information System[40] revealed social security numbers of anyone who applied to the University of Nebraska since 1985, estimated as 650,000 people. If customers can't trust a SaaS app, they will stop using it no matter what the set of features.

Performance. Performance is not a topic of focus in conventional software engineering, in part because it has been the excuse for bad practices and in part because it is well covered elsewhere. Performance can be part of the non-functional requirements and then later in acceptance-level testing to ensure the performance requirement is met.

Release Management. Plan-and-document processes often produce software products that have major releases and minor releases. Using the Rails as an example, the last number of version 3.2.12 is a minor release, the middle number is a major release, and the first number is such a large change that it breaks APIs so that apps need to be ported again to this version. A release includes everything: code, configuration files, any data, and documentation. Release management includes picking dates for the release, information on how it will be distributed, and documenting everything so that you know what exactly is in the release and how to make it again so that it is easy to change when you have to make the next release. Release management is considered a case of configuration management in Plan-and-Document processes, which we review in Section 10.7.

Reliability. The main tool in our bag to make a system dependable is redundancy. By having more hardware than the absolute minimum needed to run the app and store the data, the system has the potential to continue even if a component fails. As all physical hardware has a non-zero failure rate, one redundancy guideline is to make sure there is *no single point of failure*, as it can be the Achilles' Heel of a system. Generally, the more redundancy the lower the chance of failure. As highly redundant systems can be expensive, it is important to have an adult conversation with the customer to see how dependable the app must be.

Dependability is holistic, involving the software and the operators as well as the hardware. No matter how dependable the hardware is, errors in the software and mistakes by the operators can lead to outages that reduce the **mean time to failure** (**MTTF**)ndexMean time to failure (MTTF). As dependency is a function of the weakest link in the chain, it may be more effective to train operators how to run the app or to reduce the flaws in the software than to buy more redundant hardware to run the app. Since "to err is human," systems should include safeguards to tolerate and prevent operator errors as well as hardware failures.

A foundational assumption of the Plan-and-Document processes is that an organization can make the production of software predictable and repeatable by honing its process of software development, which should also lead to more reliable software. Hence, organizations commonly record everything they can from projects to learn what they can do to improve their process. For example, the ISO 9001 standard is granted if companies have processes in place, a method to see if the process is being followed, and record the results for each project so as to make improvements in their process. Surprisingly, standardization approval is not about the quality of the resulting code, it is just about the development process.

Finally, like performance, reliability can be measured. We can improve availability either taking longer between failures (MTTF) or by making the app reboot faster—**mean time between repairs** (**MTTR**)—as this equation shows:

$$\text{unavailability} \approx \frac{\text{MTTR}}{\text{MTTF}} \tag{12.1}$$

While it is hard to measure improvements in MTTF, as it can take a long time to record failures, we can easily measure MTTR. We just crash a computer and see how long it takes the app to reboot. And what we can measure, we can improve. Hence, it may be much more cost-effective to try to improve MTTR than to improve MTTF since it is easier to measure progress. However, they are not mutually exclusive, so developers can try to increase dependability by following both paths.

Security. While reliability can depend on probability to calculate availability—it is unlikely that several disks will fail simultaneously if the storage system is designed without hidden dependencies—this is not the case for security. Here there is an human adversary who is probing the corner cases of your design for weaknesses and then taking advantage of them to break into your system. The Common Vulnerabilities and Exposures database[41] lists common attacks to help developers understand the difficulty of security challenges.

Fortunately, defensive programming to make your system more robust against failures can also help make your system more secure. For example, in a **buffer overflow attack**, the adversary sends too much data to a buffer to overwrite nearby memory with their own code hidden inside the data. Checking the inputs to ensure that that the user is not sending too much data can prevent such attacks. Similarly, the basis of **arithmetic overflow attack** might be to supply such an unexpectedly large number that when added to another number it will look small due to the wraparound nature of overflow with 32-bit arithmetic. Checking input values or catching exceptions might prevent this attack. As computers today normally have multiple processors ("multicore"), an increasingly common attack is a **data race attack** where the program has non-deterministic behavior depending on the input. These concurrent programming flaws are much harder to detect and correct.

Testing is much more challenging for security, but one approach is use a **tiger team** as the adversaries who perform **penetration tests**. The team reports back to the developers the uncovered vulnerabilities.

Summary Given the importance of keeping the users trust, non-functional features can be more important than functional features, especially for SaaS apps.

- The Plan-and-Document processes speak little about performance, except as a potential piece of the System Requirement Specification that is later validated as part of the Master Test Plan.

- Releases, considered part of Configuration Management, are significant events in Plan-and-Document processes. A release wraps up everything about the project at that time, including documentation about how the release was made as well as the code, configuration files, data, and product documentation.

- Redundancy is the key to dependable system, with highly available systems aiming at no single point of failure. The **Mean Time To Failure** is a function of the whole system, including hardware and operators along with the software. Another way to improve availability that is easier to measure than MTTF is to concentrate on reducing **Mean Time To Repair**.

- Unlike the probabilistic basis for failures in dependability analysis, security is based on an intelligent adversary who is purposely exploiting unexpected events, such as buffer overflows.

Self-Check 12.10.1. *Besides buffer overflows, arithmetic overflows, and data races, list another potential bug that can lead to security problem by violating one of the three security principles listed above.*

◇ One example is improper initialization, which could violate the principle of fail-safe defaults. ∎

12.11 Fallacies and Pitfalls

 Fallacy: **All the extra effort for testing very rare conditions in Continuous Integration tests is more trouble than it's worth.**

At 1 million hits per day, a "rare" one-in-a-million event is statistically likely every day. 1

Activity	Added latency	Measured effect
Amazon.com page view	100 ms	1% drop in sales
Yahoo.com page view	400 ms	5–9% drop in full-page traffic
Google.com search results	500 ms	20% fewer searches performed
Bing.com search results	2000 ms	4.3% lower revenue per user

Figure 12.17: The measured effects of added latency on users' interaction with various large SaaS apps, from Yahoo performance engineer Nicole Sullivan's "Design Fast Websites" presentation[45] and a joint presentation at the Velocity 2009 conference[46] by Jake Brutlag of Google and Eric Schurman of Amazon.

million hits per day was Slashdot's volume in 2010. At 8 *billion* (8×10^9) hits per day, which was Facebook's volume in 2010[42], 8,000 "one-in-a-million" events can be expected per day. This is why code reviews at companies such as Google often focus on corner cases: at large scale, astronomically-unlikely events happen all the time (Brewer 2012). The extra resilience provided by error-handling code will help you sleep better at night.

 Fallacy: **The app is still in development, so we can ignore performance.**

It's true that Knuth said that premature optimization is the root of all evil "... about 97% of the time." But the quote continues: "Yet we should not pass up our opportunities in that critical 3%." Blindly ignoring design issues such as lack of indices or needless repeated queries is just as bad as focusing myopically on performance at an early stage. Avoid truly egregious performance mistakes and you will be able to steer a happy path between two extremes.

 Pitfall: **Thinking you don't have to worry about performance because 3-tier apps using cloud computing will "magically" scale.**

This isn't really a fallacy, because if you're using well-curated PaaS, there is some truth to this statement up to a point. However, if your app "outgrows" PaaS, the fundamental problems of scalability and load balancing are now passed on to you. In other words, with PaaS you are *not* spared having to understand and avoid such problems, but you are temporarily spared from rolling your own solutions to them. When you start to set up your own system from scratch, it doesn't take long to appreciate the value of PaaS.

 Fallacy: **Processor cycles are free since computers have become so fast and cheap.**

In Chapter 1 we argued for trading today's extra compute power for more productive tools and languages. However, it's easy to take this argument too far. In 2008, performance engineer Nicole Sullivan reported on experiments conducted by various large SaaS operators about how additional latency affected their sites. Figure 12.17 clearly shows that when extra processor time becomes extra latency (and therefore reduced responsiveness) for the end user, processor cycles aren't free at all.

 Pitfall: **Optimizing without measuring.**

Some customers are surprised that Heroku doesn't automatically add Web server capacity when a customer app is slow (van Hardenberg 2012). The reason is that without instrumenting and measuring your app, you don't know *why* it's slow, and the risk is that adding Web servers will make the problem worse. For example, if your app suffers from a database problem such as lack of indices or $n + 1$ queries, or if relies on a separate service like Google Maps that is temporarily slow, adding servers to accept requests from *more* users will only make things worse. Without measuring, you won't know what to fix.

 Pitfall: **Abusing continuous deployment, leading to cruft accumulation.**

As we have already seen, evolving apps may grow to a point where a design change or architectural change would be the cleanest way to support new functionality. Since continuous deployment focuses on small incremental steps and tells us to avoid worrying about any functionality we don't need immediately, the app has the potential to accumulate a lot of **cruft** as more code is bolted onto an obsolete design. The increasing presence of code smells (Chapter 9) is often an early symptom of this pitfall, which can be avoided by periodic design and architecture reviews when smells start to creep in.

 Pitfall: **Bugs in naming or expiration logic, leading to silently-wrong caching behavior.**

As we noted, the two problems you must tackle with any kind of caching are naming and expiration. If you inadvertently reuse the same name for different objects—for example, a non-RESTful action that delivers different content depending on the logged-in user, but is always named using the same URI—then a cached object will be erroneously served when it shouldn't be. If your sweepers don't capture all the conditions under which a set of cached objects could become invalid, users could see stale data that doesn't reflect the results of recent changes, such as a movie list that doesn't contain the most recently added movies. Unit tests should cover such cases ("Caching system when new movie is added should immediately reflect new movie on the home page list"). Follow the steps in the Rails Caching Guide[47] to turn on caching in the testing and development environments, where it's off by default to simplify debugging.

 Pitfall: **Slow external servers in an SOA that can adversely affect your own app's performance.**

If your app communicates with external servers in an SOA, you should be prepared for the possibility that those external servers are slow or unresponsive. The easy case is handling an unresponsive server, since a refused HTTP connection will result in a Ruby exception that you can catch. The hard case is a server that is functioning but very slow: by default, the call to the server will block (wait until the operation is complete or the TCP "slow timeout" expires, which can take up to three minutes), making *your* app slow down as well. Even worse, since most Rails front ends (`thin`, `webrick`, `mongrel`) are single-threaded, if you are running N such front-ends ("dynos" in Heroku's terminology) it takes only N simultaneous requests to hang your application completely. The solution is to use Ruby's **timeout** library to "protect" the call, as the code in Figure 12.18 shows.

 Fallacy: **My app is secure because it runs on a secure platform and uses firewalls and HTTPS.**

There's no such thing as a "secure platform." There are certainly *insecure* platforms, but no platform by itself can assure the security of your app. Security is a systemwide and ongoing concern: Every system has a weakest link, and as new exploits and software bugs are found, the weakest link may move from one part of the system to the other. The "arms

http://pastebin.com/tsvAfTzE

```
1   require 'timeout'
2   # call external service, but abort if no answer in 3 seconds:
3   Timeout::timeout(3.0) do
4     begin
5       # potentially slow operation here
6     rescue Timeout::Error
7       # what to do if timeout occurs
8     end
9   end
```

Figure 12.18: Using timeouts around calls to an external service protects your app from becoming slow if the external service is slow.

race" between evildoers and legitimate developers makes it increasingly compelling to use professionally-curated PaaS infrastructure, so you can focus on securing your app code

 Fallacy: **My app isn't a target for attackers because it serves a niche audience, experiences low volume, and doesn't store valuable information.**

Malicious attackers aren't necessarily after your app; they may be seeking to compromise it as a vehicle to a further end. For example, if your app accepts blog-style comments, it will become the target of blog spam, in which automated agents (bots) post spammy comments containing links the spammer hopes users will follow, either to buy something or cause malware to be installed. If your app is open to SQL injection attacks, one motive for such an attack might be to influence the code that is displayed by your views so as to incorporate a cross-site scripting attack, for example to cause malware to be downloaded onto an unsuspecting user's machine. Even without malicious attackers, if any aspect of your app becomes suddenly popular because of Slashdot or Digg, you'll be suddenly inundated with traffic. The lesson is: *If your app is publicly deployed, it is a target.*

12.12   Concluding Remarks: Performance, Reliability, Security, and Leaky Abstractions

Performance, reliability, and security are systemwide concerns that must be constantly reviewed, rather than problems to be solved once and then set aside. In addition, the database abuses described in Section 12.8 reveal that Rails and ActiveRecord, like most abstractions, are *leaky*: they try to hide implementation details for the sake of productivity, but concerns about security and performance sometimes require you as a developer to have some understanding of how the abstractions work. For example, the $n + 1$ select problem is not obvious from looking at Rails code, nor is the solution of providing hints like **:include** for association queries, nor is the use of **attr_accessible** or **attr_protected** to protect sensitive attributes from being mass-assigned by a malicious user.

In Chapter 4 we emphasized the importance of keeping your development and production environments as similar as possible. This is still good advice, but obviously if your production environment involves multiple servers and a huge database, it may be impractical to replicate in your development environment. Indeed, in this book we started out developing our apps using SQLite3 database but deploying on Heroku with PostgreSQL. Given these differences, will performance improvements made during development (reducing the number of queries, adding indices, adding caching) still apply in production? Absolutely. Heroku and other PaaS sites do a great job at tuning the baseline performance of their databases and software stack, but no amount of tuning can compensate for inefficient query strategies such as the $n + 1$ query problem or for not deploying caching to ease the load on the database.

12.13 To Learn More

Given limited space, we focused on aspects of operations that every SaaS developer should know, even given the availability of PaaS. An excellent and more detailed book that focuses on challenges specific to SaaS and is laced with real customer stories is Michael Nygard's *Release It!* (Nygard 2007), which focuses more on the problems of "unexpected success" (sudden traffic surges, stability issues, and so on) than on repelling malicious attacks.

Our monitoring examples are based on aggregating metrics such as latency over many requests. A contrasting approach is request tracing, which is used in conjunction with metric aggregation to pinpoint and diagnose slow requests. You can see a simplified version of request tracing in the development-mode Rails logs, which by default will report the database query time, controller action time, and rendering time for each request. True request tracing is much finer-grained, following a request through every software component in every tier and timestamping it along the way. Companies that run large sites often build their own request tracing, such as Twitter's Big Brother Bird and Google's Dapper. In a recent article (Barroso and Dean 2012) two Google architects discuss how request tracing identifies obstacles to keeping Google's massively-parallel systems highly responsive. James Hamilton, an engineer and architect at Amazon Web Services who previously spent many years architecting and tuning Microsoft SQL Server, writes an excellent blog[48] that includes a great article on the cost of latency[49], gathering measured results from a variety of industry practitioners who have investigated the topic.

Although we focused on monitoring for performance problems, monitoring can also help you understand your customers' behavior:

- Clickstreams: what are the most popular sequences of pages your users visit?

- Think times/dwell times: how long does a typical user stay on a given page?

- Abandonment: if your site contains a flow that has a well-defined termination, such as making a sale, what percentage of users "abandon" the flow rather than completing it and how far do they get?

Google Analytics provides free basic analytics-as-a-service: you embed a small piece of JavaScript in every page on your site (for example, by embedding it on the default layout template) that sends Google Analytics information each time a page is loaded. To help you use this information, Google's "Speed is a Feature"[50] site links to a breathtakingly comprehensive collection of articles about all the different ways you can speed up your SaaS apps, including many optimizations to reduce the overall size of your pages and improve the speed at which Web browsers can render them. The RailsLab blog[51] maintained by New Relic also collects best practices and techniques for tuning Rails apps, including screencasts on Rails tuning and how to use New Relic in development mode for profiling[52]. Be aware, though, that some of the specific code examples, especially around caching, are no longer valid because of changes between Rails 2 and Rails 3.

Understanding what happens during deployment and operations (especially automated deployment) is a prerequisite to debugging more complex performance problems. The vast majority of SaaS apps today, including those hosted on Windows servers, run in an environment based on the original Unix model of processes and input/output, so an understanding of this environment is crucial for debugging any nontrivial performance problems. *The Unix Programming Environment* (Kernighan and Pike 1984), coauthored by one of Unix's creators, offers a high-bandwidth, learn-by-doing tour (using C!) of the Unix architecture and philosophy.

Sharding and **replication** are powerful techniques for scaling a database that require a great deal of design thinking up front. While there are Rails gems to help with both, these techniques usually require database-level configuration changes, which many PaaS providers do not support. Sharding and replication have become particularly important with the emergence of "NoSQL" databases, which trade the expressiveness and data format independence of SQL for better scalability. *The NoSQL Ecosystem*, a chapter contributed by Adam Marcus to *The Architecture of Open Source Applications* Marcus 2012, has a good treatment of these topics.

Security is an extremely broad topic; our goal has been to help you avoid basic mistakes by using built-in mechanisms to thwart common attacks against your app and your customers' data. Of course, an attacker who can't compromise your app's internal data can still cause harm by attacking the infrastructure on which your app relies. Distributed **denial of service** (DDoS) floods a site with so much traffic that it becomes unresponsive for its intended users. A malicious client can leave your app server or Web server "hanging on the line" as it consumes output pathologically slowly, unless your Web server (presentation tier) has built-in timeouts. **DNS spoofing** tries to steer you to an impostor site by supplying an incorrect IP address when a browser looks up a host name, and is often combined with a **man-in-the-middle attack** that falsifies the certificate attesting to the server's identity. The impostor site looks and behaves like the real site but collects sensitive information from users. (In September 2011, hackers impersonated the CIA, MI6, and Mossad sites[53] by compromising DigiNotar, the company that signed the original certificates for those sites, leading to DigiNotar's bankruptcy.) Even mature software such as Secure Shell and Apache are vulnerable: the US National Vulnerabilities Database[54] lists 10 new security-related bugs in Apache just between March and May 2012, two of which are "high severity", meaning that they could allow an attacker to take control of your entire server. Nonetheless, despite occasional vulnerabilities[55], curated PaaS sites are more likely to employ experienced professional system administrators who stay abreast of the latest techniques for avoiding such vulnerabilities, making them the best first line of defense for your SaaS apps. The Basic Rails security guide[56] at the Ruby on Rails site reviews many Rails features aimed at thwarting common attacks against SaaS apps, and this article from CodeClimate[57] (a company that provides code metrics as a service) lists a number of important security pitfalls in Rails apps.

Finally, at some point the unthinkable will happen: your production system will enter a state where some or all users receive no service. Whether the app has crashed or is "hung" (unable to make forward progress), from a business perspective the two conditions look the same, because the app is not generating revenue. In this scenario, the top priority is to restore service, which may require rebooting servers or doing other operations that destroy the post-mortem state you want to examine to determine what caused the problem in the first place. Generous logging can help, as the logs provide a semi-permanent record you can examine closely after service is restored.

In *The Evolution of Useful Things* (Petroski 1994), engineer Henry Petroski proposes changing the maxim "Form follows function" (originally from the world of architecture) to

"Form follows failure" after demonstrating that the design of many successful products was influenced primarily by failures in early designs that led to revised designs. For an example of good design, read Netflix's technical blog post[58] on how their design survived the Amazon Web Services outage in 2011 that crippled many other sites reliant on AWS.

ACM IEEE-Computer Society Joint Task Force. Computer science curricula 2013, Ironman Draft (version 1.0). Technical report, February 2013. URL `http://ai.stanford.edu/users/sahami/CS2013/`.

L. Barroso and J. Dean. The tail at scale: Tolerating variability in large-scale online services. *Communications of the ACM*, 2012.

N. Bhatti, A. Bouch, and A. Kuchinsky. Integrating user-perceived quality into web server design. In *9th International World Wide Web Conference (WWW–9)*, pages 1–16, 2000.

E. Brewer. Personal communication, May 2012.

S. Hansma. Go fast and don't break things: Ensuring quality in the cloud. In *Workshop on High Performance Transaction Systems (HPTS 2011)*, Asilomar, CA, Oct 2011. Summarized in Conference Reports column of USENIX ;login 37(1), February 2012.

B. W. Kernighan and R. Pike. *Unix Programming Environment (Prentice-Hall Software Series)*. Prentice Hall Ptr, 1984. ISBN 013937681X.

A. Marcus. The NoSQL ecosystem. In A. Brown, editor, *The Architecture of Open Source Applications*. lulu.com, 2012. ISBN 1257638017. URL `http://www.aosabook.org/en/nosql.html`.

R. B. Miller. Response time in man-computer conversational transactions. In *Proceedings of the December 9-11, 1968, fall joint computer conference, part I*, AFIPS '68 (Fall, part I), pages 267–277, New York, NY, USA, 1968. ACM. doi: 10.1145/1476589.1476628. URL `http://doi.acm.org/10.1145/1476589.1476628`.

M. T. Nygard. *Release It!: Design and Deploy Production-Ready Software (Pragmatic Programmers)*. Pragmatic Bookshelf, 2007. ISBN 0978739213.

H. Petroski. *The Evolution of Useful Things: How Everyday Artifacts-From Forks and Pins to Paper Clips and Zippers-Came to be as They are*. Vintage, 1994. ISBN 0679740392.

P. van Hardenberg. Personal communication, April 2012.

Notes

[1] `http://www.opensourcerails.com/`
[2] `http://github.com/ucberkeley/researchmatch`
[3] `http://github.com/vinsonchuong/meetinglibs`
[4] `http://apdex.org`
[5] `http://code.google.com/speed`
[6] `http://rightscale.com`
[7] `http://github.com/capistrano`
[8] `http://travis-ci.org`
[9] `http://saucelabs.com`
[10] `https://github.com/jamesgolick/rollout`

[11]http://www.google.com/apps/intl/en/business/details.html
[12]http://newrelic.com
[13]http://pingdom.com
[14]http://sitescope.com
[15]http://analytics.google.com
[16]http://newrelic.com
[17]http://scoutapp.com
[18]http://exceptional.io
[19]http://airbrake.io
[20]http://godrb.com
[21]http://www.hpl.hp.com/research/linux/httperf
[22]http://pivotaltracker.com
[23]https://github.com/flyerhzm/bullet
[24]http://weblog.rubyonrails.org/2011/12/6/what-s-new-in-edge-rails-explain
[25]http://github.com/nesquena/query_reviewer
[26]http://apidock.com/rails/ActionController/ForceSSL/ClassMethods/force_ssl
[27]http://eval.symantec.com/mktginfo/enterprise/white_papers/b-whitepaper_exec_
summary_internet_security_threat_report_xiii_04-2008.en-us.pdf
[28]https://devcenter.heroku.com/articles/progstr-filer
[29]https://devcenter.heroku.com/articles/background-jobs-queueing
[30]http://www.huffingtonpost.com/2012/06/07/eharmony-passwords-leaked-linkedin_n_
1577175.html
[31]http://www.huffingtonpost.co.uk/2012/06/08/lastfm-hit-by-password-leak_n_1580012.
html?ref=uk
[32]http://www.zdnet.com/blog/btl/26000-email-addresses-and-passwords-leaked-check-
this-list-to-see-if-youre-included/50424
[33]http://www.neowin.net/news/main/09/10/05/thousands-of-hotmail-passwords-leaked-
online
[34]http://hothardware.com/News/55000-Twitter-Accounts-Hacked-You-Should-Probably-
Change-Your-Password/
[35]http://www.businessweek.com/technology/content/jul2009/tc2009076_891369.htm
[36]http://www.msnbc.msn.com/id/17853440/#.T9JsqxztEmY
[37]http://redtape.msnbc.msn.com/_news/2012/03/30/10940640-global-payments-under-15-
million-account-numbers-hacked?lite
[38]http://paypal.com
[39]http://stripe.com
[40]http://nebraska.edu/security
[41]http://cvedetails.com/
[42]http://royal.pingdom.com/2010/01/05/facebook-twitter-myspace-page-views
[43]http://www.slideshare.net/stubbornella/designing-fast-websites-presentation
[44]http://velocityconf.com/velocity2009/public/schedule/detail/8523
[45]http://www.slideshare.net/stubbornella/designing-fast-websites-presentation
[46]http://velocityconf.com/velocity2009/public/schedule/detail/8523
[47]http://guides.rubyonrails.org/caching_with_rails.html
[48]http://perspectives.mvdirona.com
[49]http://perspectives.mvdirona.com/2009/10/31/TheCostOfLatency.aspx
[50]http://code.google.com/speed
[51]http://railslab.newrelic.com
[52]http://newrelic.com/demos/developer-mode.html
[53]http://catless.ncl.ac.uk/Risks/26.56.html#subj6
[54]http://nvd.nist.gov
[55]http://daverecycles.com/post/2858880862/heroku-hacked-dissecting-herokus-critical-
security
[56]http://guides.rubyonrails.org/security.html
[57]http://blog.codeclimate.com/blog/2013/03/27/rails-insecure-defaults
[58]http://techblog.netflix.com/2011/04

12.14 Suggested Projects

For many of these exercises, you will find it useful to create a `rake` task that creates a specified large number of randomly-generated instances of a given model type. You will also want to deploy a 'staging' copy of your app on Heroku so that you can use the staging database for experiments without modifying the production database.

SaaS Performance and Scaling:

Project 12.1. *Seed the staging database with 500 movies (randomly generated is fine) to RottenPotatoes. Profile its deployed performance on Heroku using New Relic. Add fragment caching around the* **movie** *partial used by the* **index** *view and re-profile the app. How much improvement in responsiveness do you observe for the* **index** *view once the cache is warmed up?*

Project 12.2. *Continuing the previous exercise, use* `httperf` *to compare the throughput of a single copy of your app on the* **index** *action with and without fragment caching. (On Heroku, by default any apps on a free account receive 1 "dyno" or one unit of task parallelism, so requests are performed sequentially.)*

Project 12.3. *Use external monitoring to analyze a software design from the perspective of a significant external quality attribute such as functionality, performance, or availability. Note: The margin icon identifies projects from the ACM/IEEE 2013 Software Engineering standard (ACM IEEE-Computer Society Joint Task Force 2013).*

Project 12.4. *Continuing the previous exercise, add action caching for the index view so that if no sorting or filtering options are specified, the* **index** *action just returns all movies. Compare the latency and throughput with and without action caching. Summarize the results from all three exercises in a table.*

Releases and feature flags:

Project 12.5. *Investigate the availability cost of doing an "atomic" schema update and migration as described in Section 12.4. To do this, repeat the following sequence of steps for* $N = 2^{10}, 2^{12}, 2^{14}$:

1. *Seed the staging database with N randomly-generated movies with random ratings.*

2. *Run a migration on the staging database that changes the* `rating` *column in the* `movies` *table from a string to an integer (1=G, 2=PG, and so on).*

3. *Note the time reported by* `rake db:migrate`.

Suppose your uptime target was 99.9% over any 30-day window. Quantify the effect on availability of doing the above migration without bringing your service down.

Project 12.6. *Outline the process of regression testing and its role in release management.*

Reliability:

Project 12.7. *List approaches to minimizing faults that can be applied at each stage of a Plan-and-Document lifecycle.*

Project 12.8. *In Section 5.2 we integrated third-party authentication into RottenPotatoes by adding an authentication provider name and a provider-specific UID to the* **Moviegoer** *model.*

Now we'd like to go further and allow the same moviegoer to log in to the same account with any one of several authentication providers. That is, if Alice has both a Twitter account and a Facebook account, she should be able to log in to the same RottenPotatoes account with either ID.

1. *Describe the changes to existing models and tables that are necessary to support this scheme.*

2. *Describe a sequence of deployments and migrations that make use of feature flags to implement the new scheme without any application downtime.*

Security:

Project 12.9. *Wired Magazine's ThreatLevel column for July 2012[1] reported that 453,000 passwords for Yahoo! Voice users were stolen by hackers. The hackers said, in a note posted online, that the passwords were stored in cleartext on Yahoo's servers and that they used a SQL injection attack to gather them. Discuss.*

Project 12.10. *Describe secure coding and defensive coding practices in general.*

For the remaining projects, you will need to identify a working legacy software system that you will inspect. For suggestions, you could use the list of open-source Rails projects at Open Source Rails[2], or you could select one of two projects created by students who have used this book: ResearchMatch[3], which helps match students with research opportunities at their university, and VisitDay[4], which helps organize meetings between students and faculty members.

Project 12.11. *From the perspective of using a relational database management system, describe secure coding and defensive coding practices. Does the system you're examining follow these practices?*

Project 12.12. *From the perspective of building a SaaS app using a framework such as Rails, describe some specific defensive coding practices. Looking at Rails security guides and blogs such as the Basic Rails security guide[5], this article from CodeClimate[6], and using Google to search for recent security incidents in Rails SaaS apps, which security problems were caused by failure to follow these practices?*

Project 12.13. *Rewrite a simple program to remove common vulnerabilities, such as buffer overflows, integer overflows, and race conditions.*

Project 12.14. *State and apply the principles of least privilege and fail-safe defaults. How are these applied in our RottenPotatoes app?*

13 Afterword

Alan Kay (1940–) received the 2003 Turing Award for pioneering many of the ideas at the root of contemporary object-oriented programming languages. He led the team that developed the Smalltalk language, from which Ruby inherits its approach to object-orientation. He also invented the "Dynabook" concept, the precursor of today's laptops and tablet computers, which he conceived as an educational platform for teaching programming.

The best way to predict the future is to invent it.

—Alan Kay

13.1 Perspectives on SaaS, SOA, Ruby, and Rails

In this book you've been mainly a user of a successful distributed architecture (the Web, SOA) and framework (Rails). As a successful software engineer you'll likely need to create such frameworks, or extend existing ones. Paying careful attention to principles that made these frameworks successful will help.

In Chapter 2 we pointed out that by choosing to build SaaS, some architectural choices are made for you. In building different kinds of systems, other choices might be appropriate, but for reasons of scope, we have focused on this one set of choices. But it's worth pointing out that some of the important architectural principles underlying SaaS and SOA apply in other architectures as well, and as Jim Gray's quote at the front of Chapter 3 suggests, great ideas take time to mature.

Rails itself took off with the shift in the software industry towards Software as a Service (SaaS) using Agile development and deployed via cloud computing. Today virtually every traditional buy-and-install program is offered as a service, including PC standard-bearers like Office (see Office 365) and TurboTax (see TurboTax Online). Tools like Rails made Agile much easier to use and practice than earlier software development methods. Remarkably, not only has the future of software been revolutionized, software development is now easier to learn!

13.2 Looking Backwards

Figure 13.1, first seen in Chapter 1, shows the three "crown jewels" on which the material in this book is based. To understand this virtuous triangle you needed to learn many new terms; Figure 13.2 lists nearly 120 terms from just the first three chapters!

Each pair of "jewels" forms synergistic bonds that support each other, as Figure 13.1 shows. In particular, the tools and related services of Rails makes it much easier to follow the Agile lifecycle. Figure 13.3 shows our oft-repeated Agile iteration, but this time it is decorated with the tools and services that we use in this book. These 14 tools and services support *both* following the Agile lifecycle *and* developing SaaS apps. Similarly, Figure 13.4

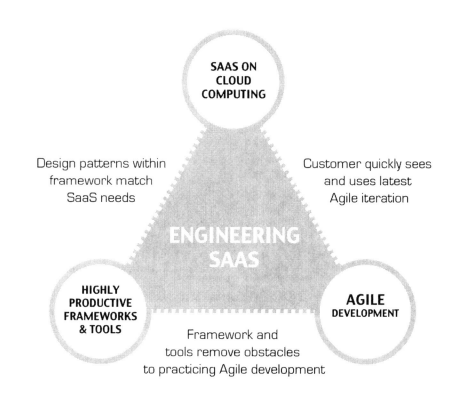

Figure 13.1: The Virtuous Triangle of Engineering SaaS is formed from the three software engineering crown jewels of (1) SaaS on Cloud Computing, (2) Highly Productive Framework and Tools, and (3) Agile Development.

Chapter 1	Chapter 2 (cont'd)	Chapter 3
acceptance test	HTTP cookie	accessor method
agile development process	HTTP method	anonymous lambda expression
automatic theorem proving	HTTP server	app root
cloud computing	interpolated	backtrace
cluster	IP address	block
DRY(Don't Repeat Yourself)	load balancer	class variable
formal methods	logic tier	closure
functional test	markup language	duck typing
integration test	master-slave	dynamically typed
legacy code	middleware	encapsulation
lifecycle	model	functional programming
model checking	multi-homed	gem
module test	MVC (Model-View-Controller)	generator
object oriented programming	network interface	getter method
public cloud service	network protocol	idempotent
regression test	peer-to-peer architecture	instance variable
SaaS (Software as a Service)	persistence tier	instrumentation
SOA (Service Oriented Arch.)	primary key	iterator
system test	public-key cryptography	lexical scoping
test coverage	push-based	looking up a method
unit test	RDBMS (relational database management system)	metaprogramming
utility computing	relational algebra	method chaining
validation	relational database	migration
verification	request-reply protocol	mix-ins
virtual machine	route	mutator method
warehouse scale computer	selector notation	poetry mode
waterfall development process	session	receiver
Chapter 2	SGML (Standard Generalized Markup Language)	reflection
action	sharding	regex
application server	shared-nothing architecture	regular expressions
client-server architecture	stateless protocol	root class
controller	structured storage	setter method
CSS (Cascading Style Sheet)	TCP port number	static variable
CRUD (Create, Read, Update, Delete)	TCP/IP (Transmission Control Protocol/Internet Protocol)	symbol
data consistency	URI (Uniform Resource Identifier)	syntactic sugar
design pattern	view	type casting
DNS (Domain Name System)	web application framework	yield
HAML (HTML Abstraction Markup Language)	Web server	
hostnames	XHTML (eXtended HyperText Markup Language)	
HTML (HyperText Markup Language)	XML (eXtensible Markup Language)	
HTTP (HyperText Transfer Protocol)		

Figure 13.2: Terms introduced in the first three chapters of this book.

summarizes the relationship between phases of Plan-and-Document lifecycles and their Agile equivalents, showing how the techniques described in detail in this book play similar roles to those in earlier software process models.

Rails is very powerful but has evolved tremendously since version 1.0, which was originally *extracted* from a specific application. Indeed, the Web itself evolved from specific details to more general architectural patterns:

- From static documents in 1990 to dynamic content by 1995;

- From opaque URIs in the early 1990s to REST by the early 2000s;

- From session "hacks" (fat URIs, hidden fields, and so on) in the early 1990s to cookies and real sessions by the mid 1990s; and

- From setting up and administering your own ad-hoc servers in 1990 to deployment on "curated" cloud platforms in the 2000s.

The programming languages Java and Ruby offer another demonstration that good incremental ideas can be embraced quickly but great radical ideas take time before they are accepted.

Java and Ruby are the same age, both appearing in 1995. Within a few years Java became one of the most popular programming languages, while Ruby remained primarily of interest to the programming languages literati. Ruby's popularity came a decade later with the release of Rails. Ruby and Rails demonstrate that big ideas in programming languages really can deliver productivity through extensive software reuse. Comparing Java and its frameworks to Ruby and Rails, (Stella et al. 2008) and (Ji and Sedano 2011) found factors of 3 to 5 reductions in number of lines of code, which is one indication of productivity.

13.3 Looking Forwards

> *I've always been more interested in the future than in the past.*
>
> —Grace Murray Hopper

Given this history of rapidly-evolving tools, patterns, and development methodologies, what might software engineers look forward to in the next few years?

One software engineering technique that we expect to become popular in the next few years is **delta debugging** (Zeller 2002). It uses divide-and-conquer to automatically find the smallest input change to that will cause a bug to appear. Debuggers usually use program analysis to detect flaws in the code itself. In contrast, delta debugging identifies changes to the program *state* that lead to the bug. It requires two runs, one with the flaw and one without, and it looks at the differences between the sets of states. By repeatedly changing the inputs and re-running the program using a binary search strategy and automated testing, delta debugging methodically narrows the differences between the two runs. Delta debugging discovers dependencies that form a cause-effect chain, which it expands until it identifies the smallest set of changes to input variables that causes the bug to appear. Although it requires many runs of the program, this analysis is done at full program speed and without the intervention of the programmer, so it saves development time.

Program synthesis may be ready for a breakthrough. The state of the art today is that given incomplete segments of programs, program synthesis tools can often supply the missing

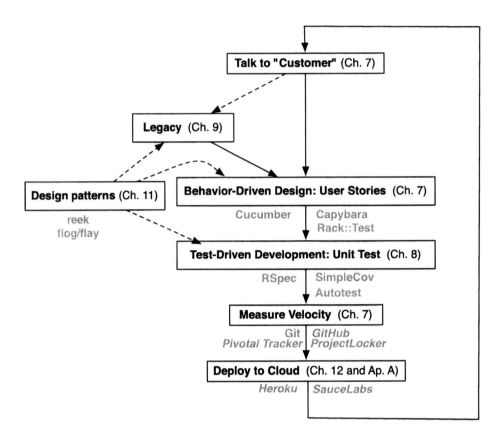

Figure 13.3: An iteration of the Agile software lifecycle and its relationship to the chapters in this book, with the supporting tools (red/bold letters) and supporting services (blue/italic letters) identified with each step.

Waterfall/Spiral	Agile	Chapter
Requirements gathering and analysis	BDD with short iterations so customer participates in design	7
Periodic code reviews	Pair programming (pairs constantly reviewing each others' code)	10
Periodic design reviews	Pull requests drive discussions about design changes	10
Test entire design after building	TDD to test continuously as you design	8
Post-implementation Integration Testing	Continuous integration testing	12
Infrequent major releases	Continuous deployment	12

Figure 13.4: While agile methods aren't appropriate for all projects, the agile lifecycle does embrace the same process steps as traditional models such as waterfall and spiral, but reduces each step in scope to a single iteration so that they can be done repeatedly and frequently, constantly refining a working version of the product.

code. One of the most interesting uses of this technology is in Microsoft Office Excel 2013, called the **Flash Fill feature**, which does programming by example (Gulwani et al. 2012). You give examples of what you want to do to rows or columns of code, and Excel will attempt to repeat and generalize what you do. Moreover, you can correct its attempts to steer it to what you want (Gantenbein 2012).

This split between Plan-and-Document and Agile development may become more pronounced with the advances in practicality of formal methods. The size of programs that can be formally verified is growing over time, with improvements in tools, faster computers, and wider understanding of how to write formal specifications. If the work of careful specification in advance of coding could be rewarded by not needing to test and yet have thoroughly verified programs, then the tradeoffs would be crisp around change. For formal methods to work, clearly change needs to be rare. When change is commonplace, Agile is the answer, for change is the essence of Agile.

While Agile works better than other software methodologies for some types of apps today, it is surely not the final answer in software development. If a new methodology could simplify including a good software architecture and good design patterns while maintaining Agile's ease of change, it could become more popular. Historically, a new methodology comes along every decade or two, so it may soon be time for new one.

This book itself was developed during the dawn of the **Massive Open Online Course** (MOOC) movement, which is another trend that we predict will become more significant in the next few years. Like many other advances in this modern world, we wouldn't have MOOCs without SaaS and cloud computing. The enabling components were:

- Scalable video distribution via services like YouTube.

- Sophisticated autograders running on cloud computing that evaluate assignments immediately yet can scale to tens of thousands of students.

- Discussion forums as a scalable solution to asking questions and getting answers from both other students and the staff.

These components combine to form a wonderful, low-cost vehicle for students around the world. For example, it will surely improve continuing education of professionals in our fast changing field, enable gifted pre-college students to go beyond what their schools can teach, and let dedicated students around the world who do not have access to great universities still get a good education. MOOCs may even have the side effect of raising the quality bar for traditional courses by providing viable alternatives to ineffective lecturers. If MOOCs deliver on only half of these opportunities, they will still be a potent force in higher education.

13.4 Last Words

Ultimately, it comes down to taste. It comes down to exposing yourself to the best things that humans have done, and then try to bring those things into what you're doing.

—Steve Jobs

Software helped put humans on the moon, led to the invention of lifesaving CAT scans, and enables eyewitness citizen journalism. By working as a software developer, you become part of a community that has the power to change the world.

But with great power comes great responsibility. Faulty software caused the loss of the Ariane V rocket[7] and Mars Observer[8] as well as the deaths of several patients due to radiation overdoses from the Therac-25 machine[9].

While the early stories of computers and software are dominated by "frontier narratives" of lone geniuses working in garages or at startups, software today is too important to be left to any one individual, however talented. As we said in Chapter 10, software development is now a team sport.

We believe the concepts in this book increase the chances of you being both a responsible software developer *and* a part of a winning team. There's no textbook for getting there; just keep writing, learning, and refactoring to apply your lessons as you go.

And as we said in the first chapter, we look forward to becoming passionate fans of the beautiful and long-lasting code that you and your team create!

13.5 To Learn More

D. Gantenbein. Flash fill gives Excel a smart charge, Feb 2012. URL `http://research.microsoft.com/en-us/news/features/flashfill-020613.aspx`.

S. Gulwani, W. R. Harris, and R. Singh. Spreadsheet data manipulation using examples. *Communications of the ACM*, 55(8):97–105, 2012.

F. Ji and T. Sedano. Comparing extreme programming and waterfall project results. *Conference on Software Engineering Education and Training*, pages 482–486, 2011.

L. Stella, S. Jarzabek, and B. Wadhwa. A comparative study of maintainability of web applications on J2EE, .NET and Ruby on Rails. *10th International Symposium on Web Site Evolution*, pages 93–99, October 2008.

A. Zeller. Isolating cause-effect chains from computer programs. In *Proceedings of the 10th ACM SIGSOFT symposium on Foundations of software engineering*, pages 1–10, New York, NY, USA, Nov 2002. ACM. doi: 10.1145/587051.587053. URL `http://www.st.cs.uni-saarland.de/papers/fse2002/p201-zeller.pdf`.

Notes

[1] `http://www.wired.com/threatlevel/2012/07/yahoo-breach`
[2] `http://www.opensourcerails.com/`
[3] `http://github.com/ucberkeley/researchmatch`
[4] `http://github.com/vinsonchuong/meetinglibs`
[5] `http://guides.rubyonrails.org/security.html`
[6] `http://blog.codeclimate.com/blog/2013/03/27/rails-insecure-defaults`
[7] `http://en.wikipedia.org/wiki/Ariane_5_Flight_501`
[8] `http://en.wikipedia.org/wiki/Mars_Observer`
[9] `http://en.wikipedia.org/wiki/Therac-25`

A   Using the Bookware

Frances Allen (1932–) received the 2006 Turing Award for pioneering contributions to the theory and practice of optimizing compiler techniques that laid the foundation for modern optimizing compilers and automatic parallel execution.

All the things I do are of a piece. I'm exploring the edges, finding new ways of doing things. It keeps me very, very engaged.

—Fran Allen, from Computer History Museum Fellow Award Plaque, 2000

Concepts

Not only is this book all about creating SaaS: it also relies heavily on SaaS, IaaS (*infrastructure as a service*), and PaaS (*platform as a service*), all of which are models of *cloud computing*. This appendix describes the cloud technologies that not only simplify your life as a student, but also are essential parts of the ecosystem you will use when deploying your real SaaS apps.

As of this writing, all of these cloud services offer a zero-cost usage tier that is sufficient for doing the work in this book.

- All of the *open-source software* used in this book has been preinstalled in a *virtual machine image*—a representation of the complete hard drive contents of a computer that would have this software preinstalled.

- To use a virtual machine image, you deploy it on a *hypervisor*. We give instructions for deploying it on your own computer using the open-source VirtualBox[1] hypervisor or deploying it on Elastic Compute Cloud (EC2), an *infrastructure as a service* cloud computing product from Amazon Web Services.

- *Secure Shell* is a widely-used protocol that allows secure access to remote services by using a cryptographic keypair rather than a password. We use it to access most SaaS services, including GitHub and Heroku.

- GitHub[2] is a SaaS site that lets you back up your *version-controlled* projects as well as collaborate on them with other developers.

- Heroku[3] is a *platform as a service* provider where you can deploy your Rails apps.

A.1   General Guidance: Read, Ask, Search, Post

Although we take steps in this book to minimize the pain, such as using Test-Driven Development (Chapter 8) to catch problems quickly and providing a VM image with a consistent environment, errors *will* occur. You can react most productively by remembering the acronym **RASP**: Read, Ask, Search, Post.

Read the error message. Error messages can look disconcertingly long, but a long error message is often your friend because it gives a strong hint of the problem. There will be places to look in the online information associated with the class given the error message.

Ask a coworker. If you have friends in the class, or have instant messaging enabled, put the message out there.

Search for the error message. You'd be amazed at how often experienced developers deal with an error by using a search engine such as Google or a programmers' forum such as StackOverflow[4] to look up key words or key phrases in the error message.

Post a question on a site like StackOverflow[5] (*after* searching to see if a similar question has been asked!), sites that specialize in helping out developers and allow you to vote for the most helpful answers to particular questions so that they eventually percolate to the top of the answer list.

A.2   Overview of the Bookware

The bookware consists of three parts.

The first is a uniform development environment preloaded with all the tools referenced in the book. For convenience and uniformity, this environment is provided as a ***virtual machine image***.

The second comprises a set of excellent SaaS sites aimed at developers: GitHub[6], Heroku[7], and Pivotal Tracker[8]. **Disclaimer:** At the time of this writing, the *free* offerings from the above sites were sufficient to do the work in this book. However, the providers of those services or tools may decide at any time to start charging, which would be beyond our control.

The third is supplementary material connected to the book, which is free whether you've purchased the book or not:

- The book's web site (`http://saasbook.info`[9]) contains the latest errata for each book version, links to supplementary material online, a bug reporting mechanism if you find errors, and high-resolution renderings of the figures and tables in case you have trouble reading them on your ebook reader

- Pastebin (`http://pastebin.com/u/saasbook`[10]) contains syntax-highlighted, copy-and-pastable code excerpts for every example in the book

- Vimeo (`http://vimeo.com/saasbook`[11]) hosts all the screencasts referenced in the book

A.3   Using the Bookware VM

Virtual machine (VM) technology allows a single physical computer to run one or more ***guest operating systems (OS)*** "on top of" the physical computer's built-in OS, in such a way that each guest believes it is running on the real hardware. These virtual machines can be "powered on" and "powered off" at will, without interfering with the host computer's built-in OS (the **host OS**). A virtual machine image is a file that contains the guest OS and a collection of preinstalled software. A **hypervisor** is an application that facilitates running VMs by "instantiating" a virtual machine image. We have packaged the software needed to do the work in this book as a VM image whose guest OS is GNU/Linux. Linux is an open-source implementation of the **kernel** (core functionality) of Unix, one of the most influential operating systems ever created and the most widely-used environment for SaaS development and deployment. GNU (a recursive acronym for GNU's Not Unix) is a collection of open-source implementations of nearly all of the important Unix applications, especially those used by developers.

The VM image can be used in one of two ways:

1. On your own computer: The free VirtualBox[12] hypervisor was originally developed by Sun Microsystems (now part of Oracle). You can download and run VirtualBox on a Linux, Windows, or Mac OS X host computer, as long as the host computer has an Intel-compatible processor. You then download the VM image file and deploy it on VirtualBox.

2. On Amazon's cloud: With this method, you don't download anything—you start an Amazon EC2 (Elastic Compute Cloud) virtual machine based on the Amazon Machine Image (AMI) VM file containing the bookware.

You can find instructions for both methods of VM deployment at http://www.saasbook.info/bookware-vm-instructions[13].

If you're thinking about installing the software yourself, be aware that the explanations and examples in each version of the book have been cross-checked against the *specific* versions of Ruby, Rails, and other software included in the VM. Changes across versions are significant, and running the book examples with the wrong software versions may result in syntax errors, incorrect behavior, differing messages, silent failure, or other problems. To avoid confusion, we strongly recommend you use the VM until you are familiar enough with the environment to distinguish errors in your own code from errors arising from incompatible versions of software components. We prepared the VM by running the `vm-setup` shell script in our public GitHub repo[14] to populate a clean Ubuntu image. You must be familiar with Unix command line utilities to attempt this process; there is no GUI.

■ *Elaboration: Free and Open Source Software*

Linux was originally created by Finnish programmer Linus Torvalds, who wanted to create a free and full-featured version of the famous Unix operating system for his own use. The GNU project was started by Richard Stallman, creator of the Emacs editor and founder of the Free Software Foundation (which stewards GNU), an illustrious developer with very strong opinions about the role of open source software. Both Linux and GNU are constantly being improved by contributions from thousands of collaborators worldwide; in fact, Torvalds later created Git to manage this large-scale collaboration. Despite the apparent lack of central-ized authority in their development, the robustness of GNU and Linux compare favorably to proprietary software developed under a traditional centralized model. This phenomenon is explored in Eric Raymond's *The Cathedral and the Bazaar*[15], which some consider the seminal manifesto of the Free and Open Source Software (FOSS) movement.

A.4   Working With Code: Editors and Unix Survival Skills

You will save yourself a great deal of grief by working with an editor that supports syntax highlighting and automatic indentation for the language you use. You can either edit files directly on the VM, or use the VirtualBox "shared folders" feature to make some directories on your VM available as folders on your Mac or Windows PC so that you can run a native editor on your Mac or PC.

Many **Integrated Development Environments**(IDEs) that support Ruby, including Aptana[16], NetBeans, and RubyMine, perform syntax highlighting, indentation and other useful tasks. While these IDEs also provide a GUI for other development-related tasks such as running tests, in this book we use command-line tools for these tasks for three reasons. First, unlike IDEs, the command line tools are the same across all platforms. Second, we place heavy emphasis in the book on automation to avoid mistakes and improve productivity; GUI tasks often cannot be automated, whereas command line tools can be composed into scripts, an approach central to the Unix philosophy. Third, understanding what tools are involved in each aspect of development helps roll back the "magic curtain" of IDE GUIs. We believe this is helpful when learning a new system because if something goes wrong while using the GUI, to find the problem you need some understanding of how the GUI actually does the tasks.

With this in mind, there are two ways to edit files on the VM. The first is to run an editor on the VM itself. We've preinstalled two popular editors on the VM. One is `vim`, a lighter-weight editor that is customizable enough to include language-aware syntax highlighting and auto-indentation. Here's a collection of links[17] to tutorials and screencasts that cover this popular editor. The other is **Emacs**, the granddaddy of customizable editors and one of the creations of the illustrious **Richard Stallman**. The canonical tutorial[18] is provided by the Free Software Foundation, though many others are available. We've included automatic support for editing Ruby and Rails apps in both `vim` and `emacs` on the VM.

vim stands for "*vi improved*," since it began as a much-enhanced version of the early Unix editor *vi*, written in 1976 by Unix legend, Sun co-founder and Berkeley alum *Bill Joy*.

The second way to edit files is to edit natively on your Mac or Windows computer, which requires setting up the Shared Folders feature of VirtualBox as explained at `http://www.saasbook.info/bookware-vm-instructions`[19]. Free editors that support Ruby include TextWrangler[20] for Mac OS X or Notepad++[21] for Windows.

Don't copy and paste code into or out of a word processor such as Microsoft Word or Pages. Many word processors helpfully convert regular quotes (") to "smart quotes," sequences of hyphens (--) to em-dashes (—), and other conversions that will make your code incorrect, cause syntax errors, and generally bring you grief. Don't do it.

A.5   Getting Started With Secure Shell (ssh)

sh was written by Steve Bourne in 1977 to replace Unix co-creator Ken Thompson's original shell. *bash* is a portable and compatible GNU replacement for *sh* whose name stands for *Bourne-Again Shell*.

The **shell** is the Unix program that lets you type commands and write scripts to automate simple tasks, and before the widespread adoption of Graphical User Interfaces, the shell was the only way to interact with a Unix system. When Unix was born, there was no Internet; users could only run a shell by logging in from a **dumb terminal** connected physically to the computer. By 1983 the Internet had reached many universities and companies, so a new tool called **Remote Shell** or `rsh` appeared that allowed you to login or run commands on an Internet-connected remote computer on which you had an account. Here is an example of using `rsh` from the command line:

http://pastebin.com/eLDdcDrz

```
1 | rsh -l fox eecs.berkeley.edu ps -ef
```

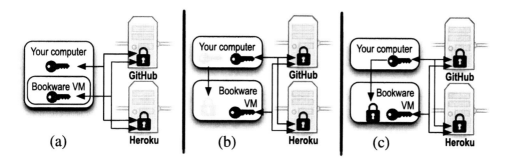

Figure A.1: Your public key is copied to the services you want to access, while your private key is stored only on the computer(s) from which you want to access them. Public and private keys for each pair are shown in the same color, with a lock indicating the public key. (a) When running the bookware VM on VirtualBox, you must copy the private key you created on your computer to the VirtualBox VM. (b) Running the bookware VM on Amazon EC2[24] also requires connecting to your EC2 instance from your computer via ssh. One way to do this in the EC2 instance setup process is to have Amazon generate a new keypair for this purpose, shown in grey. (c) Another option for EC2 is to upload your existing keypair[25] to AWS, so you use the same key for accessing both your AWS instance and all the services. In this last scenario, both the private *and* the public key end up on the VM.

This command would attempt to login as user `fox` on the computer `eecs.berkeley.edu`, run the command `ps -ef` (which gives information about which applications are running on that computer), and print the output locally. Omitting `ps -ef` would establish an interactive shell session on the remote computer.

But `rsh` is insecure: access to the remote computer usually required transmitting your password unencrypted or "in the clear" over the Internet, leaving it vulnerable to "sniffer" programs eavesdropping on the network to harvest passwords. In 1995, Tatu Ylönen at the Helsinki University of Technology developed **Secure Shell** or ssh as a secure "drop-in replacement" for `rsh`. As with `rsh`, once the connection to the remote computer is established you can either run an interactive shell or run arbitrary commands whose output is delivered securely back to your computer over the encrypted connection; in the latter case, we sometimes say the data is **tunnelled** over ssh. But rather than relying on a password, ssh relies on a keypair and key exchange using the same techniques and algorithms as SSL/TLS (Section 12.9), so your private key never leaves your computer.

Because ssh is secure, ubiquitous, and doesn't require exposing your password or any other secrets, many services rely on it for remote access, either as the default method (GitHub) or the only method (Heroku). Private and public keys come in pairs, and both halves are important. If you lose the private key paired to a given public key, any resources that relied on your possession of that key will become *irrevocably inaccessible forever.* If you lose the public key paired to a given private key, you *may* be able to retrieve a copy of it from one of the other services to which you still have access—though some services don't even allow you to view public keys you've uploaded, for added security. So treat your keypairs like a passport: personal, valuable, and long-lived.

Thus a key step in preparing your development environment is generating a keypair (if you don't already have one), ensuring its private key part is on all the computers you use for development and its public key part is added to all the services that support convenient and secure access via ssh. As Figure A.1 shows, for this book this means keeping the private key on both your computer and the bookware VM, whether deployed locally using VirtualBox or on Amazon EC2.

ssh comes from the Unix world, so it expects a Unix-like command line environment.

rsh first appeared in version 4.2 of the Berkeley Software Distribution (BSD), the open-source implementation of Unix created at UC Berkeley.

OpenSSL is an open-source volunteer-maintained library used by ssh and many SSL/TLS implementations. Fortunately, ssh doesn't use the part of OpenSSL containing the catastrophic **Heartbleed** bug discovered in 2014.

Both Mac OS X (via the Terminal app) and Linux (via xterm) have one, but Windows does not. We therefore recommend the use of the free Git for Windows[26], which provides not only superior support for the Git version control system (which we'll meet shortly) on Windows, but also provides a Windows version of bash, the Unix shell program, that provides a Unix-like environment for supporting ssh and other commonly-used commands. The rest of this section, and the online tutorials and resources to which it refers, assume that Windows users have installed this tool.

> Some people use different ssh keypairs for different services, to avoid putting all their eggs in one basket in case one private key is compromised.

If you don't already have a keypair on your computer, we recommend GitHub's excellent instructions[27] for generating a new keypair, which includes instructions for Mac OS, Linux, and Windows (with Git for Windows installed), and adding the public key to your GitHub account. (We will cover GitHub basics in Section A.7.)

■ *Elaboration: What about the Amazon AWS keypair?*

AWS|see Amazon Web Services

If you're deploying the bookware VM on Amazon Web Services (AWS) (as described on the book's web site[28]), you'll see that the AWS setup console asks you to either generate a new keypair or use your existing public key. In either case, AWS places the public key in the virtual machine (AMI) image prior to launch, allowing you to log into it via ssh with the corresponding private key. If you use AWS's Web interface to generate a new keypair, be aware that all it's really doing is running ssh-keygen for you.

A.6   Getting Started With Git for Version Control

SCM or VCS?
Confusingly, the abbreviations SCM and VCS are often used interchangeably.

Version control, also called source code control or software configuration management (SCM), is the process of keeping track of the history of changes to a set of files. It can tell who made each change and when, reconstruct one or more files as they existed at some point in the past, or selectively combine changes made by different people. A version control system (VCS) is a tool that helps manage this process. For individual developers, SCM provides a timestamped and annotated history of changes to the project and an easy way to undo changes that introduce bugs. Chapter 10 discusses the many additional benefits of SCM for small teams.

We will be using Git for version control. Cloud-based Git hosting services like GitHub, while not required for Git, are highly desirable because they enable small teams to collaborate conveniently (as Chapter 10 describes) and give individual developers a place to back up their code. This section covers the basics of Git. The next section covers basic setup instructions for GitHub, though other cloud-based Git services are available as well.

> **Linus Torvalds** invented Git to assist with version control on the Linux project. You should read this section even if you've used other VCSs like Subversion, as Git's conceptual model is quite different.

Like all version control systems, a key concept in Git is the project ***repository***, usually shortened to ***repo***, which holds the complete change history of some set of files that make up a project. To start using Git to track a project, you first cd to the project's top-level directory and use the command git init, which initializes an empty repo based in that directory. ***Tracked files*** are those that are a permanent part of the repo, so their revision information is maintained and they are backed up; git add is used to add a file to the set of tracked files. Not every project file needs to be tracked—for example, intermediate files created automatically as part of the development process, such as log files, are usually untracked.

Screencast A.6.1 illustrates the basic Git workflow. When you start a new project, git init sets up the project's root directory as a Git repo. As you create files in your project, for each new file you use git add *filename* to cause the new file to be tracked by Git. When you reach a point where you're happy with the current state of the project, you **commit** the changes: Git prepares a list of all of the changes that will be part of this commit, and opens that list in an editor so you can add a descriptive comment. Which editor to use is determined by a **configuration setting**, as described below. Committing causes a snapshot of the tracked files to be recorded permanently along with the comments. This snapshot is assigned a **commit ID**, a 40-digit hexadecimal number that, surprisingly, is unique in the universe (not just within this Git repo, but across all repos); an example might be `1623f899bda026eb9273cd93c359326b47201f62`. This commit ID is the canonical way to refer to the state of the project at that point in time, but as we'll see, Git provides more convenient ways to refer to a commit besides the cumbersome commit ID. One common way is to specify a prefix of the commit that is unique within this repo, such as `1623f8` for the example above.

> **The *SHA-1* algorithm** is used to compute the 40-digit one-way hash of a representation of the entire tree representing the project at that point in time.

To specify that Git should use the `vim` editor to let you make your changes, you would say `git config --global core.editor 'vim'`. It doesn't matter what directory you're in when you do this, since `--global` specifies that this option should apply to *all* your Git operations in *all* repos. (Most Git configuration variables can also be set on a per-repo basis.) Other useful values for this particular setting are `'mate -w'` for the TextMate editor on MacOS, `'edit -w'` for TextWrangler on MacOS, and the rather unwieldy `"'C:/Program Files/Notepad++/notepad++.exe' -multiInst -notabbar -nosession -noPlugin"` for Windows. In all cases, the various quote marks are necessary to prevent spaces from dividing up the name of the editor into multiple command-line arguments.

> Unlike MacOS, the Windows shell (command prompt) diverges from Unix conventions, so many Unix tools don't work properly. We recommend you develop using the Linux-based VM rather than Windows.

Screencast A.6.1: Basic Git flow for a single developer.

`http://vimeo.com/34754947`

In this simple workflow, `git init` is used to start tracking a project with Git, `git add` and `git commit` are used to add and commit two files. One file is then modified, and when `git status` shows that a tracked file has some changes, `git diff` is used to preview the changes that would be committed. Finally `git commit` is used again to commit the new changes, and `git diff` is used to show the differences between the two committed versions of one of the files, showing that `git diff` can either compare two commits of a file or compare the current state of a file with some previous commit.

It's important to remember that while `git commit` permanently records a snapshot of the current repo state that can be reconstructed at any time in the future, it does *not* create a backup copy of the repo anywhere else, nor make your changes accessible to fellow developers. The next section describes how to use a cloud-based Git hosting service for those purposes.

■ *Elaboration: Add, commit, and the Git index*

The simplified explanation of Git above omits discussion of the *index*, a staging area for changes to be committed. `git add` is used not only to add a new file to the project, but also to stage an existing file's state for committing. So if Alice modifies *existing* file `foo.rb`, she would need to `git add foo.rb` to cause her changes to be committed on the next `git commit`. The reason for separating the steps is that `git add` snapshots the file immediately, so even if the `commit` occurs later, the version that is committed corresponds to the file's state *at the time of* `git add`. (If you make subsequent changes to the file, you should use `git add` again to get those changes into the index.) We simplified the discussion by using `-a` option to `git commit`, which means "commit *all* current changes to tracked files, whether or not `git add` was used to add them." (`git add` is still necessary to add a new file.)

A.7 Getting Started With GitHub

A variety of cloud-based Git hosting services exist. We recommend and give instructions for GitHub. GitHub's free plan gives you as many projects (repos) as you want, but all are publicly readable. Paid plans allow you to have private repos. If you are a student or a teacher, you can get a limited number of private repos by requesting a free educational account[29].

To communicate with most cloud-based Git services, you add your public key to the service, usually through a browser-based interface. The corresponding private key on your development computer then allows you to create a remote copy of a repo there and push changes to it from your local repo. Other developers can, with your permission, both push their own changes and *pull* your changes and others' changes from that remote.

You'll need to do the following steps to setup GitHub. This section assumes you have already setup an `ssh` keypair as directed in Section A.5; you should perform these steps from any computer holding the private key from which you want to access GitHub.

1. Using the Mac or Linux Terminal or the Git Bash terminal on Windows, tell Git your name and email address, so that in a multi-person project each commit can be tied to the committer:

   http://pastebin.com/24VYTKR5

   ```
   1  git config --global user.name 'Andy Yao'
   2  git config --global user.email 'yao@acm.org'
   ```

2. To create a GitHub repo that will be a remote of your existing project repo, fill out and submit the New Repository[30] form and note the repo name you chose. A good choice is a name that matches the top-level directory of your project, such as `myrottenpotatoes`.

3. Back on your development computer, in a terminal window `cd` to the top level of your project's directory (where you previously typed `git init`) and type the following, replacing `myusername` with your GitHub username and `myreponame` with the repository name you chose in the previous step:

   http://pastebin.com/K8q7KiYy

   ```
   1  git remote add origin git@github.com:myusername/myreponame.git
   2  git push origin master
   ```

Note: If you're accessing GitHub from within an organization whose *firewall* blocks ssh connections on TCP port 22—possible symptoms include error messages such as "Connection timed out" or "Connection refused" when you perform the GitHub access commands below—this article[31] explains how you can instead perform these operations over HTTP and HTTPS, which are not blocked by most firewalls. The disadvantage is that you'll have to type your GitHub password for each operation, rather than relying on ssh key exchange. If you find it necessary to use this alternate method, you would replace the first command above with the following:

http://pastebin.com/ySXXUG80

```
git remote add origin https://github.com/myusername/myreponame.git
```

The first command tells Git that you're adding a new remote for your repo located at GitHub, and that the short name origin will be used from now on to refer to that remote. (This name is conventional among Git users for reasons explained in Chapter 10.) The second command tells Git to *push* any changes from your local repo to the origin remote that aren't already there.

These account setup and key management steps only have to be done once. The process of creating a new repo and using git remote to add it must be done for each new project. Each time you use git push in a particular repo, you are propagating all changes to the repo since your last push to the remote, which has the nice side effect of keeping an up-to-date backup of your project.

Figure A.2 summarizes the basic Git commands introduced in this chapter, which should be enough to get you started as a solo developer. When you work in a team, you'll need to use additional Git features and commands introduced in Chapter 10.

A.8 Deploying to the Cloud Using Heroku

New cloud computing technologies like Heroku make SaaS deployment easier than it's ever been. Create a free Heroku[32] account if you haven't already; the free account provides enough functionality for the projects in this book. Heroku supports apps in many languages and frameworks. For deploying Rails apps, Heroku provides a gem called heroku, which is preinstalled in the bookware VM. Once you've created a Heroku account, install the Heroku Toolbelt[33], a collection of command-line tools that simplifies Heroku access.

> The concepts in Chapter 4 are central to this discussion, so read that chapter first if you haven't already.

You first need to add your ssh public key to Heroku to enable deployment there. Heroku's instructions[34] explain how to do this once you've installed the Toolbelt. You only need to do this step once.

Essentially, Heroku behaves like a Git remote (Section A.7) that only knows about a single branch called master, and pushing to that remote has the side-effect of deploying your app. When you do such a push, Heroku detects which framework your app is using to determine how to deploy the app. For Rails apps, Heroku runs bundle to install your app's gems, compiles your assets (described below), and starts the app.

> Git branches are discussed in Chapter 10.

Chapter 4 describes the three environments (development, production, testing) defined by Rails; when you deploy to Heroku or any other platform, your deployed app will run in the production environment. There are two changes you must make to accommodate a few important differences between your development environment and Heroku's production environment.

Command	What it does	When to use it
`git pull`	Fetch latest changes from other developers and merge into your repo	Each time you sit down to edit files in a team project
`git add` *file*	Stage *file* for commit	When you add a new file that is not yet tracked
`git status`	See what changes are pending commit and what files are untracked	Before committing, to make sure no important files are listed as "untracked" (if so, use `git add` to track them)
`git diff` *filename*	See the differences between the current version of a file and the last committed version	To see what you've changed, in case you break something. This command has many more options, some described in Chapter 10.
`git commit -a`	Commit changes to *all* (`-a`) tracked files; an editor window will open where you can type a commit message describing the changes being committed	When you're at a stable point and want to snapshot the project state, in case you need to roll back to this point later
`git checkout` *filename*	Reverts a file to the way it looked after its last commit. **Warning:** any changes you've made since that commit will be lost. This command has many more options, some described in Chapter 10.	When you need to "roll back" one or more files to a known-good version
`git push` *remote-name*	Push changes in your repo to the remote named *remote-name*, which if omitted will default to `origin` if you set up your repo according to instructions in Section A.7	When you want your latest changes to become available to other developers, or to back up your changes to the cloud

Figure A.2: Common Git commands. Some of these commands may seem like arbitrary incantations because they are very specific cases of much more general and powerful commands, and many will make more sense as you learn more of Git's features.

First, Heroku needs some additional gems to support these differences. Heroku requires some specific configuration settings for your app's production environment, which are captured in a gem called **rails_12factor**[35]. Furthermore Heroku uses the PostgreSQL database rather than SQLite. The following code excerpt shows how to change your app's Gemfile to accommodate these two differences. You must do this step for *each* new app you create that will be deployed on Heroku. As always, don't forget to run bundle after changing your Gemfile, and to commit and push your changes to both Gemfile and Gemfile.lock.

http://pastebin.com/bfjxEq5r

```
1  # making your Gemfile safe for Heroku
2  ruby '1.9.3'    # just in case - tell Heroku which Ruby version we need
3  group :development, :test do
4    # make sure sqlite3 gem ONLY occurs inside development & test groups
5    gem 'sqlite3' # use SQLite only in development and testing
6  end
7  group :production do
8    # make sure the following gems are in your production group:
9    gem 'pg'                 # use PostgreSQL in production (Heroku)
10   gem 'rails_12factor'  # Heroku-specific production settings
11 end
```

After installing any needed gems, Heroku's next action on each deployment is to deal with your app's static assets, such as CSS files (Section 2.3) and JavaScript files (Chapter 6). Starting with Rails 3.1, Rails supports the higher-level language **SCSS** for creating CSS stylesheets and the **CoffeeScript** language for DRYing out JavaScript. Since browsers consume CSS and JavaScript but not SCSS or CoffeeScript, a sequence of steps collectively called the asset pipeline[36] performs the following code-generation tasks:

1. All CoffeeScript files in app/assets, if any, are converted to JavaScript.

2. All JavaScript files are concatenated into one large JavaScript file which is then **minified** to take up less space by removing whitespace and comments and perhaps renaming variables with shorter names. The resulting large JavaScript file is placed in public/assets.

3. All SCSS files in app/assets, if any, are translated to CSS.

4. All CSS files are concatenated into one large CSS file which is minified and placed in public/assets.

5. Rails arranges for the name of each of these single large files to include a "fingerprint" that uniquely identifies the file's content, allowing the static files to be cached by both browsers and servers (Section 12.7) as long as the file's content doesn't change, which in production environments only happens when a new version of the app is deployed.

6. The behaviors of the Rails view helpers javascript_include_tag and stylesheet_link_tag, which usually appear in a layout such as app/views/application.html.haml (Section 4.4), are modified to load these auto-generated files from the public directory, which in some production environments can be redirected to a separate static asset server or even a **Content Distribution Network**.

The second change you must make to your app, therefore, is to specify which of three ways Heroku should manage the asset pipeline. The first way is for you to *precompile* the assets by running the asset pipeline locally on your computer and versioning the generated JavaScript and CSS files in Git. The second is to have Heroku prepare and compile the assets at runtime, the first time each type of asset is requested. This method can cause unpredictable performance when it happens, and neither we nor Heroku recommend it. The third method, which we recommend, is to let Heroku compile the static files just once at deploy time. This method is the most DRY: since you only keep your original files (JavaScript and/or CoffeeScript, CSS and/or SCSS) under version control, there is exactly one place where asset information can be changed. It also simplifies configuration if you're using Jasmine to test your JavaScript or CoffeeScript code.

To enable Heroku to precompile your assets at deploy time, add the following line in `config/environments/production.rb`:

http://pastebin.com/7PDq3tid

```
1 | # in config/environments/application.rb:
2 | config.assets.initialize_on_precompile = false
```

This line prevents Heroku from trying to initialize the Rails environment before precompiling your assets: on Heroku, some ***environment variables*** on which Rails relies are not initialized until later, and their absence would cause an error during deployment. This article[37] contains some tips on troubleshooting asset pipeline problems at deploy time, including how to compile the asset pipeline locally to isolate problems. **Beware:** if you compile the asset pipeline locally, it will create the file `public/assets/manifest.yml`; make sure this file is *not* checked into Git, because its presence will tell Heroku that you're precompiling your own assets and don't want Heroku to do it for you!

Once you've made these two one-time changes in your app (and remembered to commit and push the results), deployment of each new app version follows a simple recipe, starting from your app's root directory:

1. **Make sure your app is running correctly and passing all your tests locally.** Remote debugging is always harder. Before you deploy, maximize your confidence in your local copy of the app!

2. If you have added or changed any gems, be sure you've successfully run `bundle` to make sure your app's dependencies are still satisfied, and that you've committed and pushed any changes to `Gemfile` and `Gemfile.lock`.

3. The *first* time you deploy an app, `heroku apps:create` *appname* creates a new Heroku application container called *appname*; if you omit the name, a whimsical name is preassigned, such as `luminous-coconut-237`. In any case, your app will be deployed at `http://`*appname*`.herokuapp.com`. You can change your app's name later by logging into your Heroku account and clicking My Apps.

4. Once you've committed your latest changes,
   `git push heroku master`
   deploys the head of your local repo's master branch to Heroku. (See this article[38] to deploy from a branch other than master, if you're following the branch-per-release methodology of Section 10.5.)

5. `heroku ps`
   checks the process status (ps) of your deployed app. The **State** column should say something like "Up for 10s" meaning that your app has been available for 10 seconds. You can also use `heroku logs` to display the log file of your app, a useful technique if something goes wrong in production that worked fine in development.

Local (development)	Heroku (production)
`rails server`	`git push heroku master`
`rails console`	`heroku run console`
`rake db:migrate`	`heroku run rake db:migrate`
`more log/development.log`	`heroku logs`

Figure A.3: How to get the functionality of some useful development-mode commands for the deployed version of your app on Heroku.

6. `heroku run rake db:migrate`
   On any deployment where you have changed the database schema (Sections 4.2 and 12.4), including the first-time deployment, this command will cause the app's database to be created or updated. If there are no pending migrations, the command safely does nothing. Heroku also has instructions on how to import the data from your development database[39] to your production database on your first deployment.

Figure A.3 summarizes how some of the useful commands you've been using in development mode can be applied to the deployed app on Heroku.

■ *Elaboration: Production best practices*

In this streamlined introduction, we're omitting two best practices that Heroku recommends[40] for "hardening" your app in production. First, our Heroku deployment still uses WEBrick as the presentation tier; Heroku recommends using the streamlined `thin` webserver for better performance. Second, since subtle differences between SQLite3 and PostgreSQL functionality may cause migration-related problems as your database schemas get more complex, Heroku advises using PostgreSQL in both development and production, which would require installing and configuring PostgreSQL on your VM or other development computer. In general, it's a good idea to keep your development and production environments as similar as possible to avoid hard-to-debug problems in which something works in the development environment but fails in the production environment.

A.9   Checklist: Starting a New Rails App

Throughout the book we recommend several tools for developing, testing, deploying, and monitoring the code quality of your app. In this section, we pull together in one place a step-by-step list for creating a new app that takes advantage of all these tools. This section will only make sense after you have read all the referenced sections, so use it as a reference and don't worry if you don't understand all the steps now. Steps are annotated with the section number(s) in which the tool or concept is first introduced.

Set up your app: (§4.1)

1. `rails -v` to ensure you're running the desired version of Rails. If not run `gem install rails -v` *x.x.x* with *x.x.x* set to the version you want; 3.2.19 for example.

2. `rails new` *appname* `-T` to create the new app. `-T` skips creating the `test` subdirectory used by the **Test::Unit** testing framework, since we recommend using RSpec instead.

3. `cd` *appname* to navigate into your new app's root directory. From now on, all shell commands should be issued from this directory.

4. Edit the `Gemfile` to lock the versions of Ruby and Rails, for example:

http://pastebin.com/6NxFRNrM

```
1  # in Gemfile:
2  ruby '1.9.3'      # Ruby version you're running
3  rails '3.2.19'    # Rails version for this app
```

If you ended up changing the version(s) already present in the Gemfile, run `bundle install --without production` to make sure you have compatible versions of Rails and other gems.

5. Make sure your app runs by executing `rails server` and visiting `http://localhost:3000`. You should see the Rails welcome page.

6. `git init` to set up your app's root directory as a GitHub repo. (§A.6, Screencast A.6.1)

Connect your app to GitHub, CodeClimate, and Heroku:

1. Create a GitHub repo via GitHub's web interface, and do the initial commit and push of your new app's repo. (§A.7)

2. Point CodeClimate at your app's GitHub repo. (§9.5)

3. Make the changes necessary to deploy to production on Heroku. (§A.8)

4. Run `bundle install --without production` if you've changed your `Gemfile`. Commit the changes to `Gemfile` and `Gemfile.lock`. On future changes to the Gemfile, you can just say `bundle` with no arguments, since Bundler will remember the option to skip production gems. (§4.1)

5. `heroku apps:create` *appname* to create your new app on Heroku (§A.8)

6. `git push heroku master` to ensure the app deploys correctly. You should then be able to visit your app's Rails splash page at `http://`*appname*`.herokuapp.com`. At this point you can safely remove the default splash page: `git rm public/index.html`. (§A.8)

Set up your testing environment:

1. Add support in your Gemfile for Cucumber (§7.6), RSpec (§8.2), interactive debugging (§4.1), SimpleCov (§8.7), Autotest (§8.2), FactoryGirl (§8.5), Jasmine if you plan to use JavaScript (§6.7), and Metric-Fu to keep track of your code metrics:

http://pastebin.com/y4MaVP72

```
 1  # debugger is useful in development mode too
 2  group :development, :test do
 3    gem 'debugger'
 4    gem 'jasmine-rails' # if you plan to use JavaScript/CoffeeScript
 5  end
 6  # setup Cucumber, RSpec, autotest support
 7  group :test do
 8    gem 'rspec-rails', '2.14'
 9    gem 'simplecov', :require => false
10    gem 'cucumber-rails', :require => false
11    gem 'cucumber-rails-training-wheels' # basic imperative step defs
12    gem 'database_cleaner' # required by Cucumber
13    gem 'autotest-rails'
14    gem 'factory_girl_rails' # if using FactoryGirl
15    gem 'metric_fu'          # collect code metrics
16  end
```

(See Section 6.7 for additional gems to support fixtures and AJAX stubbing in your JavaScript tests.)

2. Run `bundle`, since you've changed your `Gemfile`. Commit the changes to `Gemfile` and `Gemfile.lock`.

3. If all is well, create the subdirectories and files used by RSpec, Cucumber, Jasmine, and if you're using them, the basic Cucumber imperative steps:

http://pastebin.com/BvJvHezi

```
1  rails generate rspec:install
2  rails generate cucumber:install
3  rails generate cucumber_rails_training_wheels:install
4  rails generate jasmine_rails:install
```

4. If you're using SimpleCov, which we recommend, place the following lines at the *top* of `spec/spec_helper.rb` to enable it:

http://pastebin.com/G5BV1efA

```
1  # at TOP of spec/spec_helper.rb:
2  require 'simplecov'
3  SimpleCov.start
```

5. If you're using FactoryGirl to manage factories (§8.5), add its setup code:

http://pastebin.com/VDnhECsQ

```
1  # For RSpec, create this file as spec/support/factory_girl.rb
2  RSpec.configure do |config|
3    config.include FactoryGirl::Syntax::Methods
4  end
```

http://pastebin.com/Wx7veG8E

```
1  # For Cucumber, add at the end of features/support/env.rb:
2  World(FactoryGirl::Syntax::Methods)
```

6. `git add` and then commit any files created or modified by these steps.

7. Ensure Heroku deployment still works: `git push heroku master`

You're now ready to create and apply the first migration (§4.2), then re-deploy to Heroku and apply the migration in production (`heroku run rake db:migrate`).

Add other useful Gems:

Some that we recommend include:

- `railroady` draws diagrams of your class relationships such as has-many, belongs-to, and so on (§5.3)

- `omniauth` adds portable third-party authentication (§5.2)

- `devise` adds user self-signup pages, and optionally works with `omniauth`

A.10   Fallacies and Pitfalls

 Pitfall: **Making check-ins (commits) too large.**

Git makes it quick and easy to do a commit, so you should do them frequently and make each one small, so that if some commit introduces a problem, you don't have to also undo all the other changes. For example, if you modified two files to work on feature A and three other files to work on feature B, do two separate commits in case one set of changes needs to be undone later. In fact, advanced Git users use `git add` to "cherry pick" a subset of changed files to include in a commit: add the specific files you want, and *omit* the -a flag to `git commit`.

 Pitfall: **Forgetting to add files to the repo.**

If you create a new file but forget to add it to the repo, your copy of the code will still work but your file won't be tracked or backed up. Before you do a commit or a push, use `git status` to see the list of Untracked Files, and `git add` any files in that list that *should* be tracked. You can use the `.gitignore`[41] file to avoid being warned about files you never want to track, such as binary files or temporary files.

 Pitfall: **Confusing commit with push.**

`git commit` captures a snapshot of the staged changes in *your* copy of a repo, but no one else will see those changes until you use `git push` to propagate them to other repo(s) such as the origin.

 Pitfall: **Forgetting to reset VM networking when your host computer moves.**

Remember that your VM relies on the networking facilities of your host computer. If your host computer moves to a new network, for example if you suspend it at home and wake it up at work, that's like unplugging and reconnecting your host computer's network cable. The VM must therefore also have its (virtual) network cable disconnected and reconnected, which you can do using the Devices menu in VirtualBox.

 Pitfall: **Hidden assumptions that differ between development and production environments.**

Chapter 4 explains how Bundler and the Gemfile automate the management of your app's dependencies on external libraries and how migrations automate making changes to your database. Heroku relies on these mechanisms for successful deployment of your app. If you manually install gems rather than listing them in your Gemfile, those gems will be missing or have the wrong version on Heroku. If you change your database manually rather than using migrations, Heroku won't be able to make the production database match your development database. Other dependencies of your app include the type of database (Heroku uses PostgreSQL), the versions of Ruby and Rails, the specific Web server used as the presentation tier, and more. While frameworks like Rails and deployment platforms like Heroku go to great lengths to shield your app from variation in these areas, using automation tools like migrations and Bundler, rather than making manual changes to your development environment, maximizes the likelihood that you've documented your dependencies so you can keep your development and production environments in sync. If it can be automated and recorded in a file, it should be!

A.11 To Learn More

- The Git Community Book[42] is a good online reference that can also be downloaded as a PDF file.

Notes

[1]`http://virtualbox.org`
[2]`http://github.com`
[3]`http://heroku.com`
[4]`http://stackoverflow.com`
[5]`http://stackoverflow.com`
[6]`http://github.com`
[7]`http://heroku.com`
[8]`http://pivotaltracker.com`
[9]`http://saasbook.info`
[10]`http://pastebin.com/u/saasbook`
[11]`http://vimeo.com/saasbook`
[12]`http://virtualbox.org`
[13]`http://www.saasbook.info/bookware-vm-instructions`
[14]`http://github.com/saasbook/courseware`
[15]`http://catb.org/~esr/writings/homesteading/cathedral-bazaar/`
[16]`http://aptana.com/`
[17]`http://code.tutsplus.com/articles/25-vim-tutorials-screencasts-and-resources--net-14631`
[18]`http://www.gnu.org/software/emacs/tour/`
[19]`http://www.saasbook.info/bookware-vm-instructions`
[20]`http://www.barebones.com/products/textwrangler/`
[21]`http://notepad-plus-plus.org/`
[22]`http://www.saasbook.info/bookware-vm-instructions/ec2`
[23]`http://docs.aws.amazon.com/AWSEC2/latest/UserGuide/ec2-key-pairs.html#how-to-generate-your-own-key-and-import-it-to-aws`
[24]`http://www.saasbook.info/bookware-vm-instructions/ec2`
[25]`http://docs.aws.amazon.com/AWSEC2/latest/UserGuide/ec2-key-pairs.html#how-to-generate-your-own-key-and-import-it-to-aws`
[26]`http://msysgit.github.io/`
[27]`https://help.github.com/articles/generating-ssh-keys`
[28]`http://www.saasbook.info/bookware-vm-instructions`
[29]`http://github.com/edu`
[30]`https://github.com/repositories/new`
[31]`https://help.github.com/articles/which-remote-url-should-i-use`
[32]`http://heroku.com`
[33]`https://toolbelt.heroku.com/`
[34]`https://devcenter.heroku.com/articles/keys`

[35] https://github.com/heroku/rails_12factor
[36] http://guides.rubyonrails.org/asset_pipeline.html
[37] https://devcenter.heroku.com/articles/rails-asset-pipeline
[38] https://devcenter.heroku.com/articles/git#deploying-code
[39] http://devcenter.heroku.com/articles/taps
[40] http://devcenter.heroku.com/articles/rails3
[41] http://book.git-scm.com/4_ignoring_files.html
[42] http://book.git-scm.com/

Index

CPSIA information can be obtained at www.ICGtesting.com
Printed in the USA
LVOW09s1129270914

406177LV00002B/6/P